Philip Gould is a senior advise̶̶̶̶̶̶̶̶̶̶̶̶̶̶̶̶̶̶̶̶ ing and advertising executive, he runs a strategic and political consultancy with President Bill Clinton's strategy and polling aides James Carville and Stanley Greenberg. An adviser to Labour since 1985, Gould is one of the chief architects of the modernisation of the party. As well as his work in Britain and the United States, where he worked on the last two Clinton presidential campaigns, he has advised left-of-centre parties from Germany to Jamaica. He lives with his wife and two children in North London.

THE
UNFINISHED
REVOLUTION

How the Modernisers
Saved the Labour Party

PHILIP GOULD

An *Abacus* Book

First published in Great Britain in 1998
by Little, Brown and Company
This edition published in 1999 by Abacus

Reprinted 2001

A CIP catalogue record for this book
is available from the British Library.

ISBN: 0 349 11177 4

Typeset by
Palimpsest Book Production Limited
Polmont, Stirlingshire
Printed and bound in Great Britain by
Mackays of Chatham plc, Chatham, Kent

Abacus
A Division of
Little, Brown and Company (UK)
Brettenham House
Lancaster Place
London WC2E 7EN

For Georgia, Grace and Gail.

Contents

ACKNOWLEDGEMENTS

I have many debts to pay:

To Catherine Needham, who has been the book's principal researcher. Employed to help me with the book, she ended up as the linchpin of my office. But she also found time to get into perfect order van-loads of my notes, memos and documents, as well as providing background research for the entire period. She was indispensable to the book.

To Alice Miles, who helped me write and edit the book. She has an exceptional political mind and was able to make clear many of the complex issues that were confronted in the book. Just as important were her determination and commitment over many months. She drove the book forward. Without her it would never have been completed.

To David Miliband and Peter Hyman for their time and kindness. To Dennis Kavanagh, Stanley Greenberg, Clive Hollick, David Lipsey, Giles Radice and Patricia Hewitt, who provided advice and counsel. To Ivor Crewe, for his analysis of the 1983 election, and John Rentoul, for allowing me access to his notes of the Blair period. To Deborah Mattinson, who was there at the start.

To all those I interviewed, including: Simon Buckby, Colin Byrne,

Liam Byrne, Charles Clarke, David Hill, Neal Lawson, Ben Lucas, Margaret McDonagh, Adrian McMenamin, Jon Mendelsohn, Fiona Millar, Sally Morgan and Chris Powell.

To Tristram Hunt, who provided much of the historical research; to Benjamin Wegg-Prosser, who brought together the team that made the book possible; to Gordon Corera and Tom Dibble.

To Andrew Gordon, for his patience, and Philippa Harrison, for her faith; and Liz Cowen, for her help with the final draft.

To everyone who worked on the 1997 election campaign, and the two campaigns before it.

To Peter Mandelson and Alastair Campbell, who are friends as well as colleagues.

To Tony Blair, Gordon Brown, Neil Kinnock, John Prescott and others in the Cabinet and previous shadow Cabinets who were not involved in this book, but who ultimately made it possible.

Finally, to my family, who were part of this journey too. To my children Grace and Georgia, who deserve better than a father who was absent fighting an election, and then was absent writing about it. They never complained and are the best kids in the world. To my wife Gail, who has been with me through the many years when victory seemed unlikely, and my part in it less likely still. It is difficult to describe what she has had to put up with, impossible to describe how well she has coped. She gave me the confidence to start the book, the advice to get it right.

PREFACE TO THE
PAPERBACK EDITION

The New Labour enigma

This is a book about the making of New Labour. It is a personal, first-hand account of the creation of arguably one of the most successful political forces in the democratic world today. Yet New Labour remains to many an enigma. It does not conform to the traditional expectation of what a political party is, how it should behave, where it places its battle lines. Many who admire it still do not understand it. Perhaps this is unsurprising. New Labour is genuinely radical in its approach to politics, and its beliefs are often rooted in paradox: it is pro-business and yet anti-poverty; it wants taxes down for people who work hard, but public expenditure up for health and education; it seeks to be tough on both crime and its causes. These paradoxes confuse: they scramble the brain cells of many in the political class.

The confusion has been felt most painfully on the political right, where mention of New Labour is so often met by blank incomprehension, as if a vast new political Stonehenge had suddenly and inexplicably appeared in the mental landscape. A few years ago the right owned the political terrain: their view of the world prevailed, their future was assured. New Labour threatens all that. A party which was teetering on the edge of extinction is back, and back with a vengeance. That Conservative future, which seemed so certain, now appears to be lost. The essential Tory claim to power – that only they could be trusted to govern – has been exposed as an illusion. Without Labour as a demonic enemy, Conservatism lacks bearing and purpose. No wonder the right find New Labour difficult to fathom.

Many on the left also find New Labour hard to grasp. They are accustomed to the politics of the Somme: the left in their trenches, the right in theirs, with a clear unsullied distinction between the two. But New Labour is not like that: it seeks to build big inclusive coalitions; it understands the central importance of the middle class; it wants ideas which work, not ideologies which don't; it believes good government needs good presentation; it wants to keep taxes as low as possible, and is obsessively committed to economic prudence. All this can be confusing at best, alienating at worst. And yet already, after two years, the list of New Labour achievements grows longer and longer. New Labour, for all its centrism and preoccupation with the middle class, is arguably doing more that is consistent with core Labour values than any Labour government that has preceded it. No wonder the left, too, are confused.

I hope this book can help end some of the confusion and make sense of New Labour – not just how it happened, but *why* it happened. What is New Labour's character? What is it really for? *The Unfinished Revolution* does not aim to be a neutral and disinterested account of the making of New Labour. It is written unashamedly from a modernising perspective. It is at times personal. But perhaps such an account can reveal a greater truth, or at least a different truth, than more dispassionate, detached assessments. At the very least this book contains clues and insights about New Labour which only a partisan can provide.

The book is structured around two journeys. First, my personal journey from a suburban childhood to the 1997 election campaign. Second, Labour's journey from decline to recovery, and ultimately to victory. These two journeys are indivisible. Labour fell into decline because it turned its back on the kind of ordinary suburban people I was brought up with. It would recover only when it reached out to these people as a new and modern Labour Party. For me, modernisation has always been personal.

This is the first inside account of the making of New Labour. It is not authorised. All the judgements are mine and mine alone. The fact that people are interviewed in this book does not mean that they share my interpretations or opinions. I do not claim that this book is the last word on New Labour, but for me, this is how it happened. It is one person's view of a revolution.

The New Labour government

The Unfinished Revolution ends when the first modernising journey ended: with victory at the 1997 General Election. But the New Labour government has been in power for over two years now – long enough for judgements to be made, and the claims and assumptions of *The Unfinished Revolution* to be put to a meaningful test. It is reasonable to ask: was it worth it? Were the means – the long years of struggle; the constant focus on change; the slaying of shibboleths; the effective remaking of an entire political party – justified by the ends?

Labour's extraordinary victory in 1997 was a direct consequence of modernisation. This is confirmed by *Critical Elections*, the most recent and far-reaching study of the 1997 election. It states that: 'It is indubitably true that Labour's shift to the centre, and its efforts to de-ideologize British politics more generally attracted more voters to the cause in 1997'; 'Labour's modernization project was particularly successful in overcoming negative perceptions and associations that the southern voter had of the party in the 1980s'; 'The most striking finding is that in 1997 the proportion of the middle class voting Labour is far higher than at any previous point.'[1] But these gains were made without any loss of support whatever from Labour's traditional base. In fact Labour did better among its traditional supporters than at any other election since 1966.

[1] *Critical Elections*, edited by Geoffrey Evans and Pippa Norris (London: Sage Publications, 1999), pp. 135, 201.

If it was modernisation that won New Labour power, how has New Labour fared in government? In terms of public opinion this is the most popular mid-term government in modern times. Tony Blair is the most popular Prime Minister in recorded history. The figures are extraordinary: Labour's average lead in the second year of the Parliament was 27.3 per cent; Tony Blair's personal rating still over 80 per cent at the end of the second year. But that is only the start. According to NOP Labour leads the Conservatives by a 16 per cent margin on economic management, up from parity between the parties at election time. It leads by 16 per cent on the question of which party will make you better off; on taxation by 15 per cent; on interest rates by a massive 25 per cent. On taxation, on interest rates, on inflation, on basic economic competence Labour is now more trusted than the Conservatives. Maurice Saatchi once said that without the issue of taxation the Tories have nothing, and so it appears to be. Labour has won the electorate's trust where once the Conservatives were dominant, while consolidating its position in its areas of historic strength. The electoral battleground has been transformed.

It is not just the public which appreciates New Labour – the press, in their considered moments, do too. Although frequently critical in day-by-day analysis, they were almost unanimous in their mid-term assessments. Left and right consistently conceded that this was a successful government. Even the conservative papers were positive. In an April 1999 leader the *Telegraph* wrote: 'The economy has not collapsed; indeed, rather the opposite. What still remains of the left has been kept firmly under control. The unions do not run the country. Nationalisation really is dead and buried, and Britain continues to play a leading part in NATO. Most of this is because of Mr Blair. In his first two years, even his critics concede he has been a strong and skilful leader.' The *Daily Mail* too has been positive: 'Few would deny on the anniversary of his landslide that he has established himself as a remarkable Prime Minister.' Perhaps just as surprisingly the left was also fulsome: in May 1999 the *Guardian* talked of 'Labour transcendent', saying it 'could scarcely have performed much better'. The *Daily Mirror* argued that the 'New Labour government has stayed true to its pledge to concentrate on issues that matter to people like health, education, crime and the economy'.

Positive public opinion and press comment alone do not make for great government: that has to be a function of what is achieved, not what is perceived, but here too the government can claim success. The achievements of the first two New Labour years are remarkable, bearing comparison with any previous Labour government. Already, after just two years, the Scottish Parliament and Welsh Assembly are up and running; London will have a Mayor; a Freedom of Information Bill is being introduced; the New Deal has cut youth unemployment from 15 per cent to 8 per cent: there are 400,000 more people in work than two years ago; the minimum wage has been introduced; there is a minimum income guarantee for pensioners; New Labour has increased child benefit by record amounts; the government is pledged to end child poverty within twenty years; a working families tax credit and Children's Tax Credit will act directly to end family poverty; an additional £41 million has been earmarked for investment in health and education; hospital waiting lists are falling; the Bank of England has been given independence; and interest rates and inflation are approaching record lows. It seems likely that Britain will survive the world slowdown without the boom and bust that characterised the Conservative years. If this can be achieved it will be the first time a Labour government has managed to govern in its early years without constantly being pressed by economic crises, reflecting enormous credit on the Chancellor Gordon Brown.

But with the good have come difficult times for New Labour, too. Peter Mandelson is a central figure in this book, his influence stamped on page after page. But on 23 December 1998 he was forced to resign as Secretary of State for Trade and Industry because of a loan he had received for his house from Geoffrey Robinson MP before the election.

I spoke to him late on the night before his resignation and his mood was black. He had all but made up his mind to resign, judging that the media furore would not quickly subside. He recognised that he had made a mistake in accepting such a large loan, and in not revealing it at the right time. When ruling himself out of the DTI investigation of Geoffrey Robinson, he recalled how easily he could have told his officials about the loan. But he hadn't. He realised he had acted in error, and knew that he had to pay a price.

I trust this book will provide some clues into how this extraordinary turn of events came to pass. It shows the paradoxes of his personality: confident yet defensive; brilliant judgement when it comes to others, less certain judgement when it comes to himself; cautious common sense blended with an ability to take huge risks; above all, a man who appears to have the hide of a rhino, but in fact someone who is easily hurt.

Mandelson is a great talent who is missed by Labour and by the nation. I hope he will come back. But whatever the future holds he has a past to be proud of. Without Mandelson, New Labour would not have been possible, the current majority not achieved. He made a mistake, but he also helped make a new party.

The greatest crisis that the New Labour government has faced is the military campaign against Serbia: this was certainly Tony Blair's biggest test. Blair had been preoccupied with Kosovo for some time before the military action was taken, and thought no option was perfect but that the chosen one was the best. There were times in the campaign when things looked black – where success was uncertain. I have long believed that the hallmark of great leadership is the courage to take a course of action in which a satisfactory outcome is not assured. Few politicians have that courage. At these moments of blackness – the worst being after the mistaken bombing of the Chinese Embassy, when Blair appeared isolated and exposed – he never saw compromise or fudge as an option. When once or twice the situation did look hopeless to some, he kept calm, exuding confidence that we would win. This will prove a great personal milestone for Blair.

As the war ended, voting began in the European elections, where Labour was roundly beaten. A recurring motif in *The Unfinished Revolution* is the late evening drive through Whitehall to go to Labour Party headquarters on election nights, usually to lose, and only once to win. I never thought I would make that drive again knowing that I was about to watch another losing election night unfold, but I did on Sunday 13 June, during the Euro-election count. There were many reasons for the defeat: the Kosovo war, which was such an intense preoccupation for many in the government; the low turnout; the limited news coverage of the election. But for me none of those mattered: we lost, the Conservatives won, and I hate that. But defeat is salutary: it proves that politics is never predictable; it is a warning against complacency; it shows we must not take any of our voters for granted; and above all, it reminds all of us in the Labour Party how few national elections we have won this century, how bad it feels to lose, and how determined we should be to win, and win again.

The most radical option

Most reviewers of *The Unfinished Revolution* supported the central assumptions of the book, but there were dissenting voices. Although in the minority, their beliefs were passionate. The political faction Labour First was the angriest critic: 'Mr Gould should be thrown in the dustbin of history as a genuine enemy of the Party.' In a wholly negative review in the *New Statesman* David Hare wrote: 'Gould affects to be mystified by the hostility to focus groups.' Nick Cohen of the *Observer*, attacking New Labour for its concentration on the middle class, wrote: 'The turnout [in the 1997 General Election] was the lowest since democracy came to Britain. The working class and the poor, attacked by all parties with varying degrees of sourness, decided, quite sensibly, to stay at home.'

The views underpinning these criticisms may be deeply held, but they are all wrong, because they imply we were misguided in our determination to win votes. New Labour should be obsessed with winning. Winning has to be the central aim of politics, because only with power can genuine politics start. A principle without the means of its implementation exists only as an abstraction, beguiling but meaningless. Without power there can be no opportunity for change.

It is not only logic that fuels New Labour's obsession with electoral success, it is history. Not just Labour's defeat in four general elections before 1997, nor even Labour's effective loss of the twentieth century, a century it should have owned or at the very least dominated, but the fact that Labour has never, ever won two full terms in government. This is the pattern of history that New Labour is determined to break. Labour made history in 1997, but to win the next election comfortably it must defy history.

Criticism of focus groups is also misguided. It is nonsense to say that New Labour governs on the basis of opinion polls – that would be neither practical nor desirable. And few can now doubt that the government will buck public opinion when it believes it right to do so; the issue of GM food being a prime example. But with the emergence of a new and more responsive relationship between government and citizen, the public has a right to be consulted on issues that will directly affect them. If changes are to be made to the NHS or to schools, we should first listen to the people who use these services. More and more users of public services will behave increasingly as consumers: demanding the best on their terms, instead of what others think is best for them. Market research has a crucial role to play in making this process work.

The Unfinished Revolution will show how for many months before the 1997 election I was talking to voters directly in small focus groups, mainly in the suburbs of London, helping New Labour try to win their trust. After the election I felt I had a duty to go back to these voters to see if they felt their trust had been justified. So for me, rainy nights in Watford in opposition were replaced by rainy nights in Watford when Labour was in government, ensuring that the voices we listened to before victory were listened to afterwards as well. I consider those who criticise this process to be arrogant and will never make any apology for talking directly to the electorate. When governments stop listening they start dying.

The critics who attack me for overseeing – through my focus on the middle classes – an erosion of Labour's traditional base are wrong too. In 1997 Labour did do well in the centre, in the south, with the middle classes, but it did so without any loss of support whatever from its traditional base. This supports an absolutely pivotal modernising argument: that a modernising party must win more middle-class votes, as they are the emerging social force, but that winning middle-class support does not mean losing backing from the traditional working class. The middle classes are central to modernisation, but not on their own: they are part of a new 'middle-down' coalition, connecting the new middle class to the old working class, both groups linked by a shared commitment to work and the family; by a desire to improve education and the NHS; by the need to build a strong and prosperous economy; and in consequence both groups are receptive to the same New Labour message.

These criticisms, although important, are not the central critique of Labour: that in its desperation to win it has lost its soul and its purpose. In the *Times Literary Supplement* Roy Hattersley put this cogently: 'The constant criticism of New Labour both from the Conservatives and from within the party which Blair leads is the priority of place which is always given to electoral advantage and the consequent down-grading of principle.'

This is the most fundamental attack on New Labour and it has to be answered. If winning changes nothing, it is pointless. My first answer is the most obvious and the most compelling: the charge is disproved by the facts. There is no need to list again the long catalogue of radical New Labour achievements, but it is clear to most objective observers that this government is pursuing a progressive agenda of great and increasing ambition. Rather than lacking principles, New Labour offers the greatest possible opportunity for political change. The lesson of Conservative hegemony over the last one hundred years is that lasting reform requires governments that can sustain themselves in power. If we want to achieve deep, enduring change then Labour has to win again and again, and only New Labour can build the broad, inclusive coalitions that winning in modern politics demands.

But winning is not enough. The modern world demands a new radicalism in government which understands that while values remain immutable, the means of their implementation must change with the world. The best solution is the one that works best. For a progressive political party to have any authentic claim to principled radicalism it must be rooted in values, but it must also have broad appeal reaching out to middle-class voters and beyond and be flexible and competent enough to cope with ceaseless change. Only New Labour is capable of this. 'Real Labour' or 'Old Labour' may be committed to a principled radicalism, but without a consistent ability to win power and the capacity to cope with change when power is won, their radicalism is pyrrhic. New Labour is the only truly radical option.

The new incumbency

As the New Labour government moves forward, determined to break the cycle of past Labour failure, it cannot languish in the relatively comfortable circumstances of the past. New Labour operates within an entirely new environment: a context of ceaseless change and exploding technological opportunity. In his book *Business @ the Speed of Thought* Bill Gates wrote: 'Business is going to change more in the next ten years than in the last fifty. If the 1980s were about quality, and the 1990s about re-engineering, then the 2000s will be about velocity.' The impact of all this on politics is huge, not only on policy but also on the conduct of government itself. This is not a world of one or two news bulletins a day, a world in which Robin Day being gently provocative can cause a sensation and newspapers dutifully report parliamentary proceedings and political speeches. This is a world of exploding media opportunity, where news is constant, news outlets proliferate almost exponentially, where television is fragmented from two channels to two hundred, and where newspapers are governed by competitive pressures, with circulation demands that would have been unimaginable even twenty years ago.

It is a world, too, of growing scepticism about politics and politicians, in which governments are judged less by past ties and habitual loyalties, but by results: problems solved, lives improved. This does not mean that ideas and values have died in politics – this book will argue the opposite – but it does mean political choice is becoming increasingly instrumental. Governments have to deliver: they will be judged by results, as they should be.

This new context demands a different approach to government: a new incumbency which can steer, set and achieve long-term goals, which is grounded in values, which can solve problems and deliver change, but is also able to deal with a new media environment and an increasingly ferocious press. This 'total news media' tends to push coverage of politics towards the sensational and the extreme; it leads to a focus on personalities not policies; it means that issues are likely to be presented in stark one-dimensional terms; and that politicians and political parties (and other public figures) tend always to be either heroes or villains, sharply in the ascendancy or equally sharply in decline. Public figures in the new media order are 'flying or dying'. In America this new political discourse focused on personality and sensation and has been called the 'politics of personal destruction'. The American academic Stephen Carter has recently written: 'There is little coverage of the issues, there is coverage instead of

xxii   THE UNFINISHED REVOLUTION

what people say about the issues.'[1] A new and authoritative academic study, *On Message*, makes the same point from a British perspective. Writing of the 1997 election campaign, the book states: 'While the news media preferred to focus on campaign strategy, devoting roughly two-thirds of their coverage to the conduct of the campaign, opinion polls and party leaders, the parties focused on the substantive issue agenda of welfare, the economy, and education.'[2] The parties were talking about substance, the media about process.

The new incumbency means not just governing well, nor simply making a difference, but retaining credibility, trust and ultimately popularity in a media environment that is more demanding and more sensationalising than ever before. The demands of modern government fuse together the act of delivery with the communications of delivery.

This, then, is the context in which the New Labour government operates. It seeks to break the cycle of past Labour failure and it wants to introduce a new era of progressive government, and it does so in a context of swirling change. This is why so much of the criticism of New Labour is fundamentally misplaced: our critics fail to understand that what might have worked in the past will not work now. Stuart Hall in *Marxism Today* decries 'the attempt to govern by spin through the management of appearances alone. New Labour's systematic preference for media realities rather than political realities are all part of the same problem.' This critique entirely misses a central point of the new incumbency: that brilliant media relations are not somehow an appendage to good government, but are essential to it. Unless you handle the media well you cannot govern competently. This was most explicitly demonstrated in the military campaign against Serbia, when the media was more demanding and more intrusive than ever before at a time of war. The military campaign could not

[1] *Civility: Manners, Morals and the Etiquette of Democracy*, by Professor Stephen L. Carter (New York: HarperCollins, 1998), p. 130.
[2] *On Message*, by Pippa Norris, John Curtice, David Sanders, Margaret Scammell and Holli Semetko (London: Sage Publications, 1999), p. 180.

have been prosecuted effectively had the media campaign not also been successful – the two were indivisible.

Number 10 Downing Street does not need fewer communications resources, but more. It needs a state-of-the-art communications department – not to spin more, but to ensure that government is competent and effective. Misunderstanding of the demands of the new incumbency leads to the view that New Labour attempts to control too much. It is frequently argued that Downing Street seeks to impose too much discipline; that there is an over-emphasis on unity and message; that New Labour is turning into a bunch of 'control freaks'. The centre actually has far less power than is typically ascribed to it. Anyone who spends any time at Number 10 quickly realises that it is a tiny corner of a huge government machine, staffed with talented people but lacking the resources necessary to be a commanding and dominating nerve centre. The idea that officials sit at Number 10 headquarters smoothly pulling strings and levers, effortlessly controlling events, is ridiculous. For the most part they are over-worked, over-stretched and desperately trying to cope with a constant stream of difficult and challenging circumstances.

But if it is wrong to believe that 10 Downing Street has too much power, it is also a mistake to assume that a powerful core is a bad thing. Effective government in the new incumbency relies upon a centre that has the resources, the skills, the speed of response and the flexibility to cope with a velocity of events unimaginable a few years ago. A strong centre is important not just to ensure that government works competently and efficiently, but perhaps even more crucially to provide integration of policy and dissemination of information. Number 10's role is not so much to command and enforce but to integrate and inform. Unless the Prime Minister is supported by his own department that is powerful, talented and fast enough to cope with the speed of changing circumstances, then good government will become increasingly elusive.

But the demands of the new incumbency reach out beyond Number 10, they extend to government as a whole. There has to be a shift from a government built around a structure of 'silos' – huge, self-contained, autonomous departments – to a more flexible and integrated approach in which policy issues easily cross departmental barriers. A new culture of public service and excellence should develop in which outside individuals of exceptional ability fit easily into Whitehall as a normal part of a career pattern. The reverse should also be true, with civil servants having increasing opportunities to spend time working in the private sector. A new crossover culture should become entirely normal. This is not just an issue of government: in business, companies are already transforming themselves into 'restless' corporations in which flexibility and creativity are built into the organisational core. Government cannot mirror what business does, but it must react in its own way to the swirling change that surrounds it. The new incumbency makes new demands on government, and New Labour's attempts to meet them deserve praise, not scorn. Modernisation in government is as important as modernisation was in winning power.

Conclusion

I first decided to write this book in the heat of the General Election of 1992, thinking, 'If I ever manage to get out of this alive, I'll write down what really happened.' Later I came to believe that the extent of my involvement with the Labour Party from 1985 until 1997 justified a book. Finally I thought I owed it to my daughters – Grace and Georgia – to explain to them what I had been doing during the lost years when I should have been spending more time with them. I decided to write this new preface when I heard the clichéd criticisms of New Labour in opposition resurfacing as attacks on New Labour in government. In the rest of the book I have tried to explain the making of New Labour. But I hope *The Unfinished Revolution* is enjoyable as well as helpful. Politics is an extraordinary activity, fusing ideas, emotion, and long-term vision with short-term tactics, day-to-day practicalities, elation and despair. I have tried to capture some of this drama. I want you to understand New Labour, but just as much as that, I want you to enjoy the book.

'We are communal histories; communal books.'
MICHAEL ONDAATJE, *The English Patient*

INTRODUCTION: THE LAND THAT LABOUR FORGOT

Suburban dreams

As a boy I used to walk around my garden planning political campaigns. Some of the earliest books I can remember reading were David Butler's Nuffield election studies. Among the first thoughts I can remember were why Labour was on the left and the Conservatives on the right; why Labour was red, the Conservatives blue.

I knew that I was Labour, but I had little idea why. I never had any doubt that it was the right party. I was born with it. Equally, I had a visceral opposition to Conservatives and Conservatism. I am not sure where these feelings came from, but I know I had them at a very early age. My parents were Christians, and I drew my values from them: compassion; an instinctive support for the underdog; a sense that all people are born with equal intrinsic worth. But I was torn by contradiction: I wanted to protect the poor yet I wanted talent to soar; I wanted fairness yet I wanted aspiration to be uncapped.

I was not calm about all this, I was obsessed.

As time passed it did not get easier. I wanted to know why

Labour supported a liberal society and the Conservatives supported a liberal economy. I wore the grass out on this one. I simply could not understand why liberalism was right in one place and wrong in another. I could not make sense of politics, but I knew that politics was at the heart of my life.

I can remember the shame that touched my family when Suez was invaded by the British in 1956, and the shadow of fear we felt when Hungary was invaded by the Russians.

I can remember being stunned when the Conservatives triumphed in the General Election of 1959.

I can remember the excitement of early television coverage of general elections flickering through on our black-and-white screens.

I can remember the words of John F. Kennedy at his inauguration, and thinking: how could anything so beautiful come to be written? Who did it? How was it done?

When Hugh Gaitskell died I worried about who would be the best leader for Labour. I backed Wilson because I was confident that he would win, but I was not sure about his politics.

When Labour won in 1964 I felt a thrill of excitement that has never left me. I remember the pride I felt at putting Labour stickers on my school bag, and in the windows of my home.

I remember joining the Labour Party in the spring of 1965, when I was fifteen; going to my first Labour Party meeting in the small detached modern home of Terry Molloy in Highclere Gardens in Knaphill; forgetting about my O-levels and doing nothing much for a year but canvass for the second Wilson election.

I remember my first contact with the 'Reading system' of canvassing, which I never understood then and still don't now. I remember knocking on door after door and trying to persuade people to vote Labour, all the time thinking: why are people so unsure, why don't they want to vote Labour?

Above all, I remember the night of 31 March 1966, when Labour won its majority of 96. I remember the exhilaration of the result, sitting high on the balcony watching the count below, but I also remember Cranley Onslow – the soon-to-be re-elected Conservative MP – telling me that if Wilson was given enough rope 'he will hang himself'. I privately thought he was silly, but he proved to be right. Labour would not form another majority government for thirty-one years, confounding Wilson's ambition and becoming the natural party of opposition.

The people Labour betrayed

I learned my politics where I grew up, around the small town of Woking in Surrey. Not in great northern cities, the Welsh valleys or crumbling urban estates. Not in places with great political traditions and dramatic folklore.

I learned my politics in an unexceptional suburban town where most people were neither privileged nor deprived, but nearly everybody was struggling to get by – which was not pretty, and grew uglier – where people lived in unassuming council estates or in tiny semi-detached houses, where university was out of the question for most and where nearly everyone went to secondary-modern schools.

I did not have a deprived upbringing. I had an ordinary upbringing, born and brought up in a twilight suburbia, where post-war council estates nestled alongside small, detached, red-brick Victorian villas.

The party I loved instinctively was to betray the people who lived here, its natural supporters: ordinary people with suburban dreams who worked hard to improve their homes and their lives; to get gradually better cars, washing machines and televisions; to go on holiday in Spain rather than Bournemouth. These people wanted sensible, moderate policies which conformed to their understanding and their daily lives.

Labour became a party enslaved by dogma: it supported unilateral disarmament, immediate withdrawal from the Common Market, nationalisation of the twenty-five largest companies, and marginal taxation rates at 93 per cent. It abandoned the centre ground of

British politics and camped out on the margins, forlorn and useless, offering a miasma of extremism, dogmatism, intolerance and wilful elitism which put the hopes and dreams of ordinary people last.

I remember having dinner in 1983 with Michael Foot and his wife, Jill Craigie. They could not understand why the Labour Party had lost the election that June. Labour had offered education, choices and opportunities, but the people had turned on them. They read the *Sun* and abandoned the Labour Party. Yet it was not the people who had betrayed Labour, but Labour who had betrayed the people. The failures and convulsions of the late 1970s and early 1980s were so bitter as to disqualify Labour from power for a generation. Even in the 1997 General Election, an overseas observer of a focus group in Putney said to me, 'What did you do to these people that they fear you so much?'

Labour had failed to understand that the old working class was becoming a new middle class: aspiring, consuming, choosing what was best for themselves and their families. They had outgrown crude collectivism and left it behind in the supermarket car-park. I knew this, because they were my life.

The land meets the sea

I was born in 1950 in Beddington, south London, into a family with huge qualities but little ambition. This now seems derogatory; it was not then. My parents, both teachers, wanted to do what was right, not what was aspirational.

My father was not tall, about five foot nine, but he had a big voice and a strong presence. He could easily command a large audience, but was always nervous when he did it. As a child he was beautiful, and as a young man classically handsome, but he was never tidy and allowed his hair, first blond and then white, to flop carelessly around his forehead. It was always too long. His shoes were never quite clean, his suits dishevelled, and his glasses often held together with a paper-clip.

He favoured ingenious solutions to household problems:

handles were attached to doors by unlikely combinations of matchsticks and rubber-bands, shelves would be fixed with a pencil stuck in a wall. These temporary solutions, apparently too unstable to survive the day, would last for years. He was like this not out of laziness or lack of aptitude, but simply because he did not care about the ordinary workings of physical things. All he cared about were his work, his family and his mission. And his mission was clear: to use his skills as a teacher to transform the lives of the children in his care.

He was born in 1913 in a large, detached Victorian house in the centre of Ringwood, near Bournemouth, the son of a mobile tailor who travelled the New Forest measuring and making clothes. I remember him with a tape-measure always around his neck. My father was in every respect a country boy, swimming in the fast, clear water of the Hampshire Avon and able to catch trout with his bare hands. In summer he played cricket among bemused New Forest ponies in Carvers, the great playing field that extended beyond the rambling garden of his house, and in winter he played football. A local newspaper headline of the day read: 'GOLDEN GOULD SCORES AGAIN'.

He went to high school in Brockenhurst and then to teacher-training college in Winchester. His life, and his father's life before him, were centred on the New Forest. His politics were non-conformist, individualist, Liberal. Although he later joined the Labour Party, he did so only out of pity, for I had become a rather hapless secretary of my local party; desperate for members, I begged him to help.

He was a fine and talented man who would have made a success of any career he chose. But he chose to serve people, and in particular children, whom he loved. For him, to be a teacher was the summit of his ambition. It was something to strive towards, something to become. He was totally committed to the concept of public service: he believed that you did things not to make money, but because they were right; you existed to make a contribution and to serve the public.

He started teaching on the Herbert Morrison estate in St Helier, Mitcham, which gave him his first taste of urban deprivation. Unable to serve in the war because he had lost all of one lung and a good part of the other to TB, he taught in makeshift air-raid shelters as enemy bombers raided south London. He met my mother during the war when he was bombed out of his digs and arrived, unannounced and homeless, to be a lodger at her mother's house. They were married as the war ended in 1945, and then went to Barnsley for his next teaching post before returning to Beddington, where he took up his first headship at the tiny Church of England primary school. They lived in a house attached to the school, where I was born.

My mother was Dutch. Her father, an artist and a Communist, lived on a houseboat in Amsterdam. They moved to England before the war and she went to school in south London, before training to be a teacher in Chichester. She was tall and gangling, but attractive, when young; her style was fresh, clean and wind-swept. She too put service first, always wanting to teach, to contribute, but if my father's watchword was duty, hers would have been compassion. She was softer than him, more romantic about life, more optimistic about the human condition – not an English pragmatist, but a continental idealist. Her bookshelves were full of bright orange early editions of the Left Book Club. She liked ideas, she loved politics. She was a socialist.

Whatever the strange pull of destiny that brought together this odd mixture of Hampshire and Holland, it worked. He, rooted in the Hampshire countryside; she, by the waters of the Dutch canals. He, the land; she, the sea. It was not an easy marriage because both were so ill so often; she adored him and he loved her, but he was exasperated and eventually worn out by her constant sickness.

She was ill from an early age, with a degenerative condition of the brain which we never fully understood. My father said that when I was a child she would wander off and leave me to cry. My first brutal encounter with her illness came when she stumbled into our kitchen, her face covered with blood, her left hand crushed after tripping on the gravel outside. This was the first stage in an odyssey of illness which hung over my childhood and a large part of my adult life.

Periodically she would have fits, when she would lose consciousness and her breathing would slow alarmingly. Gradually she spent longer periods in hospital, the longest being at the Atkinson Morley Hospital in Wimbledon, which specialised in diseases of the brain. There, she lay in bed next to a woman who for no apparent reason, and without warning, had lost the use of her mind. Her husband came to visit her each night, desperately upset that he could no longer speak to his wife, and she looked back, her eyes small seas of panic as the words no longer came. Overnight she had become a vegetable. This was my first contact with hidden tragedy; a subterranean world of blameless people whose lives had been wrecked without warning.

My mother died on 24 June 1972 at three o'clock in the morning. I saw her last the night before, when she was gasping for her final breath. She held my hand and I said the wrong thing, that I would always love her, for it added to her panic. Somehow she turned to me and managed to say, 'Whatever you do, look after your father.' I said I would, and I did. These were the last words she spoke to me, probably the last words she ever spoke. They came back to haunt me as he fought cancer during the General Election of 1992.

My father gave me duty, my mother idealism. They gave me both the land and the sea.

A New Labour childhood

In 1954 we moved to Byfleet and then in 1957 to Brookwood, part of the borough of Woking. My father was head teacher at the Knaphill primary school, which I attended and where I was happy, although a little in the shadow of my flame-haired, ferociously successful elder sister Jill. Our summers were spent in caravans at Highcliffe or Poole, or in my grandfather's house, playing in

Carvers and sleeping in huge down beds, fishing in the same fast Avon waters which my father had swum in forty years before.

The only black cloud looming on the horizon was the 11-plus, which I had to take and was expected to pass. Every day, it seemed, the exam was mentioned, with assurances that I would do well. However, it was clear to me that my parents were bluffing and they were inwardly terrified I would fail. I was dyslexic and struggled at school. I was inundated with extra homework, old exam papers and tests to assess my intelligence. I refused to do any of it, resigned to my fate.

The day of the exam was awful. I walked into the room physically shaking, took one look at the paper and saw nothing but a blur. It was completely incomprehensible. I went home to lunch despondent but not desperate, determined to fight back in the afternoon, only to be greeted by my parents – my mother in tears, my father ashen – telling me I had failed already. I hated myself; I hated the system.

My father tried to persuade me to let him find a better school than the one I was now resigned to, but I stood by my emerging egalitarianism and insisted that I should go to the same secondary modern as all the other children. At the time this gesture seemed commendable; now it seems priggish. Either way, this was the school from hell.

First, everybody there knew they were a failure; already life had made its initial choices, and we were in the second division and not the first. Second, this was a secondary-modern school pretending to be a public school. The headmaster, a Mr Barnes, flounced around wearing his Oxford gown and addressed us daily as though we were at Eton. Life was playing a cruel trick on us: shunted into the bottom drawer, we were put into four houses – Raleigh, Langton, Grenville and Balfour – and were expected to conform to the conventions and prejudices of a genteel public school buried in the leafy lanes of Berkshire.

Third, there was the sadism. The extent of the corporal punishment is hard to exaggerate. It was like an epidemic. Boys were caned in classrooms, in rooms behind classrooms, in lockers, in the hallway. We were caned individually, in groups, outdoors, indoors, upstairs, downstairs. Whole classes were lined up in front of fences for a collective caning. And if the teachers were bad, the boys were worse. I still remember one boy in particular who acted like a young sociopath, beating me up on the bus on the way home from school each night.

Then there was metalwork. Metalwork was at the heart of the school's rationale, preparing people for life not through using their minds, but through using their hands, and we spent two full mornings a week doing it. Mostly, we filed, but sometimes we were allowed to use the lathe. Always it was grindingly, gruesomely boring. One of my favourite lines of poetry remains Henry Reed's 'Japonica glistens like coral in all of the neighbouring gardens, / And today we have naming of parts.'[1] But that was about the waste and frustration of a few weeks' military training. For most people in our metalwork class, if the school had its way, this was a sentence for life. My friends and I endured the misery of these lessons thinking, 'So, this is it, then.' Whenever I hear people talk about vocational schools as opposed to academic schools I still shudder. Most of those who claim to believe in vocational education wouldn't send their own children anywhere near it.

When I was fourteen I was taken to the Royal Aircraft Establishment at Farnborough and shown a great open space that seemed to be just one vast metalwork lesson, full of people filing and lathing and assembling and measuring. The teacher with us looked around with pride and said, 'If you do really well in your O-levels, this will be your future.' And Farnborough was for the children who did well. God only knows what the school had in mind for the majority who would pass no exams. I was horrified: I was looking at the rest of my life. I decided then and there to fail my O-levels and escape, which I did.

I do not mean to disparage those who work in places like the Royal Aircraft metalworks, or their contemporary equivalents; quite the opposite: I admire them. The people I disparage are those who fail to respect the struggle and tedium of most people's lives, which are dominated by work that is boring, unfulfilling and increasingly insecure.

At school I learned to respect people's basic impulse to work hard and try to get on. I began to understand the common-sense responses of 'ordinary' people. I developed sympathy for hard-nosed attitudes on crime and defence. David Owen, in his book *Time to Declare*, describes how, as a student working on a building site, he came to respect the tough, uncompromising views on defence of his fellow workers.[2] This sounds condescending, but Owen was right. I developed a strong populist sense at a very early age that the opinions of the majority should be taken seriously.

Whenever I hear people being criticised for their blinkered and reactionary views on crime, or welfare, or aversion to paying taxes, I always ask silently: have you known the dreadful, repetitive tedium of manual work, not just for the long university holidays, but for life; lived in cramped houses, in communities where walking the streets late at night is not a safe option; known the cancerous insecurity of work as clerks or office administrators, not poor, but never safe, and always worrying about the cost of providing for your family?

I sat in the shadow Cabinet room as the self-interest and materialism that was gripping the electorate in the 1980s was described during a polling presentation. I heard the tut-tutting of disdain from the assembled advisers and officials and thought to myself: you all live in big, comfortable houses, have Tuscan holidays and drive large cars. What do you know about the way ordinary people live?

The secondary modern lacked any ambition for its children. I was told that I did not have the ability to take A-levels. I remember talking to my friends in what purported to be the school library and somebody started to talk about university, explaining that it was a place where people like us, who attended a school like ours, never went. I had no idea what university was, but I was determined to go. Eventually I managed it, but almost no one else did, although nearly everybody in the upper streams was quite capable of doing so. The potential that this school, and others like it, killed or maimed was nothing short of educational genocide. That is why I abhor selection at the age of eleven, but also why I abhor the potential that is still being wasted by a comprehensive system that was so badly flawed in design and execution.

The best thing about school was my friends. Most of them were tough kids: Thatcher's children, although they did not know it yet. John Huntly was sensitive and intelligent and wanted to become a vet, which I am pleased to say he did. He was my fishing and country friend. Most nights we would cycle off after school and find some hidden place to fish, hoping to forget the day. He had the misfortune to be the first in our class to be caned for something he did not do.

The rest of my friends were tough-minded and thick-skinned. Roger Gosden, the son of a carpenter; William Mitchell, a plumber's son; John Stuartson, whose father worked in a factory; Barry Richardson, the son of a soldier. These were not privileged boys, not middle-class. They were what would now be called skilled working-class. They should automatically have been Labour supporters, but they were not, because their fathers all wanted to get on. Roger's dad was endlessly improving his house, adding odd bits and pieces to it that did not really work. They would buy and test the latest offerings of the emerging consumer society. They were beginning to take holidays abroad.

And they were tough about their politics. Every political judgement they made was rooted in hard, uncompromising common sense. With Brett Robinson, the son of a civil servant, I canvassed the whole of Woking, or so it felt, for the 1966 General Election. The tiny, grim, forbidding red-brick houses of Goldsworth; the bigger villas further from the centre of the town; the massive over-spill council estate of Sheerwater; the mishmash of suburban housing in Knaphill and Brookwood. Housing that was not pleasing to the eye because each owner, like Roger Gosden's dad, had tried to put their own stamp on it: small porches erected incongruously over front doors; cheap modern windows clashing with Victorian red-brick walls; different shades of paint which owed no allegiance to the house next door; little extras stuck on to make the houses look better, but making them much worse.

Even then their owners were tough on crime, tough on welfare, tough on the Soviet Union. They were fiercely patriotic, as was I. But in the course of their lives they had felt an almost tangible sense of British decline: the great post-war British confidence and achievements were ebbing away. They believed in fair reward for hard work; in responsibility; in standing on your own two feet. They wanted to get on, and they wanted a better life. Given the life they had, this was not surprising. They were early recruits to the new middle class. They might just have voted Labour in 1966, but it was easy to feel the aspirational appeal of the Conservatives. These were the voices, of my friends and their families, which the left stopped listening to. They were to become the new voice of Britain.

By this time I was enthralled by politics and would spend hours arguing with my friends: arguing for Labour, for fairness, for compassion, for society. This was grinding work – my compassionate values clashing uncomfortably with their hard-nosed ambition and unsentimental view of the world.

It was in this tension – between my soft, inner world of decency, fairness and compassion and my hard, outer world of tough-minded working-class aspiration – that my politics began to be formed. Tough and tender; strong but fair. Already I was becoming a New Labour child.

Competing trajectories

I left school at sixteen with one O-level in geography. The Friday flogger, Tom Lee, begged me to stay, but I was away, and never again – with one exception thirty years later – did I feel a breath of freedom like the one that night when I walked home from school.

Already I was obsessed with politics. I loved canvassing and telling, and attending tiny political meetings addressed by the local Labour candidate, Michael Downing, in deserted church halls. I loved the posters we used to put up, and the leaflets we put through doors. After Harold Wilson won in 1966, I attended the vast rally in the Royal Albert Hall which Wilson addressed and where Kevin McNamara was introduced after his stunning victory in Hull. But even though I loved it, I thought it could never be my life: that was for others, always on the other side of the television screen.

Instead, without any prospects, I decided to join the 1960s. I knew it was happening, and I wanted to be part of it. There was scarcely a political demonstration or rock concert I did not try to attend, a peripheral figure wanting to be part of the times. In Swansea I tried to disrupt the Springboks' rugby tour by running on to the pitch, but made it only to the perimeter fence; at demonstrations in Grosvenor Square I joined in enthusiastically, from the back; in Bath and on the Isle of Wight I sat in the mud and heard distant groans, and thought, 'Why am I here?' I joined Community Service Volunteers, working first in Pontefract with delinquent children, and then in Camberwell with recidivists recently released from long prison sentences. But the people at CSV thought I was using voluntary service as a substitute for life and threw me out. I was seventeen, with one O-level and no money.

I had no obvious prospects, but I still had a dream – a dream of going to university, that place the boys at school had talked about. It took me months of Saturdays poring over prospectuses in Guildford Library to find out that the new University of Sussex accepted students with no O-levels, as long as they had A-levels. I pounced, persuading the East London College that I needed a couple of A-levels to become a social worker. Three years later, with four A-levels and still only one O-level, I got into Sussex.

At a stroke, my life changed. The clouds parted and the sun came out. I studied politics, learned almost nothing, developed few new political ideas and refused to sit many of the exams, but this at last was the beginning of life. I dutifully attended *Das Kapital* reading classes but soon gave up. I knew that capitalism would not lead to revolution, and thought that this was a good thing. I rejected the diatribes of the student Marxists as mad nonsense, completely unconnected to the life I knew. Yet it was the International Socialists and the International Marxist Group who dominated student politics at university. In the face of their rantings I defended bourgeois democracy, even going on Sussex University television to defend the right of the Conservative MP Andrew Bowden to speak on campus. I thought free speech was indivisible and I did not believe that liberty should be so easily tossed away. I was still not fully sure what I believed in, but I knew it was not that. I managed a reasonable degree at Sussex, but I had learned little.

At the London School of Economics, where I completed my Master's degree in political theory, it was different. Here I was taught personally by Michael Oakeshott, the conservative philosopher. I studied Hegel, and for the first time found a system of ideas with which I felt comfortable. I liked Hegel for his concept of the dialectic. I was captivated by the idea of an identity evolving through contradiction and negation: 'To be what it *really* is, it must become what it is not.'[3]

Hegel helped me to resolve the paradox that had consumed my early life: the clash between the competing claims of the individual and the collective. I had explored the ideas of Hobhouse and liberal socialism, but I was unable to resolve the dilemma. Making sense of this relationship was central to Hegel: 'The human being finds his proper identity only in those relations that are in effect the negation of his isolated particularity – in his membership in a group or social class whose institutions, organisation and values determine his very individuality.'[4]

I loved Hegel's language, his ability to evoke a sense of the ebb and flow of ideas: 'When philosophy paints its grey on grey then has a form of life grown old, and with grey and grey it cannot be rejuvenated but only known.'[5] Hegel's idealism appealed to my imagination while Oakeshott's scepticism appealed to my common sense: 'Men sail a boundless and bottomless sea; there is neither harbour for shelter nor floor for anchorage, neither starting place nor appointed destination.'[6]

Hegel and Oakeshott are a good mix: the one seeing life as the unfolding of great ideas, the other as a struggle to get by in a world without meaning. In politics you need both these instincts.

Oakeshott also introduced me to the idea of 'intimation': of emerging change hinted at by early indicators, bringing to the surface deeper movements. 'Events that compose a pattern and at the same time intimate a sympathy for something which does not fully appear.'[7] This view of political change, of subtle intimations heralding the first emergence of deeper political shifts, has remained with me and I look constantly at public opinion for the first signs of subsequent, bigger change. God knows what Oakeshott would have to say about this, but it is one of the things I do in focus groups.

The London School of Economics helped me to formulate the ideas that have shaped my life, but I wanted to move on. I decided to try advertising. I did this to leave for a while the world of duty and responsibility I had come from, and to see another world: to experience capitalism in its rawest form. My father was horrified – to him it was a betrayal of my talent and a pact with the devil. But I learned to love advertising, and came to understand that, although the market is not perfect, for the most part it works reasonably well and often very well. This was the opposite of the conclusion I had expected to find. I went in sceptical of business, I came out a qualified supporter, and at least understood it first-hand.

In 1981 I started my own advertising agency with two friends, Brignull Lebas Gould Limited, which we sold after two years. I remained in advertising for a further twelve months, but I had already decided that I wanted to start working in politics. I went to the London Business School for a year as an escape route, and on 1 June 1985, two months after getting married, sat down at home in Notting Hill and declared my political consultancy open.

I had no money, no clients, no prospects, but one burning goal: to help transform the Labour Party so that it would win elections again. In all this I was spurred on by the words of the Tory PR adviser Tim Bell, who had told me just days before that there would never be another majority Labour government. I have never forgotten those words, never stopped being determined to prove him wrong.

A new Labour life

This, then, was my new Labour life.

A life begun in a land of suburban dreams, among ordinary people asking nothing more than to edge slowly forward in their lives.

A life among working people with growing aspirations, gradually emerging as a new middle class, at that time forgotten by the Labour Party, but becoming the most powerful electoral force in British politics.

A life where I learned of the daily struggle of ordinary families – silent heroes making do, getting by.

It was a life that taught me that the children from my rather shabby, second-rate school, and their children after them, had voices which deserved to be heard, and that when Labour stopped listening to them it lost power and began its long slide into betrayal and extremism. I know the suburban sprawl I came from was an ordinary place full of ordinary people. But it was my place, and they were my people. I come from the land that Labour forgot.

This book is about the post-war journey of the hard-working majority as they moved from austerity to aspiration and demanded a new politics to match their new ambition. And it is about the parallel journey of the Labour Party as it moved, over almost a century, from representing the people, to ignoring the people, to betraying the people, until finally it became the people's party again.

And in a very small way it is about my own personal journey; a journey that began in a family and a community typical of the electorate that the Labour Party had ignored and mislaid, and ended as the voice of that electorate to a party struggling to win back trust.

Mine is a very small part – without me, Labour would still have won on 1 May 1997; Tony Blair would still be Prime Minister; the majority would still be huge – but it is a part that I am proud to have played. For twelve years I was lucky enough to be a voice within the Labour Party, for this new majority in Britain. Not disadvantaged, not privileged, not quite working-class, not really middle-class – they don't even have a name. I will call them the new middle class. I first met them on the streets of Woking thirty years ago. It would take that long for Labour to become their party again.

1

THE CENTURY THAT
LABOUR LOST

The party of the night

On the night of 9 June 1983 I sat alone in my small flat just off the Portobello Road and saw the party I had supported for almost twenty years beaten into humiliating submission. Worse than that, I saw the final betrayal of the people I had grown up with, the people the Labour Party had been formed to serve but whom it had abandoned. Labour had not merely stopped listening or lost touch: it had declared political war on the values, instincts and ethics of the great majority of decent, hard-working voters. Where were the policies for my old school-friends – now with families and homes of their own – in a manifesto advocating increased taxes, immediate withdrawal from the EEC, unilateral disarmament, a massive extension of public ownership and exchange and import controls?

This assault on the hopes and aspirations of Labour's ordinary working-class supporters resulted in a massive electoral defeat. Labour lost a quarter of its 1979 vote. Its 9.3 per cent fall in the national vote was the sharpest collapse suffered by a major party at any election since 1945. At 27.6 per cent, its support was the lowest since 1918. It won only 3 of the 176 seats in the south outside London.[1] The land that Labour forgot had taken its revenge.

The result, described by Tony Benn as 'a remarkable development by any standards',[2] was in many respects the worst performance in Labour's history. Labour lost the young: the largest swing to the Conservatives was among first-time voters,[3] who were to become Thatcher's Praetorian Guard, keeping her, and the Conservatives, in power for the next political generation. It lost the working class: the swing to the Conservatives was 4 per cent among unskilled manual workers; no other social class moved as far.[4] It even lost the trade unionists, where the swing to the Conservatives was 8 per cent.[5] The party of the working class and trade unionism had driven its traditional supporters into the arms of their historic enemy.

Labour had become so disconnected from the people it sought to serve that it appeared to inhabit a parallel universe. At a time when 90 per cent of working-class voters favoured a ban on secondary picketing, 79 per cent of manual workers wanted council houses to be sold off, and 56 per cent of working-class voters favoured cuts in both social security payments to strikers' families and income tax rates for people with large incomes,[6] Labour was seen to offer higher taxes, less freedom, less wealth, more strikes, less security.

Labour damaged itself almost beyond repair in 1983. Three images of the party were dominant in the election: division, extremism and weakness. Among defectors from Labour, a third gave 'extremism within the Labour Party' as one of their reasons for voting Conservative, a quarter said 'disunity'.[7] Only 13 per cent picked Michael Foot as the best potential Prime Minister. Nearly two-thirds picked him as the worst.[8] Little can be understood about subsequent Labour politics unless the full extent of the damage in 1983 is understood. To millions of voters Labour became a shiver of fear in the night, something unsafe, buried deep in the psyche, not just for the 1983 election campaign or the period immediately after it but for years to come. Like a freeze-frame in a video, Labour's negative identity became locked in time.

For the next fourteen years, indeed until the very last days of the 1997 election campaign, Labour became a party to be feared. One woman said to me just weeks before the 1997 election, 'When I was a child there was a wardrobe in my bedroom. I was always scared that one night, out of the blackness, a monster would emerge. That is how I think of the Labour Party.'[9] This was typical. This woman was an ordinary working mother. And she was not alone in her fear. Labour had become the party of the shadows; of deep, irrational anxiety. Only modernisation would save it.

Labour's unique decline

The scale of Labour's collapse in 1983 was not only unprecedented in British terms, it was unique internationally. All around the world – from Australia to France, from Canada to West Germany – in the face of global recession in the early 1980s, incumbent governments were crashing to defeat. But in Britain the Conservatives were easily re-elected. In part this was due to the potency of the Thatcher government, recently strengthened by success in the Falklands. But the condition of the Labour Party in 1983 was just as important. The party had become an anachronism, a relic of the past trying to appeal to an electorate whose sights were set on the future. Although the post-war period had been dominated by the most extraordinary and unprecedented pace of change, other progressive parties had managed to adapt. From the 1940s to the mid-1980s, the world's leading twenty-two parties of the left lost only 2 per cent of their support. Within this, the social democrat and socialist vote fell by just 1.5 per cent.[10] Globally the left held up. It survived massive change with marginal loss of support.

The one exception was the British Labour Party. In the same forty-year period, Labour's average vote fell from 44.5 per cent to 31.8 per cent.[11] At every election between 1951 and 1983 – with the sole exception of 1966 – Labour's share of the total electorate fell. From a high point of 40.3 per cent in 1951, it had halved to 20.1 per cent by 1983.[12] The reality could hardly be starker: the British Labour Party declined faster and further than almost any other progressive party in the world.

Some of the erosion in Labour's support can be explained by the vast social and occupational changes confronting it in the post-war period. From the 1950s, the number of manual workers fell steadily while the non-manual classes grew. But the decline of Labour's working-class base does not fully explain the drop in its support. From 1951 to 1983, Labour's vote should have fallen by 11 percentage points as a result of the diminishing working class, but in fact it fell by a full 18 percentage points. Labour lost support dramatically *within* the working class: from 63 per cent in 1951 to 38 per cent in 1983.[13]

This decline reflected deeper changes in the working class: it was not only smaller, it was becoming upwardly mobile. In 1949, 21 per cent of men were in a higher occupational class than their fathers; by 1983 this figure had almost doubled.[14] And by 1983, 53 per cent of working-class fathers had sons in non-manual work.[15] The problem for Labour was that upwardly-mobile children were far less inclined to vote Labour; they felt they had moved on while Labour hadn't. The threat of occupational mobility was also linked to the challenge of geographic mobility, as people moved from the industrial north to service-based jobs in the south.[16]

The picture in 1983, then, was of a smaller, upwardly-mobile, more southern-based working class, with a vast increase in the number of routine non-manual workers. The point could not be plainer: there was a new majority in Britain – new working-class voters, new middle-class voters. And year on year Labour and this new majority were parting company. Labour was dragging behind; they were surging ahead. Labour had forgotten its purpose. As one voter in a focus group said in the early 1990s, 'Labour has left me, and I have left Labour.'[17] Most of the children I went to school with would no more have voted Labour in 1983 than flown to the Moon. Quite simply, they had too much common sense.

New times had come, but Labour was still the party of failed solutions, still the party of trade-union domination and state control. At the 1980 Labour conference Tony Benn was the authentic voice of a party trapped by its past:

> I believe that we shall require three major pieces of legislation within the first month of the election of another Labour government, and I will tell conference what I believe those pieces of legislation are. First, an Industry Bill, which will give powers to extend public ownership as requested by the GMWU [National Union of General and Municipal Workers], to control capital movements as requested by the GMWU, to provide for industrial democracy as has been suggested and demanded by the GMWU, and that Industry Bill must be on the Statute Book within a matter of days after the election of a Labour government.

He went on to demand a Bill to transfer all powers back from the Common Market to the House of Commons, and the immediate abolition of the House of Lords.[18]

Labour's failure was doubly sad because it was neither inevitable nor replicated elsewhere. All over the world progressive parties were facing comparable demographic challenges, but only the British Labour Party lost support on such a scale over such an extended period of time. This stubborn refusal to modernise was unique to the British Labour Party, buried deep in its character, its ethos, implicit even in its founding moments.

A party born old

Labour was founded in 1900 at the dawn of a new century, in which Britain and much of the world became fully democratic, people gained increasing control over their lives and mass consumption of material goods became commonplace. In the twentieth century power shifted from the privileged to the people. Yet this was the century in which the people's party was marginalised. Labour has governed for just twenty of the last hundred years, the Conservatives for seventy. And Labour has never managed a full second term.

The Conservatives stole the people's century from the people's party because they modernised while Labour did not. As Anthony Seldon has written, 'In its constant quest to gain and hold on to power, the [Conservative] party regularly adapted itself to apparent changes in public preference. The Conservatives have been far more successful in capturing working-class support than the Labour Party has been in colonising the middle class.'[19]

This echoed Disraeli, who said in a speech in 1867, 'Change is inevitable in a progressive country. Change is constant.'[20] This is the central paradox of modernisation: the party of conservatism held power because of its ceaseless modernisation, the party of radical change lost power because of its conservatism.

The answer to this paradox lies deep in Labour's past, for the seeds of its decline were imbedded in its inception. Labour was born a conservative party: it was too close to trade unionism; too obsessive about public ownership; too tied to myth; too rooted in the past. David Marquand summarises this as 'the complex mix of assertiveness and defensiveness, of secular fragmentation and group loyalty, which has shaped Labour's tradition and contributed to the paradoxical conservatism of the labour movement'.[21] The paradox of Labour conservatism flows directly from the forces that helped create it.

The first force was Fabianism: a blend of gradualism, Marxism and Utopianism which has been central in providing what has been called the 'ideology of "Labourism".'[22] Fabianism didn't make Labour a statist party, but it helped. Influenced by newly translated editions of *Das Kapital* and the writings of William Morris, Fabianism helped to ensure that Labour's dominant intellectual tendency was collectivist, squeezing out more liberal and pluralist alternatives, and leaving a progressive legacy that was unbalanced in favour of the state. Marquand describes this as 'one of the main historical causes of the decline of social democracy'.[23] An understandable emphasis on collective action in the face of poverty exposed by the recession of the 1880s 'had in practice degenerated into a bureaucratic form of social engineering'.[24] Fabianism alone was not responsible for Labour's long obsession with nationalisation and public ownership, but it certainly helped.

The second creative force behind Labour was religion. Religious language and metaphor abounded in the party's founding years. Ben Pimlott writes: 'The Socialist Commonwealth was more than merely analogous to the second coming: in the imagination of speakers and audiences there was a blurring and a merging of the two.'[25] In the view of Shaw Desmond, an early Independent Labour Party orator, Labour had become a 'faith' rather than a 'politic' movement.[26] This fusing of religion and politics generated a sense of mythic destiny: victory will be ours if no compromise is made; if we are true to our principles we will reach the New Jerusalem, not *despite* suffering and setback but *because* of them. Out of this grew the preference for glorious defeat, the fear that victory can be won only at the price of compromise.

Trade unionism was the third inspirational force. Labour was essentially founded by the trade unions to represent their interests. Marquand writes: 'In a sense not true of its social democratic counterparts on the mainland of Europe, [Labour] has been a trade union party, created, financed and, in the last analysis, controlled by a highly decentralised trade union movement.'[27] Growing rapidly in numbers, attracting thousands of working-class people, trade unions had a robustness and common sense which the other Labour organisations lacked. But they were also the source of organisational rigidity and the block vote, and they were born of cautious, defensive progress. By nature more sectional and inward-looking than their continental cousins, British trade unions were rooted in crafts not industry, battered by hostile legislation in the 1890s and in 1906. They were not intrinsically modernising institutions.

Union influence was both organisational and financial. It has been estimated that the political levy raised £35 million at today's prices between 1914 and 1927.[28] In return for this money, the unions controlled the Labour Party machinery. A majority of National Executive members were elected nominally by conference, but in reality by the unions. From its inception, the Labour Party was 'an electoral machine based on the might of the trade union finance and its block vote at conference'.[29] This had advantages, but there was a high price to pay. Discipline was gained, but flexibility and the influence of ordinary party members was weakened. The capacity to modernise and adapt was to be the ultimate casualty.

The final element in the conservatism of the Labour Party is more human, rooted in the culture and psychology of the British working class. In H. M. Drucker's view, Labour's ethos as a party – its caution, its conservatism, 'its characteristic values and traditions' – derived directly from 'British working-class experience'. 'Labour's organisational and financial procedures, its attitude towards its leaders, even the personal style displayed by its politicians – all . . . are reflections of the party's distinctive working-class ethos.'[30] According to Drucker, the defining values of Labour 'arose from a collective experience of exploitation and from the gradual construction of defensive organisations'.[31] This made the party cautious, defensive and backward-looking. Drucker believes that Labour's sense of its past is 'so central to its ethos that it plays a crucial role in defining what the party is about to those in it'.[32]

All these forces – Fabianism, trade unionism, religion and a defensive working-class culture – blended to produce a party intrinsically resistant to change. This conservatism is the ultimate explanation for Labour's failure to dominate the century. It is the reason why Labour declined in the post-war period while progressive parties in other countries did not. Marquand makes this clear: 'In world terms Labourism is the exception, not the rule.'[33] Other possible options, which were still open at the start of the century, were closed down in 1918, when a new constitution, drafted by Sidney Webb and Arthur Henderson, was adopted.

It had at its core Clause IV, with the commitment to public ownership:

> To secure for the workers by hand or by brain the full fruits of their industry, and the most equitable distribution thereof that may be possible, upon the basis of the common ownership of the means of production, distribution and exchange, and the best obtainable system of popular administration and control of each industry or service.[34]

Later in 1918, at a second conference, the party accepted 'Labour and the New Social Order', the party's first extended declaration of its aims and values. This called for 'a genuinely scientific reorganisation of the nation's industry, no longer deflected by industrial profiteering, on the basis of the Common Ownership of the Means of Production'.[35] These documents, G. D. H. Cole wrote, 'unequivocally committed the Labour Party to socialist objectives'.[36] Egon Wertheimer claimed they marked Labour's transition from 'social reform to socialism'.[37]

In establishing itself as a socialist party immutably linked to trade unionism, Labour broke with Liberalism and cut itself off from the other great radical movement in British politics. The separation of Labourism and Liberalism stopped dead the possibility of building one united progressive party, similar to the broader coalitions in the United States and Scandinavia. The division of the left gave the Conservatives a dominance in government which their electoral support rarely justified. It also meant that the collectivist instincts dominating Labourism could not be ameliorated by the individualism and plurality of the Liberal tradition. Inevitably Labour's intellectual compass became unbalanced, tilting too far towards the state, away from the individual. This had always frustrated me: I wanted Liberalism and socialism to mesh, but it took me a very long time to see how it could be done.

One further nail in Labour's modernising coffin was added

thirteen years later, in August 1931, when Ramsay MacDonald turned his back on his party and his Cabinet to form the National Government, which immediately destroyed Labour in a General Election. Described by Clement Attlee, then at the War Office, as the 'greatest betrayal in the political history of the country',[38] the National Government etched fear of betrayal deep into Labour's soul, heightening suspicion of change and adaptation.

Taken together, trade unionism, fundamentalism, utopianism and fear of betrayal were almost bound to make Labour resistant to modernisation, but they also, in another great paradox, left Labour prey to extremism. The comparative failure of Labour governments in the 1960s and 1970s was due in large measure to their inability or unwillingness to modernise either the party or the country. Yet their failure was seen by many in the party not as the failure of modernisation that it actually was but as yet another betrayal of party and principle by Labour's leadership. Their answer was not further modernisation, but yet more ideological purity, which resulted in extremism. It was perhaps inevitable that a party so infused with dogmatic certainty, so rooted in the myth of glorious defeat, would both precipitate the failure of Labour governments and then interpret that failure through the ideological prism that helped to bring failure about.

This is not to say that everything about Labour was ill-judged or reactionary – of course it was not. Labour was born from the quiet courage of generations of people who wanted the world to be a better, different place. It was born of idealism and vision and was to achieve an enormous amount. In 1945 it gave us probably the greatest reforming government of the century, which created a welfare state that gave life-changes and opportunity to millions of people. It is the party of decency, compassion, fairness and justice. But it is also a party created in a culture of caution and deference with an overbearing sense of its past: part political party, part religious movement, fuelled by a sense of destiny, accepting glorious defeat and fearing awful betrayal. For many, Michael Foot was not a leader who tried but failed woefully, but a martyr, a champion to 'the cause'. Too many saw him as Gwyn Williams did: 'There he stands, Member for Ebbw Vale, bone of our old bone, blood of our very blood, in his white hair and his cheekbones, his humanity, his generosity, his literacy and his stick, the only legitimate heir in the apostolic succession.'[39]

The circumstances of its birth made Labour a great and complicated party, earning and deserving of intense loyalty, brave in the face of adversity. But they also made it a party unlike other radical parties: conservative by instinct, destined to allow the people's century to slip through its fingers, betraying not its historic principles but the people who believed it was founded in their name.

Attlee's success

From 1918 until the fall of Clement Attlee's government in 1951 Labour's ideological consensus, which was rooted in public ownership and 'Labourism', held. The 1945 government was a massive achievement, reforming large parts of Britain's society and economy. It was able to do so because of the peculiar circumstances in which it was elected. Built on the foundations of war, national purpose, coalition and the alliance of both liberal and socialist intellectual and policy strands, it was less a Labour government than a progressive grouping which brought together not one intellectual tradition but several. Crucially, the success of the 1945 government was enhanced by its willingness to draw on the wider progressive agenda of the previous twenty years. As Tony Blair said in his speech to the Fabian Society on the fiftieth anniversary of the 1945 election victory, 'The reality . . . is that the Labour government's agenda grew out of the coalition government of the war.'[40] And it was a genuinely radical coalition that entered Downing Street. The liberal ideas of Beveridge and Keynes were the cornerstones of its reforms. The new liberal inheritance was as important as the Fabian, guild socialist or Marxist tradition. Despite the nationalisations, despite the instinct for planning, despite the singing of 'The Red Flag', the Attlee administration followed a progressive path which for a long time enjoyed the confidence of the liberal left. In many ways it was a one-nation government, utilising the patriotic fervour which had guided the war in the new campaign for social justice – 'Now Let Us Win the Peace'. For a time the Labour Party was truly the people's party, but this did not last. It was a successful government, but it survived for only six years and let in a Conservative government which lasted for thirteen. In part this resulted from exhaustion and unavoidable circumstance. But there were deeper problems related to its failure to modernise. In his speech on the Attlee administration, Tony Blair listed three main weaknesses: 'First, a failure to recognise fully the realities of the new world order, manifested in the attitude of the government towards Europe; second, a reluctance to modernise the institutions of government itself – what Kenneth Morgan calls the Labour government's "stern centralism"; and third, a tendency to look back to the problems of the 1930s, not forward to the challenges of the 1950s.'[41] Even Labour's most successful government was undone, in part, because it looked backwards and not forwards. In 1951 the radical coalition collapsed. Nye Bevan's resignation over NHS charges and ideological struggle with Hugh Gaitskell amid the dying embers of the Attlee government set the stage for the revisionist battles of the 1950s.

The first voices of modernising dissent had been heard as early as the 1930s. In 1937 Douglas Jay wrote that socialists had been 'mistaken in making ownership of the means of production . . . the test of socialisation'.[42] He was joined by Hugh Gaitskell and Evan Durbin in a group of Oxford-educated and London-based intellectuals, who met under the auspices of the New Fabian Bureau which had been founded in 1931 by G. D. H. Cole.[43]

Defeat in 1951 strengthened revisionism, the first modernising tendency within the party. Revisionism has been defined as 'synonymous with some form of reinterpretation of doctrine so critical as to amount (in the eyes of orthodoxy) to heresy or deviation'.[44] This captures the essential flavour of revisionist dissent within the Labour Party: it is not disagreement, it is heresy – a challenge to the legitimacy of the myth.

W. H. Greenleaf describes the nature of this heresy: it is the 'tendency in the Labour Party to accept that the capitalist enemy is not what it was a couple of generations ago, that the economic and social state of affairs has been so altered since the beginning of the century that it is no good continuing to apply automatically perceptions based on the old analysis but necessary rather to think out a new programme relevant to the radically changed circumstances'.[45] In other words, to look at the world afresh and with true eyes. To break through the myth into reality.

Gaitskell's failure

Revisionism proper started in the Labour Party in 1952, with the publication of *New Fabian Essays*, and gathered pace in 1956 with Anthony Crosland's major work, *The Future of Socialism*. It only gained full political expression with Gaitskell's accession to the party leadership in 1955. This gave rise to what Lewis Minkin called Labour's 'revisionist metamorphosis'.[46]

Revisionism was based around two ideas. First, it disputed the fundamentalist conception that, in Samuel Beer's words, public ownership is 'an indispensable condition and a major expression of a radically transformed economy, society and culture',[47] replacing it with Crosland's view that 'the ownership of the means of production has ceased to be the key factor which imparts to a society its essential character.'[48] And, second, it defined socialism in what have become known as ethical terms: putting values and ideals above means. In emphasising 'personal liberty, social welfare and social equality' as the true essence of socialism, collectivist means and public ownership were relegated to secondary importance.[49]

The election defeat of 8 October 1959 persuaded many of the urgent need to modernise the Labour Party. In his diaries, Tony Benn describes seeing 'Roy Jenkins on *Panorama* advocating very modestly that you should drop nationalisation, watch out for the dangers of the union links and not rule out an association with the Liberals. He dropped in here on his way back home and we had a flaming row.'[50] But Benn discovered the next day that Richard Crossman, a leading intellectual on the left, agreed with Jenkins that nationalisation would have to be abandoned.

Revisionism soon came to mean, however, more than dissenting political voices. It was encapsulated in a defining political moment: the first, failed attempt to change Clause IV. On 28 November 1959 Gaitskell made a speech which foreshadowed Tony Blair's of 1994, thirty-five long years later. Gaitskell began in modernising terms: society and the economy were changing, and Labour had to change too. Labour, he said, had to adapt itself, 'to be in touch always with ordinary people to avoid becoming small cliques of isolated, doctrine-ridden fanatics, out of touch with the main stream of social life in our time'. He argued that nationalisation was a vote-losing issue, in terms of both performance and intention. Performance, he said, was central and the people would judge Labour by it: 'Our fellow citizens are more likely to judge the value of the public sector by their experience of it than from theoretical arguments in speeches or Labour Party pamphlets.'

Gaitskell argued that confusion over policy presentation had led to confusion over intention. Countless voters had been led 'to think that we intended to nationalise any and every private firm . . . simply out of a doctrinaire belief in public ownership'. And he went on to attack Clause IV: 'Standing as it does on its own, this cannot possibly be regarded as adequate. It lays us open to constant misrepresentation . . . It implies that we propose to nationalise everything, but do we? Everything? The whole of light industry, the whole of agriculture, all the shops – every little pub and garage? Of course not.' Finally, he insisted that Labour had to be a modern, forward-looking party: it was 'no use waving the banners of a bygone age'. He urged Labour's National Executive Committee to 'try to work out and state the fundamental principles of British democratic socialism as we see and as we feel it today, in 1959, not 1918'.[51]

Gaitskell was defeated and Clause IV stood. He was beaten by a combination of fundamentalism and the block vote. Harold Wilson said, 'We were being asked to take Genesis out of the Bible.'[52] Trade union leader Frank Cousins said, 'We can't have nationalisation without socialism, we can't have socialism without nationalisation.'[53] In the face of the conservative forces ranged against him, Gaitskell had no choice but to back down.

Failure to change Clause IV was symbolic, but much more important was the general failure of modernisation to break through in the late 1950s. At the time it was clear that significant sections of the party leadership knew what had to be done. Labour had to adapt, reconnect with ordinary people and drop its dogmatic attachment to nationalisation. This happened in Germany in 1959 at the Bad Godesberg Congress, where the German socialist party renounced Marxism in favour of social democracy. The language used by Gaitskell in public and others in private is uncannily similar to that used by Tony Blair and other modernisers a generation later. But it was to take a quarter of a century and the political collapse of Labour before these simple modernising truths could be accepted. Looking back now, I still feel a lingering sadness that the people and the party came so close to connecting but then were wrenched so inexorably apart.

Wilson's fudge

The early 1960s saw modernisation trying to break free, conservatism trying to restrain it. Harold Wilson's response was to choose neither tendency but to try to reconcile them both. Essentially he chose to fudge. Wilson was the first political leader I saw speak in public and he was tremendously exciting. Remembering him now, I see him in 1960s colour, while Gaitskell remains rooted in 1950s black and white. The irony of Wilson was that he appeared modern, but was in no sense a moderniser, which made him a frustrating and ultimately unsuccessful politician.

Wilson was always trying to bridge the gap between left and right, flitting from one to the other, persuading each that his loyalties lay with them. In April 1951, he tilted leftwards by resigning alongside Nye Bevan over the 'teeth and spectacles' issue, but then he moved to the right to replace Bevan when he resigned his shadow Cabinet seat in 1954. But the Gaitskellites were wrong to see Wilson as one of them, just as the Bevanites had been earlier.

Wilson's trimming to left and right was reflected in his first Cabinet in 1964. While senior positions went to former Gaitskellites such as Jim Callaghan and George Brown, the left was also rewarded. Senior left-wingers like Anthony Greenwood, Frank Cousins and Barbara Castle all came in from the cold. During his premiership, Wilson also fostered the next generation of left-wingers, including Michael Foot and Tony Benn.

In the face of continued tension between left and right, Wilson attempted to fuse the two wings of the party with a positioning of such brilliance that it would blind anyone caring to look for the join. His central insight was to link socialism to science. Britain was undergoing a scientific revolution, unleashing vast new technological and industrial forces. As he wrote in his preface to the Labour Party document 'Science and the Future of Britain', 'The central feature of our post-war capitalist society is the scientific revolution.'[54] And this revolution had to be planned. Planning meant public ownership.

At a stroke, Wilson transformed the debate. Public ownership was new, modern, scientific, state-of-the-art. It was part of the meritocratic, technocratic revolution which would regenerate Britain. But ultimately it was all a deceit, a compromise. As Keith Middlemas observed, 'What had really occurred . . . resembled the dosing of a malarial patient with quinine: the symptoms disappeared but the party was not really strengthened, nor were its ideological fevers cured.'[55] Ironically Wilson's one great modernising act – the attempt to reform the trade unions through 'In Place of Strife', published in January 1969 – failed because it united left and right against him. The conservatism of Jim Callaghan joined forces with the leftism of Tony Benn and the new trade-union radicalism of Jack Jones of the Transport and General Workers' Union; Hugh Scanlon of the Engineers' Union; and Lawrence Daly, General Secretary of the National Union of Mineworkers.[56] Once again modernisation was smashed on the rocks. One commentator wrote of Wilson and Barbara Castle, the Secretary of State responsible for 'In Place of Strife', 'Like Gaitskell before them they underestimated both the entrenched interests of trade unions and their collective ethos of labourism which valued solidarity above everything else – even economic efficiency.'[57]

Wilson failed to modernise Labour, which put the genuine modernisation of Britain beyond his reach. His failure to resolve the competing claims of left and right, and to move beyond both to a new modernising solution, made civil war in the Labour Party inevitable.

The death march

From 1970 onwards, the left began their slow, inexorable assault. Labour's long death march had begun. The centre of gravity inside the party was shifting decisively to the left. In the following two years Labour committed itself to an enormous extension of public ownership, into areas such as banking, insurance and building societies and the construction and ship-building industries. The NEC (National Executive Committee) policy statement, 'Labour's Programme 1973', 'amounted to a clear repudiation of a revisionist social democratic approach', according to Tudor Jones, and called for 'a fundamental and irreversible shift in the balance of power and wealth in favour of working people and their families'.[58] The policy statement was described by Michael Foot as 'the finest socialist programme I have seen in my lifetime'.[59]

Enthusiasm for public ownership flourished in the 1974 manifesto and by 1976 Labour's programme demanded 'the extension of public ownership into . . . leading companies in every key sector of industry'.[60]

Meanwhile, the Callaghan government – in office from 1976 to 1979 – struggled to stay on a pragmatic course, while impotent in the face of global economic forces and domestic union power. Labour's failure to modernise reached its nadir with the strikes of the winter of 1978–79, when the dead were left unburied, leading Jim Callaghan to note, eight years later: 'Even with the passage of time I find it painful to write about some of the excesses that took place.'[61]

As the left achieved a new ascendancy, the party began to split. The summer of 1980 was a turning-point, when a special conference at Wembley in May endorsed the fiercely left-wing policy document, 'Peace, Jobs and Freedom', and booed David Owen off the podium for advocating multilateralism. In June of that year, John Silkin, Labour's industry spokesman, announced that he would propose a motion at the next party conference committing a future Labour government to British withdrawal from the EEC. After their joint, angry rebuttal of the idea, David Owen, Shirley Williams and Bill Rodgers became known as the 'Gang of Three'.

The final break came when Michael Foot was elected party leader in November 1980. 'We knew it was all over,' Shirley Williams has said.[62] David Hill, Labour's former chief media spokesperson and one of the few people to have worked closely with every Labour leader since Wilson, says it was an 'appalling' time. Labour politicians, he believes, didn't realise how serious it was: 'In the 1980–83 period everyone was at one another's throats, and everything was crisis management. It was all about Tony Benn fighting Denis Healey [for the deputy leadership of the party]. You got the most extraordinary period of conflict with a party that was unmanageable and a party which did not know how to change its ways, how to modernise itself, how to make itself unified. It needed the shock of the 1983 result to shake it up.'[63]

In January 1981 Roy Jenkins joined the Gang of Three in issuing the 'Limehouse Declaration', which established a Council for Social Democracy as a prelude to the new party, which was founded in March 1981. Within ten days the Social Democratic Party had gained over 40,000 members. 'We were pushing at an open door,' Bill Rodgers said.[64] In Brighton, in Liverpool and in Shipley, local Labour parties were taken over by Bennite apparatchiks. In Bermondsey, Peter Tatchell took over from Bob Mellish as the Labour candidate and turned a safe seat into a 9,000 majority for the Liberals. In London, Ken Livingstone ousted the moderate Andrew McIntosh from the Greater London Council. Four months after its foundation, the SDP came within 1,000 votes of stealing a seat in Warrington, a classic working-class constituency in Labour's heartland. Disenchantment with Labour had spread from the middle classes to the skilled working classes and lower middle classes. Labour's forgotten majority had had enough.

I was torn at this time, angry at the course the Labour Party had taken, understanding the frustrations of those who had left and agreeing with much of what they said. But never for a moment did I consider leaving Labour and deserting to the SDP. In part this was emotional: all my roots, all my instincts belonged to Labour. I was suspicious of the SDP, I sensed in it an elitism, the lack of a true populist politics. But most of all I believed that a new party was the easy solution, not the right one. However successful the SDP was, it could not destroy Labour but only rival it, leading to yet more fragmentation of the left. The one answer was to stay and fight, to change Labour completely and make it the fulcrum of a new progressive politics in Britain. As I sat in my flat on that awful election night of 9 June 1983, watching Labour put to the sword, I resolved that somehow I would make a difference. I would take my revenge. I knew that only modernisation could save the Labour Party – if it could only find a way.

2

SAVING LABOUR

Meeting Mandelson

I first met Peter Mandelson at a dinner party at the flat of my future wife Gail Rebuck in 1984. He was then working for London Weekend Television; I was at the London Business School. Peter struck me as charming, confident and full of life, although even then he displayed the qualities for which he would later become infamous: when another guest made a remark at the dinner table which offended him, he blanked the man for the rest of the evening. And when someone said they were considering joining the SDP, Peter commented, with threatening charm, 'Oh, no, I don't think that would be a very good idea, would it?' His opponent made the mistake of trying to argue his case, but Peter cut him dead. 'The SDP is having its moment in the sun, but it will be Labour that wins in the end,' he said, before adding witheringly, 'In politics, it is best not to follow fashion.'

A year later, at my wedding party, a friend from university, LWT executive Robin Paxton, told me Peter had just been appointed director of campaigns and communications for the Labour Party, and he had hoped to bring him along. I had recently left business school and set up my political consultancy, which I was running from a small bedroom at home. I had no clients and really wanted only one: the Labour Party. Very excited, I told Robin I was desperate to meet Peter, so he arranged a dinner for us the following week.

I went alone to Robin's house in Islington. I was so petrified I cannot even remember who was there. The evening was a complete blur. Peter says now that I didn't look him in the eye once during the entire evening. We made small talk before he turned to me and asked why I wanted to work for the Labour Party. I talked much gibberish, but somehow explained my mission: to transform Labour's image and electability by using modern marketing and communications methods. I remember thinking at the end of the evening that I had completely blown it, but I gave him an eleven-page letter I had written earlier explaining fully what I wanted to do; it was, effectively, a job application. To Peter's eternal credit he ignored my nervousness and decided to back me. 'I was thirty-two. I'd just been appointed to a job about which I had absolutely no idea whatsoever and I had no capacity or ability or experience to do it,' he says.[1] Neither of us fully understood the challenge we were taking on.

Within a few weeks I had written, at Peter's request, another detailed letter outlining some of the problems he seemed to be facing. I thought Labour was failing to get across any clear messages: their objectives seemed muddled, their communications unfocused. They were running an economic campaign at the time called 'Jobs and Industry'. I told Peter they needed to find and repeat simpler messages based around clear objectives: 'Take for example your current major campaign, "Jobs and Industry",' I wrote. 'I know very little about the perceived effectiveness of the campaign, but I would think that there is a very good chance that it will prove much more effective in stimulating support at the grass roots and with party activists, than with projecting a message to the public at large. Does this constitute success or failure? Without a decent set of objectives it is very difficult to tell.' Labour seemed to have cut itself off from the modern communications techniques at its disposal. I added, 'I think I can best help you by doing what you simply haven't time for yourself; by conducting an objective and I hope exhaustive review of all relevant aspects of your communications operation.'[2]

I started work within days. In the next four weeks I interviewed over thirty people, from politicians to journalists to advertising executives, pollsters and direct-mail professionals, among them campaign co-ordinator Robin Cook, Mandelson himself and Labour's new General Secretary, Larry Whitty. I attended campaign meetings, research briefings and presentations, examined piles of documents and publicity material and finally wrote up the report in a fortnight.

Into the abyss

On the day Peter Mandelson arrived at Walworth Road, in October 1985, an employee in the post room tried to feed a colleague rat poison. It was symptomatic of the state of the party: completely demoralised and riven from top to bottom by hatred, rivalry and dissent. Neil Kinnock, who had fought Tony Benn to be elected leader two years earlier, had done his best to modernise Labour, but it had been a slow and painful process, carried out in the face of constant defiance from the left.

When he walked into the Leader of the Opposition's office at the House of Commons after his election in October 1983, he found 'absolutely nothing', according to Patricia Hewitt, his press secretary at the time. 'We didn't inherit any kind of procedures or knowledge or view of how things were done. Literally, there was nothing. The party was a shambles. Policy was not particularly high on the agenda. What we inherited was a situation in which the party had gone off in one direction, and the parliamentary party had gone off in a totally different direction.'[3] Neil Kinnock was a moderniser, but a moderniser rooted in the valleys of Wales. He was a man who, as a boy, wanted to be a miner, and now had a home in Wales, a lovely home in west London, and children who were going to go to university. He was a part of the Welsh working class who had made good thanks to the welfare state. From the very start he had fought extremism within the Labour Party, and his hatred of extremists was to be a consistent part of his modernising identity. Where his modernisation was ambivalent was in relation to the policies and values of the party, where he was torn between the need for Labour to change and his instinctive and emotional attachment to the Labour Party of his youth.

Yet he was determined to reform Labour. In his leadership campaign speech he had identified two areas – Europe and the sale of council houses – where Labour policy had to be changed. Seeing himself as a unifying leader, he set up joint policy committees combining Parliamentary Labour Party (PLP) and National Executive Committee (NEC) members to try to make them work together. He created the Campaign Strategy Committee (CSC), which he chaired, whose membership included NEC, shadow Cabinet and PLP members, as well as trade union general secretaries. He brought in fresh, young faces to the leader's office, to create a dynamism whose momentum would, he hoped, spread and mobilise the entire party.

But before they could get to grips with anything, the miners' strike began. Charles Clarke, Neil's chief of staff, remembers Arthur Scargill coming to London to see Neil in the autumn of 1983. 'Neil said to Arthur at that time, I remember the meeting, "Have you got a strategy? Are you clear what you are trying to do?" And it was clear from that point that Arthur Scargill had no strategy to actually win the dispute, he simply wanted the dispute.' The issue ran on through 1984, dominating, with 'one member, one vote' (OMOV), the Labour Party conference that year, and only ending in March 1985. 'It made it very difficult to open up other ideological challenges in the way that we wished to do,' said Clarke. 'We were forced on to the defensive against the leftists. There was a very natural solidarity with the strike which people throughout the Labour movement felt, and it made it very difficult to promote other changes, both organisational and policy-based.' Neil had wanted to deflect media attention away from division in the Labour Party on to the policy issues themselves; the strike cost him dear in terms of time. 'It played the old aspects of the party back to their most recidivist approaches. On any issue of proposed change you had a massive coalition around the miners against that change, which in some cases threatened victory on the issue itself,' said Clarke.[4]

The strike also hurt Kinnock personally. Coming from a mining community himself, his cousins, uncles and friends were all on the picket line. 'He couldn't do anything to undermine them,' said Hewitt, 'and politically he wasn't going to do anything that would enable Scargill and the left to blame him for the defeat of the strike, although his political judgement told him from the outset that this was a strike that was going to be lost. He couldn't say any of what he felt, and you can hear it in his voice. He sounds so strangulated in the interviews.'[5]

Kinnock's leadership took another huge step back when his attempt to introduce 'one member, one vote' for selecting parliamentary candidates was defeated at the 1984 conference. His failure to change the constitution and reduce the block-vote power of the unions set back modernisation by ten years. Clarke believes it was the key issue on which the Kinnock leadership went wrong:

> We lost really by two people in the T&G [TGWU] delegation and one person in UCAT. We were complacent because shortly before the Labour Party conference in 1984, in September, Ron Todd and Moss Evans, the then General Secretary and then incoming General Secretary of the T&G, came to Neil and said, 'You don't have to worry, the T&G vote is there.' They both said it, the outgoing and incoming general secretaries, they said you don't have to worry. And we did not work hard enough at getting that vote and so we lost the vote – and that was a terrible mistake which I bear a great deal of the responsibility for. We should have won. This was 1984 remember, and it was a long time, nearly ten years, before change finally went through. That was a terrible failure.[6]

By the time of the next party conference, in Bournemouth in

1985, the fight against Militant had exploded, and Kinnock turned on them: 'Implausible promises don't win victories. I'll tell you what happens with impossible promises. You start with far-fetched resolutions. They are then pickled into a rigid dogma, a code, and you go through the years sticking to that, outdated, misplaced, irrelevant to the real needs, and you end in the grotesque chaos of a Labour council – a *Labour* council – hiring taxis to scuttle round a city handing out redundancy notices to its own workers . . . You can't play politics with people's jobs.'[7]

The party was therefore at war when Peter Mandelson arrived to run an expanded communications department. 'You had party machinery and personnel without leadership, management or purpose, which needed to be professionalised. You had a communications operation which was wholly discredited and demoralised,' Mandelson remembers.

> There was almost a complete absence of interaction between the various elements – policy, organisation, communication. The physical arrangements summed up the situation, down to the unstable chair I had to sit on at a table which had three legs and was propped up against a filing cabinet, beside which was a decaying spider plant and a World War Two-style office telephone. You went in there and it was like being hit in the face by a cross between a blancmange and a brick wall. A blancmange in the sense that you couldn't really get hold of what it was that you were working in or for, and a brick wall because it was intractable, without dynamism or momentum. That was why in the first six months I was so anxious and sleepless.[8]

The interviews I did in the autumn of 1985 revealed an astonishing morass of communications networks within the party: committee upon group upon committee, leading to a chaos of indecisiveness, one-upmanship, hedging and ultimate stagnation. The situation, two years after Kinnock's election as leader and, as it turned out, barely eighteen months before the next General Election, was ludicrous. Apart from the NEC, the CSC and the leader's office, there was a Polling Committee, a Press and Publicity Committee, a Jobs and Industry Campaign Group, a Social Policy Campaign Group, an NHS Campaign Group, the Breakfast Group – a media relations/advertising group, which did not exist officially because the NEC, in one member's words, 'does not admit of the need for advertising as yet and takes a dim view of advertising and related personnel'[9] – as well as the polling organisation MORI and the – *ad hoc* – General Election group, known as the GE Sherpas.

Advertising experts who worked with Labour at this time told me they were contacted by a variety of people from different departments, including Neil Kinnock's office, all asking them to produce unconnected advertisements with no apparent overall strategy. Mandelson had no idea Kinnock's office had been commissioning advertisements. 'Anarchy reigns,' he said resignedly when I told him. 'The leader's office thinks it's very special and over and above all forms of bureaucratic accountability and control. It is the leader's office.'[10]

'Organisational madness' was how MORI's Bob Worcester, who had worked with Labour for over ten years, described it. 'In my experience, I have had conflicting instructions from the head of press and publicity, the Prime Minister [Jim Callaghan] and the General Secretary, all of whom have told me to do something different. There are no clear lines of authority and responsibility.' The worst campaign strategically, he thought, was actually 1979, when there were two groups, one of which (the White Room group) was headed by Ivor Crewe:

> In the 1979 election, you had the White Room group who were doing some advertising [and] PR, research people, and you had the Transport House group, of which I was a part, and literally on the day before the election, this group working with the Campaign Strategy Committee, dealing with them every day, you had those guys being faced with an alternative final-day advertising strategy and set of ads. And in a room over at the St Ermin's Hotel I witnessed an industrial relations guy called Michael Callaghan

being shown two alternative advertising executions and someone saying, 'Michael, which one do you think your dad would prefer?' That was forty-eight hours before the General Election.[11]

The 1983 campaign was also a shambles: Michael Foot's driver used to wander in to the strategy meetings if he felt like it.[12] Roy Hattersley went to see Foot ten days before the election and told him he wasn't communicating for the television age. Foot told him there was no way, in the final ten days, after all these years, he could change his ways and he was going to carry on as he was.[13] A small advertising agency, Wright & Partners, was only appointed the day after the election was called, giving it no time to prepare. The election broadcasts were 'a disaster', thought Patricia Hewitt, who had unsuccessfully fought the Leicester East seat during the election. 'After Neil appointed me, I sat down and watched them, and I thought if I had actually watched them while I was a candidate, I probably would have resigned halfway through the election. They were dreadful, dire.'[14]

The press office and the publishing and marketing division were 'in mayhem', Mandelson said. The campaigns were under-resourced, the staff over-stretched and demoralised. Major speeches and policy statements were receiving little or no coverage, drowned out by the noise from Arthur Scargill, Derek Hatton and Bernie Grant, and Kinnock's attempts to fight the left. The best publicity Labour received in the whole of 1985 was Neil Kinnock's conference speech attacking Hatton and the Militant Tendency in Liverpool. But, powerful and effective though it was, it did not display a positive agenda – a reason to vote Labour. 'Why are lunatics like Derek Hatton and Arthur Scargill continually rampaging around?' Mandelson asked exasperatedly. 'They have got to be rebuffed and neutralised.'[15]

Campaigns lacked clarity, force and impact; policies were overshadowed by the actions of left-wingers. 'We've got to get away from the idea that campaigning is just about an NHS ambulance, a sticker saying "I Love the Welfare State" and the launch of a charter,' Peter told me in 1985. 'Time, political constraints, lack of intellectual rigour, distractions, being embroiled in this, that and the other – who's got the time or the will or the energy to cut through and develop one or two key thoughts, statements, messages which we want to ram home by constant repetition? The idea of image-making comes hard to the Labour Party, because they're more interested in their product, they're more interested in getting over the nitty-gritty of their social welfare policy or their investment policy, or their exchange control policy.' Health, social services, housing, law and order and benefits were all very important issues for Labour, which needed to be addressed. 'In addressing them what we have got to do is: (a) have something relevant to say by way of policy which is attractive and not off-putting – which is very hard when it comes to law and order and Bernie Grant in one sentence eclipses everything that we have to say which is worthwhile about law and order. And (b) we have to say it loudly and repetitively. And we have to present an image of the party, or messages or use language or whatever, that chimes in with what people want to think. And that's what I think we've found very difficult to do.'

He pinpointed defence and the economy as easy issues for the Tories to use against Labour. 'We've got to acknowledge our vulnerabilities. It's not just a question of having a neat little formulation extracted from some document placed before the Home Policy Committee of the NEC, or some neat way of saying: "You're number one with Labour." People are not idiots. There's going to be a lot of biting on bullets.' Mandelson was already infuriated by his lack of control over the media. 'At the end of the day our communications vehicles are TV, radio and newspapers,' he told me. 'They are the uncontrolled media. The Tories are very good at controlling them because a lot of them – newspapers – are politically committed to the Conservatives.'[16]

Although, through Steve Billcliffe at Walworth Road, the party was already doing some direct mailing, there was no targeting of marginal constituencies and the party had only just begun, reluctantly, to release money for qualitative research. Joyce Gould, the Labour Party's director of organisation, and Patricia Hewitt had asked MORI's Bob Worcester to conduct some focus group research for the 'Jobs and Industry' campaign. 'We decided we needed some focus groups on language to see if the voters were understanding a word of what we were saying,' Hewitt said.

> And Bob took out some prompt cards and stuff, and this came back with the wonderful finding that when you said 'public ownership' to the British people, they said, 'That's wonderful.' They were really in favour of public ownership. But when we asked what they thought public ownership meant, they said, 'It means privatisation – selling the shares to us, the public.' We asked what they thought about nationalisation, and they said, 'No, that's a bad idea. That's ownership by the government.' There was a wicked suggestion in one of the campaign strategy meetings that we should brief all our people to talk about public ownership rather than nationalisation.[17]

I was determined to scrap all the conflicting groups and committees and replace them with one central, integrated, professional group, which would run Labour Party communications using all the modern techniques at the disposal of the business world. Mandelson warned that we would face hostility: 'Don't forget that this is a political party. It's a democratic party. All the time in the Labour Party you are boxing with those people on the NEC – to whom at the end of the day we are all ultimately accountable below God – who do not know what we're doing, who, if they did, would oppose it, who are thoroughly ill-disposed towards all these methods and with whom you have to play it very carefully.'[18]

I also had to recommend who should head the committee. Robin Cook and Peter Mandelson had overlapping functions, and Larry Whitty was not yet confident of Mandelson, although he later backed him, quietly facilitating many of the changes Peter made. 'Larry doesn't trust Peter politically,' Whitty's political assistant Tony Manwaring told me.

Peter wasn't Larry's appointment. Larry's been increasingly impressed by Peter's managerial skills, but at a gut political level, he doesn't know whether if a real crunch issue came up – say, for example, the miners vote had gone the wrong way – there were circumstances in which Larry would have felt himself bound to argue for the party and that position against Neil. Larry does have very specific responsibilities to the party. Leaders come and go. The party doesn't, and Larry represents the party and the stability of the party. And there are a number of areas where you could criticise Neil's leadership, where things became issues and we didn't try to stamp them out before they became issues. Neil does do some pretty daft things from time to time.

Whitty should therefore chair the main communications group, Manwaring insisted, exerting some not very subtle pressure: 'I say this never to use it as a direct threat, but there is always the underlying thing: who pays the bills for an agency; who finances the whole thing; who's got to give it organisation and resources? The NEC does. And Larry is the person who will have to go to the NEC about it. I mean, you'd never actually say this, but it's an underlying truth that if it ever became an issue and Larry was against it, it would be extremely hard even for Neil to make progress.'[19]

If the interviews uncovered organisational chaos, focus group research was revealing Labour's disastrous electoral situation. On Saturday 23 November 1985, Leslie Butterfield and Paul Southgate from the advertising agency Abbott Mead Vickers, along with Roddy Glen from the Strategic Research Group Ltd, gave an all-day presentation at the offices of the advertising agency TBWA to Labour strategists, including myself, Mandelson, Cook, Hewitt, Chris Powell (managing director of BMP) and Tim Steel. Without a doubt, these research findings were the most important of any presented during the entire period I worked with the Labour Party. They displayed the fault-line between Labour and its potential supporters, the apparently unbridgeable gap between what Labour had become and what the British electorate now wanted. While

Labour was still talking the language of nationalisation, unilateralism and high taxes, the British public was buying council houses and shares in the newly privatised British Telecom and British Petroleum, and revelling in the success of Britain's born-again military might. The presentation constructed a conceptual framework of Labour disqualifying itself from potential voters because it had adopted positions that were beyond what ordinary, decent voters considered reasonable and sensible. The minority agenda of the emerging metropolitan left, of militant rights in welfare, race and gender, was completely divorced from what the British people wanted from a government.

The first key group of voters represented at this meeting – women aged twenty-five to forty-four – delivered a devastating criticism of the Labour Party. These forty-eight women gave us the first definitive proof that Labour had moved beyond the pale for ordinary people. They were frightened: they saw society breaking down and their instinct was to retreat from it into their families. 'There's no morality any more,' they said. 'It's all about greed and hate.' 'You can't trust people if you don't know them. In the old days you could trust them.' 'We've regressed: violence, rapes, murders, riots. It seems to get worse. There's something every day now.' Their response was to look after themselves.

'Where people are feeling that society is threatening and hostile, there's a feeling that the one reliable, predictable thing within such a society is "me and my immediate family",' Butterfield explained. 'A feeling that society's greater hostility means that you've got to look after number one more than ever.' Self-interest was no longer a dirty word; they admitted openly that they looked after themselves first. 'You have to look after yourself these days – no one else will.' 'Your main ambition in life is to better yourself. You can't do that if everyone lives in the same house, gets paid the same, drives the same car.' 'If everyone votes for themselves, the party that gets in will be by far the best for the majority, won't it?' And finally, 'If by voting Tory I'll get a flat or a job then I'll do it. It may be selfish, but I'm not going to vote Labour to get a job for someone in Newcastle. I don't suppose he'd think about me.'

The issues they cared about were therefore those affecting their own personal and financial security: law and order, health, education, inflation, prices and taxation. Defence and the role of minorities within society, two of Labour's big pre-occupations, were at the bottom of the list. Composite motions at party conference on unilateral disarmament and rolling back Tory trade-union legislation were not going to win the electorate over. Even more worryingly, these voters proved to us that Labour had moved itself into the unacceptable left-field of politics. The researchers produced a chart showing an 'acceptable field' of politics where these voters thought debate was reasonable. Beyond this field were the unacceptable right and the unacceptable left. Nearly all Labour's policies were in the unacceptable left-field. Nearly all of the Tories' were in the acceptable centre. The researchers reported comments like: 'The Labour Party are lunatics when it comes to defence'; 'Whenever I think of Labour I think, "Oh no, Arthur Scargill"'; 'Labour waste money on useless things'; 'It's outrageous – they're spending a million pounds on parks for gays and lesbians in Camden'; and, 'What frightens me about the Labour Party is that they are so far to the left that you get union leaders with so many thousands of block votes deciding how the country should be run.' These voters did not even have the language to describe Tory extremism, as they did Labour's. 'When you talked about what was unacceptable on the left, people very quickly translated that into socialism, communism, "reds",' Roddy Glen said. 'When we talked about what was unacceptable on the right, that did not incorporate fascism; they did not have an equivalent terminology for the extreme right in the way that they did for the extreme left.'

The Conservatives were seen as selfish, single-minded, dogmatic and determined, but people said this was what they wanted from a government. Someone like Norman Tebbit – vulgar, aggressive yet fiercely successful, who branded Church of England bishops

Marxists, told the unemployed to 'get on their bike', and attacked Kate Adie as biased – connected with an aspirational electorate as the man to get the job done. This type of strong, uncompromising, harsh leadership was what the electorate would vote for in the secrecy of the polling booth. Most of them described Labour policies in negative terms and Tory policies in positive or neutral language. 'The majority feel that there is a lack of positive policies that come from the Labour Party that relate to ordinary, working people with their own homes,' Glen said. While Labour was seen as being good for the poor, unemployed and needy, the Tories were understood to be good for everyone else – including 'me'. These women – a combination of Tory and Labour voters – no longer believed Labour represented them. And what was more, although most of them had not decided who to vote for in the next election, they were certain of one thing: they would not vote Labour. Labour had disqualified itself from consideration. 'There are too many loonies,' they said; 'They are too militant'; 'I've always been brought up as Labour, but now I'd be frightened if they got back into power'; and, 'You can't vote Labour just because they've got a heart.'

The imagery they associated with us was appalling: word association threw up 'reds', 'commies', 'you will do what you are told', 'strikes', 'Scargill' and 'Militant'. For the Tories, the words were 'Surrey', 'mortgages', 'private pools', 'private hospitals'. When asked to draw the parties, they drew a small house, small car for Labour; big house, big car for the Conservatives. Many of them drew a series of uniform little houses to represent Labour; one added a steelworks and a job centre. There were pints of beer, and a general store with prices going up all the time. Perhaps the worst single illustration of the party showed no cars, people travelling to work on the bus, houses that looked the same, no O- or A-levels, and universities closed down. The Tories held champagne glasses, Labour people wore cloth caps. The things people associated with the Conservative Party were the things they themselves wanted; all the imagery associated with them was aspirational.[20]

This was not surprising at a time when Tory privatisations were extending personal prosperity and Chancellor Nigel Lawson was overseeing a mid-1980s economic boom. Meanwhile, Labour was debating welfare support for strikers' families, the imposition of wage restraints and union-brokered incomes policies.

That was only the first of the day's shocks. A second presentation on the same day, by advertising agency BBDO to outline the attitudes of 20- to 25-year-olds, introduced for the first time the concept of 'Thatcher's Children', those who started to think about politics in the mid-1970s. Thatcherism, we discovered, was the political norm for these people – not an aberration, but the basis for their political thought. They took for granted many of its principles and any political idea was considered within that framework. 'We call them Thatcher's Children because of this,' a BBDO researcher said. 'They approve of toughness; they agree with it. They know it's tough to get on. And they all want to get on; they've all got aspirations.' They liked their leaders to be tough, and associated weakness with the unions and the welfare state, in particular social security:

> People really want to distance themselves from unemployment. They feel like if they're in a job then they've made it; they don't want to talk about people who haven't made it. Collectivism breeds weakness in their view. They've got a very crude and brutalist view of how the world works. They see all the classic institutions of collectivism as being designed to protect the weak, but by doing that somehow we're all pulled down. It's not something they can justify on an analytical level, but the more they talk about it the more they feel that individualism is the way forward. It's like a disease.

This group of young people became increasingly Thatcherite as they relaxed and felt less restrained, and the subjects that really excited them were the Falklands – 'brilliant' – business, enterprise, achievement and individualism. They admired Thatcher even if they loathed her, liked aggression, and hated Militant and other left-wing groups, whom they believed were trying to pull the country back and stop growth and efficiency. They saw tax cuts as a reward for working hard. Even unemployment came out as a Labour negative with these voters: it was a low priority, accepted as necessary, and anyway, they believed that 90 per cent of the unemployed were jobless through their own fault or choice. This, despite the fact that unemployment never dipped below 3.1 million between 1983 and 1987. 'The Labour Party they remember, in their pre-sixteen memories, is associated with inappropriateness, bad management,' the researchers reported. 'The only time the Labour Party was good was in history, what they've read at school – when the Labour Party were men in cloth caps, who spoke in funny accents, and were in Parliament getting things done for the people who voted for them. But that's not the case any more. Those images now are retrograde. Even the people we had who would be defined in demographic terms as DE, their aspirations were to be middle-class – everyone wants to be middle-class these days.'[21]

This, then, was the situation I found in 1985 – far worse than I could possibly have anticipated, far worse than many even now fully appreciate: a political party separated from its natural supporters by a chasm of fear, distrust, even anger; a campaigns and communications operation too pitiful even to begin the task of building a bridge across it; and a party not really understanding that it had to try.

My report, delivered in December 1985, ran to sixty-four pages. I criticised Labour's communications as badly co-ordinated, with unclear lines of responsibility and uncertain authority. The campaigns that Labour had run 'have not yet had any discernible effect in influencing the electorate', and the political communication from the party was overcomplicated. There was insufficient orchestration of the presentation of a policy, the press office was not proactive enough, selective targeting had been neglected and the potential of advertising under-exploited. My key recommendations included:

- The establishment of the Director of Communications as the central focus for all party communications, who would chair a weekly working group of key communicators and campaigners. A monthly Communications Co-ordination Committee with a broader membership which would co-ordinate the wider campaign effort.
- The formation of a Shadow Communications Agency (SCA), structured around the group at the Boase, Massimi, Pollitt (BMP) advertising agency which had run the campaign to save the Greater London Council. The SCA would focus and structure the professional communications expertise on offer to the party. 'Its role will be to draft strategy, conduct and interpret research, produce advertising and campaign themes, and provide other communications support as necessary.'
- Monthly qualitative research should be commissioned by the SCA, complemented by monthly MORI summaries, and both should be integrated more fully into campaign planning.
- Communications messages should be simplified, repeated and orchestrated around key themes.
- The SCA should commission a design company to examine all aspects of the 'corporate appearance' of the party, including the party logo.
- The establishment of a rapid-reactions unit to defend against 'own goals', attack those of the Tories, and exploit issues of the day.
- All campaigns should have the influence of electoral opinion as their first priority.

I also set out ten communications principles for the Labour Party, around which the communications structure and output of the party should be based:

- An agreed, early strategy
- Selectivity of target audience
- Simple message often repeated

- Orchestrated, cohesive presentation of the message
- Clear allocation of responsibility for tasks. Clear lines of authority and accountability. Adequate structures of co-ordination
- Positive, proactive press relations
- A shift in campaigning emphasis from 'grass roots'/opinion-forming to influencing electoral opinion through the mass media
- Proper use of outside expertise
- Less publicity material, used more often
- Highest-level political authority and support for the early and continuing implementation of these principles.[22]

Out of the shadows

Even as I wrote my report, a nascent Shadow Communications Agency was working on Labour's forthcoming social policy campaign. Chris Powell had offered to set up a shadow advertising agency using the same team – Alan Tilby and Paul Leeves – who produced the 'Save the GLC' campaign and who were seen as some of the best advertising people in London. I considered BMP to be the top London agency, and their best staff were Labour Party supporters at a time when advertising and PR were dominated by Tories. Peter Mandelson, aware that Labour did not have the money to employ an agency and that no agency at that time could afford to take on the Labour Party, which might have lost them business elsewhere, immediately appointed the BMP team and asked me to act as co-ordinator. Until the NEC formally approved the creation of a Shadow Communications Agency, however, we had to operate in secret.

We moved quickly from the social policy brief into all areas of Labour communications. At our very first meeting, on 19 December 1985, we decided to produce creative concepts not only for the social policy campaign but in economic areas as well, convinced that the next election would be won or lost on the question of economic management. Already we had volunteer planners and researchers working with us from the advertising agencies Abbott Mead Vickers, BMP and TBWA, as well as Chris Powell, Peter Herd and Ross Barr from BMP, Bob Worcester and Brian Gosschalk from MORI and Colin Fisher from SRU, a leading market research company. By mid-January, the SCA was effectively taking over Labour communications, although the Breakfast Group, set up by Robin Cook to bring together campaigning expertise, was still going. As well as creating the social policy campaign, we were preparing for the Fulham by-election on 10 April, working on the economic concepts, conducting focus groups and developing an overall communications strategy for the Labour Party. We had decided on our central objective for 1986: to get Labour from 35 per cent to 40 per cent in the polls. Although Neil Kinnock and Robin Cook knew we were working for Peter, only Mandelson knew the extent of our expanding communications empire.

If the first surrogate for the SCA was the Social Policy Group, set up at the end of the year to prepare Labour's 'Freedom and Fairness' campaign, the second was the Strategy Development Group, which we set up in February to cover strategic planning, design, public relations, direct mail and targeting. By the time we had moved on to creating sub-groups of journalists, PR experts and designers, the NEC finally caught up with us and officially approved the creation of a Shadow Communications Agency. Our first formal meeting was on 25 March 1986, at BMP's offices in Bishop's Bridge Road. Present were: Ross Barr, Leslie Butterfield, Robin Cook, Richard Faulkner, Colin Fisher, Brian Gosschalk, Peter Herd, Patricia Hewitt, Peter Mandelson, Deborah Mattinson, Chris Powell, Bob Worcester and myself. By June, there were seventeen projects in hand, from shadow Cabinet pairings to General Election planning, to a leaders campaign, a new corporate image and the development of a communications handbook. Twelve SCA sub-groups had been established, including a journalists' group; a writers' group chaired by Ken Follett and including Hanif Kureishi, Colin Welland and Melvyn Bragg; a broadcasting group;

a target audience definition group and a conference group. We had established a week-by-week timetable for the entire period up to the next election. We were making monthly presentations to the Campaign Strategy Committee and almost weekly presentations to Labour's policy steering committees. Research into sensitive issues like defence and the standing of Neil Kinnock was in the field. The Shadow Communications Agency was now a fact of Labour Party political life.

Yet we had stepped into a morass, entering a party at war with itself at every level. The left-dominated NEC, which had shown little interest in campaigns and communications in the past, saw us as a direct threat. Shadow Cabinet members were at best suspicious, at worst openly hostile. Labour had become so distanced from the public that we were going to have to fight the party itself over every appeal to the voters.

This is not the party I joined

The first major challenge for the SCA was Labour's 'Freedom and Fairness' campaign, launched in April 1986. Peter Mandelson wanted a communications revolution and got it. We had played a part in the Fulham by-election, conducting qualitative research, developing a campaign theme around the line 'Nick Raynsford Lives Here', and executing it. It was the first time such professional marketing techniques had been used in a by-election. They contributed to an important victory, which helped counter the growing impression that the entire Labour Party in London was in the grip of the 'loony left'. Our win suggested a new dynamism in the party, while the Tories were still getting to grips with the aftermath of the Westland crisis and were about to become embroiled in the *Spycatcher* fiasco.

'Freedom and Fairness' – the name the party adopted for the social policy campaign – was our defining test. It was planned to complement the 1984–85 economic campaign 'Jobs and Industry', that indigestible glob of a campaign which was characterised by a

huge output of paper and massive printing bills and which had
had absolutely no effect on the public.

Mandelson used 'Freedom and Fairness' as a way of saying to
the party, 'this is modern communications; this is how it works;
this is how it succeeds'. It was like a controlled explosion: this is
your future – like it or lump it. Mandelson said, 'It was absolutely
essential for our modernisation project within the party to show
(a) the relevance of communications; (b) how possible it would
be to bring about changes if other sections of the party felt good
about what we were doing at the top of the party; and (c) to get the
public starting to come back towards us.'[23] We wanted to smash
through the party's perceptions of how campaigning should be
done. My final brief for the social policy campaign – the first
complete strategy I ever wrote for the Labour Party – asked the
creative team to undertake a political communications revolution.
I demanded a campaign that was bright, modern and distinctive,
a consumer not a political campaign, using normal consumer language and not 'political' terms. I wanted language that would be
heard and understood in southern suburbs, with a visual identity
that was so different it stunned people.[24]

We developed the idea of symbolic policies – minor initiatives
like banning lead in petrol to symbolise Labour's concern for the
environment. We commissioned Trevor Beattie, who would later
become famous for creating the 'Hello Boys' Wonderbra advertisements, to create the campaign. We developed a slogan, 'Labour:
Putting People First', which was later used by Bill Clinton as his
1992 campaign theme. For the Labour Party, the leaflets and
posters were shockingly different. Mandelson loved it.

To many Labour politicians at the time, this was heresy. A
campaign was a leaflet, a march, a speech, a cause and a defeat.
Mandelson recalls showing the campaign material to Harriet
Harman, then the shadow Social Services Minister: 'And Harriet
said, are you sure that this slightly squashed-up black, grey and
silver look and print-face is quite what we're looking for, given that
it is so harsh and dark? And Trevor [Beattie] said, well yes, this

is ballsy, and that's why it's going to succeed, and there was this drawing in of breath at the word "ballsy" in response to Harriet's question. But this did make people pipe down and listen to what we had to say.'[25]

The 'Freedom and Fairness' campaign was also to prove the first test of Kinnock's own commitment to professional communications. When we took the early drafts to him in the House of Commons on 4 February 1986, he was nothing if not enthusiastic. Barely before the presentation had got under way, he grabbed hold of the advertising concepts and started to present them to himself, excitedly issuing a torrent of creative judgements. Although a bit of a shock to the professional advertising people present, it showed he cared. But Neil himself was to balk at the end result. 'I don't think he quite saw it coming together in the cohesive, all-singing, all-dancing campaign that it was, with the impact that that had,' Mandelson said. 'And when he saw it coming together he was a bit worried by the radicalness of the new look.'[26] Kinnock thought 'Labour: Putting People First' was a poor substitute for the campaign title he had chosen originally, and he wanted to stick with 'Freedom and Fairness'. 'Labour's Campaign for Freedom and Fairness had more politics in it, and was therefore more likely to appeal to and carry the party,' Mandelson said. 'I think that his caution was right. But his counselling was wrong.'[27] In the end, Kinnock refused to shift, forcing Mandelson, who was determined to retain the more voter-friendly 'Putting People First', to go out on a limb, and not for the last time.

I had not realised how much guts Peter Mandelson had until Kinnock's office called him a week before the launch. 'They said he was very worried about this, and wanted to see me. They said he wanted the whole campaign to be recast, to be changed radically. I said that's not possible, because the launch is only a week away. And they protested and said that Neil hadn't passed these things, and I said no, he did. It was approved at the meeting. They said well, he's disapproving it, and I said well, he can't, it's too late.' Mandelson went to see Kinnock personally to explain, 'one of

three occasions in my time there that I had to do that'. He took
with him the photographs, mock-ups and other materials.

> And Neil said, I just can't have this. He said the campaign name has
> to be 'Freedom and Fairness', because they are important concepts,
> important names and ideas that we have to own again. And I said
> I agreed with him, but that must come in the case we make, the
> argument we use and the language that supports that. But this is a
> piece of communication to the mass public, and whereas 'Labour's
> Campaign for Freedom and Fairness' is a party-oriented statement,
> 'Labour: Putting People First' is a public-oriented statement. We
> reached a compromise, by which I said I would overprint all our
> campaign materials with 'Freedom and Fairness', in addition to
> what was already there. We did it in very small print.[28]

The campaign was an unprecedented success – Militant called
it an unnecessary facelift, and at its launch at the London International Press Centre the left-wing MP Eric Heffer stood, horrified, at the back and moaned, 'This is not the party I joined.'
The Labour left had opposed political marketing for years. Jim
Callaghan used to dread NEC election strategy meetings in the late
1970s, as Tony Benn and Heffer consistently attacked all opinion
polling and most suggestions for advertising. But more enlightened
commentators saw in 'Freedom and Fairness' the revival of the
Labour Party. On 23 April, the day after its launch, the *Financial
Times* hailed 'Mr Kinnock's new party', writing in a leader column:
'The British Labour Party is again beginning to look like a credible
party of government.'[29] A *Daily Telegraph* story, picking up on
the grey and silver, ran: 'Labour changes colour as it sheds its
weary cloth-cap image.'[30] The tabloids hailed it as a victory for
'poster power'.[31] Even the morose *Guardian* called the campaign
'a really positive step forward in the political rehabilitation of
a party which three years ago seemed to have lost the will to
govern this country';[32] the *New Statesman* grudgingly conceded
the new style might win votes.[33] And in a more generous leader
column, *Tribune* commented, 'Freedom and Fairness could just

be the campaign that wins Labour the next election.'[34] By today's standards, the campaign wasn't much: a few leaflets, a bold image, a memorable slogan. It was never going to win the election, but it did at least prove that we *wanted* to win it.

The rose and the thorns

It was Neil Kinnock who first asked for a complete redesign of the Labour Party. He had been impressed by the Swedish Social Democrats, who had developed a new corporate identity using a rose, and he called in Mandelson and me and asked us to do the same. Peter handed the project over to me and by March 1986, when the SCA was formally set up, we were already forming a design group to prepare the new corporate image, including a logo. In April, Mandelson wrote to Larry Whitty requesting his support – both financial and personal – for the redesign. The new, sharper look of the 'Freedom and Fairness' publicity material was 'vital to reinforce the impression of an innovative party shedding old associations and image', he wrote. 'This dimension will continue to be part of our communications strategy – a fresh party, new approach, on the move. As an important basis for this I am looking at our overall "corporate" image – everything that offers a visual impression of the party.' He wanted 'an entirely new visual facelift' to launch at conference, he said. 'This exercise is an integral part of our General Election preparations. Can I continue with your blessing?'[35] Whitty returned the letter to him with a scrawled note: 'Yes. But keep me informed on design and costs. We do not yet have a General Election fund . . . LW.'[36]

Lacking the money to run a vast creative campaign, I asked Michael Wolff, founder of Wolff Olins, who had designed the Bovis 'humming bird' logo, to see what he could come up with. When I first asked Wolff for his thoughts – without telling him what Kinnock had proposed – he spontaneously suggested using a rose. Peter, Michael and I spent hours and hours in the Battersea home of Philip Sutton, the artist, surrounded by dozens and dozens of roses – a whole roomful of them. We would wander around picking up one after the other, trying to choose which was the best. 'We picked out half a dozen, ones that spoke to me, or I liked, or I thought would say something to the public,' Peter remembers. 'I had no theory to apply. I had no idea what criteria to use.'[37] Michael, Philip and designer Clare Hamilton honed these down into various designs and illustrations, which we then took to Kinnock. I made notes of the meetings on two consecutive days:

25 June 1986
Went to Philip Sutton's home in Battersea – a real artist's home. Someone called it 'a bit of Provence in the middle of Battersea'. I was nervous because the designs were a bit too wishy-washy. Philip Sutton did the illustrations. I was a bit concerned that the corporate image would end up looking all wrong. There were two or three watercolours which, although they were much less powerful than some of the others, managed to combine humanity and sensitivity with clarity as a rose – and redness of the rose. They were clearly the basis of the right sort of approach. Clare presented the type and that was absolutely right. When Michael Wolff put together the rose and the type it was quite clear that he had developed a corporate image for the party which was in the same tradition of the other work he'd done.[38]

26 June 1986
At ten o'clock we left to pick up Michael Wolff, Philip Sutton and Clare Hamilton to present the corporate image to Neil Kinnock. As I suspected, we were left outside in a corridor somewhere waiting to get in to see Neil. Eventually we go in to see him. He is wearing a light suit, which doesn't suit him, and no jacket. But he's in a good, calm, affable mood. Michael is good with him, takes his jacket off. I take my jacket off. Peter Mandelson sits next to Philip Sutton; I sit on the other side of the room. Michael says how much he hates the grey (of 'Freedom and Fairness'), Neil agrees with him, they shake hands, a good rapport is created.

The meeting goes well. Michael presents the corporate image work, which I think Neil likes. They chat about the use of hands, how to use black hands, young hands, women's hands, etc. Talk about the colour of red the rose should be. Neil looks at a photo of his son playing rugby in a red strip. He says that this red is vermilion – compared to vermilion jobs Labour will create when they get into power! Neil also made a crack about how we'll be the best-dressed runners-up, but I don't think he meant it – or maybe just a little. The critical point of the discussion was really when Patricia mentioned that the rose would be shown at conference and Neil shook his head and looked like he didn't agree with it. He said, 'I don't want that to happen.' Patricia said, 'But you agreed to it.' Neil said abruptly, 'You might have mentioned it, but I never agreed to it.' It seemed like Neil had made his mind up. But then Peter came in, he looked Neil directly in the eye, and said calmly but with enormous authority, 'Are you sure, Neil? Are you sure we shouldn't have the rose at conference?' And gradually won him over. He said that the response to the grey was really only limited, a couple of letters opposing it, opposing what had been done with 'Freedom and Fairness'. He said people would like it. Neil looked down and said quite abruptly but with good humour, 'Let's see some designs for conference.' Peter had won him over. It was a good moment for Peter and for Neil. Later I talked to Michael Wolff, who said he thought the meeting had gone very well. He'd written a letter to Neil which said: 'Thank you for your time this morning, Neil. I was looking forward to meeting you, and listened carefully to your observations and suggestions about roses and hands, and different type-faces and colours. We will now concentrate on making the whole scheme practical. I'm very excited about what I think it can achieve.' He put a quote at the end from *A Midsummer Night's Dream*. Nice, but on the whole maybe a little over the top for Neil: 'The seasons alter: hoary-headed frosts fall in the fresh lap of the crimson rose.' I'll be interested to hear how Neil responds to that.[39]

Eventually we had two drawings, which I took over to Peter Mandelson's house. Peter was in bed, ill. 'We disagreed over the length of stem,' he remembers. 'Neil wanted a short stem. I wanted a long stem. You wanted a long stem that would look softer, and in Lynne Franks' immortal words, "more Kleenex".'[40]

In the end Peter decided on the long stem, against Neil's wishes. The rose was to become so unmistakably associated with Peter and the modernisation struggle that on meeting Mandelson for the first time, Prince Charles commented blithely, 'Ah, the red rose man.'[41]

Peter himself was still having to fight petty internal battles at Walworth Road while we were working on the rose. A note I made of a conversation with him at the time records: 'PM said that Geoff Bish, Research Director of the Labour Party, had attacked and assailed him at the Monday morning directors' meeting over the size of his office, which he said was a surrogate for an attack over the publicity (about campaigning) that Peter has been getting recently and the increase in his power. He said also that the publicity was not of his doing, and just evolved around him – as indeed did the size of his office.'[42] It was a minor issue at the time: at one NEC meeting, everyone laughed when Dennis Skinner, during a discussion about where to store the Labour Party archives, suggested they put them in Peter's office as 'he won't even notice they're there'.

We decided that in addition to the rose, we would give all the delegates peach-coloured wallets to carry their conference documents around in, imprinted with Labour's new rose, to match the conference backdrop designed by Michael Wolff. When the wallets were printed a week before the conference they came out, I think, more peachy than the backdrop itself, and when Peter and I took them to show Neil and Glenys Kinnock in Neil's office at the Commons, they retreated, horrified, into Neil's room and closed the door. 'Then Neil opened the door and said "Come in",' Peter remembers. 'I went in and Glenys said, "Oh, Peter, these will never do. You'll never persuade the NUM delegation to walk around with these under their arms." And Neil was looking ashen and really, really worried. So I said I'm sorry, it's too late. They've been printed, and we're going to have to use them.'[43] I nervously watched *Channel Four News* at 7.00 P.M. on the Monday of the 1986 conference. They were doing vox pops among party

members, all of whom said the new image was fantastic. Even
the peach wallets were a huge success. They were being stolen,
begged, borrowed and bought by the end of conference week.

This was the conference at which the presentation of Labour
entered the modern era, a defining moment in the modernisation of the Labour Party. By the time delegates arrived at
conference it was a *fait accompli*. Even to the NEC it came as
a shock – they hadn't really understood what we were up to. 'We
never presented it to the NEC as a change in corporate identity,'
Mandelson said.

> At the Press and Publicity Sub-committee of the NEC, chaired
> by Gwyneth Dunwoody, in the second week of September 1986,
> I went to the committee and as part of my director's report said
> that we were introducing a new campaigning logo for the party.
> We played it down, didn't say it was a change in corporate identity
> for the entire party, merely referred to it as a logo to use in our
> campaigns. They didn't know what a logo was or anything. I passed
> it round the committee. Gwyneth Dunwoody was really brilliant,
> really protected me and us throughout. She knew exactly what
> was going on and she just allowed them to be passed round the
> committee without any further discussion. It was all sort of 'yes,
> very good' and that was it and all agreed without anyone noticing.
> Then they got to conference two weeks later and came in to the
> conference hall and there was the rose, with 'Labour: Putting
> People First'. And it was everywhere, everywhere.[44]

Neil, too, had smartened up his image: with a short haircut, dark
suits and white shirts. This was partly thanks to Joe Napolitan,
a political consultant to Walter Mondale whom Patricia Hewitt
had brought in to advise Labour. Napolitan had written a series
of hard-hitting memos on Labour's vulnerabilities, and in his first
direct note to Kinnock, in April 1986, he warned him that voters
were not convinced he would make a better Prime Minister than
Margaret Thatcher. 'You must do the things necessary to project
yourself more effectively,' he wrote. He advised him to take a
television training seminar, dry-run his TV appearances, critique

them afterwards, and 'look like a Prime Minister . . . You may truly be a man of the people – but you've got to act just a little bit different than they do.'[45] Our SCA research showed people wanted more authority, confidence and gravitas from Kinnock; although they liked him, he didn't yet measure up as a leader.

In the summer of 1986 Labour reached 40 per cent in the polls, with the Tories on 32 per cent and the Alliance on 26 per cent. At conference, delegates voted to retain nearly all the policies which had lost them the 1983 election so dramatically. Most damagingly, defence dominated the agenda as delegates and front-bench spokesmen argued over unilateralism and US Defense Secretary Caspar Weinberger argued that the party's unilateralist proposals would mean the break-up of Nato. Neil Kinnock followed with a passionate speech condemning nuclear weapons. 'I would die for my country, but I tell you I would never let my country die for me,' he told delegates.[46] At the Tory conference the next week, stunningly stage-managed by Saatchi's, ministers presented a series of new initiatives around the theme 'The Next Moves Forward'. Labour's poll ratings started to slip.

Building on sand

The 1986 conference was Labour's most successful for twenty years, but already the seeds of defeat had been sown. By the end of the year, we knew how we wanted to fight the election. We wanted to focus on television; ensure brilliant, memorable pictures; provide stories that fed into every stage of the news cycle; concentrate on the leader and a small group of key campaigners; plan the campaign around the discipline of a tightly controlled daily grid. This is how the 1987 election was fought and it is essentially how Labour has fought every national election since. 'We got ahead of the game,' Hewitt, who was on maternity leave at the time, remembers.

You [Gould] and sometimes Peter used to come down to my house, and that was when we worked on the grid for the election campaign proper. And we came up with this very simple device: we basically said, what is going to matter in this election campaign is television, and what's going to matter on television is the pictures, and we said, right, for each day there will be a theme and the pictures will be tied to the theme. And it was really simple, but nobody had ever done it.

And so we created this grid, day by day by day, and I remember sitting around my dining-room table and you saying, 'On the Thursday before election day we've got to go really big, and it's got to be health because that's our big issue,' and so we wrote in Thursday minus six or whatever it is, 'health', and that was health and it was kind of written in stone. And it was very rigid and it caused all kinds of problems when we tried to repeat it in '92, but in '87 what it did was catch the media completely unprepared, and it was only about halfway through the election that they suddenly figured out that whatever they asked Neil about, the pictures were always the pictures we wanted. And so even when we had a very nasty defence wobble right in the middle of the campaign and they were chasing Neil around the hospital trying to ask him about defence, the pictures said 'health' – hospitals, nurses, caring. And it drove them up the wall, but it was too late for them to get out of it.[47]

This approach was a revolution, not just in Labour Party campaigning but in political campaigning by any party. It was the work of two people: Mandelson and Hewitt. Hewitt provided the logistical power. By early 1986 draft timetables were in place, each election day already taking tentative shape. The degree of early planning was extraordinary for the time. Mandelson provided the combination of organisational rigour and presentational brilliance which has become his hallmark. But Mandelson also understood the essential political imperatives that were the prerequisites for election success: the extreme left had to be smashed, at best, or sidelined at worst; the party had to appear electable; we had to stop the Alliance replacing us as the natural party of opposition. As he says, 'The plan for the election, after the conference in 1986, was to show that (a) we had beaten off the hard left who had taken control of the party in the years before; and (b) either to get rid of or to make as appealing as possible the policies that we had at the time. And to use Neil Kinnock as a symbol of sense returning, the hard left being seen off, the party changing and equipping itself for serious politics. We needed to reinstate ourselves as the serious challenger to the Conservatives, and to see off the Liberal–SDP Alliance.'[48]

But although the planning was extensive, the foundations were built on sand. To will an outcome was not to achieve it. Labour was developing a surface gloss and burgeoning campaigning competence, but below the surface it was riddled with flaws. Labour looked better, but it had not become better.

Joe Napolitan had written more memos to Kinnock's office over the summer, warning of Labour's problems, which included the perception of weak and incompetent leadership; extreme leftism; the undue influence of the trade unions; racial worries; and Labour's affinity for the perceived 'undesirables'.[49] He warned of likely Tory campaign themes: law and order; 'Kinnock can't even unite his own party – how can he expect to control the country'; control of the government by the trade unions; in a time of crisis, experience counts; 'Kinnock will open the door to a flood of new immigrants'; and, most dangerously in his opinion, defence – 'You can almost see their ads now: Labour's defence policy will leave Great Britain defenceless, naked to our enemies.'[50] After the fiasco at conference, he wrote a stinging note on the defence policy, warning that it put Labour at a serious disadvantage. 'The Labour Party today finds itself in the predictable position of being on the defensive in the forthcoming campaign, primarily because of its policy on defence,' he wrote. 'Deliberate adoption of a policy that puts a party or a candidate at serious liability even before the campaign begins raises doubts about the ability of that party or candidate to accept serious strategy recommendations that might overcome the self-inflicted wound. Labour's chances of victory in the next election were, in my opinion, tenuous even before the defence policy became official party doctrine; now those chances are even less.'[51] Accepting that it was impossible to change the policy, Labour needed to try to turn it into an asset, he said, by going on the offensive, attacking the Conservatives' running down of conventional forces and accusing them of 'putting all their eggs in a nuclear basket'.[52]

Our research over the summer into attitudes towards the party's defence policies confirmed everything that Napolitan had been saying. People had a simple, common-sense view of the issue – if you have a dog, no one will attack you; if someone else has a knife, you should have a knife also. There was some support for multilateral disarmament, but none for unilateralism. People thought Labour's defence policy was throwing in the towel. And in their essential, gut responses, they were right. It is difficult now to describe the folly of our defence policy at that time. It was incredible to anyone with any vestige of common sense. Once, at a meeting, it was suggested that Labour's policy was to repel a Soviet invasion with ditches. We all laughed. Peter Mandelson commented, 'Things may be bad, but they're not that bad.' But moments later Mike Gapes, the Labour Party researcher responsible for defence (and now Labour MP for Ilford South), came into the room, shamefaced: yes, it was true. Labour planned to counter the second most powerful armed empire in the world with ditches. 'But don't worry,' Gapes added, 'they are exploding ditches.' And this at a time of East–West tension. In October 1986 the Reykjavik summit between Gorbachev and Reagan broke up acrimoniously with no agreement on disarmament.

If our defence policy implied gradual surrender, our presentational strategy for it was to go on the attack. Our proposition was not credible, but at least it was bold. It was the Tories, not us, who were weakening our defences, we argued – money spent on nuclear weapons was putting our security at risk by destroying our conventional forces. The Falklands War could not, for example, be fought today. Within two months of the end of conference we prepared a campaign, 'Modern Britain in the Modern World:

The Power to Defend Our Country', which focused on making Britain stronger and better defended, by switching from nuclear to conventional weapons.

Unilateralism would come back to haunt us throughout the run-up to the election and during the campaign itself. A trip by Kinnock to see President Reagan in Washington at the end of March 1987 rebounded when Reagan gave Kinnock less than the allotted half an hour, and his press secretary Marlin Fitzwater told journalists afterwards, in direct contradiction to what Kinnock's staff had claimed, that the President had warned Kinnock his defence policy would threaten Nato. This contrasted badly with a successful trip by Thatcher to Moscow at the end of March, when she was mobbed by cheering crowds, enjoyed eleven hours of talks with an adulatory Mikhail Gorbachev, and cemented her international image as the 'Iron Lady'. The contrast could not have been more explicit.

Defence was bad, but there was worse to come. Labour was being damned by the insane extremism of its local councils.

The Tories had begun a campaign against Labour's 'loony left', headed by Environment Secretary Nicholas Ridley, who was ridiculing left-wing councils for intimidation and political correctness. This worked partly because of the brilliance of the Conservative attack; partly because of the relentless pounding of the tabloid press; but mostly because it was true. The Tories jumped on the GLC's Section 137 rule, which allowed council funding of every special-interest group from Chile Democratic GB through Brent Friends of the Earth to the Rastafarian Society. In Liverpool, Kinnock began moves to expel the Labour group leader Tony Byrne and the group secretary Tony Hood.

In the winter, qualitative research showed that Alliance supporters – the essential election battleground – were, not surprisingly, running scared. Fear of Labour massively outweighed dislike of the Tories. It was clear that our campaign had stalled, while the Tories had successfully grabbed the election agenda – they had shifted the emphasis off Thatcher, launched a series of successful policy initiatives from more acceptable ministers, introduced a sense that the economy might be turning the corner, and maintained a sustained attack on Labour over defence, the loony left, mortgages and social ownership.

Expecting an election in the summer, I wrote that we had to begin our campaign early in the new year and that 'the focus of the campaign should be a sharp, aggressive proposition, from which all communications would flow'.[53] We did not have one, and we were not to get one. What we had was 'Investing in People'. As I wrote at the time: 'This is a convincing logic but not an election-fighting proposition. We need one with a cutting edge, if only to act as a focus for all our creative work. All PPBs [party political broadcasts] and advertisements should flow from this proposition, the prime focus of the strategy should be to discredit the government's record, and the battleground of the campaign should be Kinnock against Thatcher.' And we should use fear. 'The only realistic hope we have got of overcoming the Tory campaign of fear is a counter-campaign based on dislike and hostility of the government, and in particular Thatcher. Like it or not, it is going to be a negative campaign. If we attempt to run a positive campaign within this context we will be swamped. Our positives will not be able to defeat their presentation of our negatives.' And if we were going to fight a negative campaign, I thought we needed at least one positive, which had to be Neil Kinnock. 'Presenting Labour in a positive light will be difficult, presenting Kinnock in a positive light much less so.'[54]

I was concerned, too, that the Tories were out-campaigning us. In a note to Mandelson and Bryan Gould, who had taken over from Robin Cook as campaign co-ordinator, in December, I said we had to emulate the Tories' successful autumn offensive: 'They worked out a plan based on exploiting our greatest weaknesses, and defending their areas of vulnerability, which they then proceeded to systematically and ruthlessly implement. As Chris Powell said on Monday, when they pull the trigger the gun goes off. This is exactly what they did in 1983. In 1987 this is what we have to achieve.'[55]

But before we had a chance, we were torpedoed again. In January 1987 Deirdre Wood, a hard-left former councillor, was chosen as Labour's candidate for a by-election in Greenwich caused by the death of Labour MP Guy Barnett, against the SDP's Rosie Barnes. In the election in February we were slaughtered. Our 5,000-vote majority turned to a 6,000-vote lead for the Alliance. On the day of the defeat, Patricia Hewitt wrote a tough memo to Larry Whitty, Jack Cunningham and Frank Dobson, chair of London Labour MPs at the time. Explosively, it was leaked to the press. In it, she warned: 'It's obvious from our own polling, as well as from the doorstep, that the "London effect" is now very noticeable. The "loony Labour left" is taking its toll: the gays and lesbians issue is costing us dear among the pensioners, and fear of extremism and higher taxes/rates is particularly prominent in the GLC area.'[56] The memo caused outrage but was entirely accurate. 'It wasn't just coming up in London – it was all around the country,' Hewitt remembers. 'Charles [Clarke] and I had both tried but we couldn't get the London parties to start sorting it out. Finally, in a fury – it was a moment of ill-discipline – I wrote to Larry thinking I'll put this on paper and make it be taken seriously. And it was leaked. So that was another huge problem.'[57]

Colin Byrne began work as a press officer in Walworth Road just after the Greenwich by-election. He had read an article by Mandelson in the *Guardian* about the need for Labour to embrace modern communications and, impressed, contacted him. When he was taken on, he found the reality sadly distant from Peter's dream. 'The whole building was dismal,' he said. 'It was like starting work in a minor regional trade union headquarters in terms of morale, low quality of staff, lots of people round the place who seemed to have been there for thirty years. Literally guys in corners, smoking fags and drinking tea all day. It was very depressing, and not at all what I had expected from the rhetoric of Mandelson and modern mass communications.'[58] This was why they needed the SCA.

Kinnock made his disastrous trip to Washington in March,

against the advice of Charles Clarke and Peter Mandelson, because he hated the thought of being accused of cowardice if he cancelled. He told me: 'If you fall off a bike you have to get straight back on it.' A Commons tea-room row between John Prescott, then the employment spokesman, and former Prime Minister Jim Callaghan, over defence, overshadowed the 'New Jobs for Britain' launch. And all this against a background of a country basking in four years of sustained economic growth. Inflation had not risen above 5 per cent; average weekly earnings had risen by 14 per cent in real terms; the FTSE 100 had quintupled in value; and the basic rate of tax was heading down from 33 per cent towards 25 per cent.[59]

On 10 March, I wrote to Mandelson with the latest focus group research, from lapsed Labour voters in Camden. This research was to lead to the big strategic decisions of the 1987 campaign. People were wary of us, but they did not like the Conservatives and felt a sense of inevitable despair at the prospect of their return. This despair was rooted in deep emotions and the big social issues: health; education; jobs; crime. This was the only ground we could fight on: emotional power based on social issues. The truth is that this was an election the Conservatives should have lost. People wanted them out, but did not trust us at all. As I wrote at the time, 'If we lose this election it will not be because they have done well, but because of the failure of the opposition parties to provide a convincing alternative. The election will, in effect, be lost by default.' The line we had worked out for the creative treatments, 'Isn't it time for a change of heart?' was 'too soft and insufficiently action-based for the current mood',[60] I warned, so we decided to settle on: 'The country's crying out for change. Vote Labour.' Strangely, although Peter and I agreed this strategy and built the campaign around it, Neil's thinking was a mystery to us. It turned out that by extraordinary coincidence his timing was the same as ours, so when the first Labour advertisement using this line, and his first campaign speech using the same deeply emotional theme, appeared on the same day, it was actually unplanned.

By the end of March, we were in third place, behind the Alliance, in the polls. Over April we recovered slightly, settling at around 30 per cent, with the Alliance on 27 and the Conservatives 41. In a review of the polls, I said the consequence of these shifts 'is the poll configuration the government has been looking for before calling an election'. Post-Greenwich damage to the party might have been so great, I said, that short-term recovery was impossible. Comparisons between April and January showed an even starker picture: government approval and satisfaction with Mrs Thatcher up, satisfaction with Mr Kinnock and Labour's policies down, satisfaction with Dr Owen and the SDP's policies up. The 7,000-plus PA/Marplan poll showed Labour losing 10 per cent in the north, 12 per cent in Scotland, 11 per cent in the East Midlands and 13 per cent in Wales compared to six months earlier. Victory, I concluded, looked likely for the government.[61]

Hewitt remembers the gloom around that time:

I remember talking to Neil a week before the election was called and we had had a poll which put us in third place, or in joint third place with the Liberals, and Neil and I were talking about this and we sort of looked at each other, and one of us said, we could go into third place, and we said, once we start sliding there's no bottom to this – there's no reason why we should bottom out at 25 per cent or whatever it was we got in '83 – we could just go into freefall. And I said to him, what we've got to stop happening is this becoming the story of who is going to be in third place. And that was I think the really crucial thing that our election campaign did. It just killed the Alliance.[62]

Kinnock showed great courage during this period, but he was prone to bouts of despair. I remember an SCA journalists' group meeting at which he spent most of the evening depressed about himself and the party's prospects. One journalist had the temerity to ask him, 'What would you do if you lose? Would you resign?' Neil smashed his fist into the table, sending cutlery flying, and said, 'I will stay. I will fight on. Because only I can change the party.'

Shortly before the election, Peter Mandelson organised a presentation and dinner with Neil Kinnock at BMP's offices. It was meant to be a relaxed, friendly, morale-boosting occasion, but that afternoon we were told Neil could not stay for dinner as Glenys had planned something different. However, he stayed for the presentation. Neil was very depressed that night, full of despair about our chances in the election and blaming himself, saying, 'Your work's great, but you can't change me.' This was typical of Neil: doubting himself; concerned about letting others down; but also psyching himself up for the General Election.

Glorious defeat

On 11 May, the day the 1987 General Election was called, Peter phoned. 'Have you heard?' he said. 'Let's get on with it.' We started the election more or less as we had finished in 1983, with a 28 per cent share of the vote in an average of the first three polls, the Alliance just behind with 26.6 per cent and the Conservatives in the mid-40s.[63] It was clear that this election was going to be a battle for second place. Perhaps even worse than our share of vote were perceptions of the party: 67 per cent thought we were too extreme; 69 per cent believed our leadership was poor; 73 per cent thought we were too divided and 55 per cent said the economy would be worse under Labour.[64] This was not at all the position in which we wanted to start the election. Eighteen months of communications modernisation and war on Militant had left us barely better placed than four years ago. This election was clearly the fight for the survival of Labour as the major opposition party in British politics.

We used to meet in Peter's small office in Walworth Road, where he would sit, feet on desk, outwardly calm, always apparently in control. In some ways we were perfectly prepared, but in others we were lost. We had the grid, honed to the minute; we had advertisements fused with the grid for almost every day of the campaign; we had a series of outstanding broadcasts culminating in Hugh Hudson's Kinnock party election broadcast, perhaps the greatest party political broadcast ever made. We had schedules for our key campaigners, television pictures meshed perfectly with our chosen storyline of the day, a new corporate identity, daily opinion polls and focus groups. The problem was that we also had glaring and potentially fatal deficiencies, policies basically unreformed since 1983 including a completely untenable defence policy, and a fearsomely hostile press. Margaret Scammell has estimated that 73 per cent of the *Sun*'s election coverage, 54 per cent of the *Daily Mail*'s and 46 per cent of the *Daily Star*'s was 'Labour-knocking' copy.[65] And we had two big enigmas: one was Neil Kinnock, the other was our central campaign strategy – what we were really saying to the nation. Neil's ratings were not good going into the election. He had been set back by two US trips, by defence, by the mishaps of the spring of 1987. But he approached the campaign with an energy and power that had been waiting to be released. He would storm around the office, ranting at the iniquity of his situation, saying, 'I may be written off now, but I will destroy Thatcher and Owen with the power of my words.' His anger and intensity were awesome. His strength came from his words, he believed his power was in his rhetoric. When his words flowed, his confidence soared. In the 1987 election, the power of Neil's words saved Labour.

Although we had all the apparatus of a campaign, we lacked a strategy. We knew that in order to win we had to focus on the economy. We needed a central, compelling argument. But the setbacks of 1987 smashed these possibilities on the rocks. We could not win on the economy. We could not develop a central campaign rationale plausible enough to grab victory from the Conservatives. All we could do was to fall back on our core strengths and produce a campaign so emotional, so intense, so rooted in our heartland social issues, that we could blast the Alliance away and ensure second place. Chris Powell remembers our strategy as 'basically damage limitation, both in the sense of the fears of the potential of the SDP to take over as the official opposition party and eclipse the Labour Party for ever more, but also in the knowledge that many of the policies that Labour then had would be extremely difficult to effectively sell to enough voters to get elected. In the election itself we used advertising to try and move the agenda about, combined with the press conferences, so that we would never get pinned on one subject and have great damage done to us and get the initiative on subjects that we wanted to talk about.'[66]

There was no certainty that Neil would rise to the occasion and the strategy would work – that these two crucial elements would fuse together. For the first few days of the campaign, it seemed they might not. The Alliance started strongly and slickly; one poll had Labour in third place. People started to write Labour off. And then, in a moment of extraordinary combustion, it all came together. Neil made his Llandudno speech – 'Why am I the first Kinnock in a thousand generations to go to university'[67] – and by the sheer force of his will, the extraordinary power of his words, the election tide was turned. Visibly, tangibly, the mood changed and confidence soared. Overnight, strategy, message and leader fused, producing an incredible energy. This moment, this speech, effectively ended the ambitions of the Alliance to be the second party in British politics. Although week one saw no change in the polls, the tide had turned.

Week two saw further Labour advances. The Alliance campaign began to falter. Labour pinned the Conservatives back with a controversially worded advertisement: a broadcast remark by Norman Tebbit in 1983 saying, 'If unemployment is not below three million in five years then I'm not worth electing.'[68] Peter played this furore perfectly, constantly pouring petrol on the flames, culminating with a presentation of Tebbit's actual words on a cranky tape-recorder to the assembled journalists. Tebbit's words bore little relationship to the words on the advertisement, but it didn't matter. We had the tape, Tebbit was speaking, Peter was icily confident, the journalists were seduced.

Then came the Hudson party political broadcast, the moment,

according to the Alliance strategists, when their campaign folded. The broadcast, an emotional biography of Neil Kinnock's life using romantic footage of Neil and Glenys walking along wind-swept cliffs, was brought to Peter by Hugh late in the night two days before transmission. It ended not with the word 'Labour', but with 'Kinnock'. This was an unprecedented development – fighting an election campaign under the name of the leader and not the party. It could hardly have been more daring or controversial. But Peter backed it without a murmur. As I watched, I marvelled at its power. Despite everything, the campaign had worked. The broadcast had the most sensational impact: Neil's ratings went up 16 per cent overnight. Some people say that the broadcast had no effect, that Labour still lost. They are wrong. Almost overnight Labour had shunted the Alliance to the sidelines. By the end of the second week the polls had begun to shift. Labour was on the move.

But at the start of the third week, Neil slipped up. Asked a fairly soft question by David Frost, Neil gave the impression that Labour's response to invasion would be civil resistance. Or, in David Owen's snide soundbite, 'He wants *Dad's Army* back.'[69] The answer was not entirely Neil's fault – the defence policy was indefensible – but it was an error and Neil blamed himself terribly for it. It gave the Conservatives an opening on defence and they pounded us mercilessly. From surging forward, we were now pinned to the ropes. The Conservatives produced their one great advertisement of the campaign, 'Labour's Policy on Arms', with a hapless soldier holding his hands up. But we survived the week, Kinnock's ratings remained high, and the Alliance could not climb back. Defence was killed by a press conference devoted entirely to that subject, allowing the journalists to exhaust their interest in it and showing the wisdom of confronting serious political danger and not ducking it. Within days Labour was back on the attack, with the Conservative low point the famous wobbly Thursday, when a Gallup poll showed the lead narrowing to four points and Thatcher made a hash of health.

But this was the last good news for Labour. As we tired, the Conservatives moved into top gear. They attacked on taxation and Labour extremism, issues that were certain to hurt our vote. And they linked a massive tabloid attack with a huge advertising offensive on the classic 'Don't Let Labour Ruin It' theme. In response to this, Labour was running on empty. Peter was exhausted, drained by the awesome demands of the campaign. Roy Hattersley stumbled on taxation, which the Tory press jumped on. The *Daily Mail* denounced 'LABOUR'S LIES ON TAXATION'[70] while the *Daily Express* screamed: 'EXPOSED: LABOUR'S TAX FIASCO'.[71] Healey, put on the back foot over his wife's hip operation, fumbled on private health. We had no energy, no new ideas, no final-week burst. Meanwhile, Thatcher coolly went to Venice to meet world leaders.

The day of the election, 11 June 1987, we knew we had lost, but we couldn't predict how badly. I telephoned Peter and asked him what was the minimum acceptable result: the smallest share of the vote with which he and I could survive in Labour communications. He said 35 per cent. We got 31 per cent. I went in early that Thursday evening, and there was great optimism: a *Newsnight* poll was predicting a hung parliament. But at 9.30 P.M. a call came through from the BBC with their exit poll. Peter took the call in his office, watched in silence by myself, Deborah Mattinson, Richard Faulkner and the four Labour press officers. As he heard the poll result his face became ashen. 'It is bad,' he said, 'they're back with a majority of a hundred.' As the results rolled in, it became unbearable. I walked into the night and felt the awful pain of election defeat.

In fact, the campaign had been an extraordinary success. It had saved Labour. It need not have been so – a weaker campaign, any hint of the chaos and unprofessionalism of 1983, and Labour would have been smashed into third place, perhaps for ever. Labour's vote rose three points to 31 per cent. The Alliance vote fell almost four points to 23 per cent. A gap at the beginning of the campaign of less than 2 per cent had increased to 8 per cent: a massive shift in four weeks. Labour never looked back; the Alliance never recovered.

But it was still a crushing defeat, and on the issues that really mattered – tax, the economy, extremism – Labour had fallen back. It had modernised its communications, but not its policies or the party itself, and the best communications professionals in the world could not rescue it. 'In a way, we demonstrated the weakness of advertising and marketing,' said Chris Powell. 'It makes very little difference how well or how professionally you do the campaign if your leader and your policies are not likely to appeal to the broad mass of the population.'[72]

Yet we dragged Labour, in under two years, from a party which abhorred photo opportunities and still believed the way to address the public was to don a donkey jacket and harangue the party faithful at rallies into the glare of modern professional communications. We gave them a new identity, the red rose, the Hugh Hudson broadcast and the campaign grid. We ran a brilliant campaign and proved Labour was serious about winning and sufficiently self-disciplined to govern. It wasn't enough to win the votes we needed, but it was probably enough to secure the future of the party. Partial modernisation had saved Labour, but a basically unchanged party was still years away from earning the trust of the people.

3

The Long Decline

'Another load of bloody rubbish'

Immediately after the 1987 defeat I retired hurt to our house in Hampshire and hid, speaking to almost no one. Election defeat is like bereavement: a long, empty ache. It was not as bad in 1987 as it would be in 1992, but it was painful enough. For a couple of weeks I sat miserably alone, or took long walks around the Test Valley. I remember now only a cheerful call from Bob Worcester wishing me well.

But even as I sat and moped it became clear to me why we had lost and what we had to do next. We lost because we had not changed far enough, fast enough. The engine had been polished, but it was still a Victorian relic. I began gathering evidence for an election post-mortem which I completed in London in July and sent to Larry Whitty, Neil Kinnock and Peter Mandelson.

The strengths of the 1987 campaign were clear enough: apart from its professional organisation, it had developed a strong strategic focus – social, emotional, passionate. But there were weaknesses too. We were still fighting on our own ground, not taking back Conservative territory, or even reclaiming neutral ground. Effectively we gave up the economy, taxation and personal finance to the Conservatives, and in so doing forfeited any chance of winning the election. There was also no doubt that we tailed off in the last week. We were exhausted, we had no more strategic options. In the last, crucial few days, we lacked firepower.[1]

We had also been too vague, over-emphasising big, general themes while the Tories were precise, Exoceting the voters where it really mattered and linking the tangible benefits of voting Conservative (such as no strikes) alongside people's tangible fears (on defence, for example). On the economy we had been abstract and long-winded. I was honest about Neil, describing him as 'our greatest campaign asset', but criticising his decision to open the door on defence. His bearing had been 'oppositional rather than governmental', and misjudgements such as dancing at the final week's rally in Islington had undermined his stature.[2]

But the main conclusions of the evaluation were forward-looking and strategic. We needed to establish a planning group to examine demographic changes and how they would affect Labour; to look at changes in lifestyle, values and attitudes; to establish what the party needed to do to appeal beyond its normal demographic base.[3]

I followed the formal election review with a strategic note in late July, setting out more clearly what had to be done. Labour had been successful in regaining some heartland support, but had failed to win back key groups, particularly in the south and the Midlands. For Labour to form a government it would be crucial, I said, not only for it to appeal to its traditional support base – which came from a declining sector of the population – but also for it to attract new voters. In short, we had to reach out to the new middle classes. 'It is now essential that the party embarks on a major research project to identify why defecting groups have left Labour, and what must be done to win them back,' I argued.[4] This was the genesis of 'Labour and Britain in the 1990s',[5] the most comprehensive review of public opinion ever undertaken by Labour. It became the polling foundation upon which the party's modernisation was built.

Indications of the hostility my conclusions would face from some in the party came when Roy Hattersley, in stubbornly traditionalist mode on *A Week in Politics* in July, described equality and a freer society as the Labour Party's 'Sermon on the Mount', not to be abandoned because 'marketing men' found it wasn't attracting 'the trendy, upwardly-mobile middle classes'.[6] For me his argument encapsulated everything that had gone wrong with Labour. Fundamentalist in tone, imbuing political ideas with the power of immutable myth, resisting change, it seemed to sneer at people who wanted to get on and seek better lives for themselves and their children. For Roy, what has gone wrong for Labour is that it has capitulated to the middle classes. For me, what has gone right with the party is that it has now finally reached out to them.

We have different Labour dreams, and above all different conceptions of what and who the middle classes are: the difference between politics formed in the southern suburbs and in Sheffield's back streets. To Roy the middle classes are slick, southern, superficial. To me they are caring, hard-working, anxious, ambitious – ordinary people with dreams, living lives under the kind of pressure Roy left behind thirty years ago. They are, in one form or another, the great majority of our population and the great majority of the coalition Labour needed to build to win power. In 1987 they were Labour's future, as they are today. It infuriates Roy that Labour is obsessed with the middle classes. It infuriates me to hear progressive politicians with comfortable lifestyles pouring scorn on hard-working people who dare to aspire to a little of the same. But if Roy is resistant to middle-class politics he was kind to me: he was helpful in getting me established with the Labour Party in 1985 – something I hope he does not regret too much now.

But Hattersley was not alone. Rodney Bickerstaffe, General Secretary of NUPE, told the Labour Party conference in 1987: 'We cannot hand Labour over to marketing men to be packaged like breakfast cereal; our policies cannot be contracted out to the pick of the polls.'[7] Thankfully others, like Bryan Gould, campaign co-ordinator in the 1987 election, took a more enlightened view. He told *The World This Weekend* in July 1987: 'What we ought to be doing is looking at where policies ought to come from, what the demand is, what interests we ought to be serving. In that way we can make sure that the policy includes its popular appeal from the outset.'[8]

Mandelson himself didn't blink. Immediately he set in motion a polling and demographic review. It took four months and was chiefly carried out by Patricia Hewitt, who chaired the process; Roger Jowell of the Social and Community Planning Research; Paul Ormerod, an economist from the Henley Centre for Forecasting; Andrew (now Lord) McIntosh of IFF (a market research company); Andrew Shaw from Liverpool University and Deborah Mattinson, who had become my business partner, and was a crucial figure in Labour's communications revolution. The review was a huge undertaking; it was effectively an autopsy on the British electorate and its influence was enormous.

We presented it to the NEC and the shadow Cabinet on 20 November 1987. I introduced the meeting because no one else would. Peter and Patricia, as partisan party officials, watched from the back, not wishing to contaminate the objectivity of the findings. Speaking first was a terrifying ordeal because even at the time I was aware that this was a defining moment in the development of the Labour Party. We were about to tell the party that seventy years of history had been wrong: Labour had to take a different course; it had to modernise or wither away.

The atmosphere in the room at Transport House was tense. The room seemed vast, the audience massive. Somewhere sat Peter: insouciant and radiating a confidence I wished I could share. As I rose to speak, my knees trembled, my voice sounded hollow. I was saved by Dennis Skinner. 'Another load of bloody rubbish,' he growled. This broke the tension and lifted my nerve. At the time, I thought this was just Dennis being a Luddite; I suspect now that he was kindly rescuing me from my nerves.

I did not say much – I left that to others in a meeting which lasted three and a half hours. After it, no one who was present would feel quite the same about Labour and its future. The presentation was wide in scope and its findings were devastating: Labour's share of the vote had fallen by 17 per cent in twenty years, while the Conservative share had remained immutably solid. No single section of the population had left us more than any other. Labour had lost working-class votes as well as middle-class votes. All sections of society had deserted the party.[9]

The people who *were* voting Labour had done so out of habit: 27 per cent of its supporters voted Labour because it was the 'party of the working class'; 20 per cent because they had 'always voted Labour'. As one northern respondent said, 'I have always voted socialist. So have all my family.' But Conservative voters were more discriminating. They voted Tory because of Thatcher; because the government was doing a good job; because inflation was under control; because the Tories knew how to manage the economy. Only 7 per cent voted Conservative because they always had done.[10]

The reasons given for not voting Labour were particularly damning. Among lapsed Labour voters, extremism was the top factor; second was trade union domination and division; third, defence; and finally, weak leadership. People believed Labour would cut their standard of living and restrict their freedom to buy council houses and shares.[11]

One working-class ex-Labour voter said, 'I have changed basically because of my working position – what I want from life. I mean, eventually you want to buy a place. You want to get more out of what you earn.'[12] I wanted this voter back. Roy Hattersley was less sure.

These findings on their own were bleak. But worse was to come. The research had found that Labour's remaining support was habitual, its lapsed supporters visceral in their attitudes towards the party. But the underlying social and economic tide was making a bad situation worse. The numbers of manual workers were declining; home ownership was increasing; share-holding, private medicine and private schooling were becoming much more popular.[13]

There were some shafts of light among these damning social trends. Labour values continued to have strong support and, most important of all, less than half of the collapse in Labour support in the previous twenty years could be ascribed to demographic changes alone: most of it was the result of the policies and image of the party. If Labour changed, so could its electoral fortunes.[14]

To some this was common sense; to others, heresy. At the end of the presentation there was silence, broken by Tony Benn, who apologised for criticising our research methods in advance. Most people in the room applauded. The SCA had let off a bomb in the heart of Labour.

The lion that didn't roar

The key figure in the initiation of the policy review which followed 'Labour and Britain in the 1990s' was Tom Sawyer, then Deputy General Secretary of NUPE and, from October 1994 to October 1998, General Secretary of the Labour Party. Tom has a quiet manner, but underneath it lies real toughness. He was and is one of the genuinely modernising figures in the Labour movement. He told the Fabian Society in June 1988, 'We want to win the next General Election. And to anyone who says this is crude or unprincipled, I say that to put Labour into government, into a position where we can put our principles into practice, is the most sophisticated and principled aim that the party could have.'[15] He is also loyal. After the defeat in 1992, Tom was one of the few who stood by those who had been responsible for the campaign. He did not turn in the wind. If you put together his contribution towards the policy review and his work as General Secretary, he is someone who can genuinely claim great credit for the election of a Labour government in 1997.

Not only did Tom have the idea for the review, he was also a key figure in its gestation and development, alongside Neil. 'After the election,' Patricia Hewitt remembers, 'Tom Sawyer came to see Neil and said, this is a much bigger task than we ever thought.

We've got to go back to square one, look at aims and values, have a policy review. So it was Tom's idea. Neil bought it.'[16] They took the campaign strategy committee structure and adapted it to the policy review, with seven policy sub-committees each co-chaired by a member of the shadow Cabinet and a member of the NEC.

Neil Kinnock's two great modernising achievements were expunging Militant and ditching unpopular policies through the policy review. Many believed that Kinnock had decided at the outset the policies he wanted to emerge from the review, but he hadn't. He knew he wanted policies that would equip Labour for the future, but he was open-minded about their precise form. As Patricia Hewitt recalled:

> Neil knew in advance the outcome he wanted only in the sense that he would recognise it when he saw it. What he wanted was something that would fit the 1990s. Right at the beginning, Hattersley said there had to be a philosophical framework for this, and Neil said okay – you write it. And he wrote 'Aims and Values', but no one took much notice of it.
>
> With 'Labour and Britain in the 1990s' we were telling them why we lost the election, and how we had to change, to give a context to the policy review. And people were terrified by what we were telling them. So what Neil was saying – to the policy convenors, shadow Cabinet, NEC, party conference – was, don't worry about the old arguments, put yourself into the 1990s, the next chance we're going to have to fight an election. Stand in the future and then figure out what are the right policies for Labour to achieve its objectives. So he really gave the policy review committees a wonderful opportunity, a blank sheet of paper, and I think his overwhelming disappointment was that they didn't pick that up and run with it.[17]

The SCA was closely involved in the policy review process at all stages and undertook a research programme under Deborah Mattinson to complement the newly established policy review groups. Each group had a set of researchers assigned to it who conducted qualitative research. But polling cannot create policy, and the direct influence of the SCA on the content of the final review was less than is believed. If research had had more influence in 1988 and the people's voice had been heard more loudly, then the results would have been bolder, braver, more modern. Labour would have done better in 1992.

But in fact, with the exception of defence, where Gerald Kaufman brilliantly abandoned unilateralism, the polling evidence was largely ignored. Interesting themes and ideas that emerged through the review process tended to be blocked. We were stuck with 'functional intervention', 'social ownership' (a euphemism for back-door nationalisation), and a commitment to retake majority ownership of British Telecom and totally renationalise the water industry.[18] A highly interventionist supply-side strategy was still regarded as the only key to industrial recovery. 'I was very disappointed with the policy review,' said Charles Clarke. 'We should have been much more engaged from Neil's office. We were too respectful of the leading politicians.'[19] Most desperately, against the strongest SCA advice, John Smith was preparing benefits pledges which would trap us on tax for the next election. Although it took Labour forward, the policy review was fundamentally a missed opportunity for which we paid a heavy price in 1992.

Labour was changing too little and too slowly.

Despair

A general depression hung over the party by the end of 1987. In my diary, I wrote, 'Neil is in a malaise, which seems to be settling down over Labour Party advisers. There is exceptionally low morale at Walworth Road following re-organisation and staff cut-backs. Peter is talking about the difficulties of making progress at Walworth Road.'[20] Even some of Kinnock's closest supporters were beginning to question his leadership. Rumours that John Prescott might challenge Hattersley for the deputy leadership were rumbling on; the dispute tumbled into the beginning of the next year.

In January 1988 I wrote a private note to Mandelson warning of the dangers I felt we were facing: we lacked momentum; lacked confidence; lacked initiatives; lacked assertiveness. I warned that this could soon lead to a leadership crisis. We had to break clear of this and start looking like winners: 'At the moment I suspect that internally and externally people are sensing that Labour will not win the next election. This has to change.'[21]

But in fact things got worse. Tony Benn attacked Kinnock in a string of press releases and in March, as Nigel Lawson delivered his tax-cutting budget, slashing the top rate of income tax from 60 per cent to 40 per cent and reducing the standard rate to 25 per cent, Benn challenged Kinnock for the leadership. Defence flared up as an issue in June, after Kinnock appeared to hint first in a private lunch with the *Independent* and later in an interview on *This Week, Next Week* that he was considering a shift to multilateralism;[22] Denzil Davies, Labour's defence spokesman, resigned, accusing Kinnock of changing defence policy without consulting him. At the time, Kinnock's aides claimed he knew exactly what he was doing. Hewitt told the story of Neil's riposte when he came out of the *This Week, Next Week* studio and she said to him, 'You slayed a few sacred cows there.' Neil, she said, winked and replied, 'Just put them to sleep, lovey, just put them to sleep.'[23] But two weeks later, in an on-the-record briefing with executives of the *Independent*, he gave the impression that Labour defence policy was unchanged; unilateralism was still in.[24] Mandelson, who had no warning he was about to do this, was devastated. Shadow Cabinet members and MPs were briefing against Neil uncontrollably, and he was slated in the weekend press.

The truth is that Neil was exhausted and depressed. A fortnight later I had a meeting with two of those closest to him to discuss our Kinnock campaign. We were all concerned about him, he was under impossible pressure, much of it focused on supporting in public a defence policy he privately thought was madness. Neil had to carry within him the massive contradictions at the heart of the Labour Party, putting intolerable strains on him and his public voice.

'They mentioned two incidents,' I wrote in my diary, 'one of which was when he came out of the *Independent* interview where he did his U-turn back to unilateralism. He came out, his head spinning, apparently saying, "I don't know what I've said in there. It's all words to me. Words, just words." They also said that after the initial *This Week, Next Week* interview he came out saying exasperatedly, "What is our defence policy? I don't know what our defence policy is." In general, he appears to be in a very deep and melancholic depression and although he does seem to have come out of it now, these are exceptionally difficult times for him.'[25]

Neil was an extremely complex person, driven by a combination of courage and self-doubt. It was an essential part of his personality to express this doubt ocasionally; not a negative but a positive thing, letting rip his frustration at the confusion around him. Charles Clarke says Neil 'often became gloomy' about the state of affairs, but equally, he often became exhilarated: 'Neil was and is a very emotional politician. He felt very positively and very negatively.'[26] What happened in this period, he said, was that Neil dropped his guard a little and showed his true self to half a dozen people who hadn't seen it before. 'It started to become a talking point,' he said.

> While he may have been a bit gloomy, I don't think it was so different to what went on normally, and I think it got taken out of context. He always felt deep self-doubt about his own capacity to succeed – not for himself, I don't think he was a very personally ambitious person; I mean, obviously he has his share, as all politicians do – but he worried that he would betray the party and not bring it back to where it ought to be. He felt that he would be betraying his home, his parents, his background, his village, his constituency by not being up to it. This was his greatest fear.

The academic snobbery which started running some time during this process was very, very damaging to him, because people
believed that he was stupid and so he started to wonder, was he
stupid, which actually is the most awful untruth about him, he
is one of the most intelligent men I have ever met. But he never
believed it – if people said to him, 'actually you are very bright'
he couldn't accept it.[27]

The loss of the 1987 election increased his insecurity: 'He felt
that he had not done as well as he should have done in 1987 and
therefore his self-questioning was greater. But I don't think it was
qualitatively different to at other times.'[28]

The party looked ragged and divided. An *Observer* poll in late
June put Labour 15 per cent behind the Conservatives.[29] The press
turned on Neil, as did many of his colleagues. Joe Napolitan was
emphatic: Kinnock has to go. You can't do this sort of thing and
get away with it.[30] A *Sunday Times* MORI poll at the beginning
of July had Kinnock seventeen points behind Thatcher, an 11 per
cent fall – the largest ever in one month for a political leader.[31]
Even Neil's closest supporters began to say he should step down.
In my diary, I wrote, 'I begin to get a sense of Labour perhaps
not being able to win power.'[32]

On 16 August 1988 Mandelson wrote a long and considered
note to Charles Clarke, warning of the seriousness of the position
in relation to Neil. In it he warned that the policy review, on which
the chance of turning around the party's fortunes hinged, would
fail unless Neil became fully engaged in the process and used it
to project a new vision for himself, and for the Labour Party, and
to restore his political authority. The note read, 'Returning from
holiday I had expected the unfavourable media comment about
us to abate in August. But it has not gone away. It has dug in
rather seriously and the party, and Neil in particular, are going
to have to project a strong sense of strategy at the conference and
beyond if we are to recover fully our electoral credibility and his
political authority.'[33]

He compared the party's pre-summer recess slump with the

post-Greenwich period in 1987 – both occasions when Labour's fitness to govern became an issue:

> In 1987 we had the election campaign to re-assert our positives, all combined giving very powerful and sustained projection, chiefly of Neil. This time, though, the negatives were not countered effectively and that process of modernisation, strong leadership and 'gathering strength' which has appealed to the public, appeared to lose its impetus. Most critical of all, we know, the architect of this process himself seemed to falter, apparently becoming very indecisive on defence policy.
>
> Why did this happen? Aside from the very damaging defence imbroglio there were two other elements which could have been approached differently. The first you have already referred to is the policy review. Neil was personally not very engaged in this and was clearly disappointed by its fruits (who wouldn't be?). But I think his advocacy of the reports rather reflected this. His subsequent speeches didn't pick up on the reports in a stimulating way or with identifiable themes.

He felt also that Benn's leadership campaign had been rebutted weakly: 'In sum, this lack of visibility and projection has had an effect on the media, the public and the party. It has created a loss of strength. It meant that when defence blew us off course we were already vulnerable and didn't have strong enough organisation or communications to fight back with.'[34]

Mandelson urged Clarke to involve Kinnock more in the policy review process, and to stiffen his resolve to modernise policies on tax and spending, industrial relations, law and order and renationalisation. He wanted the national membership system to be implemented and one member, one vote strengthened in order to offset the union tag: 'We have to protect the party's constitution and rules from the ultra left.'[35]

His over-riding concern was about Kinnock himself, who had lost his identity with the electorate. He needed to re-state, clearly and repeatedly, his political goals and objectives, and find fresh goals to refer to, to update and extend the 'Kinnock agenda':

During the next year Neil's identity in the public's mind needs to be associated not just with changing the party but more directly with the country's future, the emerging economic, social and environmental issues of the 1990s and touching more politically on the 'me, my family, my hopes' concerns of the public. This, of course, is what the policy review is meant to be about. But it will not succeed unless we organise it, and Neil's involvement, differently ... I think for Neil to be seen setting out the fresh thinking and the evolving ideas of the review is essential to restoring his political authority. For Neil personally (and in all senses he is the most important element in the strategy's success) it means re-establishing the strong identity he held previously and projecting himself more actively so that it's clear what he stands for and where he's going. In particular, it means overcoming those negative attributes which have been provided by the media since June that he is a nice person but a weak leader; that he talks too much and says too little; and that his social concern is not matched by his economic competence.[36]

Finally, Mandelson lamented the lack of a strong core message and vision for Labour, one that was about the 1990s and sparked thoughts of economic competence as well as social justice. He wanted modernisation of communications, of the image of the party leadership, and of party policy itself. This was a major note setting out Mandelson's way forward, his agenda for winning the election. In the event it was largely ignored.

The remainder of 1988 saw no improvement in Labour's fortunes. Neil made a strong speech at conference but it was overshadowed by Ron Todd, General Secretary of the TGWU, who spoke at a *Tribune* rally on the same day, mocking 'sharp-suited Filofax socialists with their cordless telephones'.[37] The conference also went on to back unilateralism, although by a smaller majority than in previous years. But the low point of the period was the loss of the Govan by-election to the SNP in November 1988, overturning one of the biggest Labour majorities in the country. It plunged Kinnock – and the party – further into despair.

New Labour's false dawn

In February 1989, confronting our parlous position two years before a probable General Election, and our predicted defeat in the forthcoming European elections, I suggested a concept to get Labour on its feet again. I called it 'New Labour'. It was an idea whose time was yet to come, but I was sure even then that the party had, in some way, to demonstrate real change by being uncompromisingly new. A line had to be drawn between the old Labour Party and the new, and 'New Labour' was a way to do it. However, only for the very briefest of periods did the reality of Neil Kinnock's Labour Party match the promise of New Labour. The idea died on the vine.

On 13 February I incorporated this concept of New Labour into a campaigning note, evaluating strategic considerations for the year ahead. Labour was 11 per cent behind the Conservatives despite high levels of economic pessimism; morale was low among Labour supporters; Labour was making no progress on the key issues vital in gaining trust: extremism, high taxes, nationalisation and opposition to council house sales. Labour had gone stale. It had lost the freshness of 1985-86, when voters saw Neil Kinnock's Labour as 'new' and full of potential. It was no longer Neil Kinnock's 'new model party'. 'New Labour has lost its zest and modernity,' I wrote.[38]

I set out what seemed at the time absurdly ambitious targets: a poll lead or poll parity by the end of June; net gains in the European elections; massive shifts in attitudes to the party. I wanted people's idea of Labour to reflect the following statements:

- 'Labour has changed. Neil Kinnock has delivered a New Labour party.'
- 'I trust Labour to form a government.'
- 'Labour has sensible economic policies and the team to run them.'
- 'Labour understands people like me.'[39]

In the months that followed, Labour met its opinion poll and European election targets. But it failed utterly to meet any of these attitudinal objectives.

Our short-term objective was to prepare for the European and local elections. I argued for a continuous five-month campaign, concentrated most intensely in the two-month election period from 8 April until 15 June. At its heart was a central strategic recommendation: do not trickle out the policy review; instead, make one, big-bang presentation. Crucially, bring it forward and make it the centrepiece of the European election campaign.[40] This was in complete defiance of the previous consensus about the presentation of the review, which had been to do it late, and do it gradually, in order to minimise the possibility of backlash and dissent. My view was the opposite: people would shift to Labour only if they were sure that it had changed, and only bold, demonstrable change would convince them of that. Dissent in these circumstances did not reduce our electoral appeal, but heightened it. It was evidence of change.

When I presented the note to the campaign team the response was incredulous. Everyone fell about laughing. We were behind in the polls. We were likely to lose seats in the European elections, not win them. But I insisted: I said we had no choice, we had to win them. We had to create a sense of momentum, bringing the policy review forward so that it was out in time for the elections. Peter was with me; he had no doubts. The policy review was to be brought forward and turned into a major event.

It was published in May, following a two-day NEC meeting to approve the seven policy documents. Its title, 'Meet the Challenge, Make the Change', was conceived by Barry Delaney, a leading advertising figure and one of Labour's most talented supporters. We chose it because we wanted a title that looked both ways – to the party and to the country as a whole – and said that what we were doing for the party we would do for Britain. But although it was a clever title, it was ultimately a fudge. It hinted at change, but didn't shout about it.

Despite its limitations, the review broke through as a news story. People began to recognise that Labour was changing. Within days of publication, we were two points ahead of the Conservatives in a MORI poll, our first lead since before the 1987 election.[41] In the European elections in June 1989 Labour won fourteen seats, the Conservatives lost fourteen. Those elections saw the first public signs of the fissures at the heart of the Conservative Party on Europe. Their fiercely anti-European campaign attacking 'Diets of Brussels' alienated many within the Tory mainstream. In May Margaret Thatcher had a decidedly lukewarm celebration of her decade in power, and in October she faced her first challenge for the leadership from the stalking-horse candidate, Sir Anthony Meyer. The Tories were beginning to look fractious and stale.

This was Neil Kinnock's finest hour, the peak of his electoral achievement. From then until the 1992 election the Kinnock project went into decline. That night Neil was happier than I have ever seen him. It seemed to be the start, the prelude to other and bigger victories. But it was not to be. The splash from the policy review was enough to win the European elections, but its content wasn't deep enough to win the General Election.

We were in political decline and had reached a strategic impasse. I continued to rattle out memos arguing for modernisation as the way to take us forward. 'No party has taken the modern ground and captured the new agenda of the 1990s,' I wrote.[42] I wanted us to generate appeal by creating a sense of a modern, forward-looking party with policies to match; Labour should be open to new, radical ideas, thinking creatively and side-stepping the constraints of traditional left-wing ideology. At conference, 'We must present emphatic demonstrable evidence that Labour has changed, and that the change is permanent. Labour is the modern party of the next decade, the Tories are the party of the past.'[43]

Although the 1989 conference, based on the policy review and using the same slogan, 'Meet the Challenge, Make the Change', was successful, with the party displaying unusual levels of discipline and unity, I was still uneasy. In October I wrote a post-conference strategy note. We were failing to move towards the new agenda with any confidence, I said. 'Labour has to move as far and as fast in the next eighteen months as it has in the last four years.' Labour was still not trusted, not safe. Above all, Labour was not yet New Labour. And the electorate wanted New Labour.[44]

Although 1989 was a turn-around year, the long decline that led to defeat in 1992 had already begun. In October 1989 Nigel Lawson resigned, setting in motion a chain of events that would produce Geoffrey Howe's resignation, Thatcher's toppling and the killer electoral blow of the parliament, her replacement in November 1990 by John Major. That year also saw the killer organisational blow for Labour's campaign, with the careless loss of Peter Mandelson.

To lose both looks like carelessness . . .

Labour's internal collapse began with the departure of Patricia Hewitt to the Institute for Public Policy Research at the beginning of 1989. Patricia has her detractors, but no one can doubt her talent. She was someone whom Neil could not afford to lose, and she believed she was forced out of the office following disagreements with Neil's chief of staff Charles Clarke, although Clarke insists he would have been 'very happy' for her to stay: 'There had been for a long time a kind of head-to-head rivalry between us, which wasn't easy, but I think we had found a *modus operandi* that was okay.'[45] She kept working for the party from the outside, cutting and reshaping the policy review to meet the rushed deadline before the European elections, and later playing a linchpin role in the 1992 election campaign.

Mandelson's departure was more complicated, more painful and more protracted than Patricia's. Peter first told me that he wanted to pursue a political career over lunch in the upstairs dining room at Braganza in Soho, just round the corner from my office in

Old Compton Street, early in 1988. He believed that it was time for him to go his own way, to be his own person. He felt drained by the enormous exertions of his job, and was ready to move on. But he also felt, as Patricia did, a sense of rejection, of not being fully wanted by the leader's office or by senior party management. 'Everybody and his uncle is advising Mandelson to quit,' I wrote in my diary in January. 'He's done one good campaign, why should he try and do another which may not even be as good?'[46]

By the beginning of 1989, Mandelson's resolve had hardened. Some months after Patricia Hewitt had left, Kinnock asked him to be his press secretary. Mandelson said he would take the job but he wanted to have one chance of being selected for a seat. Kinnock refused, insisting he had to choose. He chose to stay on as Director of Campaigns and Communications and try for a seat, and Julie Hall – who eventually found the world of opposition politics frustrating and irrational – came in as Neil's press secretary.

During the European elections that June, there were rumblings against Mandelson from within Walworth Road. He gave all of his energy to that election, and delivered Labour's first major victory since 1974. But this still wasn't enough for those who were determined to undermine him. The European elections put Peter under almost intolerable strain. He had given everything. Yet a leading party official phoned him up afterwards and, instead of praising him, criticised him for his aloofness from the senior party staff during the campaign.

Although Peter wanted to leave, he could have been persuaded to stay had the will been there. After he was selected to stand for election in Hartlepool at the end of 1989, Mandelson wanted to stay on, overlapping with his successor. But Charles Clarke felt he should go immediately so that his replacement had time to get to grips with the job. 'I came to the view, which Peter didn't accept, but most other people that I speak to do think is right, that you can't have somebody who is a parliamentary candidate and is basically going to run their seat from the moment the election is called, doing the job of communications director right up until the campaign begins and then, as it were, stopping,' Clarke explained. 'Peter's view was that he could do both and that wasn't my view, and that may be a wrong view, I don't know.'[48] Colin Byrne, a senior Labour press officer at the time, believes it was a mistake. 'It was totally the wrong decision,' he said. 'Charles thought it was a betrayal of Neil for Peter to take his eye off the ball and go for a seat.' In the end Kinnock intervened, asking Peter to stay until October the following year. Clarke in turn insisted on advertising Peter's post in April, which was why Mandelson and the new Director of Campaigns and Communications, John Underwood, who was appointed by the NEC in June, ended up doing parallel jobs for four months.

And still the hostility worsened. Mandelson remembers Clarke telling him in March 1990 that if he stayed on in his job he would undermine the election effort. The bad feeling spread. In August 1990, Peter moved into a flat in north London with Julie Hall and Colin Byrne, whom Kinnock had voted for instead of Underwood to replace Mandelson. They were immediately accused of running an alternative communications base. When Julie let it be known she was going to share a flat with Colin and Peter, Charles Clarke sat her down in Kinnock's office and urged her not to. After Julie ignored him, Clarke's frustration boiled over. It looked like an act of blatant provocation by the three of them. Byrne recalls a row which occurred when Julie wanted to install a fax machine. 'Charles said if she bought the fax machine and put it into a flat where Peter was, he would refuse to pay her phone bills,' said Byrne.[48] It was out of character for Clarke, but such was the paranoia of the time that for Julie to live with Colin and share a flat with Peter was considered an act of open subversion. This sort of soul-destroying hostility nearly devastated Labour's 1992 campaign; at times we fought each other with more energy than we fought the Conservatives. Clarke felt he was in an impossible position, facing a campaign disintegrating, and a lack of loyalty in his closest team. He was a man of great intelligence and huge intensity: the driving force behind the Kinnock project. But as the campaign started to falter, his intensity sometimes turned to intolerance with the failings and shortcomings of others. Given the pressures of the time this was understandable – but not always helpful, as Charles admits now.

It was not as if our position was so strong we could afford to waste the talents we had. Although we were ahead in the polls, our position was tenuous and I continued to issue a series of stark warnings, still pleading for further modernisation. At the beginning of the year I warned in a memo that the campaign team was fragmented and did not work as a group: 'In short, Labour has stalled.'[49] In June, despite a ten-point lead in the polls, Nicholas Ridley's damaging resignation from the government, seething anger over the poll tax, and victory at the mid-Staffordshire by-election with a 21 per cent swing, I wrote, 'Labour has not changed enough . . . At the death, in the polling-booth, people may be more likely to vote for the devil they know and dislike rather than the devil they do not fully trust. As things stand the Conservatives are on course for an election victory.' I was also becoming desperate about our campaigning organisation. 'Without a campaign manager – one person in charge – Labour will find it hard to win,' I warned.[50]

Despite the poll tax and victories in the May council elections (which had been widely portrayed in the Tory press as a Conservative victory simply because Labour failed to gain Wandsworth and Westminster), we were not making any headway. I remember a meeting in Neil Kinnock's office at the House of Commons, at which Neil walked up and down talking, getting angrier and angrier as his frustration grew. Suddenly, by accident, he smashed a lamp to the floor. We all – myself, Julie Hall, Neil – tried to ignore it, embarrassed, and continued the meeting, transfixed nevertheless by the lamp on the floor. All except Peter. Without saying a word, and without looking at any of us, he crept across the room, picked up the lamp and put it back on the table, then slid back to his seat. Neil didn't pause for breath.

That summer Neil was exhausted, by constantly attempting to hold together a party threatening to fracture if he moved too far and too fast, and by the need to look restrained and 'respectable' for the press and the public – especially as the prospect of the war in the Gulf moved closer. Neil became so constrained that he began to struggle for words to express himself. He was concerned that he had lost his great power of oratory and became obsessed with the idea that he might have 'lost his words'. One of those closest to him remembers it: 'He didn't have it in him any more. After six years as leader he was emotionally and intellectually drained. The well was dry.'[51]

In fact, Neil had often struggled to find words when he was under pressure. Charles Clarke remembers when he went up to make his acceptance speech after he had been elected leader at the 1983 conference. 'He grabbed me by the shoulder, I'll never forget it, we were behind the podium and he grabbed me and said, "Charles – today of all days I haven't got a fucking speech, I haven't got a fucking speech, at this fucking conference." It was a classic illustration.'[52] Shakespeare and the Bible ran through many of Kinnock's speeches. Once, when they were looking for someone else to appoint in the office to help write them, Neil insisted on somebody who knew the Bible and Shakespeare. 'He believes that they are great texts for helping to illuminate things that go on, and he was constantly frustrated that other people were less committed to words than him,' said Clarke, who thinks Neil's attachment to words was born of his lack of self-confidence:

> They were very important to him, no question about it. Whereas I would give up after being sure I was 95 per cent there, he'd spend another five hours getting the last 5 per cent, which often made almost no difference to the way it went down. He was a perfectionist, he was a perfectionist more than anything else. He felt that people would make fun of him if he simply repeated what he had said before, and therefore this stupidity thing comes up on the agenda again.

> Neil's greatest virtue as a politician for me was that he believed

politics was generally about argument. He didn't think it was just about emotions, he believed it was about argument, so he always tried to focus on an argument and then find the language to illustrate that argument. And his language was, of course, wonderful.[53]

Although the 1990 conference theme was 'Looking to the Future', I still didn't believe anyone meant it. 'The process of modernity and change within Labour should be unrelenting,' I wrote afterwards. On the most likely economic scenario, I warned, the Conservatives would get a winning 43 per cent of the vote.[54]

And then Peter left. 'Nobody even bothered to organise a leaving party for him,' said Colin Byrne. 'It was conference, we were in a hotel in Blackpool, and it was literally Peter's last day working for the party, on the staff. And no one had even organised a leaving card. Julie Hall and I had to go off with a couple of people from Peter's staff – people like Anna Healy – and put together a little leaving drinks party. Nobody at NEC level had even thought to do that. Peter, Julie and I drove in the streaming rain to his cottage in Ross-on-Wye and he just looked utterly disappointed that people he'd worked with for years hadn't even bothered to say goodbye. It was almost like an undue haste to get him out the door, and I just couldn't understand that.'[55]

Peter came to an agreement with the research company SRU, whose managing director Colin Fisher was a good friend of Labour, that he would work as a consultant for their company two days a week, leaving the rest of his time for Labour if it wanted him. His offer was never taken up and his talents were lost.

This was the position in October 1990: Hewitt gone; Mandelson going; a party not ready to govern; a leader not trusted to become Prime Minister; an organisation not fit to win.

Mandelson into exile

I first met John Underwood, Peter's replacement, for an informal interview over lunch when it was clear that Peter was leaving. He obviously wanted to be Director of Campaigns and Communications and I was quietly impressed, believing that he could act as a consolidating figure in a rapidly deteriorating situation. He seemed a nice man and a solid manager who could build a team with Colin Byrne, the other potential candidate for the job.

I was wrong. John took the job and immediately came under enormous pressure. He felt he had been appointed not because of Neil but despite him, which was true, and this put him on the defensive with the leader from the start. He believed Peter was running an alternative power base from the flat he shared with Byrne and Hall. Byrne insists this was untrue, although he admits Peter gave him and Julie advice: 'It was just Peter trying to help out from the sidelines.'[56]

By the time Underwood took over alone, after the 1990 conference, the battle lines had been drawn: Peter, Julie and Colin on one side; John Underwood on the other; Charles frustrated with them all, and me trying to hold the whole thing together.

But it was no use: John felt constantly undermined by Peter and by the SCA, and, I suspect, by me. I would often agree to meet him and he would be very late or not come at all. He was obsessed with the idea that there was a conspiracy against him. Gradually he unpicked the communications machine which Peter and I had built up. Barry Delaney, who had produced our party political broadcasts, was dropped and a more documentary style introduced. This was laudable but lacked style. I used long-suffering Hugh Hudson to fill the gap and he produced a string of broadcasts for us. John hated the job and became more and more depressed. Worst of all, he became increasingly suspicious of me, of Peter and of Neil.

But as we fought our battles inside Walworth Road, outside in Westminster the most decisive event of the parliament was taking place: Margaret Thatcher's resignation on 22 November 1990, and her replacement by John Major. Even with Thatcher, Labour was set to lose. With Major it was almost impossible for us to win: he was the new, fresh, decent fellow people felt they could vote for. I remember hearing the result of the Conservative leadership election as I was driving back from a group discussion in Harlow. I listened to it and felt numb. I knew it was all over.

The opinion polls turned dramatically against us. There was a 9.5 per cent swing to the Tories, who shot into the lead. Even worse, there was a 24 per cent swing in perceptions of economic competence.[57] We kept fighting over the winter and spring, constantly distracted by the personal disputes in the communications team, which had started to spill into the press. Neil was becoming desperate. Colin Byrne had to remove himself to the south of France one week that spring simply to take himself off the scene for a while. Still, we did well in the May local elections and later that month we won the Monmouth by-election, orchestrated by Peter Mandelson at Charles Clarke's request, on a 12.6 per cent swing, with a majority of 2,406. Our winning claim in Monmouth, that trust hospitals would 'opt out' of the NHS, led to a massive row and Labour poll leads. The pressure we exerted stopped Major calling an election when the time was right for him: four years in, with a fresh leader, after a successful Gulf War which greatly boosted his ratings. He had his chance and he missed it.

That summer the Tories began their tax campaign, with promises to reduce the basic rate to 20p and costing Labour's plans at £35 billion, as John Smith, the shadow Chancellor, announced National Insurance increases for the middle classes. And John Underwood, who seemed to have aged about ten years in the previous twelve months, resigned. Although it was a blow to the party at such a crucial time, his departure was inevitable. He had been persuaded that too much media attention was being given to Tony Blair and Gordon Brown, whom he saw as Mandelson's protégés, and he insisted other members of the shadow Cabinet should have more exposure. I saw the end coming when he told me that he had beaten Neil once on the NEC and he would beat him again. He had the votes, he said. John was clearly walking through a minefield, and the end came soon.

His resignation in June 1991, after Kinnock refused to sack

Colin Byrne, was sad but inevitable. It was also the final straw for Charles Clarke, who had spoken to many on the NEC and was frightened that resentment and mistrust was reaching an intolerable level. He angrily told us there could be no contact with Mandelson for the foreseeable future. Peter was effectively banished. Gripped by fear, loathing and paranoia, I think we were all going mad.

Beating adversity

In the centre of all this conflict I felt I just had to make things work. I knew this would be a thankless task which would almost certainly lead to ignominy. On New Year's Day 1991 I had sat down and discussed the situation with my wife. I was sure we would lose the election; I knew that I would be blamed; and that the period before and after it would be impossibly difficult. But I had no doubt about what I had to do – I had to keep going. I felt it was my duty.

But by the time John Underwood left in June, resentment against me was growing. Walworth Road was full of people who thought they should be making decisions but were incapable of doing so – they were all too busy fighting each other. David Hill, who took over Underwood's job in July, remembers inheriting a situation – with a General Election looming – where open warfare had been declared for the past year and where nothing was in place for the campaign: 'There was an enormous amount of mistrust. There was no sense of everybody running in the same direction. People didn't know who to trust. They had clearly in the previous year taken sides. There were three groups of people, really: people who had taken the side of John Underwood; people who'd taken the side of people who attacked John Underwood; and people who had wrung their hands and said, "What on earth do we do? We don't want to be on either of these sides."'[58] Party staff at the Friday SCA meetings were also quietly seething about my influence. They resented me and what I was doing. I should have made more effort, perhaps spent more time making it work with them, but I did not. I was a man with a mission. I was going to make this campaign work and they could like it or lump it.

First, I tried meetings. The main meeting I suggested was a Thursday co-ordinating meeting, which became the Campaign Advisory Team (CAT). This was chaired by Jack Cunningham, the campaign co-ordinator, and its members included Julian Eccles, the secretary of the meeting; Larry Whitty, the Labour Party General Secretary; John Underwood (or David Hill, his replacement); Julie Hall and Neil Stewart from Kinnock's office; myself; and, later, Patricia Hewitt and Clive Hollick. The CAT met every Thursday at 9 A.M., first at the European Parliamentary Labour Party offices, then at the offices of Hollick's company, MAI, and eventually at the polling organisation NOP. It worked in the sense that it ensured the principals were in the same room and talking, and it covered all the serious planning ground. But it was based on a premise that was completely insane: it was secret. In the atmosphere of suspicion and hostility at the time, this seemed logical: we thought Walworth Road would object to our group, so we didn't tell them about it. 'There were strings of official people in the party who would have been furious,' said Charles Clarke, 'but you simply didn't have the calibre of people within the party you needed to run a major national election campaign.'[59] Now, as I write this, it seems clear that it was madness: the meeting that ran the campaign was to remain a secret to the campaign it was supposed to be running.

This was the first great flaw of Labour's strategy. Decisions were to appear as if by magic, coming from a source unknown to all but a very select few. 'We would have this secret meeting,' Hewitt remembers, 'then you would head down to Walworth Road for the official meeting. It was a joke. Parallel decision-making structures. You had a secret meeting structure with people brought in from the outside to compensate for the fact that the people on the inside couldn't do the job.'[60] Sally Morgan, now head of the political office at Number 10, who was then in charge of key seats at Walworth Road, says people 'half knew' what was going on: 'Everybody knew meetings were happening all over the place, but there was no guidance for us working at the sharp end. So some of us were just getting on and doing our own thing almost.'[61]

Gradually, I succeeded in widening the membership of the Thursday evening group. First I suggested bringing in Clive Hollick. I wanted him because he was sensible and knew about organisation; I felt that people would behave in front of him. In July 1990 he wrote a note, which was largely ignored, saying the campaign 'lacks (and needs) a unitary organisational structure'; that 'the Thursday group, by virtue of its secrecy, cannot give clear leadership'; and that it is 'vital that Neil Kinnock be involved in the process of settling the key ingredients of the campaign'.[62] None of his recommendations were implemented. The campaign never gained a unitary command structure; secrecy was maintained; senior politicians were never fully involved in the campaign; and neither, most fatally, was Neil Kinnock.

I then managed to get Patricia Hewitt involved because of her campaign skills and experience. It proved impossible, however, to get Peter in, although I mooted the idea from time to time. He had become a kind of non-person, never to darken the campaign's doors again.

The next meeting, also my idea, was a media briefing in Jack Cunningham's office at 8.30 each morning. This was attended by myself and the Director of Campaigns and Communications, and worked well enough. Jack made a big effort at this and all meetings. He did not want the job of campaign co-ordinator, but he made the best of an almost impossible situation and held together a campaign that was always close to disintegration.

On Fridays there was yet another meeting – the SCA meeting – which effectively drove and organised huge parts of the campaign. If there was a focus for criticism that the SCA was too powerful, this meeting was it. I chaired it (it was attended by representatives from BMP, NOP, the Labour press office, Patricia Hewitt and someone from Jack Cunningham's office) not because I wanted to but because no one else would. Its power grew as the collapsing campaign structure thrust increasing amounts of responsibility on to Patricia Hewitt and me. On more than one occasion Larry Whitty asked me to take even more responsibility. By now I had developed a close relationship with Larry and did not want to turn him down – I felt I had a duty to keep the campaign functioning. As time went by the SCA became increasingly influential, and Patricia and I effectively took over the operational running of the 1992 campaign. It was this that caused the greatest post-election resentment. According to our critics, the campaign had been hijacked by outsiders – unaccountable, unelected, with their own modernising agenda. It was true that Patricia and I had power beyond our formal responsibilities, but we did not hijack the campaign, we rescued it from chaos and disintegration at the direct request of the General Secretary of the party.

The final meeting was David Hill's idea. As soon as he was appointed Director of Campaigns and Communications in June 1991, he said he wanted more politicians to be involved. So we started another Monday meeting with an open invitation to all politicians to attend. The only ones who came regularly were Roy Hattersley and Gerald Kaufman. Both were bastions of common sense, but they could only advise, they could not control. At almost every meeting they asked for access to Neil, for his greater involvement in the campaign. The request got nowhere. The meeting talked sense but influenced little. I, too, tried to involve Neil in it, but this was always blocked. Clive Hollick was also keen to involve Neil. On 4 December 1990 he wrote a memo that there should be 'regular, very short, meetings with NK on Monday at which the current state of research and strategy should be presented'. Charles Clarke believed that more meetings increased the burden on Neil. I can remember Gordon Brown and Tony Blair coming only once to the Monday meeting. They took one look at the chaos and indecision and decided their talents would be better employed elsewhere.

We were not helped by an atmosphere in which every move Gordon Brown made was considered to be jostling for the leadership. Although Gordon had made a pact with John Smith in which he wrote himself out of the running, Smith's supporters, foreseeing a fight for the leadership after the election, were already going into battle. 'The whole thing was so debilitating because every time Gordon appeared on TV, someone in John's camp would say, "Look, it's another bid for the leadership,"' Patricia remembers. 'It meant David Hill couldn't put anyone up without creating problems.'[63] Thus we were being deprived of one of our best campaigners.

Despite the frustrations and the organisational morass, we did get things done. In September the SCA produced a poster campaign on the NHS with sufficient impact to persuade Major to postpone the election again. We blew Major off course and he lost his last chance of a decent majority. If the SCA did nothing else in the 1992 election, it did that.

However, I was becoming hysterical about the management of the campaign. We had no political guidance. On 8 October I wrote a memo, identifying the following problems: weaknesses in political management; weaknesses in news management; poor teamwork; inexperience in the campaign team; poor co-ordination and integration; weaknesses with campaign leadership, political integration and political strategy; shadow Cabinet splits; lack of funds and a lack of a properly functioning opposition research operation. I suggested bolstering the Thursday Group; strengthening Kinnock's office; using experienced outside help, including Peter Mandelson; involving other senior politicians, including John Smith and Gordon Brown; and establishing a core organisational team.[64]

I also tried to draft in outside help directly. Mandelson was beyond the pale and his re-entry would not be accepted. Patricia was back and the remaining big talent on the outside was Alastair Campbell, then political editor of the *Daily Mirror*. Alastair was and is a figure of immense power and ability. Peter Mandelson describes him as a 'genius'. I hardly knew him then; he had interviewed Neil for the Hudson broadcast and looked at me with the pity and contempt he reserves for people who come from professions like advertising. There was some talk he might join Neil as his press secretary, and I had lunch with him to discuss it. He wasn't keen, but he would have done it had he been asked. I didn't know it at the time, but this was another great missed opportunity – Robert Maxwell offered in 1991 to second Alastair to Neil Kinnock's office, but Kinnock and Clarke turned the offer down. More than anybody else Alastair could have helped Neil at this time, but the chance was passed over. This was a huge error, and Clarke admits it: 'We should have asked Alastair to come on board. The main reason that didn't happen was that it was a specific gift from Maxwell, and Neil didn't want to be beholden to Maxwell in any way.'[65]

Having rejected Mandelson and turned down Campbell, Labour was struggling to handle the media. Kinnock's relationship with the press was 'frozen', according to Clarke, who once went to Wapping, without telling Neil, to talk to the editor of the *Sun*. 'We simply did not tackle the media,' he said. 'I remember I went to see Kelvin MacKenzie at Wapping in January 1992. It's the only thing I ever did without telling Neil beforehand. And we had four hours at Wapping – me, Kelvin and a whole group of others going through things – and to his credit Kelvin never leaked it. And I told Neil the next day and he was furious that I had done it.'[66]

The final straw was Colin Byrne's departure that autumn. 'I saw it all fragmenting,' he said. 'I saw people starting to position themselves for jobs after an election which Labour was nowhere near actually winning, and putting more effort into that than actually keeping their eye on the ball. We should have been concentrating on big-picture politics and we were playing the sort of office politics you get in a small company.'[67] Byrne had enormous talent, experience and aggression – so much aggression, in fact, that he once tried to hit me in Westminster Hall because he felt Julie Hall, his girlfriend, was being badly treated and he blamed me. In fact Charles Clarke was letting it be known he was unhappy with her. Byrne left disillusioned and depressed. It was a terrible blow to the campaign.

On 12 December, I delivered the 1992 'War Book': the complete campaign plan for the election. I said our first weakness was tax, our second, lack of trust. The Tories' core message would be 'You can't trust Labour'. Their key attacks would be on tax, followed by Neil Kinnock, trade unions and extremism, and the core themes would be Kinnock against Major and high-tax Labour against low-tax Conservatives.[68]

By the end of 1991, the Labour campaign was in crisis. Planning for the election itself was in hand, but the pre-election period was empty of any content. There was no timetable; no day-by-day campaign grid; no strategic plan. I phoned Patricia at home and said we had to fix it. In her office in the attic of her house we planned a grid every week for the period from 1 January until a likely election in April or May. I then took this grid and forced it through the party machine, getting it approved in January. I was resented for this as well, and distrust of me increased. The seeds of campaign confusion were being sown.

Less than four weeks after I wrote the War Book the Conservatives hit us on tax, with the 'Tax Bombshell' campaign on 6 January 1992. I was out of the country and heard the news over the telephone. As the news went on and on – National Insurance, top rate of tax, £1,000 per family – I knew we were finished. And less than three months later the Tories launched their election campaign, with the slogan 'You Can't Trust Labour'.

We slogged on. The grid that Patricia and I had drawn up was pretty much implemented, and we did what we wanted to do, fighting long and hard through the spring. Gradually we crawled back to level-pegging with the Conservatives and then nudged ahead. We were going to meet our first election objective, which was to go into the campaign ahead in the polls.

But by the start of the election a campaign machine that had been brilliant in 1987 and strong in 1990 had weakened almost to breaking-point. Peter had gone; Patricia had left her formal position; Alastair was not used properly. 'By the time we had moved into the period of the election campaign proper, we were exhausted and jaded,' says David Hill.[69] Charles Clarke agrees: 'Energy is very important, and we were lacking energy. Everybody was tired.'[70] The campaign team was riven with suspicion bordering on paranoia; lines of command were confused; and the leader of the party was isolated from his own campaign team.

But organisational collapse was the symptom, not the cause. The truth was that Neil's brave, necessary, crucial modernising project had been in political decline since 1989 and was now exhausted – physically, intellectually and emotionally. The policy review failed to be the modernising document the nation needed. Our defence policy was transformed but on trade unions, on public ownership and above all on tax and spending, essentially we were still stuck in the past.

For much of that year Neil's confidence was low and his colleagues were constantly at odds. Alastair Campbell, a close friend of his, remembers it: 'There wasn't much of a team effort going on. I think that made Neil quite angry and resentful. You never found the shadow Cabinet really pushing in the same direction at one time. They were pretty disparaging of Neil privately, which I think is unforgivable.'[71] Neil was in despair about this. At dinner during the 1991 conference I said to him, 'Why don't you talk to your colleagues and get them to act as a team?' He smashed the table and replied: 'If you're so bloody clever why don't you talk to them, and see how far you get?'

This was the state of Labour as it approached the election: falling apart together.

4

LOVE AND ANGER

Taxis

I spent hours and hours of the 1992 campaign in taxis, running between endless meetings at our three campaign headquarters – Walworth Road, Millbank, where we had a suite of rooms behind the main press conference venue, and Transport House, where the Shadow Communications Agency had its offices. The meetings started at 6.30 A.M. and recurred at what seemed like hourly intervals through the day, ending with a campaign strategy meeting on the top floor of Walworth Road at 7.00 P.M., when it seemed as if anyone who wanted to turned up. Notes of these meetings include strings of references to people who were missing, briefings lost in other offices, a driver being unable to find the shadow Cabinet member due at the press conference in half an hour's time. It was madness to separate us like this, but Neil's office decided at the last minute that it was a security risk to have us all at Millbank as planned. When the decision was announced by Charles Clarke at a Thursday CAT meeting, I lost my temper. I knew it would be a disaster, and the confusion it created led directly to our ignominious retreat from the battle of 'Jennifer's Ear'.

The SCA was housed in the room at Transport House in which press conferences had been held in 1987. I had a desk on one side with my assistant Kathryn Smith, who was brilliant beyond words. Patricia Hewitt's desk was on the opposite side of the hall. She was helped by Julian Priestley, now Secretary General of the European Parliament and a man of outstanding competence. The room between us was full of people: researchers, volunteers, helpers of all sorts. In an annexe Deborah Mattinson oversaw a complete polling operation. Our position in Smith Square, opposite Conservative Central Office, meant the Tories would regularly send in spies to see what we were up to: but as they wore tweed jackets and looked nervous it was easy to throw them out. The press, too, tried repeatedly to get in. The SCA, secluded in its own building, had an aura of quiet, mysterious power.

Without Peter, I felt personally accountable for the conduct of much of the campaign and I knew that our chances of reaching the finishing-post without major mishap were very slim. I had one simple objective: to be ahead in the polls on election day, and I did not think we would be able to achieve it. The responsibility felt overwhelming.

No election campaign has been more misunderstood than Labour's in 1992, and no account of it has been fully accurate. Our preparation had been extensive, but less effective and sharply honed than in 1987. I had in mind a campaign with three aspects: slickness, energy and fierce, relentless attack. In the event we only really achieved the first. For most of the time the campaign was slick and professional, but it lacked passion, anger, attack. Because the 1987 campaign lacked an overall theme and jumped from subject to subject on an almost daily basis, I had designed a campaign that unfolded in four phases: the economy; health, as our best attacking issue; education, to give Neil the chance to take off; a last week that recapitulated all three issues. The press conference sets, designed by Wolff Olins, were very beautiful. They were rosy pink at the bottom, merging into a soft blue at the top. The colours grew in intensity as the campaign developed. The campaign line was borrowed from the Australian Labor Party: 'It's time.' This line also unfolded as the campaign developed: 'It's time for health; it's time for education', and so on.

But when the election was called, at one o'clock on Wednesday 11 March, I sat alone in my office in Soho and felt a terrible sense of foreboding. I remembered the same moment in 1987, when I had thought we were facing certain defeat but I knew we were ready and would do our best. The atmosphere had been defiant and resigned, with a sense of camaraderie. In 1992, the mood was very different: the team was divided; the polls were extremely close, with Labour just ahead; people expected us to win; the press expected us to win. And I didn't think we would. What's more, I was alone. I telephoned Peter and we talked briefly about the fight in 1987, but I could tell that mentally he had already left London and was fighting Hartlepool. I picked up the phone and called David Hill, collected my papers, and hailed a taxi for Walworth Road.

Taxation

The first issue that dominated Labour's campaign in the 1992 election was tax. Maurice Saatchi told a friend after that election that the only issue the Tories had was tax, and that Labour gave it to them: 'If they'd dealt with it, we had nothing else.'[1] It is to my credit that the SCA tried to kill it, to my discredit that we failed.

In a brilliant move just before the campaign started, the Tories destroyed us in the Budget of Tuesday 10 March. This was partly our fault because we had already announced too many of our tax and spending plans: we were committed to raising taxes for the middle classes to pay for child benefit and pensions increases; we had said we would reverse any Tory income-tax cuts and we had only one surprise up our sleeves for our shadow Budget the following week – a fall in National Insurance. This was our sole escape route from accusations that we were hitting the middle classes. On Budget Day the Tories cut it off.

'I go to hear the Budget in the shadow Cabinet room,' I wrote in my diary.

It was full of the economic advisers to the party, to the leader, to John Smith. It could hardly have been more tense. It was like walking into a Gold Seal battery, it was so charged. John Eatwell [economic adviser to Kinnock since 1986] sat on his own table to the left, with a large sign saying 'reserved'. I crouched at the back out of the way, so tense I could hardly talk. By the time Lamont got to tax, David Hill and I were pacing nervously at the back of the shadow Cabinet room, waiting for the knockout blow. I was saying: '2p [tax cut]. It's got to be 2p.' David said: 'No way. They're not going to do it.' And then at the end, when there had been absolutely nothing, David said to me, 'You're right, it must be 2p.' But Lamont announced: 'There's going to be no cut in the basic rate of income tax. We're going to introduce a 20p band.'

John Eatwell, who had been glued to the screen in silence throughout, looked up, flung his papers over the table, and said: 'We can't respond to that. That's it. It's all over. We've got no money to spend. Neil's got no speech.'[2]

And he was right. The budget totally undermined our strategy. The Tories had looked at our figures and worked out that the way to kill us off on tax was a 20p band. No one had any idea how to respond. The room was in chaos. And I had an advertisement to produce – fast; it was going into the papers the next day and the concept I had prepared was based on the assumption that the government would cut income tax. The headline was, 'Georgina Norris died because the NHS is short of money. Meanwhile the Tories are cutting taxes to keep their election hopes alive.' The question was: was the new 20p band a tax cut? 'I asked David Hill: "Is it a tax cut or isn't it? Will we reverse it or not?" No one knew; it was pandemonium. Neil fudged the answer in his reply. By the time the politicians returned, John Smith storming through, Neil following looking drained, they had decided. They swept us into their office and told us they would reverse it.'[3]

When things had quietened down a little, I went in to see Neil alone. 'How was it?' he asked. I thought he was referring to the Budget, so I said, 'I thought it was a pretty poor Budget.' 'He looked nervous,' I wrote in my diary, 'and started to look at the floor. He said: "I didn't mean that; I meant how was my speech?" Well, I hadn't seen the speech because I was so wrapped up with this wretched advertisement, so I said lamely: "Very good." Then everybody else swarmed in and said: "Bloody good speech, Neil. Bloody good." Everybody was there. Roy was there. Everybody was drinking champagne. Everybody was happy. We thought that the Tories had messed up.'[4] That was our big mistake.

That was the last I heard about the Budget for a couple of days. On Thursday evening, the day after the election had been called, David Hill and I were discussing leaflets when a panic call came through for me to go immediately to Neil Kinnock's office in the House of Commons. As I passed the office of Jim Parish, the senior campaign officer, he gave me the front cover of the manifesto to look at. It was terrible, and since it was going to press the next day, I had to stay and fight the design company over the phone to get it changed – this was to be the mood throughout: chaotic and panic-stricken. I reached the House of Commons finally at 10.30 and made my way to the shadow Cabinet room, which was in half-darkness. Patricia Hewitt, John Eatwell and a few others were already there, shadowy figures in the half-light. You could almost touch the gloom.

The problem we faced was appalling and insoluble. The central premise on which the shadow Budget was based had been that the Tories would cut at least 1p off income tax. Our central proposal in response was to reverse the tax cut but drop National Insurance by 1 per cent, from 9 per cent to 8 per cent, which was the equivalent of an income-tax cut of 1p. The point of this was twofold: it would soften the blow of Labour's policy of lifting the National Insurance ceiling for those earning more than £22,000, and it would mean an effective tax cut for those earning less than £22,000. By introducing a 20p band, Lamont had presented us with an impossible dilemma. If we reversed the 20p band and cut National Insurance by 1 per cent, higher-income earners would be slightly better off, but around three or four million people earning between £3,000 and £10,000 would be worse off. On the other hand, if National Insurance was not cut and measures were taken instead to prevent lower-income earners being hurt (i.e. by increasing personal allowances), middle-income earners at £22,000-plus would be hit.

There had been almost non-stop meetings for the previous two days and no one had found an answer. Alastair Campbell, then still at the *Daily Mirror*, had been helping, and remembers it as the worst example of the chaos of the 1992 election. 'It just wasn't stacking up,' he said. 'I was helping them the night before the shadow Budget and you had a sense of this thing being put together at the last minute, which of course it was.'[5] In that dark, gloomy room, at eleven at night, we had to choose: hit the poor, or hit the middle classes. Patricia, David and myself argued strongly that Labour should cut National Insurance and take the risk with lower-income earners. But Neil believed Labour could not go into an election threatening to raise taxes for the poor. We shouldn't have had to do either, but the mess we had got ourselves into meant we had to choose. 'If we don't do something for the middle classes, we will lose the election,' I warned.[6] But Neil refused to hit the poor. We were trapped by the Tory strategy and by our own foolish pledge to raise the National Insurance ceiling to pay for child benefit and pensions. We were going to hit the middle classes.

The tragedy is that Neil had never wanted to raise taxes for middle-income earners and had tried to get the policy changed. By the time of the election, even John Smith, who was responsible for the policy, had reservations, but he would not or could not change it. They had left themselves only one escape from the tax trap – the National Insurance cut – and when the Tories closed that off they were snared. The meeting in the shadow Cabinet room went on until the early hours of the morning, but could find no escape.

These policies had never made sense and the SCA had consistently opposed them. They had their genesis in the policy review, which had failed to modernise Labour's tax and spend policies sufficiently and had also committed the party to publishing details of its tax policies in advance. In effect, it had committed Labour to the idea of a shadow Budget and to what its contents would be. I had tried to prevent it, and had repeatedly warned the policy review groups and John Smith of the consequences if Labour entered the election with a policy of raising taxes.

From November 1987 until April 1988, we had commissioned research on tax and benefits as the basis for the review of Labour's tax policy. The findings, which were presented to John Smith at the time, were emphatic. People were hostile to the principle of paying taxes which they felt did not benefit them directly. Recipients of benefits were often seen to be 'scroungers', with high levels of concern about fraud. There was intense anxiety about Labour and tax.[7] In April 1988 the SCA presented polling which said, 'Respondents thought Labour would increase taxes for everybody, with the result that the rich would be driven abroad, ordinary people would be worse off and there would be no incentive to work. Ultimately the country, in the words of one respondent, "would face ruin".'[8] This research should have persuaded John Smith of the extent to which Labour's loss of the lower-middle-class vote was related to its attitude to tax.

The research cut little ice in the policy review process. John Smith thought it inconceivable that we could go into an election without pledging to put a fixed amount on the basic benefits; any alternative wasn't even considered. 'He felt that by committing the party very soon after 1987 to the same level of increase as we'd promised in 1987 – not to have to put it up in line with inflation or anything – he'd pulled off an amazing piece of modernisation,' Hewitt said. 'It was just extraordinary – and that was the most you could possibly expect the party to agree to. It meant that as early as 1988 we were stuffed on tax for the next election.'[9]

At the beginning of July 1988 I wrote in my diary, 'We can see the last two and a half years as an oscillation between the social agenda, which is positive for us; defence, which is negative; and the economic agenda. We have to sort out the economic agenda because we lost the last election partly because of an economic failure on our part and partly because of the economic credentials of the government. We must sort out the economic policy as almost a discrete, separate product, sorted out and got right, and made into the bedrock of our credentials for government.'[10]

During the next four years the SCA had issued a series of increasingly urgent warnings on tax policies and the economic agenda. In December 1989 BMP had developed the concept of the 'aspirational classes'.[11] They argued that the key determinants of the next election would be 'financial well-being: spending power, taxation, interest rates'.[12] Qualitative research conducted at the time showed that despite the recession, Labour was seen as more likely to accentuate economic difficulties than the Conservatives.[13] The key target group was the aspirational classes – working-class achievers and the middle class under pressure. This is the group I came to call the new middle class. I define them as those people who call themselves middle- and upper-working-class, estimated by the British Social Attitudes survey to comprise 50 per cent of the population.[14] I came from this class and believe I understand it. It is the pivot around which progressive politics must revolve.

In January 1990 I had warned, 'Labour has had a successful year but is not on track to win an election. Labour lags behind on the key issue of economic competence; and while the Conservatives need a moderate performance to win, Labour needs an exceptional performance.'[15]

The council elections in May 1990, in which the Conservatives held Wandsworth and Westminster with very low poll tax rates, showed the importance of financial self-interest in determining voting intention. I wrote to Peter Mandelson: 'The Conservative device of comparing at all points the financial advantage of voting Conservative with the financial disadvantage of voting Labour was starkly effective. The most important lesson is that in the General Election financial comparisons will be used and will be effective. We must avoid any policy commitments that exacerbate such a comparison and maximise any financial incentives which alleviate it.'[16]

Two weeks later, on 24 May 1990, 'Looking to the Future', Labour's early manifesto, was launched (amid a row over whether the document was too glamorous because the woman on the cover, posing with my daughter Georgia, wore earrings). In it Labour said it would raise £2 billion in its first year of office by raising the top rate of tax to 50 per cent and removing the National Insurance ceiling to pay for pensions and child-benefit increases.[17] The die was cast.

A few days later I wrote another note to the CAT: 'The policy review has fallen short of expectations. In the key areas of trade unions and taxation Labour has not moved fast enough. A majority believe that Labour would raise tax for middle-income earners.'[18] The next month a survey of 1,200 people rammed home the same points: 'Tax was raised as a central problem for Labour'; 'Concerns about economic management magnify concerns about tax'.[19]

A few months before Mandelson left, at his request, Deborah Mattinson bravely presented to the shadow Cabinet in the summer of 1990 a presentation warning that a substantial majority of those polled – 70 per cent or so – believed they would pay more tax under Labour.[20] John Smith deeply resented it, saying he wouldn't be lectured to by 'admen and pollsters'. A period of estrangement between John Smith and the SCA resulted, although at the time I was urging Peter to give John a higher profile: 'The shadow Chancellor has high credibility in the economic area and this should be maximised.' But John was furious, both at the presentation and because I had recently discovered that the threshold for paying more tax was very low – about £16,000 – and was telling anyone who would listen that if this wasn't increased Labour would lose the election. 'John has got to hear about it and is very cross with me indeed,' I wrote in my diary. 'But I am trying to rebuild the relationship, although I keep telling him and David [Hill] that we will definitely lose with these tax policies.'[21]

Eventually John did realise that Labour was highly vulnerable on tax and that the recession made Labour's tax policies increasingly untenable. But he believed that his reputation for integrity was essential to our chances of re-election: that, given the other reforms Kinnock had introduced, Labour's standing would be destroyed if he, Smith, committed a U-turn on tax policy. 'All we have in politics is our integrity, and if we lose that we lose everything,' he told me. 'Neil's changed so much, I can't change at all.'[22] Although he understood the dangers of the policies and intended to use the shadow Budget to confound his critics and cut National Insurance, he was essentially committed to them and, in particular, believed as a matter of faith in the moral case for increasing benefits. His position was that the strategy should be amelioration of the policy, not abandonment of it.

Gordon Brown, then shadow Trade and Industry spokesman, took a wholly different view. He felt that the very idea of a shadow Budget was insane, and gave the Conservatives all the weapons they needed to attack us. He said, 'I think John's making a mistake, he shouldn't be giving any figures away at all. But we're stuck with it because we've committed ourselves to this pension and child-benefit rise.'[23] Neil also opposed the policy, but could find no way out of it. When he later floated the idea of phasing as a solution, it exploded in his face.

Tax was the key strategic and tactical issue in 1991. All through the year the SCA presented polling which warned of the dangers of tax. In an opinion poll on 24 April, tax was identified as the main reason not to vote Labour, with 54 per cent giving it as the primary reason.[24] This was fed into the campaign team and the appropriate politicians. Yet on 5 May, John Smith announced on *Frost on Sunday* that employees earning over £20,300 a year would pay extra National Insurance contributions to raise an extra £2.5 billion.[25] Three days later the Tories announced their aim of reducing basic-rate tax from 25p to 20p.[26] In June the Tories started their long tax campaign, with David Mellor costing Labour's tax plans at £35 billion.[27]

To make absolutely sure the politicians were getting the message, the SCA prepared a separate presentation for Labour's economic spokespeople – John Smith, Margaret Beckett, Tony Blair and Gordon Brown. The presentation, which was in the autumn, could not have been clearer or more emphatic. It was long and very forceful. It showed that tax was the top reason for not voting Labour, with 65 per cent agreeing with the statement that Labour will raise taxes for everyone. That figure increased to 72 per cent in the key C2 group: 'To the public, Labour is the party of high taxation. The fact that the lower end of the social spectrum feel that they will be taxed heavier is a matter of where they see themselves aspiring to as much as where they are currently.' We also told them Labour would have great difficulty winning the election with its current tax policies and urged them to broaden the argument on tax to include VAT, poll tax, interest rates and inflation.[28] The presentation made the politicians angry. Tony Blair and Gordon Brown were frustrated that we were in a position where our policy was both untenable and highly unpopular; John Smith, knowing what we said was all true, simply walked out.

Labour's senior figures were so divided, their truce so finely balanced, that it became almost impossible to get anyone even to listen to our pleas. Patricia Hewitt prepared a paper that autumn for the CAT on Labour, taxation and public spending, which once again spelled out the realities of the situation. 'The public,' she wrote, 'and especially target voters, believe that Labour will increase taxation for everyone. Fear of taxes is the single most important reason for not voting Labour.'[29] Qualitative research found that a threshold of £21,000 was not seen as particularly high – especially in the south east: 'Nobody wants to pay more tax.'[30] Charles Clarke saw the paper before it was presented and exploded. 'You don't fucking understand. We can't discuss it,' he shouted at Patricia.[31] It is difficult to describe how angry he was. Terrified of re-opening the issue and destabilising the careful truce reached between Neil and John, he insisted that all copies of the paper be returned and destroyed. 'I was very nervous about a dispute with John,' Charles explains, 'that's certainly true. I mean, I had a stand-up row with John at the shadow Cabinet away day in January, when he was not producing what Neil wanted him to produce. I felt very nervous about the relationship with John. I felt that that was a very flawed state of affairs. And it was a very febrile relationship.'[32] Neil considered sacking John. 'I think that he didn't feel strong enough, I mean we went through a whole series of processes, called emergency meetings of the shadow Cabinet and all the rest of it to instruct John. At the end of the day Neil had the decision to either sack John as shadow Chancellor or not. I think it was a straight stand-off, and John believed rightly that he was strong enough to resist Neil,' Clarke says.[33]

Despite this, tax wouldn't go away as an issue. Rational strategic planning dictated that if we couldn't change the policy, we should launch an initiative announcing our existing tax plans on our terms and before the Tories attacked us. The SCA produced scripts for a tax broadcast that would spearhead our economic broadcast and act as a pre-emptive tax attack. Neil didn't like them. I wrote in my diary, 'It was done in a way that was creative and intelligent, but nonetheless the policy was exposed, and Neil clearly didn't like the policy. You could feel it.'[34] Other politicians who were shown the script reacted with horror; they hated the policy, so they hated the broadcast. 'When they were shown the policy in the raw – that we were raising National Insurance by a very substantial amount for people earning over £21,000 to pay for child benefits and pensions – they realised that it didn't make political sense. Blair and Brown felt this most. They asked questions about who developed the policy; where had it come from, and so on,' I wrote. 'Neil's view was that these broadcasts were all very well and good but the key was that before we presented our economic case, the tax case was put, and put by John Smith, in December. This was absolutely Neil's view, that John had to do that.'[35]

However, John was unsure about announcing our tax plans early. He said to me: 'Why in politics do something that would make you unpopular? Why take the risk?'[36] His view was that tax for Labour was rather like the NHS for the Conservatives – if you raise the issue, it just gets worse. Patricia Hewitt said, 'We spoke to John about it, saying the tax attack would come, and we tried to work out a line – something like an early version of "eight out of ten people will be better off under Labour". But John wouldn't go for that because he kept saying, with some justification, until he saw the 1992 Budget, he wouldn't know what our figures would be.'[37]

I kept hammering away at John, trying to get him to address the tax issue properly. This tactic drove Charles Clarke to distraction and he eventually turned on me in the corridor outside the leader's office. 'You're getting a reputation for crying wolf,' he said. 'You're going on and on about this tax attack. It's never going to happen.'[38] To my eternal discredit, in the face of Smith's stubbornness and Clarke's antagonism, I lost heart and, temporarily at least, gave up. Four weeks later, in January 1992, the Tories launched their 'Tax Bombshell' campaign; our rebuttal, Norman Lamont as 'VAT-man', went up a lamentable four weeks later.

In the week after the tax bombshell dropped on us, Neil wrote a letter to John arguing the case for phasing in the higher National Insurance contributions, and then mentioned the option to journalists at a dinner at Luigi's restaurant in Soho. 'Neil's view was that we ought to make commitments about not raising tax,' said Clarke. 'That's what led to the Luigi's problem. All Neil's instincts led him to believe that we were going to raise taxes too much.'[39] Neil was anxious; an ICM poll had put Labour behind after the tax attack, and since the phasing idea had been floated already he decided to mention it. It leaked out the next day, just as Smith received Neil's letter proposing the idea. At our regular Thursday meeting the next morning, the atmosphere was explosive. 'Charles Clarke was emphatically of the view that we would make it clear that we were not deviating from policy. Julie [Hall] was of the view that we should say we are deviating from policy,' I wrote in my diary.[40] It was chaos. John Smith was furious and his confidence in Neil – never high – dropped further. Right up to the election he kept referring back to the Luigi's incident. When David Hill and I told John that Neil was going to attend the shadow Budget (this was very controversial at the time because of worries that Neil would be asked questions which were unanswerable), John was dismissive and came out with a typically sharp rejoinder: 'Dressed as a waiter from Luigi's?'[41]

After the election I wrote in my diary, 'This was a core disability at the heart of the Kinnock leadership, because the fact that he and Smith did not get on meant they never got to grips with the tax problem. If, before the election, they had been able to discuss it, they might have been able to solve it. But the relationship was not there and instead they accepted an uneasy compromise, their advisers kept them apart, and we were left with no big economic story to tell the voters.'[42]

After the election we were criticised for not using John Smith more, but there wasn't much he could say and he was occasionally unable to attend press conferences because of his health. However, this wasn't always the reason. In my diary, I recalled one press conference, on housing repossessions in London, which 'John refused to do because he wouldn't have been able to promise interest-rate cuts; Neil had pushed him to support entry to the ERM, which tied us to high interest rates'.[43] When I gave John the draft manifesto, the only comment he made was that he wanted a whole paragraph on an independent National Statistical Office – he was absolutely obsessed with having an honest system. Clarke believes Smith thought he could 'busk' it: 'John Smith fundamentally believed that the policy of "just leave it to him and he could busk it" would carry us through, and he believed everybody else was a combination of stupid or tactically inept in the way they handled things.'[44]

For all these reasons, the day after the 1992 General Election was called, John Eatwell, Patricia Hewitt, Neil Kinnock and I found ourselves late at night in the gloom of the shadow Cabinet room trying to decide whether to hit the poor or the middle classes in the shadow Budget in four days' time. And Neil insisted on protecting anyone earning under £22,000. The shadow Budget at the Institute of Civil Engineers the following Monday was an incredible political event. 'We arrived early and the atmosphere was extraordinary – tense, but exciting, electric,' I wrote in my diary. 'The whole place was packed full of journalists and hangers-on, business people who had been invited along. It was as though electric currents were being passed through everyone. I stood at the back. John Eatwell was behind me. He was so nervous he was rendered inarticulate. I have never known such an atmosphere, such a sense of occasion. Clearly, this was going to be the decisive moment in the election campaign.'[45]

Clive Hollick saw John Smith just days before the shadow Budget and asked him whether he was worried about the electoral impact of his proposals. 'No,' John said, 'we won't implement half of them anyway.'[46] It must have been the first occasion ever when a political party planned to break its pledges on tax the wrong way around, promising tax increases it never intended to deliver.

At first it seemed that the shadow Budget had killed off tax as an issue. Although the tabloids attacked it – and Anatole Kaletsky wrote in *The Times* the next day that it was the largest increase in tax for middle-income earners there had ever been[47] – initially it went down well with the broadcasters, who reported it favourably. But the Tories came back to hit us hard that weekend with a savage attack: having costed Labour's mani-festo, they announced: 'The Price of Labour – £1,250 a Year for Every Family', to complement the notorious 'Labour's Double Whammy' posters.[48] The BBC's political correspondent John Sergeant reported that tax was the defining issue of the campaign and Bryan Gould, at a campaign strategy meeting, said the election was stuck on tax, tax, tax. I had a plan to get off it. It was called 'Jennifer's Ear'.

'Jennifer's Ear'

I accept full responsibility for 'Jennifer's Ear'. I was always hawkish on health, believing it was an election-winning issue which should be played very hard. The Conservatives' NHS reforms were a particularly explosive area. They led people to believe, and allowed Labour to claim, that the NHS as we knew it was under threat. But although fears about the NHS reforms simmered away, the issue flared up only if there was a specific controversy – for example, over the concept of 'privatisation' – or where real events demonstrating under-funding and chaos intruded. For the 1992 campaign, I wanted to produce a health broadcast so controversial, so shocking in its impact that it would turn the election for Labour. 'Jennifer's Ear' was not that broadcast, it was a softer version of the really shocking one. At the beginning of the campaign, we didn't even plan to use it. But I firmly believe it remains one of the most effective and successful party election broadcasts ever shown. The chaos around it was caused by organisational confusion and a communications breakdown for which I alone was not responsible. That party election broadcast forced the Tories out into the open on health. They stood there, exposed and vulnerable. And in an act of stunning feebleness, we walked away.

In the year before the election, powerful negative health campaigns by Labour had twice shaken the Tories, demonstrating its weight as an issue. The Tory counter-attack also shook Robin Cook, who was targeted by a relentless press campaign. The first decisive campaign was at Monmouth in May 1991, where Peter Mandelson had returned to mastermind the by-election fight. Going to visit Peter, who had reconstructed his old team and his old methods, was like seeing a campaigning king in exile – there was an energy, an organisation and sense of purpose that had been quite lost in Walworth Road. Peter had found an issue to fight the by-election on in a local hospital which was reported to be considering trust status. He invented the idea that trust hospitals had 'opted out' of the NHS and built the campaign around it. Labour won, health exploded as an issue and the Conservatives became convinced that Peter had black skills. Their defeat was instrumental in persuading the Tories not to go to the polls that autumn.

After the Monmouth by-election, qualitative research started to throw up the idea that the NHS was being made private. I turned this into privatisation, which seemed to me to be a killer concept. But privatisation was not a word that Labour's then shadow Health Secretary Robin Cook was happy to use. He was uneasy about it, often moving towards it but then pulling back. Harriet Harman, his deputy, had no such inhibitions and, displaying some guts, used the word with alacrity.

Labour's good spring turned into a bad summer. The Gorbachev coup of August 1991 gave John Major the chance to dominate the news, and the Conservatives edged ahead in the polls. We decided to run a ferocious health campaign to back the Tories off from an autumn election. During the summer, I developed, with BMP, the idea of exploiting voters' privatisation fears on a poster symbolising the horrors of a Tory fourth term. This was the second decisive negative health campaign. The poster was ghoulish, with four skeletons lined up against a black background. Around each skeleton was a sign: privatise the NHS; privatise the education system; raise VAT to 22 per cent; increase unemployment to three million. The headline read: 'How many more have the Tories got in their cupboard?' It was a brilliant poster, truly frightening. Unfortunately we only had the money to put one up. But one was enough. As it was being launched in September by Harriet and Robin, a journalist told me that John Major had made a comment about private insurance which poured petrol on the privatisation issue. The poster and the news joined to make NHS privatisation a massive issue. It dominated the news and Labour crawled back into the lead. This was a decisive moment because it finally persuaded the Tories not to call an election in the autumn, a fatal error as their lead in the marginal constituencies evaporated in a winter of recession. After the election, their pollster Robert Waller told me that an election called in September or October 1991 would have given them a lead of over 60 seats. Once again, health had turned the tide.

Although health worked well as an issue for us, it was always rough because the Tories had to fight so hard on it, and it was roughest on Robin Cook. He entered a period of campaigning purdah for four months because he was under constant attack for not having positive proposals. He decided to come back in February with plans for a new health offensive. In preparation for the campaign he phoned me up to say he wanted a graphic and a line. I arranged a meeting with Robin and Chris Powell, who was responsible for our advertising, but it went badly: Robin said he needed a proposal, Chris said he needed a brief, but eventually we got a graphic – a stethoscope in the shape of a £ sign – and a line: 'If you want to be well, you had better be well off'. Robin also approved a poster showing William Waldegrave as a highwayman with the line: 'Your money or your life'. A series of press conferences in February went well, but the newspapers were starting to dig into case histories we had given them. They found some flaws and went after Robin.

Gradually it became clear that the Conservative tabloids were seeking to destabilise him. Soon he came under further fire. A major document on under-funding had been leaked to us from the Department of Health, and the 'mole' had been found. His career was about to be destroyed and the tabloids were camping outside his home. The mounting tension erupted at the Park Lane Hotel on 13 February, where Labour was holding a gala dinner. David Hill, Gez Sagar, the Labour Party's chief press officer, and Robin went to a private room so David could explain to Robin what was happening. Robin had asked me to join them but Gez, who resented my influence, blocked the way. I barged past him and went to talk to Robin, who had just been told about the discovery of the mole. Understandably he was very upset, and felt responsibility for what had happened. The atmosphere was angry and emotional, typical of what was to follow.

The effect of the attacks was that Robin, who was now aware there seemed to be a tabloid offensive against him, felt undermined and keen to be more positive about health. However, I was unremitting in my insistence on attack. At a meeting with Robin I told him of my intention to produce a 'shock horror' broadcast on health, for use in the fourth of our five party election broadcast slots. BMP were developing two alternative concepts: one used real case histories, the other was based around a Ridley Scott reconstruction of a futuristic privatised hospital. Robin seemed nervous, but agreed.

BMP was also producing another broadcast, on privatisation – of health and education. It was about two children, one who used private health and education, the other who used state provision. We didn't know when or if we would use it. It was too complicated, not enough about privatisation and opting out. John Webster, the writer, went away and turned it into a straight health broadcast based around a girl with ear-ache, and linked it to a letter that had been written to Robin Cook by a man called John Bennett, who had a five-year-old daughter called Jennifer who had acute tonsillitis which was linked to grommets. The broadcast graphically showed the difference in treatment provided by the NHS and private healthcare.

I had also prepared the 'Georgina Norris' advertisement for use the day after the budget, about an eighteen-month-old girl with a serious heart condition who had died following several cancelled NHS operations. Thus, on 11 March, the day the election was called, we were already fighting on health. It was a very tough advertisement, one of the toughest ever to run in Britain. I phoned Mrs Norris many times to confirm that she was happy with it, and that the facts added up, and Cook agreed to go with it. But it was heavily attacked by the press, becoming known as the 'dead baby ad', and Robin was shaken again.

The following Tuesday, we held a meeting to discuss the main health campaign, which was being launched in a week's time. Robin came with his researcher Geoff Norris and Sam Etherington, a GP who had been advising Robin for some time and was also helping us with 'Jennifer's Ear'. We discussed the health launch and my proposed 'shock horror' broadcast for the fourth slot, in particular the one based on real cases. Robin was queasy about using real cases, but I presented qualitative research which showed that the public would support advertising based on case histories, providing the evidence stacked up.[49] We did not discuss 'Jennifer's Ear' because it was only one of many broadcasts floating around which I did not think we would use. We also assumed Robin knew about it, which was a huge error. BMP believed throughout that Cook had endorsed the 'Jennifer's Ear' broadcast because of Etherington's involvement in the shoot and because they had been given copies of Mr Bennett's letter to Cook. But, as it turned out, Robin knew little or nothing about it.

On Saturday 21 March, David Mellor launched the big Tory attack on Labour's tax and spending plans. The media loved it and it was clear we were going to be slaughtered in Sunday's papers. I began to think about upweighting the launch of our health campaign on Tuesday, as a way to turn the coverage. We had a PEB (party election broadcast) slot then, the second in the series, and we planned to show a 'switchers' broadcast in it: real people who had turned from the Tories to Labour over the previous four years. I considered scrapping this, or putting it on hold for later, and strengthening the health campaign launch with not just a poster, as we had planned, but backed up by the 'Jennifer's Ear' broadcast. We were still holding back the real 'shock horror' health broadcast until the last week of the campaign. I watched 'Jennifer's Ear' with David Hill and, in fact, thought it soft, and not controversial. We recorded Neil as a voice-over for the end of the broadcast and he saw and approved it. John Bennett came up to London on Saturday to record his letter to Robin Cook as a voice-over for the broadcast.

We weren't planning to use this; it was just an insurance policy. About this time, something about the broadcast began to make me nervous. Over the weekend I phoned John Bennett and all sorts of alarms went off. I did not find him convincing. I immediately made sure that his voice-over was not used and sent a note to the press office, insisting that no connection be made between the broadcast and the Bennett family. 'The idea for the broadcast came from a letter sent to Robin Cook by a worried father . . . [but] Philip is keen that Mr Bennett's case is not confused with our PEB,' Kathryn Smith wrote to Labour press officer Anna Healy.[50] The film stood alone without the Bennett family, and it had been developed independently of them. At that time it was actually called 'Mandy'; 'Jennifer's Ear' was a press description that came later.

On Sunday the press was terrible: 'Kinnock's middle-income massacre' – *Sunday Express*;[51] 'Gunning for Labour on tax' – *Sunday Telegraph*;[52] 'Labour's direct taxes give advantage to the Tories' – *Sunday Times*.[53] Even the cartoonists were at it: later in the campaign Jak in the *Mail on Sunday* drew a series of posters reading: 'More tax please we're British – Vote Labour'; 'Give more to the tax man with Labour'; '80 per cent tax under Labour – Glad to pay! Want to pay!'[54] And that afternoon, 22 March, I got a call from Robin saying he wanted to postpone the whole health initiative: he wanted to be positive. I didn't agree and said it was too late to postpone the launch.

The next morning, the day before the health launch, the tax attack was even worse. The Tories had launched the 'Double Whammy'/'Price of Labour – £1,250 a year' attack. The coverage in the mid-market press, whose readers we had to win over, was horrifying: 'Beware Labour's tax on ambition' and 'Lamont tots up Labour's incredible shopping list' – *Daily Mail*;[55] 'Why Labour have got it all wrong' – the *Sun*;[56] 'Labour's 50p tax shambles' – *Today*;[57] 'Labour's tax lies exposed' – *Daily Express*.[58] I thought again about using 'Jennifer's Ear' instead of the 'switchers' broadcast to add weight to the health launch. Robin had still not seen the broadcast, and I planned to show it to him that Monday evening. But then fate intervened: I had a phone call from an old schoolteacher of mine, Mrs Hockley, to say that my father had been taken seriously ill and was in hospital in Weybridge. I went to Patricia, explained the situation, and effectively handed the whole campaign over to her. She just took it all on; she didn't flinch. Patricia was extraordinarily strong and brave during this period. It was a campaign of intense pressure, far more than the election campaigns that preceded and followed it. And for a while I was effectively disabled. But she just took the responsibility and soldiered on.

I was driven down to see my father. I had not seen him in six weeks and he was a changed man, wasted and neglected. He was clearly dying. The hospital said that he had cancer. I was overwhelmed. I felt an immediate sadness but also a determination to go on, for him, for what he represented. But I also heard my mother's last words, 'Whatever you do, look after your father,' and so every day until polling day, late in the evening after the campaign had effectively gone to sleep, I visited him. I did not know if this affected my judgement or my energy. I did not know if it was the right thing to do or not, but I was determined to do it.

The following morning, Tuesday, I went to a research meeting at which there were conflicting views of how well 'Jennifer's Ear' had researched. Nick Moon from NOP said it was the worst broadcast he had ever tested. Deborah Mattinson said it was one of the best. But the 'switchers' broadcast had tested worse, so we finally decided to go with health. Robin had still not seen the broadcast and I tried to get him to watch it, but he didn't have time; he was frantic about the press conference. He agreed to go ahead with it nonetheless, and we decided we would take the line that it was not based on a real case. I thought we were safe.

The poster was unveiled in pouring rain and in front of a demonstration by Militant. It did not augur well. We had planned to show the broadcast at a special press conference, and the pre-conference briefing meeting was a mess; we had little time, everybody was tense. And then we had the phone call from hell. It was Lesley Smith, a press officer, who told Anna Healy that Julie Hall, who was travelling with Neil, had read out John Bennett's letter to journalists travelling with the Kinnock entourage. Lesley was shaken – she thought it was a mistake. Julie came to the phone and strongly defended what she had done. It was typical Julie – bold, gutsy and risky – but I knew we were in serious trouble. Somehow Julie had not been told by the press office that my office in Transport House had advised against making any connections between the Bennetts and the PEB.

We showed the broadcast at the press conference and it was as if a bomb had gone off. The effect was devastating. The press clamoured for details. Under pressure we started to offer them information about the case. We had a Campaign Management Team meeting that night, and afterwards Gez Sagar asked if the family concerned was the Bennetts. He said the *Independent* and the *Express* had details of the case and the consultant involved was saying our claims about the story were false. I remember frantically trying to contact Kathryn Smith to get the complete file on the broadcast, but I couldn't find her; she was still over in Transport House. I tried to track down the health team, but they had all disappeared. The press office was being overwhelmed with enquiries. In fact the BBC *Nine O'Clock News* and ITV's *News at Ten* were very positive – the best reports of the entire campaign. I phoned Mandelson in Hartlepool and told him we were besieged. He said whatever we did we must keep the details secret. But it was too late: we were leaking information.

The next day the *Daily Express* front page read: 'EXPOSED: LABOUR'S SICK NHS STUNTS'.[59] Their story was based on a claim by Jennifer Bennett's consultant that the delay in treatment had been due to an administrative breakdown and not, as we insisted, to under-funding. But the consultant, Mr Ardouin, had clearly blamed under-funding in a letter to the Bennetts a month earlier. He had said nothing at all about administrative failure. We still had the ground to fight on if we had the guts to do it.

As I thought controversy was necessary in order to move the agenda off tax and on to health, I was not unduly worried by the *Express* story. But I was about the only person who wasn't, and the campaign went on the defensive. The next day I was in a meeting with Hugh Hudson about the final campaign broadcast when I got a phone call saying that Jennifer's mother and grandfather had condemned 'Jennifer's Ear'. They were both Tories. I watched the news, Mr Bennett supporting the broadcast, Mrs Bennett denouncing it. By now I was hearing whispers, too, of a briefing against the SCA to some journalists, from someone within the Labour Party. Tension was mounting. Throughout all this Neil showed tremendous guts, spirit and loyalty, as did Charles Clarke, who said he thought the controversy was helpful.

That Wednesday, Peter Hitchens from the *Daily Express* jostled with Neil in the post-press conference scrum. The story moved on to Labour's campaign being knocked off balance, which unsettled the press office. They thought smooth campaigns won elections; I knew this wasn't necessarily true.

By the next day we had won the battle over under-funding, so the press moved its attention to finding out who had released the information identifying Jennifer Bennett. At our press conference in Nottingham Neil Kinnock denied it was Julie Hall. Then Julie put her hand up: she wanted to ask a question. Roy Hattersley, who was chairing the meeting, studiously and sensibly ignored her. Roy has a lot of experience, but a question from our own press staff was new to him. Robin Cook gave a very long answer to try to get past the situation. But Julie would not be stopped and marched up to the microphone to make a ten-minute outburst admitting she had released some information, but denying it was sufficient to identify Jennifer Bennett. It was a débâcle. This was our low point.

Later that day, at a Conservative press conference, we were offered a way out. William Waldegrave, the Tory Health Secretary, revealed that the consultant had contacted Conservative Central

Office, who had put him in touch with the *Express*, before the broadcast had even been shown. So it was a stitch-up between the *Express* and Conservative Central Office – who had been warned by Jennifer Bennett's grandfather about the broadcast days earlier – and, more to the point, the Conservatives had been complicit in releasing confidential medical information to the press. Their culpability had been exposed, and we should have gone on to kill them. After the election I attended a seminar with Shaun Woodward, the Conservative Director of Communications at the time, who said the Tories knew about the release of information and were terrified about the consequences. He thought we should not have let up. At that moment we were ahead in the 'War of Jennifer's Ear'. But the ferocity of the attacks on us had unnerved too many people. We needed courage and we needed Mandelson, and we had neither.

Instead, we had another cock-up. On Thursday morning we released a health dossier of ten people who suffered from NHS under-funding out of the thousands who had contacted the party with similar stories. The tabloids examined them and claimed that most were inaccurate, and at the time the press seemed to be right. In fact, most of the cases stood up to scrutiny. Anyway, I didn't care; I still thought all the publicity was good. But other people were alarmed by it.

Robin came in at eleven for the briefing meeting. He was spitting blood, shouting at Patricia and me: why had we let out a dossier based on inaccurate cases? Why had we produced a broadcast based around a family, in which the mother and grandfather were Conservative? I talked to him later, quietly, about it all. I took responsibility for the broadcast, but not the dossier, which had nothing to do with me. We agreed to have a Health Service press conference the next morning, by which time the tabloids were in full flow disproving all the cases. I wrote about the morning in my diary:

6.45 A.M. – usual media meeting. Robin Cook storms in, face

absolutely black, saying he has spoken to Neil Kinnock and he has agreed that whoever is responsible for the release of the dossiers must leave the campaign. There is silence: no one knows who is responsible. Then Neil storms in, equally angry. He is awesome, terrifying, shouting at the meeting. He wants to speak – now – to whoever is responsible for speaking to the consultant in the first place (which someone on the campaign did). At which point everyone starts to squirm under the table and hope that whatever it is that has been done, they didn't do it. The tension in the room is overwhelming. This is the most bloody and brutal meeting of my life. Patricia breaks into tears. Peter Herd, the account director, silently vows never to work in politics again. Gez, who I had not been getting on with during the campaign, has the balls to admit that it was him, he spoke to the consultant. He leaves the room with Neil, certain to die. It can't get any heavier or nastier than that. Throughout it all Charles Clarke is completely relaxed.[60]

We then gave up on health. I didn't want to, I thought we had the advantage, but the campaign was drained emotionally. It wanted to move on.

'Jennifer's Ear' was considered a disaster, and it was messy beyond words. I was attacked from all sides in the press that weekend (although not as heavily as I would be later), and an anonymous campaign colleague claimed in the *Sunday Express* that I was 'fighting for [my] political life'.[61] But it broke the stranglehold of tax, which never recovered as an issue in the rest of the campaign. Taxation increased by only 5 per cent as an issue of concern during the campaign. But health jumped from 32 per cent to 51 per cent, dwarfing all other issues.[62] Up and down the country, health and waiting lists dominated the local news. NOP polls showed 62 per cent claiming that health was the most important issue in deciding how to vote.[63] It is also true that tax and the economy were the most important unprompted issues in deciding the vote,[64] and of course they were fundamentally much more decisive. But in so far as it was possible to pull a campaign away from tax and on to health, that broadcast did it. Of course, the better way would have been to win the argument on tax, but that had to wait.

One final footnote. The polls throughout were very close, and obviously wrong, but the only time they showed big Labour leads was after the 'Jennifer's Ear' broadcast. I remember sitting in a café on the last but one Wednesday of the campaign, a week after the broadcast, waiting for the opinion polls. One put Labour ahead by 7 per cent, another 6 per cent, a third by 4 per cent.[65] For the first time in the campaign I felt a glimmer of happiness and vindication. It was a false dawn, but it indicated that whatever our true position 'Jennifer's Ear' had not hurt us – it might even have helped. Sometimes you have to go nuclear.

Kinnock

After tax and health, the third big issue of the campaign was Neil himself. There are two views of his electoral significance. The first was put without sentiment by Joe Napolitan in a memo dated 8 March 1991, which said, 'The worst thing that happened to Labour was the ousting of Margaret Thatcher. With Kinnock as the candidate, Labour cannot win the next General Election.' He continued: 'Comparing the candidates directly is a lost cause. When the survey was taken in early January, Major's favourable/unfavourable balance was +55 per cent. Neil Kinnock's was –12 per cent. This gives a 65-point spread in Major's favour.'[66]

Anthony King and Ivor Crewe put a more considered view in *Labour's Last Chance*, in which they conclude Neil Kinnock's image and identity could only have lost the Labour Party under 0.5 per cent of the vote. One analytic model they developed of the 1992 election showed Neil adding 0.4 per cent to Labour's votes. Another contradictory model suggested that 'Major's net pulling power' in 1992 was in fact 0.5 per cent greater than Kinnock's. The latter is more likely to be right, but it is a very small amount which would still have left the Conservatives with a crushing lead. They made a telling point: 'It is worth emphasising again the importance of indirect leadership effects . . . Kinnock's importance to Labour almost certainly lay in his effect on the party's policies and image.' Furthermore, they argued, 'John Smith is a considerably more highly regarded Labour leader than his predecessor, Neil Kinnock, was; yet Labour's standing in the polls under Smith in the mid-1990s . . . was no higher than it had frequently been under Kinnock.' In summary, they thought Neil lost Labour votes because he lacked voter appeal, but added them because of the changes he made to the party and its policies.[67] And in the final analysis, Labour under John Smith was no more popular than it was frequently under Neil Kinnock.

I have enormous respect for Neil Kinnock. Without him, there would be no modern Labour Party, no huge Labour majority. He was and is a giant of a man who through the power of his personality lifted Labour into the modern era. He made the first great modernising breakthrough. He took Labour from the pathetic, unelectable shambles he inherited in 1983, with a Conservative majority of 144, to a party on the brink of government just 20 seats short of a hung parliament. Charles Clarke says of Kinnock:

> Neil was elected with one ambition in mind – to make Labour electable again and then hopefully get it elected. When he became leader after the 1983 defeat there was a real prospect of Labour never being electable again, of being a party which disappeared out of British politics. Certainly Neil felt that. His job, duty, responsibility was to make Labour electable again. And I think that's what he did. Not well enough to win the 1992 election, or to take, even, victory from the Tories in the 1992 election, which was a different thing, but well enough to lay the path for Labour to win the 1997 election in the way that it did. That is what I think Neil was about. But his achievement was fragile enough even after 1992 that we might not have won 1997. It needed the modernisation agenda to continue, which is what Tony did, to a fantastic triumph.[68]

Neil Kinnock did not change the Labour Party far enough, fast enough. This was his essential failure. He himself believes now that he should have moved more quickly, but the miners' strike, the one member, one vote defeat and Militant slowed him down right from the start. He became more cautious about taking on the party. 'There were some of us who thought that he could have moved faster,' said Charles Clarke. 'There were various organisational issues where he went for caution, and it is easy with hindsight to say we should not have done so. But it still remained the case that the main inhibition against moving more quickly was the fact that you immediately turn the party back to splits, with senior party people conducting battles in the media against the leadership. I myself thought we should have gone faster, as did Patricia, and we could have gone faster in certain ways, but to say absolutely categorically with the benefit of hindsight that going faster would necessarily have got us to where we were now a lot quicker is not absolutely convincing.' Those early errors fatally damaged Neil's leadership, he believes: 'The failures of the end were the failures of the beginning.'[69]

Alastair Campbell believes Neil was a little ambivalent about modernisation:

I think there was a tension. Neil knew that the party had to be modernised and that modernisation was essential to any develop-ment of its electoral appeal. I think he knew that there were an awful lot of things in the Labour Party that were wrong, but he also had a sentimental attachment to some of the things that were wrong as well. He was deep-rooted in that sort of sentimentality, but nobody can say he didn't challenge it. He did challenge it, but time wasn't on his side to get the changes through. He did actually get an awful lot of changes through. It's hard to tell [if he could have moved faster] because you can't tell what he could have got through the party. I think he could probably have moved things more quickly on certain fronts, but you don't know. It's easy in hindsight to say that.[70]

Public perceptions of Neil Kinnock have been the basis of some of the most concerted attacks on the SCA, and also on me. After the defeat, and after John Prescott's attacks on the 'beautiful people'[71] who had hijacked the campaign, John and I had a reconciliation lunch at L'Amico in Westminster. John was very warm and for me it was a very moving occasion. His most consistent criticism was: why did you not present private polling about Neil Kinnock to the shadow Cabinet? There is still, today, a feeling that the SCA and I, in particular, represented the leader rather than the party; that by withholding information in some way we interrupted the democratic process. If they had had the full information, they could have acted against him.

On one level I can dismiss this attack lightly. As an election adviser it wasn't part of my brief to go to the shadow Cabinet and present polling information that undermined the party leader. It was not part of my role to get involved in internal party politics. It is also true that there is nothing in private polling that cannot be found in public polls.

But on another level my defence is weaker. It is true that I presented without compromise all negatives about all other aspects of Labour but not about its leader. I went pretty far, but not the whole way. I put loyalty to Neil first; but Neil knew from the start that the public didn't warm to him as a leader. There was no need for me to tell him. He agonised about it, he felt the pain of it constantly. Before the election, he considered standing down on more than one occasion. Patricia Hewitt believes he would have done so if he thought it would work. 'He talked about it,' she said. 'He was very down in the winter of 1991–92. He was demoralised by eight years of the press and most of his colleagues telling him he was as thick as two short planks. But he just couldn't see a way by which he could stand down.'[72] After the 1987 election he told me he felt that the better course might have been to have stood down.

On balance, I think he was right to remain party leader. Good leadership is not just how you appear on television, it is what you do. And while it is true that it would have been almost impossible to have won the election with Neil, it would have been little better with any other leader. It is easy to claim that a shift to John Smith would have significantly improved our position, but research carried out when he was leader showed he made little difference to Labour's image. The press were building Smith up as an alternative leader, but, if they had had their way, they would have turned on him before the election. 'I believe that Neil had decision-taking qualities,' said Charles Clarke:

> Neil was not a fudge leader. His sharpness could be wrong, of course. But he was about addressing issues, going in and getting things done. John believed you had to position things. He had a very good media image. And it's just conceivable that if you'd changed leader at the beginning of the campaign itself then it might have been okay, because by that stage the whole thing was so much in shape that his lack of leadership qualities wouldn't have come through. But if you'd done it significantly before, even as late as January 1992, I think that his weaknesses would have been viciously exposed. It's the same reason that when people say today that John Smith could have won the 1997 General Election, I don't believe it. I believe that the capacity of leadership that is required to win these things is exceptional. And there are not many people who have that. And John was the classic consensual person, who could have become Prime Minister if he'd inherited the job from the previous Labour Prime Minister, *à la* Callaghan. He never had the leadership quality that was required to *grasp* leadership.[73]

Had Smith been leader, the media could have put him under enormous pressure on tax and Labour would not have changed its tax policies as much as it did under Kinnock. It would have been impossible to have formed a majority; the only likelihood would have been a hung parliament with Labour perhaps 6 per cent behind the Tories. Labour would have been forced to put up taxes, forced out of the ERM. It could easily have seen Labour defeated again in months rather than years. The process of history would have been cheated. We would not have won in 1997 with a majority of 179.

Neil Kinnock deserved that last chance and it was right that he had it. History was not short-changed, Labour advanced. The Conservatives took another course, dumping their leader to win short-term success. They won the election, but have lost power for a generation. The Conservatives still suffer from that one internecine act.

I asked John Smith after the defeat if he had considered trying to replace Neil before the election. He was appalled by the thought: it was Neil's right to be leader in 1992. Yet the British people never really took to him as leader, and there was nothing he could do about it. There was much talk after the election about how Neil was constrained by his advisers, that if he had been his natural self he would have done better. But this was not true. Nothing Neil could have done would have endeared him to the voters. We had a plan called Operation Liberation, in which Neil would cut loose, and become his real self. But it didn't work because his real self had changed, become older, wiser, different. In the run-up to the election, Alastair Campbell remembers the strain Kinnock seemed to be under: 'You got a sense of Neil trying to hold it together and you could feel the tension. He hadn't run out of steam, but there was a lack of cohesion, lack of drive. It wasn't a question of Neil – Neil had drive – there was just no sense that you'd got a machine on the march. It wasn't there.'[74]

Neil remained isolated from his campaign team. This, perhaps, is the greatest misunderstanding about the campaign. When I had lunch with John Prescott I explained, as best I could, what had happened in the campaign, much of which was new to him. But what he really couldn't understand was the estrangement between the campaign-team leadership and the party leader. He had thought that there was constant interaction between Neil and the campaign team, that the leader and key campaigning personnel were effectively operating as one integral unit. John thought he had been shut out while we were locked in.

This wasn't true. John had little access to Neil, nor did we. For the last six months or so before the campaign started I hardly saw

Neil and there was never, as far as I can recall, a time when he and his campaign team sat down and discussed the planning and operation of the election. The Thursday Group was in one place, Neil in another. We were all asking constantly for contact with the leader, but we never got it. The reason given was always the same: 'It would add to his burden, increase pressure on him, lead to endless demands that he would be unable to meet.' I don't know if Neil knew he was being protected in this way; I suspect not. Once I picked up a ringing phone in Neil's office and it was Neil. We started chatting and immediately it became clear that he was desperate to hear about what was happening on the campaign, of which he knew almost nothing. He wanted to know more and more. We talked for a very long time and could have talked longer. Neil was a man trapped in a glass prison. Whether he made the prison himself, or others made it for him, I do not know. Charles Clarke denies he was being over-protective: 'I think Neil was very focused on his own performance as he went up to the election, getting his own speeches right and so on. I think that time was very much at a premium. I certainly felt that a general run around the course in a rather vacuous way wouldn't help very much. Now, that certainly was not intended to be over-protective.'[75] I saw far more of John Smith in the period before the campaign. I worked with him closely and I hope warmly during this time, after he overcame his initial resentment at my criticism of his tax plans. But Neil was isolated from his campaign team, from the planning of his campaign, even from his senior colleagues.

However, although I saw little of Neil in the pre-election period, I saw a huge amount of him during the four-week election campaign itself. Still haunted by his hunt for elusive words, I remember him, head in hands, saying, 'Words: where can I get words? I must have words.' It is difficult to describe his courage and dignity during the campaign. He had a cold, he was very tired, but he fought and fought and fought. 'He had guts,' said Campbell. 'He's somebody who went into politics because he was genuinely motivated by a belief that politics was the way to get a better way of life for the sort of people he grew up with. And allied to that was a real sort of passion, temper – call it what you want – which had a good side and a bad side. The good side was that he actually got angry about things, but that also led to all sorts of problems for him as well, because a temper you can't control can become a problem. But he was properly motivated – he was, I think, a straightforwardly decent kind of bloke, soundly motivated throughout.'[76]

And he was always kind. He never blamed me for 'Jennifer's Ear'. Talking to him privately later in the campaign, I referred to the strain and trauma of that week. He said simply, 'That's what politics is about, Philip; love and anger.' Once when I brought my daughter Georgia into the campaign, he found the time to sing the whole of 'Georgia On My Mind' to her. He did every single thing expected of him, and just made one mistake when, at the Sheffield Rally, overwhelmed by the occasion, he was over-enthusiastic in greeting the crowd. And he still bitterly regrets that mistake. Nothing will have replaced for Neil the sense of loss he has about losing the 1992 election. He is the kind of man who will carry it with him always. But he need not and should not. He is the rock upon which the election triumph of 1997 was built. He is a modernising hero.

The Sheffield Rally and proportional representation

Of the many that have been given, the Sheffield Rally on 1 April 1992 is the least convincing reason for losing the election. Bob Worcester calls it the turning-point. That is nonsense. It was barely on the news and was hardly noticed. It did Labour little or no harm. The voters had bigger fish to fry. That said, it was a mistake – it looked over-confident, the politicians were over-exuberant and it was too American and glitzy – but this time it was not my mistake. It was a good idea which went wrong.

Charles Clarke had wanted a last-week rally to end all rallies.

The idea floated around for some time and I went to various meetings before it floated off to Jim Parish, the senior campaign officer, who had the monumental task of organising it. Strategically, its point was to give Labour a major lift going into the last week, assuming we would be behind, or neck-and-neck. It was not designed for a situation in which Labour was 6–7 per cent ahead, when the rally would be useless. I still think the concept was sound; we couldn't have predicted the polls.

Parish's only instructions were to give it dignity and style, and for the shadow Cabinet not to walk with Neil across the stadium hallway because we did not want it to look triumphalist. On the day after the 'Jennifer's Ear' broadcast, at a meeting about the rally, I said it must have dignity and integrity throughout, and not look too much like an American convention. In the end the rally failed on all these counts and the walk happened, but I do not blame Jim. It was a great effort of organisation to have got it done at all.

Jim and I worked closely (at least I thought we did) through the election period. He was considered difficult, but he had real talent and I often defended him. But after the election he wrote a memo, which was leaked to the press, blaming the SCA for all the campaign's failings and me personally for the mishaps of Sheffield, simply because the rally started late, and that was my fault. I expect it did not matter very much. The later the better, probably.

The Sheffield Rally started late because I had reached an agreement with Robin Cook that 'Jennifer's Ear' would be expunged from the rest of the campaign; but I had forgotten about the video for the rally, which Hugh Hudson had produced and which contained an excerpt from 'Jennifer's Ear'. Somehow Anna Healy heard about this, and mentioned it to Robin. She was not being unkind, she was trying to be helpful. But Robin erupted – understandably – and I had to get 'Jennifer's Ear' out. I phoned Hugh, who was travelling to the rally, and begged him to take it out. He shouted at me, too – also understandably – but said he would try. As he was sitting next to Robin on the train, I don't expect much was said about me that was complimentary.

Meg Clark, Hugh's assistant, saved me, sending new pictures to Sheffield by satellite. I was panicking badly; this was the final straw. The video was due to introduce Neil and he was delayed waiting for it. When the video spluttered into life without 'Jennifer's Ear', I couldn't believe they had managed it. All I saw of the rest of the rally was a couple of clips on the news. And that's all the public saw.

Proportional representation is a more difficult issue. Peter Mandelson thinks it cost us dear in the last week, and so does Gordon Brown. There is little evidence that it did, but it was not the ideal way to end a campaign. Patricia has been blamed for this – unfairly, I think.

The drive towards proportional representation came from a belief that it was the only certain way to make Labour safe. If you have PR, Labour can never govern alone. It will always be neutered, a consensus not an extreme government. Tony Blair had always opposed the idea of using PR to emasculate Labour. If you want to make Labour safe, change the party – don't duck out of the issue with PR. Blair believed that only when the party itself was safe would people vote for it. But that option was not available in 1991, and PR seemed a reasonable alternative; post-election research showed that the need to make Labour safe had been a key campaigning requirement. Neil supported the idea of a referendum on it, and this was included in the manifesto.

Post-election criticism focused less on the inclusion of a referendum on PR in the manifesto and more on the way it was raised at the end of the campaign. Patricia remembers: 'When we were planning the campaign, we knew that there was going to be this Charter 88 Democracy Day on the Thursday before polling, so David [Hill], Charles [Clarke] and myself agreed a form of words, which we cleared personally with Roy Hattersley.'[77] We knew the issue of PR would be raised and we had no power over it. It is almost certainly true that we should have tackled it earlier, but that said, there is no evidence that it harmed Labour in the end. Post-election qualitative research found people thought it made

Labour safer, and Labour's lead gradually increased from 1 per cent to 3–4 per cent over the six days after the issue was raised (causing the Tory tabloids to turn viciously on Ashdown).[78]

The question was raised at the press conference on the Charter 88 Democracy Day. Neil read out the answer, which made people suspect the question had been planted, and also raised the profile of the issue. 'Neil was so determined and worried about saying the wrong thing, and because he pulled that piece of paper out, it looked like a plant and it absolutely wasn't,' said Hewitt. 'He pulled out a piece of paper and read the form of words so it looked as if Elinor [Goodman, political editor of *Channel Four News*] had been set up to ask the question, and it looked as if he was making this great big initiative.'[79] Kinnock's answer was precisely that agreed previously with Roy Hattersley, then Labour's Home Affairs spokesman, and only pushed the boat out a tiny way, inviting the Liberal Democrats to join a working party to consider PR. It then took off as an issue, and Neil was embarrassed on the *Granada 500* programme four days later when he refused to say whether he was for it or against it. He actually hadn't worked out what he would say if asked. I had wanted us to concentrate in the last week on the recession and health, but we could not begin to break through with the message. It was too late, the agenda had moved on, PR had become the story. It became an issue less because of its intrinsic merits, more because a hung parliament seemed likely. I do not think it was wrong to open the debate on it, given that it was bound to be raised, and indeed I believe that if Labour had lost by 7 per cent and we had not nodded towards some form of electoral reform the campaign would genuinely have been open to criticism.

Into the night

Nineteen ninety-two was the toughest campaign I have ever been involved in. It stretched all of us to breaking-point. It was a campaign always close to cracking, conducted in an atmosphere of tension and mistrust. The tension was eating people up; personal relationships were sour. I said afterwards that anyone who hadn't gone through that election couldn't understand what it was like, and that was true. It was less an election campaign, more a collective trauma. Yet, despite all this, we all believed we could win. Not that we would, but that we could. The polls – all of them – said we could do it. But the polls were wrong.

At an SCA lunch on the Friday before polling I asked the researchers who had been conducting the focus-group discussions if we would win. Yes, they said: we are absolutely certain. I remembered this after the election and vowed I would do the focus groups myself for the next election, which I did. Even the cautious Roger Jowell predicted a hung parliament. Some people have claimed that I said Labour could not lose the election, but this is wrong. What I said to the Campaign Strategy Meeting at the end of the campaign was: 'The Conservatives have lost the election. We have yet to win it.' This was true. People didn't want to vote Conservative, but they were not yet prepared to vote for us. The polls led me to believe we might win, but I could never actually see it: I couldn't imagine Neil Kinnock in Downing Street. Nor could the electorate.

Neil said later he became convinced he would lose over the last few days. I am not sure if this is true. I spoke to him often towards the end and he said: be cautious; play safe; avoid mistakes; we will just make it. I think he thought we were just ahead and the key requirement was not to blow it.

This illustrates the greatest mistake we made in the campaign. We allowed ourselves to become the incumbents: to take on the attributes of the government, rather than the opposition. This was largely the result of the polls, and the small leads they gave Labour throughout. We sat on our lead and acted with governmental caution; the Conservatives, a couple of points behind, fought like tigers and behaved like the opposition.

But that was only the first effect of the polls getting it wrong. The second was much more important: because Labour was ahead and assumed by much of the press to be the next government, thousands, perhaps millions, of voters were motivated to come out and stop us. This was partly because of the strength of our campaign; we persuaded voters we might win. If we had been behind in the polls the Conservative vote would have been lower. David Hill believes it was the polls and not Sheffield that seemed to turn the votes against us in the last few days: 'The day before Sheffield the opinion polls had shown us well ahead in three polls; they suddenly alerted the electorate to the fact that we might win. That was a problem.'[80]

My overwhelming feeling during that last week was complete exhaustion. I was aching with fatigue and nervous about the result, although on the evening of Tuesday 7 April I walked up to John Major to try to cheer him up. It was quite late and Patricia and I were walking from Millbank back to the SCA headquarters in Smith Square. John Major's battle-bus was parked outside Tory Central Office and standing in front of it, looking sad, dejected and defeated, was Major himself. He appeared to have been abandoned. Patricia and I felt sorry for him, so we walked towards him and he brightened as we approached, putting on a smile. But as we got closer he recognised us and his smile became fixed, then disappeared altogether. We didn't know what to say, so we just shook his hand and walked away, leaving him as forlorn and lonely as when we had arrived.

But when I saw the newspaper headlines the next day I knew it was Labour that was in trouble. I arrived at the Millbank media centre at 6 A.M. and saw articles which were not so much negative as apocalyptic. The *Daily Express* headlines screamed of mortgage rises, race riots, chaos in the NHS and higher costs for six out of ten households if the 'shallow man' Kinnock was let in. 'Don't throw it all away,' it urged in a front-page opinion.[81] The *Sun* destroyed Neil and Labour with an eight-page attack entitled 'NIGHTMARE ON KINNOCK STREET', warning, 'He'll have a new home, you won't', 'A threat to proud history', 'My job will go', 'Prices set to jump', 'Do not trust his judgement or his promises', and 'Lest we forget – Hell caused by last Labour government'.[82] It delivered the final knock-out blow a day later with its front-page headline: 'IF KINNOCK WINS TODAY WILL THE LAST PERSON IN BRITAIN PLEASE TURN OUT THE LIGHTS'.[83] And on it went. The *Mail*, with 'Labour would have to raise loan rates' and 'Warning: a Labour government will lead to higher mortgage payments. There is no doubt about it. Interest rates will rise within days of Kinnock entering Number Ten.'[84] The *Express*: 'Can you really afford not to vote Tory?'[85]

I looked at those papers and silently wept. I could feel the fear of our voters: we would lose them in the ballot box, as I had predicted two years earlier – 'At the death, in the polling-booth, people may be more likely to vote for the devil they know and dislike rather than the devil they do not fully trust.'[86] I went home that Wednesday night and saw the polls reported on the *Channel Four News*, our lead melting away like snow. We had achieved our objective and got to polling day ahead in the polls, but only just. I knew that I had done my best in an almost impossible situation and helped to get the campaign through.

But I also knew that it wouldn't be enough, and I hardly slept that night. The next morning I voted very early and expected an empty polling station. I was shocked to find it packed – packed with hordes of elderly voters, one with a zimmer frame, all clearly come to stop us getting in. I knew then we had had it and phoned David Hill and others. We are, I told them, undone by the zimmer-frame vote. I was desperately sad. I had no doubt that we were finished. I stayed at home for the rest of the day, sleeping intermittently and fretting, getting the occasional hint of news about the exit polls, most of it good. David Hill phoned me just before nine o'clock and said the exit polls showed a hung parliament, but I was not convinced. I took a taxi to Walworth Road and, as I had done in 1987, made it drive by Downing Street, but I had the same certainty as then: we would not be in there tomorrow.

I went the press office and the exit polls had worsened. Inside I felt numb; I knew what was coming. I went upstairs to Kinnock's office and they were convinced they were going into Downing Street. Neil Stewart, Kinnock's policy adviser, was certain: 'Tomorrow I will be in Number 10,' he said. Peter phoned, wanting to know if we had won this bloody election or not. No, I said. As the night progressed the polls got worse, and I knew it was all up. The Basildon defeat was clearly the end. For a brief period I went to the party at Millbank to show my face. I felt that was the least I could do. But the mood there was complete desolation. I returned quickly to Walworth Road. Peter phoned, distressed. You didn't deserve this, he said. Everything you did was better than 1987, and you deserved to win. It was not true, but he was being kind. After Basildon I said to my wife Gail, we are beaten, let's go home. I walked out of Walworth Road into the cold night, looking and feeling totally dejected. A lone reporter asked if I had any comment. I said, 'There will be another day.' I went home numb and defeated.

The next morning was worse. Major was triumphant. Labour had snatched defeat from the jaws of victory.

And then the recriminations began. People who had supported us, praised the campaign, worked alongside the SCA and agreed with everything we did, turned on us in defeat. I had seen this coming: I knew the reputation of the campaign was going to be torn to shreds. To lose once and receive credit for running a good campaign is possible; when you lose twice the knives come out.

It began with the press. *Tribune*, which had praised Labour's campaigners throughout and in its election-day editions, saying there was plenty of room for pride in a job 'done as well as it could be done',[87] turned immediately, taking revenge on the SCA and in particular Patricia Hewitt and me. Its former editor, Phil Kelly, who had fought and lost a seat in the election, took aim at the 'elitist and manipulative' techniques which Kinnock and his 'tight clique of supporters' had espoused. 'The glitz and gloss approach, far from enabling Labour to compete on equal terms with the Tories, positively obscured our message' and created 'alienated bewilderment' among voters, he wrote. 'At least the

1992 result means that Labour can dispense, lock, stock and barrel, with the well-meaning, metropolitan, middle-class ministrations of the Shadow Communications Agency and go back to real politics.'[88] In a vitriolic attack on Labour's 'image-makers' or 'party strategists' headlined 'LOOKING BACK IN ANGER', in *Tribune* in June, John Booth attacked Patricia and me personally ('Are we seriously expected to believe that we will win if Dennis Skinner has his humour honed by Patricia Hewitt . . . and should we all ask Philip Gould for the number of his hairdresser?'), demanded to know how much the SCA had been paid and for what, and concluded: 'Let us never again allow ourselves to be convinced that because some people get to the top they know what they are doing.'[89]

Vincent Hanna made a television programme claiming that the monitoring unit (a group of volunteers, including Glenys Thornton, who monitored grass-roots opinion) had been making constant protestations of disaster which the campaign leadership ignored. This was completely untrue. The last report of the group had said: 'With a little more effort this week, we may be able to win over the last 2 per cent we need to get a majority.'[90]

And then the big guns lined up: in an influential piece in the *Independent*, Anthony Bevins argued that Labour need not have lost, but had done so because of the arrogance of the campaign leadership, in particular the SCA. It quoted anonymous senior Labour politicians as claiming they hadn't even known we existed until they saw televised news clips of us working on the campaign, and effectively accused us of inventing Labour's manifesto behind the backs of the shadow Cabinet.[91] This broke the dam and open season was declared on the SCA. The conventional wisdom became that we, in particular Patricia and I, had hijacked the campaign while the politicians had been marginalised. And a lot of it came from the politicians themselves, who felt, understandably enough in the circumstances, that control of the campaign had been ceded to unelected advisers.

John Prescott was our most outspoken critic. In June, as the party prepared for an official post-mortem on the election, he demanded that the NEC reassert its authority over 'out-of-control' advisers, saying the campaign 'had a complete mess at the heart of it, particularly in the last week', with strategy made 'on the hoof' by unaccountable outsiders.[92] On *Frost on Sunday*, he added: 'For far too long [the party] has been controlled by a few people who abuse some of the authority given to them.'[93]

Clare Short said the campaign had relied too much on 'glitz' and opinion polling and claimed people had not voted for us because 'Labour was seen as having lost its soul, its identity, its integrity.'[94] A 'senior NEC member' attacked the SCA in the *Guardian*: 'Peter Mandelson invented this Frankenstein's Monster and it's out of control.'[95]

It became a fact. We lost because the SCA had ousted politicians and party officials. Then Jim Parish joined in the fray. Andy Grice of the *Sunday Times* phoned me the Saturday before the NEC's inquest into the election defeat and said he had bad news for me. Parish had written a report for the NEC inquest blaming the entire failure on the SCA and claiming we had mounted a 'wholesale takeover' of the campaign. His attack was bitter and personal: the SCA was 'a small team consisting of two [very] successful businessmen and another adviser, herself well-off . . . a group more remote from the people we had to convince it would be difficult to find.' He concluded: 'A future campaign must not be handed over to people who offer magic means of winning elections that ultimately ignore political realities.'[96]

People I barely knew even approached me in the street, insulting or blaming me. But a few offered encouragement. Tom Sawyer took me for coffee in Old Compton Street and showed me copies of the left-wing press that had been praising the campaign just hours before the defeat. 'You almost did it, son,' he said. He thought we were finished, our time had gone. I was deeply pessimistic. In July I wrote to Dennis Kavanagh (now Professor of Politics at Liverpool University, and the co-writer of the Nuffield election studies that had been my bible in my youth), reflecting that in

1987 I had said: 'You can't win a campaign in four weeks, but only in four years.' Now I was forced to admit: 'After four years' continuous campaigning, that excuse is no longer available.'[97]

But I did not stop, and I did not give up. I commissioned research immediately after the election to find out why we had really lost. And of course the normal reasons given – 'Jennifer's Ear', or the Sheffield Rally, or PR – disappeared under the weight of the evidence. The polling was clear: Labour lost because it was still the party of the winter of discontent; union influence; strikes and inflation; disarmament; Benn and Scargill. It lost because people thought they had left the party, and the party had left them. Labour and the voters were facing in different directions. The electorate looked 'onwards and upwards; they work hard; they want to do better for themselves and their families'. Labour looked downwards: 'Clawing back; turning the clock back; for Militant; anti-home ownership; strife; strikes; inflation. Not for me.'[98]

The conclusions were dramatic: if Labour was to have a chance of winning, it had to change completely. It should consider all options, including dumping the name. I had some sympathy with this view. I told the playwright David Hare a few months after the election: 'It is very hard for supporters to understand the word "Labour" belongs to the past.'[99] New Labour was eventually to provide a solution.

This research could not have been made clearer. The cleavage between people and party which opened twenty years before, and reached its peak in 1983, had still not closed. Labour was still not the people's party. It was still the prisoner of the past. Labour lost not because it had changed too much, but because it had changed too little. It lost because the process of modernisation had been too slow. I was asked by the General Secretary to present the research on why we lost to the NEC inquest on 18 June. Of all the presentations I have made, this was the worst. Bryan Gould, David Blunkett and John Prescott had said they would question me at the meeting. I was dreading it and asked Alastair Campbell to write an article in the *Daily Mirror* in my defence the day before the ordeal.

'It threatens to be one of the most explosive and nasty National Executive meetings since the days when they were all explosive and nasty,' he began. He printed the SCA's analysis of why Labour had lost the election, under the headline, 'Labour must look to the future – NOT for election scapegoats.' He criticised the politicians who were seeking to hide behind campaign officials, arguing: 'If politicians lost control of a political campaign, that is the fault of the politicians.' And most importantly, he argued for further modernisation, not retreat: 'Labour lost not because they changed, but because they didn't change enough.'[100]

Underlying all the criticism had been the basic political sentiment that we lost because we modernised, we lost because we sold out to the polls and the public. The next day I walked through the ranks of press and photographers and up the steps of Walworth Road like a condemned man. I told the NEC that campaign mistakes had not helped us, but that we had lost because we were still not trusted, still not changed enough. I presented the post-campaign research in its unvarnished form. Left-wingers including Joan Lestor and Tony Benn argued that modernisation had been tried and failed, and existing policies should be consolidated rather than dismissed as 'baggage', as some modernisers were suggesting. Paul Anderson wrote in *Tribune* that week: 'The whole approach adopted by Labour from 1987 to 1992, designed *precisely* to address lack of trust in the party and its perceived obsolescence, failed miserably to achieve its objectives.'[101]

The aftermath was almost over, but not quite. I spent the summer writing a series of campaign evaluation documents that took an endless time to prepare and compile. This was hell. All the time I was thinking: one percentage point. Just one. But I wanted to leave a legacy. I wanted the party to know what had really happened. I said that Labour must become the party 'of achievement and aspiration for ordinary working people'. Labour needed to become a mainstream, not a minority party. Labour should have the courage to say that it had changed.[102]

I spent much time with my father, who by now was staying with my sister. I fished in the local river, thinking of when he and I had fished the Avon all those years before. I felt remorse. I felt guilt. I did not answer the criticisms hurled at me because I felt I would have taken the credit if we had won, so I should accept the blame now we had lost.

I was with my father when he died. The last words I heard him say were, 'That is my son and I am proud of him.' I was determined to justify that pride. I would not stop fighting until Labour won.

5

A LINE IN THE SAND

Into the wilderness

The decline of the Kinnock project and the compromises that followed saw a split in the ranks of the modernisers. Peter Mandelson and I had become professionally estranged, impeding our mutual effectiveness. I had stayed at the centre of the campaign, close to Charles Clarke, who was the strongest figure in the team, its fulcrum. As Clarke and Mandelson fell out, this led to divided loyalties, and the distance between Peter and me had grown. But after the campaign, I decided that never again would I allow this to happen: good or bad, I would stick with Mandelson, stick with modernisation and never compromise. It was clear to me that Labour had to modernise completely or eventually it would die.

We were going to have to wait, however. John Smith wanted to heal the party, not reform it. His instinct was for consolidation, not modernisation. During the leadership campaign following Neil Kinnock's resignation after the 1992 election, fought between him and Bryan Gould, he expressed his reservations about the modernisation process: 'If radical change involves the Labour Party subverting its principles and aborting its mission, then I'm conservative in that very narrow sense.'[1] I knew my project wouldn't get far with him. He didn't want Mandelson either. Peter spent the two years of John's leadership kicking his heels in London and Hartlepool. On one occasion, he recalls saving a visit to the supermarket so that he would have something to do on a Sunday. But there was no question that I would give up, or let the 1992 election defeat stand. I decided, instead, to leave Britain and learn more about campaigning; find out how other parties were modernising; discover how to win.

I was determined to remain privately and publicly loyal to John Smith. I believed modernisation was the only way forward, but I also believed it was time to be quiet. At a low level, behind the scenes, I helped John whenever he asked me to. From time to time I conducted focus groups for him, but I was clearly, and rightly, at the very fringes of the Smith leadership: out in the cold.

The SCA was closed down after six years. Its demise became public in October 1992 when party officials confirmed in *Campaign* magazine that they would 'wind up the team of volunteers who ran the last two election efforts'. A party official was quoted as saying: 'The relationships we had at the last election no longer exist, so we are in the process of seeing what else is on offer.'[2] We became non-people. A chapter was closed; it was time to move on.

Four weeks in Little Rock

I had begun to develop links with the Democratic Party in the United States in 1986, when its consultant Joe Napolitan started to help Neil Kinnock. Although Neil always refused to meet him, once deciding against seeing Joe when he was already halfway down the long corridor to Neil's office in the House of Commons, Joe was the doyen of political consultants, one of the first and one of the best.

After the defeat of Michael Dukakis in 1988, I visited the United States to talk to people who had been involved in the campaign, all of whom were feeling terribly the burden of defeat. It was quite clear where they had gone wrong: they had capitulated to the awesome Republican attack and they had failed to connect to the great American middle class. I visited the Democratic National Committee with Peter Mandelson the following year. In a long, rambling and not very successful meeting, Peter turned to me and said in his typical stage whisper: 'Do you know what the best thing about this meeting is, Philip? I will tell you. The best thing is the doughnuts.' I also organised and partly financed a trip with Jack Cunningham and Ken and Barbara Follett to learn about fundraising techniques.

Both Bob Shrum, a leading media consultant in the United States, and Mark Mellman, an American pollster, helped with the British election in 1992, although they were not paid. Bob wrote the final words of Neil's last conference speech in 1991: 'It is time to start transforming Britain from the country it has become, into the one we know it can be.'[3]

But I never met James Carville, who was later to manage Bill Clinton's election-winning campaign, and I met Stanley Greenberg, pollster to Clinton in 1992, only briefly, on a trip to garner polling advice in 1990. I am embarrassed to say that I neglected to take up Stan's offer of polling help at that time. But a connection was made, and one that obviously stuck in Stan's mind, because at the beginning of September 1992 I received a memo from his office which read: 'Stan is anxious to meet you here in Little Rock, Arkansas, at the Clinton Campaign Headquarters. We are anxious to have you observe the campaign, and to hear about your efforts.'[4] For me at that time – depleted, dejected, depressed – this fax was like water in the desert.

I took the first flight I could get to St Louis, then on to Little Rock. Before the flight, and at the stopover, I was being nagged by Bennett Freeman, a volunteer on the campaign: 'Get here faster, it's urgent, they want you to appear in a press conference.' The reason for their alarm was that the Bush campaign appeared to be trying to steal Conservative tactics and apply them in the States. An attack by Bush over a Russian trip of Clinton's seemed to echo the 'Kinnock: the Kremlin Connection' smear by the *Sunday Times*.[5]

The Bush campaign had issued a press release saying: 'Back in the USSR. Six weeks after he organised a massive anti-war protest in London, then student Bill Clinton turned up at the Soviet Union for a visit during the dead of winter.'[6] The Republicans were also developing their own 'tax bombshell' attack.

The Clinton campaign's anxiety was partly rational, partly emotional. They had been following our campaign closely and felt dismayed and let down by our defeat. At a meeting the day after, someone from their campaign had said, 'We are on our own now.' There was a fear that somehow the same thing could happen there: the Labour jinx might cross the Atlantic.

I travelled to Little Rock with trepidation. I was the architect of a defeated and discredited campaign. My esteem was low, my confidence shot. What could I offer them? I expected them to be dismissive and arrogant, but I could not have been more wrong. Arriving at that campaign was like leaving the shadows and coming into the sunlight. I was greeted with more warmth than I imagined possible, certainly more than I deserved. I was told repeatedly, 'Everyone here has been defeated two or three times in presidential elections. Defeat is how you learn. We want to learn from you.' The campaign was not only friendly, it was also awesomely efficient: a great, co-ordinated, self-confident machine which was trampling Bush to defeat. It was like entering a different world. That campaign saved me professionally and, in a different way, personally. Their warmth that autumn began my recovery from defeat.

I wrote in my diary in early October:

Arrived at Little Rock. Two taxi-drivers playing dice under a tree. Flat, vast country. Small pink barns and farmhouses. Take a cab to the Capitol Hotel. Old Southern style: the best hotel in Little Rock. Am met immediately by Bennett and Tom Hagemann [another campaign volunteer]. Agree a memo on the Kremlin connection smear story. Arrange to have dinner at 9 P.M.

Oversleep and am woken by Bennett on the phone. James Carville and George Stephanopoulos are waiting downstairs and

Michael Foot as deputy leader of the Labour Party in 1980, addressing an anti-nuclear rally in Hyde Park.

After the 1983 defeat: Neil Kinnock and Roy Hattersley, the new leadership of the party, in Brighton on the last day of the 1983 conference.

What a difference a year makes: the conference platform in 1985 (above)
and 1986 (below) – the first time the rose logo appeared at conference.

Roy Hattersley, Neil Kinnock, Denis Healey and Gerald Kaufman at the launch of the manifesto for the 1987 General Election campaign.

Patricia Hewitt (right), Neil Kinnock's press secretary from 1983 to 1989, with Harriet Harman.

Peter Mandelson, Julie Hall and Philip Gould at the 1990 party conference in Blackpool.

The 'skeletons in the cupboard' poster used during the 1992 General Election campaign.

A still from the infamous 'Jennifer's Ear' party election broadcast.

Neil Kinnock concedes defeat in the 1992 election.
The Tories, this time under John Major, had won their fourth victory in a row.

John Smith, elected leader of the party after Neil Kinnock's
resignation following the 1992 defeat.

Tony Blair and Gordon Brown at John Smith's funeral in May 1994.

The New Labour Party: Blair's first conference speech as leader, October 199

where are you? James is getting angry. I am in a blind panic, and am totally disorientated. I am naked; jet-lagged; half-asleep. All this way and I am blowing it. I rush downstairs and they have gone. Except for Bennett who takes me to a restaurant where they all wait. Half-asleep I give a rambling account of the UK campaign. Then Carville asks a *Washington Post* journalist what he is writing tomorrow, and the poor man says it is a story about Clinton being a KGB spy. Carville gets extremely angry. He shouts abuse at the reporter and gets up and leaves. George follows. The journalist sits there, ashen-faced. I have a drink at the bar and go to bed.

The next day I get up at 6 A.M. and go to the 7 A.M. meeting. This meeting happens every day, but is a little later on Sundays. I enter a large cluttered room where all the key operators and players are working. This is known as the 'war room'. At the centre of the room is a huge desk in front of a vast sofa. This is where Carville sits. It is the epicentre of the campaign. The room fills with young, bright, attractive campaign workers – Kennedy volunteers thirty years on. Eventually almost the entire campaign is jammed into that one room. No one is excluded, everyone is invited. At the stroke of 7 A.M. Carville walks in. Huge denim jacket with 'Clinton '92' written on the back. Denim jeans, white T-shirt. Hard eyes. Rugged face.[7]

In a campaign, Carville is a towering, raging man, breaking the back of his opponents by force of will: accepting no setback, no mistake, no retreat. In his book he quotes a Vietnamese battle cry: 'Follow me if I advance, kill me if I retreat, avenge me if I die.'[8] That sums up his view of how to conduct an election campaign.

I continue in my diary: 'George Stephanopoulos follows. Small. Smart. Bright-faced. Attractive. Cool. Confident. Their entry produces hush and awe.' George in an election campaign is deeply pessimistic. He predicts the worst, believing in some semi-religious way that this will somehow stop the worst happening. He charms while Carville cajoles. Despite, or perhaps because of, their dissimilarity, they function brilliantly as a team.

The meeting starts. What's Bush doing today? An aide reports, and so it goes on. I am billeted to the debate prep room to be near Bennett Freeman, but I have no desk. I spend the day preparing a dossier on the Tory campaign. We take it to George Stephanopoulos. He sits cool behind his desk, constantly on the phone. He uses a miniature headset phone that means he talks to you and his caller at the same time.

At the 6.45 P.M. meeting there is far more detailed coverage of the campaign. Suddenly and without warning Rick Steidman, the Press Director, announces that Philip Gould is going to make a short speech identifying the differences between the UK and the US situation. I do this pretty well and they applaud. I feel I am on the way back.[9]

The press release I had worked on was covered the next day by the *Washington Post*: 'Bush, according to Clinton aides, is borrowing almost all his campaign strategy from British Prime Minister John Major. In interviews and in internal analyses of the similarity between the two campaigns, Clinton aides noticed the close resemblance between Bush's television ads charging that Clinton would raise taxes and ads run by the Conservatives against Labour earlier this year. More pernicious, the Clinton camp say, is the Bush campaign's effort to put a dark spin on a trip Clinton took to the Soviet Union . . . They argue this was a smear modelled after a similar attack on Neil Kinnock.'[10]

The British connection became a cottage industry in the campaign. Bennett Freeman is a former Rhodes scholar and committed Anglophile. He wrote a series of brilliant memos exploring the Bush–Major connection and analysing Labour's campaign failures. And it was certainly true that Bush was drawing extensively on the Major campaign. There was much talk of meetings between Conservative officials, including Sir John Lacey, in Washington. Shaun Woodward, the Tories' Communications Director in the 1992 campaign, later told me that senior Bush officials visited him in London 'and left his office bare', they took away so much material.

Bennett Freeman and I called ourselves the 'British operation'. One week after my arrival I wrote a long memo developing the similarities between the two campaigns and the dangers for Clinton. I said, 'It is the last week that counts; forget the plaudits, concentrate on the smears; fear builds slowly, and only shows in the vote; tax and trust are the only issues that matter.'[11] This note was the genesis of the defensive strategy used by the Blair campaign five years later.

But a week into the campaign my confidence was fading. 'I do not know how long I can stay, or how long I should stay,' I wrote in my diary.

> I have no desk, I sit in the cafeteria. But I am not giving up. Bob Boorstin takes pity on me: 'Get a desk. You are now part of the campaign.' I grab a desk in the debate room and try to feel at home.
>
> The whole campaign is preparing for the debate. Bennett is entrusted with the job of personally travelling to the debate headquarters with a copy of the *Penthouse* interview with Gennifer Flowers, which also includes many revealing photographs. After much deliberation he decides to carefully cut out the photos for reasons of delicacy. He flies to St Louis and delivers by hand this copy of *Penthouse* cut to ribbons. The Governor just grunts.[12]

The atmosphere changed on the day of the first television debate between Bush and Clinton:

> Enormous tension about the debate. The war room is cornered off. A large TV screen is moved to the rest room (the campaign headquarters café) and as the debate gets closer people get tenser. Preparation for the debate has been incredible. Twelve vast books contain every rebuttal fact about Clinton, every attacking fact about Bush. This is all also on the computer, but the computer is too slow. The books are faster. Every time any claim has to be rebutted the relevant page of one of the books is torn out, and given to Bob Boorstin, who types in the rebuttal note. This is all done incredibly fast, and at incredible pressure. The rebuttal note and a line to take on the debate is finished and sent out to 200,000 media and other outlets before the debate has even finished. It is clear that Clinton

has won the debate and relief flows though the campaign. George comes on to the speakerphone the next morning: 'You were great last night.'[13]

When the debate season finished, Carville and Stephanopoulos returned to the campaign. 'James carries in a bright orange basketball. George warns about complacency. Some words are barred: "mandate"; "transition"; "White House". James supports him: "They will not go gently into the good night."'[14] One week before polling day I have to leave, to meet my family in New York. 'James greets me warmly as I go: "We are going to win this one for you guys." Bob Boorstin takes me to the airport. I am very moved. In New York I see the polls are close and get nervous. CNN has the gap at only 2 per cent. I am fearful that there will be some terrible repeat of the British election.'[15]

Five days before polling day I wrote a last-week warning memo to Stan Greenberg and Bob Boorstin from my New York hotel. It said the Clinton campaign should 'reawaken anger about Bush's record and maximise fear about a Bush second term. Only fear of Bush will overcome anxiety about Clinton. You have to shift the question in the next few days back to Bush's record. This has to be done with all the aggression and toughness that is necessary. You will lose more by not being tough enough with Bush than you would gain by being above the fray. Clinton must fight back on character. Voters expect it. Advertising must be tougher and more aggressive.'[16] I got no response and assumed the memo had been buried somewhere.

On Saturday 31 October I returned to Little Rock. Bob Boorstin sought me out and congratulated me on my memo. 'It has determined last-week thinking,' he said. Michael Waldman, who was working in the press office before moving to the White House, said that Stephanopoulos told him the memo had 'provided the basis for the last-week strategy'. I simply could not believe he had said this. I stood there open-mouthed.

On Sunday I went to see George. He said the campaign team

had been in a full-blooded argument with Clinton, who was on a plane. The campaign wanted to attack Bush, the Governor wanted to stay above the fray. 'As this argument was going on my memo arrived and they read it over the phone to him, and it won him over.'[17] I doubt my memo actually made much difference, and I am sure its influence on strategy was exaggerated, but I didn't care. I may have failed to win a majority for Labour in Britain, but I had made some slight difference in the greatest electoral contest there is. This was a turning-point for me in every way. It restored my faith and gave me the will to go on.

Later I talked more to George. He was very nervous and asked me if this was what it felt like on the last Sunday of the Labour campaign. I said it was a different world.

On the eve of polling there was one last war-room meeting. The room was so crushed people were standing on desks, clutching on to each other to avoid falling off. George spoke briefly, emotionally, and introduced James, who made a remarkable speech:

> I think we are going to win tomorrow, and I think that the Governor is going to fulfil his promise and change America, and I think many of you are going to go on and help him. I'm a political professional; that's what I do for a living. I'm proud of it. We changed the way campaigns are run. Used to be there was a hierarchy. If you were on one floor, you didn't go to another floor . . . Everyone was compartmentalised. And you people showed that you could be trusted. Everybody in this room. Everybody. I was thirty-three years old before I ever went to Washington or New York. Forty-two before I won my first campaign. And I'm happy for you all. You have been part of something special in my life, and I'll never forget what you all have done. Thank you.

He broke down in tears, unable properly to finish his speech. As he sat down the whole room shouted: 'One more day. One more day.'[18] The room was hot with bodies and emotion.

On election day the exit polls came early and it was clear by eleven o'clock that Clinton was going to win a massive victory.

That night I stood for hours in front of the Old State House waiting for Clinton's acceptance speech. It was freezing cold. I was waiting with Martha Kearney of the BBC, who was doing a programme about the election. She asked: 'When is this going to happen for Labour? When will a Labour leader be making an acceptance speech?' I answered: 'When Labour has got rid of high taxes and trade-union dominance. When we have changed as the Democrats have changed.' She smiled politely at me, as though I had gone temporarily insane. Eventually Clinton came out and made his speech, accepting the presidency on behalf of the people. I felt proud but determined that one day I would hear a Labour leader make a speech accepting victory and determined that I would be part of it.

The next night I attended the campaign dinner in the back room of Doe's Eat Place, the now legendary steak restaurant in Little Rock. Bob Boorstin rose and made a toast: 'To Philip Gould and the British Labour Party for all their help.' Those Little Rock days were relatively brief, perhaps five weeks in total, but they changed me, and I like to think they changed – in part, through me – the subsequent course of progressive politics. Nothing would ever be the same again. Progressive parties would stop being victims and start to be aggressive; they would regain contact with the values and hopes of middle-class and working-class people; they would develop campaigning techniques that meant the left started to win elections far more often than they would lose; above all, they would regain the confidence and self-belief which had drained away in two decades of defeat. That night – 3 November 1992 – was the moment the era of conservative electoral dominance ended. As John Major watched these scenes in Downing Street he was seeing his own future.

There would be other times when I would have the opportunity to help Bill Clinton. The most decisive came in November 1994, when the modernising project in the United States was set back by awful defeats in the mid-term elections. At the end of October, a week before election day, I took my family to meet the President at the White House, and each of my young daughters said, as they had practised, 'Good afternoon, Mr President.' He had just flown in from the Gulf and wanted only to know about the state of the election. His eyes looked distant and watery: he expected the worst. Later we saw Vice-President Al Gore, on crutches because of a torn ligament. He chatted to my daughter Grace and laughed that her second name was Atlanta, making a perfect pairing with my other daughter's name, Georgia. I discussed the elections with George Stephanopoulos in his office next to the Oval Office. George was always relaxed. He would sit there with his feet on the desk as if he had all the time in the world. His room was always untidy, and he had Greek icons on the wall. He is religious. We discussed the defeat and thought about examples of politicians who had turned defeat into victory. François Mitterrand came to mind, and George asked me to write a memo on this and to send him some books. I did both, and wrote a note called 'Winning from Cohabitation'.

In it, I suggested Mitterrand's cohabitation strategy should be the model for Clinton. 'Mitterrand carefully positioned himself as the arbiter President, above the political fray . . . He was careful to intervene only when he had the support of a majority of the electorate. He did this by effectively vetoing unpopular legislation. He always used the national interest as the basis of his intervention.'[19] Thus was born the cohabitation strategy, which many believed helped save Clinton's presidency.

Middle-class dreams

Bill Clinton's election in 1992 showed the world that the left could win, and it showed the left *how* it could win. It was the moment the tide of history and events tilted from right to left. It was a victory founded on the ideas and characters of the three principals.

George Stephanopoulos was in charge of rapid response for the 1988 Dukakis campaign, but realised that in the face of the remorseless negativity of the Republicans a response unit was pathetically inadequate and the whole campaign had to become one large rapid-response unit. George handled the press cleverly during the campaign. His charm and personality meshed the campaign together, fusing its members into a team. He is a rare example of someone in politics who has real integrity, and because of that he inspires enormous loyalty.

James Carville was the Democrat who drew a line in the sand and stopped the Republicans advancing one step beyond it. Until 1991 the Republican advance had appeared unstoppable. Walter Mondale was blitzed; Michael Dukakis was humiliated; Democrats appeared too liberal to get elected, too soft to fight. First with Senator Harris Wofford's campaign in 1991, and then with Governor Bill Clinton, Carville turned the Democratic Party from victim to aggressor. Almost through the sheer brute strength of his personality he stopped the Republican advance. He revolutionised campaigning methods. He developed the concept of the war room (all the key campaign players in one shared physical space); he created flat, faster, more flexible campaign management structures to replace the previous orthodoxy of campaign hierarchy; he involved all members of the campaign in planning meetings; he genuinely changed the way people campaigned.

But it was Stanley Greenberg who – with others – broke the new strategic ground. He was able fully to articulate what I had always instinctively felt and had begun only falteringly to describe: that the left could only win through modernised parties, reclaiming values believed by many to be owned by the right, and most important of all rooted in the hopes and aspirations of ordinary working people.

Greenberg began his career as an academic at Yale, and then set up his own polling company. From the start he sought to refashion a new progressive consensus rooted in the middle class. Like Stephanopoulos, Greenberg knew what Dukakis had to do, but was unable to get him to do it. In a memo to Governor Dukakis in September 1988, Greenberg wrote: 'The swing segments of the electorate, particularly the Reagan Democrats, are looking for Michael Dukakis to speak to them in terms that demonstrate a real identity with the middle class.'[20] Greenberg did not give up after Dukakis ignored his advice and crashed to defeat. He wrote repeatedly about a new politics of the middle class. The article I read most often – so frequently, in fact, it became a kind of defining text for me – was called: 'Reconstructing the Democratic Vision', written for *The American Prospect* in 1990. It was Greenberg's attempt to draw up a strategic manifesto for the 1992 presidential elections. It started with a harsh attack on Dukakis. He 'did not articulate any set of principles, offered no special perspective, and invoked no deeply resonant historical experience. The public was left by default with a savage caricature created by Lee Atwater, Republican campaign strategist: a Democratic Party short on patriotism, weak on defence, soft on criminals and minorities, indifferent to work, values and the family, and, inexplicably, infatuated with taxes.' Greenberg was describing Michael Dukakis and the Democratic Party, but he may as well have been describing Neil Kinnock and the Labour Party in 1992.

This was the right analysis, as insightful in relation to the UK as the US. The beneficiaries of progressive politics in America 'no longer appeared to be the broad working population, but rather the poor', and the poor alone. The answer to this, he went on, is 'the middle-class project'. This meant: 'The Democrats need to reassert their claim to represent the majority of working Americans. The working middle-class needs to figure at least as centrally in the party's identity as the traditional blue-collar imagery of the New Deal coalition, because in our time the working middle-class constitutes the broad majority. To reach the middle class today Democrats need to accommodate "middle-class consciousness", containing three primary and interconnected principles: work, reward for work, and restraint.' This brought together the values of opportunity and ambition with the values of responsibility.

But Greenberg's central insight was that reaching out to the middle class does not exclude the poor; in fact, it does the opposite: 'Most poor people also work, or want to work, and identify strongly with middle-class aspirations of security and upward mobility.'[21] By reaching out to the middle class it is possible to build a coalition that includes the poor and is able to help the poor by winning government. More than anyone else, Stanley Greenberg gave life to the idea of a middle-class politics, and the possibility of a new progressive coalition which had the middle class at its heart. In his book, *Middle-Class Dreams*, Greenberg developed his analysis: 'Democrats cannot aspire to dominate this period and lead the country unless they re-invent their links with and regain the confidence of downscale voters – working and middle-class voters – who want nothing more complicated than a better life. Democrats will never renew the bottom-up idea unless they begin with middle-class America as the centre of their discourse.'[22] Greenberg was not saying that the middle class are the end-point of progressive politics, but that they are its starting-point. If the left wants to build a coalition which can be sustained in power, and which can implement over time a progressive agenda that will really help the poor, it must begin with the middle class. That is true in the United States, and it is equally true in the United Kingdom.

It was Bill Clinton who gave public voice to the new politics of the middle class. In July 1992 he made a speech encapsulating all that I had always believed: 'In the name of all those who do the work and pay taxes, raise the kids and play by the rules – in the name of the hard-working Americans who make up our forgotten middle class, I proudly accept your nomination for the presidency of the United States. I am a product of that middle class, and when I am President you will be forgotten no more.'[23]

British politics are not American politics. The American middle class is not the British middle class. But when Clinton spoke in this way, he spoke also for me, and for the people I had come from.

The land that Labour had forgotten, the forgotten middle class. Both casualties of progressive politics gone wrong.

Back to stagnation

As soon as I returned to London from the 1992 Democratic victory I wrote a long document summarising the Clinton campaign, and Labour's strategic position, and sent it to the party leadership. Party staff say that it went down 'like a lead balloon'. It argued that Labour was perceived to be looking 'downwards not upwards', and 'backwards not forwards'; it was for 'minorities and not the mainstream' and it was 'not trusted to run the economy properly'. Organisationally, Labour was slow to adapt and had divergent structures of accountability. In terms of campaigning it lacked 'executive capacity; message; a persuasive economic argument; an effective rapid response and attack capacity; flexibility; integration; resources'. Finally, there was a lack of 'mutual support, openness and honesty'. The document argued for 'an agreed, unified decision-making structure; a rapid-response capacity; the development of a war room where all key campaign functions are included; the establishment of task forces and task leaders; the use of outside expertise; a new culture that is honest; supportive; trusting'. It called for comprehensive change in the campaigning capacity of the party – 'sticking-plaster solutions are not adequate'. Politically I argued that 'Labour needs a proper connection with the aspirations of ordinary working people'. It needed to be 'associated with improving the life of ordinary voters, not penalising them'. The document called this a 'new populism'. Labour needed a new relevance, shifting from being a party associated with the past to being a party associated with the future. Above all Labour needed a fresh start: 'A changed Labour Party is the basis of a new relationship of trust with the British electorate.' And this change must be open: 'Labour has not changed until it announces that it has changed.'[24] This was exactly what the Democrats had done when they called themselves the 'New Democrats'. This document was private, but in public too I was beginning to put my case. Patricia Hewitt and I worked together on an article for *Renewal* magazine in January, which argued that Labour 'should emulate Clinton's success in discarding the Democrats' image "as the party of the poor and of the past" by forging "a populism of the centre rather than the left"'.[25]

I went further, and organised a one-day Clinton conference at the Queen Elizabeth II Conference Centre in Westminster, with two unlikely co-sponsors, the TGWU and the *Guardian*. This conference included most of Clinton's major personnel, and caused a few waves within Labour. John Prescott objected to the Clintonisation of the party, and John Smith sent me private messages asking me not to be disruptive. But the conference went ahead. Stan Greenberg talked of the need to broaden class appeal and of opposition to the term 'middle class', as it was thought by many Democrats to be disparaging to the working class and the poor. Carville's partner Paul Begala spoke of Clinton being willing and eager to use the media. Elaine Kamarck, an adviser on the Clinton campaign, talked of a new Democratic Party relevant to the twenty-first century, which had moved beyond the left–right divide and excessive political correctness. The conference was ahead of the mood of the party leadership, but it was influential. Peter Mandelson was there and sucked it all in. *Tribune* attacked the conference and those who sought to learn from it, warning: 'The self-styled modernisers having nothing more substantial to offer than making Labour even more bland in pursuit of elusive affluent working-class and centrist middle-class voters . . . have failed to see that the main reason for "lack of trust" in Labour is that people can see through politicians who appear to be all packaging and no substance.'[26]

I was not a lone voice for Clinton within Labour. Margaret McDonagh, John Braggins and Alan Barnard, who were to hold senior positions in the 1997 election campaign, were all working in one capacity or another for Clinton. Jonathan Powell, then working for the British Embassy in Washington, now Tony Blair's chief of staff, was observing the Clinton campaign at first hand and building links that were later to prove priceless. Out of all this was born Millbank Tower and the 'war room' it housed; rapid rebuttal and the Excalibur computer; an obsession with message; and a tough, unremitting focus on hard-working people and their concerns.

Clive Hollick had also visited the Clinton campaign, and upon his return wrote a memo called 'Campaign '96', in which he argued for a 'new Labour Party, new policies on tax and trade union links'.[27] He presented these findings at a meeting with John Smith, Murray Elder and David Ward – respectively Smith's chief of staff and policy adviser. Smith's reply was telling: 'This is all very interesting, but I think you will find that it will be our turn next time.'[28]

At the time the message of Little Rock was not heard, but it could not be silenced. The Clinton experience was seminal for the Labour Party. Within five years almost everything that was written in my document had been implemented. Modernisation of Labour did not depend on Clinton, it would have happened anyway, but his election did give modernisation a road map. Above all it offered hope.

But for the moment, Labour was stuck. In May 1993, just a few months after the Clinton conference, I wrote to Murray Elder to reiterate that 'qualitative research shows no real improvement in Labour's position. In fact it is possibly weakening through an increasing sense that Labour is losing its relevance to ordinary people.' Worse, 'Labour's core level of support is eroding through demographic and ideological changes. Most estimates put it at between 30 and 35 per cent and reducing on an annual basis. To win, Labour has to gain new support from new groups. Labour has to move forward just to stand still.'[29]

In June I wrote an even tougher memo: Labour was most associated with trade unions; least associated with successful businesses, a clear vision of the future, and getting ahead. It had not gained sufficiently from the demise of the Conservatives. Its share of the vote was too low: 'Labour is not trusted; it is not relevant.' John Smith had yet to break through. He was 'legal; decent; honest and truthful', but was an 'invisible man', not 'dynamic or charismatic'. He was 'less well-received now than as shadow Chancellor or as newly elected leader'. The explanations I gave included: 'Distrust of the Labour Party influences perceptions of the leader. Labour is believed to be difficult and unmanageable. This undermines all Labour leaders.'[30] Clearly, changing the leader was no substitute for changing the party. 'John was essentially a fudge leader,' said Charles Clarke. 'Tony Blair was the linear descendant of Neil Kinnock as a modernising Labour leader. John Smith was not.'[31]

I don't believe John Smith took any notice of the notes I wrote him, but although he did not move, others did. Gordon Brown and Tony Blair were changing the party. Brown, now shadow Chancellor, was ditching Labour's tax and spend policies, refusing to allow us to get boxed into any spending commitments or tax-raising proposals, later promising that 'a Labour government would not "tax for its own sake".'[32] Blair, shadow Home Secretary, was modernising Labour's approach to law and order, producing a new emphasis on the balance between prevention and deterrent: 'Tough on crime, tough on the causes of crime.'[33] He also began the process of reconnecting Labour to its heartland values. In February 1993 he said, 'If we do not learn and then teach the value of what is right and what is wrong, then the result is simply moral chaos which engulfs us all . . .'[34] Later that year he told the Police Federation annual conference, 'If we dare not speak the language of punishment then we deny the real world.'[35]

I worked far more with Brown than Blair at this time, conducting focus groups and writing strategy notes for him, because I believed that modernising our tax and economic policies was the crucial task. In September I wrote a strategy note flowing from two group discussions. I was not optimistic: 'Those respondents with direct experience of economic uplift had already drifted back to the Conservatives.' Respondents preferred an improved performance by the Tories to the upheaval of a new government – 'Better the devil you know' still ruled their votes. 'Labour was the party of minorities; not those on welfare; not for ordinary working people.'[36]

In this note I recommended what Dan Clifton, the broadcasting officer at Millbank during the 1997 election, calls the worst campaigning line ever written: 'Stop the rot, and start to build.' But I also argued for a focus on tax and a continuing theme, using the line: 'You can't trust the Tories on tax.'[37] I wanted revenge.

It was clear that, despite reasonable polling leads, Labour was not on course to win next time around. Tony Blair and Gordon Brown knew that and chafed at their constraints. They believed only modernisation would save Labour. Blair repeatedly pushed John Smith on the issue of one member, one vote and the trade union link, and John always pushed him back. Patricia Hewitt remembers Tony Blair saying, 'We have to make changes *now* and be vocal about it despite our leader, because otherwise there will be nothing to inherit.'[38] Gordon Brown also tried to push Smith hard on OMOV and was 'vehement' in his opposition to the compromise which Smith finally brokered.[39]

Labour had a new advertising agency, Butterfield Day Devito Hockney, which did a good job, but campaigning and polling had regressed. I was invited to attend a vast polling meeting stuffed with academic experts, who said that we had no gender problem and we could safely put taxes up. I couldn't stand it and left. Merely an observer, I couldn't bear to watch.

Fighting the fear factor

As there was still no place for me with Labour, I took my memos to Europe, where Julian Priestley asked me to co-ordinate the European election campaign for the member parties of the Socialist Group in the European Parliament. This was a great strain on my family. I was working in Brussels from Monday until Friday and living in a hotel. My children were young, but I was determined – it seemed the next logical step.

The first part of the project involved a review of the political situation of all the socialist and social democratic parties in the European Union, based on interviews in all member nations. This was a massive task and the findings were predictable: progressive parties were losing ground because the demographic tide was against them; if they did not change they would face further continual decline. The conclusions could not have been more gloomy and I presented them to a massive audience of MEPs at a conference in Aix-en-Provence.

It was also clear that the EU was out of touch with public opinion almost everywhere, and the campaign theme had to reflect that. I devised the notion of a 'People's Europe', which was used by all members of the Socialist Group except the British Labour Party, who thought it too populist. I developed a new corporate identity for the Party of European Socialists; set up a Europe-wide rapid-response unit; arranged for focus groups to be conducted in all European countries; and had a television commercial made by Jacques Seguéla, media adviser to President Mitterrand, which was applicable in all nations.

This was a lot of work, but it gave me an insight into European politics. I was not impressed. There was little evidence of fresh thinking, new ideas or a drive to modernise. European progressive politics had gone stale. People accuse me of looking to the United States rather than to Europe, and it is true, I did. But this was not because I wasn't interested in what progressive parties in Europe had to offer. I did look, but I found little there. All the new thinking was being done in the United States. I became increasingly certain that uncompromising modernisation was the only answer for the left. In this Julian Priestley was a wonderful ally. He has impeccable modernising credentials.

I got the chance to put my new campaigning ideas into practice in elections across Europe. In Sweden, Norway, Greece and Holland, progressive parties won elections using Clinton's ideas.

My central premise was that the right's main technique was the use of fear, and progressive parties had to learn how to fight it. I wrote all this down in a document called 'Fighting the Fear Factor', which was my campaigning bible. It argued that modern electorates are insecure, uncertain and anxious. They 'are more afraid of things getting worse than they are hopeful of things getting better'. This mood of anxiety about the future allowed the right to use the tactics of fear, enabling them to dominate politics for the 1980s and early 1990s. To defend against attacks rooted in fear, progressive parties had to respond instantly when challenged; establish war rooms to co-ordinate the campaigns; fight hard and with conviction and concede no ground; win on tax and the economy; avoid being caricatured as the incumbent. Above all, they had to 'change and admit they had changed'; only modernised parties would be safe from attack.[40]

But although Europe was welcoming me – and winning – I was still trying hard to bring these ideas back home. I wrote a very long memo on 9 May 1994 called 'The Labour Party: Preliminary Campaign Observations'. It stated that, tactically, Labour must develop a completely new campaigning capability: it must gain confidence, conviction, attacking capacity, rebuttal, flexibility, speed, integration. Strategically, I said Labour must become modern and relevant; win the economic battle; reconnect with its voting base. 'Labour must become once again the political instrument through which ordinary working people achieve their ambitions and reflect their opinions. This means developing policies that will persuade ordinary working people that they will be financially better off under Labour; connecting with the populist instinct of voters through policies that are tough on crime; opposing welfare fraud; supporting individual responsibility.' I said Labour's message should be based on a series of choices: social cohesion versus social disintegration; democracy versus centralisation; the people versus privilege; New Labour versus old Conservatism.[41]

I took it to Tony Blair the day before John Smith died. He was impatient. He held the document in front of him. 'This is all very well,' he said, 'but as far as I can see Labour will only win when it is completely changed from top to bottom. That is the beginning and the end of it.'

Tragedy

On 12 May 1994, Peter called to tell me there was something wrong with John Smith. We didn't think it was serious. A few minutes later I heard on the TV that he had died. I phoned Peter. He was devastated, as was I.

John's death had a profound effect on the British electorate. Not really connecting with him when he was leader, they missed him greatly when he had gone, and they recognised him as a politician who commanded enormous, widespread respect. In death the public revered him and through his death they started to feel differently about the Labour Party. They saw once again its deeper, finer qualities, so long submerged by failure and strife. John Smith healed a party that had become ill at ease with itself. He widened democracy in the party. But most of all, through the extraordinary national response to his death, he gave back to Labour the confidence and pride it had lost for so long.

Peter and I did not speak for some time after we had heard of his death. It was a shattering moment, but in the unspeakable cruelty of politics it was clear that private grief would soon mix with the public reality of a world moving on, and that the battle for the succession would soon begin.

6

Electric Shock Treatment

Blair emerges

Alastair Campbell saw leadership potential in Tony Blair at their very first meeting in the Members' Lobby at the House of Commons in 1983, soon after Blair's election as an MP. 'He was bright, personable, clever, witty, with a sense of what he wanted to do. A very strong sense. If you had said to me then: is this the kind of guy whom you would consider could one day be leader of the Labour Party, I'd have said yes. When did I actively start to think that he would be leader? I suppose it was a slow process really, but it was somewhere in the back of my mind while Neil was still leader.'[1]

Campbell and Blair used each other's skills:

I was a journalist and he was one of the politicians I would go to for insights into politics. Where I found Tony useful, as a journalist, was actually he was very good at analysing the weaknesses of his opponents, the Tories. He was very good at setting a political context for things. I would construct whole columns and magazine features around the things he would articulate. So that is what he's always been good at. He had the ability to make sense of complicated situations, articulate them simply and do it in a way that made people feel reassured by him. For someone who was then quite young he was really quite a reassuring figure, and I think I saw him as the kind of rounded, full personality who has an innate understanding of what makes people tick. He's kind of plugged in to them.

He remembers Tony Blair and Gordon Brown working as a team: 'I was always struck by Tony and Gordon and their ability to have ideas that would then be seen through the media. They did it pretty well together.'[2]

I first met Blair and Brown during the 1987 election, but I recall them only as fleeting shadows. The faces who dominated that election were Kinnock, Hattersley, Healey and Bryan Gould. Blair and Brown were hardly on the radar.

Yet soon after the election they moved from peripheral to central positions. They immediately knocked Bryan Gould into the margins. Bryan feels very bitter about this, and blames Peter Mandelson, but this is wrong. Bryan lost his way after the 1987 election. He was the public face of that election, and as such was brilliant. I remember one occasion when we had organised a press conference to show Hugh Hudson's final broadcast for the campaign – the press had arrived, but the broadcast had not. It got later and later, but Bryan kept completely cool. About twenty minutes after the broadcast was due to be presented he turned to me and said, 'Well, Philip, what is this broadcast about?' I told him, and without any sense of panic he walked towards the press, prepared to re-enact the broadcast to them in full as if this were a giant game of charades. Fortunately the broadcast arrived at the very last minute, but he would have done it. That kind of pressure takes its toll. The 1987 election campaign knocked the stuffing out of Bryan and he never fully recovered.

Blair and Brown had ability; they were a breath of fresh air; they were attractive on television. In 1988 Blair appeared in two consecutive broadcasts and in 1990 he and Brown, interviewed by Fiona Millar, who is now Cherie Booth's press adviser, appeared in a ten-minute film directed by Hugh Hudson. Fiona

Millar describes the interview: 'We started out at Tony's house in London with the kids running in and out. There was a huge dilemma about whether we'd use the kids in the film, and he was just warm and nice.'[3]

At this time we occasionally used 'people metering', a research technique in which groups of people use dials to respond instantly to politicians speaking on television. A line appears on the screen indicating immediately how warmly or coolly the group is responding to what is being said and to the person saying it. We tested almost all the shadow front bench and the person who scored highest was Tony Blair. Even when he was faltering or not at his best, the line would shoot up when he started to speak. I remember thinking that the public response was disproportionate: Blair was good, but not that good. He seemed to be able to connect with the public in a way that transcended rational explanation. It was a response qualitatively different from that to any other politician.

This quality, which is hard to pin down, was central to Blair's emergence as eventual leader of the Labour Party and to some of the frustrations resulting from the contest for the leadership. Its very elusiveness meant that several people close to him missed it completely; they did not understand how this young, unseasoned politician, who was utterly unlike any previous Labour politician, could have such an extraordinary impact. Consequently, while some were convinced from as early as 1989 – much earlier than conventional wisdom would have it – that Blair was emerging as the natural choice as next leader of the Labour Party, others missed it completely.

Also central to Blair's political personality is a feeling that he can leave politics; his existence does not depend upon it. Over the years he has said repeatedly that he does not need to be a politician, that if it doesn't work out, he can leave and turn to another career. His family and his faith give him a breadth of experience and vision which takes him outside politics. This makes him an unusual politician.

The first time that I really thought Tony Blair might become leader was during his speech to the 1990 Labour conference, as shadow Employment Secretary. His autocue stopped working, which he was furious about afterwards, revealing his ambition and his impatience. But the early part of the speech, before he lost his place, proved he had a natural command of an audience and showed oratorical strength. Already Brown and Blair were eager to get on. I went to Brown's room during the 1990 conference and they were both there, the carpet littered with speech drafts, the atmosphere charged, both almost frenzied in their desire to get things moving: 'Why aren't we doing more, faster?'

As the times began to favour Blair, Brown was entering choppier waters. He had been the next natural leader of the party for so long that a backlash was inevitable, and it came. Several of the politicians I worked closely with in the pre-1992 election period began to grumble about Brown behind his back. Resentment and jealousy grew. Blair, on the other hand, was being spoken about in a different light: his colleagues were describing him as a future leader. In 1991 I would sometimes talk to Jack Cunningham about the next leader and he was certain: it would be Smith, then Blair. And at a party to launch Robert Harris's book, *Fatherland*, in 1992, when Mandelson, Blair and Brown entered as a group, Roy Hattersley looked at Blair, nodded at him and said, 'That is the man who will save the Labour Party.'

Just after the 1992 election, as part of my ritual post-election-defeat humiliation, I had to speak to the 1,000 Club of big donors to Labour at Millbank. I mumbled my analysis of why we had lost, nervous and faltering, hating every minute. Philip Hughes, the painter (and now my neighbour), gave me a particularly hard time. But Blair, confident and inspired, electrified the meeting. We lost because we did not change enough, he said; we would only win again when Labour had changed completely. His speech convinced both my wife Gail and I that he would be leader one day. Gail had gone to the meeting depressed and despondent but left thinking anything was possible – Blair had totally changed her view of the future. And it was this mantra, of modernisation and renewal, which Blair would bravely take from studio to studio after the 1992 defeat. When I showed him the post-election polling in his Parliament Street office, which proved Labour had lost because the process of modernisation had been too slow, he became manic: you must get it out, he said, people must know. So, for the one and only time in my political career, I leaked research to a national paper; the *Sunday Times*.

After the US election in 1992, Blair was disappointed in me because I did not use my Clinton campaign experience to push the case for modernisation harder. I had written an article for the *Guardian*,[4] which he thought pulled its punches, failing to make explicit the importance of modernisation to Clinton's victory. However, I was still feeling responsible for the 1992 defeat and thought I owed John Smith loyalty.

Despite Blair's emergence as a leadership candidate by 1992, at that time Gordon Brown was still ahead of him. Brown was the senior figure, and his period deputising for John Smith during Smith's first heart attack in September 1988 had marked him out as a true star. Had one of the modernising candidates stood in 1992, it would have been Brown and not Blair. Blair had wanted this to happen. A close aide of Blair's at the time says, 'Tony's view was that Gordon could have beaten Smith and that they should have run against Smith: Gordon as leader, himself as deputy. Tony's view was that Gordon would have won. He would have run as an out-and-out moderniser, and said that Smith was a conservative. Tony's view was that the party wanted to be led, it didn't just want to be sleep-walking, and if you sold it an out-and-out modernising message it would take it.'[5] Yet Brown did not stand against Smith, out of loyalty to Smith, just as he would not stand two years later.

I saw more of Brown than Blair from 1992 to 1994 partly because of work, partly because of temperament. While Blair was clearly going to flourish as shadow Home Secretary, I thought all the pressure would fall on Brown, shadowing the Treasury. It was clear he would be under immense strain and that if he sank, all hope of modernising the party would sink with him. I went to see Blair and said that for the next two years what time I had would be concentrated on Brown. He agreed that this was right. He thought Brown's task was massive.

It was not only political imperatives which pushed me towards Brown. I found it easy to connect with him. Whenever I saw him, and see him now, my heart warms to him. He came to my home occasionally and Gail was fond of him. She would feed him books, which he would devour. He was always demanding: more ideas; more input; more focus groups. I often phoned him at home in Scotland to discuss strategy.

I felt slightly less at ease with Blair. He was a different kind of politician. I felt he had about him a sense of destiny, and this unnerved me a little. I did not see him a great deal socially, and when we did meet he had no time for small talk. He wanted only to know: how are we doing? Why are we moving so slowly? His preoccupation with Labour's unfitness to govern was continuous and intense. He was demanding, but in a different way from Gordon: he had a habit of asking the most difficult question, the one you didn't want to hear. And he expected an incisive answer.

Although I did not work closely with him during this period, I watched his progress. He was repositioning Labour as a party that would be tough on crime, which connected directly with my suburban populist instincts. This repositioning was classic Blair. One of his close aides at the time describes the process: 'What was fascinating about the way he approached it is that he said nothing, read a lot, thought about what the strategy should be, and then hit it.'[6] Blair's speech in Wellingborough after the murder of James Bulger in February 1993 was the point at which this strategy broke through. It attacked directly the liberal individualist consensus that had developed over crime, using the language of punishment, and right and wrong. Perhaps more than anything, this change in perspective towards crime reconnected Labour with its electoral base. Most people believe in punishment, they believe in right and wrong, they believe in discipline and order. That for so long Labour denied this, that they sought to excuse the inexcusable on grounds of education, class or other disadvantages, was unacceptable to large numbers of the electorate who suffered the consequences of crime on a daily basis. Now, what Blair said seems common sense; then, it seemed, in the annals of many on the left, iconoclastic. Although Blair was certain of what he felt, he was concerned about making a public speech on such a great personal tragedy as James Bulger's killing. He agonised long and hard about the speech and in the end released only a one-and-a-half-page press release after making it; it had enormous public impact.

However, it was his work on one member, one vote which really made the difference to his leadership credentials. Shifting decision-making within the party away from union block votes towards individual party members had long been an aim of the modernisers. Kinnock had attempted to bring in OMOV at his first party conference in 1984, but he had failed to build up a big enough coalition of support and the motion was defeated. He had been able to push through a compromise after the 1987 election, under which individual party members could vote on the selection of parliamentary candidates, but two-fifths of votes remained in the hands of local trade union branches. This 'unsatisfactory hybrid'[7] had remained in place until after the 1992 General Election. During the leadership election which followed Labour's defeat, both John Smith and Bryan Gould made clear their support for OMOV, and the pressure for change was intensified by Kinnock. One of his last actions as leader was to ask the NEC to set up a sub-committee to look at replacing party decision-making at conference by block votes with OMOV.

Blair joined the sub-committee (the union links review group), in October 1992, but was endlessly frustrated with the pace of change. He was continually pushing forward, much to the annoyance of John Smith, who was trying to pull him back. Smith wanted progress, but he also wanted unity; he feared nothing more than a divided party. Smith was constantly telling Blair to slow down. He would say, 'Tony, you are being too intellectual about this,' when Blair started to talk about OMOV. Sometimes Blair would let his real feelings show. His *On the Record* interview in January 1993 on party modernisation was about as bold as it was possible for a Labour politician to be at that time,[8] and went too far for Smith, who asked Blair to rein in his modernising instincts. One of Blair's aides remembers, 'Blair was fantastically politically frustrated. He was banging his head against the table after coming back from shadow Cabinet meetings. He basically said to Smith: "You've got to give us a lead, you've got to tell us which way you are going." Margaret Beckett was chairing the OMOV committee, but nobody in the committee had any idea what the Smith line was, or where he was trying to get to.'[9] The union links review group made its final report in July 1993. At last Smith had taken a stance on OMOV and forced the union representatives on the group to accept a compromise, giving more power to individual members but allowing the union block vote one-third of the votes in the election of party leader. This compromise was passed at conference in 1993, although there was union opposition up to the last moment and Smith was forced to threaten to resign if his OMOV plans were defeated. Even so, the vote was won only by a margin of 3.1 per cent.

Blair thought the settlement was too timid. 'He thought talk about ending the block vote would disappear once people realised that the unions still had all these votes, that they could continue to vote as a block. He thought there was an opportunity after 1992 to have a real symbolic break with Labour's past, and that opportunity wasn't being grasped. His feeling about the 1992 election was that we were always going to lose, because we hadn't shown how different we were. He felt that we were about to make the same mistake.'[10]

Although his position was more extreme than his colleagues would have liked, and it irritated them, he won their respect, especially John Prescott's. He was also a member of the union links review group and appreciated Blair's determination to resolve the inconsistencies in the party's internal democracy.

Blair's frustrations with the slow pace of change were shared by Brown. According to one of Blair's aides, 'The two of them [Brown and Blair] were at the end of their tether at the inability of most of the people in the party, and most of the leadership, to see that the party needed to change and that it wasn't just the fact that we had got close and therefore would win next time. Blair's view of Kinnock was that Kinnock had done great things to reform policies, had taken on the left, but had done nothing to change the culture of the party.'[11]

Although both Blair and Brown were frustrated, Brown's frustrations went deeper. Brown was making extraordinary changes shadowing the Treasury, abandoning the shadow Budget and the old policies of high taxation and high spending. He had allowed one opportunity to be leader to pass him by, and must have felt the tide of events moving slowly against him. Blair sensed this too, says one of his advisers: 'Tony's view of Gordon was that people go up and down, and that at that time Gordon was going down just as he was coming up. His view of Gordon was that he just had to stick to changing the economic policy, take the flak and not be downhearted. Gordon was becoming a bit depressed because of the internal party flak he was taking, and was not being seen as a great performer in public.' The two men worked closely together. Their offices were next door to one another: if Norman Lamont (then Chancellor) was making a statement, Blair would help Brown. If the Home Secretary (Kenneth Clarke) was making a statement, Brown would help Blair. 'Blair was incredibly supportive about how to rebuild Gordon, but Gordon was getting himself into a very black mood.'[12]

Brown's frustration was understandable. He had been fighting to modernise the party for almost a decade. He was changing the crucial policy areas of taxation and the economy, despite fierce and consistent opposition, and yet he wasn't getting the political credit he felt he deserved. A political trajectory that had been upwards until 1992 had now stalled, while Blair's, which had been behind Brown's until 1992, was edging past him. And this was happening within a political relationship that was and is as close as a political relationship can be. Blair certainly understood what was happening, and it was impossible for Brown, with his extraordinary political insight, not to know that events were slipping away from him.

This reveals a basic truth about politics. It is not always fair. At any time before 1992, including the 1992 leadership election, Brown would have been the natural modernising candidate. Around the middle of 1993 the mantle passed to Blair. Succeeding to political leadership requires a conjunction of two events: you must have the talent to meet the moment, but you must also have the moment that meets your talent. For perhaps four years Brown was ready, but the moment was not there. In 1992 it might have been, but loyalty stopped him attempting to grasp what was probably only half a chance. When the modernising moment finally came, when the music stopped, the moment was Blair's and not Brown's.

Both Tony Blair and Gordon Brown have outstanding qualities, but they are different. Gordon Brown is a dynamic political strategist, surveying the political terrain, spotting every movement, anticipating every consequence. He is almost impossible to defeat in argument. He lives in a world of ideas and has constructed a complete political philosophy, nurtured in Scotland and Scottish universities. His values are anchored in a passion to end social injustice and to create equal opportunity. He has restless, impatient energy, and is never satisfied. He moves from great warmth with flashes of charm to dour introspection and a strength of character that can sometimes appear brutal. He has a dogged, enduring courage. He achieves his ambitions the hard way.

Tony Blair is a brilliant strategist also, but of a different sort. He sets contemporary politics into a vast sweep of history that goes back to the Liberal–Labour split and forward into the next century. He wants to remake the big picture but carefully, combining long-term radicalism with short-term common sense. He cuts immediately to the quick, seeing instantly the essence of a situation, of an idea, of a person. He will follow his instincts whatever the consequences, leading sometimes to stubbornness and inflexibility. His values are rooted in community and Christianity: he is not afraid to talk about compassion. He has a sense of the destiny of the nation, and of the pulse of the people. In this he is like Margaret Thatcher. He can move quickly from a caution that frustrates to a daring that alarms. He has a confident, winning quality which makes life appear easy. Both these men could have been leader, but in July 1994 it was Tony Blair's time. The moment and his abilities matched. In as cruel an outcome as could befall Gordon, for a second time he saw his chance of leadership slip through his grasp.

The music stops

There was a moment on 12 May, perhaps two hours after we had heard that John Smith had died, when I began to feel a sense of foreboding about the battle ahead. There was obviously going to be a fight for the succession. It was a time of crisis for the modernisers. Everybody was deeply shocked by John Smith's death, yet it was inevitable that the future would quickly intrude on the past and our thoughts would move to who the next leader would be.

For Brown and Blair, of course, the situation was even worse. With grief over the loss of a father-figure came the realisation that only one of them could succeed him. Time was a luxury they did not have: non-modernising candidates were understandably considering their position, and within hours of Smith's death the media were discussing the potential candidates for the leadership.

Alastair Campbell was in a car leaving the BBC, where he had been reviewing the papers, when a message came to call his office. They told him that there was a rumour John Smith had died. He phoned Hilary Coffman in the Labour press office and could tell from the way she was talking that something was terribly wrong. He recalls:

> I then went straight to the Commons and made a few phone calls and spoke to Jack Cunningham, who told me John was dead. At that time I was on my way to ITN at Millbank to do something on TV and I was in the extraordinary position of knowing he was dead but not being able to say that because I was doing this thing on television. I then went off and spent most of the day just doing the rounds and doing obituaries about John and I think, like a lot of people, I was quite shocked by how upsetting I found it all. I don't even know if I spoke to Tony that day, I might have done, I can't remember. There was a general understanding that people would not talk about what would happen next. I did an interview on *Newsnight* and I think there was an understanding with Mark Mardell that he wouldn't ask me. Not an agreement, but just 'that's off-limits' kind of stuff. Right at the end of the interview he said: 'Who do you think is the next leader of the Labour Party?' and I said Tony Blair. I don't think there was a moment's doubt.[13]

Blair had doubts, however. On Friday Campbell travelled to north Wales for a funeral: Glenys Kinnock's mother had died. Campbell spent much of the long and difficult drive on the phone: 'I was getting all sorts of calls from people, friends of Tony's, saying you have got to speak to him because he is basically saying it's got to be Gordon. Now I don't know how much he was constantly testing the argument. I think parts of him did feel the fact that they had come up together, and it had generally been accepted that Gordon was, as it were, the senior of the two.'[14] But Blair soon came to the conclusion that he had to stand. When I spoke to him a few days later he was already clear that he had no choice, and I reinforced that view. I do not know how Gordon Brown saw those first few days. He has not discussed it with me. However, from conversations with his friends and colleagues, I am sure that he was confident he would become leader. Yet within a very short time Brown would see the massive momentum building up behind Blair and watch his own leadership ambitions evaporate.

Part of the problem for him was the suddenness: John Smith's death froze a moment in time. The music stopped and the political ether set solid. Intimations, moods, tendencies, trends which had been discernible but not yet irrevocable were suddenly set in concrete. Although it had been clear to some of us in the year or so before John Smith's death that Blair had replaced Brown as the natural choice for the next leader, it was not yet an accepted fact and was certainly not clear to everyone. But within hours of John Smith dying a new political reality emerged, and there was nothing anyone – not Tony Blair, not Gordon Brown, not Peter Mandelson, not Alastair Campbell – could do about it.

I never doubted that Blair was the right candidate, but I knew also the huge personal crisis this would pose for Gordon Brown. I phoned him on Sunday 15 May, three days after John's death. We talked for a while and then with great courage he asked me the question he must have dreaded: who should it be, who would have the best chance of winning? I said Tony, without hesitation. Gordon asked me why, and I replied that Tony not only met the mood of the nation, he exemplified it. He would create for Labour and for Britain a sense of change, of a new beginning, which Gordon could not do. When he asked me if he should stand down, I replied, only if he could live with the consequences of doing so. It was not a question of personal ambition, Gordon said, but of giving up the chance to implement his ideas – ideas he had spent a lifetime developing. He said this with sadness and resignation. It was clear to me that he would not, in the last resort, stand against Tony. That he did not, that he stood down and gave way, was the action of a brave man.

The truth at that time was simple: Blair had no option but to stand. On 18 May I wrote a memo to Mandelson: 'Post John Smith there is only one viable strategic opportunity for Labour, and that is to become a party of change, momentum and dynamism. This is most certainly the mood of the country, and probably of a majority of the party. At this time Tony exemplifies this mood more completely than any Labour leader since Wilson. Gordon has prodigious strengths, but will be seen as an interim leader, half-way between John Smith and Tony Blair. At this time all strategic decisions must be taken on the basis of this national and party mood.'[15]

I considered the possibility of Blair standing down, but said that if he did there would be enormous disappointment in the country and the party. There would be a backlash against Labour and a belief that Labour was only prepared to take half a step forward; then a backlash against Gordon as the candidate who stopped Tony. The backlash would harm Gordon immensely. 'It is possible for Tony to win both in the technical sense of winning the election, and also in the broader sense of creating Labour as a party of change. By this standard it is almost impossible for Gordon to win. Any win for Gordon in these circumstances would carry a huge cost. The relationship with Tony would be damaged. The modernisers' cause would be damaged. The public would be dismayed and Gordon's chances of winning a subsequent General Election would be greatly harmed.'[16]

Writing a memo like that is easy; giving up the ambition of a lifetime is very hard. I realise now that I – and others, I am sure – underestimated the difficulty of Gordon's decision. To me, Tony was the natural choice as the next leader. But for Gordon it was about ideas and the long haul, and the huge strength of support for Tony must have seemed unaccountable. Our certainty, our view of the world, was not his. He did not know until the very last moment that time and chance were not to favour him.

Anyone who doubts Gordon Brown's stoicism should have seen him late on the evening of 20 July 1994, the day before Blair was officially declared leader, but when it was certain that he would win. Tony's acceptance speech was not finished, and Gordon was working on it in his office in Millbank. If you want to know what real loyalty is, it is this: Gordon Brown late in the evening, cursing, muttering, arms flailing as he punched words into a computer, writing the speech that just a few weeks earlier he believed he would be making himself.

Although it was clear to me, and to Alastair, that Tony Blair should be the next leader of the party, others saw it differently – and not only Gordon Brown's supporters, but also Peter Mandelson. Mandelson had always seen Brown as the natural successor to Smith:

> Anyone who had any contact with me in the years preceding John Smith's death knows how committed I was to Gordon Brown. I worked for him day in, day out. I was his adviser. When I was Director of Communications, and beyond that, when I stopped in 1990, right up through the General Election of 1992 and beyond, I made sure that the machine served Gordon Brown. But I also made sure that the machine served Tony Blair as well, because they were both leaders of the modernisers, manifestly the most competent and able, and they were both superb performers. But nobody who knew me and knew the situation could seriously argue that I didn't put Brown before Blair right up until 1994. It was always Brown one, and Blair two.[17]

I know this to be true from endless conversations I had with Mandelson over this period. When the election for leader came, he was torn: 'When John Smith died both their standings were incredibly high, but within hours of Smith dying, the whole world had gone to Blair. It wasn't something that could be organised, managed, manipulated, it just happened,' Mandelson says. 'It could have turned into the most awful mess, but I didn't let go of Gordon, and didn't let go of the possibility of Gordon, until well into the next week.'[18]

This is consistent with my dealings with Peter at this time. From the moment of John's death he was hopelessly divided between his loyalty to Gordon and friendship with Tony. Quite simply he did not know what to do. Every day we would talk; usually several times a day. He wanted to be loyal to them both. I told him constantly the candidate had to be Tony, but he would not have it: Gordon and Tony both had claims and he would respect both. He wrote to Gordon on the Monday, a week after John Smith's death. His letter started by praising Brown's abilities, making it clear that although he had the qualities needed to be leader of the party, that was not the issue. It had become a question of presentation and media and public acceptability and the need to win the south. Tony Blair was now so far ahead that he could not withdraw. The only option would be for Gordon to stand as well, which would weaken Tony and might open the door to a new non-modernising candidate. If Gordon stood, it would need a massively upweighted media campaign and outstanding media-management skills, which Mandelson said he would be prepared to provide. This letter lent itself to different interpretations, but I think the central thrust was pretty clear: Mandelson was saying to Brown, you could run, but it would damage Tony; I would help, but it would be better if you did not stand. I do not see this as duplicitous: it was Mandelson trying to square an impossible circle. He kept on repeating, 'There will only be one candidate,' but in the early days he refused to say who it should be. Soon, he came to realise it would be Tony, but the change was gradual.

When I went into Peter's office on Tuesday 17 May he said, 'It is time we got down to work.' For Tony, I assumed, but I was wrong. Peter asked me to write a briefing note on how best to present Gordon in the campaign. He was determined to keep Gordon's leadership chances afloat so that time could be bought to make a calm and rational decision. He wanted to be fair to both. He would not allow a word to be said against Gordon. When Harriet Harman came into his office and said, 'It has got to be Tony,' he barked at her, 'That is not decided yet.'

At the time Mandelson said that he thought the best course might be to leave the stage for a while, and adopt a neutral, disinterested position. But he admits that was never really an option: 'I knew I could not get out of it because I was both their best friends and I was looked to by the media the whole time to represent what was going on among the modernisers. I was the agent, the publicist, the spin-doctor of the modernisers' cause.'[19]

After it became clear that Tony was going to be the modernisers' candidate, Mandelson says, 'I worked with Gordon to devise the best possible exit strategy for him that I could, which I did, which I think I managed incredibly well right up until the last moment. Gordon's people never wanted Gordon to exit, but Gordon knew he had to. I was the constant intermediary between him [Brown] and Tony, organising right down to the last word of the briefing statement that we put together for the day that Gordon withdrew.'[20] I was not party to these discussions: Mandelson was under huge strain, and would not talk openly about what he was doing.

The leadership election produced a breakdown in the previously very close relationship between Mandelson and Brown, although not between Blair and Brown. The bitterness after the election focused on the followers, not the leaders. Blair and Brown speak only warmly of each other and their relationship retains its strength, but the campaign did leave its mark. Part of the problem now is that there is no shared consensus about what happened. The account that I have given above is simply not believed by many who were involved. And my perspective is limited: I only saw my small part of the events. But I am certain of some things. I know that Gordon Brown acted with great courage in standing down; that Tony Blair had no option but to stand and did everything he could to support Gordon; and that Peter Mandelson was caught between two loyalties and tried to make the best of a difficult situation. Not everyone sees it this way. Bitterness remains, but not between the two principals. Campbell says, 'I was struck by what Gordon did. It was a difficult thing to do. It was a ballsy thing to do. But I think they have managed to hold their relationship together. It is a very powerful relationship and a very powerful motor within government, and some people around them find it very difficult to fathom how it works, but it does. I think that's because they have been through quite a lot together. They are both basically decent blokes.'[21]

The leadership campaign

On the Monday after John's death Anji Hunter, head of Blair's office and an absolute linchpin in his political life, contacted me to ask if I would help on Tony's leadership campaign. I phoned Tony at home. He was anxious, needing reassurance about whether or not he was right to stand. I said he had no choice, he had to do it. He invited me to his house and when we talked in his kitchen he had become more settled about standing. He was determined to go ahead, but was very worried about Gordon. Already, however, he was thinking about fighting the Tories in a new way. He did not want to get trapped on their ground: he said we should concede and move on – agree with the Conservatives where we could only lose, fight only where we could win.

Very early on I wrote a strategy note for the campaign, dated 17 May, called 'Strategy for the Leadership Election and Beyond', in which I identified a new political map and a new political mood. 'The electorate has lost hope, lost trust, and lost the confidence that things can improve. It has become sullen, resentful, unbelieving.' There was 'a lack of confidence in Britain, what is happening to it, and what is its place in the world. Britain in this mood is crying out for the right kind of leadership. This strategic opportunity can only be grasped by a shift from a strategy of consolidation to a strategy of change.' The strategy of consolidation was based around 'consensus and compromise' and 'would have produced a Labour vote of around 37–9 per cent: a low downside, a low upside.' This approach could not work now, I argued: we had to move to a strategy of change, based upon 'party unity through momentum', 'direction and dynamism'; 'electoral appeal through excitement, modernity and renewal'. 'The upside of this strategy is higher, perhaps 42–3 per cent of the vote. But so is the downside.

A strategy of change is risky, but there is no other choice, and nor should there be.'[22]

The strategic components of this new approach were:

> Change, which is a complete political project . . . a new approach to politics, and a political leader who embodies that approach. It is about radical ideas and fresh new solutions; it is about excitement and momentum . . . That is at the heart of the modernising project. For Labour, and for Britain.
>
> Populism, which means Labour becoming once again the instrument through which ordinary people believe they can achieve their aspirations. We have to make it clear to working people that we understand their aspirations and that we want to make them better off; that we are against taxation for its own sake; that we are tough on crime; that we stress individual responsibility.
>
> A new Labour Party: we must at some appropriate point say to the public – and to the party – that we are a new Labour Party. Radical in intent, driven by change, underpinned by conviction, confident in our beliefs and ready to sweep the Conservatives away.[23]

I typed the note in my office in Brussels and began to shuttle between the two campaigns: the leadership campaign in London and the European election campaign in Brussels. Until Europe went to the polls on 9 June, I often had to commute between the two cities in one day: London in the morning, Brussels in the afternoon.

Once the European elections were over, the official leadership contest began. The ban on campaigning, which all candidates (Blair, Prescott and Beckett) had observed since Smith's death, ended. I attended Blair's campaign meetings, which were held at 8.30 A.M. in Jack Straw's office in Parliament Street, just along the corridor from Tony's. Anji Hunter had been keen for me to be at these meetings, but I was very cautious about re-entering British politics. I had been hit so hard after 1992. Anji insisted and gave me tremendous support and encouragement, so I arrived for my first meeting early. Jack Straw, an early opponent of Clause IV, welcomed me. Others then drifted in: Alun Michael (Tony's deputy on shadow Home Affairs); Peter Kilfoyle, a Liverpool MP with impeccable working-class credentials; Mo Mowlam, a politician who always spoke her mind regardless of the consequences; and Barry Cox, Tony's close friend and treasurer of the campaign. I said almost nothing, but I no longer felt a pariah, and from then on I attended the meetings every day.

I was uneasy about the way the as-yet undeclared campaign had started, and on 20 May spelled out my concerns: 'There is no sense as yet of the party falling in behind Blair; there is already a media backlash; and most dangerous of all there is already a media consensus on his weaknesses: that he is soft; that he may not be strong or tough enough to lead the party and the country . . . Only a campaign that is ruthless in maximising Tony's strengths will succeed.'[24]

When Gordon stood down for Tony on 1 June the atmosphere cleared. The next day I wrote a further memo: 'Last week was probably the most dangerous of the campaign, and TB came through it well. However, apart from the simple need to avoid complacency, there is progress to be made and the campaign must keep pushing ahead.' Blair's political identity had yet to be established: 'It can either be the agent of change and renewal or the combination of Bambi and Bimbo the media is trying to create . . . TB must make a speech that makes it clear that it is he, and not his opponents, who represents the real aspirations of working people. However, TB must go beyond this and build a broader coalition, including many of the middle class, because the desire for change, renewal and community does not stop at Birmingham or end at £35,000 a year.'[25]

In early June Blair wrote a memo summing up his themes for the campaign. It is astonishing, reading it now, how clear he was about his aims even then. This was, in effect, an early Blair testament. On the personal front, his first point was 'strong convictions based around Christian socialism; came to party through belief not background. Values at heart of his policies', followed by, 'family; more to life than politics'. He then highlighted guts, consistency and commitment to Labour, and an open and friendly style of leadership. Under a second heading, 'Strategic Principles', he wrote:

> Change and Renewal: a new direction for the country; traditional principles but modern application; honouring the past but not living in it. Smith's legacy to us unity based around consensual and open style of leadership. This will be Blair's style. But without Smith we are going to have to be bold advocates of change rather than cautious . . . Excitement, inspiration, visionary: engendering new political mood . . . Ideas: a bold new agenda for the left. Breaking through old left/right barriers. Radical but modern, redefining what being left of centre means . . . Conviction: Blair believes in what he says; says what he believes.

Under a third category, 'Policy Framework', he outlined what he called a Basic Principle:

> Socialism is not a set of rigid economic prescriptions but a set of values based around a belief in society and community: i.e. individuals prosper best within a strong and cohesive society, where opportunity and obligation go hand in hand. We have to renew Britain as a strong society – one-nation socialism – but do it for the modern world. This will mean a new direction for the country.

He then listed a series of new policy directions:

> On society – to re-create terms of community and social cohesion, based on welfare whose purpose is not to create a set of dependants but to provide the opportunity for self-improvement; on the economy – economic regeneration through investment, and a revolution in skills; on the Constitution – a new settlement between society and individual, devolved power, individual rights; on Europe – Britain leading in Europe but re-shaping path of

co-operation; on politics – change in style and manner: pluralist, open, inclusive; on party – transform party organisation towards campaigning and mass membership.[26]

This document underlines the constancy of Blair's ideas, and of his grounding principles. I added a section on message. These themes governed the leadership contest and dominated the next three years and beyond.

Blair's leadership campaign was anchored around a manifesto and six major policy speeches. Peter Hyman, who has worked for Blair since the leadership campaign, spelled out the thinking behind it:

There was a conscious decision by Tony that the campaign had to take Labour a strategic step forward; that we shouldn't just win, we should make use of the heightened exposure of the leadership campaign, which was unusual for a party in opposition. The cameras were on us rather than the Tories, so this was an opportunity to give out different messages about Labour. We did this not just through 'Change and Renewal' [the campaign document], which was a kind of surrogate manifesto, but also through five or six substantial speeches, which staked out a new territory for the Labour Party.[27]

On 6 June I conducted focus groups for Tony Blair, the first of many I was to do for the Labour Party in the period up to the 1997 election. Almost all of these were with one key group: 1992 Conservative voters who were considering switching to Labour. From them I constructed profiles for all the main political leaders. Major's negatives were terrible: he was considered 'weak, out of his depth, not up to the job'. The European election campaign had exposed the hollowness of his leadership and the growing ideological chasm at the heart of the Conservative Party. Clarke was disliked, Portillo seen as sinister. Only Heseltine had any kind of popularity. On Labour's side John Prescott was 'very popular', considered 'honest, blunt, straight-talking and no-nonsense'.

Before television exposure Tony Blair was 'liked and considered a different sort of politician', although some – particularly men – thought he was too young. However, exposure to Blair on television transformed perceptions. They liked him, 'his charisma, his message of pulling together, and the sense of a new kind of politics. And a new politician.'[28]

Labour won a massive victory in the European elections on 9 June, and the Socialist Group retained their majority in the European Parliament. The next day I wrote a leadership election campaign document. I showed it to Tony, Peter and Mo, but Peter would not allow me to show it to the campaign team. He thought it would overwhelm them. It was long – fourteen pages – but I expect they could have coped with it. It brought together everything that had been written to date but included a new section on developing Blair's identity: 'The media want a beauty contest. Tony Blair must insist on a contest of ideas. The media want a nice, cuddly, telegenic family man. Tony Blair must give them an uncompromising champion of change.'[29] A day later, nervously, Tony announced his candidature to a packed meeting at Trimdon Labour Club in Sedgefield, the heart of his constituency.

On Thursday 23 June, Blair launched 'Change and National Renewal', his campaign manifesto. This was the first time he had pulled together his ideas into one coherent statement. It has been criticised for its 'thinness'[30] but that is harsh; it is better described as uneven, yet it laid the foundations for much of what was to come. David Miliband, now head of the Policy Unit at 10 Downing Street, says of it: 'I think that the first and last pages are very good. Where the Tories have gone wrong – economic and social failure, insecurity, which affects us all. You've then got New Labour's prescriptions. It's fairly basic, it's what appears in Clause IV, pretty much word for word. Then you have got the policy agenda which was stuffed in at the last minute. And then there is the Challenge for Labour, which is pretty good.'[31]

The document opens with a critique of the Conservatives: they failed because they 'saw all forms of social co-operation as inherently wrong, fit not for reform but for demolition. As a result the Conservatives consistently ignored the central importance to any successful country of ensuring that society works together to advance the interests of the individual'. The result of this was 'to tear apart the social fabric and encourage a narrow view of self-interest which was both selfish and ultimately self-defeating'. The document includes a paragraph which is a reasonable definition of Blairism: 'The simple case for democratic socialism is that individuals prosper best within a strong, active society, whose members acknowledge that they owe duties to each other as well as themselves, and in part at least, depend upon one another to succeed.' This was the basic sentiment behind the new Clause IV.

Although these principles were right and enduring, they had to be re-interpreted for a new age: 'The principles are timeless, but we should not merely accept as necessary, but advocate as desirable, the application of those principles to new circumstances.' This led to the need for renewal: 'economic renewal', 'social renewal', 'political renewal', 'international renewal' and 'party renewal'. The last was central to Blairism: reform of the nation required reform of the party; the one was dependent upon the other.

Blair ended with a re-statement of his basic approach to politics: Labour had to win at every level. 'To win the trust of the British people, we must do more than just defeat the Conservatives on grounds of competence, integrity and fitness to govern. We must change the tide of ideas.'[32] This was not simply rhetoric. It was central to Blair's beliefs, and he would repeat it often in the three years before the General Election.

To drive home his insistence that Labour had to win the battle of ideas, Blair followed his manifesto with a series of considered and fairly heavyweight speeches. David Miliband was chiefly responsible for drafting the education speech, delivered on 24 June; Derry Irvine, the constitution speech; Gordon Brown, Andrew Smith (a shadow Treasury minister) and David Miliband drafted the economy speech; and Peter Hyman worked hard on the welfare speech. All these speeches mapped out putative New Labour positions. They were tentative, but they began to set a new direction.

The leadership election was not free from anxiety. Blair did not perform at his best either in an interview with David Frost on Sunday 12 June, or in a *Panorama* televised debate on 13 June. On both he looked ill-at-ease and under-prepared.

By the end of June, however, the campaign feedback reports were making it clear that Blair was going to win. In fact, they attacked him for appearing complacent: 'Two respondents said that Tony was not perceived to be campaigning hard enough. He is taking victory for granted.'[33] He wasn't, of course. In my meetings with him at his home he never took victory for granted. This was a continuing characteristic of Blair's, which resurfaced in the 1997 General Election campaign, when he would continually warn against complacency despite the poll leads.

Many people display a surface confidence that betrays inner insecurity. Blair is quite the opposite. He can often appear anxious about the outcome of events, but inwardly be absolutely confident, as in fact he was in 1994. It is this inner confidence that makes him so unusual as a Labour politician. When I visited him at home during the leadership campaign, he would appear outwardly nervous about winning, but when the point was pushed he would be unequivocal in his confidence that he was going to do it.

The leadership election was held during a sunny early summer, just as the election was three years later, and Blair liked to sit outside his house, lounging in a garden chair. He dislikes formality. I have never seen him work behind a desk. Usually, as Leader of the Opposition and as Prime Minister, he works from a sofa with his papers on a coffee table in front of him. But his casualness is deceptive. He moves suddenly from relaxed chat to a pointed question, and without warning will want to move on, often ending a conversation abruptly, as though you had suddenly said the wrong thing.

On 21 July 1994 Blair won a massive victory, with 57 per cent of the vote. John Prescott, always Tony's preferred choice, was elected his deputy. Once, when I suggested to him that the focus groups might favour another candidate, he brushed me aside, saying, 'I suggest you go away and refocus your focus groups.' Blair made a formal speech of acceptance at the Institute of Education, the speech which Gordon Brown had been working on so late at night. He then came to an upstairs room at Church House opposite Westminster Green and made a short, emotional speech of thanks. In it he thanked 'Bobby', a reference to Peter Mandelson, who had been his surrogate campaign manager. Mandelson's involvement had been kept secret because of supposed animosity towards him in the Parliamentary Labour Party. Mandelson says of this, 'Bobby was a sort of joke, but it was a private family joke. I was the sort of invisible linchpin of the campaign, and orchestrated it through Anji [Hunter], Tim [Allan] and Peter Hyman, without the campaign committee apparently realising it.'[34] This was not really true, because they knew Mandelson was the campaign's hidden guiding hand, but felt it best just to keep going as though he wasn't there. The secrecy was a hangover from the bitterness of Kinnock's years. It would have been better to have been open about it.

Blair's victory was the decisive moment in the 1992–97 parliament. Labour's lead in political identification, which is the key measure of electoral support, immediately increased from around 2 per cent under Smith to around 12 per cent under Blair, where it stayed until the 1997 election. Even more importantly, Blair's victory marked the point at which economic optimism and the Conservative share of the vote diverged.[35] For almost all the Conservatives' years in office they had been in tandem: the more optimistic people were about the economy, the higher the government's support. But Blair's election ended this connection. The public grew ever more optimistic about the economy, while support for the Conservatives remained static. Labour might have won under John Smith, but it was not a certainty and we would not have won by a landslide or anything like it: probably, we would have scraped home. But the majority would have been small, and a hung parliament not impossible. It was Blair who changed the political map.

Hitting the centre ground running

Blair wasted no time moving the party into the mainstream. Three days after his win he was interviewed by Brian Walden and, risking the wrath of the liberal consensus, made it absolutely clear that for most children he believed having two parents was better than having just one. Blair asked and answered his own question: 'Do I believe that it is best, it is easiest, that kids are brought up in a normal stable family? The answer is yes, I do believe that.' He then went further. When asked by Walden whether he thought it was wrong for women to choose to become mothers before they were in a stable relationship, he said, 'Yes. I disagree with what they have done.' He then made the essential populist point, the point that I had been waiting twenty years for a Labour leader to make: 'Can I tell you what is extraordinary, is the degree to which people have ended up associating the left with certain thoughts that are a million miles away from ordinary people.' 'Whose fault is that?' responded Walden. 'Maybe there is a bit of fault on both sides, but I tell you this: what is absolutely essential is this is the type of Labour Party that there really is today, where we know the importance of strong family community and family values.' He went on to say that the family was the 'essential, stable social unit'.[36]

Two days later Blair demonstrated a clear intent to persuade Conservative voters to switch to Labour. The heart of his General Election strategy was this: 'Many of those who voted Conservative are now asking serious questions about their quality of life and living standards and prospects for their children under the Conservatives. There is a great mood in this country for fresh thinking, for a new start.' He then made another decisive statement: 'There was a point in the 1980s when we went badly wrong and there is no harm in admitting that.'[37]

The *Daily Mail*, then the key influencer of middle Britain, ran an extraordinary editorial that day praising Blair. 'This paper is not in the habit of congratulating leaders of the Labour Party, but then few politicians recently have spoken with the courage and conviction of Mr Tony Blair.'[38]

Just two days later, on 28 July, and still only a week after his election as leader, Blair smashed more shibboleths, this time on education. The party was launching its education policy White Paper at the Institute of Civil Engineers. Blair had discussed this with David Miliband beforehand. He had made it clear to Miliband that he was going to make education a central priority of his leadership and that he intended to use this launch to refocus Labour's education policy away from vested interests and towards standards. He took over the press conference from then shadow Education Secretary Ann Taylor. When pressed hard on selection he denied that he would abolish it, a clear difference from the content of the policy document being launched at the same time, which stated, 'Labour rejects any system in which a few are selected at the expense of the vast majority.'[39] Pressed further about the content of the document, Blair replied with a smile, 'I think the document will repay very, very careful reading.' On the BBC *One O'Clock News*, when asked what the main points of the document were, he went even further, saying that his first point was that unfit teachers would be sacked.[40] Blair didn't like the party's policy document and was not afraid to say so.

On 29 July Blair went on holiday, but he had done his work. He had made it absolutely clear that he was setting the party on a new path. He had signalled a determination to ditch the old party and bring Labour back to the hopes and values of ordinary voters. But this was only a small step forward; Blair had a far bigger project in mind.

Building New Labour

On 22 July I wrote a 25-page memo – 'Consolidating the Blair Identity. Rebuilding Labour; Demolishing the Conservatives' – laying out the groundwork for a new Labour Party. This was a long and comprehensive document, which I wanted Blair to read on holiday.

First I spelled out the strengths and weaknesses of Blair's position. His strengths were 'freshness and a sense of change; confidence and self-assurance; that Tony Blair is a new kind of politician; that Blair changes what it means to be Labour.' His weaknesses were that he could be perceived as 'over-smooth', 'too soft and not tough enough', and 'inexperienced'. In response to this, 'Tony Blair should not be what he is not. This will not work and it will be counterproductive. He should not try to avoid the problem of youth by behaving with excessive gravitas. Nor try to avoid looking soft by behaving with excessive aggression. What he must do is build on his strengths, and build an identity as a politician that is of a piece with the political positions he adopts. He must be a complete, coherent politician who always rings true.'

The problem was that Labour lacked defining positions and in the rest of the document I attempted to remedy this. I argued that the real political agenda was a combination of right and left. It was right-wing on crime, welfare, immigration, discipline, tax and individualism, but left-wing on the NHS, investment, social integration, opposition to privatisation and unemployment. People wanted change, but they didn't yet want Labour. 'People have had enough of the Conservatives but they cannot understand why . . . whatever they think about the Tories they are not in love with Labour . . . There is still a lurking fear about unions and the loony left; there is potential concern about Labour because of its liberal social positions; there is anxiety about tax; there is almost no idea what Labour stands for.'

Worse still, there was a 'Conservative hegemony': 'Conducting these [focus] groups I am struck by the extent that the confidence and consistency of fifteen years of Conservative government . . . has established the framework through which these voters see the political world. Their scepticism of government action, their belief that everything has to be paid for, their social conservatism, their dismissal of so much that the left has to offer, shows the difficulties we will have in developing an alternative framework of ideas.'

Labour's only chance was to rebuild completely from the ground up. This meant: 'New foundations: a reason for its existence as a political party; a new structure, a central message to help change the political map; a new superstructure: defining positions supported by defining policies.' This reflected my belief that we would only win an election on the basis of a complete political project: starting with the foundations and then building upwards. Substance had to come first.

For me the foundations of the party were the people it was created to represent. Labour existed to be the party that must 'reflect the real interests and attitudes of working voters, not the left-wing myths about what working people want . . . it must reconnect with both "working-class" and "middle-class" voters'. I then wrote what I suppose is the heart of my political beliefs, a statement born explicitly of the politics of the suburbs I came from: Labour must recognise that 'what most voters want is, over time and without greed, to advance and improve their lives. In short, to become better off. This is absolutely critical. The progress and well-being of individuals and their families [should be] our central reference point in making sense of politics. It allows Labour to respect the value of work, which is, after all, the original reason for its existence.' The ultimate foundation of the Labour Party is not dogma, or even values, it is the hopes and aspirations of ordinary people. My instincts are populist: I put the people first.

Next I moved on to what I called New Labour's structure, the values and principles of the party. Labour had to be the party of 'change and renewal'; of 'the community advancing individuals'; and of 'a new Labour Party: beyond left and right . . . Labour must say that it is a new Labour Party, that is left-of-centre, but which has moved beyond old left–right boundaries. This means being tough on crime, welfare waste, standards and discipline, while also committed to the community, investment, and rebuilding the NHS.' Last was Labour's 'superstructure' – its defining positions – in which I started to lay out Labour's new dividing lines: welfare for independence not dependence; rebuilding the NHS but with modern application; influence, not isolation, in Europe.

This then was what I wanted New Labour to become, but that was only half the story. The other half was demolishing the Conservatives. 'Just as Labour has to be rebuilt, the Conservatives have to be demolished. It is clear that dissatisfaction with the Conservatives has not translated into enduring reasons for not voting Conservative. This has to change in an exercise in demolition that matches Labour's reconstruction.' The essence of the attack I laid out was this: 'The Conservatives are out of touch with ordinary voters and do not represent their interests. The Conservatives have made ordinary working people worse off. The Conservatives cannot be trusted. They have lied before, and will lie again.' I ended the document by saying that Blair must make 'a conference speech that should in effect rebuild the Labour Party'.[41]

These, then, were my strategic goals in the summer of 1994: the complete reconstruction of Labour and the total destruction of the Conservatives. I remember thinking as I wrote: this may be a trifle ambitious. But, more or less, it was achieved. I gave the document to Blair to read while he went on holiday in Italy and France. Out there he met up with Alastair Campbell and tried to persuade him to become his press secretary. Blair was staying at the house Alastair's family had rented in Flassan, with Cherie, their three children and, for a while also, Neil and Glenys Kinnock. The house was not large and the atmosphere was close and occasionally explosive. Blair had talked about the job of press secretary with Alastair just before the holiday, and Alastair had phoned me up to discuss it. He said he wasn't sure, but he seemed to want to do it. I told him it had to be his decision. He asked me what Labour's chances were of winning. I said I was certain Labour would win, a remark he threw back at me often in some of the dark days ahead. Campbell, who had by then been a political journalist for eight years, describes his uncertainty at the time:

Sometimes if you have been doing something for a long time you can't necessarily imagine yourself in a different role. What was good in a way was that I was driving down – Fiona was flying down with the kids – so I had a long time to think on my own. I had two impressions which came to me through the whole holiday – I literally took the whole holiday to think about it, which was a month. But two things came back to me the whole time. The first was that we lost the election and I was there thinking I could have made a difference. And the other was that we had won and I could have been part of it. Fiona was basically hostile, she felt it was too much. Neil was totally hostile and he was there on holiday for part of the time and was saying it will completely ruin your life. It will ruin your family's life, it will ruin your health. Life as you know it is over, forget it, don't do it. And then Tony appeared, stayed for a few days and we talked about all sorts of things, but in the end it was me thinking, you can't really say no to this, so I just had to go through the process of finding the rationale for it.

Central to his rationale was the importance of the media:

Tony was completely seized by the importance of how to get a better press than we'd had before. It was one of the things I used to argue with Neil about – and I completely understand why he found it difficult, because they were complete bastards to him – but I held the view that, however bad the press is, it can be worse, and it can be better, and you have got to work at it all the time. I think that was allied to a sense that I was thirty-six and that I'd pretty much done all I could do where I was and this new adventure could come up. There have been some absolutely awful moments along the way, but I haven't regretted it. There are all sorts of things I would have done differently and you do have to make sacrifices, but I don't regret it at all.

One of the other things Blair discussed with Campbell was Clause IV:

> We had a long discussion, partly in the sitting-room, but we also went for a long walk and he was going through the kind of changes he wanted to bring in, and he said – he swore me to secrecy – for example, I am thinking about scrapping Clause IV. And I said that would be pretty bold and it did have a certain appeal. Not because of any ideological bent. Although I have always been keen on the modernising thing, there has always been a heavy traditionalist streak in me. So I wasn't thinking great, let's smash up Clause IV. What appealed to me was the sheer boldness of it and the fact that this was someone who wasn't going to mess about.[42]

Over the summer Blair also spoke to Gordon Brown and Peter Mandelson about the abolition of Clause IV. Mandelson was keen, but typically cautious: 'I strongly supported it. It didn't take me long to make up my mind, but I did think about it. I always think about things. I never say yes immediately. I have my instincts but then I reflect.'[43] Campbell could not wait to get started. He wrestled with his decision all summer, but once he had made it he was impatient and he cut his holiday short. He phoned me on his return and told me of his decision. He sounded completely determined, as if nothing would stop him.

I went to see Tony Blair on 6 September and he asked me to work with him. He was in Neil's old office, having rejected John Smith's as too grand and detached from his staff. It was strange seeing Blair in Neil's old office: the same place, but a different era. For Blair, opposition was already a waste of time: something to be finished with as soon as possible. He paced around the room and wouldn't sit down. He could not have made his intentions more clear. 'Past Labour leaders lost because they compromised,' he said. 'I will never compromise. I would rather be beaten and leave politics than bend to the party. I am going to take the party on.' He was pleased Alastair had joined him, confident about the future, but tense, wired, impatient to get started. I wrote to him afterwards, confirming how much I wanted to help him. I started the letter plaintively (but I meant what I wrote and it was absolutely true): 'All I have wanted since I was a small boy was the chance to have a campaigning role in electing a Labour government, and this time I am sure I will get that chance.' Further on, I wrote (underlined to make the point): 'I am completely confident that Labour will win, but only if Labour is completely remade . . . Just as important as remaking Labour is the trust they place in you. Again, I am absolutely certain that if you are consistent, clear, tough and honest over the next two years, you will win their trust.'[44] On the same day Blair visited the TUC and briefed journalists that he would 'treat [the unions] in the same way that Labour treated business'.[45] This is typical Blair, boldly heightening the impact of a remark by cutting directly against the expectation of the context in which it is made. In America they call this 'counter-scheduling'.

The following day, Alastair Campbell was officially appointed Blair's press secretary. Two days later, on 9 September, Blair held his first extended 'brainstorming' session at the Chewton Glen Hotel in Hampshire, organised by Colin Fisher, managing director of the market research company SRU. There was the usual endless prevarication about who should attend. In the end, as well as Blair and Brown, there was Campbell, Mandelson, myself and Michael Wills, then a television producer, now an MP. I had written another huge document for this event, running to thirty-six pages. After receiving it, Tony told me tactfully that he preferred to have his memos on a single sheet of paper.

This document was grounded in a historical analysis of the double betrayal of the electorate by the two major parties. Post-war British politics had been dominated by two themes: the 'need for national renewal and modernisation; and the emerging individualism, consumerism and aspirations of working-class voters'. On both counts the Conservatives had done better than Labour. In the 1950s, 'the washing machines and welfare decade', the Conservatives had begun to identify themselves as the party of working-class aspiration. In the 1960s Labour had power, but Heath made the killer point in 1965: 'I would like to associate with a government which gives ordinary people the opportunity of leading fuller lives.' And, 'Labour are the true conservatives.' In the 1980s the Conservatives reached out and grabbed our territory and our voters. Thatcher started to renew Britain, and where the Conservatives were succeeding in taking Labour's ground as the party of the people and the party of renewal, Labour was failing on both counts. The party had gained the unenviable position of being both extremist and at the same time timidly conservative. Labour had 'failed spectacularly in 1978–82, but these events were not an aberration in the development of the Labour Party, but the culmination of a long-standing failure of the Labour Party to either implement a consistent project for national renewal or represent the aspirations of its natural constituency.' The language is overblown, but the sentiments were right.

But in the 1990s the Conservatives had crashed too: 'They have lost their reputation for competence; their capacity for national renewal . . . and they are no longer the party of the aspirational working class or even the middle class.' It is extraordinary to contemplate just how incompetent John Major's administration was. By 1994 it had suffered a massive devaluation, the rebellion of forty-one MPs over the Maastricht Treaty and the loss to the Conservative Whip of a further eight, and the humiliating dismissal of the Chancellor of the Exchequer Norman Lamont, the man who had run Major's leadership campaign.

I continued: 'Deep-seated suspicion of Labour, which has yet to rebuild itself, and the crash of the Conservatives mean that the electorate has lost trust not only in the effectiveness of the two major parties, but in the process of politics and the effectiveness of politics itself.' Labour had 'not only to rebuild itself, but to rebuild the relationship between the electorate and the government. The issue is not just trust in Labour, but trust in government and politics itself.'[46]

Most of the Chewton Glen brainstorming session was dominated by Blair's insistence on arriving at new positions, new dividing lines, and working out what New Labour was. Brown's focus then, as now, was on opportunity. This has always been his guiding concept. Blair is anchored in community, Brown in opportunity for all. These are complementary concepts, but they are different; they give a different shade to their politics and their policies. Before lunch we walked in the sun, getting used to a new political reality. Neither Blair nor Brown looked fully comfortable in his role yet.

For me the day is memorable for one defining moment: in the queue with Tony, waiting for the buffet, we talked about the need for rapid change and Blair turned to me and made one of the most compelling political statements I have ever heard: 'Conference must build New Labour. It is time we gave the party some electric shock treatment.' Labour had to be made new. And Blair was going to do it.

In mid-September, when interest rates rose by 0.5 per cent to 5.75 per cent, Blair redirected Labour's approach to economic affairs. Instead of immediately condemning the rise in rates, as Labour politicians were expected to do, he indicated a shift towards fiscal conservatism by avoiding direct criticism of Kenneth Clarke's decision. In an interview in the *Financial Times* the next day he said 'inflation is the symptom not the disease'.[47] He went further on Radio 4's *Today* programme, claiming to James Naughtie that he could run the market economy better than the Conservatives. Naughtie was amazed: 'It is a long time since a Labour leader has said: "Vote for me because I know more about a market economy than the Tories."' Blair didn't flinch: 'But it is absolutely true,' he said.[48] Although he had been leader for just a matter of weeks, and spent a good part of that on holiday, Blair had already made huge strides in repositioning the party: bad teachers should be sacked; two parents were better than one; Labour had made grievous errors in the past; business was as important as unions; Labour could run a market economy better than the Tories.

By now, New Labour was an accepted figure of speech – at least among ourselves. On 1 September I had written a summary note with the heading: 'New Labour; Right as Well as Left'.[49] I do not claim the credit for inventing New Labour. I had first mentioned it as a concept in the spring of 1989, and it had stayed in the ether in the years to 1992. But it really became the natural next step in the modernisation of the party after the success of the New Democrats in the United States, when Blair grabbed the idea with both hands. He knew that only by contrasting 'new' Labour with 'old' Labour explicitly would the electorate believe that Labour had changed and could be trusted. But it was Alastair Campbell who turned the term 'New Labour' into an entirely new identity for the party. We wanted a slogan for conference. I favoured 'A New Approach from Labour', which I am the first to accept was a dreadful line. Alastair was working on some alternatives. We were in a meeting and Alastair, as is his way, scribbled down several lines, which he showed to me. One was: 'New Labour, New Britain'. He liked it best, but I thought it too crude. On 25 September, the Monday before conference, Jackie Stacey, who was in charge of presentation, including the platform set, was chasing Peter Mandelson for a decision about the slogan. We had both been cautious about the 'New Labour, New Britain' line. But Mandelson asked me, 'Which line will truly connect with the electorate?' In the course of a long, restless night worrying, I had decided 'New Labour, New Britain' was after all the right line, and so we agreed on it. Walworth Road stirred into mild rebellion: Karen Buck and Matthew Taylor from the campaigns unit, and others, were nervous. They were worried that the party would revolt, delegates might walk out of the conference hall. Alastair had to sit at the desk of Kate Garvey, Blair's able and effervescent diary secretary, and fight for his line. Putting New Labour in massive letters in front of hundreds of delegates was effectively renaming the party. It was a huge risk. But the slogan was used and there wasn't a murmur from the conference. This was the moment New Labour became a reality.

In late September I went to see John Prescott to present to him the results of focus-group research. He was in John Smith's old office. Wary at first, he asked me everything about New Labour. He wanted to know where it came from, what the voters thought of it, whether it was necessary. After half an hour he seemed convinced and his attitude became warmer. His main concern was that we were ditching what was good about our past, but he was persuaded that fear of Labour was so entrenched that a clear dividing-line was needed. That was typical of John: wary then warm; apparently traditional, but a force for change. However much he might hate it being said, John Prescott is at heart a moderniser. He is not frightened of reform, in fact he welcomes it, provided there is evidence to support the need for it. And most important, he is a genuinely populist politician who has the instincts and aspirations of working people close to his heart. He is also fair. He was the only one of my critics in 1992 who actually took the trouble to seek me out and ask me what had happened.

He was not so convinced by the plan to ditch Clause IV. He was troubled, but open to persuasion: if it was right he would support it. John may be a reluctant moderniser, but he is a moderniser nonetheless.

On 27 September Blair made his first important speech as leader, at the National Film Theatre, opening Labour's seminar on the global economy. It was an explicit attempt to redraw the dividing-lines in economics and an unambiguous rejection of 'tax and spend'. By now conference was upon us. One week before it, on 23 September, I had written to Tony begging for boldness. Not that I needed to. I said his speech should be 'so bold, so clear, so uncompromising, that [it] confounds the electorate, forcing them to change their minds . . . This is a risk, but it is the least risky course. If perceptions about Labour are not radically improved, Labour will lose.'[50] The days before the conference, when we had to take the final decision on whether or not to go for the reform of Clause IV, were confused and uncertain. Alastair Campbell recalls: 'In the days up to it [the conference] when we hadn't decided whether to do it or not, you were having different meetings with different people about the speech, some of whom knew, some of whom didn't, and sometimes you would forget.'

John Prescott's agreement was essential to the success of the Clause IV strategy. Campbell reflects:

There was no way we could have done it without John Prescott – not just John reluctantly agreeing, but John actually giving his blessing to it. The night before I was practically up all night, up and down the stairs to John's room, and going through it. In the end it was John who said: if you are going to do this, you have got to say it, you can't bugger about. That was when we wrote in right at the last moment to review our constitution for a new age. That actually came from John – we were going to skirt around it. You can argue that we skirted around it anyway, but the fact is that at one point we were not going to mention the constitution at all. I can remember there was a moment of extreme tension because Tony had to broaden the circle of people who knew.

Early on Tuesday morning, around 1 A.M., Campbell called all Labour's press officers into a hotel bedroom and announced that the next day Tony Blair would ditch Clause IV. People started to hyperventilate. Campbell recalls, 'I was in this room – it was a difficult situation, I was still officially a political journalist – and there were people there telling Tony it was the end of the Labour Party and making it clear it couldn't be supported.'

The period from then until the end of Blair's speech was the most uncertain in his political career. He could have been destroyed by the conference. Campbell says: 'I remember Tony saying to me, what's the chance that by 5 P.M. tonight, after the speech, that we are completely dead in the water? I think I said 5 per cent.

Yes, there's a chance, isn't there.'[51] That morning saw a continual flow of shadow Cabinet members coming to Tony's room to be informed of what he intended to do. I had to be kept hidden; the change to Clause IV was combustible enough without my involvement in it being too apparent. Once, I hid in a wardrobe. Alastair left out the last few pages of the speech when it was handed out to the press to maximise impact and minimise risk.

Blair rose to the occasion, holding the audience so closely with him that they did not fully realise what had happened until the speech was over and the press office had begun to give briefings. By then it was done: New Labour; new constitution. As Campbell says, 'Within five minutes of the speech starting I knew it was going to work.' The change to Clause IV 'was so overwhelmingly, blindingly obvious when you think about it: one, that it had to be done; two, that it was something that could be really useful in terms of the overall message of what we are trying to do'.[52]

The speech was important for more than just Clause IV. It saw Blair begin to articulate a new voice for Labour:

> To parents wanting their children to be taught in classrooms that are not crumbling, to students with qualifications but no university place, let us say, the Tories have failed you, we are on your side, your ambitions are our ambitions.
>
> To men and women who get up in the morning and find the kitchen door smashed in again . . . the video gone, again . . . to pensioners who fear to go out of their homes, let us say, the Tories have abused your trust, we are on your side – your concerns are our concerns.
>
> To middle- and lower-income Britain, suffering the biggest tax rises in peacetime history to pay the bills of economic failure, let us say, the Tories have betrayed you, again . . . Labour is on your side . . . your aspirations are our aspirations.
>
> We are back as the party of the majority in British politics, back to speak up for Britain, back as the people's party.[53]

This at last was the authentic voice of Labour: becoming once again the party of aspiration for the working majority, for the new middle class. But Blair wasn't stopping. On 8 November in a speech to the Per Cent Club – a group of business people who pledge a percentage of their earnings to charity – he said, 'Our country needs . . . enterprising entrepreneurs.'[54] He promised that the basic elements of Conservative trade union law would remain; that Labour understood the disincentive effects of high marginal tax rates; and that the minimum wage would be set at a level that 'avoids any adverse impact on jobs'.[55]

Six focus groups in November showed how far the party had moved. On 11 November I wrote, 'There is clear evidence of a real improvement in attitudes towards Labour in comparison with the Kinnock, Smith, and even the early Blair period . . . The most common response is, "I am going to give them a go." This may not sound much, but it is a lot. There is a definite sense that Labour may now be able to address the problems of Britain. Even the beginnings of hope. I have never before felt this in any previous period.'

The reasons for the change were, I wrote, a new Labour Party, the Blair leadership and the Blair–Prescott joint leadership. 'Tony Blair is a surprising choice as leader of Labour. He forces people to reassess their view of Labour. John Prescott is extraordinarily popular. Almost everybody likes him because of his honesty and directness . . . he and Tony Blair are considered a team that works, each mutually enhancing each other.' Finally, 'Blair and Prescott connect in a way John Smith never did. He was trusted but did not really impact on people in the way that the current leadership does.'[56]

Later that month the *Financial Times* published a leaked Conservative Central Office paper by John Maples, which was consistent with my own poll findings. 'If Tony Blair turns out to be as good as he looks, we have a problem,' he wrote.[57] Maples' analysis of the problems facing the Conservatives was accurate and insightful. The Tories were disliked because they were perceived as arrogant and out of touch. At least someone was telling the party leadership the truth, and at this stage it was still not too late for the Conservatives to change. Perhaps too late for them to win, but certainly not to avoid landslide defeat.

On 1 December the *Daily Mail* announced that the Blairs had chosen to send their son Euan to the London Oratory school. The headline said: 'Labour leader ignores party policy and puts family first.'[58] Blair was due to appear on *Good Morning With Anne and Nick*, where he was forced to defend his decision by saying that he wanted maximum choice for everyone. This was the point of most intense disagreement between Blair and Campbell. Tony and Cherie Blair believed that the London Oratory is a state school and a religious school and that it was the right choice for their son. As Blair had no intention of closing grant-maintained schools he did not believe he was being hypocritical. He also believed that this sent a signal out to parents everywhere that Labour was now on the side of those who wanted the best for their children.

Alastair Campbell saw it differently. He and Fiona are passionate believers in comprehensive education and felt that the decision to send Euan to the London Oratory would have a huge political fallout, as it did. The disagreement between Campbell and Blair was heated. But Blair would not be shifted. On grounds of principle, as a parent and politically, he was sure he was doing the right thing. His decision had a mixed political effect. Some of the electorate thought he was a hypocrite, others welcomed the clear signal that Labour wanted educational excellence, not educational mediocrity. In the event the decision was – just – more electorally helpful than not, but that didn't matter to Blair. He was convinced he was doing the right thing, in every sense, while Campbell remained unhappy about it.

On 12 December I wrote Blair a note confirming the improvement. Public opinion 'is now becoming settled in Labour's favour'.[59] On 15 December this poll report was given electoral substance by Labour's victory in the Dudley West by-election, in which the swing to Labour was 29 per cent – the largest since 1933.

These polls proved Blair's decision on the Oratory had no effect on Labour's ratings.

In my last note of 1994 I wrote that at last we had a message: 'People versus privilege'.[60] Gordon had developed his 'fat cats' attack on the excessive salaries of the privatised utility bosses, and this gave substance to our message. It was not complete, but it was a start. The next twelve months would see us struggling to break through with a broader message encapsulating all that New Labour now stood for.

Winter doubts

In January 1995 the tide of public opinion turned a little. This happens sometimes almost by osmosis: as if one entity, the electorate changes its mind. I wrote a note warning, 'In comparison with pre-Christmas there was less enthusiasm for Labour . . . less anger with the government . . . Tony Blair is not connecting with the strength and immediacy of the pre-Christmas period.'[61] A series of policy confusions, over VAT on school fees, devolution and nuclear energy, had sapped momentum and fostered doubts. The first attack came from Ken Coates, Labour Euro MP, on 13 January: 'This young man [Blair] has not the faintest idea of how socialists think, and does not begin to understand the mentality of the party which he has been elected to lead.'[62] On 15 January Roy Hattersley argued for consensus: 'I have learned, during the forty years since Clement Attlee was Prime Minister, that the party does best when it is at peace with itself.'[63] On 21 January TGWU General Secretary Bill Morris said in a speech that he had seen nothing from Blair which would satisfy the wishes of the trade unions.[64] Blair was being attacked from left and right: different ideological perspectives linked only by conservatism. January also saw the arrival of Blair's new chief of staff, Jonathan Powell, who had been a diplomat in Washington. He added new skills to the operation: he understood government and how it worked and was vital in making Labour's transition to power so smooth.

On 15 February Blair took on the 'One Nation' mantle at a speech at the Newspaper Fund Lunch, and on 27 February Joy Johnson was appointed director of campaigns, media and elections. It was not to be a happy appointment.

By March 1995 the electoral situation had got worse. 'Support for Labour is highly fragile,' I wrote. 'It could collapse at any point . . . commitment to Labour is based on no real knowledge of the party or what it will do. No one has any idea of Labour's policies . . . [Support for Labour] is a leap of faith driven by desperation. This faith could be shattered at any time. It is vulnerable to attack from the Conservatives on the hard economic issues and the usual fears. It is certain that many of these switchers will return to the Conservatives . . . If Labour wins it will be on probation. With these voters Labour has come a long way, but it still has a long way to go . . . Labour is still definitely more of a risk than the Conservatives.'[65]

At an all-day meeting at Chris Powell's house at Fritham on 3 March, I brought all these concerns together. I listed Labour's weaknesses: 'Competence – can Labour really govern Britain? Labour is still feared and will be feared at the election . . . Labour is highly susceptible to negative campaigning . . . deep down people do not really trust Labour on the economy.' Labour will find it hard to win, I argued, because 'the British electorate is probably the most cautious in Western Europe . . . Labour's base is eroding; Labour carries massive historical baggage and deep-rooted fears; changing to Labour is a major upheaval. The Conservatives are nearly always the safer choice.'[66] The most noticeable policy insight of the day was that Gordon Brown and his team were keen, even at that early stage, for a degree of independence for the Bank of England. Ed Balls, Brown's economic adviser, presented these plans to the meeting at great length. John Prescott was not invited to Fritham, and when he found out about the meeting several weeks later he was furious that he had been excluded.

As the electorate started to get nervous about Labour, I became increasingly concerned about our campaigning capacity. Even the Clause IV campaign seemed to have ground to a halt. 'Our campaigning is a bit of a mess,' I wrote at the beginning of the year. 'What was working in 1994 has stopped working now.' This was because of 'policy uncertainty; defensiveness; campaigning gridlock; lack of preparation; a slow start to the Clause IV campaign'.[67] It seemed as if we were losing control of events. By this time – spring 1995 – I was attending Tuesday, Wednesday and Thursday meetings at 8.45 A.M. in Gordon Brown's office in Millbank. A large number of people went to them: Gordon Brown, Labour chief whip Derek Foster, Jonathan Powell, Peter Mandelson, Brown's press secretary Charlie Whelan and policy aide Ed Miliband. The meetings started well, with Brown scouring the news, anticipating Tory intentions and generating an attack or response from Labour. But after a while they became bogged down and cracks started to appear.

Alastair was beginning to get nervous. 'I think we started to have a few problems – things started to get slightly ragged. I think some of the relationships became difficult. I've got to be honest, deep down I had doubts about whether we were going to win. Although I was always miserable and pessimistic, it was also part of my professionalism: thinking of all the things that could go wrong. I had a kind of sense that we were going to lose.' It was true that he could get gloomy. My family's nickname for this was 'the glums'. But he always had the capacity to come through it.

I've always noticed that when things get slightly rocky, when they're starting to get out of control, I know that I can find it within me to get the towel around my head, to work out how to sort it out. On a grander scale that is what Tony can do. Whenever things have gone slightly wrong, when there have been a few days when we're feeling a bit off-balance and not quite so sure what to do, then – and it's often after a weekend, often after a holiday, often after something cataclysmic that brings everything to a head – he will just sit down and instead of him lounging back like he usually does, he sits forward with a bit of paper in front of him and goes through things, one, two, three, four, five. And he will have worked it out and it will be clear. Now I think that is leadership.[68]

Concern was growing, too, about Clause IV. The *Guardian* had reported on 30 December 1994 that Blair had become alarmed about the strength of opposition to its reform, which was true. Blair simply did not have the means to deliver the Clause IV vote in the party at large or even within the NEC.

Sally Morgan, head of Blair's political office in opposition and at Number 10, started to work for Blair at the beginning of 1995:

> From conference to Christmas nothing much happened. There was a general feeling that the thing was drifting and turning against us. Then we took a grip on it, a small group of us. But first of all we had to get the actual [Clause IV] position through the NEC. This took a lot of cajoling and talking. It took a lot of hours. Endless one-to-one discussions between me and them. Bringing them back on board. First of all I had to get them on board to support modernisation, because it had been bounced on them and they didn't know anything about it. They'd had no role in trying to convince the party of it, so we had to win a majority of them over to start being part of the solution, rather than being the opposition.[69]

Margaret McDonagh, General Election co-ordinator at Millbank and now General Secretary of the Labour Party, confirms this view: 'Between October and Christmas 1994, to be honest, everybody's eye was taken off the ball. Nothing happened. There was no campaign. I was rung at home over Christmas 1994–95 and asked to come into the office to organise the campaign, and there was just nothing there. There was no infrastructure. There was no reaching out, getting the message to all reaches of the party, and I suppose for me it was quite an eye-opener about how we all had to work together.'[70]

McDonagh and Morgan, with Anji Hunter and others, put

together a highly effective campaign team that turned the tide. Derek Draper, formerly Mandelson's research assistant and founder of modernising magazine *Progress*, helped with the campaign in the constituencies. Blair began to meet party members in open forum. This type of interactive campaigning – direct contact between politician and voter – is an essential part of representative democracy. It enables politicians to be held to account, and the public or party members to be heard.

On 13 March 1995 the new Clause IV was presented to the party. Its development had been tortuous. Blair's policy unit worked on the first draft from October 1994 to January 1995. This was much shorter than the final version, and David Miliband thought it was pretty good. Most of the drafts were sent to me for comments. When the penultimate draft arrived I panned it, urging Blair to write it himself instead. Matters came to a head one Sunday afternoon with Tony Blair sitting on his bed, Alastair Campbell, Jonathan Powell and David Miliband perched around the room, while Blair's daughter Kathryn's party went on downstairs. In the end Blair wrote it himself, with one line – 'power, wealth and opportunity in the hands of the many not the few' – surviving from the policy unit draft. That was the work of Peter Hyman.

I liked the last and final draft and said so. The main sentence is long, but has power: 'The Labour Party is a democratic socialist party. It believes that by the strength of our common endeavour we achieve more than we achieve alone, so as to create for each of us the means to realise our true potential and for all of us a community in which power, wealth and opportunity are in the hands of the many not the few, where the rights we enjoy reflect the duties we owe, and where we live together, freely, in a spirit of solidarity, tolerance and respect.'[71] This is the essence of what Tony Blair has always believed: individuals should be advanced by strong communities, in which rights and responsibility are balanced.

Blair was also uncompromising on the economy: the new Clause

IV calls for a 'dynamic market economy'; the 'enterprise of the market and the rigour of competition'.[72] It was a massive step forward.

The new Clause IV was adopted by a special conference at Westminster Central Hall on 29 April. The vote for the new clause was 65 per cent. But while 90 per cent of constituency parties had voted in favour, only 55 per cent of Labour's affiliated organisations, including the trade unions (most of whom had not balloted their members) had supported it.[73] This incensed me: either we were a democratic party or we were not.

Despite the success of the Clause IV campaign I was still not happy. In April I wrote to Jonathan Powell that our campaigning needed 'dramatic improvement. Walworth Road is effectively useless as a decisive campaigning machine; there is a lack of follow-through; our opposition research/attack/rebuttal operation is not effective.'[74] During the winter and early spring I took a settled view: Labour was not yet ready. It had to change more. One week before the Clause IV triumph, to date modernisation's finest hour, I sat down and wrote a document. It was called 'The Unfinished Revolution'.

7

THE PROJECT

Winning the battle of ideas

If the period from 1994 until the Clause IV ballot in March 1995 was about electric shock treatment, jolting the party into the future, then that from May until the 'stakeholder' speeches early in 1996 was about giving substance to the New Labour concept.

This was partly a political project: making New Labour a party that could win elections and hold power, which was the focus of 'The Unfinished Revolution'. But principally it was an intellectual project to make choate the ideas, values and principles that comprised New Labour. We had lost two elections, partly because we changed the appearance of what we were without transforming Labour's substance. This time it would be different. New Labour would be a new party, built on firm intellectual foundations.

Tony Blair was obsessed with winning the battle of ideas. He believed New Labour would be nothing, could be nothing, without ideas at its heart. If a political party is not founded on ideas which have the power to dominate the political agenda, it is unlikely to win a convincing or sustainable electoral victory. Ideas matter in politics. Although it is claimed of New Labour that it won by adopting Conservative ideas, what was, in fact, central to

Labour's success in 1997 was a belief among ordinary voters that something was profoundly wrong with the basic tenets of modern Conservatism. People felt society mattered and that society was deteriorating. They wanted to live in more decent, more caring, safer communities, but they needed to know that the price of a decent society was not an inefficient and cost-laden economy. This shift in public mood was as marked as the shift eighteen years earlier away from the state and towards the individual. In both years election results reflected changes in the intellectual *Zeitgeist*. Not just in the pages of the broadsheet papers, but in the homes of millions of ordinary citizens.

By the time of Blair's election as leader I could not claim to have anything approaching a coherent set of political ideas, but I had several guiding principles. I was passionately opposed to Conservatism. Instinctively rooted in the values of compassion and fairness, I was determined to help rebuild Labour as a new party, articulating the hopes and aspirations of a new middle class. I wanted a new, radical politics that would remove poverty but also encourage aspiration, respecting the individual while strengthening the community. Above all, I wanted to help develop a new progressive majority, holding power not just for one election, but for many. It was these principles that had given me the strength and desire to work with Labour for the past nine years and would keep me with it until its victory in 1997.

Blairism

Tony Blair arrived as party leader in July 1994 certain that Labour needed a new political identity. Even in 1992, after the election defeat, he had made this completely clear: 'Labour does need a clear identity, based on principle, not a series of adjustments with each successive election defeat. But the identity should be one for the modern world not a throwback to a romanticised view of the past.'[1]

He was also clear about the political identity he wanted Labour to have. As is well-known, it was deeply rooted in his Christian faith and his experience at Oxford. Here he had been introduced to Peter Thomson, an Australian mature student, by Geoff Gallop, another Australian and a Rhodes scholar. Blair once described Peter Thomson as 'the person who has most influenced me'.[2] Through Thomson Blair discovered the work of the Scottish philosopher John Macmurray, who was Grote Professor of Philosophy at London University in the 1930s. Thomson says of Macmurray: 'I was into this bloke called Macmurray. I think he was one of the most important British philosophers this century. And he was on to a concept of community. He used to say that the noblest form of human existence is friendship, and instead of being on a debt and credit ledger of "If you do this for me, then I'll do this for you," we ought to develop a sense of community where people were committed to the welfare of one another.'[3]

Macmurray's stress on the importance of the community grew out of the English idealist tradition. In the 1880s and 1890s the Oxford philosophers T. H. Green and Bernard Bosanquet inspired a generation of students to understand their experience through the spirit of community. Hegel's notion of civil society, combined with Plato's belief in the ethical nature of citizenship, helped produce a new philosophy which rejected the *laissez-faire* stance of Adam Smith and the individualism of the Utilitarians. In its place stood the concept of community through which the individual could realise himself. The concrete result was a series of Settlement Houses, where Oxford undergraduates taught and mentored deprived communities at the turn of the century. The most famous – Toynbee Hall – was where Clement Attlee's social conscience first emerged (and where I later went to college to study for A-levels in 1968).

The idea that individuals are defined by their relationship to the community, not in isolation from the community, is Blair's grounding idea, his core political insight. As he said at Wellingborough in 1993, 'We do not lose our identity in our relations with others, in part at least we achieve our identity through these relations.'[4]

The point is not that individuals are subsumed within a community and should be dominated by that community, but that individuals can exert an identity only through their relations with others, and that strong communities do not impede the development of the individual – rather, they assist it. This view connects back also to L. T. Hobhouse, the liberal socialist, himself influenced by T. H. Green, who wrote, 'The individual cannot stand alone, but that between him and the state there is a reciprocal obligation.'[5] The relationship between the individual and the community can never be fully resolved, because it is a relationship that by definition is always evolving. What is important to understand is that the relationship is intrinsic to people's existence, and that strong communities advance, rather than constrain, strong individuals. This was Tony Blair's intellectual heritage: not classically social democratic, but every bit as radical. Explicitly linking the individual to the community, implicitly connecting the Labour and Liberal intellectual traditions: a body of ideas destined to remake progressive politics in Britain.

Blair's commitment to the community found full voice during his time as shadow Home Secretary. He made a number of speeches analysing the condition of Britain, the most compelling of which came in the aftermath of James Bulger's murder:

The importance of the notion of community is that it defines the relationship not only between us as individuals, but between people and the society in which they live, one that is based on responsibilities as well as rights, on obligations as well as entitlements. Self-respect is in part derived from respect for others, the notion that we are not just buyers and sellers in some market place, or individuals set in isolation, but that we are members of a community that owes obligation to others as well as ourselves and that depend on others to succeed and prosper. It is easy to deny the idea of community and some may feel unhappy with it. But call it community values, family values, or even spiritual values: what they all have in common is something bigger than me.[6]

Community was vital to Blair, but only part of his political project. The idea of national renewal was also central: of a new national identity for a new era. From the start Blair had wanted to make Britain a renewed and modern country: 'Rebuilding Labour as a strong community, with a modern notion of citizenship at its heart, is the political objective for the new age. Labour must transform itself into a credible vehicle for achieving it. The project of renewal for Labour mirrors that for Britain. What the country wants is what Labour needs.'[7]

The 'Third Way' emerges

Community and national renewal were Blair's defining political ideas, the one being linked to the other. But Blair wanted to go beyond this, to create an entirely new approach to progressive politics, which he called 'new dividing lines'. On 28 January 1993, he made explicit this new approach:

This is a time when the fundamentals of political debate can move. There are new dividing-lines opening up in British politics. In them lie the opportunity for Labour, not just to punish the Conservatives for their mistakes but to establish its own credentials to govern. These new points of definition encompass both social and economic policy, from issues of economic management through to policies on family and crime . . . Let us be clear as to what divides Tory and Labour. It is not that they believe in personal responsibility and we do not, but that we recognise that personal responsibility is more likely to be furthered in a strong and cohesive society.[8]

This approach, which refused to accept the old Conservative dividing-lines and created new ones, metamorphosed in Blair's thinking into the 'Third Way'. It is possible the first use of the term 'Third Way' was by Pope Pius XII in the late nineteenth century, when he called for a third way between socialism and capitalism. But it was Tony Blair and Bill Clinton who re-invented the phrase, both separately developing a new politics that moved beyond left and right. Bill Clinton used the phrase in his State of the Union address in January 1998: 'My fellow Americans, we have found a Third Way. We have a smaller government, but a stronger nation.'[9]

Earlier, in an address to the Democratic Leadership Council in Cleveland on 6 May 1991, Clinton had said, 'People do not care about the rhetoric of left and right and liberal and conservative, and who is up and who is down and how we are positioned. They are real people, they have real problems, and they are crying desperately for someone who believes the purpose of government is to solve their problems and to make progress.' Although he did not use the term 'Third Way', he talked of a 'new choice' that 'plainly rejects the old categories and false alternatives'.[10] And he was not alone in thinking this. The Democratic Leadership Council, an organisation founded by Al From to make the Democratic Party more centrist and mainstream, was also trying to forge a new Democratic politics. In its 1990 New Orleans declaration the DLC continued to press for new, progressive direction: 'We believe the purpose of social welfare is to bring the poor into the nation's economic mainstream, not maintaining their dependence . . . We believe in preventing crime and punishing criminals, not explaining away their behaviour . . . We believe in the moral and cultural values that most Americans share: liberty of conscience; individual responsibility; tolerance of difference; the imperative of work; the need for faith; and the importance of the family.'[11] E. J. Dionne, the progressive political commentator, wrote, 'The "great American middle class felt cheated" by a liberal creed that "demeaned its values" and a conservative one that "short-changed its interests".'[12]

Tony Blair's thinking was entirely complementary to this. While Clinton was advocating a 'new way', Blair was talking about breaking the old left–right barriers. In his leadership campaign notes he made explicit a series of dividing-lines – 'breaking through old left–right barriers'.[13] In his speech to the National Film Theatre in 1994 he rejected the divisions set down by the Conservatives. 'The right were able to pose as the party of the market, enterprise, successful business, low inflation, low interest rates and prudent spending. The political dividing-lines were put in place entirely to suit them.' Blair was anxious to erect new political divides: 'The left-of-centre response should not therefore be to adopt Tory policies. That would be foolish because they have failed. But it should put in place the dividing-lines in better and more accurate places . . . The divide on the market is not that the right believes in it, and the left doesn't, but between the *laissez-faire* market approach of the right and the left's commitment to investment in industry and education . . . On tax the dividing-line is not between high and low taxes, but rather fair and unfair, coupled of course with the central tenet that "tax and spend" questions cannot be divorced from the state of the economy.'[14] A year later, on 30 November 1995, Blair reinforced the point: 'New Labour is neither old left nor new right. We understand and welcome the new global market. We reject go-it-alone policies on inflation and the macro-economy. We stand for a new partnership between government and industry.' He continued: 'We recognise, just as our founding fathers did, the need to pursue the common good, the belief that as individuals we do best in a fair and decent society where we look after others as well as ourselves. This does not represent a choice between self-interest and the interest of others. It is enlightened self-interest.'[15]

The 'Third Way' is a label, but it is also an approach that is rooted in the modernising tradition and in the themes of this book. I sensed in the playground of my secondary-modern school a clash between my soft compassionate values and the harder, common-sense attitudes of my friends. It has always been an intrinsic element of my approach to politics to connect my basic values of compassion and fairness with the understanding that people want to advance themselves with better houses, better holidays, better lives. As I grew older, I learned from direct experience the need to link my commitment to fairness with the imperatives of business and the market. Both were needed in the modern world.

The 'Third Way' appears to be an abstract idea, light years away from the hard lives of ordinary working people. But this is not so. Working people hold instincts that draw from both left and right, but move beyond them both. On a basic level people are tough on crime but supportive of a strong state role in education and health. They want a decent society but understand the need to compete and win in world markets. They want this now, but it is also what people were saying and thinking twenty or thirty years ago. People outgrew left and right long before the politicians did.

These new dividing-lines were a continuing obsession for Blair. His speeches from well before he became leader, his strategy notes, his conversation, were all infused with the need to remake the political map, to put new dividing-lines in place.

Blair had built the basis of a coherent intellectual approach based on three defining ideas – the community, national renewal linked to party renewal, and new dividing-lines, later to become the 'Third Way'. Each of these were eventually articulated in the new Clause IV. But despite this progress, the real work of rebuilding Labour had only just begun. Ideas were crucial, but so was building an election-winning and power-sustaining political machine.

The political project

The first pressing need of the project was therefore to turn new Labour from brilliant concept to concrete reality. This was the point of my document, 'The Unfinished Revolution', a graphic and sometimes raw account of the changes Labour had to make to become a party of government capable of winning not just one election but many, dominating the twenty-first century as the Conservatives had the twentieth. The document was a war-cry for total modernisation.

'The Unfinished Revolution' was written on 23 April 1995 and was sent to only a very few people. It was never leaked. What was leaked to the press was a shorter, summarised version, which also had a restricted circulation. Its full title was: 'The Unfinished Revolution: Winning Power, Sustaining Power, Transforming Britain'. It started with an introduction that is a modernising credo: 'Labour has not just to win the next election: it must win a working majority; it must have a project and policies that will transform Britain over an eight-year period; it must have a campaigning machine that will sustain Labour in power; it must become a party of sufficient structural and ideological coherence to support Labour in government, without splitting and without sabotaging. It must be aiming to achieve in the next century what the Conservatives have achieved in the last . . . New Labour is still a party in transition: midway through its revolution.'[16]

I had in mind Anthony Seldon's *The Conservative Century*: 'The Conservative Party's very pragmatism and adaptability will allow it to overcome the severe internal and support problems it faces in the 1990s and will in all probability ensure that the cycles of Conservative dominance will be repeated well into the twenty-first century.'[17] I was determined this would not happen – the next century would be Labour's.

I argued that the real tests for Labour lay ahead. 'Labour is always fighting the battle in hand, not the battle that is yet to come. For the great majority of the last ten years Labour has been comfortably ahead in opinion polls, but at decisive moments Labour has been found wanting. Labour wins the battle of the moment, but fails the ultimate test.' There were three measures by which to assess Labour's preparedness for the battle ahead: first, 'the state of the Conservative Party in 1979, the last time an opposition party won an election in the UK'; second, 'the state of the Clinton campaign in 1992, the last time a major progressive party won power from opposition'; and third, 'the likely state of the Conservative Party in 1997: the enemy that we will face when it matters, not the one we face when it doesn't'.

Labour fell short on all these measures:

> New Labour is not yet a cohesive, integrated political party sharing the same political ideology. In reality New Labour is a new party created within the structures of the old, like a butterfly trapped within its own chrysalis. This problem will become painfully apparent at the 29th April [Clause IV] conference, when the 30 per cent who were balloted will be for Blair, when around half the unions will be opposed. 30 per cent trapped within 70 per cent.
>
> New Labour does not have the flexibility, adaptability, capacity for innovation . . . that is the hallmark of a successful political organisation . . . Labour does not yet have a political project that matches the Thatcher agenda of 1979, nor will be able to sustain Labour in government and transform Britain . . . New Labour is behind Clinton in almost all aspects of campaigning and campaign preparation. In addition, Labour must expect a Conservative recovery just before, or soon after, the next election.

Labour had to move on. It must complete its revolution. And to do so it needed a revolution in its structures: 'The new party must become the whole party. New Labour must escape from the 30 per cent/70 per cent trap. In the short run the union proportion of the conference vote should be reduced . . . In the long run Labour has to become a genuinely one member, one vote party. That is the only ultimate future for Labour.'

I added a recommendation which was to become highly controversial: 'Labour must replace competing existing structures with a single chain of command leading directly to the leader of the party. This is the only way that Labour can become a political organisation capable of matching the Conservatives. It will be more effective, and in a one member, one vote party, more democratic.' This offended everybody. It was in part a response to my short-term concerns about campaign organisation, but at root the point was much bigger than that: I felt then, as now, that only a unitary system of command could give Labour the clarity and flexibility it needed to adapt and change at the pace required by modern politics. This seemed to me to be a key element in the speed and success of Conservative adaptation in this century. Conservative leaders had always had a powerful capacity to direct their party. Labour's structure had become too diffuse, with power shared between the NEC, the PLP, the conference, the unions and the constituency associations.

With that in mind, I believed all Labour's organisational structures should be transformed. 'Within the context of a new unitary command structure, the organisation must become flexible, responsive and innovative. It needs fewer people but better people; it needs flatter management structures; it needs a new culture rewarding risk and excellence; and it needs a new building.'

Labour had to revolutionise its policies: 'We must develop a Blair political project and a Blair policy agenda that is sufficiently bold, radical and robust to be capable of both sustaining Labour in government and transforming Britain.' This meant we needed a 'definitive Blair/New Labour document that matches and beats the "Right Approach" [Margaret Thatcher's policy paper of the mid-1970s] by spring 1996'. And we needed 'a policy agenda in place for conference 1996 that is more radical, more modern, more innovative than anything the Conservatives offer, and anything most of us currently envisage'.

Finally, Labour needed a revolution in its campaigning: 'The TB campaigning operation has been effective and successful. It has been well supported by the GB attack on tax and trust and excess pay. But the wider campaigning operation is simply not equipped to fight and win a competitive election in 1997. Walworth Road is effectively useless as a decisive campaigning machine at the national level; there are competing campaigning power bases; there is an enormous lack of trust; there is a lack of strategic preparation for initiatives, and when they are made there is a lack of follow-through: our rebuttal/opposition research operation is not working.' My solution was to focus all campaigning through the leader's office: 'There must be one ultimate source of campaigning authority, and it must be the leader . . . The operational heart of the campaign should be unambiguously established in the leader's office.'[18]

Other recommendations in the 26-page document included the suggestion that the daily media-management meeting be reconstituted and held in the leader's office, chaired by Jonathan Powell. This advice was wrong, and Blair rightly ignored it. Gordon Brown continued to chair the daily meetings throughout the campaign. I was being too purist: I wanted a unitary system of command, and that was the end of it. The system we developed was messier, but worked in part because of that. Blair was not interested in straight lines on organisation charts. He wanted the best talents at his disposal and he wanted those talents to work together, whatever the cost. This made the process more difficult but produced a better outcome, and his instincts were vindicated by the effectiveness of the campaign and the eventual result. In my quest for Leninist simplicity I had missed the bigger point.

With that one exception, I believe every word I wrote was correct and I would retract none of it. On 24 April I wrote to Blair, 'I have written a document called "The Unfinished Revolution", which spells out the challenges facing us and what we need to do to meet them. It is fairly bold and highly sensitive.'[19]

Peter Mandelson phoned me at home a few days later, wanting a summary to read. He needed it very quickly and I dashed off a two-page synopsis in less than an hour. For this summary, and only in this summary, I added the words: 'Labour is not ready for government: it needs to complete its revolution.' I sent the summary to Peter Mandelson, Jonathan Powell and Alastair Campbell. That was the last I heard of 'The Unfinished Revolution' for several months.

The intellectual project

'The Unfinished Revolution' was a private enterprise, written by me and me alone. It was the product of obsession, which explains its rawness, but sometimes in politics directness and obsession are essential to achieve change. I was determined not to dilute 'The Unfinished Revolution'; I wanted to write something with an explosive power capable of changing events. However, it was about structure and politics, and not ideas. And winning the battle of ideas was central to everyone, not just Tony Blair himself.

For the rest of 1995 this was my central preoccupation, as it was other people's. I spent much of my time talking to, and working with, David Miliband, Blair's head of policy. David is the son of Ralph Miliband, who wrote what proved to be an influential text for much of my generation: *The State in Capitalist Society*, which was one of the most widely read books among politics students when I was at Sussex.

Ralph Miliband must have been a wonderful father as well as a brilliant polemicist, because his sons Ed (who works for the Chancellor) and David are two of the most decent, kind and intelligent people you could wish to meet. David is always courteous and behaves with personal integrity; he does the right thing in all circumstances, public or private. He is fearsomely clever and easily grasps the post-war intellectual terrain, understanding in depth all the major current policy issues.

For much of the period – from the party's approval of changing Clause IV in April 1995 through Blair's stakeholding speech in January 1996, and until the launch of Labour's early manifesto, 'New Life for Britain', in July 1996 – David and I were engaged in constant dialogue. What is Blair's defining insight? How do we reconcile modernisation and community? Is it possible to conflate both concepts into one unifying idea? How do we reconcile populism which is for a majority of the people – most, but not all – with concepts of community and one-nation which appear to include everyone? David and I were obsessed with building a new, election-winning politics based on principle. Many of our conversations took place in a cafeteria in the House of Commons. We would sit and talk about New Labour and Blairism as the coffee machine hissed and gushed steam and we talked, I am sure, much hot air.

In this tortuous way we worked towards our new political project. Slowly Blair was giving substance to his ideas, fleshing them out. By the end of it, he would have five priorities for government based upon his analysis of the problems facing Britain: lack of a first-class education for the majority of children; community disintegration leading to crime and pressure on families; the poor performance of the economy, and the unstable relationship between government and business; a centralised and secretive political system; and isolation and lack of influence overseas.

Blair made several big speeches in the early part of 1995 that pushed the project forward, gradually making his dividing-lines clearer. On 22 March he gave his *Spectator* lecture, fleshing out his beliefs about the community, stressing the need for responsibilities as well as rights.[20] On 22 May he delivered his annual Mais lecture which set out how macro-economics dedicated to stability needed to be combined with an energetic and radical micro policy. The speech was suffused with new dividing-lines:

> As in the 1970s, we now need to recognise that a new approach is needed . . . a macro-economic framework to keep inflation low and stable is even more important now than was said in the 1980s. Far from being an alternative to Labour's long-term investment strategy, controlling inflation is an essential part of it . . . Too much reliance has been placed on deregulation alone to improve the supply side of the economy. There is an active role for government – particularly in, though not confined to, the improvement of human capital . . . Much of the current debate on taxation and spending is parochial and sterile . . . The key question therefore becomes not how much to spend, but what to spend it on, and how to improve the performance of the economy . . . I came into politics because I believe that a fair society and a more efficient one go hand-in-hand. By providing long-term economic strength and by raising the standard of education and opportunities of our citizens, we can achieve the stronger and more cohesive society I want to see. Social aims without economic means are empty wishes. By uniting the two we can build a better future for all our people.[21]

The War Room at Millbank Tower during the 1997 General Election campaign.

Peter Mandelson in the War Room, April 1997.

John Prescott on the hustings during the 1997 campaign.

Gordon Brown as shadow Chancellor, in his office at Millbank.

Margaret McDonagh, General Election Co-ordinator, at Millbank.

Philip Gould and David Bradshaw (right) in the War Room during the 1997 campaig

FRED JARVIS

Peter Mandelson and Charlie Whelan at Millbank, overlooked by the 'Demon Eyes'.

TOM STODDART/IPG/KATZ

Tony Blair and Alastair Campbell on board the campaign bus during the 1997 election.

The final Sunday: Blair reviews the papers with David Miliband (top),
Anji Hunter (middle) and Alastair Campbell (bottom).

Tony Blair flying from Sedgefield to London after the polls had closed; during the flight it became clear that Labour had won a massive majority.

Tony Blair and Cherie Booth at the Royal Festival Hall, 2 May 1997.

The new Prime Minister in Downing Street, 2 May 1997.

In each area of economic policy there was a new dividing-line, a new way forward. Here was another early 'Third Way' speech. Blair was rewarded with a *Financial Times* leading article, which said: 'There is now a coherent vision of what a left-of-centre government should do,' consisting of 'low inflation, fiscal prudence, increased competition, and long-term investment in education and infrastructure'.[22]

Later in the year, at the News Corp Leadership Conference on Hayman Island in Australia, Blair made even more explicit his new dividing-lines and commitment to a 'Third Way'.

> My case therefore is that neither old left nor conservative new right can provide the framework for the solution of the central question. If – and I accept this is the real challenge – the left can liberate itself from outdated preconceptions, strip its essential values out from the means of their application relevant to another part of their history, then a modern left-of-centre is the best able to provide security amid change. Let me make that case and in doing so demonstrate also why this new left-of-centre is not simply an accommodation of the right, but how it tries to move the political debate beyond the old boundaries between left and right altogether.[23]

Blair was feeling his way towards an explicit 'Third Way' philosophy.

The Conservatives blink

On 22 June 1995, John Major resigned as leader of the Conservative Party. I was in a meeting with Gordon Brown, Tony Blair and others when we heard. The moment it was announced, Blair asked us to leave so he could consider the new situation quietly. Gordon Brown and Alastair Campbell stayed, and later Peter Mandelson joined them. Blair hates big meetings at the best of times, certainly at moments of crisis. Joy Johnson – the party's communications director – was enraged at being ejected from the meeting: she wanted to be at the heart of things.

This was a moment of potential danger. Apart from economic recovery, the one anxiety I had about our election chances was that the Tories might ditch Major and elect a new leader. It seems that this was Major's feeling also, and so he embarked on the Doomsday scenario of seeking re-election. He challenged his chorus of internal opponents to 'put up or shut up'. To his amazement, Secretary of State for Wales John Redwood did 'put up'. Although losing Major could not have had the electoral impact of ditching Thatcher, Michael Heseltine as Tory leader would have posed a much more formidable threat. What Major did was the worst possible course of action for the Tories. When he announced the election the Conservatives' position strengthened – people welcomed the idea there was going to be a change. They couldn't believe that the Tories would re-elect Major. Their mood held throughout the campaign but the moment he *was* re-elected, it collapsed. The election had promised change but delivered the status quo, and the impact was almost all bad for the government. In a focus-group report of 6 July, I wrote, 'People felt used, and they felt manipulated . . . some thought the whole thing was a con, a charade, that Redwood had been put up to it . . . their resolve to vote Labour had been stiffened. One said: "I was nervous about voting Labour, but now a third of the Conservatives have voted against their own leader, so can I."'[24] What looked good in the short term, in the long run made things worse. It was a classic Major miscalculation.

It seemed that the Conservatives might be starting to crack. The night of Major's victory I had dinner with Maurice Saatchi, to celebrate the publication of a novel by his wife, Josephine Hart, which was being published by my wife, Gail. Maurice was cock-a-hoop about the leadership election and the result, which he had clearly been closely involved with. I told him he had just won the election for Labour. For a moment his confidence flickered and a trace of doubt crossed his face. This contrasted with his attitude the night Britain was forced out of the Exchange Rate Mechanism. Despite the appalling defeat this represented for his party and our country, he had been brimming with confidence. 'We will be able to keep Norman in for as long as we want,' he said, a comment which was probably as good an omen as any of the hubris that would be the Tories' undoing.

The project under pressure

August and early September saw the New Labour project come under pressure. On 11 August Richard Burden, MP for Birmingham Northfield, wrote in the *New Statesman* that he was 'ashamed' of the Littleborough and Saddleworth by-election (in which Chris Davies, the Liberal Democrat, won with less than a 2,000 majority over Phil Woolas, the Labour candidate). Peter Mandelson and I had both been heavily involved in this campaign and had hit Davies hard on his record, particularly on his attitude to the liberalisation of drug use. Burden went further, criticising the centralised power of the 'inner sanctum': 'I thought that kind of approach to political leadership went out of fashion when the Berlin Wall came down.'[25] His protest set off a period of carping about the style of Blair's leadership.

Then, on 12 September, a summary of my document 'The Unfinished Revolution' was leaked. The first indication I had that something was wrong came when my pager buzzed at 5.50 P.M. on 11 September: 'Call Alastair urgently.' This meant trouble. When I phoned him, he said, 'It's a bugger, this.' My heart sank. 'They have got one of my memos,' I said, thinking, 'Pray God may it not be "The Unfinished Revolution".' Alastair said, 'The *Guardian* has got the worst one. They've got "The Unfinished Revolution".' I just said: 'Oh, my God.'

When we had finished talking I got a copy of the memo out. The long document I had did not match the description Alastair had given to me. There was no reference in it to Labour not being 'ready for government', the phrase he had mentioned, and I assumed that the *Guardian* had not got a copy of the document but had been given a verbal briefing on its contents. I had momentarily

forgotten the synopsis I had written. The BBC journalist Peter
Kellner phoned from Brighton, where the TUC was meeting.
Blair was speaking to the conference the next day. The timing
could not have been worse. Kellner was going to cover the leak
for *Newsnight* that evening and wanted to confirm details of what
was in the memo. Inadvertently I misled him because I had the
long document and he was working from the summary.

The moment you are the centre of a bad news story, you become
a person apart. Even though people are helpful, an invisible glass
wall separates the person who has caused a problem from those
who are trying to contain it. This has happened to me on three
occasions: 'Jennifer's Ear', 'The Unfinished Revolution', and the
leak of the 1997 election War Book, which I had largely written.
Peter Mandelson phoned up and offered support. But I waited for
Newsnight like a condemned man. Kellner came on in Brighton,
being as supportive as possible but bursting with the excitement
of a good news story. My picture popped up on screen, and
then words from my memo appeared. I still thought it was a
briefing, as the words Kellner was using didn't fit my document.
I went to bed feeling sick, got up at five the next morning and
bought the *Guardian*. 'LABOUR'S SECRET STRATEGY', read the
splash. 'Party not ready for government. Call for central control by
Blair.' The front-page lead by Seumas Milne read: 'A confidential
strategic plan drawn up Tony Blair's closest advisers warns that
New Labour is not ready for government and calls for a centralised
command structure under the personal control of the leader . . .
The report, passed to the *Guardian* by a senior Labour source,
was written by Philip Gould, the Labour leader's campaigns and
strategy consultant. It is understood that Peter Mandelson, the
Hartlepool MP and Mr Blair's most trusted political confidant,
collaborated in the report.' This was untrue, but the attempt
to suck Peter into it indicated that he was possibly the target
of the leak rather than me. Colour pictures of Campbell, Blair
and Mandelson were splashed across the page.

Inside was the synopsis in full. I had forgotten I had written it, but the *Guardian* had it. The *Guardian*'s political correspondent Patrick Wintour detailed the damage the memo would do to Tony Blair: 'Disenchanted left-wing activists are likely to see it as confirmation that Mr Blair has a near-presidential agenda.' He described it as 'intemperate even for an extremely private document'.[26] I waited for the first news of the day on the BBC. Sure enough, the memo was the lead story. I watched, stunned, then went into work, knowing I would be doorstepped by television cameras. I did my best with them and went into my office to hide. Throughout the day the news coverage continued unabated. I received a stream of telephone calls with conflicting advice from various Labour officials: 'Do a doorstep' – David Hill; 'You shouldn't have done that' – Alastair Campbell. I was told that John Edmonds – General Secretary of the GMB trade union – was so rude about me in one interview that his comments could not be broadcast in full.

The next day was worse. The *Guardian* headline ran, 'SECRECY ROW SHAKES LABOUR'. Now I was getting really worried. For a moment it did look as though the New Labour project might be falling apart. Mandelson phoned and said, 'We are going to have to fight hard to get out of this one.' Inside the *Guardian* I was described as 'rumpled' and 'naïve', and not in it for personal publicity.[27] This was certainly true; I was hating it. The story was in all the papers and making headlines in some of them. *The Times* was sniffy about the memo,[28] but the *Independent* was supportive. Its leading article – 'From Molotov to Mandelson' – read, 'Mr Gould is right, of course. And not only is he right, but it is encouraging that the Blair entourage seems to recognise these problems.'[29] I don't know who wrote that article, but I thank them. I don't know either – and nor do I care very much – who was the senior Labour source who leaked the summary of the memo, although I have my strong suspicions. I know that it was not one of the small number I sent it to personally, and I suspect it was stolen off someone's desk. This was not something to be proud of.

Tony Blair went to Brighton and, typically, turned the incident to his advantage. Campbell recalls, 'For a few hours it was a bit of a disaster, but all the media attention meant that by the time we got to Brighton people wanted to hear what Tony had to say. Tony always has a glint in his eye at these things – I am the same – I really like these big moments. The media think you are going to lose it and in fact you go there and stick it up them. Tony did a big, ballsy, barnstorming, off-the-cuff speech. We'd gone down to Brighton with people saying we were going to end up 5–0 down, and in fact we won 2–1.'[30]

Despite this, I sent a note of apology to Tony; he telephoned on Wednesday and was supportive: 'You said things that were true; it will work out in the long run.' But he was critical of my 'unfit to govern' comment. This is typical of Blair: I had just given him the worst two days since he was elected leader and he phoned me up to offer support. This quality isn't often found in politicians.

The affair hadn't quite blown over yet. I was told that the *Guardian* had a second memo, which they were going to leak before Tony's speech at conference. They didn't do it, but it made conference week uncomfortable.

The young country

Despite the summer turbulence, David Miliband and I, along with other people, were still trying to develop New Labour thinking, now focused on the 1995 conference speech.

On 18 August I wrote a note, 'Winning the Trust of the Centre Without Betraying the Left', in which I argued that we should reclaim the centre: 'Building a governing coalition does not just mean putting roots down on the left. It also means reclaiming the centre.' This meant being explicit about our centrist position: pushing the Conservatives to the right; pushing the Liberals to the margins and the left. But it also meant 'giving ourselves a real anchor on the left' by 'taking our "for the people" positioning and establishing it as the grounding principle that divides us from the Conservatives'. I summed it up in one phrase – 'Labour's new coalition: anchored in the left, owning the centre, underpinned by a commitment to govern for all the people.'[31]

A week later I wrote another document, called 'What is New Labour?' I answered that it was the response to two challenges: the need to build a new Britain, and the need to build a new model of social democracy. Renewal was straightforward – we needed 'to build a new Britain with a new identity and a new self-confidence: our economy; our society; our politics all must be renewed'. The complicated part was rebuilding social democracy, which I argued was under threat because 'vast areas of our lives that were the traditional province of government are now being served by market solutions . . . global markets minimise the space for government intervention . . . demographic trends work against social democracy'. I asked, 'How far must modernisation go to meet these new conditions? Should it reform and modernise the existing model of social democracy, or should it reconstruct a completely new model?' Predictably, my answer was that New Labour must construct a completely new model of social democracy. 'Halfway solutions linking old models don't work,' I wrote. 'New Labour must be positioned in the centre.'[32]

However, we were still short of compelling concepts. It took Blair himself to provide them. Earlier in the year I had been chatting to him at a party Anji Hunter gave at her house in the country. It was a lovely summer's day and we were talking in the garden. As I spoke to Tony, my daughter Grace and Tony's young daughter Kathryn held hands and trailed behind us, talking about God knows what. After the normal niceties about how we needed to do more to win, Blair said he wanted to base his conference speech around the concept of 'one nation'. He had mentioned this as a theme in his leadership campaign notes, but I had forgotten. I did not like the idea much, nor did anyone else – it seemed too abstract – but he would not let go of it and as the conference speech came closer it became clear that this concept met the moment. It was centrist, and in origin it was a Conservative concept. Benjamin Disraeli first used the idea in his novel *Sybil, or, The Two Nations*: 'Two nations between whom there is no intercourse and no sympathy . . . THE RICH AND THE POOR.'[33] But the one-nation philosophy is as relevant now as it was in the 1840s. It articulated Blair's concept of community in a new way, which it linked to a new patriotism. But it left unanswered the problem of renewal. This had to wait longer and only in the final hours before his conference speech that year did he develop the idea of 'young country'. These two concepts, 'one nation' and 'young country', were the pillars of his 1995 conference speech. In my view, this was the strongest of Blair's pre-election conference speeches. Certainly it meant the most to me. It started with a passage linking Blair's political beliefs to his Christian principles: 'The simple truths. I am worth no more than anyone else. I am my brother's keeper. I will not walk on the other side. We aren't simply people set in isolation from each other, face to face with eternity, but members of the same family, the same human race.'

These were also my most basic beliefs. He then talked directly to his and my generation: 'Let me tell you about my generation. We grew up after the Second World War. We read about fascism, we saw the Soviet Union, and we learned to fear extremes of left and right. We were born into the welfare state and the NHS, and into the market economy of bank accounts, supermarkets, jeans and cars. We had money in our pockets never dreamed about by our parents . . . We enjoy a thousand material advantages over any previous generation, and yet we suffer a depth of insecurity and spiritual doubt they never knew.'

This too I found very moving. A final key passage linked the values of community to the necessity for renewal:

Let's build a new and young country that can lay aside the old prejudices that dominated our land for generations. A nation for all the people, built by the people, where old divisions are cast out. A new spirit in the nation based on working together, unity, solidarity, partnership. One Britain. That is the patriotism of the future. Where never again do we fight our politics by appealing to one section of the nation at the expense of another. Where your child in distress is my child, your parent ill and in pain, is my parent, your friend unemployed or homeless is my friend; your neighbour my neighbour. That is the true patriotism of a nation.[34]

In a few sentences Blair brought together his core values, his commitment to community, his demand for renewal, and finally his patriotism. Although incomplete, these were the beginnings of a new progressive approach. The next day the press recognised that Blair was redefining social democracy – perhaps not quite the Bad Godesberg Congress, but potentially as seminal for British progressive politics.

Stakeholding: a first attempt at synthesis

New Labour was beginning to take real shape: a new constitution, big themes, positioned in the centre of British politics, pushing the other parties to the margins. But we still lacked one big, unifying concept.

I was determined to integrate Labour's one-nation message with its economic message. David Miliband and I spent weeks batting ideas back and forth on the theme of one-nation economics, and came up with a string of concepts. In a note on 12 November 1995 I proposed the theme: 'Efficiency and society are not mutually exclusive, but mutually dependent. For New Labour, society is a benefit, not a cost. The alternative view is put with brutal clarity by Maurice Saatchi when he says: "The choice is between the Conservatives, who are cruel but efficient, and Labour, which is caring but incompetent." We have to say that "cruel is efficient" is a fundamentally wrong view: "Efficiency needs society".'[35] I hardened this line on 9 December: 'The central insight of one-nation economics is that social capital and social cohesion enhance market efficiency and economic strength; social division and the depletion of social capital impair market efficiency, weaken economics.'[36] Here Miliband and I drew heavily on Francis Fukuyama's *Trust*, and the Harvard political scientist Robert Putnam's work on social capital and civic society. We needed a concept to unite the belief that efficiency and society are complementary. We needed to synthesise these apparent opposites and made some suggestions: 'One-nation economics; social capitalism; stakeholder capitalism; a cohesive market economy.' David Miliband wanted a 'stakeholder Britain that combines one-nation society with one-nation economics'.[37]

On 8 January 1996 Blair made his famous 'Stakeholder Economics' speech in Singapore. It burst through the media. I believed it pulled together many other themes and ideas that had been emerging not just over months, but years. Crucially, it linked the values of community to the imperative for efficiency: 'We need a new relationship of trust not just within a firm but within society. By trust I mean the recognition of a mutual purpose for which we work together and in which we all benefit. It is a stakeholder economy in which opportunity is available to all, advancement is through merit and from which no group or class is set apart or excluded. This is the economic justification for social cohesion, for a fair and strong society.'[38]

Alastair Campbell describes the circumstances of the speech:

The stakeholder speech was one of the most important. [Blair] was delivering it at the High Commissioner's Residence in Singapore. Jon Sopel from the BBC was the only journalist travelling with us. On the plane down we wrote the stakeholder speech and I had a real sense, as did Tony, that this speech would make a real impact. The night before I contacted two local stringers from the *Telegraph* and the *Guardian* who were there and I briefed them on the speech, telling them that this was the big idea. All I was trying to do was get the speech up overnight, to alert the London media to it. I then got Sopel in for a briefing, and it led the *Today* programme. But the trouble was that Tony was making the speech

at a lunch to an audience of just forty local movers and shakers at
the High Commission, which was meant to be private. This clearly
could have been a problem, so in the end I persuaded Sopel that
he could film the event on the condition that the cutaways did
not expose the smallness of the event. We had a backdrop made
up, with Tony standing up on the podium with a lectern and
microphone in a room no bigger than a kitchen.[39]

This speech immediately gave New Labour its defining idea,
but unfortunately it ran into difficulty just as quickly: it was open
to attack as being corporatist, just when corporatist solutions
appeared to be failing in Europe and non-corporatist Asian tigers
were starting to roar. Gordon Brown did not like stakeholding as
an economic idea. He felt it was a hostage to fortune, exposing
Labour to the risk of attack on grounds of social costs, and he
queried the sense of adding to our strategic burden.

In its way it was a classic 'Third Way' speech, spelling out
the need to mesh the impact of economic globalisation with
the rights of social citizenship. The language of stakeholding
may have withered, but the new approach underpinning it has
prospered.

On 29 January Blair developed his political philosophy further,
in a speech in Southwark Cathedral in which he gave full voice
to his deepest beliefs, returning, without mentioning him, to the
philosophy of John Macmurray. In a way this speech saw the
closing of the intellectual circle – Tony Blair, the Labour leader,
articulating the ideas of Tony Blair, the student:

I start from a simple belief that people are separate economic
actors competing in the market place of life. They are citizens
of a community. The identity of an individual comes through
his relationship with others. We are social beings, nurtured in
families and communities and human only because we develop the
moral power of personal responsibility. Our relationships with and
commitments to others are not add-ons to our personalities. They
make us who we are. Notions of mutuality and interdependence
are not abstract ideas: they are facts of life.[40]

In little more than a year, New Labour had moved decisively towards becoming a coherent political project. We had become the one-nation party: a party anchored in the centre, a modernising party determined to rejuvenate Britain, determined to fuse efficiency with community. We had set out new dividing-lines laying the basis for a 'Third Way', now arguably the dominant political approach throughout the world. Much had been done, and there was more still to do. But it was time to start winning the election.

8

REASSURANCE, REASSURANCE, REASSURANCE

Still unsafe

Nineteen ninety-six was the year we had to gain the voters' trust. Reassurance became the public face and strategic anchor of our campaigning as Blair, Brown, Campbell, Mandelson and I struggled privately in meeting after meeting to hammer out our campaign strategy and message, in what sometimes appeared to be an endless, frustrating process. And as we fought to reassure them, the public, faced with a steady drip of controversies from a series of shadow Cabinet members, including Clare Short on tax and Harriet Harman on education, began to lose faith. The year-long battle to keep their trust began with plans for the 'Road to the Manifesto', through its launch, the pledges, conference, and was only won when, finally, we reassured them that Labour would not raise income tax.

During 1995, while we modernised the party, we had still not persuaded the public that we had changed completely. Labour faced the same old problem: lack of trust. In the first memo he wrote to Tony Blair, on 8 June 1995, Stan Greenberg, who was helping Labour on a committed but unpaid basis, spelled out the need for reassurance. 'New Labour is defined for most voters by Tony Blair's willingness to take on and master the unions,' he wrote.

> In the focus groups the switchers spoke of little else, because this is what qualifies Labour as a plausible electoral option. Blair and his party were seen to control the unions; the unions no longer seemed to control Labour. But voters need relentless reassurance. Almost a third of Conservative defectors to Labour worry about excessive union influence. The women defectors in the focus groups mostly shifted back to the Tories after a fairly moderate attack on Blair focusing on union influence. For the Liberal defectors, the reining-in of the unions allowed them to feel comfortable with a Labour vote.
>
> 'Change' voters are turning to Labour, not because of Labour, but because of their disaffection with the Tories. Our main task is to make sure that is as easy a choice as possible. This means reassuring these voters that Labour is 'safe', even though most of these voters are inclined to see Labour as 'dangerous'. The Labour leadership needs to reassure these voters again and again.

He listed a number of problems that needed to be addressed if Labour was to continue to be seen as 'new'. The major concern was taxation: 'Labour is not trusted on taxes: 42 per cent of the electorate believes they will raise taxes for everyone. 57 per cent of Conservative defectors believe Labour will betray them on taxes.' And also important, still, was what Greenberg called 'the basics': 'One of the pre-occupations of Old Labour was a preoccupation with what the public often saw as "bizarre" issues: homosexuals, immigrants, feminists, lesbians, boroughs putting their money into peculiar things. Voters think that a serious party that represents the ordinary person focuses on things that matter to people in their lives, "addresses things that concern us".'[1] After ten years of reform and modernisation, and despite the great strides taken by Blair, Labour was still a prisoner of its past.

This is what many commentators never understood. They saw

a big Labour lead, thought Labour was certain to win and therefore accused us of being too cautious. But the truth was more complicated. Conservative defectors and centrist, floating voters were always nervous about Labour, regarding it as potentially unsafe. This was true until the very last days of the 1997 election campaign. And it was only Labour's strategy of relentless reassurance that turned opinion-poll leads into a real majority.

Tony Blair had no illusions about the fragility of the electorate's trust in Labour. Polling towards the end of 1995 had shown voters shifting back towards the Conservatives and looking at us more critically. I reported on Conservative-to-Labour switchers in focus groups who were saying: 'Tony Blair is all right, but what about the rest of the party?'; 'They don't agree with him; they are biting their tongues, biding their time'. 'People want to be convinced that the party genuinely supports its leader,' I wrote. 'Many of these voters are now facing the real prospect of a Labour government, and this is scaring them.'[2] At one of our weekly campaign meetings at the beginning of January 1996 I asked Tony what the heart of his strategy was. His reply was emphatic: 'Reassurance, reassurance, reassurance.' From then until election day, we would fight to convince the country we could be trusted.

The endless grind of meetings

If 1996 was about trust, it was also about endless meetings. Early in the year we moved our daily media meetings to Millbank Tower, which was now creeping open for business. I was based there full-time from the beginning of January; Peter Mandelson started to move in gradually soon after.

But the weekly meetings with Tony Blair, Gordon Brown, Alastair Campbell, Peter Mandelson, Jonathan Powell and others, myself included, continued in Blair's office in the House of Commons. Blair had wisely ignored my advice in 'The Unfinished Revolution', and kept the same basic structure in place: Gordon

Brown in overall charge of the campaign and of strategy, Peter Mandelson in charge of campaign management and Millbank.

These meetings and the campaigning process they exemplified were never easy. For the entire pre-election period the process of strategy development and campaign management was frustrating, difficult and strained. This was partly because of relationships. The leadership election had led to a breakdown in trust between Brown and Mandelson, which sometimes improved, sometimes worsened. And from time to time other relationships suffered, which was inevitable given the pressures of the situation.

But there was a second, deeper reason why the process was so frustrating – the participants had different views of the campaigning process and all these had to be resolved.

Gordon Brown is constantly looking to anticipate the news and use it. He thinks that modern campaigning is news-driven or it is nothing; that the political landscape is constantly changing, always fluid – what is down now will be up soon. He thinks that you need permanent momentum. There is no end-point; you don't arrive; you are sailing constantly in a changing sea. Peter Mandelson can see the chaos, but wants to create order out of it. He wants defining landmarks, clearly delineated campaigns, events that can be planned and executed with consummate professionalism. He wants impeccable, perfect order. Alastair Campbell wants boldness: the audacious, unpredictable coup – the *Sun* coming out for Labour; Alan Howarth defecting.

Tony Blair combines intellect with instinct. He is forever seeking clarity: the single insight that explains a situation. He demands strategy constantly: his principal explanation for any failure is lack of strategy. But he also relies powerfully on his instincts, and he will back them in defiance of conventional argument. Once, after a long and convincing case against a controversial decision about funding the unions was put to him, and everyone in the room had agreed such a decision would be untenable, Blair looked at us all and said, 'But why can't we just do it?' He trusts his common sense and damns the consequences. Over the reform of the union 'closed shop', over Clause IV, over choosing his son's school – he knew what was right and did it, despite myriad conflicting voices.

I was seen as the voice of the electorate, and usually the voice of pessimism, and I was obsessive about the need to develop and repeat consistent messages. I wanted us to agree a campaign rationale and stick to it.

This makes a potent brew for any campaigning meeting: several different and often competing perspectives, and a time horizon that moved from the next day, or even the next hour, to the next year or longer. No wonder the meetings often seemed to go nowhere. But gradually, over time, a strategy and message were agreed and developed. It was tough, but we got there. I began to understand that good campaigning is, by definition, a struggle. There is no right way to do it, no one perspective that is always correct. Politics is so complicated you see from all sides of the mountain. You need conflicting views, different insights. And you need a process that is interactive, challenging, sometimes competing. This is easy to understand now, but it was hell at the time. Alastair Campbell describes the process:

> He [Blair] used to come in sometimes with a clear idea of what we were going to do that day, sometimes not. In terms of devising strategy I would say he relied, in terms of who he needed in the permanent orbit, on Gordon, Peter and myself. He relied upon you [Gould] for a strategic input which he valued for the fact that you were slightly outside, not in the maelstrom of activity the whole time. But we used to have these conversations that you just felt were going round and round in circles, because we were all saying different things, but we were pretending we were saying the same things. I think you were right, we did have different views. But in the end we were complementary. In the long build-up to the campaign I felt physically and mentally like a racehorse. I felt that we were testing the whole time, training, trying things out, building up stamina, finding out the things that could be rejected and working out the things that had to be developed, and by the time we got to the election – I feel we timed everything about right. Now you could argue about where all that came from, but

I think probably it came from all those hours. If you had a camera in there people wouldn't have dreamed of voting for us – it was ridiculous, circular conversations – and yet there was discipline in the end. We were honing all the time. But at times it was bloody grim, because you felt the election wasn't coming, because Tony and I were constantly telling each other that the Tories were doing well – partly it's a defensive thing, we had to build them up the whole time so we could get a proper sense of how we could do them in.[3]

If this pre-election process was grim for Campbell, it was worse for Mandelson, dealing with the tensions of the relationships. 'It was a nightmare, just a nightmare. It was a fruitless, demoralising, agonising, dreadful waste of energy – truly draining. It was like moving with a huge boulder dragging behind you.'[4] Nineteen ninety-six was exhausting. Progress was slow and often painful, but gradually we moved ahead. And we did address, in turn, all the big strategic issues. In the end it was Tony Blair who kept the show on the road. He trusted everyone in his team, and they all trusted him. The problem was that the electorate did not yet trust us.

'The Road to the Manifesto'

Lack of trust was not only a problem for Labour. The legacy of betrayal by both major parties meant politicians generally were not trusted by the public. The voters were reeling from Conservative U-turns on tax rises; the September 1992 devaluation of the pound; the 'Back to Basics' hypocrisy; Conservative misinformation over the length and depth of the recession. All were combining to induce an almost unshakeable contempt for the political process. This was one of John Major's most damaging legacies. Typical comments about the Conservatives from members of focus groups made this sense of betrayal vivid: 'cutting the throats of the home-owner'; 'fallen down on their promises'; 'I own a small business. They cut me off at the knees'; 'I opted to own my own council house. I ended up losing it'; 'They used working-class people'; 'They were always for the rich – we just fell for it'.[5] It was clear that the Tories had broken their contract with the British people. They had lost the people's trust, but in doing so had undermined public faith in politics and politicians generally.

I was becoming certain that the only way we could persuade the electorate that Labour as a political party had *really* changed was to take our manifesto to the party and ballot them on it. This would have two consequences. First, it would persuade the electorate that New Labour was real – that it was not just about Tony Blair, but a political project supported by the majority of the party. This would solve what Blair called the 'head and body' problem: that Labour's head, represented by him and other modernising leaders, believed one thing, but its body, represented by the party, appeared to believe another. And second, a ballot, as a real event and not just a rhetorical device, would help break through the wall of cynicism surrounding the voters. They were not impressed by words alone, they wanted actions and preferably actions involving conflict and opposition. Only then would they believe something had actually happened.

I first jotted down this idea in a note on 3 December 1995: 'We need a major new policy-based initiative in the spring. Words alone are not enough. They won't break though electoral scepticism and resistance. The best way of moving from words to action is to take our policy positions directly to the party, and win their support. It will kill the sense that the party and leadership are in a different place, and it will bring back the sense of crusade and mission we had with Clause IV.'[6] Three days later I wrote to Tony Blair directly: 'TB needs to go beyond rhetoric to action. This means, for example, taking a policy programme or statement directly to the party, overcoming opposition, winning their support.' Without conflict, I said, 'people are simply not convinced'.[7]

Later in the month I went to Blair's house for a polling meeting with Stan Greenberg. Blair at home is almost always the same: relaxed, friendly, casual. His children wander in and out of meetings. Once, at a weekend strategy meeting at his house, a series of loud and disconcerting noises emanated from a computer game which Euan was playing in the corner of the room. This was annoying other members of the meeting, but Blair didn't mind. He just ignored it. Sometimes Kathryn would wander in, asking for help with her homework. Cherie would often be there and would always be warm and supportive. Despite coping with the kids, coping with her job, coping with Tony, she still always finds time to be friendly. With Cherie there is no side: she is genuinely the person she appears to be.

On this occasion, Tony heard the polling and we discussed what we could do to bring the head and the body together. He had long been committed to direct consultation with the whole party membership and he decided – I think there and then – that balloting the early manifesto was the way forward. He had been searching for a mission for 1996, and this would be it.

On 19 December I wrote a longer end-of-year document – '1996: The Year Labour Changed Politics'. It was built on two premises: that the public still thought Labour a risk, and that Labour had 'to face and overcome a wall of cynicism'. I warned that Labour was not connecting with the electorate:

> In part this is because our positive messages in 1995 lacked the demons that give fire to our party reform messages: unions; nationalisation; old left. But it was mainly because our message now is not going beyond words to action as it did through [the abolition of] Clause IV. 'Modernisation of Labour' the message became 'modernisation of Labour' the fact. This illustrates a central truth of modern campaigning: that the scepticism of the electorate is now so advanced that words alone are not enough: message must be meshed with action.
>
> This means that we need a new approach to politics in which we actively engage the electorate, not talk to them as passive recipients of a message.

I called this new approach 'Partnership With the People'. Its centre-piece would be April–May onwards, 'when Labour takes its policies to the party and the people. The rhetoric of "partnership with the people" becomes reality. Labour takes its policy statement to the party and the country, not just listening but challenging and engaging. New Labour will achieve in 1996 with policy what it achieved with Clause IV in 1994.'[8]

'Partnership With the People' quickly became a central focus for our political strategy. In a note written in mid-January Tony Blair set out his strategy for 1996. He would write strategy notes every six weeks or so. This one said, 'We want to end by summer/autumn in the following position: a draft manifesto – "Partnership With the People" – which is effectively our contract with Britain. This should be a challenge to the party and to the country. It must be the campaign around which we hang policy, communication and maintain momentum. It should allow us to resolve any remaining policy positions; and be, in certain areas, both provocative and controversial. Besides "Partnership With the People", our attacking and positive messages should be honed, disseminated to the party and PLP and understood in the country.' He continued: 'We must definitely be New Labour, not old. A further raft of internal reform, if necessary, should be put together. Energy. Ideas. Vitality. The future not the past. We must be in the centre ground: the real one-nation party.' His note went on to outline New Labour's key themes and the 'attack on the Tories, depicting them as the party of the privileged few, not of ordinary people'. By hand Tony added: 'Most of all a complete and compelling dissection of their economic record. This is paramount.'[9]

It is difficult to believe the hours we spent discussing this note. Before we could move on to the plan we had to agree the note, and we never could. Sometimes we would get tantalisingly close, but we never quite made it. The note is not agreed even now, but it did contain two of the three defining themes of our election campaign – the future, not the past; the many, not the few – and the hours spent discussing strategy paid off in the end. We did – just about – arrive at an agreed and tightly honed set of messages, but the process was endless, and is probably still not completed. At a meeting to discuss the referendum for an elected assembly in Wales after the election, the Prime Minister decided to give the participants a short seminar on the long and tortuous process of message development before the election campaign. 'It took hours and hours and hours of discussion to get it right,' he said. Long pause. 'And I am not sure we ever really finished it, or ever got it completely right.' I groaned. Alastair put his head in his hands, moaning, 'No more, no more.' This illustrates a central campaigning insight: the process is as important as the end-point. Often discussing a note is as important as the contents of the note itself.

The note also gave the green light to 'Partnership With the People', which Alastair turned into 'The Road to the Manifesto'. This was agreed by the NEC on 27 March 1996, and announced to a surprised press conference immediately afterwards. It was breaking new ground for a party to put its manifesto (even in early form) to a plebiscite of its members. But the idea had its roots in the very first note Tony wrote in his leadership campaign, when he called for ballots of the whole membership on policy issues. 'The Road to the Manifesto' was a series of policy statements and initiatives. Robin Cook was delegated to write it, and David Miliband used to meet him regularly to discuss its contents. Sometimes I would attend too. We met in Robin's Parliament Street office and went through a long and involved drafting process. I had no responsibility for policy, I dealt with message and thematic structure. In the end it was largely Blair who wrote it, working from Cook's draft.

The document, launched on 4 July 1996, was called 'New Life for Britain', a title invented by Alastair Campbell as he sat with me in a bar on a long beach in Majorca. As usual Alastair was sitting in the shade complaining about the sun. On holiday he is a creature of habit, liking to sit in the same place, wearing the same clothes, drinking a huge mug of tea. But he does write brilliant political lines – and very quickly.

The night before its launch Peter Mandelson, David Miliband

and I were up most of the night proof-checking 'New Life for Britain' in a design studio besides the Thames. We also did some last-minute rewriting. The most difficult decision was whether or not to include stakeholding as a section heading. Stakeholding had fallen out of fashion somewhat, but for reasons of continuity we felt it better to keep it in.

'New Life for Britain' was Labour's early manifesto, but it had another important element: after some struggle, it contained Labour's 'five pledges', later to become the centrepiece of our election campaign.

The pledges

The pledges had no single point of origin. They emerged over many months, following literally scores of meetings with politicians and dozens of focus groups. In one sense they emerged almost by accident. For about a year I had been taking out to focus groups rough summary copies of what I estimated rival manifestos would say. I anticipated the Conservative pledges would be: a referendum on the EU; no social chapter; no minimum wage; 'two strikes and you're out'; a grammar school in every town. Labour's, I guessed, would include more bobbies on the beat, cutting waiting lists and reducing class sizes. The Conservative one would be populist and right-wing; Labour's would contain very simple, very basic claims. After a while I noticed that the simpler the claim, the more powerful the communication. People wanted smaller promises that they could believe in, not larger ones which seemed incredible. I also found that if we said how the promise would be paid for, the power of the pledge was enhanced enormously. As our policy developed, we tested and re-tested it, with rival manifestos, until gradually the core promises began to emerge.

Although this was interesting, it was not taking us anywhere. The true parent of the pledge was Peter Hyman. Hyman had been a research assistant for Gordon Brown, then Donald Dewar, before working for Tony Blair. He was a communications zealot;

obsessed with campaigning. He thought David Miliband and I lived in a world of abstract indulgence: stakeholding, one nation and renewal were all well and good, but they would butter no voting parsnips. We needed messages that were stark, clear and populist. Above all, we needed an offer: something concrete, tangible and desirable that we could hold out to the voter to match the Tories' promise of tax cuts. He was obsessed with this. For weeks he could talk about little but 'the offer'. Hyman says: 'Up against tax cuts it was not good enough to say merely your health and education may get better, you may have a more decent society. We needed to give people an offer. We needed to get people to say, "I want that; I will go out and vote for that," and "I can see what it is, and it is achievable, and it is costed".'[10] Hyman's relentless pursuit of populist communications paid off. In the election campaign it was us and not the Tories who had the simple messages and an offer people really wanted to hear.

Hyman and I both knew, therefore, that to break through the barriers of distrust we had to offer the electorate a simple contract: elect me and if, in five years' time, I have not delivered, then sack me. In developing the pledges there was constant interplay between Peter, myself, David Miliband and Matthew Taylor, head of policy for the Labour Party. The actual wording took weeks to agree, and Hyman spent hours developing alternatives. He recalls:

First of all, there were many more than the five final pledges which we dropped either for good policy reasons or because the shadow Cabinet member wasn't happy defending them. Although the pledges seemed very simple, we needed to come at them from a hell of a lot of different angles: would outside experts think they were do-able? Were they do-able for the costs? Would the Tories attack them in the election campaign? Would they just fall apart? We had endless meetings in Tony's room, with Gordon and you [Gould] and Peter, going through exactly the arguments, what was feasible, could you get waiting lists down by more than that, was thirty and under exactly the right wording. There were a hell of a lot of considerations.[11]

The pledges were tested exhaustively. Four were agreed fairly early on: class sizes, jobs for the young, fast-track punishment, and cutting waiting times. The fifth was the problem. I tested several options: the university of industry, help for small businesses, cutting the starting rate of tax to 10p, a pledge that we would be tough on the economy, or just having four pledges instead of five.

I strongly favoured a pledge promising toughness on the economy. In a memo of 6 June 1996 I noted, 'The last ten groups have all shown a marked increase in economic optimism.' I also wrote that MORI had recorded a massive 19 per cent increase in economic optimism among switchers to Labour: 'There is no doubt that economic optimism among our core target is rising rapidly and is slowly affecting their vote.' I argued that 'The Road to the Manifesto' document should offer 'tough targets; financial discipline; no uncosted promises; prudence tax restraint . . . there is a case for a genuinely bold and startling manifesto commitment in the money area . . . a kind of mini-Clause IV for financial competence . . . Even if this is not done, the fifth pledge must be a money pledge. 10p [starting rate of tax] is our best offer but financial prudence is even more important.' Polling confirmed these instincts. 'The economic-prudence pledge provided massive reassurance, almost physical relief,' I wrote. 'Every respondent selected this as their first pledge.'[12] People wanted to be able to trust Labour on the economy.

I was pushing at an open door. Gordon Brown was obsessive about financial prudence and his adviser Ed Balls drafted the last pledge. This was not easy, and took dozens of drafts, but it was finally agreed: 'Labour will set tough rules for government spending and borrowing; ensure low inflation; strengthen the economy so that interest rates are as low as possible.'[13] Inelegant, possibly, but a quantum leap from where we had been in 1992, and a crucial building-block for election success. We also ensured that each of the pledges included details of how it would be paid for, which was as important in reassuring the public as the pledge itself. People took our promises much more seriously when they knew we could pay for them. Reassurance, reassurance, reassurance.

As early as June 1996 we were testing a pledge not to raise income tax, but Gordon did not want to show his hand until much later. For the later election pledge card we included our commitment not to increase income tax, and we inserted in the advertising a promise to hold a referendum on membership of the European single currency. This eliminated another attack the Tories were planning to use. An increasingly Euro-sceptical Tory party would no longer be able to accuse Labour of 'selling out' British sovereignty. Tony Blair was slowly reappropriating Labour's patriotic heritage.

The pledges worked better than anything else I have ever tested in politics. Nothing else came close. They worked because they connected immediately to people's lives; because they were relatively small, which gave them credibility; because they were costed; and because they were an explicit contract between the voter and Tony Blair. The fact that it was he who made the promise, he who offered the contract, added enormously to their power.

But although people loved them, politicians and media commentators did not take to them easily. The idea met with enormous resistance. Politicians just didn't see their point. They thought they were too small, too insignificant to base an election campaign on. But they missed the point: to the voters they represented substantial and real improvement in their lives. The fate of the pledges hung in the balance for weeks, until eventually it was decided to give them a go. Even then they were called 'early' pledges because the politicians wanted to make clear that other promises would be made later. They were finally turned into a credit-card-sized pledge card, with a picture of Tony Blair on one side and the pledges on the other. The card also included the crucial words: 'Keep this card, and see that we keep our promises.' Margaret McDonagh had first seen a card like this when she was working on the Clinton campaign in California. It was used to support 'Proposition 186' in a state referendum on health care. It had the four benefits of voting yes on the back. Peter Hyman went on to develop the card idea, and BMP made a mock-up. McDonagh still keeps the 'Proposition 186' card in her wallet.

The pledges survived months of relentless attack by the Conservatives, who were unable to break them down. Now they are central to government. They are being used by the people and the media to hold the government to account, which is how it should be. When Labour meets the pledges, a contract will have been kept, trust in politics restored a little.

Some people may be horrified that it required so much research to find out what people wanted, but they misunderstand. For election after election Labour has offered better hospitals, better schools, more jobs, but it has never been believed. The issue is not the promise, but *making the promise credible*. What research revealed was that the public wanted smaller, more concrete pledges, they wanted them costed and they wanted them presented in the form of an accountable contract. The result was more honesty, less fudge, more trust. Much of the media sneered, but it was the electorate who showed common sense and maturity, and I am glad they were consulted.

The pledges were included at the end of 'New Life for Britain'. Peter Hyman was furious. As far as he was concerned, they were the only real point of the document and they were buried at the back. He was right, and his fury continued unabated for some days. Peter was often furious, which is a good thing – good campaigners need passion and anger, and Peter is a very good campaigner. His desk was close to mine at Millbank. It was always surrounded by monstrous piles of discarded documents and memos. He would rush back and forth feverishly between my staff and the advertising executives with new ideas, new strap-lines, new visuals; that is, when he wasn't hurling derogatory comments at the latest Tory spokesman defending the indefensible on the news.

In its way 1996 was the year Labour changed British politics. The pledges have established a new pattern which will not be broken: hard, concrete, accountable promises that are, effectively, a binding contract with the electorate; manifestos not just agreed by a few politicians in smoke-filled rooms but agreed by the party. This is the way of the future, it is the way trust in politics will be restored. But in 1996 trust in Labour was still not secured. Labour had had other problems on the home – and school – front.

'Why should we trust you?'

Harriet Harman's decision to send her son to the selective St Olave's school in Orpington, Kent came after Tony Blair had chosen to send his sons to the 'opted-out', grant-maintained London Oratory. That Blair sent his children to a grant-maintained school was an issue, but not as big a one as commentators made out. In any event the controversy missed the point. As Blair put it later, it was not an eleven-year-old boy who had destroyed our education system, but a seventeen-year-old government. Some people thought he was being hypocritical, but many, including – crucially – most of our core group of previously Conservative voters now considering voting Labour, thought it demonstrated a commitment to parental choice in education. What the public thought or said on this matter did not influence Blair. He and Cherie wanted their children to go to religious state schools, and the one they and their teachers thought would be best was the Oratory. Blair knew the choice would be unpopular, but he was determined to do it anyway. This is a vital part of his character as a politician: he follows his instincts, and damns the consequences. And his instincts are, by and large, the people's instincts. He connects to a rich vein of empirical common sense that has always been central to the British people. Once his mind is made up, almost nothing can change it. Alastair Campbell and others warned him that sending Euan to the Oratory could lead to media attack, but he would not be swayed. He thought it was the right thing to do.

Harriet Harman was in a different position. One of her children was already at the Oratory, which was just within the bounds of public and party acceptability, but sending her second son to a grammar school crossed a different line. Opposition to grammar schools was an act of faith for Labour, and the idea of selection at eleven was anathema to almost everyone in the party. Many, probably a majority of even Blair's office, thought she was wrong.

When the decision was announced on 19 January it led to a media firestorm. I was in Blair's outer office the evening that media and party baying was at its height. The atmosphere was all gloom. Enormous pressure was building for Harman to go. She had little support except from Peter Mandelson, myself and a few others who felt that if she went, New Labour lost. A signal would be sent to every voter in the land that Labour punishes parents who want the best for their kids. Blair asked me in to see him. We were alone. He sat on his sofa, tie loosened, feet on the table. Should she go or should she stay, he asked. It was a rhetorical question: he had already made up his mind. I said, 'She has to stay. We cannot allow old Labour to win.' This was his view too, and nothing, not the combined forces of every paper and every member of the PLP, would shift him from it. He had said he would not compromise and he meant it.

The focus groups were bad. In one meeting, on 22 January 1996, all eight members of the group thought Harriet Harman had done the right thing as a mother, but six out of the eight thought she had done the wrong thing as a politician. As Harriet remarked poignantly, 'It's easier to go through the eye of a needle than be a good mother and a good politician.'[14] I wrote, 'The damage to us is: honesty; trust; sincerity.' There was immediate damage to Blair: words like 'insincere' were being used to describe him, which had not happened for a long time.[15] I phoned Blair at home to tell him. He always insisted on getting bad news immediately.

He was philosophical and said simply, 'Why can't people get a sense of perspective? This is just a mother sending her son to a state school.' The findings did not influence his course of action one jot. He had decided to stand by Harriet, he believed that to be right and that is what he did.

I thought we had been feeble in our response to the attacks. I wrote on 28 January to Blair and Brown, 'There are a lot of lessons to be learned from last week, but the most immediate was that once again, under real pressure, our message crumpled and we failed to retaliate effectively . . . If we do not fight [the continual Tory attacks], they will work and once again the electorate will awake blinking on a Friday morning not quite believing that they have elected them again . . . We are not tough enough, not hard enough, not brutal enough.' We had to fight back, accusing them of trying to hide their failure as a government behind spurious attacks on Labour front-benchers, I said, suggesting the following line of defence: 'As a parent Harriet Harman is making the best of a bad system; in government she will make sure all children get the best. What Britain needs is more politicians who face the real dilemmas of daily life, because they are best able to change the lives of ordinary people.'[16] But this was a week too late. I was too slow, we were all too slow. We failed to get our retaliation in first.

The spring continued to go badly for us. There was persistent sniping about Blair from disgruntled Labour MPs; growing resentment over the power of his office and 'spin-doctors'; some fierce and well-directed attacks by Major on whether New Labour would be 'tough on hypocrisy, tough on the causes of hypocrisy'.[17] Then, finally, came the resignation of Joy Johnson as Director of Campaigns and Communications. The only stories in the press were about splits and policy U-turns. By the beginning of March we were running into very choppy water. I wrote a note on 3 March called 'Fighting Back: Step by Step', trying to bolster confidence. Most of the campaign team were getting disheartened. Alastair Campbell was fed up. 'We are not in tailspin,' I said, 'we are not falling apart; we have taken a hit; and we are going to win.' And: 'Perseverance: we have to just battle this bad patch.'[18] The knock-on effects of Harriet Harman's decision had still not gone away a month later, when I broke the period down into two phases: 'Phase 1: Pre-Harman – very positive: mood almost matched Clause IV period. Stakeholding positively received. Phase 2: Post-Harman – breakdown in trust. TB not listened to with the same confidence. New Labour: just another party.'[19]

And while the voters continued to question whether they could trust us, we did even more to unsettle them, Clare Short was reported as saying on GMTV's *Sunday* programme on 14 April 1996 that 'under a fairer tax system people like her would pay a bit more tax'.[20] This shot through the electorate like a forest fire. On 1 May I summarised two groups conducted in Watford. 'These groups confirm the shift in mood against Labour since the Clare Short tax controversy,' I wrote. 'When prompted, everybody knows about the remarks of Clare Short. Several people believed that Clare Short had said that people earning £30,000 would be clobbered. The issue here is about trust as much as tax levels.'[21]

The voters were also confused by our announcement on 19 April that we were considering the abolition of child benefit for children over sixteen. I attended the meeting at which it was agreed that this was the correct thing to do: it sent out a tough, strong message. But it was a risk. I supported the decision completely and still do. Gordon Brown thought it essential to make and demonstrate tough choices. Unless we did this we would never be taken seriously on the economy. It was the right decision, but it was not popular.

By mid-May the voters were worried about splits within the Labour Party. In a note to Peter Mandelson I wrote: 'We are now in the most serious situation that we have faced since Tony became leader. If we continue to implode and disintegrate we can still lose.'[22] The first real evidence of economic improvement in June created a further increase in doubts about Labour: on 6 June I warned that these were two sides of the same coin – as things got better, people were more aware of the risk of Labour.[23] Opinion polling confirmed this trend. On 29 July Stan Greenberg wrote a report on a Labour Party poll conducted the month before: 'The survey does suggest some slippage in Labour's support over the last three months. On party identification Labour has lost 3 per cent of its net advantage . . . intense negative feelings about the Conservatives are down sharply: "cool" sentiments have dropped from 60 per cent to 53 per cent . . . There was also weakening of support within the Labour voting block, and that too is worth paying attention to. Intense support has fallen off somewhat.' The drop-off of Labour's vote and intense support was concentrated in 'volatile segments of the electorate', he said – voters under forty-five, and women. And central to the weakening in Labour's support was the strengthening economy: 'The changing perceptions of the economy are real, substantial and important strategically. An increasing number of people believe the economy is strong and a declining number describe it as weak.' This was a 'pretty dramatic change from April: an 18 per cent swing towards those thinking the economy is strong'.[24]

On the same day I reported on two focus groups among Conservative switchers to Labour, which confirmed a continuing trend back to the Tories:

The economy has improved a little . . . people are frightened of losing the small gains they have made. In effect they are saying: 'Now that we are off the floor and things are a little better, we have something to lose, and Labour may put that at risk' . . . This small improvement colours their view of Labour. They are now far more likely to talk about Labour's past. They are convinced Labour failed economically in government. They think interest rates and taxes soared. That Britain under Labour was a bleak, strike-ridden place. Almost a kind of dark age for Britain. (This is not an exaggeration: a myth has developed about Labour in the past.) This makes a future Labour government a risk. Everybody in these groups thought taxes and interest rates would go up under Labour.[25]

The local election results on 3 May were good but not spectacular: Labour's share of the vote was actually down two to
three points, the Conservatives up, and the Liberal Democrats
marginally up. But the changed political weather was not going
to deter Blair. The next day, in an interview with the *Independent*'s
Tony Bevins, he positioned Labour right on Conservative turf:
'Politics will alter dramatically in the next few years. But I cannot
foresee exactly what shape it will take. There is no doubt that
if we continue to occupy the centre ground, if we become the
one-nation political party, if we attract support from the centre as
well as the centre-left, then we will be able to benefit significantly.
Many Conservatives have probably got a lot more in common with
us than with those who have taken over their own party.'[26]

On 15 May Blair dismissed talk of splits as 'tittle-tattle'.[27] But
it was clear that this was a period of potential danger for New
Labour. The economy was improving, doubts about Labour growing, 'better the devil you know' was becoming almost a mantra in
the groups. We were vulnerable in the spring and early summer,
but the situation was to get worse. In high summer Labour came
under massive internal attack and the Tories moved in for the
kill. The battle was joined: would the New Labour line hold?

Demon eyes

'SHORT FLAYS BLAIR'S "DARK MEN"' ran the *Guardian* headline
on 8 August. 'Clare Short, the controversial shadow Cabinet
minister, last night accused her leader's advisers of jeopardising
Labour's chances of victory at the General Election and threatening its existence,' the article began.[28] Her accusations had been
made in an interview with the *New Statesman*, in which she focused
on 'Blair's misguided strategy'. She described his advisers as 'the
people in the dark', whose 'obsession with media and focus groups
is making us look as if we want power at any price'. She said,
'These people are making a terrible error. They think that Labour
is unelectable, so they want to get something else elected, even

though really it's still the Labour Party. This is a dangerous game which assumes people are stupid . . . They are saying, "Vote for Tony Blair's New Labour. We all agree that the old one was absolutely appalling and you all know that most of the people in Labour are really the old one, but we've got some who are nothing to do with that, vote for us!" One, it's a lie. And two, it's dangerous.'[29]

It wasn't an isolated attack. The week before, Joy Johnson had attacked Tony Blair in the *New Statesman* for his use of 'stilted language', like 'young country', 'the British dream', and 'stakeholding'. She continued, 'For New Labour it is time to drop the "new"' and start 'speaking the language of the people'.[30] On 28 July Ken Livingstone, writing in the *Mail on Sunday*, compared Labour under Blair to 'the old Soviet Union'.[31] Roy Hattersley joined in, writing in the *Observer* on Sunday 11 August that 'Miss Short's attack rightly or wrongly reflected what a lot of rank and file members are thinking . . . There are immense dangers in dismissing all that happened before the spring of 1994 as based on an outdated ideology which had nothing to do with New Labour.'[32]

The Conservatives reacted immediately with the most famous advertisement of the campaign. It appeared on the same Sunday in the *News of the World*, the *Mail on Sunday* and *Sunday Times*, and portrayed Tony Blair with red, demonic eyes, alongside the caption: 'One of Labour's leaders, Clare Short, says dark forces behind Tony Blair manipulate party policy in a sinister way.'

I heard about Clare Short's interview and the 'Demon Eyes' advertisement while I was on holiday in France. I thought the interview was a problem, but the Conservative advertisement an over-reaction. When Alastair Campbell came to visit us on holiday I put a copy of it outside so he could find the house. Alastair was not in good humour. He was having the holiday from hell, having given up his lovely house in Flassan for a cheaper one further north, which was noisy and had its entry barred by two dangerous dogs. On top of that, Fiona was ill. He was furious about everything.

He thought the advertisement was effective, and said Tony was worried about it. He recalls, 'The holiday from hell was very difficult. It was the low point. I felt that you can do so much, but there are plenty of people out there who can undo it.'[33]

Back in London, Peter Mandelson was having to cope with it all. From France, I imagined him padding round his Millbank office, shoes off, phone glued to his ear, barking orders with his eyes fixed on the TV. His immediate instinct, which was the right one, was to react and not to ignore it. His strategy was to twist the advertisement from being a depiction of the dark and sinister forces behind Tony Blair, into portraying Tony Blair as satanic, which was incredible and would rebound on the Conservatives. For this he needed a bishop to condemn it. Peter Hyman discovered that the Bishop of Oxford was outraged by the advert and had put out a strong quote condemning the Tories for accusing Blair of being the devil. Hyman faxed it to Campbell, who said it was the one thing to make him smile that holiday. The advertisement was immediately rebranded on our terms. Not sinister forces manipulating Blair, but the desperate Tories labelling Blair as the devil. Ironically, Saatchi's now say that the eyes behind Blair were supposed to be Mandelson's, but he was too quick for them to be able to establish this.

Mandelson's strategy was high-risk. It made the advertisement famous, handing millions of pounds of free publicity to the Conservatives, and was considered internally and externally to be a mistake. Many in Millbank thought we should have kept quiet about it. It led *Campaign* magazine to give 'Demon Eyes' the award for advertisement of the year. But Peter was right and his critics wrong. Blair manipulated by sinister advisers ran the risk of being believed if the Tories were able to press it home; Blair as the devil did not. It positioned the advertisement to the British people in a way that was implausible and offensive. They felt a line had been crossed, and it began to make them angry: if all the Conservatives could offer the British people was an advertisement depicting Tony Blair as the devil, then they were not worth re-electing.

At the time, the advertisement appeared to be the high-point for the Conservatives and Saatchi's in the campaign, but in fact it was the point at which their advertising and communications strategy was exposed as terminally flawed. They should never have conceded New Labour was a reality, they should have been apologising not attacking, and they should have claimed the credit for the economic recovery.

In France, Alastair, Fiona and his children moved in with us for a few days to escape the dogs. The mood was strange. Peter Mandelson was engaged in trench warfare with the Tories, but for us it was the final interlude before war began. We discussed the conference speech a little, but did not get very far. All Alastair wanted was to get back, to get into the fight. He was intensely frustrated about his aborted holiday and the situation at home. He spoke to Tony Blair once or twice and to Peter Mandelson every couple of days. I was calling Mandelson often, but when you are so far away it is hard to give useful advice. Peter felt under extraordinary pressure, dealing with a serious crisis while almost every other senior politician and campaign member was away. Once or twice his voice sounded strained, although he was clearly relishing the fight.

At our house in France that summer, though, the mood was glum. Alastair wanted to leave early and at five one morning he drove off with his family to start the journey home. There was a sadness about his departure, a sense that before us was the battle to decide all our futures. After years of waiting, it was upon us.

'Better the devil you know'

When I got back, posters were up spelling out New Labour's pledges. They were not inspired but they did what was required: they helped to brand us as the positive party, the Tories as negative and destructive. Mandelson had had a controversial summer, but he had been strategically skilful. The first twelve groups I did after

the holiday showed 'a strong and probably strengthening resistance to the government'.[34] Labour had survived the assault. The
conference that year was disciplined and brilliantly orchestrated.
Margaret McDonagh did a superb job. Blair's speech received an
extraordinary response. The theme of 'Labour's Coming Home'
tapped cleverly into the feel-good mood engendered by England's
soccer success in Euro '96 but, more to the point, fused directly
with my sense that Labour had finally reconnected to the people
it was created to represent. As in the previous year, the leadership
was not defeated once. This was due to the extraordinary work
of John Cruddas, assistant to Tom Sawyer, Pat McFadden, from
Blair's political office, and Sally Morgan, who were in charge of
political relations with trade unions and the party. They have a
fixed way of working which is to say, perhaps three months before
conference, that every vote will be lost, before gradually conceding
that we have the chance with the odd one or two, before eventually
winning every vote. John Cruddas is the master of this: he turns
pessimism into an art form. The Conservatives also had a good
conference, with John Major looking relaxed in a shirt-sleeved
question-and-answer session, and the lead narrowed. In a post-
conference evaluation document I wrote, 'The Conservatives are
recovering on the back of the economy . . . but they will not
recover to victory. There is a vast constituency of voters out there
who are sick of the Conservatives, want change. They will see the
Tories out.' I wanted to make people perceive the Tories as a risk:
'Transferring the burden of risk to them is the key to victory.' We
had to build a 'devastating fifth-term campaign . . . A Major fifth
term must not be allowed to become a comfortable option.'[35]

Late autumn saw doubts growing again about Labour, and
also about Tony Blair. This may have been a consequence of
the 'Demon Eyes' attack, but more probably it was just that he
had now been leader for over two years and the electorate had got
used to him. We had always been concerned about this. The long
three-year period leading up to the election gave time for voters'
normal cynicism to return. This was most pronounced among

women: on 28 November I wrote, 'Women are far more nervous of Labour, appear to have less idea of what we will do, are more sceptical of our promises . . . The problem for us is that they see the election in terms of a single dimension: a contrast between the Tory record, and the threat of a Labour government.' I argued that the answer to this was to pose the threat of a Conservative fifth term, for when women were confronted with the prospect of a Conservative fifth term they were 'shocked or dismayed at the prospect of them getting back. The change in the dynamic produced by this shift to the Tory future is remarkable. Women who were drifting back to the Tories came straight back to us. This is not just a question of fifth-term fear, it is an issue of incumbency. As long as we allow the re-election of the Tories to be a gap in the voters' minds, we are allowing ourselves to be painted as incumbents once again, they escape as the challengers.'[36] Findings like this led to a series of meetings arranged by Sally Morgan and Anji Hunter, including Liz Lloyd from the policy unit, that focused specially on the concerns and anxieties of women. This linked to other initiatives including the 'Winning Words' campaign of Clare Short, Patricia Hewitt, Deborah Mattinson and Carmen Callil that tried to develop language that women could relate to. Women were always a central priority in the campaign. This paid off: the gender gap was closed.

Although I wanted to use fifth-term attacks, Tony Blair and Gordon Brown were uneasy: they wanted to fight the Tories on their record, what they had done, not what they might do in the future. Blair was also beginning to feel that we needed to become more positive and less negative in our campaigning. His speech to the Commonwealth Parliamentary Union in South Africa, fleshing out his conference speech idea of the 'decent society', was part of that positive programme.[37] Most of all, he was concerned about the tenor of our advertising, being prepared to accept the attacking posters of the forthcoming spring, but wanting to move ultimately to using positive advertising. His instincts told him the nation wanted it. We seasoned campaigners used to scoff at him for this, but in the end we came round to his point of view. Brown also held a fixed campaigning belief that every attack had to be balanced by a positive initiative – otherwise the media would not use it and the voter would resist it. Negative messages needed positive messages to make them work. The Conservatives would have done well to heed this advice. In the end we compromised. We would start the year with the launch of a positive policy document and then move into a major fifth-term attack.

Thus the new year began with the launch of a new policy document, 'Leading Britain into the Future', and our fifth-term attack based around VAT on food, with a poster showing an egg being smashed. Both Blair and Brown disliked this poster and were relieved when it came down. Even Alastair Campbell lost faith in it. But it worked. It pushed the Tories on to the defensive on tax; Kenneth Clarke was forced to come out and rebut it. At the same time the Tories attacked us with a new advertising campaign, using a blood-red tear, and slogans like 'New Labour, New Mortgage Risk'. But it was lame – light-years away from the potency of 1992's 'Tax Bombshell'.

In the event none of this mattered to the electorate. It passed them by completely. On 9 January I wrote, 'There was almost no awareness of the campaigning initiatives of Monday, Tuesday, Wednesday. Even when shown coverage of these events people were unable to recall them.' However, a sense of '"Better the devil you know" was widespread. Typical comments were: "I am frightened about a leap in the dark"; "I feel comfortable now"; "Can I move to what I don't know?"'[38]

With less than four months to go before the most likely date of a General Election the voters were still nervous: it was time to deal with tax.

Winning the tax war

Tax was central to our strategy of reassurance. If the election campaign had one crucial battle, one defining fight, it was over tax. We lost the 1992 election and won the 1997 one in large part because of tax. Tony Blair and Gordon Brown both believed the shadow Budget in 1992 had been a mistake: it revealed our hand and raised taxes for middle-income earners. Brown had thought the basic election strategy wrong: he believed we should have focused remorselessly on the recession – 'It's the economy, stupid'. For three years he had been arguing persistently that we shouldn't make public expenditure commitments which could only be met by increased taxation. Once he became shadow Chancellor under John Smith, there was never any doubt that Labour's tax and economic positions would change.

Reforming tax-and-spend was the central modernising task at the time. It was not simply a question of tactics or election strategy, but a matter of political principle: it was simply wrong. Brown and Blair thought the idea of solving problems by spending money raised through taxes was unsustainable in a modern global economy. It was impossible to compete and succeed if tax increased continually as a proportion of GNP. In the long run, sustainable additional resources for education and health had to come through reducing the cost of welfare, increasing investment to increase the rate of growth, through 'save and invest' not tax and spend. Blair had joined Brown in sounding the death-knell for old-style Labour economics in his 1995 Mais lecture when he said, 'No one wants a return to penal taxation, and of course the objective of any government is to lower rather than increase the tax burden on ordinary families.'[39] Blair and Brown had a gut feeling that hard-working families paid enough tax; why should they pay any more? Paul Keating, when he was Australian Prime Minister, once told Blair, 'Whatever you do, promise you will not go into the election promising to raise income tax.'[40] Stanley Greenberg explains why tax is so important:

Taxation was the symbol of an out-of-control Labour Party. When Labour was last in government a vast array of things were out of control. Public spending, strikes and taxes were symbols of that, and were the way people felt it most directly. And just for voters to hear Labour say that it would not raise taxes and – probably more importantly – hear Labour attack the Tories for their twenty-two tax rises, says to them that this is a Labour Party which understands the financial burdens of the ordinary citizens, this is a Labour Party that is able to rein in government spending and operate within limits. And therefore this is a Labour party that will not jeopardise the living standards of mainstream Britain.[41]

Soon after the 1992 election Brown scrapped the shadow Budget and began reassuring the public on Labour's economic competence and its tax plans. Helped by massive tax increases piled on to the electorate by the Tories in their first post-election budget, we slowly began to win the battle. For five years Brown largely took this upon himself; it was our most daunting task, our toughest issue. It put him under massive pressure: after the 1997 election he looked a different man, as if a weight had been lifted from his shoulders.

My first big meeting with Brown after the 1992 election was in spring 1993. He had publicly ditched Labour's election manifesto tax-and-spend plans in November, and the Tories' reputation for economic competence had been severely damaged by their forced withdrawal from the ERM and the tax increases they had introduced in Norman Lamont's March Budget of 1993, which had introduced the largest tax rise in peacetime history. Lamont also slapped VAT on fuel, something the Tories had explicitly ruled out during the 1992 election campaign. Brown had launched a series of withering attacks under the theme, 'You Can't Trust the Tories'. In a large conference room in 1 Parliament Street, where Brown used to have his office, next door to Tony Blair, I met with Brown's economic team and representatives from Butterfield Day Devito Hockney, Labour's advertising agency at the time.

Across a large table were sprawled dozens of advertisements and posters depicting various ways of attacking the Tories on tax. Our problem was that there was no consistency; we had no one way of describing the Tory tax increases. Some advertisements suggested income per family per week, others per year; some, total tax increase; one included a multitude of different designations. I remember saying angrily that we had to agree on one line of attack and one way of depicting the Conservative tax increase. I wanted revenge for 1992; I said we should take their 'Tax Bombshell' poster and ram it down their throats.

Our goal was to put the government on the defensive about tax increases as well as presenting an alternative to their policies, but throughout the summer and autumn we had trouble getting our message through. In June we were still considered untrustworthy and irrelevant; Labour's support was losing ground in the face of the Conservative betrayal, because of a feeling that we would do worse. We needed, I said in a note on 22 June, 'a complete party identity that suggests greater economic competence' and 'sensible, plausible, non-penalising policies, particularly in the area of tax'. I added, 'Nothing is as important as the message. Message development and delivery are Labour's greatest long-term failing, particularly in the economic area.'[42] The situation hadn't improved by September 1993: two focus groups in Northwood Hills, north London, showed women were angry, but believed a new Tory leader would rectify the situation. Men believed the economy was recovering. They showed no awareness of Labour's attacking arguments. 'Those respondents with direct experience of economic uplift had already drifted back to the Conservatives,' I wrote. 'Both groups preferred an improved performance by the Conservatives to the upheaval of a new government.' Our economic message was being impeded by cynicism about politicians in general and Labour in particular, 'a view that Labour is for the unemployed, the poor, and not for ordinary people in work'.[43] I wanted to develop a continuing theme – 'You Can't Trust the Tories' – with two specific examples to back it up: VAT on fuel and £8.50-a-week Tory tax increases. In October a group in Harlow insisted they had 'no choice' but to vote Conservative; they could not run the risk to their personal finances of a Labour vote. The ERM débâcle would have been handled 'much worse' by Labour, they believed. 'It would have been a disaster,' said one.[44]

During the winter of 1993-94 and the next spring, Brown took huge strides in transforming our position on tax, relentlessly attacking the Tories for breaking their election promises, accusing them of hypocrisy and beginning to position Labour as the sensible spending party. He had drawn up plans to cut VAT on domestic fuel to 5 per cent and proposed public–private partnership extending into hospitals and schools. Yet when I conducted focus group research in July 1994, I found not only resentment and anger at the Tory tax increases, but the belief: 'Still, after all this, Labour will raise taxes more.'[45] And at the beginning of the following year, despite Tony Blair's election as leader, quantitative research showed the position getting worse, not better: in February 1994 Gallup had 58 per cent believing taxes would rise under Labour; by early 1995 it had risen to 65 per cent.[46] We still had a long way to go.

Throughout the spring and summer of 1994, as Labour announced it would not reverse any tax cuts brought in by the Tories before the next election and Brown began to set himself up as the financially prudent 'Iron Chancellor', I worked on developing an economic message. The Tories had come to be seen as the party of the rich and privileged, and not of the working majority. But 'support for Labour remains soft', I wrote on 14 July; 'fear of reversion to old Labour remains strong; tax cuts and an expanding economy will pull significant numbers back to the Tories'.[47] I warned that the number of voters not trusting us on tax and the improving economy were forming the basis for both a Tory recovery and their future election campaign. We had to give ourselves economic credibility, I urged.

That autumn I warned Brown we still had taxation problems: 'Large numbers think that a higher-rate band, even when set at £100,000, is a tax on success. And there is a deep-seated unease with such a tax: to many it seems punitive rather than fair. Almost all voters think that although they believe Labour should oppose Tory tax cuts, if they do . . . they will lose the election.'[48] And 50 per cent of people still believed Labour would put up everyone's taxes. Economic optimism under the Tories was also beginning to rise.

We had been trying to undermine people's confidence in the economy, using the device of Britain slipping to eighteenth place in the league table of national wealth. But as the economy appeared to strengthen, this claim lost credibility and Brown felt it impossible to communicate fundamental weakness in the face of the public's growing economic optimism. I wanted to continue to attack on the real economy, but Brown and his team felt they had to move on to a new strategy of making trust the key issue that divided the parties. If the public trusted Labour, then however economically confident they became they would still feel safe switching to us. Labour would float up with the economy.

Gradually a strategy began to take shape. For the last year before the election, almost all of our advertising and broadcasts featured tax in some form. In May 1996 we launched 'The Tories Hit You Where It Hurts', a poster featuring a twisted man with money falling out of his pocket and a PPB with a giant smashing up the country. The summer saw 'Same Old Tories, Same Old Lies' – posters carrying a red warning triangle. In September our first pledge posters went up. Just before we launched the 'Enough is Enough' campaign at the end of November, focus groups in Bury and Bolton showed deep mistrust of the Tories over tax, although it was still linked to anxiety about Labour on the same issue: we had moved on, but not enough. 'The improving economy is by far our largest problem,' I wrote. 'Better the devil you know' was still a common comment.[49]

In November 1996 the Conservatives attacked us with a new 'tax bombshell' campaign. Conservative Central Office re-ran their 1992 formula by producing a hundred-page document listing all Labour's alleged spending pledges and costing the total at £30 billion, which they translated into £1,200 a year in tax for the average family. The *Daily Telegraph* and *Newsnight* had warned the night before that it was to happen, and we were prepared. The document was rushed back from the Westminster launch to Millbank. There it was instantly distributed to all the relative policy personnel, who had facts and figures waiting to rebut it. 'When the Tories threw the tax bombshell at us, that showed Millbank at its best,' remembers Liam Byrne, a management consultant who had been seconded to Labour. 'All the politicians were there. People divided up the labour very quickly. Everyone processed a little bit. They brought it back together and rebutted it within three hours.'[50] The Tories launched their document in the morning, and by the time we called a press conference that afternoon the *Evening Standard* carried the headline: 'TORY TAX BOMB LANDS ON TORIES'.[51] 'That was when Central Office first faltered seriously,' says Byrne. 'They threw this stuff at us that had clearly been supported by the full mighty weight of the British Civil Service, and this small band at Millbank took it, caught it and turned it around within hours. They had the line ready for the early evening news. It was poetry in motion. It was tremendously exciting.'[52] We hit back again with '22 Tory Tax Rises Since 1992', a poster showing grabbing hands with the line, 'Enough is Enough', and, following the Budget at the end of the month, a poster proclaiming, 'Still £2,120 Worse Off Under the Tories – Enough is Enough.'

Our attacks were gaining ground, but we still had to deal with the problem of trust: the only way we were ever going to reassure the voters was to unveil our tax plans. There was never any question whether the basic rate should rise; it would have been political suicide. As far back as November 1995, Brown had announced proposals to drop the basic rate to 10p 'when affordable'.[53] That left only the top rate. Throughout 1995 and 1996 I conducted regular focus groups on this issue and the findings were always the same: people were wary of any increase in the top rate. When I suggested to respondents at a group in Watford on 1 May 1996 that the extra money from higher taxes on those earning over £100,000 could be spent on education, they were uneasy at what they saw as a tax on the rich. Suggestions that it could be used to fund a middle-income tax cut also met a wary response.[54] I never had any doubt: increasing the top rate put us at political risk. But there were other arguments: putting up the top rate of tax would make it clear where at least some of the money was coming from to pay for our spending plans. Blair was always instinctively against raising the top rate, Brown more inclined to keep the option open. In meetings they would discuss it as a matter of principle: did increasing the top rate reveal your instincts as a tax-raising party, or did it not? Blair thought it did, Brown thought it did not.

The Tories launched another attack on us on 6 January 1997, which we countered with a picture of John Major: 'Why trust him on the economy after 22 tax rises?' And two weeks later Brown, in an audacious coup, announced, first on the *Today* programme and then in a speech to Labour's Finance and Industry Group at the Queen Elizabeth II Centre in Westminster, that neither the basic nor the top rate of tax would go up under Labour. The Tories were pole-axed. It was as though a political mallet had been smashed through their heads.

It took some time for the tax pledge to break through, and it needed a national poster campaign, launched on 14 February, to do it, but our pledge turned the national mood and even by the beginning of February confidence was rising. 'These were the most encouraging female groups this year,' I wrote on 5 February. 'They did express worries about Labour: mainly interest rates, and fear of the unknown, but these doubts were containable.'[55] At the end of February I wrote, 'There is some evidence of a hardening of an anti-Conservative sentiment. The sense is of an electorate who spent the first six weeks of the year focusing (and worrying) about Labour, reshifting their focus on to the Conservatives and liking them even less.'[56] On 18 March, Stan Greenberg announced tax victory: 'Labour has won the tax issue and is making further gains. Labour is now trusted over the Tories on taxes by 11 per cent.'[57] This was an amazing victory and an extraordinary contrast to the tax débâcle of 1992. Labour had done what five years before had seemed impossible: it had beaten the Tories on tax. And without tax, as Maurice Saatchi said, they had nothing.

9

THE DARK ARTS

For the many not the few

I have once described political campaigns as acts of war, but they are acts of principle also. They are the way that progressive values can become progressive realities; they are the means by which progressive ideas can prevail and conservative ideas can be defeated; they are the instrument that can turn a compassionate instinct into lives made better.

For as long as I can remember I have believed that there is a continuing battle between progressive and conservative forces. For most of this century conservative forces have won in Britain, and for much of the 1980s they were winning across the world – winning (in part) because the right could campaign well, and the left could not. I felt humiliated by these defeats, but it wasn't me that was hurt: it was the millions of ordinary working people who deserved a better life, but who were repeatedly let down by progressive parties which campaigned poorly and did not seem to think that it mattered.

In 1985 I decided it was time to try to make a difference. I believed it was time that the progressive forces started to win. I was not alone: all over the world, but particularly in the United States, people were starting to say, 'We have to fight back.' So at the age of thirty-five I left a very well-paid career in advertising to set up a one-person consultancy with little money and no clients but with one aim: to use my communications skills to help the left beat the right; not just in Britain, but across the world. Two things were formative in my decision. One was Labour's appalling defeat in 1983. The other was a *Panorama* programme called 'The Marketing of Margaret',[1] showing the extraordinary, ruthless professionalism of the Conservatives and making it clear that unless Labour completely transformed its campaigning it could never hope to win.

I believe in the ascendancy of progressive ideas and progressive values. I believe in political parties that serve the people and advance their hopes. And I believe that it is the responsibility of all of us involved in progressive politics to advance our case with the greatest skill and professionalism. The people we seek to serve would expect nothing less, and our opponents will do nothing else. There is no reason why the interests of the rich and the powerful should be advanced by the ruthlessly professional techniques of campaigning, while these are denied to the poor, the disadvantaged, and the hard-working majority. We should be proud that in Britain, and increasingly across the world, progressive parties have now established themselves as the better campaigners. Political campaigning skills are not 'black arts', as they have been described, but a body of expertise that has every right, probably more right, to belong to the many, and not to the few.

This is a chapter about the entrails of campaigning. It is about the extraordinary preparations made by the Labour Party to secure victory in 1997 and about the skills and contribution of those who helped to make Labour's campaigning machine so formidable and so effective. It is also about my own personal view of campaigning – how I approach it, what I believe in. It is about those hundreds and thousands of campaign workers and helpers in the 1997 General Election who made sure that conservatism was beaten, and progressive principles could finally win.

Campaigning principles

There are few, if any, fixed rules of campaigning. My approach to political campaigning is dynamic and based on the need for constant change, continuous reassessment, and the resolution of contradictions, while always seeking to connect ideas to experience. I hope that this book as a whole is more able to articulate what I believe about campaigning than these few paragraphs can. But the following ten basic campaigning principles run through it.

1: Campaigning is holistic. It is a complete activity involving every element of the political experience. Successful campaigns must get not just a single element right, they have to get everything right. They have to be rooted in substance, in ideas, in values, in principles: these in turn have to connect to organisation and structure, which in turn must connect to message and to the delivery of the message, to every detail of every leaflet, to every performance on television. A campaign is like a vast, multi-dimensional structure moving forwards and backwards, upwards and downwards, meshing abstraction and concreteness, policy with presentation, future to past. The art of campaigning is to take this complication and make it compellingly simple.

2: Campaigning is dynamic. Campaigning is not static, it is the continuous unfolding of interconnecting events. A campaign is a fluid, interacting sequence stretching indefinitely into the distance. It is necessary to anticipate events and the consequences of those events; not just what will happen, but what will happen as result of it, and how this will influence us and what we should do next. It is essential in campaigning never to assume that the prevailing situation will continue, for it may not. It is also imperative to understand that what has worked before may not work again, what was successful in the last election may be stale or ineffective in the next. The soapbox was astoundingly effective for Major in 1992, laughable five years later.

3: Campaigning is about momentum. In politics either you have momentum or you are losing momentum, there is no middle way. Politics does not accept a condition of stasis, in which both parties are in equal and continuing balance. In a campaign you must always seek to gain and keep momentum, or it will pass immediately to your opponent. Gaining momentum means dominating the news agenda, entering the news cycle at the earliest possible time, and repeatedly re-entering it, with stories and initiatives that ensure that subsequent news coverage is set on your terms. It means anticipating and pre-empting your opponent's likely manoeuvres, giving them no room to breathe, keeping them on the defensive. It means defining the political debate on your terms. Every political debate can be seen in two ways: one that will favour you, and one that will favour your opponents. It is essential that your definition prevails. Momentum is especially vital at the end of the campaign. Although it was clear that Labour would win the 1997 election, a week before polling day the size of the majority was uncertain. The last few days of the campaign, when Labour stormed to a crescendo and the Tories slunk away, lost the Conservatives dozens of seats.

4: Campaigning is about message. People think message just means a few words, often repeated, but message is much more: it is the rationale that underpins your campaign. It is your central argument, the reason you believe that the electorate should vote for you and not your opponents. This rationale is the most important thing to get right in a campaign. You must be clear about why you are seeking to form a government, or why you wish to be Prime Minister. A message can be formed in part by opinion polling and the attitudes and values of the electorate, but it must also come from the substance of what you represent: what is true about you, as a party or a politician. In the months leading up to the 1997 election, more time was spent developing the right message than doing anything else. The messages that emerged – enough is enough; Britain deserves better; people not privilege; future not the past; leadership not drift – appear very simple and uncomplicated, but they took years to develop. They were compelling to the electorate, but they were also true to New Labour.

5: *Campaigning is about speed*. The British electorate, like almost every electorate in the world, is subject to a continual assault by news. On radio and television news is broadcast every hour at the very least, often far more often. Almost everyone reads one or more newspapers which are competing in ferocious media markets and where the demand for news is insatiable. Any political assertion, however false, can spread through this media jungle with the speed of a panther. The world of politics is littered with assertions that are untrue, but are believed to be true because they were not effectively answered. An unrebutted lie becomes accepted as the truth. You must always rebut a political attack if leaving it unanswered will harm you. And you must do it instantly, within minutes at best, within hours at worst, and with a defence supported by facts. That is what the computer Excalibur and the Rapid Rebuttal Unit at Millbank were about. The first big Tory tax attack in November 1996 was smashed back within three hours with a convincing rebuttal document, and that effectively was the beginning of the end of the Tories' tax campaign.

6: *Campaigning is about endurance*. People who have not been involved in political campaigns do not understand the sheer physical toll they take. Campaigns now go on not just for weeks, but for years. Perpetual, continuous campaigning has become the norm, and this exacts an enormous physical and mental cost. In the 1997 election the Conservatives believed that by calling the election at the last possible moment and by having a long, six-week campaign, endurance would take its toll and Labour would slip up. There were moments when the election seemed an eternity away, but Labour absorbed the pressure better than the Conservatives and the long campaign simply heightened the demand for change. But the capacity for endurance – not just to keep going, but to make good, sensible, fast decisions when almost dropping with exhaustion – is an essential quality in campaigning.

7: *Campaigning is about trust*. Trust is the vital ingredient of modern politics, and it is also the most elusive: hard to win, almost impossible to get back once lost. People have stopped trusting politicians, they have become increasingly sceptical, they feel alienated and disconnected. To win trust we will need new and different ways of communicating and campaigning. The old ways will not do. This means moving from rhetoric to action. Not just saying things, but doing them. Changing Clause IV and balloting Labour's early manifesto are good examples of this. It also means entering into new and more accountable relationships. Increasingly politicians and parties will have to establish what are in effect contracts with the electorate. The pledges were the first example of this, but they will not be the last. The electorate will no longer accept the old rhetorical politics, it wants to hold politicians to account.

8: Campaigning is about beating fear. Almost always the electorate hovers between hope and fear. In the last election the electorate wavered continuously between a desire to get rid of the Conservatives and anxiety about a Labour government. In the referendum on the Good Friday agreement in Northern Ireland, on 22 May 1998, the Protestant electorate hovered tantalisingly between genuine fear of what the agreement might bring, and the hope that it might usher in a better future. In both cases hope won, but fear will not diminish as a factor in modern politics. Modern societies and modern economies mean more change, less continuity, and, inevitably, insecurity and anxiety will increase. Electorates will be less certain, more anxious, more fearful about the future.

In general, over the last two decades, the right has campaigned on a basis of fear, the left on hope. Almost invariably fear won. Fear is a more compelling emotion, more easily provoked. Reagan in 1984, Bush in 1988, Thatcher in 1987 and Major in 1992 all used fear shamelessly as a weapon: fear of taxation, fear of communism, fear of crime. But progressive parties have learned to defeat fear, through rebuttal, counter-attack, more aggressive, less passive campaigning, with an emphasis on message which connects directly with the insecurities of working families. Increasingly the electorate rejects purely negative attacks and demands more positive campaigning. It is now almost impossible to present a negative message without a positive message to complement it. The Conservative negativism of 1997 probably lost them scores of seats. Labour used only positive posters during the six-week campaign. But in an increasingly fast-changing world, insecurity is likely to grow, and with it the potential for fear-based campaigning. Progressive parties will have to fight harder to combat it.

9: Campaigning is about substance. However good your campaigning, you will not win, at least not comprehensively, if your campaign is not based on substance. Even brilliant presentation cannot sell a dud product. Labour lost in 1987 despite a brilliant campaign, and in 1992 with a creditable campaign, because it had not changed enough. The electorate knew this. It always does. It senses if politicians are not real, understands when policies or positions are bogus. Because voters get their information about politics largely from television, they search for clues to reveal the real character of politicians. They are always looking for indications of what is really true, what lies beneath the surface. They admire politicians who show courage, who do brave and unexpected things, who take tough and unexpected decisions, who do not back down under fire. Tony Blair was made as a politician by the courage he showed in ditching Clause IV. The electorate is now double- and treble-guessing politics and politicians all the time. Voters are desperate to get beneath the surface to the substance. The same is true of policy pronouncements. Media scrutiny of politics still concentrates on spin-doctors and sound-bites, while the electorate and most thoughtful politicians are moving on.

10: Campaigning is about a dialogue with the people. The most important thing a party must do in a campaign is listen to what the voters are saying. This does not mean doing what they say, it means knowing what they are thinking and feeling, and respecting it. In a media age new forms of dialogue must be created. Focus groups and market research are an essential part of this dialogue. So too are interactive party broadcasts, and 'Town Hall' meetings, at which politicians can be questioned and held to account. British Telecom logged 230,000 people who responded to an invitation to talk to Tony Blair following the broadcast that launched 'New Life for Britain' on 4 July 1994. The number gives some idea of the pent-up demand for involvement in the political process. People want to have their voices heard. This is not just about developing winning strategies or compelling messages, it is about paying proper respect to the opinions of the public and involving them in the political process. If this is not done, people will either switch off or start to reject the political process altogether. A political campaign should be a partnership between a political party and the people.

Millbank

Campaigning principles are one thing, but putting them into practice is quite another. Peter Mandelson's central preoccupation during the eighteen months before May 1997 was preparing the election campaign. He dedicated most of his energy and intellectual capital to this one task. He had found managing the 1987 election draining and he did not look forward to 1997. In the intervening ten years, campaigns had become incomparably more complex, the media more extensive and demanding: Sky has continuous twenty-four-hour news coverage which, although not watched by millions, spots errors and is monitored by journalists. The BBC and ITV have news bulletins throughout the day; news radio has become ubiquitous; the press are facing ever greater competitive pressures. This is why Millbank was such an essential innovation.

The idea of moving Labour campaigning to one modern, central space came from those of us who had worked on Clinton's campaign in 1992. The contrast between that integrated operation and our scattered campaign force in the British election began a drive for the creation of a similar 'war room' from where we could fight the next election. Tom Sawyer, General Secretary of the Labour Party, took the idea and pushed it through the NEC, which in September 1995 approved the £2 million budget to rent and refurbish a new campaigns and media centre at Millbank Tower. After the rabbit warren of Walworth Road, Millbank was like a breath of fresh air. Instead of endless, scurrying corridors we now had a single, open-plan office floor. People could talk to each other and communicate effectively – a far cry from the ghastly 'meeting rooms' of John Smith House. It was bright and professional, and had stunning views over the Thames. Its openness promoted a sense of community. I believe it played a significant part in reducing the wrangles and arguments which had bedevilled Labour's previous campaigns. This was a cultural revolution for many in the Labour Party: over the next year the headquarters at Walworth Road were marginalised, and our entire campaigning operation expanded and moved into the vast new office space, with a converted cinema downstairs for press conferences. We set up rebuttal and attack teams backed up by computerised research systems, reporting to a unified command structure under the tight control of Peter Mandelson. A lot of people's noses were put out of joint, but many others were forced to embrace the changes and admit that the way they had done things in the past was wrong. The smoothness of the operation owed much to work done quietly behind the scenes by Tom Sawyer, who was unobtrusive, diplomatic and sensitive. He was supported by Fraser Kemp, then General Election Co-ordinator and now MP for Houghton and Washington East.

The press office was the first team to move in, at the beginning of 1996, with Margaret McDonagh, then head of the campaigns unit and later to become General Election Co-ordinator when Kemp stepped down in October. Various task forces and groups followed over the next few months.

I arrived in February 1996; Peter Mandelson spent the mornings at Millbank from January but only moved in fully in March. The atmosphere was depressed. Joy Johnson had recently left her job as Director of Campaigns and Communications after a difficult twelve months. A former BBC political reporter and a forceful proponent of news-driven, story-led campaigning, she had been appointed to give our campaigning drive and energy, which she did. She also introduced some good initiatives like the daily brief sent out to all Labour MPs, candidates and councillors, but she was never at ease with Alastair Campbell and Peter Mandelson and she was never completely behind the modernisation project. She understood very well how to manage the news, but she was less comfortable organising a department. This was a difficult time. No one was in effective command. I used to hold regular weekly meetings in Walworth Road at which I invariably lost my temper. The atmosphere was too close to 1992 for my liking.

After Joy Johnson resigned nobody was appointed to replace her; Peter took over most of her responsibilities when he moved into Millbank Tower. 'It was like moving in as a liberating army,' he says. 'There were people cheering and waving flags, putting up the bunting and opening cheap red wine.'[2] Millbank was a mess: the campaigning team lacked cohesion and didn't work properly; the move from Walworth Road combined with the lack of leadership had created a sullen mood about the place. Peter was gloomy. Expected to take over the whole operation, he was unsure what to make of this vast space full of people he didn't know. I, on the other hand, loved it. After working for so long in small, isolated offices, I enjoyed working with so many people in such an unfettered environment.

The campaign headquarters was on two levels. The lower level was the main room, a vast space bordered on one side by huge windows which were covered by blinds for security reasons. There was no dedicated 'war room' in the Clinton manner, just one open space containing all the elements of the campaign. On the right immediately as you entered was Jackie Stacey, who was in charge of the presentation of the party: design, press conference sets, and so on. She has been working tirelessly as a communications moderniser since 1985, and is one of New Labour's true stars. She appears timid, but is fierce in her dealings with senior politicians, not afraid to tell them exactly how long they may speak at conference, for example, and is quite prepared to turn off the microphone if they overshoot their time limit.

At the centre of the floor was a collection of desks which became the campaign hub, where the chief media spokesman David Hill, Margaret McDonagh, Matthew Taylor (head of the policy task force), Peter Mandelson, Peter Hyman, Charlie Whelan (Gordon Brown's press secretary), Tim Allan (one of Tony Blair's press officers) and I sat during the election. But at the beginning we were scattered at different points around the vast floor. Immediately behind the central tables, so close that our chairs were always clashing, stood the Attack Task Force or Rapid Rebuttal Unit. Next door to them – in a separate, heavily locked room – the Excalibur database computer system whirred quietly. Beyond that lay media monitoring, who told us what the papers were going to say the next day, followed each nuance in the different editions, gave regular updates on all the news bulletins, and monitored every interview, story and speech on radio and on television.

Policy, led by Matthew Taylor, was to the side, by the river. With a policy officer covering every area of Labour's manifesto, they were crucial in putting out documents refuting the latest Tory allegations. Their phones never stopped ringing. One moment it could be a worried local agent from Bristol, the next Robin Cook about to go on *The World at One*, both demanding the last detail of Labour's programme. They rarely made mistakes; if they did, the fallout could be terrible. My area, which was a combination of strategy, polling and advertising, was in a corner on the opposite side from the river. My staff and the BMP team, when they arrived, huddled here.

Peter Mandelson had his own office, which he shared with Benjamin Wegg-Prosser, his able research assistant, who organised his life for him. There was a large conference room, which was too hot in the summer, too cold in winter, and in which the acoustics were so bad that discussion was impossible unless you shouted. Tom Sawyer and John Prescott had offices at the far end of the floor. The campaigns unit (responsible for co-ordinating the campaign from a national to a local level), led by Margaret McDonagh, was clustered around the conference room.

Above the main room was a smaller, second level, reserved for Tony Blair and his office. It was largely empty until the election, when it became very crushed. In one room, pressed together like battery hens, was the whole policy team, plus extras like Derry Irvine, who managed to find some space in between the head of policy, David Miliband, and policy adviser Liz Lloyd. Yet Blair's office didn't seem to mind their cramped accommodation. It created a new sense of camaraderie that had been lacking in the Leader of the Opposition's sprawling Westminster offices.

Peter Mandelson had been asked by Blair to get a grip on the campaign and he swiftly accepted an offer from Liam Byrne, from Andersen Consulting, to come and help. 'It was a mess,' Byrne, who arrived in April 1996 and was seconded to us until the election, remembers.[3] 'You had a random collection of people. They had what theoretically looked like a good organisational structure but no one really knew what they were doing and crucially it lacked leadership. There were lots of people in different units drifting along without anyone pulling them together. There didn't appear to be any strategy.'[4] Like an organisation after the chief executive has just left, it was spinning around and everybody knew it was a problem. We expected the election to be called in October, in six months' time.

First of all we got to work on Millbank's fabled rapid rebuttal system, in which we had invested £500,000 and which had become a complete shambles. At its centre was Excalibur, a computer with a huge capacity and the ability to read articles and documents and feed them directly into its memory like a photocopier. Unfortunately this capacity had been used indiscriminately, and it had collected a vast amount of data, including random pieces of MPs' correspondence, all of which were unfiled, unstructured and unprioritised like a massive electronic dustbin. Excalibur had to be emptied and the process of electronic gathering began again. During the heat of the campaign, the Attack Task Force often found it more convenient to use the paper files hanging on the wall than to trawl through the computer.

While we sorted out rapid rebuttal, which took several months, Mandelson attacked the campaign structure, which had been set up by Tom Sawyer, Fraser Kemp and Margaret McDonagh, and consisted of twelve task forces, ranging from logistics to attack, through the leader's tour, campaigns and message delivery. This in itself had been a small revolution for the Labour Party – the move from a directorate to a task-force structure. Mandelson used this as his way in, and worked punctiliously through each of the task forces. This is how Peter works: slowly; painstakingly; calmly; step by step. He likes to get the small things right. He thinks political success and failure rest on detail and planning.

'The building was great, like a great new toy,' he remembers, 'but I felt I had to be careful. I didn't want anyone to think I was moving in, sweeping up, hiring, firing, etc. I played it very slow, very long. The key thing I proposed to Tony was that in the whole political campaigning structure there had to be a General Election planning task force that we should ring-fence. That whatever messing around went on by anyone else in relation to any of the rest of what we were doing, the General Election planning should be sacrosanct and protected and chaired by me.'[5]

When the work on Excalibur was finished, Mandelson asked Byrne to spend a month on a full-scale operational review of Millbank. Byrne reported in August that, although the infrastructure was good, Labour lacked the political management structure to run the operation effectively. The campaign needed underpinning with strong political support and a decision-making structure that was clear, agreed and unambiguous. Decisions were not being taken because there was no clear political command structure. This was a very difficult message for politicians to swallow. The lack of communication and co-ordination meant we were unable to sustain a coherent message. No matter how many initiatives we took, our message wasn't getting across.

'There was no chief operating officer,' said Byrne. 'We didn't have someone who pulled everyone together, who sat everyone down and said, right, you do this, you do that, what are the problems, let's sort them out, now go away and do it. We didn't have someone who could do that.'[6]

As a result, Margaret McDonagh was appointed General Election co-ordinator in October, and helped Mandelson enormously. Initially their chemistry was not ideal, but they were an excellent match: both were good at different things. McDonagh made things happen for Mandelson. 'There were sometimes complaints about Margaret from other senior managers,' Byrne said. 'People found her brusque, but I remember sitting in a meeting with Peter and Peter, as he often does, just sort of summed it up. He said the one thing about Margaret is at least she gets things done. And in a party which is short of finishers, which is short of implementers, Margaret stands out as someone who gets things done quickly, effectively and without fuss. She doesn't mind, she doesn't complain when she's been given a difficult job to do. She doesn't start grumbling or machinating. She just picks up the phone and gets on with it.'[7] Mandelson gave the whole place shape, coherence and direction, but McDonagh was crucial as his lieutenant. 'In an organisation as complicated as an election HQ, where speed is of the essence, you need someone who is going to act quickly and who is not going to second-guess you or question you or cause trouble or procrastinate,' Byrne said. 'When you give an order you need it executed. I mean, this was war.'[8]

The other major problem was the political leadership of the campaign, which was not cohesive and would not become so until the election period itself, when it did fuse. Gordon Brown was in political control of the campaign, Peter Mandelson in charge of Millbank. Relationships between them were not warm, often prickly, sometimes difficult. This was hard for both Mandelson and Brown, and difficult for the rest of us. Partly this was a matter of temperament and a once-close relationship which had been badly bruised, but it was also because of a difference in approach. The most telling example of this was the campaign grid. Peter had spent weeks working on this. Entire weekends were spent by him crafting a perfectly designed campaigning plan, replete with every detail for every day.

Finally he presented it to Brown, who resented and resisted it. He felt that news should dominate the election, and news by definition could not be foretold. It was fluid, unpredictable, impossible to pin down. It would escape from the constraints of any campaign grid. Peter understood the value of news, but felt deeply that without order and discipline there was chaos. His fear of disintegration and disorder in a campaign is almost visceral – it is an abyss we cannot slide into. The lessons of 1992 were engraved on everyone's mind. The truth is that both Brown and Mandelson are right: you need structures and you need flexibility. Labour's 1997 campaign was effective because these two impulses were married, but it was not an easy match and only happened after a long and difficult period of tension and disagreement.

That is how successful campaigns are built: on the synthesis of contrasting ideas and contrasting policies. One of Blair's great strengths as leader is that he understands this, and is able to make it work. He wants the best and he wants ideas and strategies to be tested and debated. He is only confident in an idea or a person if it has come through the fire. This is as true for himself as for others; he distrusts people who agree with him, he wants to be taken on. His view of the management of the campaign was simple. Brown and Mandelson are the best. They have brilliant but different campaigning skills, and he wanted both of them. In the short term it was difficult, but in the long run it paid off. He would not compromise on ability for the sake of harmony. In fact, the search for perfect team harmony is a fantasy in politics. Neil Kinnock's senior politicians were often at odds and this sometimes led him to despair. Throughout my twelve years working with the Labour Party, conflicts and tensions between senior politicians were a fact of life. The challenge of leadership is to accept this and to transcend it, and this Blair did brilliantly well.

Two other areas needed strengthening: message development and story development. Peter Hyman was moved from Blair's office to work in Millbank full-time in order to strengthen the message, and Brian Wilson MP was moved across to work with the rebuttal team on a full-time basis. Brian enjoyed a warm friendship with Adrian McMenamin, who headed the team, which was staffed also by Richard Elson, Tristram Hunt, Adam Bowen and Will Parkes. The deputy political editor from the *Daily Mirror*, David Bradshaw, was recruited to develop material for the press office to send out. He also made sure that every important regional newspaper had at least one article a week from Tony Blair or a shadow Cabinet member.

Matthew Taylor was head of the policy task force, and a central figure. He used to exasperate me, primarily because he used to challenge everything I said. I find this annoying at the best of times, but with Matthew it was doubly irritating because he was so often right. He did the same with Mandelson, who took it better than I did. But he was always thinking, always protean. He had a new idea, fresh insights, almost daily, and would tell everyone about it. He was always trying to ridicule and humiliate me. He began to develop a tracking chart correlating my faith in opinion polls against the strength of Labour's lead. He would mimic my excessive delight if a poll was good, my manic despair if it was bad. I grew very fond of him.

Of equal importance was Labour's polling director, Greg Cook, with whom I worked closely. He transformed Labour Party polling, which had been in a mess before he took over. He took care to ensure that polling information came in from many sources and not just one. He assembled a complete picture. Tony Blair used to call on him often for polling information during the campaign.

Yet another hidden star was Alan Barnard, a big, fair-haired, often quiet but suddenly outspoken man, who is now in charge of campaigns. He combines nitty-gritty, street campaigning skills with an understanding of the needs of the modern media. Alan was the kind of man to drop everything to go and heckle John Major at an open-air press conference.

Slowly, very slowly, it all began to work. Margaret McDonagh fought to bring everything together. 'Everything in the Labour Party's difficult,' she said. 'It's meant to be like that. You're talking about a hundred-year-old organisation that's very conservative and had to be changed root and branch.'9 She adopted a holistic approach, integrating all the elements of the campaign. There were regular meetings between the task-force leaders, to communicate to them what was going on, and give them information on polling, message or whatever. These meetings were integrated with staff meetings, so the process was very open and people could contribute. Margaret introduced telephone conferencing to include constituencies and regions, assigned politicians to each of the regions, and gave each of the regional offices a politician to deal with to make everyone feel that they were part of the effort. McDonagh had learned the strength gained by integration at all levels when she worked on the Clause IV campaign – 'Ultimately, the party member knocking on the door would be saying the same as Tony Blair on *News at Ten*,' she said. 'I think that that is the one thing we did achieve in the election campaign.' Whatever was happening nationally would be mirrored locally:

Generally now when you talk to people about the General Election, when you talk to anybody, whatever part of the party, whether they are a member, a member of staff in the regions or here, people always tell you about their contribution. They feel that they made one. They understood what their part was in the overall structure – they were a piece of the jigsaw and I think that that's just amazingly important for people. Also there was a realisation of the different roles between politicians and staff. Politicians behaved like politicians, they made political decisions, whereas in the past because the political decisions have been difficult to make they have concentrated on the detail or gone

off into trying to run the organisation. This time they accepted
the responsibility that they had to make political decisions. People
like you, Philip, and me to some extent, kept throwing it back
to them saying, no, you've got to make a decision on that; no,
you've got to make a decision on taxes; no, this is what is happening on Europe. I think they were challenged. Yes, they did
deliver.[10]

It was a fraught twelve months. We all argued for much of
the time. At no point in 1996 did Peter Mandelson or I believe
Millbank was really working. Alastair Campbell never had complete confidence in it either, and was always complaining about
it. For him, the progress being made was too gradual and too
slow. He thought the organisation was poor and this made Blair
anxious. Campbell often complained that decisions were being
made when he wasn't there, which was true. It was particularly
true of advertising, about which he considered himself an expert.
And in the final analysis, the advertising owed as much to him as
to anyone.

But in the first two months of 1997 things came together. The
daily meeting at 8.30 A.M. moved to Millbank from Brown's office
in Parliament Street, which was inconvenient for him but made
Millbank feel that it was the genuine centre of the campaign. The
place started to hum: the numbers had swollen to 250 and the
operation became bigger, noisier, more exciting. Liam Byrne
compared it to a City trading floor. 'For a whole generation
of comparatively young people it was one of the most exciting
things they'd ever done,' he said. 'People were desperate to get
in. It was a very young, very vibrant place.'[11]

A system called Lotus Notes was introduced in the press office
– all the policy documents and press releases there at the touch of
a button. It provided a rolling agenda of breaking news stories,
a 'line to take' for all press staff, and a politician to call on. It
was invaluable. Key campaigners out on the road were linked by
fax and pager to Millbank, where each had their own political
lieutenant so if there was a problem their lieutenant could literally

walk up to Peter Mandelson and explain the confusion and clear a line within seconds.

On the ground, workers overseen by the key campaigners unit set up by Margaret McDonagh a year earlier had built up detailed databases of switchers, so that Millbank had a national database of key voters, largely people who were Conservative or Liberal in 1992 and who were saying they had now switched. They were our primary targets, together with voters who were Labour but unlikely to vote – largely young people. We meshed the information gathered on the ground with the electoral register and census details and sent out direct mail which was innovative and precisely targeted. On the morning after the election was called, 3.2 million items of direct mail were delivered.

Somehow, when the campaign started, Millbank swung smoothly into action. 'I just feel very proud for the organisation staff and members and what they did,' said McDonagh. 'The organisation was completely transformed, and often we brought people in here during the campaign, trade union leaders or business people or whatever, and they were really shocked about how it ran, really. During the election campaign, in this space you had 310 people and they all knew what they were doing and I think they knew at every level in the party what they were doing. I think we reached out much more. We were more confident. When you're not very confident about what you're doing, it all becomes secretive.'[12] We had moved a long way since the days of the secret campaign team in 1992.

The War Book

The strategic anchor of any campaign is the War Book, so called because an election campaign is like a surrogate war. In my interview with David Hare for his play *The Absence of War*, I said, 'Political statements are not acts of sense, they are acts of war,'[13] which sums up my feeling about a campaign: it is a fight to the political death, with only one winner. Central to the War Book and one of my core beliefs is that you must be absolutely honest about your opponent's strengths, and your own weaknesses, and that you should put them in writing. It is a risk putting sensitive information down on paper, but in my view unless you document hard campaigning truths they will never be fully taken into account and will run the risk of being dodged or discounted.

In this I took my lead from Joe Napolitan, who told me: 'If a strategy is not in writing, it does not exist.' Unless strategy and the inputs into strategy are written down and agreed, they will not be there. They will be just an impression of a strategy: you will think you have it, but under the pressure of campaigning it will melt.

There are other views, of course. When Labour's 1997 War Book was released by the Tories in the middle of the campaign I was accused by them of naïveté in writing it all down. They were wrong. The truth may well be embarrassing, but in the long run, it is essential for the growth and development of any organisation that it is known, disseminated and can be read. Vital to political success is a complete understanding of your weaknesses. The odd leak is small change compared with that and, in any event, the leaked truth can not only help prod an organisation in the right direction, but also tell the world that it is still listening, it still cares.

The War Book is not just a matter of writing down party strengths and weakness and mapping out likely campaign manoeuvres. It is also about re-enacting or simulating the campaign with real voters. It is always essential to try to produce the most damaging campaign that your opponents are likely to come up with and then to expose it to the electorate, to gain their response, and to find the most effective defence against the likely attack.

I started to do this in the middle of 1995. In the beginning I used to focus on the likely Conservative manifesto at the time of the election, and see how it compared to the one I expected us to produce. But I also tested rough advertisements that simulated the Conservative campaign. By early 1996 I was testing 'New Labour,

New Danger' in focus groups, because we had been informed that it was their probable campaign slogan. We also did quantitative polling on it. We would constantly be testing their best attacking arguments, and our best defences to them. Although it had the potential to hurt, I was confident about the deficiencies of 'New Labour, New Danger' before a single member of the public had seen it. It legitimised New Labour, but more than that it was too negative. It was simply not possible to inject this message into the political bloodstream without it being preceded by a massive positive campaign.

Peter Mandelson asked me to start work on the War Book in early summer 1996, and I jotted down an outline summary on 10 June. In July, I booked a room at a hotel and spent the day with Peter Hyman and Liam Byrne attempting to predict the election. The first draft, dated 1 July, was flimsy. It had both Labour and Conservative strengths and weaknesses and predictions of how both major campaigns might unfold. But, as Peter Hyman says, 'It was just a first trawl over the campaign battlefield.'[14]

This was one of many drafts. We ended with version three, number two, which was the one that was leaked. It had a summary of our message at that time: 'Two futures: a future of hope with Labour, a future you cannot trust with the Conservatives.' It pulled absolutely no punches. It started with Labour and Conservative strengths and weaknesses. Our strengths were Blair, newness and the future, the many not the few. Our weaknesses were tax, interest rates, inflation, hidden left, fear of change. Conservative strengths were the strengthening economy, patriotism and security – 'better the devil you know'. Their weaknesses were 'in office too long', for the few not the many, betrayal and trust, drift and weak leadership, education and health.

I summed up the threats facing us: 'The economy; fear of Labour; Major; Europe.' The opportunities were: 'Blair/New Labour; business; tax; education; fear of another Tory term.' I then spelled out in some detail the election battleground – staking out the competitive positions of both parties. For example, Labour would say, 'Major is weak', the Conservatives would say, 'Phoney Tony'; Labour would say, 'The Tories have been in power for too long', the Conservatives would say, 'Don't take the risk of change'.

The War Book then mapped out the Conservative campaign: a negative campaign based on the claim that Labour was dangerous; a positive campaign based on the proposition that this was the strongest economy in Europe. I assumed that the positive and the negative campaigns would be equally important in Tory tactics. In the event they fatally downplayed their positive campaigning. The likely Conservative campaign plan was mapped out too: each month we anticipated what they would do. This was not that difficult, as we had their advertising schedule and they almost never deviated from it.

Labour's campaign was also set out in detail. Blair wanted to structure our message around three anchors: Remind (about their record); Reassure (that Labour is new; that we have safe, common-sense policies); Reward (through the pledges). By November the War Book had our final dividing-lines in: leadership not drift; for the many not the few; the future not the past. These became a mantra. For the first time in perhaps thirty years Labour was getting a genuine message that would be used repeatedly by politicians. Eventually these were augmented by the culminating message of our campaign: 'Enough is Enough: Britain deserves better'. These messages appear very simple but they are the result of months of work, taking New Labour's big themes and making them completely accessible to the public.

At the cutting edge of our campaigning were what we called 'offers to the electorate': our positive offer – the pledges, and our articulation of what the Conservatives had to offer – the dark side of a Tory fifth term. Our offer was: 'Labour's pledge for a better future: cut waiting lists; cut class sizes; ban knives and guns; young people into work; strong economy, cut VAT on fuel'. We contrasted this with a Tory pledge for a future you could not trust: 'VAT on food; running down the NHS; continued decline in schools'. There was no mention of pensions in this: it was included only after Peter Lilley published his pension-plus proposals, and only after it became clear that the Conservatives were planning to end the state pension as we knew it. The pledges connected straight back to our need to build trust, to enter into a new and more accountable relationship with the electorate.

The War Book then went on to the target audience. We had five groups. The first were swing voters: switchers from Conservative to Labour were our key group and our primary focus by a long way. For example, almost all (over 90 per cent) of my focus groups were conducted within this group. But we also targeted women because of Labour's continuing gender gap in favour of men; first-time voters; the DE social grouping, our historic base; and the Pennine Belt, our key group of marginals. In the event we were successful among all groups. Over one and a half million voters made the direct journey from the Conservatives to Labour, a staggering figure. We closed the gender gap, we got 58 per cent of first-time voters, and we won every target seat in the Pennine Belt. The War Book also contained an extensive campaign grid, which was not filled in for security reasons, and a final section summarising our messages and pledges.[15]

Our War Book was comprehensive, but not yet decisive. Paul Begala, a senior consultant to Bill Clinton in 1992, wrote a penetrating critique of it, arguing for more focus, more attack. It is true that it was too long, but I believe that just as you must be honest about weaknesses, you must embrace complication before you can become simple and single-minded. Politics is complicated, multi-layered and dynamic. To make true sense of it you must respect its complexity, but then turn its complication into simple, sustainable, communicable truths. But this means a massive amount of work, and a huge process of distillation. If you just reach for the easy, shallow simplicity it will not last a week before it crumples under scrutiny. By the end of the campaign our message was five lines plus the pledges. It could all be written on the side of a match-box, but it took three years, several versions of the War Book and a small rainforest to get there.

Labour advertising

There is a myth about political advertising, largely spawned by the success of Saatchi's. The Conservatives won four elections in a row, and Saatchi's produced advertising for all the campaigns. Often it was very good, sometimes it was brilliant. Understandably, a winning election campaign and good advertising points intelligent minds to cause and effect: good advertising produces election victories. But this is nonsense. Advertising has an effect, but it is small and rarely decisive. For example, it is certain that in four of the last five elections advertising did not materially influence the result. The one possible exception is the 1992 election, where it can be argued that the 'Tax Bombshell' had some effect on the electorate. But even this is highly debatable. Labour lost that election because it was not yet electable. Its tax plans and tax reputation were the real issue, not the advertising attack. Almost always the role of advertising is marginal. How does one explain otherwise the fact that in 1997 the Conservatives spent millions more on advertising than in 1992, but won 171 fewer seats in the election? This marginality applies in Britain, where TV advertising is banned, but not, of course, in the United States and elsewhere, where unlimited campaign advertising is permitted. There, advertising can change the dynamics and the results of elections.

But advertising does have a role in Britain and it can be significant. It can help to set agendas. It can concentrate minds and force parties to agree on the one thing they want to say. It can capture the popular mood and express it in a single, memorable image or line: 'Labour Isn't Working' in 1979; 'Like Your Manifesto, Comrade' (comparing Labour and Communist Party programmes) in 1983; and 'Labour's Policies on Arms' in 1987 were good examples of this. Advertising is not vital, but it is important.

In the past Labour had produced successful campaigns, but not in the 1983 election where Johnny Wright, working in impossible circumstances, produced the lamentable 'Think Positive, Act Positive, Vote Positive' campaign.

In 1984 the left hit back with brilliant advertising developed by BMP for the 'Save the GLC' campaign. It focused on the one issue generated by the abolition of the GLC which could unite all groups: they were taking away your right to vote. Their 'Say No to No Say' campaign was outstanding (although it did not save the GLC). Because it was supported by Ken Livingstone (MP for Brent) it gave advertising credibility on the left, softening its pariah status.

I always wanted BMP to do Labour's advertising, but for commercial reasons they were unable to in the beginning. So in part I recommended setting up the Shadow Communications Agency as a front organisation for BMP. This worked, and in 1987 BMP produced some visible and intelligent advertising. The advertising in 1992 was not as good, and when the SCA died, so did BMP's involvement with the party. I then recommended that Leslie Butterfield of Butterfield Day Devito Hockney be appointed. Leslie is a brilliant advertising planner (advertising's word for a strategist). He produced what I consider to be the single most influential piece of research ever conducted for Labour during my period of involvement (the 'Beyond the Pale' research of November 1985).[16] They did well, but when Blair became leader Mandelson and I thought it was time for a change: Peter wanted someone bigger. He needed to have confidence in the capacity of Labour's agency.

In the late autumn of 1994 I bumped into Peter Gatley, who was head of art direction at BMP. He was taking his son to the sandpit next to the Serpentine as I was taking my two daughters. He was desperate to work with Labour and felt that after all this time BMP deserved another chance. I thought he was right, and gradually the idea of re-appointing BMP took shape. The core of BMP, as far as Labour is concerned, is Chris Powell, its chief executive. Powell goes back further than anyone. He first offered his advertising help in 1972, and replaced David Kingsley as the third man of the three wise men who advised Harold Wilson. The other two were Peter Lovell-Davis and Denis Lyons. Powell did not work in the 1979 election, but had some involvement in 1983. He was responsible for getting Johnny Wright selected: 'All I did was dump poor old Johnny Wright with it – poor sod.'[17]

In 1987 Powell and the SCA had a successful campaign with a series of clever advertisements. One was based on Margaret Thatcher's stone heart – Peter Gatley spent weeks getting the actual stone carving absolutely right. In a series of presentations to the economic team in 1992 he pressed home our acute vulnerability on tax and interest rates. He says: 'The frustration we all had in 1992 was the failure to take action against what was obviously going to hit us. Between us we put together a strategy for responding, but no action was taken for dealing with it.'[18]

But returning in 1995 was not easy. 'I think our role changed enormously between 1985–87 and 1997. In 1985 in a way we were showing Peter Mandelson how to do it because he was new to it, but by 1997 he knew how to do it in his sleep. So where we had a central role in 1987 we had a far less central role in 1997. On top of that, rather than being Bryan Gould, Peter Mandelson and Philip Gould, you had a complete army of people all with different opinions in a general mêlée without a particular command structure.'[19] A typical meeting would include Peter Mandelson, Alastair Campbell, Margaret McDonagh, Peter Hyman, broadcasting officer Dan Clifton, Jackie Stacey, any number of strange young helpers and myself from the Labour side, and from BMP's side, Chris Powell, John Webster, Daryl Fielding, occasionally Simon Buckby, Gail Nutney, and various researchers – anything up to twenty-five people. Simon Buckby, the producer of the broadcasts at BMP, describes a typical meeting: 'This meeting would sometimes consider the slogan on tax and a really big decision needed to be taken – would we go with twenty-two Tory tax rises? – and sometimes this very same gathering would be looking at whether or not the shade of a leaflet needed to be a slightly different magenta to that presented by the agency. So these meetings had sprawling and huge agendas and they would genuinely consider what time train people needed to get in order to be at a poster launch with Tony Blair three weeks away, while at other times they would be saying, should we or should we not spend x million pounds on this poster?'[20]

Relations between politicians and advertising agencies are never easy, and as well as the ridiculous rows there were some moments when the two cultures clashed exquisitely. One day the new director responsible for the Labour Party account wrote a memo introducing herself, which began: 'Now we've been talking the talk, it's time to walk the walk.' This was enthusiasm, which we desperately needed, but it was not language that the Labour Party easily understood.

There was continual internal controversy about our advertising right up to election day itself. The BMP team never clicked with the Labour campaigners at Millbank, as it had when it worked through the SCA in earlier years. Younger members of Labour's team wanted newer, more fashionable agencies. Peter Hyman thought BMP lacked the political nastiness and killer instinct we needed. Millbank wanted hard, ruthless professionalism. They wanted an agency that would do exactly what it was told. Alastair Campbell just felt he could do it better. The BMP people had a hard time and they battled on. And they did keep us focused on tax.

BMP was also under occasional predatory attack from other agencies who wanted to work with us. Ironically, the agency we used most other than BMP was the old Saatchi & Saatchi, which Maurice and Charles Saatchi had left. They developed the 'Enough is Enough' line, and pushed our thinking towards being more positive and less negative.

We struggled to make our advertising arrangements gel, in awe of the Conservative advertising power. They had a huge amount of money to spend and we were at first fearful of their reputation. Whenever they launched a new advertising initiative we waited for the explosion and the damage it would cause – like war-time families in air-raid shelters in the last days of the war, awaiting V1 and V2 rockets. But after a while it became clear that the Tories were firing blanks. Their adverts, as Blair said, were everywhere: every street in every town had a Tory poster in it, or near it. It was like being occupied by an invading propaganda army. But I didn't think it was working.

In contrast to the Conservatives, whose advertising flowed off the production line according to a carefully worked-out plan, we never had the same campaign twice. We were groping our way towards solutions. Our advertising chopped and changed in style, design and theme, although for the most part we had one central message: tax. Jackie Stacey used to put them all up on the wall next to her desk to humiliate me. We started with 'Tories Hit You Where It Hurts' in spring 1996; moved on to 'Same Old Tories, Same Old Lies' in the summer; moved again to the pledges, virtually unvarnished, in September 1996; and finally developed the device of John Major facing both ways, with one side of his face saying, '1992: Tax Cuts Year on Year' and the other side saying, '22 Tax Rises Since 1992'. This was the best single attacking advertisement of the campaign. It hurt the Conservatives without damaging us because it was factual and people did not think we were being unfair. We followed it up with the tax pledge poster which was the most effective advertisement of the campaign. It calmed the mood of the electorate, pouring reassurance on them.

Tony Blair was never really happy with our advertising. He was always tetchy about it and wanted to be more positive. In the spring he started to talk about dropping negative advertising. At first Peter Mandelson and I thought he was mad, but gradually, because of the complete failure of the Conservative campaign, we came round to the same view. The Conservatives had yielded all the political ground associated with hope and positivity, and it was ours to grab.

In the end, because the final advertising plans for the election campaign seemed to be stuck, I arranged a meeting with only Peter Gatley and Alastair Campbell. Peter and Alastair clicked, and gradually we came to the conclusion we should be positive not in a timid way, but an intrusive and dominating way. I suggested bright, bold colours. Peter Gatley came back with stunning posters using vivid, unusual colours and the single line: 'New Labour, New Britain'. Gatley said this advertising would break new ground and he was right. It was positive, it was bright, it exuded hope. Internally, reaction to it was very mixed, but Alastair and I loved it.

I did not, however, want to use the line 'New Labour, New Britain', preferring our campaign line, 'Britain Deserves Better', which captured the national mood perfectly: everybody felt they deserved better. But Peter Gatley hated this, he thought there was an innate contradiction between using positive colourful posters and a slightly negative line. In fact, he hated it so much, he resigned from BMP when I insisted on using it – at least, this was the reason he gave. Such is election madness. The next stage of the advertising was planned to be the colours plus the pledges. Finally, we would have a picture of Blair with the line: 'Vote Today. Because Britain Deserves Better'. Peter Gatley hated this too, and tried dozens of alternatives based on various clever lines. But I wanted to close the campaign as it started, with 'Britain Deserves Better', and a reassuring picture of Tony Blair. I didn't want to be clever, I wanted to win.

The election advertising and the tax advertising which preceded it worked extremely well, and in the case of the 'colours' posters broke new ground. It may not have received the recognition it deserved or the plaudits given to Saatchi's in earlier years, which is unfair on BMP, but a majority of 179 is its own reward.

PPBs and PEBs

Party political broadcasts and party election broadcasts, often dismissed as silly, irrelevant, dull and ineffectual, are in fact both powerful and important. They are a democratic asset, giving all parties the chance to put their case fairly, and their demise would be a loss to democracy. We put enormous energy and care into our broadcasts in 1997, producing, I believe, the best series of election broadcasts ever made.

There are two major problems with PPBs. The first is the 'turn-off' factor. Viewing figures for PPBs, even outside election times, can reach between eight and ten million, and during elections this rises. They are shown at prime times on BBC1 and ITV just before the main evening news, as well as on BBC2. This assures them of a huge audience. However, although a lot of people start watching, often caught unawares, our minute-by-minute breakdowns taught us that they rarely watch the whole broadcast, especially on the BBC, where they are least expecting it. They watch the first forty-five seconds or minute, then they turn over and surf around, then they come back, thinking perhaps it has ended, and watch another forty-five seconds before surfing some more only to return again, maybe watching the last forty-five seconds while waiting for it to end so they can watch the news.

The research we did showed how crucial it was to ensure our broadcasts were entertaining and engaging as well as informative. It also persuaded us not to make a five-minute film which told one story as a complete narrative, but to segment it and tell the same story again and again, so that people got the whole story in their forty-five-second block. We applied this model to virtually all the PPBs that we made.

The second problem with PPBs is that although their budgets are tiny – we had £35,000 for each one during the election – the viewers see them as regular current affairs TV, and there-fore expect the same production values. They should not appear cheaper, nor should they be too glossy, otherwise viewers become wary. Therefore we banned 'Film on 4'-style 'arty' broadcasts, because people are suspicious of this and feel it is elitist. We made them to the same production standards that people might expect when they were watching the news or *Panorama*, adding a commercial element by repeatedly re-stating our brand identity –

either our message, or a visual slogan, or Labour's own mnemonic. This combines a TV programme with an advertisement, which is basically what a party political broadcast is.

For the 1997 election, for the first time, we also planned our broadcasts as an integral part of the overall campaign, so that when, for example, we were banging home the message about 'Tory Tax Lies' in autumn 1996, the PPBs did the same: same message, same concept, same slogan, even the same typeface. Simon Buckby at BMP, a former television reporter and adviser to John Prescott, was responsible for them:

> The first 'Tory Tax Lies' broadcast is a very good example of splitting the five minutes into four segments telling a very strong message but in a humorous way. We chose to use the *Spitting Image* characters. In one segment after another we basically said, here is the 'Tory Tax Lie' on health, education, crime and tax. You only needed to watch one of those four segments to get the whole message, which was that the Tories can't be trusted because they betrayed their promises. The message was really hard – they are lying – but because it was told through identifiable characters, with humour, you could get away with saying something so much harder than if you simply had a talking politician saying: 'The Tories are liars.' All the evidence suggests that this was the most-enjoyed PPB we've ever made, because people just laughed at it.[21]

For the next broadcast, '22 Tory Tax Lies', in November, which helped launch the '22 Tory Tax Rises' part of the campaign and went hand-in-glove with the 'Enough is Enough' posters, we went for an entirely different approach and produced a pastiche of a horror film, portraying five typical families in five different situations, with a hand stealing money from them. There was, for example, a pensioner sitting by her gas fire which was going off because her money was being stolen. It was very hard-hitting. And in January we had the 'Oxo Mum' broadcast – a female, a typical *Daily Mail* reader whom our target audience would be able to identify with – going through four different segments of the five minutes to reveal the hurt and damage she had felt over the previous five years: education, health, crime, and finally, of course, tax rises.

Probably the hardest-hitting tax broadcast we produced was the next, shown in the middle of March just before the election was announced. I had been concerned that John Major had developed 'Teflon' qualities over broken promises and I wanted to connect him to his record. We again portrayed him as two-faced, saying one thing before an election but doing another after it, promising lower taxes and then raising them twenty-two times. It was hard, but it was accurate and fair.

Going into the election campaign, viewing figures for the broadcasts started to rise, and the segmented approach became less important. The first of our five election broadcasts, on 10 April, was deliberately reassuring and positive, coinciding with the launch of the business manifesto. We had business people such as Anita Roddick, Terence Conran and Gerry Robinson endorsing us as 'a party that business can do business with'. Margaret McDonagh met the participants, and Simon Buckby interviewed them, with a friend of his holding the camera.

Our second PEB was the famous 'bulldog' broadcast, interspersing shots of Tony Blair talking about his hopes and ideas with pictures of him meeting world leaders, and clips of Fitz the bulldog. It was a bold stride across Tory territory – Labour re-awakening national pride to make Britain great again. It was centred on a line from Blair, 'The Tories say Britain's good enough. We say Britain can be better.' This broadcast was planned over a long time, about six months. I tested an animatic – a cartoon replica – of the broadcast in focus groups and it researched well. There had been fears that it might alienate women because it seemed so aggressive, but that didn't happen. There were endless discussions about whether it had to be a formal interview with Blair or with him on the move, and how you could cut between the dog and Blair. And before we actually got agreement to film Fitz, we commissioned what turned out to be two or three months' worth of intensive filming between the documentary-maker Molly Dineen and Tony Blair. By February we had spent a lot of money and had set up Ridley Scott Associates to shoot the dog (on film), but still had no agreement to go ahead with it. Simon Buckby and I were very keen, others wary. BMP had to make a big presentation at Millbank before Mandelson and Campbell would agree to let them film the broadcast. Blair and Brown were nervous too, and Blair only agreed to proceed with it after seeing an animatic of the broadcast in his office.

Film of the dog was all cut and ready by the end of February. The problem then arose that the footage Molly Dineen had shot did not work with the film of Fitz: in black and white, lethargic and gloomy at first then rising and trotting happily away, symbolising the renewal of Britain. Molly had been filming for two months and had forty tapes of Tony Blair. She edited them down to 8–10 minutes of highlights, which were gritty and personal but which just wouldn't fit with film of the dog. We needed new film of Blair 'rousing' the dog as he spoke, and it was agreed that Alastair Campbell would interview Blair in his house in Islington. 'For some reason, possibly because Tony felt too comfortable with Alastair, it didn't work,' said Simon. 'It didn't look powerful or strong enough.'[22] By now it was the beginning of April, in the middle of the election campaign.

At a heated meeting that included Alastair Campbell, Peter Mandelson, Margaret McDonagh, Simon Buckby and Dan Clifton, it was agreed to make two separate films – to ask Molly Dineen to continue cutting her forty hours into ten minutes, and to try to get some different footage of Blair for the Fitz broadcast. 'Molly was left to go and shoot her own film,' Simon said, 'and we agreed that Tony needed to have somebody who maybe he knew but was a bit more distant from than Alastair to interview him, so I did it. And we went to somebody's house in Wandsworth and shot it and there was something wrong with the colour. It was too pink.' We had to get it shot yet again, on the Saturday morning, 12 April, three days before it was due to be broadcast. Buckby and Mark

Lucas, Labour's head of film production, went to Blair's house in Islington, 'and we shot him really quickly this time because he had a bloody good idea what he wanted to say and how he wanted to say it. And it worked. And Mark and myself went to the editing suite and edited overnight and chucked the pictures against the dog, took it back to BMP who rejected it because they preferred the original pink version and Alastair's interviews.'[23]

John Webster, the long-suffering director, cut another version of the film, which was a combination of Buckby's interview and Campbell's interview, and both films were brought to Mandelson and me on Monday morning for us to choose. We watched the version combining the two interviews, and it looked terrible. One moment Blair was sitting in front of this brightly lit window in Islington, the next he was obviously somewhere completely different, back-dropped by pink curtains. We chose Buckby's version. It was a wonderful PEB. When the music by Michael Nyman, from the film *Carrington*, came in at the end, you got a soaring sense of opportunity, of hope and prospect in the future of a Labour government. It created a sense that Britain could be better. It had been hard work, but it was worth it.

Our third PEB, on 21 April, was another classic example of humour allowing you to say something on television that you simply couldn't do in print. We wanted to portray the Tories as so out of touch that they had done things – and would continue to do things – that hurt the target electorate. BMP came up with the idea of showing the Conservatives at the end of conference singing 'Land Of Hope And Glory', looking ecstatically happy and pleased with themselves, cut against pictures of real Britain – powerful images of people living in the real world, with captions explaining what the Tories had actually done. So at the beginning, as the Conservatives rose up to sing, you saw old people in homes, moving into the rundown NHS, overcrowded schools, people being mugged on the streets, women with families not being able to afford food because of VAT, all ending in an amazing crescendo as the sea washed away a sandcastle as if Britain were being destroyed by the Tories. It was powerful television, directed by Simon Kellen Jones, who also made *Our Friends in the North*.

Molly Dineen's film of Blair came next. I had been sceptical of it, but Alastair Campbell and Molly were keen, and they were right to be: its honest, glitz-free, fly-on-the-wall approach broke through the scepticism of the electorate, at a time when they were fed up with the whole campaign, making it probably our most effective broadcast.

Our final broadcast on the Monday before polling day summed up all our earlier messages. We returned to the traditional story-telling format, but again segmented into four sections. Directed by Stephen Frears, it starred Pete Postlethwaite as a taxi-driver picking up a father and his young daughter, who has been in casualty for six hours with a broken arm. The message of the film was blunt: vote, and vote Labour, or here's what the Tory fifth term will look like. In the film the taxi-driver picked the pair up after the polls had closed and explained to the father that he should have voted because of what was going to happen to his daughter's future, running through crime, education, tax and health. At the end the clock turned back, the taxi-driver told them they still had time to vote, dropped them off outside a polling station and drove off, showing a glimpse of his angel's wings. There was a lot of opposition to those wings: Campbell naturally hated them and wanted them cut out; I wanted them in. In the end Peter Mandelson took the video to Tom Sawyer, the General Secretary, who liked the wings, so they stayed. And these things stick. In January I was doing a focus group when someone said, 'I voted Labour because of the taxi-driver who had wings.'[24]

Reading all this, the rows, the pettiness, the trivia, it's easy to think: what is the point? It's all ridiculous, why does it matter so much? But that misses the point. Of course, when highly creative people meet highly political people the odd lapse into absurdity is inevitable, but the hours and hours spent getting every last detail right matter. Most obviously, if our communications are professional, then it reassures people that we will be professional and competent in government. More importantly, it means that we are taking the electorate seriously, not taking them for granted. This came through as an important difference between the two campaigns: Labour seemed to be making an effort to win support, the Conservatives hardly trying at all. Making an effort, being a perfectionist over small details gets through to the public. They need signals that tell them: this party cares about me. And in the end, if we believe we are right, and they are wrong, we have a responsibility to present that message with the greatest skill and professionalism we can muster. Saying the right thing but saying it badly is an indulgence. We have a duty to do the best we can.

Focus groups and opinion polling

With the exception of 'spin-doctors', no campaigning phrase has been imbued with a greater air of nonsensical mystique than 'focus groups'. Why focus groups should have gained this elevated position I cannot tell. Old-fashioned qualitative research, another name for the same thing, has not taken off in people's imaginations in the same way, nor has quantitative opinion polling, which is now incredibly sophisticated and potentially much more influential.

Focus groups are important to me. The mystique surrounding them is ridiculous: they are simply eight people in a room talking. Their importance in modern politics is that they enable politicians to hear directly the voters' voices.

I first came into contact with focus groups, or qualitative research, or group discussions as they were then known (and still are to many research practitioners) when I worked in advertising in the 1970s. In those days the moderator, the person who conducts the groups, would also prepare the evaluation and write the report. I was soon dissatisfied with this and wanted to attend. When I did I found it fascinating, gaining an understanding which immediately transcended that given by the moderator's report.

When I left advertising and started to work with the Labour Party they were already using qualitative research. In November 1985 some of the finest researchers in Britain presented ruthlessly damning findings on the unelectability of Labour.

At that time I did not conduct groups, but often sat in on them and always found them the source of enormous insight. This worked well until the 1992 campaign, but then research failed Labour. Both our quantitative polling, and to an extent our qualitative polling, failed to gauge accurately the public mood. All, or certainly most, of our researchers believed that Labour was heading for a hung parliament at worst, a small majority at best. I attended no groups during the 1992 election and I bitterly regret it. I decided there and then that I would conduct all my own groups, and that if I ever had a chance to work in another election I would conduct group discussions every single night.

I took my courage in my hand and conducted my first group. No one trained me, I just did it. And I loved it. I loved the direct contact with the electorate, the way that I could put arguments, hear arguments, confront arguments, develop ideas, feel the intensity of a point of view and hear the opinions, attitudes and emotions of ordinary members of the public.

I nearly always conduct focus groups in unassuming front rooms in Watford, or Edgware or Milton Keynes or Huddersfield, in a typical family room stacked with the normal knick-knacks and photos. The eight or so members of a group will have been recruited by a research company according to a formal specification: who they voted for in a previous election, their age, their occupation. They often begin nervously but then relax and talk freely, and usually do not want to stop.

I never analyse a group in isolation. I see them in relation to the other groups I have conducted, to the direction and purpose of the campaign, to the concepts that I and others may be developing at the time. In no way is this a passive process. I do not just sit there and listen. I challenge, I argue back, I force them to confront issues. I confront issues myself. I like to use the group to develop and test ideas.

I nearly always learn something new and surprising. People do not think in predictable ways or conform to conventional prejudice. In a group it is possible to test out the strength and depth of feeling around an issue, which can be more difficult, although not impossible, in a conventional poll.

Above all, what I get from focus groups is a sense of people's dignity, of the hard and difficult lives they lead. Most people work very hard and usually both parents work. They often feel insecure about their jobs, and are always worried about crime, the NHS, and schools for their children. Most people lead lives under pressure. They are sceptical about politics, but pleased that some-one is prepared to listen to their views. Such is their scepticism and alienation that they cannot believe that a political party is interested in what they have to say. Sometimes at a focus group I would say that I was conducting this group for Tony Blair and its members would be astonished. Tony Blair cares what I think? He does care, and so do I. Focus groups do not of necessity involve dilution of principle or compromise – to say that implies that the voters are fools, which they are not. They want politicians who are tough, honest and courageous, and who govern with principle. That is why they respected Margaret Thatcher and in the end lost faith in John Major. The public want leaders who lead, they want governments that tough it out. But they also want to be heard. Of course, governing with principle and yet in a continuous dialogue with the voters is complicated. But modern politics is complicated. The electorate is more demanding and is right to be so. It is up to us to meet the new challenge. I do not just see focus groups and market research as campaigning tools; increasingly I see them as an important part of the democratic process: part of a necessary dialogue between politicians and people, part of a new approach to politics.

Not all groups work as they should. On one occasion two

strangers seduced each other as the group was going on. Everyone pretended not to notice. Sometimes people get too angry, but mostly they work well.

For the three years before the election I did focus groups about once a week. For the six and a half weeks of the election I conducted them six nights a week. Mostly I focused on 1992 Conservative voters who were considering switching to Labour, our prime target group.

Focus groups in London

To give the flavour of a typical focus group of switchers from Conservative to Labour, here are some comments from verbatim transcripts, literally picked at random from a huge pile near my desk. These groups were conducted in Edgware:

April 1996: 'Why have you stopped supporting the Conservatives?'

- 'I've lost a lot of money. I have got severe negative equity on a flat that we bought about two years ago. I have lost about half the value of it so we had to go to the building society to ask to borrow more. It's upsetting to say the least. It did come quite close to losing our house at one stage, but we were lucky we could pull through.'
- 'Overall we have gone back to the dark ages here. The NHS system here is just a complete, total nightmare.'
- 'I just feel that we are going backwards – they certainly aren't taking us forwards. Crime is rising, the NHS is going to pot.'[25]

May 1996: 'What do you feel about voting Labour?'

- 'I have thought about it. But Labour has got to be very careful over the next few months. They are being careful, but they have got to continue being careful. I don't really trust Labour.'

- 'There has been a huge success in how Labour has improved their image and they've done a lot of work. About ten years ago I wouldn't have touched them with a barge-pole, but now I just might. You do hear how Labour MPs are sponsored by the unions and you do wonder, though, just how in their pockets they are and how extreme they are. You still would be a little bit scared.'

- 'After the last time they were in, everyone had a bad feeling – a bad taste in their mouth. They can't completely change all their policies. They were so extreme that they really did have to move towards the centre, and I'm just not convinced that they truly have.'[26]

These answers give a clear sense of the dilemma facing these switchers: disillusioned with the Conservatives but wary of Labour. This mood remained until the end of the campaign.

Focus groups in the United States

As a comparison between focus groups in the United Kingdom and the United States, below is a diary account of focus groups conducted in Los Angeles in February 1995 by Stanley Greenberg for the President, which I attended along with George Stephanopoulos:

23 February: Arrive LA mid-afternoon. Palm trees in the airport. Fast transfer. My driver waits. Tousled hair, jeans, bright shirt: 'Hi, I'm Mike.' Guided tour through the sprawl of outer LA. Long drive to focus groups. Long detailed questionnaire. Women college graduates. The respondents introduce themselves. 'Hi, I'm Karen. I'm an actress. I just had a part in *Murder Incorporated*' (low gasps of admiration). 'I've had silicone implants, but they have inflated, poisoned my body, gave me rheumatism, but I struggle on' (moans of condolence). 'Hi, I'm Carol. I think criminals should have their hands cut off' (general assent).

Strongly pro-choice. Tough on welfare, didn't like Gingrich, but he has made his mark. Dole: Boring. Bureaucratic. Warm to Clinton: for the middle class. Tries hard. Done a lot.

Response to Clinton not at all like Major. No sense of betrayal. Not for the privileged. No extremism.[27]

24 February: The female groups are the same as last night. Concerns about crime, violence, having to work too hard. Clinton liked: decent, on our side, understands us, for the middle class, tried to get health care through: but ineffective, has not done anything for us. The women, as yesterday, were more self-contained, more optimistic, less beaten down than many British women I have spoken to in groups.

The men looked like a six-pack platoon. Uncompromising. Unattractive. They were everything you imagine US blue-collar voters to look like. They were concerned about the same things but again not as angry as in Britain. They liked Clinton, but less strongly.[28]

25 February: Black groups in downtown LA. These groups were extraordinary. The black males were initially hostile: 'Who are you, sister?' 'Is this a black research agency?' The start was very aggressive. But then they soften and occasionally dissolve into farce. Tony the aggressive Afro-American poet from New York trying to develop a relationship with the moderator. They are open about their lack of knowledge and impressively supportive of the less articulate members of the group. They are angry, clearly feeling themselves the victims of racism, which is often subtle. 'They told me I couldn't have a car-washing job because I didn't have the experience. Only afterwards did I realise you did not have to have experience to wash cars.'

They are polar opposites of the blue-collar males. They appear almost impossible to contain in the same coalition. George Stephanopoulos is witty about his boss, the President: when one of the women says Clinton procrastinates, George says, 'You got that one right.'

The women were very impressive. They were intelligent, warm, supportive, honest, informed. They liked Clinton, they thought he was trying, particularly on health care, but he changed his mind too often, has not delivered. They were optimistic, strong, and put the white groups to shame.[29]

Alastair Campbell did not believe in focus groups, but he does now: 'Well, before I went to them I thought you were a bit of a nutter, frankly. But I never went to a focus group where I didn't get some sort of insight that was useful. I think one of the great dangers of politics is the sort of level you are at, either in opposition or in government. It is very easy to lose track, and the people who were talking were the people who had to vote for us, so you had to listen to what they were saying. Sometimes it was depressing because there you were working your balls off trying to communicate what you were all about and they knew bugger-all about it and yet they had opinions about it. Very strong opinions.'[30] Bruce Grocott MP (Blair's Parliamentary Private Secretary) was another convert. He was against the whole idea, but attended a couple of groups and became an addict.

Focus groups are only part of the polling programme. Equally as important, probably more important, are quantified opinion polls with samples of over 1,000. Political polling is far more advanced in the United States than in the United Kingdom for obvious reasons: the USA has dozens and dozens of elections, with large budgets for polling and media.

For the election and pre-election period we were lucky to have the voluntary assistance of Stanley Greenberg. Greenberg has taken quantitative research to new heights. Polls are no longer snapshots of public opinion, they are incredibly perceptive measures of where public opinion is, using long questionnaires with subtle and intelligent questions. Greenberg likes quantitative research because the process of writing the questionnaire forces strategic choices to be taken. After the poll has been conducted it is subject to a level of statistical analysis that transforms your understanding of the data. This is strategic research at its best, and it is incredibly valuable to a political campaign. Greenberg says of the use of modern polling techniques in political campaigning:

It doesn't need defending. It is part of the democratisation of modern elections. Just as governments have changed, just as parties have changed, campaigns have changed. Democracy has changed. The institutions that used to be effective in mediating popular sentiment have atrophied, and have lost their ability to articulate. So the trade unions, for example, just don't have the kind of base that they used to have. If you want to know what working people think, you can't turn to these organisations which can effectively represent their members and so there is no choice but to go to people directly through these means. Politicians have always used various instruments to try to judge where the public stood. And now polls and focus groups are the best available means.[31]

In Millbank Greg Cook co-ordinated the whole polling programme with great skill. He made sure that as well as the opinion polls and focus groups, vast party telephone banks were in constant contact with switchers to Labour. Deborah Mattinson also conducted intensive polling in the key area of the Pennine Belt. It was a highly sophisticated polling operation, and a great credit to Cook.

Spin-doctors

The only campaigning phrase more abused than focus groups is 'spin-doctor'. It is used by the media without thought or understanding. Initially, 'spin' was a term reserved for the practice of putting the best possible gloss on an event breaking in the news. Typically, after a US presidential debate, James Carville and George Stephanopolous for one side and Mary Matalin, now Carville's wife and a spokesperson for Bush, for the other would rush – literally, run – to the awaiting media corps to give their line on the debate.

This was called 'spinning': putting your perspective on what happened. In 1996 I was in the media area after a presidential debate. It had a huge sign over it saying SPIN CITY. The moment the debate started it was as though the floodgates opened and dozens of spokespeople from both Dole and Clinton rushed into the room. The place was in complete turmoil – crushed, heaving, shouting, maniacal. At points just yards apart campaign representatives were spinning, putting their views of the debate. Above each of Clinton's team an assistant carried a prominent sign with the name of the person doing the briefing: 'Leon Panetta' (Clinton's chief of staff), 'George Stephanopolous', and so on. By the next debate the Republicans had caught up: they had their signs, too.

From 'spinning' grew 'spin-doctors', which is just a fancy name for media spokespeople. But from there somehow the name came to include anyone or anything included in what are believed to be the 'black arts' of campaigning. This is just media nonsense. If a 'spin-doctor' exists at all, he or she is someone responsible for media relations for a political party. This is a longstanding and completely unexceptional activity. In a world in which political parties, and other high-profile organisations, are under twenty-four-hour media attack, it is common sense to employ people to put the view of the party or organisation and to do it to best effect. In a modern media environment, competence and good communications are inseparable: you cannot have one without the other.

Of course, some media spokespeople do this with greater skill than others. Because of his long background in the tabloids, Alastair Campbell understands the needs of the press. He knows that unless you constantly feed the media stories, they will gobble you up. He thinks it a point of professional pride that he has to make the best case for Tony Blair: after all, that is what he is there for. Campbell is more than just a media spokesperson. He is also an outstanding strategist, but above all he has the presence and qualities of endurance which made him, in effect, the rock of the campaign. He has received much credit for the 1997 victory but he is still in some ways underestimated. Campbell is hard to get to know, difficult to break down. He tends to be suspicious of people, and categorises them into either a very small group who are acceptable or a very large group who are not. But when he does accept someone he is loyal to them: particularly if they work with or for him.

David Hill, until recently chief media spokesperson for the Labour Party, and another highly skilled and highly rated 'spin-doctor', describes how he works:

> The first rule is you have to understand and know the people you are dealing with. You have to be robust. You have to never tell a lie – telling lies is disastrous, because one of the most effective elements in being a spin-doctor is that they believe what you are saying to them. Because if you kill a story and then they find out that you are lying and in fact the story is true, you've had it in the future. So you've got to be robust, you've got to understand your journalists, you've got to never lie to them, and you have got to recognise what they want. You have got to have speed, because if you don't get your strike in first, or if you don't follow something up quickly, then you get left behind. You must provide words, because they always need words. What you have got to do to be an effective spin-doctor – someone who can really do the business on behalf of the party – is be someone who the media can go to and say: 'Although I have got a story, if I've spoken to you I know the status of an issue. I know where it is taking me, I know whether it is going to take off or not.' Then you will have created a relationship with the journalists which is pivotal.[32]

Putting the best progressive case to the media should not be a reason for criticism, but a cause for pride. The ability to handle the media is essential in opposition and government. It is one of the ways progressive parties advance their cause, and serve the public well.

The grid

The grid is the heart of an election campaign. It is the point at which strategy, message and logistics all gel on one single piece of paper. A grid is not just a timetable – where leading politicians will be on every day of the campaign – but outlines the strategic and message imperatives that connect with the planning logistics.

Most task forces in Millbank drew up their own election grids. Jackie Stacey's team had compiled a detailed day-by-day plan of Blair's and Prescott's nationwide tours. Dan Clifton spent a great deal of time filling in a schedule of all the radio and television programmes that were planned for the campaign. Faz Hakim and Ian Howarth in 'Key Campaigners' drew up campaign diaries for all the shadow Cabinet visits. However, these grids stood alone and often did not relate to each other. They needed an overall masterplan to defer to and into which they would slot, giving the campaign shape, cohesion and a central message. Following the launch of 'Leading Britain into the Future' in early January 1997, Mandelson knew that the clock was ticking and that he had to get something down on paper, both setting out the structure of the campaign day and drawing up an early grid. He went to Waheed Alli's house in Kent on the weekend of 25–26 January, armed with his laptop and a warm jumper.

Mandelson spent the whole weekend in the living-room by a log fire, with his computer on his lap, bashing out notes to Tony Blair on a proposed daily structure of meetings and, more importantly, drawing up the first draft of the 'message grid'. Each day was allotted a separate page, with simple sections typed into the margins, including details of the morning and afternoon press conferences, the whereabouts of Tony Blair, the main photo of the day and key broadcast appearances of shadow Cabinet members. Each page contained only eight or nine simple facts, but they provided the umbrella for all the logistical and media scheduling. When Peter returned from Kent, he and Alastair went over it together before distributing it to Tony Blair's office, Gordon Brown's office and key staff at Millbank. Over the next three months it was discussed at countless meetings and went through a dozen redrafts. It was finally taken to a series of early morning meetings with Tony Blair and Gordon Brown at Millbank.

There was never a final draft of the grid. It was refined through-out the campaign, with Mandelson clipping new sheets into the purple folder which accompanied him to every campaign meeting. It now sits on the top of his bookshelf in the study of his London home.

The grid was brought to life by a series of late-night meetings organised with great skill and gusto by Anji Hunter. These meetings showed Anji at her best: she powered through them, mowing down anyone who was slow or unco-operative. There was no chance of an early night: pizzas arrived at about midnight and the grid would be finished come what may. These meetings started in early 1997 and continued almost until the election. They were crucial in making the grid real: agreeing events, locations, opportunities for photographs. They key participants – in addition to Anji – were Margaret McDonagh; Jan Royall, veteran grid organiser and longstanding senior aide to Neil Kinnock; Peter Mandelson; Alastair Campbell; Peter Hyman; and Blair's official photographer for the campaign, Tom Stoddart.

The grid is the heart of the campaign, bringing together all elements of strategy on one sheet of paper. Without a grid, the campaign cannot really be said to exist.

The Conservative campaign

We believed we were up against the most formidable political fighting machine in the world. We were – at the start at least – in awe of Saatchi's and their destructive potential. Jonathan Powell employed Jon Mendelsohn – former adviser to Greville Janner MP – on what was effectively a Saatchi-watch, virtually full-time. We wanted to know everything the Tories were going to do, before they did it. Jon used to write long and vivid reports about how we would be bludgeoned into defeat. 'I was trying to get a full handle on the Tories' *modus operandi*, to analyse what they were doing, how we should respond to it, what we should or shouldn't take seriously,' he said. 'I found this a very, very interesting duty at the beginning. I took a long time studying a large part of the Tory organisation, the personalities, the key figures involved.'[33]

Very early on in 1996 their complete media plan was leaked to us, and this was genuinely scary. First of all, they had a plan; second, they kept to it; and third, they had huge amounts of money – upwards of £10 million. It was all there: the launch of 'New Labour, New Danger' in July; then 'New Labour, New Danger' versions one, two, three, four and five, and so on and so on. Their plan was so reliable you could set your watch by it.

However, although we were in awe of the Saatchi/Central Office machine at the beginning, our respect soon waned. From the start the Conservatives had not known how to react to New Labour. Initially they had three positions: Labour hasn't changed, it's still old Labour; Labour has changed, but it's just a carbon copy of the Conservatives, so why not stick to the real thing; Labour has changed, but is still as dangerous as ever. Maurice Saatchi explained these options to me in 1995 and moaned about the failure of the Conservatives to make a decisive choice. Eventually they did choose, but they chose the wrong one. They decided to concede New Labour and try to link it to 'new dangers'. This was a mistake. Conceding New Labour as a fact gave it the credibility it needed to be believed by the electorate. It made New Labour real. And the 'new dangers' of New Labour were spurious. Nothing frightened the voters about New Labour at all – all that frightened them was old Labour: unions, taxes, extremism. There was no way that their strategy could work. What the Conservatives should have done was try to present New Labour as a sham, and maintain that old Labour and old dangers were still lurking. That they did not is amazing. Saatchi's now say they were influenced by a survey conducted by Richard Wirthin in 1995, which claimed that New Labour was accepted by the electorate as an irreversible fact and that Conservative strategy therefore had to be built on that. If this was so, then this poll must have been conducted in a parallel electoral universe because the electorate was nervous about old Labour right up to the end of the campaign, and it has taken a

Labour government to dispel these fears finally and completely.

But the Tories' worst error was to launch an attacking strategy too early. For the Conservatives to have any chance of winning they had to follow a strategy of three A's: Apologise; Achievements; Attack. They did make some sort of apology – 'Yes it Hurt. Yes it Worked' – but it was too partial and too arrogant. Major should have looked the voter in the eye and said, 'Yes, we made mistakes. Yes, we caused you pain. And we are sorry.'

Next they had to take credit for the economic recovery, as Clinton had in the United States. Throughout 1996 they should have been advertising positively on the economy: linking the economic upturn with their performance in government. That they did not do this was the biggest strategic error of the campaign. Sir Tim Bell wanted to, as did Saatchi's, but Brian Mawhinney panicked, believing the Conservatives needed an attacking campaign to build morale and stop infighting. The result was that they got no credit for the recovery and alienated the electorate by the negativism of their approach. The more negative they were, the more voters felt they had nothing to offer.

The irony for the Conservatives is that all the elements were in place for electoral recovery: the economy was strengthening, doubt about Labour growing. But they missed their chance. A positive campaign in 1996 followed by a 'Don't Let Labour Blow It' campaign focusing on old Labour would have reduced Labour's majority.

From the summer of 1996 it became clear that the Conservative strategy was not working. Although it was creating some doubt about Labour, it was causing greater resentment towards the Conservatives. In mid-1996 Jon Mendelsohn had reported huge strengths in their campaigning machine. 'It soon became quite apparent actually that I was pretty wrong in the analysis, and it started tailing back quite considerably from that period to looking at their weaknesses,' he remembers.[34] The Tories had given up any claim to exemplify the future or hope or any kind of positive value. This left a vast space in the political landscape for Labour to occupy. Labour could be positive; Labour could represent the future. Blair understood this instinctively. The rest of us had to catch up, but in the end we got it right. The Conservative advertising was a gigantic own goal.

As the campaigning months passed, Mendelsohn's notes became less frequent. He found it harder and harder to say constructive things about what the Tories were trying to achieve. They were also hindered by a largely ineffective media operation. Charles Lewington, Sheila Gunn and the others who made up their press corps were simply no match for Millbank. They tried hard, but they were doomed. By January Mendelsohn had decided that the Conservatives' only remaining strength was fund-raising; the rest was worthless. Then John Major talked about 'two futures' in his New Year address and I began to suspect that the Tories had a copy of my War Book, as indeed it later turned out they had. I noticed soon after that we were being attacked by Brian Mawhinney for scare-mongering on lines closely related to those in the War Book. I was sure they had it, and I phoned Peter from holiday to tell him. Jon Mendelsohn spent weeks trying to find out who leaked it, but he never succeeded. Yet despite having the War Book, with all the polling information about target voters it contained – and the Tories did not do much effective polling themselves – as well as the complete list of Labour's weaknesses as we ourselves perceived them, they had continued to produce advertising that influenced no one but their own hard-core supporters.

'By about February 1997 I had become the personal punching-bag of Philip Gould, and every time he kept on turning to me and saying, "What are they going to do now? They're stuffed. Tell me what they're going to do,"' Mendelsohn remembers. 'At which point I think I developed myriad pathetic excuses for the paucity of the Conservative position ranging from "structurally they're not so bad, it's just the politics really" to even more embarrassing conclusions. Essentially, from January we knew they had completely screwed it because they had no understanding whatsoever of the electorate, the polling, of us, of themselves.

They had no understanding of where it all stood and they could not mount a credible attack on us.' In the end Jon was forced to admit it. 'They have blown it,' he wrote.[35]

The final phase

Just as the election was about to be called, everything started to come together. Alastair Campbell, always sceptical, admits that at the end it all worked: 'If you ask me now how it was all put together I could not tell you, but it was.'[36] Peter Mandelson had a grip on the task forces and on the structure and organisation of the campaign. Margaret McDonagh was in effective charge of the logistics, which meant things worked. We had our messages and a theme, and BMP produced advertising expressing the line and the pledges in the brightest of colours so that Labour became the positive party. The grid was finalised. The sets were agreed. Peter Mandelson joined us all to sit at the central table in the middle of Millbank. I used to sit directly opposite Margaret McDonagh. 'Will we still be friends by the end?' she asked at the beginning of the campaign. We are. Gordon Brown and his team moved in. We were ready to go.

And then there was a strange lull. 'My overwhelming sense was of waiting,' said Liam Byrne.

There was a point in about January–February when things looked as if they were suddenly coming together and I felt for the first time that we were going to be okay. There were so many differences of opinion about who was going to be in charge and what everyone needed to be doing, but in January–February everything suddenly came together. Then my sense was of waiting, waiting for the Conservatives to really hit us hard – and we kept waiting. I remember there was a period of two days – the only time I ever came close to hitting a panic button – when they hit us on trade unions because this was a real business issue that we needed to win. I think it's true to say that we wobbled for a day – for about a period of twenty-four hours, we wobbled. We then fully expected them to come and hit us with a couple more good right hands, and it never came. I remember talking with the business unit – we were expecting the great adverts, you know, Tory battalions to charge into us, and it just never came. We had just cut the ground from under them.[37]

Every week, and perhaps twice a week as the election drew closer, I conducted focus groups in London and the north-west. Afterwards I would phone up Tony Blair and talk to him about the voters and their mood. The closer the election got, the more reflective he became. Often I would call and interrupt him gently strumming on his guitar, calm, focused, preparing himself. He was ready for the fight. So was Millbank.

10

LANDSLIDE COUNTRY

Week one: Losing the election campaign

Monday, 17 March

W e knew Major would call the election that day. Of course people were excited, but it was actually very calm in Millbank as we watched Major's election announcement outside 10 Downing Street. Everyone knew exactly what to do. Tony Blair did some interviews at lunchtime from a school. He looked nervous, but carried it off. Alastair Campbell was with him and remembers a sense of victory: 'We had done an awful lot of preparatory work, that school had been set up for weeks and we always said the minute the election was called we'd go to a school. And we fixed up live – Tony did a storming interview, absolutely storming. He looked right. I could sense then we were going to do it.'[1]

In Millbank, Peter Mandelson and Gordon Brown called a staff meeting of everyone in the building. The room was packed. They outlined the seriousness of the task ahead, that this was the moment everyone had been working towards.

That night I went to do my first focus group of the election. I had decided to conduct them every night for the next six weeks, except Saturdays. I was afraid of exhaustion. I took Labour's election campaign with me to be tested – every advertisement, every poster, about twelve of them. I bought a coffee and a chicken burger at Euston Station, as I have done dozens of times before, and got on a train to Watford feeling a settled calm: we are off, it is going to be okay. I then sensed that something was missing, and realised I had left Labour's entire election campaign by the Burger King at Euston Station. Desperate panic overcame me. I had no phone. I was compounding idiocy with idiocy. The thought crossed my mind that, for me, 1997 could become some terrible replay of 1992. 'GOULD LEAVES ELECTION CAMPAIGN ON EUSTON STATION.' I reached Watford and phoned Margaret McDonagh, hyperventilating – 'I have made a terrible mistake' – and explained what had happened. She was calm, talked me down. 'It will be all right,' she said. But the moment she was off the phone she screamed at one of my assistants to 'get down to Euston now'.

My wife was at home with the children. I got her down to Euston as well. Then I rang directory enquiries to find the telephone number of the Burger King; the only one they had was at Paddington. I arrived at the house where the groups were being held and stumbled through the first minutes, semi-hysterical. Then my pager buzzed: 'Posters found'. I relaxed. This is an omen, I thought. This time the gods are with me.

The gods were not with John Major. He was mauled in the focus groups. I went home and did what I would do virtually every night of the campaign: I wrote two notes, one to the campaign team – Tony Blair, Gordon Brown, Peter Mandelson, Alastair Campbell, Jonathan Powell, Anji Hunter and Margaret McDonagh – and a second, personal one to Tony Blair. This took until quite late, perhaps one or two in the morning. I was up again at five. This was not exceptional: most of the other people involved in the campaign worked these kind of hours.

I frequently phoned Alastair Campbell with findings from the groups. That night he told me that the *Sun* had come out for

Labour. Stuart Higgins had paged him while Blair was doing a question-and-answer session in Gloucester earlier that evening. 'I knew instinctively what it was,' he said.[2] This was a sickening blow to Tory morale so early in the campaign.

The night's findings were clear: 'On the basis of these groups Labour won the day. Fourteen out of sixteen respondents thought TB was the most effective performer on the basis of news coverage. Major did most badly with women, who thought him arrogant and lacking in humility.' They particularly disliked him describing the election as 'fun'. 'Major's problem as a campaigner is that he is soiled by his record. In 1992 his approach was new and he had no baggage. Now he has a record of failure. Last time the mood was: "Give him a chance". Now the mood is: "He has had his chance". The soapbox worked then, it does not work now.' And Labour's message – that Britain could be better – 'overwhelms the Tory message that Britain is good enough'. The Conservative message – 'Eighteen years has transformed Britain. Don't take the risk with Labour' – only reminded people they wanted change.[3] I wrote to Blair, 'You beat Major today.'[4]

Tuesday, 18 March
I went to have acupuncture at seven. In my taxi to the office I got a call from Blair. 'How was I?' he asked. How was what? I thought. It turned out that he had been interviewed for the *Today* programme on Radio 4. He was full of nervous excitement, desperate to get going. Unable to face the humiliation of saying I was having acupuncture at the moment the leader of the Labour Party was giving his first major interview of the campaign, I lied and said I was at the gym. Blair groaned. I squirmed with embarrassment. 'You too?' he said. He had phoned Peter Mandelson for his reaction to the interview and Peter really *had* been at the gym. Blair and Campbell both thought we were completely pathetic.

Blair was anxious about the result. I decided to suppress my usual pessimism and said we should be aiming for a 10 per cent, hundred-seat win. I said it was certain we would win comfortably. I phoned Peter. We both felt foolish.

I arrived at Millbank where we were still on the nine o'clock morning meeting schedule. We did not move to seven o'clock starts until after Easter. Millbank was starting to fill up. Peter Hyman had moved on to the central table, along with, occasionally, Alastair Campbell. Margaret, who had saved my life the night before, suggested possibly I needed more sleep. 'She thinks I am cracking up,' I thought.

In an annexe to the main campaigning space, shadow Cabinet researchers were assembling. A 'Reflections' group had been formed to give dispassionate strategic advice.

Blair's office was moving in upstairs, including Derry Irvine (Lord Irvine of Lairg) who was a huge figure in the campaign and who formed a special bond with Stanley Greenberg and myself. He was especially fond of Stan, and consulted him often, like a doctor. Working with Derry was one of the pleasures of the campaign. He combined a boyish sense of humour with a rather grand manner that I found both endearing and entertaining in a long, gruelling campaign. He was in Millbank to offer his forensic legal mind and to make sure the relationships worked. He was soon in action helping to dig us out of trouble on the issue of union recognition.

Peter Mandelson was cooler and calmer than in 1987. He sat at his desk, feet on the table, listening to the radio through earphones, watching television, ready to pounce. He rarely lost his composure: he was controlled and measured throughout. This is only one side of Mandelson. He is a balance of outward control, genuine self-confidence, lurking vulnerability and a biting sense of humour, and he normally moves quickly between these mooods. His greatest quality is his courage – often when a situation looks parlous he will ratchet it up, take a few more risks. He likes to be on the edge. But he also wants to have fun, squeezing the irony out of people and situations. During this campaign, however, he stayed in one mood: clinical, detached, in control, pacing himself and the campaign.

For most of the weeks that followed, I hated the 1997 campaign. It was a dreadful ordeal from beginning to end. I wanted only one thing: to win, to win massively, and for no one, not one single person, to say, 'We could have done better.' I was going to exorcise the ghosts of 1992. I knew that this degree of focus, this obsession, verged on a kind of madness, but I believe that many campaigners are in their way slightly mad. Through the force of my will, I wanted to drive the Tories into the ground. But one day, as I was wandering off to a focus group clutching my art bag and wearing crumpled, dishevelled clothes, Tony Blair's Jaguar swept past me with Blair, Campbell and Anji Hunter laughing at my apparent eccentricity, and I thought perhaps I was going too far.

The *Sun* dominated the mood on Tuesday. Robin Oakley, political editor of the BBC, poignantly described the dismay of the Tories: 'Old friends are passing them by on the other side of the street.'[5] At the morning press conference, Gordon Brown came under pressure for refusing to name the companies that would be affected by windfall tax. After the conference the BBC filmed Charlie Whelan briefing frantically in the foyer of the media centre, leading Peter Mandelson to give an order that no one was to brief inside the centre, because of all the cameras. We had a better afternoon: the Liberal Democrat MP Simon Hughes asked a question about the Downey Report into alleged corruption by Neil Hamilton and others at Prime Minister's Questions, and we realised sleaze could be catapulted to the top of the agenda again. The Scottish MP Brian Wilson was sent off to tour the Press Gallery to talk up the story. David Hill immediately got on to John Prescott to get him to front our end of the attack. 'We didn't want the Liberals at the forefront of this anyway, but also it was a disadvantage because it wouldn't have the same impact,' he said. 'So I immediately contacted John Prescott and said, "You have got to front this tomorrow morning. You have got to go and kick the shit out of the Tories over the latest developments in Tatton and Hamilton." And he went on the *Today* programme the following morning, after I had told everybody it was going to happen, so the story ran overnight and built up massive momentum. Prescott was on at ten past eight and went for them very effectively. It just took off.'[6] It was classic Prescott – funny, bombastic, hammering the Tories again and again. Sleaze was up and running.

The focus groups that night were good: 'All these respondents have hardened in their support since they were last interviewed (around a year ago). Their position going into the election is clear: the Conservatives are finished, Labour should be given a go. This does not mean the election is a formality: it is a test that Labour must pass.' Labour had won the day, 'but by a closer margin than yesterday. Respondents did not really understand the windfall tax. It did not break through today.'[7] To Blair I wrote: 'You are beating Major comfortably. Seven of the eight respondents say you are outscoring him.'[8]

Wednesday, 19 March

The windfall tax was extensively covered in the broadsheets, but the Downey Report dominated the news. We had been preparing for a Tory attack on the latest jobless figures, which showed a substantial reduction in unemployment, but they were completely overshadowed by sleaze. All anyone wanted to know was why they had not published the Downey Report before the election. Michael Heseltine called the BBC news agenda 'a scandal'.[9] Brian Mawhinney toured the TV studios accusing us of mischief-making and attempting to cover up the good unemployment figures. Millbank staffers stood around the TV screens cheering as Mawhinney got more and more irate. It was being claimed that the election was called early to avoid publication. I did not believe it. Our intelligence had always been that Major wanted a long campaign, which was another of his appalling errors. All the long campaign did was make people fed up and heighten their desire for change.

The focus groups showed this was another strong day for us. 'This group was very good for us indeed. We still face campaigning challenges, but they can be dealt with.' However, the voters were already beginning to get impatient with the campaign: 'Women all used the same word – "muddle" – to describe the campaign. Men think the campaign is still in its slow early stages: the first ten minutes of a football match.'[10] To Blair I wrote, 'Your own position is remarkably strong,' but at the moment, 'you are our campaign; nothing else is on the radar'. I was convinced that we should be positive; the electorate was screening out negative messages. There were some worries too: our campaign 'is liked and admired' but 'lacks content and definition'; 'Europe is mentioned a few times – people want reassurance on it. If the Tories got the right message they could make progress on the economy.'[11]

Thursday, 20 March

The focus was all on sleaze. At the daily eleven o'clock strategy meeting, which had a large cast but did not always make much progress, Gordon Brown had one of the most brilliant ideas of the campaign. He wanted the Labour candidate in Tatton to stand down and for an independent to stand against Hamilton. The first time he said it, he mumbled it a bit and no one really listened. He repeated it and this time they took some note. It seemed like a Brown long shot: it was not really going to happen. But Gordon was a man with a mission: if he could, he was going to keep sleaze running until polling day. The more Hamilton and his wife appeared on TV, the less chance the Conservatives had to campaign on their agenda. Prime Minister's Questions had Blair and Major face-to-face in combat. Blair was angry, Major vicious. An interim report into the sleaze allegations was published, leaving a question-mark hanging over ten Tory MPs.

But out in Northwood, where I did my focus groups that night, the election was already going off the boil. People were starting to lose interest: they were using words like 'boring' and 'bickering'. 'Day-one excitement has fizzled out,' I reported.[12] These groups did not warm to Blair either: 'Five of the eight did not like you.' But, 'The crucial point of this group is that they are natural

Conservatives who have had enough . . . It would take a lot to get them back to the Tories.' The risk to us remained the same: 'The Tories have potential on the economy and Europe but are as yet unable to unpick it.'[13]

Friday, 21 March
More sleaze, more boredom in the focus groups. The *Guardian* front page – 'Sleaze: the evidence' – was dominated by revelations that Major knew of £25,000 bribes paid to Tim Smith MP, but allowed him to remain as Northern Ireland Minister. This story dominated the news bulletins all day. Gordon Brown was waiting impatiently to see if the Labour candidate, Jon Kelly, would stand down in Tatton. Kelly was considering it, but the Liberals had to stand down too. I was already getting exhausted. I had doubts about whether I could keep doing groups every night. Margaret said I should ease up, but I was determined to keep going. My exhaustion was matched by the voters' boredom. 'The election has become a bit of bore. People are starting to switch off. Most women have very little sense of anything happening at all. Most men think it has been a slow start. This is in marked contrast to the sense of excitement and anticipation that was felt on Monday.' Meanwhile things were getting worse for the Tories. 'It is clear that sleaze is really starting to hurt them. In the short run because they [the voters] are starting not to believe Major, but more crucially because it connects directly to their recent history of incompetence and dishonesty. They are branding themselves as a government you cannot trust.' In response we had to be 'a positive voice in a sea of sleaze and cynicism'.[14]

Weekend, 22–23 March
On Saturday I went into Millbank for a short time. Peter was there and we chatted for a while. He was calm, reflective. I simply felt intense relief that I had got through the first week. I went home and collapsed.

On Sunday evening I drove out to do a focus group in Carpenders

Park, close to Watford. It was a beautiful sunny evening and I had a sense of elections past. This one felt calmer, almost serene. The woman hosting the groups was friendly and kind; she was certain we would win. But the group dispelled my confidence: 'This group was far more uncertain than earlier groups this week, and gave much better guidance on how the Conservatives could mount a strategy of recovery. The best way back for the Conservatives is the economy. The basic premise of their poster "Britain is Booming/Don't Let Labour Ruin It" has the power to connect. To be effective the strength of the economy has to be linked to fear of Labour. If they can make the economy a risk, they can make progress. Anxiety about Labour focuses on the unions, interest rates, inflation, tax, Europe, inexperience.'[15] This response was typical and showed the folly of the Conservatives' strategy. As the campaign developed, more and more people became convinced that Britain was booming. A positive strategy from the start would have put the Tories in a different and stronger position.

I wrote to Blair, 'We are in the right place but they are not dead yet. We must watch the economy like a hawk.'[16]

Week two: Field of dreams

Monday, 24 March
The Tories began to do the right thing and attack on the economy, using better-than-expected trade figures to support their 'Britain is Booming' claim. John Sergeant on the BBC lunchtime news accurately observed that 'Tory guns are pointing in the right direction on the economy.' The proposed televised debate between Blair, Major and Ashdown was heating up as an issue. Michael Dobbs, the Tories' negotiator, attacked us for 'hiding behind Liberal skirts on this one'.[17] Matthew Taylor was angry over a briefing someone had given to the *Independent* that we would save £2 billion by merging the management of NHS trusts. More seriously, the *Daily Telegraph* splashed with a story on Labour's

plans for union recognition at the workplace. They had a leaked draft of our business manifesto and claimed we had duped the CBI over union recognition rights.

Two focus groups in Slough showed people losing ever more interest in the campaign: 'Every day that passes leaves people more and more disconnected from the campaign.' I wrote that, 'We easily won the news. Seven out of the eight thought Labour was most impressive. This was because Major looked tired and carping. TB was fresh, confident and positive. This contrast swamped the Tory message.'[18] This note has a trace of complacency. It was tempting fate: this was to be our last good day for a while.

Tuesday, 25 March

The Conservatives dropped their education press conference and started attacking us on unions instead. The *Daily Mail* followed up the previous day's *Telegraph* story on the unions with a classic piece on how Labour would return Britain to the 1970s – coupled with lots of gritty images of the Grunwick dispute. The paper produced a list of sixty-three firms which would, they claimed, be dragooned into recognising unions. The Tories had picked up on it. In response, Gordon Brown made a small mistake in answering a question on unions, suggesting that a judge be involved in the adjudication process. He was angry with himself, but anyone answering questions in a General Election press conference is massively exposed, and he was given the wrong information. I was concerned. Fear of trade-union domination was probably our greatest single vulnerability: if we lost ground there, we would lose ground everywhere. The later news bulletins were dominated by Labour's proposals to hold workplace ballots on union recognition, and we were unable to hold to a consistent line. We changed our position three times that day when asked who would define 'workplace': first we said a judge, then, after someone discovered we did actually have a policy on this which everyone had forgotten about, we said some sort of arbitration committee, and finally we put the two together, by saying the committee would be chaired by a judge. Within one 'clarifying' telephone call to a journalist, David Hill had to change his line of argument three times after the intervention of the employment policy officer, Nick Matthews. Derry Irvine immediately called for all the requisite papers. The situation was getting out of control, and the shadow Employment Minister, Stephen Byers, was dispatched to the studios to calm things down.

Tony Blair was wandering around Millbank that night and saw a BBC *Nine O'Clock News* bulletin implying that Labour would surrender to the unions in office. Blair went over to Dan Clifton and said: 'You've got to get a grip on this, this must stop.'[19]

Meanwhile, the negotiations over the leaders' TV debate continued. There was ambivalence in the campaign about it. We were confident Blair would win, but were uneasy about it becoming a distraction, in effect sidelining the rest of the campaign. The Tories shared this ambivalence, which is why in the end the debate didn't happen. We had more negotiating firepower than the Tories: Campbell, Mandelson and Irvine up against Michael Dobbs. In the end the Tories blinked.

In the focus groups that night, unions were hurting us: 'Labour's union recognition proposals are a problem for us, potentially a very serious problem. This is because: unions plus Labour equals danger. Union domination is people's core fear of Labour. The proposal [for union recognition], however sensible and rational it might be, means more union power.' They were scared it would be the thin end of the wedge: ' "Will it lead to me being forced to join a trade union if one is recognised?" Will pressure be brought to bear on them? People do not like the element of compulsion: that they will be forced to join trade unions.'[20] I had no doubt at all about what we should do: 'We must close this down immediately. There is no point in trying to hide it, or evade it, we have to confront it and kill it off as an issue.'[21] It did not need me to tell Tony Blair that.

Wednesday, 26 March

At the morning press conference Blair bided his time before moving in for the kill, appearing to go through the motions of the conference but really waiting for his moment: 'Anyone who thinks Labour has made changes in the party to give it all away to the unions or anyone else does not know me.'[22] This was enough to reassure the voters, effectively killing the story stone dead. 'It was a very uncertain time for about twenty-four hours,' David Hill remembers:

> Very uncertain. It was one where it was quite difficult to actually answer the questions. But Tony came back and did a press conference the day afterwards and was stunning. He put it to bed. This was one moment during the campaign when I thought all the theatre coupled with all the authority of the leader came together, when all the people in the campaign were working in unison. Tony arrived for the morning press conference, and I actually can't tell you whether what he said was 100 per cent accurate, I can't tell you whether he put it to bed because his forensic skills on the subject were so stunning that there was no answer to what he said – what I can tell you is that his demeanour, his arrival, the theatre of his performance, the authority of his performance that morning meant it was put to bed – and that's all that mattered.[23]

It showed in the groups: 'TB's words were enough to reassure them. These words certainly stopped or at least massively reduced damage today,' I wrote. But I was relentless: 'We must be emphatic that we will not in any way be pushed around by any union. Fairness not favours; no turning back. The bottom line is simple: provided people think that this proposal is the end of it, then we are – just – safe. If they think that this is the first of many, or even of any, concessions, then we are in very serious trouble.'[24]

But even as the Conservatives put us under pressure on unions, they crashed into sleaze again. Tim Smith – one of the MPs being investigated in the cash-for-questions affair – resigned after it was revealed that he had accepted several thousand pounds for asking parliamentary questions. Major was having no luck. Or as David

Hill ironically put it, 'God is a switcher.'[25] After a nasty couple of days, the tide had turned again. Hamilton and Smith were having an impact – and we had yet to hear of Piers Merchant.

Thursday, 27 March

The Tory MP Piers Merchant dominated the news. The *Sun* had caught him kissing a seventeen-year-old nightclub hostess. This was a terrible day for the Tories, made worse when Heseltine went on the radio and said Merchant should resign, which Merchant refused to do. It emphasised the weakness of the Tory leadership and also killed the unions as a story.

Late in the day Michael Dobbs miscalculated in the debate negotiations. Mandelson and Campbell had put him under intolerable pressure, and he over-reacted, toughening his negotiating stance. No sooner had he done this than the Press Association had our response: 'The debate is dead in the water.' Campbell was not unhappy. 'I felt that if we weren't careful, because the media is obsessed with itself, there would have been focus on nothing but the debate and we actually wouldn't get through to the public and it would become a barrier. So to be perfectly honest I was not disappointed when the whole thing collapsed. Next time though, things may be different.'[26]

Progress was being made with the anti-sleaze candidate in Tatton. The Liberals were coming on board, an announcement was imminent. But in Carpenders Park the voters had had enough: 'The overall mood is clear. People are getting fed up and frustrated with this election. Too much bickering, too much sleaze.' However, the Conservatives were 'getting credit for the economy' and our greatest danger remained 'interest rates and inflation'.[27]

Easter weekend

On Saturday Jon Kelly stood down as Labour candidate in Tatton. We were searching for someone to stand against Neil Hamilton, to force him to resign – none of us thought he would tough it out. We assumed that the Tories would push him if he didn't jump. I went away for the weekend with my family. On Saturday I watched the news and saw the chairman of the Scottish Conservatives, Sir Michael Hirst, being forced to resign because of an alleged homosexual relationship. However, it soon transpired that this had more to do with internal Tory party ructions in Scotland than sexual misconduct. For a moment I felt pity for them, but only for a moment. They were dying, but not yet dead.

On Sunday I wrote my first long strategy note of the campaign. 'The electorate are not connecting with the election and do not understand most of the issues. They find news bulletins fragmented and confusing.'[28] This last point was important. Night after night I would show people the news, and they would not understand it. This was most true of the BBC, partly because their news is delivered at a level of abstraction that loses many people, but mostly because they insisted on editorialising continually. It was always over to Huw Edwards (or whoever it was) for his view of the election. Sky, who played it straight, were most easily understood, and connected best. The BBC let down their viewers.

I said we were vulnerable on 'taxes/interest rates/inflation, Europe, unions', any signs of 'cock-ups' or policy confusion: 'This election is a test of our competence.' I was certain we should remain positive for now: 'We must have a positive core to our campaign . . . we need positive policies, initiatives. Otherwise the electorate will turn away from us. They want us to take them seriously.'[29]

I also wrote to Alastair Campbell about the launch of our posters on Monday. It was his idea to have dozens of multi-coloured posters, all displaying our 'Britain Deserves Better' message, parked in a field in Kent. Tony Blair was to stand in front of them, making a speech. Alastair called it 'the field of dreams', the name he gives Turf Moor, home of Burnley Football Club, which he supports. I called him and talked about the campaign. I said we should try to turn a corner strategically by saying we were fed up with negative campaigning and were going to go positive.

We needed to lift ourselves out of the sleaze quagmire which was tarring all the parties, and position ourselves as the positive force in the election. My note was in the same vein: if we needed to refer to sleaze we should do it in 'sadness and a non-partisan way . . . We must try at all times to be positive.'[30]

On Easter Monday, as Blair was launching the pledge posters, David Blunkett was facing down the unions, addressing the NUT annual conference where a year before he had been jostled by angry delegates. He warned them that New Labour would govern for the whole of Britain, and not 'those who threaten and bully'.[31]

That night I conducted a focus group among men in Merton. They were certain to switch to Labour: 'They have made up their mind, and there wasn't much point in following the election closely.'[32]

Week three: The nation switches off

Tuesday, 1 April

Although we had been slugging it out for two weeks and I had already endured fourteen focus groups, the real election had not begun. The public was starting to go mad with boredom. We began our meetings at 7 A.M., with a daily press conference at 8.30 A.M. Our first press conference of the campaign proper had Alan Howarth, Tony Blair and Gordon Brown. There was a live link to John Prescott in Cornwall, with a Cornish pasty, surrounded by people in the sunshine. It all looked very happy and breezy. The leader's tour began, with three coaches, one for Tony Blair and his team, the others for the press. Alastair had slogans painted on them which linked sequentially: 'Leading Britain . . .', 'Into the future . . .', '. . . with Tony Blair'. This showed our attention to detail. We spent hours discussing it, worrying about getting the buses in the right order. Alastair particularly liked the idea of journalists paying to be part of a gigantic moving advertisement.

I went to College Green in Westminster to see the buses off. There was some excitement, but only a little. I was rocking with tiredness, blinking in the sunlight.

The results of our first tracking poll came in. Our heavily adjusted lead had us stable at 20 per cent. But the economy was strengthening at an alarming rate: a net 41 per cent believed the economy was strong. This was up 8 per cent on our poll just two weeks earlier, and compared with a net minus 24 per cent just one year before. Agreement with 'the Conservatives have messed up the economy' was a net zero; it was a net minus 50 per cent a year before. Improving perceptions of the economy were beginning to have a political effect. Increased numbers thought the economy would be worse under Labour, and Labour's advantage on offering the best standard of living had slipped.[33] Slowly but surely, the Conservatives were gaining an economic foothold. But Blair was moving further ahead of Major. Stan Greenberg in his polling summary wrote, 'Major is clearly being hurt by sleaze and the negative quality of his campaign, particularly among women.'[34] The Conservatives were moving ahead with real power on the economy but were crippled by sleaze. I discussed the research with Blair, who was concerned about the economy factor.

Focus groups in Watford showed sleaze was becoming an even more serious issue for the Conservatives: 'It has become trashy and tabloid. Dominated by sex and the *Sun*.' And there was a new shift in the mood: people had 'increasing fifth-term fears about the Tories. The view of these voters is that if the Tories can win after all their lies, their incompetence, their corruption, then they will not have learned their lesson and be capable of anything.'[35] This was one of those moments when the national mood changes: the Conservatives did not deserve to get back, and if they did, who would control them? It became a refrain for the rest of the election.

Wednesday, 2 April
The Conservatives launched their manifesto. I watched it on television in Millbank and thought it could hardly have seemed

more stale. It looked as if Major, the only one who spoke, was barely trying. Meanwhile, Tim Bell, John Gummer and Maurice Saatchi stood on the sidelines of the press conference, looking over-pleased with the result. Their manifesto was a scatter-gun of uncosted proposals and contrasted badly with our far more specific five early pledges. We spent all day trying to push the Tories on how they would pay for the manifesto proposals, which worked to a limited extent, but we kept coming up against the problem that everyone seemed to have written them off so no one really cared. I knew the manifesto launch would die in the groups that night, and so it did: 'The manifesto did not connect with any of the group. It lacked life, excitement, energy, impact. The two words used to describe the launch were "desperate" ("They dreamed up these ideas ten minutes before the press conference") and "apathetic" ("They weren't really trying").' It could not have been worse for the Tories, but it gave us a chance. I wrote, 'I think we have a real opportunity tomorrow. Tonight's group covered every age and class. They all voted Tory in 1992. Were not that keen on us, but today's [Conservative] manifesto launch convinced none of them . . . This masks a deeper dynamic that is beginning to dominate the campaign. Increasingly we are coming to represent hope, new ideas, a fresh approach, the future, while they are mired in the past. Tomorrow we must drive this contrast home: we are energy, verve, leadership, hope.'[36] To Blair I wrote: 'You are killing Major in this campaign.'[37]

Thursday, 3 April
There was no 8.30 A.M. press conference as everybody was preparing themselves for the manifesto launch. Margaret McDonagh, Jackie Stacey and Jocelyn Hillman, who was responsible for Labour Party publications, had spent weeks on the design of the manifesto, keeping it carefully under wraps. The manifesto was called 'Because Britain Deserves Better', and featured a cover photograph of Blair taken by Snowden. The content was based largely on the earlier manifesto. Originally it was intended to base the chapters on

the ten parts of the 'Contact' (a list of ten vows that Labour would uphold in government introduced by Tony Blair in his conference speech in 1996), but this idea was felt to be too restrictive and was dropped. In the event the contract was included at the beginning of the manifesto. On the Sunday before the launch, I read the draft introduction and did not like it. I noted that the first page included the words: 'anger, despair, appalled, distressed, ashamed, repelled'. This was not the tone needed to reach out to wavering Conservatives. Blair rewrote the introduction himself and Alastair asked him to write out the ten-point contract in long-hand. This appeared – with corrections – over all the next day's press.

Peter Hyman had his way and the pledges were at the front. The manifesto did not contain many new ideas, but that didn't matter; the ideas it had were what the voters wanted and what New Labour stood for. It was launched at the Institute of Civil Engineers in Great George Street. Blair performed brilliantly, playing down expectations. He refused to smile when holding the manifesto for a photo-call, he talked about the need to make promises reliable rather than overblown, and he talked of the pledges: if at the end of five years Labour had not fulfilled them, it deserved to be voted out.

At the end of the launch Gore Vidal, who was making a film for *Newsnight*, held an impromptu press conference of his own in front of the stage, but he was quickly bundled away by Millbank Tower press officers and was pretty scathing about the way he had been treated.

Outside, the Conservative chicken (another failed and pathetic Conservative stunt, attacking us for not doing the TV debate with Major) was chased by a headless chicken from the *Mirror*. The actor who had to play the part of the Tory chicken was to suffer a great deal more abuse during the campaign. One particularly nasty moment occurred in Edinburgh when an ugly crowd ripped off his head and started chasing him along Princes Street. He soon acquired a personal bodyguard.

The manifesto was a complete success in the groups that night.

Typical responses were 'not too radical, sensible, promising, common-sense, achievable'. 'It broke through their considerable barriers of scepticism, and it did not raise huge worries about: "Where's the money coming from?"' I wrote. But the voters were becoming increasingly fed up: 'People are tending to switch off political news.'[38] In a separate note, I wrote to Tony Blair and Alastair Campbell, 'We have to respond to the scepticism of the electorate, who seem increasingly to be switching off from the election. We are not yet being hurt, but we must find a way of connecting more effectively.'[39]

Friday, 4 April
The day after the manifesto launch, we entered our first real election storms. In an interview with the *Scotsman* newspaper, Blair made a comparison between the tax-raising powers of the proposed Scottish Parliament and a parish council, which was presented as a downgrading of the importance of the Parliament. Donald Dewar was in Millbank that day and was greatly agitated by this. The press jumped on it as a major 'gaffe', and the Scottish media in particular went into overdrive. A press conference the following day was like slow torture for Blair as the journalists harried him relentlessly over the comments.

The Tories were quick to attack. At an election rally at the Royal Albert Hall, Mawhinney held aloft the *Evening Standard* headline, 'BLAIR'S FIRST CLANGER', to the cheering audience. Some Labour staff felt deflated by this – the manifesto launch had put them on a high and now they crashed back to earth. I didn't mind the story so much, but it did blow up and for the first time in the election we were hurt by the news: 'Scotland was perceived as TB on the defensive, the party divided, the whole situation confused.'[40] I wrote to Blair: 'This was not a good day for us, probably the least successful day of the campaign. People felt you looked defensive and momentarily wrong-footed.' I continued, 'This one incident is not a problem for us, [but] if a pattern develops of Labour policy uncertainty . . . we will be harmed.'[41]

Weekend, 5–6 April

On Saturday we discovered that Charles Lewington, the Tories' director of communications, was briefing the Sunday press that Blair had to be told what to do by Peter Mandelson. Central Office was suggesting that he wore an earpiece at press conferences giving him answers down the line. They tried to suggest he was cracking under the strain. This truly was madness; if anyone was cracking up it was them.

But the *Sunday Telegraph* led with the headline, 'BLAIR: WE'LL PRIVATISE EVERYTHING'. The *Sunday Times* claimed that Blair had changed his mind not only on tax-raising powers for Scotland, but also on unions and privatisation. Privatising air-traffic control was raised as a possible Labour policy. This was the unfortunate result of some over-zealous briefing, an attempt to rebut the allegations that Labour had a 'black hole' in its spending plans. Unfortunately, the media soon found a clip of Andrew Smith at the 1996 party conference denouncing Tory plans for the sale of air-traffic control, saying repeatedly, 'Our air is not for sale.' Gordon Brown appeared on *The World This Weekend* to announce that in government Labour would compile a list of all public assets with a view to disposing of the 'inessential' elements.

Over the weekend Alastair Campbell told me that the BBC journalist Martin Bell was going to stand in Tatton. We assumed Hamilton would stand down; Gordon Brown did not believe the Tories could possibly be so stupid as to keep him in. But Central Office was not as tough as Christine Hamilton. Despite furious reports that Major wanted Hamilton to go, the Hamiltons stuck it out. The Tories then had to deny that they wanted to oust Hamilton, and instead had to support him as the official Tory candidate.

But John Major hit Blair hard on trust, and on *Breakfast With Frost* the Tories developed a 'Three U-turns' theme. Major accused Blair of 'slithering and sliding around' in a highly personal attack. We were now under pressure on three fronts: the unions, Scotland and privatisation.

But our second tracking poll showed us with a 22 per cent lead, a 2 per cent improvement on the last poll. Most importantly, our position on the economy was strengthening despite further improvements in economic optimism.[42] Greenberg explained this in his report on the poll:

On the key contested issues – particularly the economy – Labour is making gains, despite the still growing perceptions of a good economy. Labour has regained its lead on managing the economy (plus 5 points, up 5 points this week) and preserving the economic recovery (plus 3 points, a gain of 5 points). The worry that the economy could weaken under Labour has in fact dropped by 3 points this week. The Tories are failing to make gains on the economy because their posture is completely out of touch with the electorate. In the focus groups, the Tory defectors said with some passion the economy is doing better but not their 'standard of living'; the economy is 'lean and mean'; you now work 'under pressure'; more and more people have 'temporary contracts'; the economy is good because 'we're cheap'. In short, these voters are articulating our primary economic message: the economy is not working for the hard-working families of Britain.[43]

This poll exposed probably the most important dynamic of the election campaign: the Conservative failure to turn an improving economy into increased electoral support. But it also demonstrated why we could never for a moment relax: with the economy that strong, a Conservative breakthrough was always possible.

Week four: 'A horrible week'

Monday, 7 April
Blair made his big economic speech of the campaign in the City, which was well received, but we were entering what Mandelson believes was the worst week of the campaign. 'It was a horrible week,' he said, 'the only bad week, very difficult. We seemed

to be on the run. The media felt they had got their teeth into something.'[44] The focus groups revealed the first real doubts about Labour: 'The U-turn attack, which was already a problem, now has real legs. U-turns are a trust problem, but also a competence problem.' The Tories, helped by the *Daily Mail* and the *Telegraph*, had us on the defensive for the first time. In response I argued that 'we must get our message right on privatisation. Our position must be distinctive from the Tories. We must establish a clear dividing-line. It must be rooted in values and what works best for people. We must kill off the U-turns attack. Step by step we must get back our reputation for consistency and conviction. We must stand firm in the face of new attacks.'[45]

In my note to Blair I wrote, 'Somehow or other a combination of Scotland, the unions and now privatisation has got us into the wrong place on the campaign. We have allowed ourselves to be associated with the most unpopular policy of the government, while simultaneously getting a reputation for U-turns.'[46] I was concerned that we might be losing control of the campaign. Blair had to intervene that week to tighten things up at Millbank. Charlie Whelan was moved to the centre table, together with Tim Allan.

That night Blair appeared on *Panorama* and was put under intense pressure by David Dimbleby in an exceptionally aggressive interview.

Tuesday, 8 April

Tatton dominated the news. Martin Bell was ambushed by Neil Hamilton and a huge media entourage, and when asked by Hamilton's wife whether he believed Hamilton was innocent, he replied, 'Yes.' The campaigners watching in Millbank threw up their hands in horror. After that we sent up a member of staff to try to sort things out for Bell. Adrian McMenamin, the head of rebuttal, produced a list, at Derry Irvine's request, of five or six things everyone knew Hamilton had done wrong. We quickly faxed it up to Bell's rather ramshackle operation in Tatton.

The group that night was a follow-up group of switchers from a year earlier. Six of the eight had stayed with us, but they were 'feeling increasingly disconnected from the election'. They felt 'Bell and Hamilton was a farce, but will seriously hurt the Tories because Hamilton and his wife are arrogant; because people believe they are guilty; because it makes Major look weak and pathetic'.[47] I wrote telling Blair that response to his *Panorama* interview was not positive. Half the group had seen it and tended to think he looked 'defensive' in an interview they conceded was aggressive and unfair.[48]

Wednesday, 9 April
Our ICM poll lead was down to twelve points, the Conservatives attacked us on air-traffic control, but Neil Hamilton was re-selected in Tatton. GMTV described this as 'Major's worst nightmare'. Millbank was jubilant, pictures of Neil and Christine were being pinned up across the office. Later in the day, an Institute of Fiscal Studies Report was published, showing that since the last election the tax burden under the Conservatives had increased by £11.5 billion.

I was spending more and more time with Derry Irvine; the more pressure we were under, the more you wanted someone like Derry around. He was constantly asking us how big the majority was going to be. Stan Greenberg always said massive – he thought 10 per cent was the minimum. Derry asked repeatedly, 'But is your track record any good?'

The groups that night clearly indicated a change of mood. 'Until last Friday the dynamic of the electorate was fixed and favoured us. People saw us as a beacon of positiveness in a sea of sleaze, and blamed negative, lacklustre campaigning from the Tories. The events of the last few days have changed this: people have lost some confidence in us; they are getting fed up with the campaign and disconnected from it. They see it as over-managed, over-packaged, and obsessed with point-scoring. People are thinking we are taking victory for granted . . . they want to see more fight and grit from us.' I added, 'People want to renew their faith in Tony Blair. They want to see him tested in real situations, facing real pressure.'[49]

Thursday, 10 April

Tempting fate, Blair took a question from the *Express*'s Peter Hitchens, who asked about the London Oratory and wouldn't shut up. Hitchens had been a problem for us in the 1992 campaign – a key player in the 'Jennifer's Ear' saga, making strong and repeated attacks on Labour. A talented columnist but fiercely right-wing, his question dominated the news until lunchtime.

Air-traffic control exploded as an issue when a trade union leader – Joe McGee, from the IPMS – said he had received written assurances from Labour as late as March that air-traffic control would not be privatised. The Tories were accusing us of U-turning. In fact they were right that we had altered our policy, but it hadn't happened that weekend, as they were alleging – it had been decided in January not to rule out privatisation. But it was a problem for us; we had floated the possibility of privatising it to plug a gap in our finances – the so-called 'black hole' which the Tories were shouting about, but which left us open to accusations of a U-turn. There was no way out.

'In a way, the air-traffic-control issue was the most difficult one for us throughout the campaign,' said David Hill. 'It was the most difficult one because there was no way we could just kill it, because if we killed it then the issue immediately came back to, well, how are you going to make good the gap in your accounting? If we didn't kill it, though, we were susceptible to accusations of a serious U-turn in the space of less than twelve months, and I am afraid that the tactics we used were the only tactics we could use. Which is that we complained and moaned and let it run and hoped that something would emerge that made it fizzle out.'[50] The BBC would not let the issue go and we went to war with *The World at One* for leading on the story. Hill accused them of setting themselves up as the official opposition to Labour.

That night the story broke that the junior Agriculture Minister, Tory MP Angela Browning, had announced she would be standing on an anti-single currency platform, in an attempt to blunt the appeal of the local Referendum Party candidate. We were going to be delivered from the air-traffic-control row. This was the moment Adrian McMenamin had been waiting for since the campaign began: anti-single currency election addresses had been a private obsession of his for months. It had been only a matter of time before one of the Euro-sceptic Tories came out of the woodwork and split from the carefully worked-out Central Office line. We had been monitoring all the constituencies thought likely to produce Euro-sceptic manifestos. No one had imagined Browning would be the straw to break the Tories' back.

The group that night suggested people were still unimpressed: 'Too much bickering and slagging off.'[51] The events of the last week had irritated them, but they hadn't moved from us.

Friday, 11 April
Friday saw the launch of our business manifesto, which was central to our strategy of reassurance. We had set up a business unit in Millbank the summer before to get the business community on-side. All Britain's top businessmen, and many in the small business community, had been invited to party events highlighting our issues – Europe, entrepreneurs, small business – and asked for their comments for our business manifesto. Even Alan Sugar and John Harvey-Jones gave us advice about what we should be doing. We followed it with the PEB that night.

The launch of our business strategy was overshadowed by the Tory implosion on Europe. We were scouring the country for Conservatives who would oppose the single currency in their election addresses. Whenever one was found, Adrian McMenamin would proudly parade their name around the office. Brian Wilson said Angela Browning 'came like a vision from the night' to help Labour.

The groups that night were mainly C2s and Ds – skilled and

unskilled working class. 'The women were totally confused by the election and felt completely cut off from it. They find election news negative, complicated. It in no way speaks to them. And because they find the news incomprehensible and negative they assume that all politicians are lying.' I thought this gave us an opportunity: 'The Tories are now seen to offer nothing but negativism and scares; Labour is the party of hope. To capitalise on this we must find ways of breaking through the news with positive stories and positive messages.'[52]

Weekend, 12–13 April
Sunday saw Tony Blair launch the pledge posters in another of Alastair Campbell's 'field of dreams', near Milton Keynes. After the poster launch Alastair briefed that we were moving away from the current slanging match to a more positive campaign; Blair wanted to inject 'fresh vision, passion and conviction'. He was, Campbell declared, determined to grab the campaign by the scruff of the neck after the distractions of the previous week. The briefing got slightly out of hand, ending up with unwelcome 'LABOUR CAMPAIGN IN U-TURN' headlines. Unfortunately, John Prescott was alleged to have told a journalist, 'You can't tell the truth all the time. Nobody does,'[53] and the Tories tried to play it up. But Prescott's reputation as a man who always speaks his mind was too well-known and limited the story's potency. It wasn't going to run.

Research that night showed that the Liberal Democrats were capturing the change of mood better than us: 'The women's view of the campaign was that it was almost wholly negative, and both sides were to blame. This led to confusion, uncertainty, and made Paddy Ashdown a sensible, positive, appealing alternative.' The men thought similarly: 'They felt that Labour had wobbled on Scotland, *Panorama*, and privatisation, and that Paddy Ashdown was a strong, no-nonsense politician with a clear political message.'[54] This was the start of a long, good run for Ashdown in the campaign.

Week five: Don't bind my hands

Monday, 14 April
At the morning press conference Labour focused on education. At lunchtime Tony Blair said Labour was prepared to be isolated in Europe over fishing quotas. In the afternoon he returned to education, delivering a lecture at Birmingham University which led the evening news.

The day's most important development was yet another Tory flouting the 'wait and see' policy on the single currency. This time it was the vice-chairman Dame Angela Rumbold. They were falling thick and fast now.

The groups were more settled: 'Four quiet days have calmed them down. No one mentioned privatisation or U-turns.' The dynamic of this group followed an increasingly familiar pattern: 'The group started with fairly strong commitment to Labour. It then went on to an exhaustive period of discussion about Labour and the risk associated with it, but finally decided that despite everything it was time for the Tories to go.'[55]

Tuesday, 15 April
The *Daily Mail*'s front page screamed: 'The battle for Britain. There is a deafening silence at the heart of this election and its name is Europe.' Angela Rumbold said, 'Integration has gone far enough.'[56] The Conservatives tried to say Labour was gagging its candidates, while they were allowing theirs to speak out. Two government ministers, John Horam and James Paice, became the most senior Conservatives to break ranks. Tony Blair and Alastair Campbell were in a hotel in Southampton, waiting to record a radio interview. They had just been to a pub. First, they heard a rumour that a government minister had resigned and then, later, they got the proper story. Blair, in his dressing-gown, said, 'They can't come back from this.'[57]

Peter Mandelson paraded around the green outside Millbank with Fitz the bulldog, the star of that night's broadcast. The dog had already caused some difficulty: Mandelson was at first under the impression it was called 'Fritz', and had been trying to work out how to present a German dog as a British symbol. Its genitals had had to be airbrushed out of the broadcast because of their excessive size. It was Peter's first formal election photo-call, the biggest public event he was involved in during the election. 'Peter was rather dreading it. It had all the ingredients for a disaster, but he pulled it off,' said Benjamin Wegg-Prosser, Mandelson's researcher.[58] I missed this, but was allowed to meet Fitz, who was temporarily kennelled in Blair's private office with a bowl of water and an air-conditioning unit to cool the dog down in case he overheated. I rather took to him. His visit was planned by Mark Lucas with military precision. Mark had arranged a very sophisticated travel plan to make sure no one spotted the dog.

Fitz was a rare moment of light relief in a campaign that had to be suffered rather than enjoyed. It was not as hard, perhaps, as 1992, but was very tough in its way. It was about focus and endurance and never making a mistake. It takes courage to fight from behind, but it takes courage also to stay ahead. If we had slipped up, history would never have forgiven or forgotten. Everybody knew that. The price of failure would be unbearable. This feeling hung around Millbank like a dark cloud. I enjoyed almost none of the campaign, experiencing constant tiredness, and a ruthlessness that I had never known before. The Tories had to be finished off, battered to the ground. There could be no moment of weakness, no chance for them to come back from the dead. The journey had been too long for us to falter at the last. So I went through the campaign as a kind of living-dead person: emotionally numb, physically numb, spiritually numb, consumed completely by the will to win.

The groups that night were bad. The first was a set of Liberal and Conservatives voters who would not consider voting for us, but the second was a follow-up group of switchers to us, who had tended to move away from us: 'The election has been confusing, and confusion creates doubt; we have been under attack and look defensive.' Worse, Ashdown had moved on to our pitch: 'Ashdown and the Liberal Democrats are exacerbating our weaknesses and clouding our message. We claim to be the party of education, but they will spend more. We claim to be honest, but they say where the money is coming from. We are starting to lose some ground to the Liberals.'[59] Our mid-week tracking poll confirmed this trend. Greenberg wrote, 'Paddy Ashdown in particular, but also the Liberal Democrats, are making important gains. Their vote has climbed 2 points to 16 – up 4 points this last week. Warm feelings about Ashdown have gone up 5 points this survey.'[60]

Wednesday, 16 April

Europe was building up as a major issue. The papers were running stories saying that between 140 and 200 Tory candidates would come out against the single currency. The Conservatives were losing control. At their press conference, Major made his extraordinary 'Like me or loathe me, but don't bind my hands' speech, and the election burst into life. It was an incredible performance and I watched it in the media centre, transfixed. On the ITV news Michael Brunson described him as 'fighting like a tiger'. It made me nervous. I thought it could shift the dynamic of the campaign, and begin to unlock the hidden potential of the improving economy. Campbell, typically, thought him pathetic. Major cancelled his planned PEB that night and went straight to camera with the same argument.

Major's performance helped him and the Conservatives. For a few days it shifted the mood. The focus group that night liked him: 'Aggressive, confident, direct: a decent man, finally showing some spark. Trying to get control of his party.' And they were getting worried about Labour: 'There is uncertainty about us. People do not know what we stand for. We do not look confident enough.'[61] I was still arguing that we should be relentlessly positive for now, but the time was getting close when we should change direction and turn on the Tories. This was clearly a point of uncertainty and fluidity, a turning-point that would favour either them or us.

Thursday, 17 April

This was the day Blair reached full power. His team had been depressed since the *Panorama* interview, feeling they weren't connecting; the campaign was going well enough, but there was no feeling to it any more. 'Tony was basically in good shape throughout the campaign,' said Campbell. 'Nothing really went badly wrong during it. I thought generally we were in pretty good nick. There was a low point in the couple of days before the Edinburgh speech, when we weren't connecting, the media were bored and we weren't breaking through. We decided Tony should do the speech in Edinburgh and completely let rip. That was important.'[62]

It was a turning point for us. As Major went back to Europe, holding out the promise of a free vote on the single currency, and again being undermined by stories that three more ministers had expressed their hostility to the single currency, Blair was in the Usher Hall, Edinburgh. He upped a gear and, in a mesmerising performance, threw away his notes and spoke off the cuff. Major might have had a good day yesterday, but Blair was closing in for the kill.

John Major's bubble of popularity was already beginning to burst: 'This was a much less good day for the Conservatives than yesterday,' I noted. 'They looked divided and confused. Major looked weak.'[63] Major's audacity had helped, but division was undoing them.

Friday, 18 April

The Conservatives, still convinced Europe was a winning issue, scored another spectacular own goal, producing an advertisement initially sketched by Michael Heseltine which depicted Blair as Helmut Kohl's puppet. In a reference to the forthcoming Amsterdam Summit negotiations, the caption ran, 'Don't send a boy to do a man's job.' I thought this was ridiculous and would rebound, but Blair was worried about it and came on the conference phone at the morning media meeting. We all tried to reassure him, but he remained concerned. Major came under pressure all day to apologise for it.

Major was also in trouble for hinting that any vote on a single currency would be a matter of conscience for MPs outside government. Unfortunately, he developed this policy on the hoof, without consulting Kenneth Clarke, who immediately distanced himself from the idea. The Tories were coming apart at the seams.

I was worried that I was missing out on some target voters, so I changed my recruitment criteria for the groups to people who were basically Tories. The results were extraordinary, and began to finally convince me that we were going to win. For the previous ten days I had been talking to people who had started the campaign intending to vote Labour, but were now having doubts. This evening's groups, though, showed me there was another dynamic at play: 'Tories are leaving [the Conservatives] because of the negativity of their campaign. Almost all members of both groups believed that they would end up voting Conservative at the outset of the campaign. They had doubts but they felt the power of the campaign would persuade them to once more vote Tory.' In fact, the opposite had happened: the campaign had turned them off because the negativity and abuse of the campaign had persuaded them that the Conservatives had nothing new to offer.

'All this was eloquently summed up by one female respondent, who said, "I wanted to stay a Tory voter but I feel that in all conscience I cannot do so given the nature of the campaign they have fought."'[64] The Conservative campaign was losing them votes. Our voters might be getting nervous, but theirs were feeling completely alienated.

Weekend, 19–20 April
Our weekend tracking poll showed that my suspicions that Major's 'Don't bind my hands' speech would shake up the election were valid. Greenberg wrote:

The dynamic of the race is changing – which will require a pointed response from Labour. Labour's lead has dropped from 21 points to 16 points in this survey. The Labour slippage was due entirely to the consolidation of the Conservative vote. There is considerable cause for alarm in these numbers. The bloc of solid Labour voters has dropped to 35 (down 6 points), when it should have been solidifying. Among women the rise in uncertainty is very dramatic, with solid support dropping 12 points. The explanation for this is the economy. Perceptions of a good economy have risen from 68 to 72 per cent. Voters now believe the economy will be *weaker*, not *stronger* under Labour (by 10 points). The cause of this shift to the Tories is an improvement in perceptions of John Major: his job performance jumped 6 points; he gained 8 points on 'leadership' in comparison with Blair, and 7 points on strength.[65]

All this was a direct consequence of Major's speech, lifting perceptions of Major and allowing the Tories to start gaining credit for the strength of the economy. The Tories put this down to Europe. In fact, what mattered was that Major had finally shown some strength. Europe wasn't the issue; it was leadership.

On Saturday Kenneth Clarke waded into the Europe row, saying people who thought Europe was a threat – including, therefore, Michael Howard – were talking 'paranoid nonsense'.[66] The press office wanted to play this up, but Gordon Brown wasn't keen: Europe was closer to their agenda than ours. Focus groups on Sunday continued to show our female voters getting nervous. The men were all right, they saw the Conservatives falling apart, but 'the women were getting nervous about change as the election drew closer'.[67] This was inevitable. My view was that it was getting close to the time to attack, and that we had to be ready with fifth-term fears.

Week six: The War Book

Monday, 21 April
Jacques Santer, President of the European Commission, entered the fray with an attack on Euro-sceptics, for 'unjustified and

misplaced' attacks on the EU.[68] This could have been a bigger problem for us had he done it earlier in the campaign; it gave the voters and the Tory Party a common enemy. The Tories could even have started to unite around it. Malcolm Rifkind, the Foreign Secretary, certainly tried to make the most of it. He attacked Blair for his 1996 conference speech, in which he had declared that he would 'never allow this country to get isolated' in Europe. But it was too late. Blair turned the issue around to leadership, flaying Major in an attack on his authority. Yet Millbank was wary about the Tory return to Europe – we knew it was a potentially vulnerable area. We got the *Sun* to run an article by Blair the next day, promising that he would 'slay the Euro-dragon'.

The focus groups thought Blair was 'strong and sincere', Major weak. And at last Ashdown, whom we had been attacking for four days, was running into the ground: he was described as 'an old bore'. Ashdown had started well but had been unable to develop his message: he needed to move from 'a plague on both your houses' to a political offering of his own: this he was unable to do. Blair was back in the saddle.

It was now time to attack: 'We have got to confront the voters with the possibility of another Tory term. Our positive credentials are well-established. Ashdown is faltering. Attacks will get it up in the news. We must use our advantages: energy, strength, dynamism. We must power our way through the next ten days.'[69]

Tuesday, 22 April

All day there were rumours of a very bad poll for us and we were desperate to get hold of it. Strangely, Adrian McMenamin, who went to the Tory press conferences every day (as they sent someone to ours), had been approached by their research director, Danny Finkelstein, that morning. Finkelstein asked him, 'How are your plans to get Frank Dobson elected as a Cabinet minister going?' McMenamin replied, 'If the polls are to be believed, quite well I think, thank you.' Finkelstein said, 'You won't be saying that this evening.'[70] I don't know if he knew about the bad poll or not. There was a black shadow over the day, and at five in the afternoon the poll came in: ICM in the *Guardian* had us just 5 per cent ahead. Our leads on economic competence and Europe were slashed. Mandelson looked at me coolly and said, 'I thought we were supposed to be doing well in this election.' But people kept very calm; we suspected at once it was a rogue poll. Margaret said, 'I don't care what the poll says, I will fight them on the streets and get our voters out one by one and door by door if I have to.' She was tough. Blair heard about the poll in a hotel in Luton. He suspected it was wrong, but decided to take it at face value in order to smash complacency and to remind the electorate that the Tories could still win. He went immediately on to the attack in a speech in Stevenage, and decided that soon we would need to focus on the risks of a Conservative fifth term.

That night we got the most important private poll of the campaign, saying Labour was up 1 per cent with a 17 per cent lead. This meant that the Tory advance had been checked. It also meant the ICM poll was wrong. But it showed, too, that the Tory gains revealed in our last poll had largely been held.[71] Greenberg reported: 'The survey sends mixed signals. On the one hand, the poll offers a sense of relief that the drop last weekend was really a movement to a lower plateau and not the first signs of a collapse. On the other hand, the race has changed in important ways. Major and the economy have both achieved a higher standing which lessens the desire for change and allows worries about Labour to matter more. This argues for a greatly increased focus on fifth-term worries.'[72]

I conducted two groups that night, and though there were some doubts, it was clear they were going to hold. The response to Blair on the news was very strong.

I wrote a note that night to Blair that exposed the ruthlessness and obsession that had consumed me during the campaign: 'You have spent five weeks building up your positive credentials and you are now able to go after him. You can hit him on Europe, you can hit him on education, health, crime. You have to hunt him down and finish him off.'[73]

I spoke to Blair and told him not to worry about the ICM poll. I said it was hopelessly wrong and should be discounted.

Wednesday, 23 April

Our lottery day. We held a special press conference to announce plans for a 'people's lottery'. It took off well, according to David Hill. 'It was a really big-impact story and it went like a dream,' he said.[74] This was a proper, positive story, which was good because trench warfare recommenced only hours later. Early in the day Peter Hyman, who like me was obsessed with bringing home to voters the dangers of a Tory fifth term, jokingly suggested, 'Why don't you write a really lurid fifth-term memo and have it leaked so we can get the fifth term up as a story?' There was no need – the Tories were about to do it for us. Sitting in a strategy meeting in the late afternoon Alastair Campbell's pager went off. He made a call in the meeting room and gave me a quizzical 'you've done it again' look. The Tories had my War Book, and they were distributing copies of it outside Central Office.

I knew this was embarrassing, but didn't feel it was terminal. Gordon Brown was very concerned because it contained our weaknesses as well as our strengths, and these focused on the economy. His face blackened when he read what I had written. I felt a glass wall surround me once again. It was the lead story on Sky News and Radio 4's *PM* programme, and once again I watched myself at the centre of a storm. Judith Dawson, senior political correspondent on Sky News, said, 'I cannot for the life of me understand why these callow youths write this stuff down.' Alastair was angry on my behalf and stormed off to the lobby to do a briefing. He saw the leak as an opportunity rather than a threat:

I don't think you should advertise your enemy and what the War Book was, was our strategy. And one of the developments in modern media is that it is interested in strategy – it reports strategy. I felt that there was nothing for us to lose in this. Once you get over the fact that the media is obsessed with leaks and the fact that leaks happen, so what? I felt the document actually was a coherent case for the campaign strategy that we were doing. So while we were talking about it, I said get me enough copies and I'll go round to the press gallery and do a briefing on the basis that they've made a terrible mistake, because what they've done is drawn attention to our strategy. I'll say this is where we are, and you'll see that unlike them we've got a clear strategy, we've followed it all along the way, and we're now looking at an attack on the fifth term.[75]

By the time the briefing was over the press began to believe we had leaked it.

I had forgotten they had the War Book, and the leak surprised me. This time I wasn't named, but the media came hunting for me anyway. I slipped out to my focus group by the back entrance, feeling uncomfortable.

The groups that night showed increasing momentum towards us: 'TB is breaking through more strongly than ever. We are starting to surge, they are starting to sink. For the next few days we can attack as it gives us power, differentiates us from the Tories. But from about Monday we need to make a turn and move to a message of hope.'[76]

Thursday, 24 April

This was our final-week launch, again held at the Institute of Civil Engineers. The strategy was stark: five positive pledges versus five fifth-term fears, one of which was that the state pension would be abolished. This was true. Under the Tories' own proposals state pensions would in time be scrapped.

I had wanted to attack the Tories on fifth-term pension fears for two years, but neither Blair, Brown nor anyone else would have it. It was too incredible. When Peter Lilley announced what was, in effect, privatising pensioner care and introducing private pensions for young people, their resistance collapsed. The Tories were announcing what I had been blocked from predicting. On that Wednesday morning, Adrian McMenamin was sitting next to Baroness Blatch, one of Major's personal aides in the campaign, at the Tory press conference. Norma Major came in and sat behind him and began chatting with Blatch. Earlier Norma had been talking to Alastair Goodlad, the Tory chief whip, who had told her how he had been producing a whole load of leaflets on pensions because they were very worried we would attack them on it. Adrian heard all this, then reported it back to us at Millbank, and we thought it ought to be followed up.

Even so, pensions would not have taken off as they did had the Tories not leaked the War Book that afternoon; the issue was suddenly given currency and saliency. 'The War Book was very important,' said David Hill. 'They launched it, Mawhinney comes on the *PM* programme, says, "This shows how appalling they are," and then says, "We are launching this to reveal the gutter politics that the Labour Party is undertaking, the sort of things they are saying about pensions" – and I said, "Go for it." And I kept saying "Go for it" all the time – "Go for them on pensions, they are terrified on pensions." Then we went for it on Thursday morning and changed the press conference, and on the Friday I remember saying, "Go for it again." I was like a dog with a bone.'[77] Rather than let the issue die, the Tories kept attacking us, which poured petrol on the flames. They held a bizarre press conference, headed by Stephen Dorrell, with a picture of Tony Blair as a chameleon changing colour under the banner, 'You can't believe a word Blair says'. They attacked Blair for 'telling bare-faced, despicable lies' over pensions. They went into a tailspin. It was madness.

The groups that night were again typical: 'nervous about us' but unlikely to return to the Tories.[78] I wrote to Blair and told him our latest poll gave us a 19 per cent lead, but also noted that 'it is absolutely essential we do not slacken off in the face of this improvement but that we drive this dynamic home. Momentum is all in the closing days. You are already performing at a superb level but you still need to build more as polling day approaches.'[79]

Friday, 25 April

The *Independent* was conducting some focus groups of its own, which they claimed showed the election was going to be close. They were misreading the responses: doubts about Labour do not always turn into Tory votes.

Labour led on crime, and ITN's Michael Brunson reported: 'Pensions has been fought to a draw.' The *Daily Telegraph* ran the headline: 'LIAR, LIAR, ELECTION'S ON FIRE'. Blair was unhappy about the way the pensions issue was portraying him. It was probably the first time in history Labour had fought so aggressively. Our claim that the Tories would abolish the state pension sooner rather than later was justified by what they had said in the past; we never actually said pensioners would lose their pensions, but that was how our attack was interpreted. When Blair was asked directly, 'Are you saying pensioners will lose their pensions?' he simply replied along the lines of, 'I would never tell anybody to trust the Tories about anything.' He refused to withdraw 'one iota' of Labour's allegations.

Both the Tories and the press were astounded at how hard we were fighting. Not content simply with winning, we were beating them to a pulp. 'This is all in the context of an election which is palpably won and comfortably so,' said Hill. 'It knocked the Tories all over the place. They were stunned at the strength of what we were doing. They were stunned that we stuck to it.' Even the journalists were shocked that morning. Hill recalls:

I had the most extraordinary exchanges with journalists and broad-casters on the Friday morning. Tony was very calm at the press conference and did a tremendous job, and I then came out and had Adam Boulton [Sky News political editor], Robin Oakley [BBC political editor] and various other people saying, 'What on earth is going on here? Why are you deliberately misleading the general public?' etc., etc. I said, 'What the hell's wrong with you lot? Why are you getting so steamed up about this?' And they said two things: 'One, you're so far in front you don't need to get rough like this. Secondly, we don't expect things like this from you.

These are the sort of things that only the Tories do.' And I thought that was fascinating, having been around for so long that even given this steely leadership of Blair, the fact that there were people like Mandelson and Brown at the political helm, there were people like Alastair Campbell and myself who have got a reputation in terms of the way we deal with the press – even with that team in place in terms of the public image of the party, there was still this perception among these journalists that Labour played as the gentleman and the thugs were the Tory party. That was still there right at the end of the campaign.[80]

In the groups that night, the issue was finely balanced but we were just ahead: 'Pensions mostly works for us. In terms of who is believed, Major and Blair are about equal. However, the gain for us is that it makes us look strong, rooted in conviction, different from the Tories.' Our current attacking strategy, I said, had strengths and weaknesses. 'The strengths are many: it keeps the focus on them; it stops us being the incumbent; it shows TB to be strong; it gives us momentum; but it makes us vulnerable to Lib Dem erosion; and it means that we are not offering a reason to vote for us. But on balance it is working.'[81]

Maurice Saatchi has said that pensions turned the tide, that the lead was falling to 5 per cent and pensions pulled it back up.[82] This is nonsense – a post-election Tory myth. Our lead fell a little after Major's 'Don't bind my hands' press conference on Europe, but it picked up before pensions were on the map. Pensions helped us a little, but made no substantive difference to the result of the election.

I tried to keep the pressure on Blair: 'In general your attacking stance of the last week has been effective. But soon you must make the turn and focus on your positive message. In general your position is very strong. But it is not yet secure. This is for two reasons. There are millions of voters out there who have yet to make up their minds. And the election is not just about winning, it is about winning a big majority. For both these reasons it is essential that we do not slow down, but speed up. The party with momentum at the end will make disproportionate gains. We must keep momentum, we must stop the Tories getting it.'[83]

That afternoon, Neil Kinnock came into Millbank, at Peter's invitation, to address us. It was an emotional moment for Neil and the staff. He said he wished that he could have had this dedication, these skills in 1992. The battle was now between 'the desperate and the determined'. But there was no malice, no rancour, only the hope that we would finish the job that he had started in 1985.

That night we had the results of another tracking poll, which showed us rallying again. Greenberg wrote, 'The survey shows a strengthening of Labour's position at the current level and a weakening of the forces that destabilised the race a week ago. With exactly a week before the election, confidence in Major's leadership and the economy have fallen back. Labour is holding stable at 45 per cent. Labour has been tested, and has come through stronger.'[84]

Weekend, 26–27 April

Late on Saturday evening I went into Millbank. Peter Mandelson was there. We talked calmly about the prospects. After twelve years, we were close. We had almost done it.

The Sunday papers were excellent, with the *News of the World* coming out for Labour and the *Sunday Times* leading on an anti-Tory story. Even the *Observer* was at last being supportive. The polls were strong, with ICM giving us a fifteen-point lead. The news also had shots of Blair with Richard Branson, in contrast to Major ambling around Huntingdon like a retired gardener.

I wrote a 'last four days' note to Alastair Campbell. I said that our lead was down to 16 per cent and economic optimism was up. Major was up on his job approval. In focus groups there was absolutely no perception that there would be a landslide. 'Everybody believes the election will be close. Tony's tone was not right in some of the bulletins. It is absolutely essential that no impression is given that this election is won. We should never discuss Friday, even in terms of humility. TB must repudiate any sense that there is going to be a landslide. He must throw the idea out. Instead he should connect with the real feelings of the people: the election will be close; every vote needs to be won.'[85]

Final week: Into the sunlight

Monday, 28 April

Today the Conservatives started to die. Blair phoned me and was nervous about the last few days, getting the tone right. I told him that Stan Greenberg was confident of a landslide. Blair's message was now spot-on. 'This is not a landslide country,' he repeated throughout the day. I think it was Alastair's line, although he only remembers 'a blur' by then.

Major went on a meandering tour of parts of the country, his passion gone. He returned to College Green at Westminster to warn the assembled journalists that 'We only have seventy-two hours to save the Union.' The old 1992 attacks just weren't working. He was fading. Blair was brilliant in the East Midlands. The atmosphere in Millbank became almost relaxed; Major's flying tour looked ridiculous and desperate and Blair just kept improving. He was at the best he has ever been that week – he just got better and better.

The groups that night were the moment I had been waiting twelve years for: 'There was a definite sense tonight that the final mood is shifting to Labour. Taken as a whole, these women gave out a tangible sense that a collective decision was being taken to vote Labour. One said, "My friends are voting Labour, so I shall."'[86] The earth had moved, we were going to do it. I wrote to Blair, 'You got your message and tone absolutely right. Battling for every last vote in the country is absolutely the right message. There is a discernible sense of a deeper turn towards us. You could almost feel them tilting towards us as the election comes to an end. They still have doubts, but they are going to do it. For the next two days you must keep battling for every last vote.'[87]

Tuesday, 29 April

The final press conferences of the campaign. Labour returned to its ten-point contract. Major was limp, Blair fantastic in Bristol. Even Alastair Campbell began to feel optimistic:

> You couldn't tell, the longer the campaign went on. You get all the data and things, but frankly, polls have been wrong before, you do have to rely on your gut sense of where things are. I can remember Glenys [Kinnock] coming back one night in the 1992 election campaign from Basildon and saying, 'They're just not looking me in the eye.' And I felt in those last few days that we were just connecting in a way that was extraordinary, really getting through to people. Everywhere you went people were warm, they had a sense that something was happening. These public meetings we were doing, you know normally you'd get a bit of aggro and there just was none of that those last few days. Very warm, big crowds. You could sense as well in terms of the media that things were moving. In terms of the message it was really important that we kept going, we kept saying it was close, we kept saying we were fighting for every vote.[88]

The media seemed to swing behind us in those last few days. No longer interested in making Blair look silly, they ran fantastic pictures, for example, on polling day, in the market in Stockton-on-Tees, standing above a sea of heads, pointing, looking like the next Prime Minister.

Campbell was increasingly disappointed at the lack of Tory fight. He recalled afterwards, 'I'll tell you what was interesting in terms of the campaign, it was like being a boxer and you've psyched yourself up to go the fifteen rounds and at the end of the thirteenth round your opponent, who you've battered into the canvas, just gets up and walks away. And for the last few days while we'd been keeping up this relentless pressure, they'd gone.'[89]

The groups confirmed the choice the nation was making: 'These groups offer more evidence of a tilt in mood towards Labour. There appears to be a growing consensus even among nervous

Labour voters that Labour is going to win. This is giving comfort and support. The single biggest failure of the Tory campaign is that they have offered nothing to their lost supporters; no promise; no reward; no positive future; just relentless negativity.'[90] To Blair I wrote, 'You have been fantastic these last few days. Both days have been clear wins for us. We have exactly the contrast we want in the last few days: they are tired and sagging, we are urgent, surging.'[91]

Wednesday, 30 April
The final day. Stan Greenberg wrote a memo predicting Labour would get 43 per cent and the Conservatives 31 per cent.[92] He got it right to the point. Later he talked to me about the election campaign:

> There were two dynamics. One centred on the Tories, their time in power, the state of the economy. Very important to that was, I think, a public impatience, a public who were tired with the Thatcherite project of simply dismantling the state as the response to current challenges. The other side was Labour able to finally communicate through an election that it had settled the issues that had created so many doubts about the social democratic project in Britain. I think that most of the elections of the '70s, '80s and '90s were not about the Conservatives, not about Thatcher. It was the reputation of the Labour Party and its project that scared people. The country had moved on, the Labour Party had not. Labour had gone through perhaps two elections where it was trying to address these issues, but not with the drama that Tony Blair addressed these issues. There was a finality about the way he addressed them. In this election, I don't think the voters were constantly agonising over whether this was a tax-and-spend Labour Party which would drive the economy into the ground at the behest of the trade unions. I think these issues were largely resolved, and the voters were able to look forward.[93]

Millbank thinned out as staffers headed for the key marginals to work on the ground on polling day.

I knew we would win by a huge margin. Around midday I slowly packed up my papers and my personal belongings and left Millbank for the last time as a member of the campaign team. It was over for me. For a moment I felt pure, undiluted happiness. I knew we had won, I knew the long journey was over. I walked to my wife's office and arrived unannounced, carrying my bag and my belongings. I said to her, we have won, and it will be a landslide, before falling asleep on her sofa.

But I was not quite finished yet. That night I did the last focus group, a follow-up group of 1992 Conservative voters who had switched to Labour. They had remained 100 per cent solid for Labour, were certain to vote for us. The journey was finally coming to an end. The circle had closed. Those terrible focus groups when Labour was a pariah – unelectable, for the past, for extremism, for the minorities – had gone. This group was voting Labour. Adrian McMenamin went to canvass the next day. He panicked when he saw the kind of people going out to vote: 'When you've done this for fifteen years you think you know what a Labour voter looks like,' he said, '[and] I thought we were going to lose the election. I was leaving my daughter with my mother that night and said to her, "We're going to lose, it's a disaster." I was really convinced of it. But the truth was, these people were Labour voters; they just hadn't voted Labour in the last sixteen years so they looked different to me.'[94]

I wrote one last polling report:

People are going to vote Labour tomorrow. They have some doubts, but they are going to do it. The respondents have connected to almost all elements of our strategy: business reassurance, health, education, strong leadership, our positive approach. They saw the campaign as a test and Labour has passed it. The Tories are clearly in trouble. But in the last days the Libs have also started to fade. Ashdown looks tired, their message has become confused. There will be no last-minute panic rush back to the Tories. Some nervous switchers, undecideds will go back, but they will not affect the result to any material extent. But we must retain the right note throughout tomorrow. People are still deciding. We must take nothing for granted. The winning margin should be around 10 per cent. I cannot see any circumstances in which it will fall below the 5/6 per cent we need for a reasonable working majority.[95]

It was done. I wrote to Blair, saying he would win by at least 8/9 per cent. But still I pushed him: 'Even today you should not let up, people will be making their minds up. You are still taking nothing for granted, you are still dismissing the possibility of a landslide.' I talked of Labour in power. 'In government the cynicism will start working for you. People expect promises to be broken, so that if you keep any of your promises, let alone all of them, faith in politics will be restored. You must never deviate from your New Labour project. You should not shrink from unpopularity, you should not court it either.'

I closed on a personal note: 'It has been a great privilege to have had the opportunity of working with you during this period. You have been a great leader of the opposition, and will, I think, be a great Prime Minister. Today marks the end-point for me. The election of a Labour government has been the prime purpose of my life for the last twelve years. Best of luck today and in the coming years. You are going to win.'[96]

Much later, Sue Nye, Gordon's assistant and someone else who had worked for so many years to get Labour elected, called. She had Gordon on the phone. He was worried. The vote in Scotland seemed soft. Could it all go at the last? His voice was tired and warm. I reassured him: this time, the fates would not deny him. Tomorrow he too would win. I sat up late into the night, thinking of the past.

Thursday, 1 May

I voted and waited. At lunchtime I went to a local café and got the first exit polls at 2 P.M. – we would win by a landslide. I had dreamed of that exit poll showing us ten points ahead for ten years, but when it came, nothing happened. I couldn't feel anything. I spent most of the rest of the day in a state of shock, a kind of emotional paralysis. I phoned Jonathan Powell, who was at Tony's house in Sedgefield, and told him the exit-poll result. He took it to Tony Blair and Peter Mandelson, who were talking in the garden. 'I felt relief, some excitement,' said Peter, who was expecting a majority of about seventy. 'Tony was quite elated but, you know, it's not over till the fat lady sings. He didn't yell or anything, but he went, "God, do you think it could be true?" I said I hadn't a clue and I will not presume or bank on anything until we get the votes.'[97] After I'd spoken to Jonathan I went home and called James Carville, who was waiting by the phone. 'For these few moments,' he said, 'you will breathe pure oxygen for the one time in your life.' I phoned George Stephanopoulos. 'Good news, I hope,' he said.

At 9.30 I drove into Millbank past Number 10, as I had in the last two elections. At Millbank I met up with Stan Greenberg and Paul Begala, who was here to observe Blair's victory. The later exit polls came out – we had won by a huge margin. When the results came in, it was like a dream. Blair and Campbell, in Sedgefield, had done little all day, waiting, people telephoning, friends coming in and out. They didn't watch the television, except for the exit poll. 'Everybody said, "Oh, isn't it great" and all that,' Alastair remembers, 'and I was miserable by then. Really miserable. And Tony was saying, "Is it real?" There was a wonderful moment when he made me phone Millbank and tell them to stop being so happy.' It only dawned on them that it was for real when they were at the count. 'That was the only time we watched the telly and a whole series of Tories just fell,' Alastair said. 'And I remember at one point Tony turning to me and saying, "What on earth have we done here?" It was when Forsyth went.'[98] Michael Forsyth, Secretary of State for Scotland, had just lost his Stirling seat with a swing to Labour of nearly 8 per cent.

In Millbank, Alastair's message had come through – you are being too triumphalist; the election is not won yet – and was met with the derision it deserved. We heard the Tories were briefing that we would get a majority of seventy. We drove to the Royal Festival Hall, where a victory party had been quietly organised by Margaret McDonagh, who sat within three feet of me, without me even knowing.

I walked in, and people started to clap me on the back and shake my hand in a way I could never have imagined happening. Less for what I had done, more because I had just stuck with it all these years. I was in tears. I can't actually remember very much; it was too much to take in. Peter arrived and immediately started to do interviews. I joined him. We both felt completely vindicated; the long fight was over. Blair was on his way down in the plane with Alastair Campbell. 'People find this odd, but it was quite subdued,' Campbell remembers. 'There's some pictures of this, where Tony and Cherie are sitting there, and Fiona and I are sitting here. And my pager was on the table and it was going, like, every five seconds, with another Labour gain. It was getting ridiculous. And we were just sort of talking away quietly.'[99] They scribbled some notes for Tony's speech, arrived at Stansted airport and drove into London.

We waited outside as the dawn gently broke. In front of the Festival Hall a huge stage was erected, waiting for Blair. On Waterloo Bridge the traffic stopped, buses were stationary, people waited. Every physical space was filled. For the first time I felt exalted. 'It did start to build up on the way from the airport,' said Campbell, 'but then we got stuck in a one-way street for about twenty minutes, listening to the radio saying, "and we hear that the Prime Minister is just a couple of minutes away" and we could hear "Things Can Only Get Better" [Labour's campaign song] and we were stuck in a one-way street.' Eventually they arrived. 'Tony and Cherie were in the car in front, Fiona and I were in the second car, and I had his notes in my inside pocket. So we get up the ramp and see all the crowds there and he jumps out of the car and is running off and I think, "Oh shit," so I jumped out of the car while it was moving and the wheel went over my ankle.

I thought it was probably broken. For weeks I had this kind of bruise right across my foot, and I had to run up and get to him and give him the notes.'[100]

Blair made his speech: 'Truly it is a new dawn. I said that if we had the courage to change we would win, and we did.'[101] Neither Alastair Campbell nor Tony Blair enjoyed the party at the Royal Festival Hall much. Alastair says, 'We went upstairs somewhere quiet after Tony did his speech, and I said to him, what did you make of that? And he said, "God, I'm jealous. Weren't you?" And I said, "yeah", because I didn't feel any of it at all. I was in this mode where if anything infringed upon it, like people being happy or all this stuff, it just didn't get through. I feel really bad about it.'[102]

Later Blair made a speech to a smaller audience, thanking everybody. I saw Alastair, looking like a man possessed, still totally focused. He rushed towards me and we hugged. Then Cherie spotted me, pulled me across and I hugged her and Tony too. It was over, we had done it. I walked with Gail into the morning sunlight, this time, at last, a winner. I thought of my children waiting at home, still not really believing, still nervous that victory would somehow slip from our grasp as it always did. I thought of my father who had hoped for this moment, but doubted it would come. Most of all I thought of the quiet suburban street that I had come from, and felt pride that people from that street, and millions like them, had dared to vote Labour, and were forgotten no more.

AFTERWORD: THE PROGRESSIVE CENTURY

Winning in the suburbs

We took the newspapers home with us to persuade my daughters, Georgia and Grace, that Labour had finally done it. They had been up most of the night, worried, not really believing it. A few hours later, at half-past eleven on 2 May, I waited with the children and hundreds of others outside the gates of Downing Street. At first the police refused to let anyone in, which caused a bit of a row, but eventually the gates opened and the crowd rushed through, feeling like a small liberation army. At first most of us were Labour Party workers, who had fought for this moment for many years, but soon other people arrived and the atmosphere became carnival-like, euphoric. Anji Hunter was cheered as she arrived and went into Number 10. Then the Prime Minister and Cherie Booth began making their way up Downing Street, greeting the crowd, thanking people, to chants of 'Labour's coming home'. I was so exhausted I barely took it in. Alastair Campbell followed, looking proud but shattered. Tony Blair stopped in front of Number 10 and spoke: 'I say to the people of this country – we ran for office as New Labour, we will govern as New Labour . . . For eighteen long years my party has been in opposition. It could only say, it could not do. Today we are charged with the deep responsibility of government. Today, enough of talking. It is time now to do.'[1] I shook Alastair's hand but he hardly noticed, he was already gone, on to the next challenge. The door to Number 10 opened, and he slipped inside.

I went home and collapsed in a fog of exhaustion. The first dramatic days of the Blair government were a background blur. A few days later I went back to Woking to pay respect to my parents, who had missed this moment. At first much appeared to be the same: tiny red-brick Victorian villas still fighting with post-war semis, but now they had tiny conservatories and satellite dishes added on. The cars were better and newer, and the shops were full of microwaves and videos instead of black-and-white televisions and unwieldy tumble-dryers. The suburbs had changed, but this time Labour had changed with them. I went to the house that I had grown up in, and saw the large garden, now overgrown, in which I had first dreamed of working in political campaigns, first worried about what I really believed in. My journey was over.

Labour's journey was over too. It had won an extraordinary victory on 1 May. The statistics of success were a mirror image of the failure of 1983, the election that had finally persuaded me to get involved. In 1983 Labour had lost by 144 seats, in 1997 it won by 179 seats: a shift of 323 seats in fourteen years. In 1983 the swing to the Conservatives had been 6 per cent, in 1997 the swing to Labour was 10.3 per cent.[2] Tellingly, a Conservative lead of 8 per cent among skilled working-class voters had been turned into a Labour lead of 21 per cent.[3] And most satisfying for me, 1.8 million Conservative voters in 1992 were estimated to have switched to Labour in 1997.[4] This scale of direct switching had been deemed impossible by many commentators, but was at the heart of New Labour's election strategy. These were the voters I had spoken to weekly, then daily, for three long years. Labour, a party almost dead in 1983, was now reborn. Labour did not win in 1997; New Labour did. Only when Labour had been completely modernised – and signalled this change through what was effectively a new name for the party – could dissatisfaction with the Conservatives be turned into positive support for us. Those 1.8 million Conservative voters in 1992 would not have switched had Labour not modernised; nor would white-collar workers have moved to Labour in such huge numbers; nor would Labour have won back the great mass of working-class support which had switched to Margaret Thatcher in 1979 and 1983. In focus groups across England, Wales and Scotland, among all social classes, it was the fact that Labour had become New Labour that gave people the confidence to make the change. New Labour was the last line of defence against people's fears and memories, their images of extremism and failure. It was a line that held.

The progressive century

Although May 1997 was an end-point, it also marked the beginning of a new journey. Labour had won its greatest election victory, but it has never won a full second term. More than that, Labour has never been able to establish itself as the dominant party of government, or even as a consistent governing party. This is New Labour's next challenge: to hold power not just for one or two terms, but to build a progressive coalition which dominates the next century as the Conservatives have commanded this one. David Marquand calls this the progressive dilemma: 'How to transcend Labourism without betraying the labour interest; how to bridge the gap between the old Labour fortresses and the potentially anti-Conservative but non-Labour hinterland; how to construct a broad-based and enduring social coalition capable of not just giving it a temporary majority in the House of Commons, but of sustaining a reforming government thereafter.'[5] This is the test by which the New Labour government should be judged. When critics attack New Labour for caution, for failing to be radical enough, early enough, for making tough economic decisions, for trying to impose order and discipline, they are trapped in the conservative mind-set that kept Labour in opposition for so long. If a progressive coalition can govern Britain for a majority of the time then more poverty will be removed and more real change implemented than could ever be achieved by short, sharp, occasional spasms of radicalism. Lasting change can only happen over time, as part of a progressive project for government. The alternatives have failed Britain and its people. We lack schools that are good enough, hospitals that are modern enough, streets that are safe enough. The British people lack skills, opportunity and ambition. Our public infrastructure has been allowed to crumble, our national identity is uncertain. We have let people who do not use our schools run our education system, and people who do not use our health service run the NHS. This is the price Labour has paid for losing the last century. We need a new long-term radicalism, to ensure that progressive instincts become rooted in the institutions of the nation, just as conservative instincts were in the past. New Labour may have won an election, but now it has to win a century.

A new progressive politics

Labour lost the last century because it failed to modernise, and lost connection with the people it was founded to represent. It was a party trapped by its past, even at the moment of its birth. If Labour is to win the next century it needs a new progressive politics: welcoming change; reaching out to the new middle class; reshaping the political map.

Managing change: the progressive opportunity
In the twenty-first century the pace of change will be so fast, so all-embracing, that it will in effect be an age of permanent revolution. In the economy, increasing globalisation will mean that the whole concept of national businesses and national markets effectively disappears. Competition will intensify, information will flow so quickly that any new business development or insight

will be known by competitors within minutes, possibly seconds. Technological advances are going to take our breath away.

This will have enormous social impact. The changes that have already happened have left most people in developed democracies feeling insecure. The idea of a job for life has gone, the hope of a job for a decade is fading. Families will face increasing strain as both parents work, the pressures on communities grow and traditional bonds and values further erode. The external environment will appear increasingly hostile. In 1985 people in focus groups described the world out there as dark and menacing, but a world that could be blocked out by shutting the front door. Eleven years later the viability of this form of defence had collapsed. One woman in a focus group in 1996 described the world outside 'like a black slime that could seep under your front door'. The menace of 'outside' could no longer be stopped by slamming the door in its face, it was too pervasive. Change is everywhere: always unsettling, sometimes threatening.

Labour failed in the twentieth century because it retreated from change. It can only win the next by embracing it. Working people and their families will choose parties of the left which seek to equip them to manage change, rather than parties of the right which expect them to cope with it alone. Tony Blair describes this process: 'Ordinary people see change happening at a pace and depth they find frightening. They seek security amidst the whirlwind. They try to regain some control over their lives as change hurls them this way and that. Our task as modern governments is to help them do it. But here is the dilemma. People know that change cannot be resisted. There is no comfort in isolation. It doesn't work. But neither do they want change to control them, to rule them. So: our task is to equip people for change, to shape its impact, to make sense of it, to embrace it in order that we make it work for us.'[6]

This is modernisation for the many. Modernisation which gives to hard-working families the tools and resources they need to advance and prosper. Modernisation which meshes the values of community with the imperative of efficiency in a way that understands the necessity of both as well as their mutual dependence. Modernisation which knows that we cannot enter the new world of change without the capacity to compete, but nor can we enter it without strong and decent societies, because if we do, the strain of change will be unbearable, the cost unacceptable. This is the progressive opportunity.

The new middle class: the heart of the new progressive coalition

Over 60 per cent of people now believe that they are, to one degree or another, middle-class. This new middle class does not just include people in white-collar jobs: 50 per cent of people in skilled manual occupations consider themselves to be to some extent described by the term 'middle-class'.[7] The middle class can no longer be viewed as a small, privileged sub-sector of society. Mass politics is becoming middle-class politics. Winning the century means winning middle-class support.

The new middle classes are the aspirational working class in manual occupations, and the increasingly insecure white-collar workers with middle- to low-level incomes. These are the children I was brought up with, the people of the suburbs. They do not lead easy lives but lives of struggle and hard work: wanting little more than a better life for themselves and for their families. In the past Conservatism has claimed them with promises of individual freedom, lower taxes, a reduced role for the state, unfettered aspiration. But changing times have made middle-class voters wary of the ideology of the right; social breakdown has exposed the limits of individualism, emphasising the importance of the family and the community. Change is the basis of a new progressive coalition because it affects the old working class and the new middle class, both insecure in the face of change, both wanting an active government that will make change work for them, and not against them. Change is the lever that is increasingly pulling the new middle class away from the parties of the right as voters realise that only progressive governments can be trusted to manage it for them. Stanley Greenberg describes this new coalition: 'The new popular progressive majority will be built broadly among working middle-class families, shaped by the new task of helping people of ordinary luck to achieve a better life in a world of unimagined changes and of growing economic and family pressures.'[8] The new middle class is the key to the progressive century.

A new political alignment, a new progressive map
The progressive dilemma will only be resolved permanently when an enduring alliance is created, bringing together all those with progressive instincts into one broad, pluralist political grouping – the party Labour could have been had it not split so fatally from the Liberals almost one hundred years ago. Only then will the left finally be completely trusted, only then will a progressive century be assured. It is time to heal the rift between the Liberal and Labourist traditions in British politics. Throughout the century the split in the progressive forces has impeded the left and assisted the right, and never more so than in the ten years after the formation of the SDP, when a divided left allowed Thatcherism to flourish long after it should have met its demise.

But the schism also cut Labour off from a body of ideas which would have broadened its base and widened its appeal. It is no coincidence that the most successful Labour government – 1945 to 1951 – owed much to the thinking and planning of two Liberals, Keynes and Beveridge, and to its one-nation characteristics drawn from wartime coalition experience. The split between the Liberal and Labour parties not only led to divided progressive forces, it led to divided intellectual traditions, separating Liberalism, with its emphasis on individualism and tolerance, from Labourism, which stressed solidarity and social justice. The result left Labour as a dogmatic, statist party, ignoring and marginalising the core liberal concepts of individual responsibility, self-reliance and civic rather than state action.

Tony Blair has done much to reconcile these two traditions; bringing together the ideas of community and the individual, and understanding their interdependent relationship, has always been central to his politics. Self-reliance, duty and responsibility are core Blair concepts. But in order to build a progressive alliance that lasts, either the Liberal Democrats and Labour will have to converge – effectively becoming one party – or New Labour modernisation will have to accelerate, broadening the party's appeal so that the Liberals are driven to the margins and New Labour alone becomes the broad progressive church of British politics. The better course would be for Liberalism and Labourism to unite.

But this will not be easy. It will require the Labour Party to be generous, to reach out to a smaller party when in a position of great strength. It will require the Liberal Democrats to show the discipline and responsibility necessary to enable them to move from the margins to the mainstream of British politics.

The prize is great. If a new progressive politics can be realised, a new progressive century can be won: New Labour confirmed as a modernising party constantly adapting to change, and helping hardworking families to adapt too; providing a new way forward, linking the values of community to the exigencies of a modern age; building an enduring coalition of government centred on the new middle classes; reaching out to the liberal tradition which has long been its rival; and ending the debilitating split within the progressive forces in British politics – Labour reborn genuinely radical, almost one hundred years after its birth as a party rooted in conservatism.

The unfinished revolution

This is the boldest and most radical agenda in British politics today. It is the radicalism of the long term, of deep-rooted and enduring change.

It is a long way from the political settlement of 1918, and from Labour's terrible defeat in 1983. It is far removed from the days of the forgotten suburbs. It is the agenda of a modernising revolution not yet finished. But if this agenda can be achieved, the goal of a progressive century is within our grasp: a century in which progressive politics can take hold, and in which the great majority of working people are helped and supported by the Labour Party, not now and again, but again and again. This is why the Labour Party was formed. This is what it forgot for so long. We must win the next century as surely as we lost the last.

NOTES

Further publication details can be found in the Bibliography.

Introduction

1. Henry Reed, 'Lessons of the War: 1. Naming of Parts', *The Oxford Book of Twentieth-Century Verse*, p. 478.
2. David Owen, *Time to Declare*, p. 39.
3. Herbert Marcuse, *Reason and Revolution*, p. 124.
4. Ibid.
5. G. W. F. Hegel, *Elements of the Philosophy of Right*, p. 23.
6. Michael Oakeshott, *Rationalism in Politics*, p. 129.
7. Ibid, p. 124.

1: The Century That Labour Lost

1. Ivor Crewe, 'How to Win a Landslide Without Really Trying', p. 2.
2. *Guardian*, 20 June 1983.
3. Crewe, op. cit., p. 14.
4. Ibid., p. 15.
5. Ibid.
6. Crewe, 'The Labour Party and the Electorate' in Dennis Kavanagh (ed.), *The Politics of the Labour Party*, p. 27.
7. Crewe, 'How to Win a Landslide Without Really Trying', p. 25.
8. Ibid., p. 23.
9. Focus group, verbatim transcript, 17 February 1997.
10. Crewe, 'Labour Force Changes, Working-Class Decline and the Labour Vote: Social and Electoral Trends in Postwar Britain' in Frances Fox Piven (ed.), *Labour Parties in Post-Industrial Societies*, p. 23.
11. Ibid.
12. Ibid., p. 26.
13. Ibid., pp. 36–7.
14. Ibid., p. 38.
15. Ibid.

16. Ibid.

17. Focus group, verbatim transcript, 12 September 1991.

18. Michael Cox, *Labour and the Benn Factor*, pp. 74–5.

19. Anthony Seldon, *The Conservative Century*, pp. 13, 18.

20. Benjamin Disraeli, speech in Edinburgh, 29 October 1867, quoted in *The Times*, 30 October 1867.

21. David Marquand, *The Progressive Dilemma*, p. ix.

22. A. J. Davies, *To Build a New Jerusalem*, p. 49.

23. Tudor Jones, *Remaking the Labour Party*, p. 109.

24. Ibid.

25. Ben Pimlott, 'The Labour Left', in Cook and Taylor (eds), *The Labour Party*, p. 180 (quoted in Jones, *Remaking the Labour Party*, p. 15).

26. Shaw Desmond, *Labour: The Giant With the Feet of Clay*, p. 197 (quoted in Jones, *Remaking the Labour Party*, p. 15).

27. Marquand, op. cit., p. 17.

28. Davies, op. cit., p. 119.

29. Ibid., p. 120.

30. Jones, op. cit., p. 9.

31. Ibid.

32. H. M. Drucker, *Doctrine and Ethos in the Labour Party*, p. 25 (quoted in Jones, *Remaking the Labour Party*, p. 9).

33. Marquand, op. cit., p. 17.

34. Labour Party Annual Conference Report, January and February 1918, Appendix I, Constitution of the Labour Party, Section 3 (d).

35. *Labour and the New Social Order* (quoted in Jones, *Remaking the Labour Party*, p. 5).

36. G. D. H. Cole, *A History of the Labour Party from 1914*, p. 56 (quoted in Jones, *Remaking the Labour Party*, p. 5).

37. Egon Wertheimer, *Portrait of the Labour Party*, p. 50 (quoted in Jones, *Remaking the Labour Party*, p. 5).

38. Davies, op. cit., p. 213.

39. Hilary Wainwright, *Labour: A Tale of Two Parties*, p. 82.

40. Tony Blair, speech to the Fabian Society commemoration of the 1945 General Election, 5 July 1995.

41. Ibid.

42. Douglas Jay, *The Socialist Case*, p. 195 (quoted in Jones, *Remaking the Labour Party*, p. 27).

43. Jones, op. cit., p. 26.

44. W. H. Greenleaf, *The British Political Tradition, Vol. 2*, p. 475 (quoted in Jones, *Remaking the Labour Party*, p. 25).

45. Ibid., p. 476.
46. Lewis Minkin, *The Labour Party Conference*, p. 125 (quoted in Jones, *Remaking the Labour Party*, p. 26).
47. S. H. Beer, *Modern British Politics*, p. 237 (quoted in Jones, *Remaking the Labour Party*, p. 27).
48. Anthony Crosland, *The Future of Socialism*, p. 41 (quoted in Jones, *Remaking the Labour Party*, p. 27).
49. Jones, op. cit., p. 27.
50. Tony Benn, *Years of Hope: Diaries, Papers and Letters, 1940–1962*, p. 318.
51. Labour Party Conference Report, 1959, pp. 109–13 (quoted in Jones, *Remaking the Labour Party*, pp. 46–8).
52. Davies, op. cit., p. 294.
53. Ibid.
54. Ibid., p. 302.
55. Keith Middlemas, *The Politics of Industrial Society*, p. 417 (quoted in Jones, *Remaking the Labour Party*, p. 86).
56. Crewe, op. cit., p. 28.
57. Davies, op. cit., p. 330.
58. Jones, op. cit., p. 91.
59. *Guardian*, 3 October 1973 (quoted in Jones, *Remaking the Labour Party*, p. 92).
60. Jones, op. cit., p. 102.
61. Davies, op. cit., p. 365.
62. Patricia Sykes, *Losing from the Inside*, p. 37.
63. Interview with David Hill, 13 March 1998.
64. G. L. Williams and A. L. Williams, *Labour's Decline and the Social Democrats' Fall*, p. 113.

2: Saving Labour

1. Interview with Peter Mandelson, 18 March 1998.
2. Letter to Peter Mandelson, 1 November 1985.
3. Interview with Patricia Hewitt, 13 October 1997.
4. Interview with Charles Clarke, 23 March 1998.
5. Interview with Patricia Hewitt, 13 October 1997.
6. Interview with Charles Clarke, 23 March 1998.
7. Neil Kinnock, speech to the Labour Party conference, 1 October 1985.
8. Interview with Peter Mandelson, 16 October 1997.
9. Private information.
10. Interview with Peter Mandelson, 9 November 1985.

11. Interview with Robert Worcester, 12 November 1985.

12. Interview with Patricia Hewitt, 13 October 1997.

13. Interview with David Hill, 13 March 1998.

14. Interview with Patricia Hewitt, 13 October 1997.

15. Interview with Peter Mandelson, 9 November 1985.

16. Ibid.

17. Interview with Patricia Hewitt, 13 October 1997.

18. Interview with Peter Mandelson, 9 November 1985.

19. Interview with Tony Manwaring, 10 November 1985.

20. Transcript of presentation by Leslie Butterfield, Paul Southgate and Roddy Glen, 25 November 1985.

21. Transcript of presentation by BBDO, 25 November 1985.

22. Philip Gould, 'Report on Labour Party Communications', 18 November 1985, p. 16.

23. Interview with Peter Mandelson, 16 October 1997.

24. Gould, 'Social Policy Campaign – Final Brief', 4 February 1986.

25. Interview with Peter Mandelson, 16 October 1997.

26. Ibid.

27. Ibid.

28. Ibid.

29. *Financial Times*, 23 April 1986.

30. *Daily Telegraph*, 23 April 1986.

31. *Sunday Mirror*, 27 April 1986.

32. *Guardian*, 23 April 1986.

33. *New Statesman*, 25 April 1986.

34. *Tribune*, 23 April 1986.

35. Letter from Peter Mandelson to Larry Whitty, 7 April 1986.

36. Ibid. (response from Larry Whitty handwritten at bottom of letter).

37. Interview with Peter Mandelson, 16 October 1997.

38. Author's diary, 25 June 1986.

39. Ibid., 26 June 1986.

40. Interview with Peter Mandelson, 16 October 1997.

41. Ibid.

42. Author's diary, 23 June 1986.

43. Interview with Peter Mandelson, 16 October 1997.

44. Ibid.

45. Memo from Joe Napolitan to Neil Kinnock, 15 April 1986.

46. Kinnock, speech to the Labour Party conference, 30 September 1986.

47. Interview with Patricia Hewitt, 13 October 1997.

48. Interview with Peter Mandelson, 16 October 1997.

49. Memo from Joe Napolitan to Neil Kinnock, 3 August 1986.
50. Ibid., 27 June 1986.
51. Ibid., 13 October 1986.
52. Ibid.
53. Gould, memo to the SCA Management Group, 17 November 1986.
54. Ibid.
55. Letter to Peter Mandelson and Bryan Gould, 12 December 1986.
56. Memo from Patricia Hewitt, 26 February 1987.
57. Interview with Patricia Hewitt, 13 October 1997.
58. Interview with Colin Byrne, 20 March 1998.
59. Gould, memo to Jeremy Kane, 3 March 1987.
60. Letter to Peter Mandelson, 10 March 1987.
61. Gould, memo to Jeremy Kane, 25 April 1987.
62. Interview with Patricia Hewitt, 13 October 1997.
63. Gould, memo to Jeremy Kane, 2 May 1987.
64. Ibid.
65. Margaret Scammell, *Designer Politics*, p. 140.
66. Interview with Chris Powell, 19 March 1998.
67. Kinnock, speech to the Llandudno Labour conference, 15 May 1987.
68. David Butler and Dennis Kavanagh, *The British General Election of 1987*, p. 114.
69. David Owen, *Time to Declare*, p. 693.
70. *Daily Mail*, 5 June 1987.
71. *Daily Express*, 6 June 1987.
72. Interview with Chris Powell, 19 March 1998.

3: The Long Decline

1. Philip Gould, 'SCA Campaign Appraisal and Next Action', 12 July 1987.
2. Ibid.
3. Ibid.
4. Gould, 'Research Note', 29 July 1987.
5. Labour Party NEC, 'Labour and Britain in 1990s', May 1988.
6. Colin Hughes and Patrick Wintour, *Labour Rebuilt*, p. 39.
7. *Campaign*, 2 October 1987.
8. Quoted in Hughes and Wintour, op. cit., p. 38.
9. Labour Party NEC, 'Labour and Britain in 1990s', p. 5.
10. Ibid., p. 9.
11. Ibid., p. 10.
12. Ibid.

13. Ibid., pp. 16–21.

14. Ibid., p. 24.

15. Quoted in Hughes and Wintour, op. cit., p. 103.

16. Interview with Patricia Hewitt, 13 October 1997.

17. Ibid.

18. Interview with Patricia Hewitt, 13 October 1997.

19. Interview with Charles Clarke, 23 March 1998.

20. Author's diary, 24 January 1988.

21. Letter to Peter Mandelson, 12 January 1988.

22. Hughes and Wintour, op. cit., pp. 84–6.

23. Interview with Patricia Hewitt, 13 October 1997.

24. Hughes and Wintour, op. cit., p. 90.

25. Author's diary, 17 July 1988.

26. Interview with Charles Clarke, 23 March 1998.

27. Ibid.

28. Ibid.

29. Author's diary, 28 June 1988.

30. Ibid., 30 June 1988.

31. Ibid., 3 July 1988.

32. Ibid., 5 July 1988.

33. Letter from Peter Mandelson to Charles Clarke, 16 August 1988.

34. Ibid.

35. Ibid.

36. Ibid.

37. Hughes and Wintour, op. cit., p. 97.

38. Gould, '1989 Campaigning Strategy Considerations', 13 February 1989.

39. Ibid.

40. Ibid.

41. MORI political polling, 18–22 May 1989.

42. Gould, memo, 12 September 1989.

43. Ibid.

44. Gould, memo, 14 October 1989.

45. Interview with Charles Clarke, 23 March 1998.

46. Author's diary, 24 January 1988.

47. Interview with Charles Clarke, 23 March 1998.

48. Interview with Colin Byrne, 20 March 1998.

49. Gould, 'Current Strategic Position', 10 January 1990.

50. Gould, 'Winning the Election', 13 June 1990.

51. Interview with Patricia Hewitt, 13 November 1997.

52. Interview with Charles Clarke, 23 March 1998.

53. Ibid.
54. Gould, 'Post Conference Note', 8 October 1990.
55. Interview with Colin Byrne, 20 March 1998.
56. Ibid.
57. Gould, 'Summary of Research and Strategic Implications', 20 December 1990.
58. Interview with David Hill, 13 March 1998.
59. Interview with Charles Clarke, 23 March 1998.
60. Interview with Patricia Hewitt, 13 October 1997.
61. Interview with Sally Morgan, 19 March 1998.
62. Clive Hollick, memo to Thursday Meeting, 30 July 1990.
63. Interview with Patricia Hewitt, 13 October 1997.
64. Gould, memo, 8 October 1991.
65. Interview with Charles Clarke, 23 March 1998.
66. Ibid.
67. Interview with Colin Byrne, 20 March 1998.
68. Gould, 'War Book', 12 December 1991.
69. Interview with David Hill, 13 March 1998.
70. Interview with Charles Clarke, 23 March 1998.
71. Interview with Alastair Campbell, 17 March 1998.

4: Love and Anger

1. Private information.
2. Author's diary, 20 April 1992.
3. Ibid.
4. Ibid.
5. Interview with Alastair Campbell, 17 March 1998.
6. Author's diary, 20 April 1992.
7. SCA, research into attitudes to taxation, 12 April 1988.
8. Ibid.
9. Interview with Patricia Hewitt, 13 October 1997.
10. Author's diary, 5 July 1988.
11. BMP research for the SCA, December 1989.
12. Ibid.
13. Ibid.
14. SCPR, 'British Social Attitudes' survey, 1996.
15. Gould, 'Current Strategic Position', 10 January 1990.
16. Letter to Peter Mandelson, 10 May 1990.
17. Labour Party, 'Looking to the Future', 1990.
18. Gould, 'Presentation of the Policy Review', 23 May 1990.

19. SCA, 'Campaigning Until the General Election', 26 July 1990.
20. Deborah Mattinson, presentation of SCA reseach findings on taxation, 25 June 1990.
21. Author's diary, 20 April 1992.
22. Ibid.
23. Ibid.
24. SCA, 'Campaigning in London', 24 April 1991.
25. ITV, *Frost on Sunday*, 5 May 1991.
26. *Guardian*, 9 May 1991.
27. David Butler and Dennis Kavanagh, *The British General Election of 1992*, p. 36.
28. SCA presentation, 12 November 1991.
29. Patricia Hewitt, memo to the Campaign Advisory Team, 29 October 1991.
30. Ibid.
31. Interview with Patricia Hewitt, 13 October 1997.
32. Interview with Charles Clarke, 23 March 1998.
33. Ibid.
34. Author's diary, 20 April 1992.
35. Ibid.
36. Ibid.
37. Interview with Patricia Hewitt, 13 October 1997.
38. Author's diary, 20 April 1992.
39. Interview with Charles Clarke, 23 March 1998.
40. Author's diary, 20 April 1992.
41. Ibid.
42. Ibid.
43. Ibid.
44. Interview with Charles Clarke, 23 March 1998.
45. Author's diary, 20 April 1992.
46. Interview with Clive Hollick, 2 July 1998.
47. *The Times*, 17 April 1992.
48. Butler and Kavanagh, op. cit., p. 105.
49. SCA, 'Summary Qualititative Research', 21 February 1992.
50. Letter from Kathryn Smith to Anna Healey, 24 March 1992.
51. *Sunday Express*, 22 March 1992.
52. *Sunday Telegraph*, 22 March 1992.
53. *Sunday Times*, 22 March 1992.
54. *Mail on Sunday*, 5 April 1992.
55. *Daily Mail*, 23 March 1992.

56. *Sun*, 23 March 1992.

57. *Today*, 23 March 1992.

58. *Daily Express*, 23 March 1992.

59. *Daily Express*, 25 March 1992.

60. Author's diary, 27 March 1992.

61. *Sunday Express*, 29 March 1992.

62. Gould, '1992 General Election: Evaluation and Implications', 22 September 1992.

63. Ibid.

64. Ibid.

65. Gould, 'Post-Election Evaluation of Party Election Broadcasts', April 1992.

66. Memo from Joe Napolitan, 8 March 1991.

67. Heath, Jowell and Curtice, *Labour's Last Chance*, p. 139.

68. Interview with Charles Clarke, 23 March 1998.

69. Ibid.

70. Interview with Alastair Campbell, 17 March 1998.

71. *Independent*, 25 May 1992.

72. Interview with Patricia Hewitt, 13 October 1997.

73. Interview with Charles Clarke, 23 March 1998.

74. Interview with Alastair Campbell, 17 March 1998.

75. Interview with Charles Clarke, 23 March 1998.

76. Interview with Alastair Campbell, 17 March 1998.

77. Interview with Patricia Hewitt, 13 October 1997.

78. Gould, '1992 General Election: Evaluation and Implications', 22 September 1992.

79. Interview with Patricia Hewitt, 13 October 1997.

80. Interview with David Hill, 13 March 1998.

81. *Daily Express*, 7 April 1992.

82. *Sun*, 7 April 1992.

83. *Sun*, 8 April 1992.

84. *Daily Mail*, 8 April 1992.

85. *Daily Express*, 8 April 1992.

86. Gould, 'Winning the Election', 13 June 1990.

87. *Tribune*, 9 April 1992.

88. *Tribune*, 17 April 1992.

89. *Tribune*, 26 June 1992.

90. Memo from Glenys Thornton to Patricia Hewitt and Philip Gould, 6 April 1992.

91. *Independent*, 25 April 1992.

92. *Independent*, 18 June 1992.
93. *Independent*, 22 June 1992.
94. *Tribune*, 3 July 1992.
95. *Guardian*, 18 June 1992.
96. *Sunday Times*, 21 June 1992.
97. Letter to Dennis Kavanagh, 7 July 1992.
98. Gould, '1992 General Election: Evaluation and Implications', 22 September 1992.
99. Interview with David Hare, 15 July 1992.
100. *Daily Mirror*, 17 June 1992.
101. *Tribune*, 26 June 1992.
102. Gould, '1992 General Election: Evaluation and Implications', 22 September 1992.

5: A Line in the Sand

1. Jon Sopel, *Tony Blair: The Moderniser*, p. 135.
2. *Campaign*, 16 October 1992.
3. Neil Kinnock, speech to the Labour Party conference, 1 October 1991.
4. Letter from Dianna Wentz, Greenberg–Lake Analysis Group Inc., 25 September 1992.
5. *Sunday Times*, 2 February 1992.
6. News release, Bush–Quayle campaign, 5 October 1992.
7. Author's diary, 6 October 1992.
8. Mary Matalin and James Carville, *All's Fair*, frontispiece.
9. Author's diary, 7 October 1992.
10. *Washington Post*, 8 October 1992.
11. Gould, 'British Parallels', 10 October 1992.
12. Author's diary, 11 October 1992.
13. Ibid.
14. Ibid., 20 October 1992.
15. Ibid., 21 October 1992.
16. Gould, 'The Final Week', 29 October 1992.
17. Author's diary, 1 November 1992.
18. Matalin and Carville, op. cit., pp. 461–2.
19. Gould, 'Mitterrand: Winning from Cohabitation', 13 December 1994.
20. Stanley Greenberg, 'The Dukakis Message, Speaking Middle Class', 20 September 1988.
21. Greenberg, 'Reconstructing the Democratic Vision', *The American Prospect*, No. 1, Spring 1990.

22. Greenberg, *Middle-Class Dreams*, p. 305.
23. Bill Clinton, speech to the Democratic Convention, New York, 16 July 1992.
24. Gould, '1992 Campaign Evaluation and Implications', 9 December 1992.
25. Philip Gould and Patricia Hewitt, 'Lessons from America', *Renewal*, January 1993 (quoted in Sopel, op. cit., p. 145).
26. *Tribune*, 8 January 1993.
27. Clive Hollick, 'Campaign '96', 28 July 1992.
28. Interview with Clive Hollick, 2 July 1998.
29. Gould, 'Assessment of Current Position', 20 May 1993.
30. Ibid.
31. Ibid.
32. John Rentoul, *Tony Blair*, p. 274.
33. Tony Blair on BBC Radio, *The World This Weekend*, 10 January 1993.
34. Rentoul, op. cit., p. 290.
35. Ibid., p. 160.
36. Gould, 'Strategy Note', 10 September 1993.
37. Ibid.
38. Interview with Patricia Hewitt, 19 March 1998.
39. Rentoul, op. cit., p. 327.
40. Gould, 'Fighting the Fear Factor', 8 February 1994.
41. Gould, 'The Labour Party: Preliminary Campaign Observations', 9 May 1994.

6: Electric Shock Treatment

1. Interview with Alastair Campbell, 17 March 1998.
2. Ibid.
3. Interview with Fiona Millar, 17 March 1998.
4. *Guardian*, 13 November 1992.
5. Private information.
6. Ibid.
7. John Rentoul, *Tony Blair*, p. 313.
8. BBC TV, *On the Record*, 17 January 1993.
9. Private information.
10. Ibid.
11. Ibid.
12. Ibid.
13. Interview with Alastair Campbell, 17 March 1998.
14. Ibid.

15. Philip Gould, 'Negative Consequences of a Two Horse Race', 18 May 1994.

16. Ibid.

17. Interview with Peter Mandelson, 18 March 1998.

18. Ibid.

19. Ibid.

20. Ibid.

21. Interview with Alastair Campbell, 17 March 1998.

22. Gould, 'Strategy for the Leadership Election and Beyond', 17 May 1994.

23. Ibid.

24. Gould, 'Leadership Election: Tony Blair Campaign', 20 May 1994.

25. Gould, 'Blair Campaign: Moving Forward', 2 June 1994.

26. Tony Blair, 'Themes', 2 June 1994.

27. Interview with Peter Hyman, 24 March 1995.

28. Gould, 'Focus Group Debrief', 6 June 1994.

29. Gould, 'Leadership Election, Blair Campaign, Campaign Strategy Document', 10 June 1994.

30. Rentoul, op. cit., p. 394.

31. Interview with David Miliband, 24 March 1998.

32. Blair, 'Change and Renewal – Leadership Election Statement', 1994.

33. Feedback Report, 28 June 1994.

34. Interview with Peter Mandelson, 18 March 1998.

35. I am indebted to Peter Kellner for this analysis.

36. Blair, interview with Brian Walden, 24 July 1994.

37. *Daily Telegraph*, 26 July 1994.

38. *Daily Mail*, 26 July 1994.

39. Labour Party, 'Opening Doors to a Learning Society', 28 July 1994.

40. BBC TV, *One O'Clock News*, 28 July 1994.

41. Gould, 'Consolidating the Blair Identity: Rebuilding Labour; Demolishing the Conservatives', 22 July 1994.

42. Interview with Alastair Campbell, 17 March 1998.

43. Interview with Peter Mandelson, 18 March 1998.

44. Letter to Tony Blair, 14 September 1994.

45. Jon Sopel, *Tony Blair: The Moderniser*, p. 267.

46. Gould, 'Destroying the Conservatives, Rebuilding Labour', 9 September 1994.

47. *Financial Times*, 13 September 1994.

48. BBC Radio 4, *Today*, 13 September 1994.

49. Gould, 'New Labour; Right as Well as Left', 1 September 1994.

50. Gould, 'Next Two Weeks', 23 September 1994.

51. Interview with Alastair Campbell, 17 March 1994.

52. Ibid.

53. Blair, speech to the Labour Party conference, 4 October 1994.

54. Blair, speech to the Per Cent Club, 8 November 1994.

55. Ibid.

56. Gould, 'Where Labour Stands', 11 November 1994.

57. *Financial Times*, 21 November 1998.

58. *Daily Mail*, 1 December 1994.

59. Gould, memo to Tony Blair, 12 December 1994.

60. Gould, memo to Tony Blair, 19 December 1994.

61. Gould, 'Urgent Action Resulting from Focus Groups', 20 January 1995.

62. *Daily Telegraph*, 13 January 1995.

63. *Observer*, 15 January 1995.

64. *Sunday Telegraph*, 22 January 1995.

65. Gould, memo to Tony Blair, 21 March 1995.

66. Gould, 'Where We Are, Where We Should Be Going', 3 March 1995.

67. Gould, 'Where Our Campaigning is Going Wrong; What We Must Do About It', 12 January 1995.

68. Interview with Alastair Campbell, 17 March 1998.

69. Interview with Sally Morgan, 19 March 1998.

70. Interview with Margaret McDonagh, 13 March 1998.

71. See the Appendix in Rentoul, op. cit., p. 495.

72. Ibid.

73. Tudor Jones, *Remaking the Labour Party*, p. 146.

74. Gould, 'Draft Notes on the Next Steps', 20 April 1995.

7: The Project

1. Tony Blair, 'Why Modernisation Matters', *Renewal*, 4 October 1993.

2. John Rentoul, *Tony Blair*, p. 38.

3. Ibid, p. 42.

4. Blair, speech to the Wellingborough Constituency Labour Party, 19 February 1993.

5. L. T. Hobhouse, *Liberalism* (quoted in Blair's speech, 'Faith in the City: Ten Years On', 29 January 1996).

6. Blair, speech to the Wellingborough Constituency Labour Party, 19 February 1993.

7. Blair, 'Why Modernisation Matters', *Renewal*, 4 October 1993.

8. Blair, speech at Durham University, 28 January 1993.

9. Bill Clinton, 'State of the Union' address, 27 January 1998.
10. Clinton, Address to the Democratic Leadership Council, Cleveland, 6 May 1991 (quoted in Stanley Greenberg, *Middle-Class Dreams*, p. 276).
11. Democratic Leadership Council, 'The New Orleans Declaration: A Democratic Agenda for the 1990s', New Orleans, 24 May 1990.
12. E. J. Dionne, Jr., *Why Americans Hate Politics*, pp. 11–12 (quoted in Greenberg, op. cit., p. 277).
13. Blair, 'Themes', 2 June 1994.
14. Blair, 'New Policies for a Global Economy', 27 September 1994.
15. Blair, 'Time', 30 November 1995.
16. Philip Gould, 'The Unfinished Revolution', 23 April 1995.
17. Anthony Seldon, 'The Conservative Century' in Seldon and Ball (eds), *Conservative Century: The Conservative Party Since 1900*, p. 65.
18. Gould, 'The Unfinished Revolution', 23 April 1995.
19. Gould, memo to Tony Blair, 24 April 1995.
20. Blair, *Spectator* lecture, 22 March 1995.
21. Blair, Mais lecture, 22 May 1995.
22. *Financial Times*, 23 May 1995.
23. Blair, speech to the NewsCorp Leadership Conference, Hayman Island, Australia, 17 July 1995.
24. Gould, 'Focus Group Report', 6 July 1995.
25. *New Statesman*, 11 August 1995.
26. *Guardian*, 12 September 1995.
27. *Guardian*, 13 September 1995.
28. *The Times*, 13 September 1995.
29. *Independent*, 13 September 1995.
30. Interview with Alastair Campbell, 17 March 1998.
31. Gould, 'Winning the Trust of the Centre Without Betraying the Left', 18 August 1995.
32. Gould, 'What is New Labour?', 25 August 1995.
33. Benjamin Disraeli, *Sybil, or, The Two Nations*, pp. 65–6.
34. Blair, speech to the Labour Party conference, 3 October 1995.
35. Gould, 'How Can We Expect the People to Understand What We Stand For, If We Don't Agree Among Ourselves', 12 November 1995.
36. Gould, 'One-Nation Economics', 9 December 1995.
37. David Miliband, notes on stakeholding, 13 January 1996.
38. Blair, speech to the Singapore Business Community, 8 January 1996.
39. Interview with Alastair Campbell, 17 March 1998.
40. Blair, speech, 'Faith in the City: Ten Years On', 29 January 1996.

8: Reassurance, Reassurance, Reassurance

1. Stanley Greenberg, 'Strategic Observations on the British Elections', 8 June 1995.
2. Philip Gould, 'The Tony Blair Problem', 6 December 1996.
3. Interview with Alastair Campbell, 17 March 1998.
4. Interview with Peter Mandelson, 18 March 1997.
5. Focus group comments, May-October 1996.
6. Gould, 'Campaigning Note: The Budget and After', 3 December 1995.
7. Gould, 'The Tony Blair Problem', 6 December 1995.
8. Gould, '1996: The Year Labour Changed Politics', 19 December 1995.
9. Tony Blair, 'Forward Strategy', 16 January 1996.
10. Interview with Peter Hyman, 24 March 1998.
11. Ibid.
12. Gould, 'Strategic Findings', 6 June 1996.
13. Labour Party, 'New Life for Britain', 4 July 1996.
14. John Rentoul, *Tony Blair*, p. 430.
15. Gould, 'Focus Group Report', 22 January 1996.
16. Gould, 'Fight Back Now', 28 January 1996.
17. John Major, Prime Minister's Questions, 23 January 1996.
18. Gould, 'Fighting Back, Step by Step', 3 March 1996.
19. Gould, 'Strategic Appraisal and Next Steps', 4 April 1996.
20. GMTV, *The Sunday Programme*, 14 April 1996.
21. Gould, 'Focus Group Report', 1 May 1996.
22. Gould, 'How You Can Get Out of This Mess and Start Enjoying Your Life Again', 14 May 1996.
23. Gould, 'Strategic Findings', 6 June 1996.
24. Report by Stanley Greenberg, 29 July 1996.
25. Gould, 'Focus Group Report', 29 July 1996.
26. *Observer*, 4 May 1996.
27. *The Times*, 16 May 1996.
28. *Guardian*, 8 August 1996.
29. *New Statesman*, 9 August 1996.
30. Ibid., 2 August 1996.
31. *Mail on Sunday*, 28 July 1996.
32. *Observer*, 11 August 1996.
33. Interview with Alastair Campbell, 17 March 1998.
34. Gould, 'Focus Group Report', 6 September 1996.
35. Gould, 'Conference Evaluation', 17 October 1996.
36. Gould, 'Beating Fear of Labour', 28 November 1996.

37. Blair, speech to the Commonwealth Parliamentary Union, Cape Town, South Africa, 14 October 1996.
38. Gould, 'Top-Line Findings', 9 January 1997.
39. Blair, Mais lecture, 22 May 1995.
40. Interview with Alastair Campbell, 17 March 1998.
41. Interview with Stanley Greenberg, 2 July 1998.
42. Gould, 'General', 22 June 1993.
43. Gould, 'Economic Campaigning', 14 September 1993.
44. Gould, 'Focus Group Report', 17 October 1993.
45. Gould, 'Taxation and the Economy', 10 July 1994.
46. Gould, 'Economic Campaigning – Key Facts', 12 March 1995.
47. Gould, 'Developing an Economic Message', 14 July 1994.
48. Gould, memo to Gordon Brown, 12 October 1994.
49. Gould, 'Focus Group Report', 17 November 1996.
50. Interview with Liam Byrne, 13 March 1998.
51. *Evening Standard*, 20 November 1996.
52. Interview with Liam Byrne, 13 March 1998.
53. *Independent on Sunday*, 19 November 1995.
54. Gould, 'Focus Group Report', 1 May 1996.
55. Gould, 'Focus Group Report', 5 February 1997.
56. Gould, 'Voter Mood, Election Strategy', 27 February 1997.
57. Greenberg, 'The Pre-Election Survey', 18 March 1997.

9: The Dark Arts

1. BBC TV, *Panorama*, 'The Marketing of Margaret', 13 June 1983.
2. Interview with Peter Mandelson, 18 March 1998.
3. Interview with Liam Byrne, 13 March 1998.
4. Ibid.
5. Interview with Peter Mandelson, 18 March 1998.
6. Interview with Liam Byrne, 13 March 1998.
7. Ibid.
8. Ibid.
9. Interview with Margaret McDonagh, 13 March 1998.
10. Ibid.
11. Interview with Liam Byrne, 13 March 1998.
12. Interview with Margaret McDonagh, 13 March 1998.
13. Interview with David Hare, 15 July 1992.
14. Interview with Peter Hyman, 24 March 1998.
15. War Book, version 3.2, 13 December 1996.

16. Leslie Butterfield, Paul Southgate and Roddy Glen, 'Towards a Communications Strategy for the Labour Party', November 1985.
17. Interview with Chris Powell, 19 March 1998.
18. Ibid.
19. Ibid.
20. Interview with Simon Buckby, 19 March 1998.
21. Ibid.
22. Ibid.
23. Ibid.
24. Focus group, verbatim transcript, 24 January 1998.
25. Ibid., 18 April 1996.
26. Ibid., 5 May 1996.
27. Author's diary, 23 February 1995.
28. Ibid., 24 February 1995.
29. Ibid., 25 February 1995.
30. Interview with Alastair Campbell, 17 March 1998.
31. Interview with Stanley Greenberg, 2 July 1998.
32. Interview with David Hill, 13 March 1998.
33. Interview with Jon Mendelsohn, 17 March 1998.
34. Ibid.
35. Ibid.
36. Interview with Alastair Campbell, 17 March 1998.
37. Interview with Liam Byrne, 13 March 1998.

10: Landslide Country

1. Interview with Alastair Campbell, 17 March 1998.
2. Ibid.
3. Philip Gould, 'Focus Group Report', 17 March 1997.
4. Gould, note to Tony Blair, 17 March 1997.
5. BBC Radio 4, *Today*, 18 March 1997.
6. Interview with David Hill, 13 March 1998.
7. Gould, 'Focus Group Report', 18 March 1997.
8. Gould, note to Tony Blair, 18 March 1997.
9. BBC Radio 4, *Today*, 20 March 1997.
10. Gould, 'Focus Group Report', 19 March 1997.
11. Gould, note to Tony Blair, 19 March 1997.
12. Gould, 'Focus Group Report', 20 March 1997.
13. Gould, note to Tony Blair, 20 March 1997.
14. Gould, 'Focus Group Report', 21 March 1997.
15. Gould, 'Focus Group Report', 23 March 1997.

16. Gould, note to Tony Blair, 23 March 1997.
17. BBC Radio 4, *Today*, 24 March 1997.
18. Gould, 'Focus Group Report', 24 March 1997.
19. Private information.
20. Gould, 'Focus Group Report', 25 March 1997.
21. Gould, note to Tony Blair, 25 March 1997.
22. Tony Blair, Labour Party press conference, 26 March 1997.
23. Interview with David Hill, 13 March 1998.
24. Gould, 'Focus Group Report', 26 March 1997.
25. Interview with David Hill, 13 March 1998.
26. Interview with Alastair Campbell, 17 March 1998.
27. Gould, 'Focus Group Report', 27 March 1997.
28. Gould, strategy note, 30 March 1997.
29. Ibid.
30. Gould, note to Alastair Campbell, 30 March 1997.
31. BBC Radio 4, *The World at One*, 31 March 1997.
32. Gould, 'Focus Group Report', 31 March 1997.
33. Labour Party, Campaign Poll 1, 1 April 1997.
34. Stanley Greenberg, 'The First Campaign Survey', 31 March 1997.
35. Gould, 'Focus Group Report', 1 April 1997.
36. Gould, 'Focus Group Report', 2 April 1997.
37. Gould, note to Tony Blair, 2 April 1997.
38. Gould, 'Focus Group Report', 3 April 1997.
39. Gould, note to Tony Blair and Alastair Campbell, 3 April 1997.
40. Gould, 'Focus Group Report', 4 April 1997.
41. Gould, note to Tony Blair, 4 April 1997.
42. Labour Party, Campaign Poll 2, 6 April 1997.
43. Greenberg, 'The Latest Tracking and Other Matters', 5 April 1997.
44. Interview with Peter Mandelson, 18 March 1998.
45. Gould, 'Focus Group Report', 7 April 1997.
46. Gould, note to Tony Blair, 7 April 1997.
47. Gould, 'Focus Group Report', 8 April 1997.
48. Gould, note to Tony Blair, 8 April 1997.
49. Gould, 'Focus Group Report', 9 April 1997.
50. Interview with David Hill, 13 March 1998.
51. Gould, 'Focus Group Report', 10 April 1997.
52. Gould, 'Focus Group Report', 11 April 1997.
53. *Sunday Times*, 13 April 1997.
54. Gould, 'Focus Group Report', 13 April 1997.
55. Gould, 'Focus Group Report', 14 April 1997.

56. BBC TV, *Newsnight*, 14 April 1997.
57. Interview with Alastair Campbell, 17 March 1998.
58. Interview with Benjamin Wegg-Prosser, 20 March 1998.
59. Gould, 'Focus Group Report', 15 April 1997.
60. Greenberg, 'Tracking Two Weeks Out', 15 April 1997.
61. Gould, 'Focus Group Report', 16 April 1997.
62. Interview with Alastair Campbell, 17 March 1998.
63. Gould, 'Focus Group Report', 17 April 1997.
64. Ibid., 18 April 1997.
65. Greenberg, 'The Changing Campaign', 21 April 1997.
66. *Independent on Sunday*, 20 April 1997.
67. Gould, 'Focus Group Report', 20 April 1997.
68. Nicholas Jones, *Campaign 1997*, p. 232.
69. Gould, 'Focus Group Report', 21 April 1997.
70. Interview with Adrian McMenamin, 16 March 1998.
71. Labour Party, Campaign Poll 7, 22 April 1997.
72. Greenberg, 'The New Plateau', 23 April 1997.
73. Gould, note to Tony Blair, 22 April 1997.
74. Interview with David Hill, 13 March 1998.
75. Interview with Alastair Campbell, 17 March 1998.
76. Gould, 'Focus Group Report', 23 April 1997.
77. Interview with David Hill, 13 March 1998.
78. Gould, 'Focus Group Report', 24 April 1997.
79. Gould, note to Tony Blair, 24 April 1997.
80. Interview with David Hill, 13 March 1998.
81. Gould, 'Focus Group Report', 25 April 1997.
82. *Spectator*, 22 November 1997.
83. Gould, note to Tony Blair, 25 April 1997.
84. Greenberg, 'An Increasingly Stable Labour Vote', 25 April 1997.
85. Gould, note to Alastair Campbell, 27 April 1997.
86. Gould, 'Focus Group Report', 28 April 1997.
87. Gould, note to Tony Blair, 28 April 1997.
88. Interview with Alastair Campbell, 17 March 1998.
89. Ibid.
90. Gould, 'Focus Group Report', 29 April 1997.
91. Gould, note to Tony Blair, 29 April 1997.
92. Greenberg, 'A Stable Close to the Campaign With Some Chipping', 28 April 1997.
93. Interview with Stanley Greenberg, 2 July 1998.
94. Interview with Adrian McMenamin, 16 March 1998.

95. Gould, 'Focus Group Report', 30 April 1997.
96. Gould, note to Tony Blair, 30 April 1997.
97. Interview with Peter Mandelson, 18 March 1998.
98. Interview with Alastair Campbell, 17 March 1998.
99. Ibid.
100. Ibid.
101. Blair, speech at the Royal Festival Hall, 2 May 1997.
102. Interview with Alastair Campbell, 17 March 1998.

Afterword
1. *The Times*, 3 May 1997.
2. David Butler and Dennis Kavanagh, *The British General Election of 1983*, p. 336, and Butler and Kavanagh, *The British General Election of 1997*, p. 295.
3. Butler and Kavanagh, *The British General Election of 1983*, p. 296, and Butler and Kavanagh, *The British General Election of 1997*, p. 246.
4. Labour Party, *The General Election Report 1997*, p. 31.
5. Quoted in Tony Blair, speech to the Fabian Society commemoration of the 1945 General Election, 5 July 1995.
6. Tony Blair, speech to the French National Assembly, 24 March 1998.
7. NOP private poll, July 1998.
8. Stanley Greenberg, 'Popularizing Progressive Politics', in Stanley Greenberg and Theda Skocpol (eds), *The New Majority*, p. 297.

BIBLIOGRAPHY

Beer, S. H., *Modern British Politics* (London: Faber & Faber, 1982)

Benn, Tony, *Years of Hope: Diaries, Papers and Letters 1940–1962* (London: Hutchinson, 1994)

——, *Arguments for Socialism*, edited by Chris Mullin (London: Penguin, 1980)

Blair, Tony, *New Britain* (London: Fourth Estate, 1996)

Butler, David, and Kavanagh, Dennis, *The British General Election of 1983* (London: Macmillan, 1984)

——, *The British General Election of 1987* (London: Macmillan, 1988)

——, *The British General Election of 1992* (London: Macmillan, 1992)

——, *The British General Election of 1997* (London: Macmillan, 1997)

Callaghan, James, *Time and Chance* (London: Collins, 1987)

Cole, G. D. H., *A History of the Labour Party from 1914* (London: Routledge & Kegan Paul, 1948)

Cocks, Michael, *Labour and the Benn Factor* (London: Macdonald, 1989)

Crewe, Ivor, 'How to Win a Landslide Without Really Trying: Why the Conservatives Won in 1983' (Colchester: University of Essex, 1984)

——, 'Labour Force Changes, Working-Class Decline and the Labour Vote: Social and Electoral Trends in Postwar Britain' in Frances Fox Piven (ed.), *Labour Parties in Post-Industrial Societies* (Oxford: Polity Press, 1992)

——, 'The Labour Party and the Electorate' in Dennis Kavanagh (ed.), *The Politics of the Labour Party* (London: Allen & Unwin, 1982)

Crick, Bernard, 'Britain's "Democratic Party"', *The Nation*, 10 December 1960

Crosland, Anthony, *The Future of Socialism* (London: Jonathan Cape, 1964)

Davies, A. J., *To Build a New Jerusalem* (London: Abacus, 1996)

de Crespigny, Anthony, and Minogue, Kenneth (eds), *Contemporary Political Philosophers* (London: Methuen, 1976)

Desmond, Shaw, *Labour: The Giant With the Feet of Clay* (London: Collins, 1921)

Dionne, E. J., Jr., *Why Americans Hate Politics* (New York: Simon & Schuster, 1991)

——, *They Only Look Dead* (New York: Simon & Schuster, 1996)

Disraeli, Benjamin, *Sybil, or, The Two Nations* (London: Penguin, 1980)

Drucker, H. M., *Doctrine and Ethos in the Labour Party* (London: Allen & Unwin, 1979)

Fielding, Steven, *Labour: Decline and Renewal* (London: Baseline Books, 1995)

Greenberg, Stanley B., 'Reconstructing the Democratic Vision', *The American Prospect*, No. 1, Spring 1990

——, *Middle-Class Dreams* (New Haven, CT: Yale University Press, 1996)

Greenberg, Stanley B., and Skocpol, Theda (eds), *The New Majority* (New Haven, CT: Yale University Press, 1996)

Greenleaf, W. H., *The British Political Tradition, Vol. 2: The Ideological Heritage* (London: Methuen, 1983)

Heath, Jowell and Curtice (eds), *Labour's Last Chance* (London: Dartmouth, 1994)

Hegel, G. W. F., *Elements of the Philosophy of Right* (Cambridge: CUP, 1991)

Hobhouse, L. T., *Liberalism and Other Writings* (Cambridge: CUP, 1994)

Hughes, Colin, and Wintour, Patrick, *Labour Rebuilt* (London: Fourth Estate, 1990)

Jay, Douglas, *The Socialist Case* (London: Faber & Faber, 1937)

Jefferys, Kevin, *The Labour Party Since 1945* (London: Macmillan, 1993)

Jenkins, Roy, *A Life at the Centre* (London: Macmillan, 1991)

Jones, Nicholas, *Campaign 1997* (London: Indigo, 1997)

Jones, Tudor, *Remaking the Labour Party* (London: Routledge & Kegan Paul, 1996)

Kavanagh, Dennis, *Election Campaigning* (Oxford: Blackwell, 1995)

—— (ed.), *The Politics of the Labour Party* (London: Allen & Unwin, 1982)

Labour Party, 'Labour and Britain in the 1990s' (London, 1988)

——, 'Meet the Challenge, Make the Change' (London, 1989)

——, 'New Life for Britain' (London, 1996)

——, 'Leading Britain into the Future' (London, 1997)

Marcuse, Herbert, *Reason and Revolution* (London: Routledge & Kegan Paul, 1941)

Marquand, David, *The Progressive Dilemma* (London: Heinemann, 1991)

Matalin, Mary, and Carville, James, *All's Fair* (London: Hutchinson, 1994)

Middlemas, Keith, *The Politics of Industrial Society* (London: André Deutsch, 1979)

Miliband, Ralph, *The State in Capitalist Society* (London: Quartet, 1977)

Lewis Minkin, *The Labour Party Conference* (Manchester: Manchester University Press, 1980)

——, *The Contentious Alliance* (Edinburgh: Edinburgh University Press, 1991)

Oakeshott, Michael, *Rationalism in Politics and Other Essays* (London: Methuen, 1962)

Owen, David, *Time to Declare* (London: Michael Joseph, 1991)

Pimlott, Ben, 'The Labour Left', in C. Cook and I. Taylor (eds), *The Labour Party* (London: Longman, 1980)

Rentoul, John, *Tony Blair* (London: Warner Books, 1997)

Routledge, Paul, *Gordon Brown* (London: Simon & Schuster, 1998)

Scammell, Margaret, *Designer Politics* (New York: St Martin's Press, 1995)

Seldon, Anthony (ed.), *How Tory Governments Fall* (Oxford: OUP, 1994)

——, *Major* (London: Weidenfeld & Nicolson, 1997)

Seldon, Anthony, and Ball, Stuart (eds), *The Conservative Century* (Oxford: OUP, 1994)

Sopel, Jon, *Tony Blair: The Moderniser* (London: Michael Joseph, 1995)

Sykes, Patricia, *Losing from the Inside* (Oxford: Transaction Books, 1988)

Wainwright, Hilary, *Labour: A Tale of Two Parties* (London: Hogarth Press, 1987)

Wertheimer, Egon, *Portrait of the Labour Party* (London: Putnam, 1929)

Williams, G. L., and Williams, A. L., *Labour's Decline and the Social Democrats' Fall* (London: Macmillan, 1985)

Wright, Tony, and Carter, Matt, *The People's Party* (London: Thames & Hudson, 1997)

INDEX

References in **bold** denote major section devoted to subject.

the occupied cities of Palestine. www.palestinelitfest.org.

Cairo

MEMOIR OF A CITY TRANSFORMED

Ahdaf Soueif

BLOOMSBURY

LONDON · NEW DELHI · NEW YORK · SYDNEY

First published in Great Britain 2012
This paperback published 2014

Copyright © 2012, 2014 by Ahdaf Soueif
Maps by Omar Robert Hamilton

The moral right of the author has been asserted

No part of this book may be used or reproduced in any manner whatsoever
without written permission from the Publisher except in the
case of brief quotations embedded in critical articles or reviews

Bloomsbury Publishing Plc
50 Bedford Square
London
WC1B 3DP

www.bloomsbury.com

Bloomsbury Publishing, London, New Delhi, New York and Sydney

A CIP catalogue record for this book is available from the British Library

ISBN 978 1 4088 3050 5

10 9 8 7 6 5 4 3 2 1

Printed and bound in Great Britain by CPI Group (UK) Ltd, Croydon CR0 4YY

For the young people of Egypt;
the shuhada who died for the revolution,
and the shabab who live for it

CONTENTS

A NOTE ON SPELLING ARABIC SOUNDS IN LATIN CHARACTERS

Writing some of the sounds of Arabic in Latin characters has been an issue since the Middle Ages. Systems of transliteration vary, along with their levels of complexity.

What I've chosen here is to adopt a new system that was, I believe, initiated by Arab bloggers. It's very simple:

1. Where there is a traditional accepted—and unique—spelling in Latin letters for an Arabic sound, I retain it. As in: *gh* for غ —like the French *r*; *kh* for خ—as in the Scottish *loch*.

2. Three sounds are written as numerals:

    The hamza, ء, pronounced as a glottal stop in the middle or at the end of a word, is written as a 2. So if we were doing this in English, the cockney *butter* would be written *bu2er*. The ain, ع, a soft vibration in the back of the throat, is written *3*. The *heavy h* ح, is written *7*.

    However, where words already have an image and a presence for the reader of English, I've kept them as they are. So *Tahrir* has not become *Ta7reer*, *Ahmad* has not become *A7mad*, *Aida* has not become *3aida*, and so on.

EMBABA

ZAMALEK

OUR HOUSE

The hospital where I was born

15th May bridge

SIMONDS

BOULAC

AGOUZA HOSPITAL

MASPERO

ATABA

6th october bridge

TAHRIR SQ

qasr el nil bridge

ABDEEN

qasr el eini st.

LAZOGHLI

CAIRO UNIVERSITY

university bridge

← PYRAMIDS

ABBASEYYA

COPTIC
HOSPITAL

AIRPORT

N

CEMETERY

CAIRO

1 MILE

1 KILOMETER

PREFACE

Almost twenty years ago I signed a contract to write a book about Cairo; my Cairo. But the years passed, and I could not write it. When I tried, it read like an elegy, and I would not write an elegy for my city.

Then, in February 2011, I was in Tahrir, taking part in the revolution and reporting on it. Alexandra Pringle, my friend and U.K. publisher, called me; this, she said, must be the moment for your Cairo book. I fought the idea. But I feared she was right.

I say "feared" because I wanted more to act the revolution than to write it. And because I was afraid of the responsibility. Jean Genet, in his book that I most admire, *Un captif amoureux*, writes: "I am not an archivist or a historian or anything like it. . . . This is my Palestinian revolution told in my own chosen order." I cannot say the same. This story is told in my own chosen order, but it is very much the story of *our* revolution.

It proved impossible to sit in a corner and write about the revolution. What was happening needed every one of us to be available at all times to do whatever the—let's call it "the revolutionary effort" might need, whether it was marching or standing or talking or mediating or writing or comforting or articulating or . . . So I tried to "revolute" and write at the same time, and I soon realized two things: one, that I could not write what was fast becoming the past without writing the present; and two, that for this book to be as I wanted it to be and believed it should be, an intervention rather than just a record, it needed to take in—and on—as much of this present as possible.

And so I wrote *Cairo: My City, Our Revolution*, which was published in hardback in the UK in January 2012. The "present" that it took in went up to October 2011. And the structure, the storytelling mode, that seemed truest to the story then, showed the period from 12 February to 31 October as an "interruption" to the course of the revolution. It was still possible then to believe that the revolution as we knew it, as we had lived it, would continue, and that we would pick up from where we had left off.

Now, over a year later, we can no longer believe this. What we are living now can no longer be seen as an interruption; we are living the revolution in the course and the form it has had to take. Our revolution does continue, but it has become bigger, harder, more real(istic), and more diverse; it has lost a lot of its innocence and may, perhaps, have to lose even more.

And once again, it was a friend and publisher who made me deal with this change: LuAnn Walther, my U.S. editor. So this, the paperback edition of my book, takes in this later period: the winter, spring, and summer after October 2011. In preparing it, I was tempted to tidy up the story, to make it more streamlined, to sweep through our Egyptian story from January 2011 to "now" in chronological time. But the story resisted, and something in me resisted. Because the story I've been writing is not just about the events that took place, but about how I, how we, perceived and felt and understood them. And it's also a story about me, my family, and my city—told to a reader, a friend, out of a particular moment, a particular emotion.

And so I have preserved the integrity of my text. I have not rewritten it but have let the past remain unchanged and carried on with it in the only way I could: picking up the story from where I had left it before. The revolution is not an event but a process, a process we're all going through, and this book is going through it with us, fitting itself to the altered forms of the revolution and to the transformations of the city.

And at its heart there are those eighteen golden days, eighteen days that were given to us, when we all pulled together to get rid of the head of the regime that was destroying us and our country and everything we held dear; eighteen days that brought out the best in us and showed us not just what we could do but how we could be. And it was this way of "being," as well as what it achieved, that captured the imagination of the world, that made the Egyptian revolution an inspiration for the people's movements that are crystallizing across the planet. Every Egyptian I know is both proud of this and humbled by it. I know I am.

Cairo, December 2012

REVOLUTION I

Eighteen Days

25 JANUARY–11 FEBRUARY 2011

The river is a still, steely gray, a dull pewter. Small scattered fires burn and fizz in the water. We've pushed out from the shore below the Ramses Hilton and are heading into midstream. My two nieces, Salma and Mariam, are on either side of me in the small motorboat. As we get farther from the shore, our coughing and choking subside. We can draw breath, even though the breath burns. And we can open our eyes—

To see an opaque dusk, heavy with tear gas. Up ahead, Qasr el-Nil Bridge is a mass of people, all in motion, but all in place. We look back at where we were just minutes ago, on 6 October Bridge, and see a Central Security Forces personnel carrier on fire, backing off, four young men chasing it, leaping at it, beating at its windshield. The vehicle is reversing wildly, careering backward east toward Downtown. Behind us, a ball of fire lands in the river, a bright new pool of flame in the water. The sky is gray—so different from the airy twilight you normally get on the river at this time of day. The Opera House looms dark on our right, and we can barely make out the slender height of the Cairo Tower. We don't know it yet, but the lights of Cairo will not come on tonight.

A great shout goes up from Qasr el-Nil. I look at Salma and Mariam. "Yes, let's," they say. I tell the boatman we've changed our minds: we don't want to cross the river to Giza and go home. We want to be dropped off under Qasr el-Nil Bridge.

And that is why we—myself and two beautiful young women—appeared suddenly in the Qasr el-Nil Underpass among the Central Security vehicles racing to get out of town and all the men leaning over the parapet above us with stones in their hands stopped in midthrow and yelled "Run! Run!" and held off with the stones so they wouldn't hit us as we skittered through the screeching vehicles to a spot where we could scramble up the bank and join the people at the mouth of the bridge.

That day the government—the regime that had ruled us for thirty years—had cut off our communications. No mobile service, no Internet for all of Egypt.[1] In a way, looking back, I think this con-centrated our minds, our will, our energy: each person was in one place, totally and fully committed to that place, unable to be aware of any other, knowing they had to do everything they could for it and trusting that other people in other places were doing the same.

So we ran through the underpass, scrambled up the bank, and found ourselves within, inside, and part of the masses. When we'd seen the crowd from a distance, it had seemed like one bulk, solid. Close up like this, it was people, individual persons with spaces between them—spaces into which you could fit. We stood on the traffic island in the middle of the road. Behind us was Qasr el-Nil Bridge, in front of us was Tahrir, and we were doing what we Egyptians do best, and what the regime ruling us had tried so hard to destroy: we had come together, as individuals, millions of us, in a great cooperative effort. And this time our project was to save and to reclaim our country. We stood on the island in the middle of the road, and that was the moment I became part of the revolution.

✓✓✓✓

A month before, a week before, three days before, we could not have told you it was going to happen. Yes, there had been calls to use National Police Day on 25 January as an occasion for protests, but there had been so many protests and calls for protests over the years that it hadn't seemed special. Those of us who were in Egypt intended to join, for form's sake and to keep up the spirit of opposition. Those of us who weren't, well, weren't.

Me, I was in India, at the Jaipur Literary Festival. Late on the twenty-fourth, I did an interview with Tehelka TV:

For a very long time now, our perception is that [Egypt] is not being run in the interests of the Egyptian people. The primary motivation of the people who are governing us is that they should remain in power in order to continue ransacking and looting the country. Now, the main support that they have is, of course, the Western powers—particularly the United States. And the price that they pay in order to be supported is to run policies that favor Israel.

We've been watching what's been happening in Tunisia and we've been very excited by it. You hear: now, will Egypt move? And you hear: Egypt is too big . . . too heavy.

It really does not look as if the government is going to allow a peaceful and democratic change. So . . . what's going to happen? Will we get a situation where people . . . sort of, erupt? And will you get . . . blood on the streets? Will the army come down? Nobody knows. It feels very unstable. And it feels dangerous. And all the activism that happens is in specific areas. And it's all young people and it's all really without a leadership . . . but it's there. It's keeping the streets alive. We've never had as much civil unrest in Egypt as we've had in the last five years. And that is good. That is good— but, how will it coalesce? And what shape will that take?[2]

We now have this information—you, my reader, in more advanced form, as you read these words, than I as I race to write them in the summer of 2011. I won't try to guess at what's on your news bulletin today—but whatever shape Egypt is in as you're reading now, this is the story of some of the moments that got us there.

And it's also, in a small way, a story about me and my city, the city I so love and have so sorrowed for these twenty years and more. I am not unique, but Cairo is. And her streets, her Nile, her buildings, and her monuments whisper to every Cairene who's taking part in the events that are shaping our lives and our children's futures as I write. They whisper to us and tug at our sleeves and say: This is where you were born, this is where a man, a boy, first reached for your hand, this is where you learned to drive, this is where the picture in your schoolbook shows Orabi facing down the Khedive Tewfik, this is where your mother says she and your father stood in '52 and watched the fire take hold of Cairo. The city puts her lips to our ears, she tucks her arm into ours and draws close so we can feel her heartbeat and smell her scent, and we fall in with her and measure our step to hers, and we fill our eyes with her beautiful, wounded face and whisper that her memories are our memories, her fate is our fate.

For twenty years I have shied away from writing about Cairo. It hurt too much. But the city was there, close to me, looking over my shoulder, holding up the prism through which I understood the world, inserting herself into everything I wrote. It hurt. And now, miraculously, it doesn't. Because my city is mine again.

Masr is Egypt, and *Masr* is also what Egyptians call Cairo. On Tuesday, 1 February, I watched a man surveying the scene in Tahrir with a big smile: the sun was shining and people were everywhere, old and young, rich and poor. They talked and walked and sang and played and joked and chanted. Then he said it out loud: "Ya Masr, it's been a long time. We have missed you."

/ / / /

It was evening on Tuesday the twenty-fifth when I realized something was happening back home. On my Jaipur hotel TV, I could only get CNN, but there the Americans were, transmitting from Tahrir, and the whole world was wondering what was going on, and the spokesperson for the Egyptian government, Hosam Zaki, was cheerily dismissing the crowds on the screen and reassuring the world that our government and our people were very close and that the government knew the people and knew what they wanted and would supply the bits of it that it saw fit. This was the line that the regime was unable to let go of; throughout the three weeks of the confrontation, every speech given by (now-deposed president) Mubarak or his vice president, Omar Suleiman, or any member of his party or regime, maintained the patronizing "we know what's best for you" stance that had been so roundly rejected by the people.

What transfixed me so completely was that the picture on the screen was from Tahrir. Unmistakably from Tahrir. Midan el-Tahrir—

I prefer the Arabic word *midan* because, like *piazza*, it does not tie you down to a shape but describes an open urban space in a central position in a city, and the space we call Midan el-Tahrir, the central point of Greater Cairo, is not a square or a circle but more like a massive curved rectangle covering about 45,000 square meters and connecting Downtown and older Cairo to the east, with the river and Giza and the newer districts to the west; its southern boundary is the Mugamma3 building and its northern is the 6 October Overpass—

The Midan has been our Holy Grail for forty years. Since 1972, when (then-president Anwar) Sadat's forces dragged the student protesters at dawn from around the empty plinth at its center and into jail, demonstrations and marches have tried and failed to get into Tahrir. Two years ago we managed to hold a corner of a traffic island in front of the Mugamma3 building for an hour. We were fewer than fifty people, and the government surrounded us with maybe two thousand Central Security soldiers, the chests and shoulders of their officers heavy with brass.

Since Egypt's ruler, Khedive Ismail, established it in 1860—its core modeled on Paris's Étoile, six main roads leading out of its center and a further six out of the larger space surrounding it—control of Tahrir has seemed central to controlling the country. Ismail stationed the Egyptian army and the Ministry of Defense here, and when the British occupied Egypt in 1882, their army took over the barracks and the ministry on one side of Qasr el-Nil Bridge, and they put their embassy on the other. The Americans were to follow suit and put their increasingly fortresslike embassy next to the British. Then in Nasser's revolutionary times, Egypt put a statue of Simón Bolívar between the two embassies; the Arab League building and the headquarters of the Arab Socialist Union went up in place of the British barracks, and the Ministry of Foreign Affairs faced them from the (nationalized) palace of the Princess Nimet Kamal across Tahrir Street.

But as well as housing the symbols of military and political power, Tahrir is home to the civic spirit of Egypt. The Egyptian Antiquities Museum (1902) marks the northern end of the Midan, and when in 1908 the Egyptian national movement founded—through public donations—the first secular Egyptian University, they rented the palace of Khawaga Gianaclis—now the old campus of the American University in Cairo—at the other end. In 1951 all government departments that came in direct contact with the citizens were consolidated in one huge new building: Mugamma3 al-Tahrir. And early in the 1952 revolution, the small mosque near the Mugamma3 was enlarged and dedicated to Sheikh Omar Makram, the popular leader against Napoleon's French Expedition in 1798, against the British "Fraser" Expedition of 1807, and later against Muhammad Ali himself when Sheikh Omar felt the ruler was taxing the people unfairly. Omar Makram died in exile, but his statue is part of our revolution; a meeting place, an inspiration, a bearer of flags and microphones and balloons.

In 1959 the first modern international hotel in Egypt, the Nile Hilton, opened in Tahrir, next to the Arab League. A decade later, on the evening of 27 September 1970, and having just closed the two days of negotiations and arm-twisting that ended Black September and would kill him, President Gamal Abd el-Nasser—whose picture was raised by many during the revolution—stood on the balcony of the thirteenth-floor suite he had occupied for a few nights and gazed at the Nile. He turned, smiling, to Abd el-Meguid Farid, the secretary to the presidency: "How come I've never seen this amazing sight before? Look at it! I'm buried alive out in Heliopolis." Then he went home. And it was from a window in the Arab Socialist Union building next door that, two days later, his wife and daughters watched his funeral surge across Qasr el-Nil Bridge toward Tahrir. The ASU building became Hosni Mubarak's National Democratic Party headquarters—the only building in Tahrir to be torched by the revolutionaries.

The Hilton—now bearing the Ritz-Carlton sign—has been undergoing renovation for years. In front of it is a waste ground surrounded by sheets of corrugated iron—which we will use in the battles for the Midan. This massive space in the central *midan* of our city has been in a condition of ruin for twenty years. We're told it's to do with the construction of the Metro. Also to do with the Metro, we're told, was the removal of the empty plinth in the middle of the garden of the central roundabout, the plinth around which the students gathered in 1972 on the night Amal Dunqul immortalized in "The Stone Cake":

> *Five o'clock struck*
> *with soldiers a circle of shields and helmets*
> *drawing closer slowly . . . slowly . . .*
> *from every direction*

and the singers in the stone cake clenching
and relaxing
like a heartbeat!
Lighting their throats
for warmth against the cold and the biting dark.
Lifting the anthem in the face of the approaching guard.
Linking their young, hopeless hands
a shield against lead
lead
lead.
They sang.

Now the whole country is gathered around that central, plinthless garden. In one of the most moving moments of the revolution—and there were to be many—the people's delegations that had come in from the cities and the provinces of Egypt set up their banners around the garden and set up the chant "El-shar3eyya m'nel-Tahrir"—legitimacy comes from Tahrir.

I drove to Delhi in the morning and, next day, caught a plane that put me in Cairo on the evening of Thursday the twenty-seventh. From the airport I called my sister, Laila, and asked, "Where's the revolution? Should I go to Tahrir?" She said I should call her daughter, Mona, and Mona said there was nothing in Tahrir, but I might, possibly, see some crowds if I went to Midan el-Sa3ah in Nasr City or if I drove through Abbaseyya. But there were no crowds. I saw two charred and overturned Central Security Forces trucks, but the city was, if anything, quieter than was normal for a Thursday evening. The revolution was up and running in Suez and Alexandria; in Cairo it was gathering its breath, getting ready for Friday.

FRIDAY, 28 JANUARY, MIDDAY

Embaba, on the western bank of the Nile, five minutes and one bridge from my home on Gezira Island. For a long time, all I knew of it was the name of its main bus stop, the Kit-Kat, and attached to the name a black and white image of British johnnies staggering out of shady doorways, drunk, into the street, hushed families watching them from darkened rooms, their faces lined with the light from streetlamps falling through drawn blinds. The Kit-Kat, I seemed to know, was one of the many sleazy nightclubs that had sprung up in Cairo to cater to the Allied forces stationed there in the West's second great war. Now if you say "el-Kit-Kat," everyone thinks of Daoud Abd el-Sayyed's 1991 film, with the opening shot of Mahmoud Abd el-Aziz weaving through Embaba market on his motorbike. A long, ongoing shot—and sometime during the course of it, you realize the biker is blind.

Embaba has a small airport from where you can go gliding. When my first marriage was breaking up, we flew from there, in a glider, I and my just-become-ex-husband. He was at the controls. I can't think why we did that. For clarity, maybe? We—I—didn't find it. Even the amazing spread-out fields below, the river, broad and still and—from here—docile, were dimmed by my unease.

And Embaba is known for three hospitals. One is a specialist rehabilitation center where they taught Ali, the five-year-old son of Um Nagla, our help, to speak. My father snatched him back from the jaws of a "fraudulent charlatan" who, he said, was about to send him off for electric shock treatment—and sent him to Embaba instead. He's now fifteen and speaking plenty. Ali says he'd carry on going to school if there were any use, but he's not learning anything, and the teachers are only there for the cash from the private lessons. The only thing that might be useful now for his life is the revolution. He berates his mother for being prepared to believe that Hosni Mubarak is "sorry" and will give back our stolen money. "Ali," she tells me, "Ali says of Mubarak and all his men: 'Before they open their mouths, they're liars; they breathe lies.' And this," she adds, "is Ali-who-couldn't-speak."

The second is the Embaba Fevers Hospital, which used to rival the best in the world. The third is the new Emergency Hospital, where construction was stopped when its riverfront position caught Mrs. Mubarak's eye, and the government decided to turn it into a luxury residential block. The latest scandal of this kind is the Madin'ti Project, where eight thousand acres were sold at so much lower than market price that the courts estimated the loss to the Egyptian treasury at billions of pounds. Today as our protest passes the hospital project, the crowd starts up the chants against corruption: "A bowl of lentils for ten pounds—a Madin'ti share for fifty p."

We've been walking the streets of Embaba for two hours. My friend Mamdouh Hamza brought me here and left me in a small coffee shop by the local mosque. MH is a celebrated civil engineer who's been in charge of some of Egypt's major construction projects. I'd known he'd been lending his support for a while to some of the revolutionary shabab, the young people. "Something will begin here," he said, and went off to distribute banners. It was the usual pleasant, the world-is-on-pause feel of Friday prayer time, and I watched women chatting in front of shops, the winter sunshine falling on them through the colorful clothes displayed above their heads, men sitting at cafés, others spilling out of the mosque, praying on green mats in the road. In my coffee shop, a young man is sitting in the corner; something about his stillness, his quality of concentration, stays with me.

Prayers finish, but the imam solicits blessings. And blessings. And more blessings. Men start folding their mats, putting on their shoes. Suddenly the young man from the coffee shop is above the crowd, on top of it. People shift and stir, there's a buzz like in the theater at the moment the curtain starts to rise, everyone looks, people come out of shops: the young man's arm is in the air, his hand is reaching to the sky, and then there comes the loud, carrying voice: "Al-sha3b yureed isqat al-nizam!" There it was, no lead-up, no half-measures; the young man on the shoulders of his friends; a loose knot of some fifteen young people: "The people—demand—the fall of this regime!" We start to walk.

Later, we will learn that similar marches started after prayers in every district of Cairo and many other cities. We will know this young man as Khaled el-Sayyed, one of the three hundred young people who organized these first marches. Up there, his still concentration has transformed into energy, his back is straight, his arm movements are precise. Again and again the call goes out, and the crowd responds: "Your security, your police—killed our brothers in Suez." We walk, and the numbers grow. Every balcony is full of people; some just watch impassively, some men look uncomfortable. "Come down from the heights / Come down and get your rights." Most women are smiling, waving, dandling babies to the tune of the chants "Eish! Horreyya! Adala egtema3eyya!" Bread. Freedom. Social justice. Old women call, "God be with you! God give you victory." For more than two hours, the protest walks through the narrow residential lanes, cheering, encouraging, instigating: "Prices up and no one cares / Next you'll sell your beds and chairs." We pass the offices of the Land Registry. In 2008 I'd visited it to get some papers relating to my mother's estate. I failed to get them. At the next window a man remonstrated that this was the fifth time he'd been and that he no longer understood what he was required to do to get the stamp he needed on his papers. Then he lost it: "Yel3an abu Hosni Mubarak!" he bellowed. God curse him curse him curse him! He slammed his files rhythmically on the countertop as he cursed out the man at the head of the system that, here and now, in this local specific manifestation of petty bureaucracy and corruption, was frustrating him to insanity.

"Eish! Horreyya! Karama insaneyya!" Bread. Freedom. Human dignity. Kids run alongside the march: "The *people—demand—* the fall of this *regime—*" In the eighties and nineties, at the time of the big expansion of the Islamist currents, Embaba came in for some particularly harsh treatment. The Dakhleyya (Ministry of the Interior) stopped policing Embaba itself but set up border stations at its exits; every male going in or out was subjected to stop and search. Anyone not carrying his ID was detained, and "detained" meant beaten—sometimes tortured. Several times during today's march, sweeping up people from the neighborhood, the cry rises, "To the police station!" and each time the march's leaders deflect it.

Later I will find out that my sister, Laila, MH, and various other friends are all on this march. But it has grown so big, we don't see each other. By the time we wind onto a overpass to head for Downtown, we are easily five thousand people or more.

As we descend from the overpass, I recognize that we're in Ahmad Orabi Street. This is where my beloved Khalu, my mother's brother, ever present though gone now these eighteen years, used to live. His wife still lives here. I glance up at her plant-filled balcony, and I can't resist. I slip away from the march and up the five floors to her flat, where I find cousins and friends—all slipped away from the march for a few minutes' rest and to find out the news. We'd woken up that morning to find the Internet down, and by eleven a.m. not a single mobile was working. Landlines were all we had, and even there the international lines had been taken down. We knew then that this was a regime fighting for its life. We sat around in Tante Nahed's home and used her landline to phone and check up on friends and family. Most homes had arranged to have one person stay in by the landline and act as liaison. My brother, when I called him, said his daughters wanted to join the action, and would I take them? This would be their first protest. Tante Nahed gave us tea and juice. The last time I'd sat in her living room was two years ago, and I had been looking through the results of a survey she'd just published: *The Problems and Discontents of the Egyptian Citizen.* Unemployment consistently scored highest on the list of people's personal problems, second was housing, and third was education.

4:00 P.M.

My brother, Ala, and his wife, Sohair, and their daughters Salma and Mariam, pick me up. As we drive, we pass protests heading to Tahrir. Ala and Sohair have brought bottles of water and hand them out. Months later my brother—an IT man and an Egyptologist—will, with friends, put together an initiative to dismantle the security establishment, another to overhaul pre-university education, another to set up a national employment bureau. . . . Today this is his and his wife's first action for the revolution.

Salma and Mariam and I decide we'll walk across 6 October Bridge and up the Corniche into Tahrir, so my brother drops us off in Agouza, at the foot of the steps leading up to the bridge. We run up the steps and find ourselves facing a cordon of Central Security soldiers blocking our way. The bridge crosses Gezira Island and passes over the Gezira Club. My nieces, twins, had both been champion gymnasts in their childhood and teens, and the Gezira was their club. Now twenty-two, they could easily still pass for seventeen. I take their elbows and stride up to the line of soldiers: "Excuse us, my daughters are late for their training—" pointing below us at the club grounds. The line opens courteously.

I love these young men. And I don't want them to be part of Central Security. In fact, we've got a case in court arguing that using conscripts for Security is unconstitutional; conscription may be necessary to protect the country against invasion or aggression. But to use conscripts to protect the government of the day against the people cannot be right.

We get to the middle of the bridge before we realize that there are no cars, that the air is dim and fumy, and that the few people around us are not moving forward. There's something of Dante about the spectacle. Isolated figures drift. Smoke drifts. Everything is slowed down and dim. A young man comes up and gives us tissues, then sprinkles vinegar over them. "Hold them over your nose," he says, "a tip from our Tunisian friends." In Palestine they use onions. We can't yet smell the gas. I see a friend, Lena, and her husband, and we drift together, embrace, and stand silently watching a man wearing a large brown paper bag over his head rotate slowly on the narrow traffic island at the center of the bridge. He's turning in slow motion, and as he faces us, we see the slits for the eyes and the large, red question mark starting on the forehead and running down the nose with the dot at the mouth. Later I note this as my first experience of spontaneous, revolutionary street theater. Now it just adds to the weird, dreamlike feel of the scene. A heavy thudding thumps rhythmically through the smog. Lena says it's guns. Across the water, we can see that the real action is on Qasr el-Nil Bridge. We've started to feel the gas, but Salma and Mariam and I decide to follow our plan and run the hundred meters or so to the bridge's exit by the Ramses Hilton, get down, and run along the river to Qasr el-Nil.

Tear gas! This was a gas that made you feel the skin peeling off your face. Later, when we saw the canisters, we found it had passed its expiry date. You'd think that would make it less painful, but apparently it makes it worse. We run blind; I can't even open my eyes to see what's going on. When I do force them open for a second, I see that Mariam, the more delicate of the twins, has stopped in the middle of the bridge, her eyes streaming and shut tight, one of her shoes lost, her arms held out helplessly. She's saying something but so softly I can't hear. Salma and I run back for her. "I can't," she's whispering, "I can't." We find her shoe, grab an arm each, and run. We run down the slope of the bridge and straight into another cordon of Central Security soldiers. They're meant to block the way. We are three women, disheveled, eyes streaming. We run right up to them, and they make way. "Go!" they urge us. "Quick!" Eye to eye with one of them, young, brown, open-faced, Egyptian, I pause, just for a second. "What can we do?" he shouts into the smoke. "If we could take off this uniform, we'd join you!"

Stuck. Stranded. For a moment, as I was running down the slip road with my eyes closed holding on to my nieces, I had the—typical—thought that we might nip into the Ramses Hilton and wash our faces, maybe even get some tea. Down on the embankment, with the soldiers facing us and behind them the Corniche road littered with stones and charred cars and the Hilton dark and shuttered, it is clear that a five-star interlude is out of the question. We run down the embankment steps and jump into a boat: "To Giza, please. Drop us next to Gala2 Bridge." We'll go home.

But: as we get farther from the shore, our coughing and choking subside. We can draw breath, even though the breath burns. And we can open our eyes. And when our eyes meet, we change direction and head, again, to Tahrir.

////

On the traffic island at the Qasr el-Nil entrance to Tahrir, you turn 360 degrees and everywhere there are people. I cannot tell how many thousands I can see. Close up, people are handing out tissues soaked in vinegar for your nose, Pepsi to bathe your eyes, water to drink. I stumble, and a hand under my elbow steadies me. The way ahead of us is invisible behind the smoke. From time to time there will be a burst of flame. The great hotels: the Semiramis Intercontinental, Shepheard's, the Ramses Hilton, have all darkened their lower floors and locked their doors. On the upper-floor balconies, stick figures are watching us. At the other end of the Midan, from the roof of the American University, the snipers are watching us, too. Silently. Everywhere there is a continuous thud of guns and, from time to time, a loud, intermittent rattling sound. We stand. That is our job, the people at the back: we stand and we chant our declaration of peace: "Selmeyya! Selmeyya!" while our comrades at the front, unarmed, fight with the Security Forces. From time to time, a great cry goes up, and we surge forward: our friends have won us another couple of meters, and we follow them and hold our ground. We sing the national anthem. Eight months ago some young protesters from the 6 April Movement were arrested in Alexandria for singing the national anthem; it was "instigator," the prosecution said. We sing it. On 28 January, standing at that momentous crossroads, the Nile behind us, the Arab League building to our left, the old Ministry of Foreign Affairs to our right, seeing nothing up ahead except the gas and smoke and fire that stand between us and our capital, we stand our ground and sing and chant and place our lives, with all trust and confidence, in each other's hands.

✓✓✓✓

Some of us die.

✓✓✓✓

Many of us have not yet truly realized what we are engaged in; what the country is engaged in. We know that Suez has been under siege for three days and people there have been killed. We know Alexandria is up, and news is coming in of other cities. But we are still calling what we are doing "protesting"—and we have been protesting for ten years. I think that over the last decade, every time I've arrived in Cairo—and that's three or four times a year—I've joined my sister and various friends on protests: marches to support the Palestinian Intifada, marches against the war on Iraq, protests against our rigged elections, against our co-opted judiciary, against the plots to perpetuate the regime by slithering Gamal Mubarak into power, against corruption, and against police brutality. The government was vicious in dealing with all of them. It knew that a demonstration for Palestine or Iraq would sooner or later turn its attention to the Egyptian regime, and that a demonstration against the regime would count its role in Palestine and Iraq among its sins.

Looking back now, we see the progression, from small groups collecting medicines for the Intifada, to the civil movement Kifaya hitting the streets, to the massive workers' strikes in Mahalla, to the point where every sector in civil society—judges, lawyers, farmers, teachers, pensioners, journalists, tax collectors—is fighting with the government. And I see it, too, in my family. Like so many politically engaged Egyptian families, it's now in its third generation of activists—and this third generation, in their twenties, are more clever and cool and effective than we ever were. We, the older revolutionaries, have been trying since '72 to take Tahrir. They are doing it. They're going to change the world. We follow them and pledge what's left of our lives to their effort.

FRIDAY, 28 JANUARY, 10:00 P.M.

Four army tanks are on the Maspero[3] Corniche, the run of riverside from Boulac to the Ramses Hilton on the eastern bank of the Nile, five minutes and one (different) bridge from my home on Gezira Island. They're blocking the road in front of the Radio and Television building (also known, through metonymy, as Maspero) where, when I was a student, I had my first job. I played "Laila" who, with her brother "Ahmad," appeared in weekly episodes of a sitcom designed to teach English to schoolchildren. Sometimes we filmed on location, but mostly we worked in a studio in Maspero. This was in the early seventies, and the cavernous and freezing Studio 6 had no editing facilities. Each episode was twenty minutes long, and we had to record it from start to finish without stopping. If someone made a mistake or missed a cue or got the giggles, we had to start from the beginning. And if our booked time ran out, we had to vacate the studio and wait till a free slot came up and try again. So I've spent many, many hours loitering in this area, warming myself, drinking tea and chatting and hanging about and catching up on essays and assignments. And now it is dark and deserted, and there are four army tanks outside the building, and MH is distributing molasses sticks both to the soldiers on the tanks and to the revolutionaries on the street "for energy."

In the weeks to come, I will understand why revolutions and coups always rush to seize the radio and television facilities. Our revolution seized the main *midans* of our cities and went on to deal with the strongholds of the most hated parts of the regime: its party and its brutal security establishment. Next day there was talk of Maspero, but trying to take it would have meant engaging not the police or Central Security but the military.

At six p.m., Hosni Mubarak had declared a curfew. Nobody paid attention. At seven, while the battle for Tahrir was raging, a cry—a jubilant warning—had gone up: "El-geish nezel!" The army had deployed. We saw the first open four-man vehicle arrive on the Corniche by Qasr el-Nil Bridge and just about caught a glimpse of the red berets of the Military Police before the welcoming, co-opting crowds closed in on the vehicle.

Now, at ten, we walk past Maspero and past the darkened Ramses Hilton. In the eighties it was a novelty to zoom up thirty-six floors and watch, from Windows on the World, as night fell and strings of city lights blinked on and light-encrusted boats darted about on that central darkness that was the river. Five days from now the regime will barricade the world's media correspondents in this hotel while it calls in its cavalry and makes a desperate stand against the revolution. But we don't know that yet. Ahead of us a huge cloud of black smoke rises to the sky: the National Democratic Party headquarters has been set on fire; flames leap from its windows and the windows of Suzanne Mubarak's Specialist National Councils. Hundreds of people on Qasr el-Nil Bridge are holding up mobile phone cameras. But next door, around the Egyptian Museum, the young people, the shabab,[4] have linked arms and are surrounding the building, cordoning it with their bodies. When the fire broke out next door, even young people who had left the Midan came back to protect the museum. At this point, none of us knows that the regime's snipers are concealed on its roof. We don't know that the army will use it as a holding pen and a fast-torture location. The young revolutionaries just know that this is their museum and they have to protect it; they will not move until they have handed it officially to the army. They even make the brigadier with his tanks show ID before they'll give him the building.

When I'd gone home to drop off Salma and Mariam and to write and file copy, my aunt Laila Moussa (Lulie) said that Mona and some of her friends had stopped at the house and taken some clothes and papers and that they're locking themselves away in someone's mother's unused apartment. They've managed to establish a connection to the Internet. The young man who hacked through to the Internet is blind. Mona is twenty-four. Throughout the revolution, she will race between Tahrir, her genetics lab at Cairo University where she's finishing her M.Sc., and the secret location where she and her band of friends become the central nerve in the great communication effort that keeps the revolution linked to itself and to its comrades in the world outside. Now Lulie says Mona has phoned on the landline to say that there is a small

mosque in the Tahrir area that is receiving the wounded and anyone who can help in any way should go there. Lulie is a doctor, but
we persuade her to wait, wait till morning before trying to go out.

MH insists that we skirt Tahrir, so we go down Mahmoud
Bassiouny and Talʒat Harb to get to the back of the Midan, and
here, as we walk through Downtown, the sense of being in a film
hits me: one of those urban apocalypse movies where the familiar features of Manhattan—it's generally Manhattan—are eerily
recognizable through the flood/hurricane/nuclear destruction.
The streets, the buildings are the same, but they're dark and semi-
empty. The shops are shuttered. Litter seems to be floating around
at knee level. There's rubble on the streets, and the lights are
out, and there's no police: no traffic police, no guards on banks,
nothing.

In neighborhoods across the country, through the night of this
Friday that will become known as the Friday of Wrath, the regime
kills hundreds of Egypt's young. Police and Security men drive
cars and trucks into groups of protesters.[5] Snipers shoot young
men and women from the rooftops of the Ramses Hilton, the
American University, the Egyptian Museum, and the Dakhleyya.
Troops fire on them with shotguns and rifles and automatics, and
the thug militias, the baltagis, burn them with Molotov cocktails
and batter them with stones, ceramics, and marble.

Soldiers break down and cry and are comforted by the revolutionaries.[6] Families will spend months of heartbreak finding out
and trying to prove how their children were killed. Brave doctors and lawyers will speak up for them. The Dakhleyya will
continue—as I write—to deny responsibility.

Now, in the darkened and derelict heart of our city, we arrive
in Midan Bab el-Louq. And because we're out of communications, we don't know that, three streets down, the young people,
the shabab, are taking on the well-hated Dakhleyya, attacking

the massive, fortified building in Lazoghli with their bare hands, improvised weapons, and the anger of many years.

////

When my aunt Awatef (Toufi) got married, she moved into a flat in Lazoghli. I was eight years old, and I used to go and stay with her often, and so, alongside Ataba and Abdeen, my childhood landscape acquired the oddly named Lazoghli. Odd because of the tickly effect of the heavy *z* and the *gh* so close together, and because—unlike *Ataba* and *Abdeen*—it wasn't a word that meant anything in Arabic. Soon I learned that *oghli* is Turkish for "son of"; I would demonstrate precocity in front of my parents' leftist friends by saying I was staying at "Lazovitch."[7]

Unlike Ataba (which was always connected with bustle and commerce) and Abdeen (which was the royal and then presidential palace), exclusively Lazoghli for me was the bridal setting-up of a new home, a home that was an alternative to how my parents did things.

When my mother was twelve, she fell ill with rheumatic fever. This meant that she got to lie on sofas and read while her nine-year-old sister had to step into the traditional domestic role of eldest daughter. These roles were to last all their lives: Fatma ("Fifi," later, "Mama Fifi") the brainy intellectual, Toufi the keeper of tradition.

So when she married and moved to Lazoghli, Toufi's flat was a demonstration of the proper way of doing things. Though small, it had a *salon* (drawing room) and a *sofrah* (dining room)—the two pillars, it seemed, of every Egyptian household (except my parents'), and whose very names reflected the two dominant cultures to which the Egyptian bourgeoisie was in thrall: French and Turkish.

The drawing room chairs were upholstered in pale blue bro-
cade, and the windows had soft white cotton curtains—which, a
few years into their marriage, when Toufi and her husband moved
back into the family home to look after my grandfather, had to
be extended by double their length to fit her old windows. When
she died nine years ago, and we had to dismantle the Ataba house,
and I washed and folded the curtains, I realized that the repeated
pattern of three slim horizontal pleats halfway down each curtain
had been her solution to disguising the joining seam. I sat with the
curtain on my knee and the pleat between my fingers and thought
how she had always done that: made do and patched up and fixed
the world with results of originality and elegance.

But Lazoghli, most important, had a balcony where, on summer nights, we had a full view of the screen of the open-air Cinema
Lazoghli. No bedtime, no restrictions on what you could watch—
the absence, when it came down to it, of my father's regulations:
Lazoghli was freedom with a prime seat at a summer cinema every
night. From here I watched *River of Love*, *The Other Man*, *Rumour
of Love*, *A Beginning and an End*. . . .

My aunt, as I said, later moved back to Ataba, and Lazoghli
dropped off my map for decades. Until, in 2000, when Egyptians
started mobilizing in support of the Palestinian Intifada, it came
back: now Lazoghli was disappearances, Lazoghli was torture,
Lazoghli was the Dakhleyya and the State Security Intelligence
Bureau, the Mabahith Amn el-Dawlah. It was also the Coroner's
Office, which habitually covered up the crimes of the Dakhleyya
and the State Security Intelligence Bureau.[8] Now—unbeknownst
to us in Bab el-Louq, three streets down—the young revolutionaries are attacking Lazoghli, and the security establishment, about
to lose the streets of the country, is determined to keep it. Five
snipers are on the roof, snipers whose existence the ministry will
deny despite their images captured on film.[9]

As we stand in Bab el-Louq, I can hear a voice over a *tannoy*.

I can't make out the words, but the voice is repeating them and repeating them, and it sounds like an appeal. It comes from the Midan end of Tahrir Street, where I expect Mona's mosque to be, so I start walking up toward it. It's dark, and the shop on the corner with the best carob juice in town is shuttered. MH has gone to hunt for a truck that will agree to come here and transport the wounded. Men walking down warn me to turn back. I can hear the shots and smell the acrid smoke, but a lesson learned from time spent in Palestine is that unless there's an insurmountable physical obstacle (and that includes a man or woman with a gun), keep going. So I keep going and find that the voice is coming from Amir Qadadar Street to my left: "This is a house of God. A house of God and a hospital. There are wounded people here and doctors trying to help them. You must not attack this house. Your brothers and sisters are here. This is a house of . . ."

It's an entrance you might easily miss. One of the magical architectural features of downtown Cairo is the pedestrian passages that run at street level between or through buildings. My grandfather's house had one of those. You walk through them, under cover, linking from street to street. Some of the wider passages have stalls or shops. This entrance is to a passage that links Amir Qadadar Street to Tahrir. I didn't know it existed, and I only see it because of the knot of people and cars outside it. "This is a house of God— and a hospital—" the voice declares, and there's rubble and smoke, and the only people in the street are around that small entrance almost hidden by a large sign for mobile phones, so that's where I go. I edge past the hurried toing and froing, and I'm inside, and the space is maybe twenty meters long by eight meters wide. If I walk straight through, I'll come out on the east side of Tahrir, but to my left there's a waist-high railing that runs the length of the passage, and the space beyond it—a width of some six meters—is a small mosque. Well, not a proper mosque but a space that has Quranic verses hanging on the freshly painted walls, and a prayer niche to guide you toward Makkah, and rows of prayer mats on the floor, and on the mats lie young men covered in blood, and other young men are running in through the Midan entrance carrying yet more young men covered in blood and lowering them carefully onto the mats, and by the walls figures are stretched out, shrouded in dark blankets and then I see a white light at the center of it all, and it's coming from a slight figure crouched on the floor doing something to the chest of a young man, and the figure has a face of such intent seriousness and compassion that I cannot look anywhere else, and I stand and watch her until she finishes and straightens up and is revealed to be Mona Mina. Mona is the founder of the activist group Physicians Without Rights. She's a friend of my sister and the mother of Salma Said, a fiery and popular activist. As I step toward her, a young man runs up between us and puts his head in my eye line. I say "journalist," but he's already asking: "Is the pellet still there? Can you take it out, or should we leave it? I have to get back to the shabab." The shabab are storming the Dakhleyya. Mona tells me she knows two of the young fighters: "Two weeks ago they were scared to report that their boss was bullying them. Look at them now!"

I look. Wounded young men everywhere. And other young men and women tending to them. Medicines and dressings stacked in neat piles by the walls. People come to talk to me. I write fast; their message is urgent: they're using live ammunition. They're using shotguns. Look: empty cartridges, *Made in the USA*. Look. Look: his legs aren't working. Two others have died. No one wants to go to hospital because they report them and they get taken away. Eye injuries. Head injuries. They're shooting to kill. Then the tear gas floods in again, and the exhortations on the loudspeaker grow louder, disbelieving, angry: "Soldiers of Egypt! Police of Egypt! Your brothers and sisters are in the protection of this house. . . ." Young men try to carry the wounded out into the air through the back. Someone gives me a gas mask. Someone else gives me two empty cartridges. They'll sit on my mantelpiece. "This is what we get from USAID. This is the 'aid' they hold over us." The gas clears. A collapsed Central Security soldier is carried in. He's given emergency treatment, and his weapon is emptied before he's set free. He sobs as an older man pats his shoulder. Weeks from now we'll find out that soldiers went AWOL and lived on the Midan until the military broke the sit-in. I make a list of things the hospital needs: Betadine, dressings, spray anaesthetic, sutures, needles, surgical gloves, painkillers . . .

✦ ✦ ✦ ✦

At midnight I'm standing outside the pharmacy on the street corner opposite my house waiting for the pharmacist to bag the things I've bought and for MH to come back from his search for sutures and needles. We suspect we won't get these because pharmacies are not allowed to sell them except to hospitals. We drove to a couple of hospitals, and they wouldn't let us in. The central twenty-four-hour emergency pharmacy is closed. So we've gone round collecting things from any neighborhood pharmacy that's open. There are no streetlights. And no police.

The Dakhleyya, thoroughly beaten by the protesters in Alexandria and Suez and about to lose Cairo, has pulled all its men from the streets. The accepted figure for the personnel of the security establishment is about 1.5 million. They have received orders to withdraw from duty. Our government has switched off the lights and gone away. Actually, no, they've not gone away: in the dark they've thrown off the camouflage and transformed into the occupying force they always were.

Word is coming through that the Dakhleyya is opening up selected jails and police stations across the country and letting— or even throwing—violent criminals out. In el-Wadi el-Gedeed prison, all the cells were opened except for one that held thirty-six newly detained Islamists; then the prison was set on fire. A group of convicted criminals risked their lives to break open the cell and set the new prisoners free. We'll find out later that General Muhammad al-Batran, the Dakhleyya's chief of intelligence of prisons, has been battling to keep order. General Batran has a reputation for fairness. Yesterday he visited Fayyoum prison and established peace there. It will turn out that at the same moment that I'm standing here, on the corner, waiting for the medicines, he's on the phone to his sister. He is enraged. He tells her that Habib el-Adli, the minister of the interior, has closed down seventeen police stations and is determined to set the whole country ablaze. Tomorrow General Batran will go to Abu Za3bal prison and restore order. Then he'll go to Qatta prison and talk to the prisoners, and they will agree to return to their cells—and then he will be shot and killed by the inspector in charge of the jail. His sister, Manal al-Batran, will pursue his killers in the courts for months—perhaps years.

I glance up, and my balcony, on the sixth floor, draws my eyes to its light, its trellises and plants. I always leave the light on at night, so that I, coming home, or someone coming to visit, can glance up and feel an early welcome. Now I question whether it's a good idea.

Karima comes to talk to me. She's my age and is the daughter of the greengrocer under my building. He, the greengrocer, used to sit quietly in the corner all day with a cigarette-full of hashish while Karima's mother ran the shop and the children. When I was small, I used to watch their fights from the balcony—enthralled. They were a mother and a father with two daughters and a son. Just like us. But instead of the tight lips, the silences, the "withdrawal of affection" that signaled anger or displeasure in our household, their emotions and exchanges were all out there: yells and wails and tantrums, the mother chasing the kids with a bamboo cane, the kids screaming and running and dodging behind startled passersby, the street intervening, cuffing them on the head, enforcing peace. I was sure I preferred their style to ours. The parents are dead now, and the brother runs the greengrocer's. He still gets into fights, and the classy glass front he's put up for his shop is often smashed. But Karima owns three hardware and general stores on the street and holds court from a stool on the corner. When her children were young, you saw them stop by her, composed and well dressed and always carrying books.

She comes to talk to me and says she's worried. "They drove round and collected all the guards from the embassies and the banks," she says, "and it's not only that; they've turned their baltagis loose on the streets. How can we live without security?"

"Don't tell me you're afraid?" I joke.

"Of course I'm afraid."

"Well, seriously, don't be. You could take on a hundred baltagis."

The baltagis are worse than the regular forces. They're men— and recently women—with a record of violent crime, who're trained and paid by the Dakhleyya and used for special assignments, like beating up people at elections, dispersing protesters, etc. A baltagi is mercenary and without honor. A baltagi is violent and loud but ultimately a coward; his speciality is bullying the weak. And Karima is not weak.

Two weeks later, when Mubarak falls, she will take off her *galabeyya* and veil and put on a loose trouser suit and a scarf. When I grin, she'll shrug: "Just a bit of a change." But now, at midnight on 28 January, we stand together and watch three young residents armed with sticks take up position outside my apartment block. "Where are your children?" she asks. "They're coming," I say. I don't tell her that I've made my youngest, Ismail Richard, stay put in London to circulate information and help organize the protests there—and finish his M.Sc. But my older son, Omar Robert, is, in fact, trying to come home. Two nights from now he will join these young men at the barricades.

As we'd driven from Tahrir to my neighborhood, Zamalek, to look for pharmacies, news was coming through of the police withdrawal. By the time we'd finished buying the medicines and were heading back to Tahrir, we passed three citizen checkpoints in Zamalek alone. In every district people came down from their homes and set up neighborhood watches, Popular Committees. They invented barricades out of tires and chairs and lengths of wood and blocks of stone and traffic barriers. The characters of the checkpoints varied with the neighborhoods: in the villages they were farmers with axes and hoes; in the poorer neighborhoods they wore *galabeyyas* and carried sticks; in the posh districts they had walking canes and golf clubs; at one Zamalek checkpoint there was a lady in a camping chair holding a glass of gin and tonic. Kids played in the streets.

For a week the city will be policed by Popular Committees. They will have fun, checking ID and licenses and ushering cars through with a theatrical flourish. Everywhere they are courteous and apologize for the inconvenience. And we are courteous right back and thank them for protecting us, thank them for giving us our city back. Everybody ignores the curfew. People, especially women, say they've never felt safer. We joke, seriously, that we can save the eighteen billion pounds the Dakhleyya costs us every year and put it into something more useful. In the daytime the shabab will run the traffic and collect the litter. Revolutionary graffiti will start to appear everywhere and become more confident and more sophisticated each day.

2:00 A.M.

It is quieter at the mosque. I deliver the supplies, add them to the neat mounds that other citizens have brought in, then sit with an exhausted young doctor who tells me he'd come down with four of his friends from Minya to join the protest. They lost each other and, with no mobiles, couldn't communicate. Then the shooting started, and he knew what he had to do. He has been working nonstop for ten hours. I ask if he knows where he'll sleep. My brother, who's come down with more medicines and a car, takes him to the Hisham Mubarak Legal Center, which is now functioning as a shelter and food kitchen as well as providing legal backup for activists. The center was set up by my sister's husband, Ahmad Seif, and a group of friends in 1999 and named after one of the group, Hisham Mubarak, who'd been thirty-five when he died of a heart attack ten years earlier.[10] Tonight its floors and sofas are home to scores of Egyptians from outside Cairo who've come to join the revolution.

Before I leave, I ask the name of the mosque. It is the Mosque of Ibad al-Ra7man, the Servants of the Compassionate.

Hundreds die that Friday night. And thousands are injured, and many will die later of their wounds. Their smiling, hopeful faces will be everywhere. Our shuhada: our martyrs of the revolution, who walked in peace and died before they could live the lives they dreamed of. Their song will become our anthem.[11] We will march in their funerals and promise, "We'll get what they died for / Or die as they died." If we tire or our hope dims, if our optimism for a moment falters, we will open our hearts and they will come to us: their bright faces, their hopes, their lives, their parents, their children. This is now our life's work: we will create the Egypt they died for.

3:00 A.M.

On my way home I walk again through Cairo's darkened streets, through the rubbish, past the shuttered shops and the closed hotels and the smoldering party headquarters and the charred, upturned personnel carriers, and it all seems apt. It's not a film anymore. This is the reality that we've been living for decades, finally risen to the surface. At last our capital reflects the true condition of the country and of our lives: burned and broken and almost ruined. And now we'll have to save it.

I come again to the four tanks on Maspero. The soldiers in camouflage are still standing on top of them; I wonder if they have to stand there all night or if they may at least sit down. Behind one of them is the sign of the Paprika restaurant, and as I look at the restaurant's darkened window I see—so clearly that my breath catches—I see my younger self, ablaze with love and poetry and the stormy, dusty *khamsin* winds, sitting, leaning across the table from the man I love, the man who has followed me from London to Cairo, allowing him to hold my palm to his mouth, to kiss it under the gaze of all the waiters standing by.

〜〜〜〜

For our honeymoon we drove up the length of the Suez Canal and discovered we were on a military road only when we hit the first checkpoint and it was too late to turn back. The soldiers fetched the colonel. I gave him our passports, our story, our marriage certificate from the day before. He stared for a moment at the silent foreigner in sunglasses sitting in the passenger seat, then said "Mabrouk" and let us pass. We went through at least ten check-points before the road gave us an option to exit.

Four months later our London wedding, for good or ill, took place on the anniversary of Nasser's 1952 revolution. And my life became Cairo/London, London/Cairo. And both cities changed, but I liked—on the whole—the changes that happened to London: the view from Waterloo Bridge, more exciting every year, the blossoming street markets, the angel alighting once more on the dome of our local theater. In Cairo, every time I went home, home got a bit more bitty on me.

I came home and found the old mysterious villa on the corner of our street gone. One of my classmates used to vanish into it at the end of every school day; now the wrought-iron railings, the dense trees, the lights shining far within: all gone. In its place, this pharmacy.

I came home, and they'd pulled apart my beloved Abu el-Ela Bridge and built the ghastly 15 May Overpass in its place. No more strolls to Maspero, to Boulac, to the Shagara Café. The overpass (named after the 1971 coup—the "Corrective Revolution," with which Sadat consolidated his power and got rid of what was left of Nasser's men) runs across Zamalek and turned its high street into an instant slum.

In Ataba, the other main theater of my life, the changes were more radical. A super-ugly iron walkway circumambulated the *midan*: Midan el-Ataba el-Khadra, the Place of the Green Threshold. Step through the threshold, east into the heart of the old city, west into the heart of Haussmann's late-nineteenth-century creation, both hearts centered on commerce. Everyone here was in small industries and trade. But they used to have style. My grandfather's home was here, his business a five-minute walk across Shari3 el-Azhar. But he was dead, and Khalu, my uncle—because of the Mafia-style practices of the tax authorities—was shifting the business from wood to aluminum. The showrooms and workshops, soon to be sold, were in the massive Italianate terrace on the eastern side of the *midan*. Look at the confidence of it! Of the National Theater, and the Khedivial Post building, and the block that held Matatias's coffee shop, where Khalu played chess every night.

And the house: a solid Mediterranean-style apartment block fronting on a quiet courtyard on Shari3 el-Geish. The fun thing was to approach it from the other side, from the Ruwei3i market. You walked through the busy street past Alf Sanf w'Sanf, the piled-high toy store from which we bought all my toys and my brother's and sister's toys. Alf Sanf w'Sanf furnished me one day with the sudden aperçu that the accurate translation of *Alf leila w'leila* was not the literal "a thousand and one nights" but just "a thousand nights"—or even "lots of nights." Anyway, past the toy store and through the cool passageway that ran under the building, and you emerged in a courtyard with notices and banners hanging out to dry outside a calligraphy workshop, then you turned right into the spacious entrance with the old black and white marble floor and the stately wooden lift. This was the landscape that furnished my imagination and kept me going through the cold years of the Ph.D. in the north of England. When I came back, I fought my way through the Ruwei3i market to find my aunt, Toufi, fighting a battle with rising garbage and falling plaster and smashed marble. The lift had been overpainted with brown lacquer, and street vendors run by the local MP were using the entrance as storage. Of our neighbors, older people were dying, their children moving into the new districts, away from the center, their apartments taken over by local bosses who used them as storage for cheap goods, and baltagis.

Cairo/London, London/Cairo, and Cairo was being constantly downgraded. Despite the new luxury multipurpose blocks, the marble shopping malls, the $15 million apartments, the city was disintegrating. Partly through neglect and partly, we felt, on purpose. Streets were dug up and left unpaved. Sidewalks vanished. Prime and historic locations—like the site of the burned-down Opera House just off Ataba—became car parks. Streetlights dimmed. Nothing was maintained or mended. Old houses were torn down and monstrous towers built in their place. Public transport became a joke. And in a noose around the city, they built luxury gated communities on virtually stolen land, adorned them with water-guzzling golf courses, and called them "European Countryside" and "Beverly Hills."

And through it all, I loved her and loved her more. Millions of us did. We'd wake up one morning and find a just finished underpass dug up again, more marble and ceramics brought in to line its walls. We'd check out which MPs traded in marble and ceramics (the same MPs who would send truckloads of baltagis with marble and ceramic shards to crack open our heads in the streets of the revolution). Traffic signals were burned out and bent, and we'd wake up another morning to find the city had sprouted plastic palm trees festooned with winking red and green lightbulbs. They'd really scored there: not only made money but made Cairo into a clown. We apologized to her. Among ourselves and in our hearts. We told her we loved her anyway, told her we were staying. I felt a rush of love every time I passed the strange, creamy house with the rotting turrets that they hadn't yet pulled down; the great art deco cinemas, flea-ridden and on their knees but still there. The day the Cairo Tower lost its discreet white uplighting and was caught in a net of flashing colored dots, I cried. They dammed sections of the Nile to create new waterfront residences (the ministers of housing responsible are now being tried) and land was sold from under residents' feet to foreign "investors." Cement was poured into every public construction project, including disastrous restorations of thousand-year-old mosques. The cement factories ran on subsidized fuel and made a profit margin of 65 percent. In Muqattam the sewage from a new, wealthy development on the top of the hill eroded the rock on which Dwei2a, the old poor district below, was precariously perched and sent it crashing down the jagged hillside. (The residents are now camped in protest in front of Maspero, their wretchedness displayed for all to see.) A quarter of a million children lived on the streets, and some people set up shelters for them, and some made films about them and some stole their kidneys and corneas. Police officers ran protection and drug rackets. People regularly fell out of windows during questioning or had heart attacks in police custody. There was a video of a woman hanging upside down and begging, begging. . . . there were protests, marches, demonstrations every day. There were flash screenings of torture videos. The top judges of the country stood for two hours in silence in the street outside the Judges' Club with their sashes and ribbons and medals on their chests. We knew then that judgment would surely come.

Degraded and bruised and robbed and exploited and mocked and slapped about: my city. I was ashamed of myself for not saving her. Every one of us was. All I could do was look and listen and stay and march and insist that I loved her. And she acted like she didn't care. She unraveled with bravado. Every thread of that once tightly ordered pattern breaking loose: blue and green and red and black and every shade and texture, all sprung away from the tapestry, in disarray, tangled, knotted, vivid, sizzling, present. The city stayed awake longer, put more people on the streets. It threw up new haphazard districts, and when the government would not supply them with water or electricity, people stole them from the mains. It opened special restaurants and started special services to cater to the new Gulf tourists. Including agencies for seasonal marriages to young, pretty, impoverished Egyptian women.

Small art galleries opened, and tiny performance spaces; new bands formed across the musical spectrum. Mosques and cultural centers clutched at the derelict spaces under overpasses. Green spaces vanished, but every night the bridges would be crammed with Cairenes taking the air. We suffered a massive shortage of affordable housing, but every night you'd see a bride starring in her wedding procession in the street. Unemployment ran at 20 percent, and every evening there was singing and drumming from the cheap, bright, noisy little pleasure boats crisscrossing the river.

Trees that were not cut down refused to die. They got dustier, and some of their branches grew bare, but they grew. We looked out anxiously for the giant baobab in Sheikh Marsafy Street in Zamalek, for the Indian figs on the Garden City Corniche, for what my kids called the Jurassic Park trees by the zoo. If they cut a tree down, it grew shoots. If they hammered an iron fence into its roots, the tree would lean into the iron, lean on it. If a building crowded the side of a tree, the tree grew its other side bigger, lop-sided. I knew trees that couldn't manage leaves anymore but put all they had into a once-a-year burst of pink flowers. And once I saw a tree that seemed looked after, that had just been washed: it couldn't stop dancing.

I loved her. I would wake up in my London bed convinced that as my front door opened onto Wimbledon, my garden door opened onto Zamalek. Until one day, when I was neither in Cairo nor in London but in Jaipur, the shabab of Egypt decided they would no longer allow their lives to be stolen, and in every district in the country they got up and walked into the hearts of their cities. They chanted, "We're your sons / And daughters too / What we're doing is for you," and we came down from our houses and walked with them. They marched for bread, and they marched for freedom, for social justice and for human dignity. We followed them, and we marveled at them, and we stood shoulder to shoulder with them, and every so often—more often than they wanted, for sure—we'd grab one of them and hug them and shake their hand and thank them. Yes, we would thank them for lifting the burden of failure from our backs, for ridding our hearts of their load of sorrow, for stepping forward and sweeping away the question that tormented each one of us: *What manner of homeland, what manner of future am I leaving my children? What have we allowed to happen to our country? To our world?* We're taking care of it, they said, just stay with us: "Parents! Friends! Draw close to us!" And we did.

SUNDAY, 30 JANUARY

MH has turned his office into a revolutionary headquarters, and this is a meeting of some of the older figures of what you might call the establishment opposition to the regime of Hosni Mubarak. Most are over sixty-five. They sit in a big circle, and the buffet man goes round with coffee. They talk above each other and listen only long enough to pick up a line and go with it themselves. An unkind thought crosses my mind: *This is the political leadership that failed.* They talk about the necessity of creating a patriotic front to fill the vacuum created by the fall of the National Democratic Party, about the need to call for the election of a founding committee to write the constitution—and the conversation/argument has the same theoretical feel as the ones we've been listening to for thirty years: lists of things we need to do. But our host has promised us a visit from some of the young leadership of the revolution; when they come in, an energy comes in with them. Six young men, all in their twenties. They're like a football team; they huddle and confer quickly, they "pass" to each other with a nod or a look. They're concise, self-deprecating, firm, and courteous. They say that if they claim any credit, it will be for 20 percent of the people who came out on the twenty-fifth; the rest has been spontaneous, organic—as surprising to them as it was to everybody. When the Khaled Said[12] Facebook page received over 300,000 responses to the call to come out on the twenty-fifth, eleven other groups decided to meet and coordinate. They met physically (and secretly) and organized themselves and their friends. They are about three hundred, and no, they don't all know each other. They won't give information about how they operate, but they want to put it on the record that, were it not for all the protests and writings and activism of the older leadership, they would not have been able to do what they're doing now. "We've learned from you," they tell the room, "and we're building on what you've accomplished." There's a silence, and then one of the older people says simply: "Whatever you want us to do, we'll do."

I go out onto the porch. If I walk across Mesa7a Street, to the right, I'll come to a house we lived in briefly when I was three. A memory of riding a blue tricycle down a paved slope into a—living room? My mother at a sideboard wearing a full-skirted dress in blue and white pencil stripes. The walls were ablaze with paintings, and in the living room my parents' friends, the authors of these paintings, all in their twenties, were laughing and arguing and waiting for the mini-sandwiches my mother was preparing at the sideboard. This is the university neighborhood. Just down the road there's the Cairo University Faculty Club—the Union. We used to come with my parents when we were children and play in the garden while they socialized or organized. My parents taught at Cairo University all their lives, and Laila, my sister, followed them—only she specialized in maths. In 2006 she was one of the group that founded the 9 March Group for the Independence of the Universities—and she and her comrades started contesting the Union. As she told of stormy meetings, of regime-rigged elections, of being locked out of the building and holding alternative meetings on the pavement outside, I would try to imagine all this happening in the quiet, lofty rooms with their dark furniture, their rugs, their discreet lighting that spoke so sonorously of stability and scholarship and calm.

And now, just as my eight-year-old self is peeping round a heavy wooden door into a book-lined room, I hear an earth-shaking roar. I look up. Low down in the clear, blue winter sky, four F-16s are dipping and swooping. They circle several times. In Tahrir, I will learn later, people start to dance. "He's gone crazy! He's gone crazy!" they sing, and dance the crazy dance.[13] A man who works for MH comes onto the porch. "Don't go to Tahrir," he warns. "Go home and stay there. This whole story they're talking about inside isn't going to work." I remind him there's a call for a mil-lioneyya[14] tomorrow. He says he has a friend in the innermost cir-cle of the Presidential Guard. "They have a plan for this. They've been getting ready for this for a long time, and now," he says, "they have orders to put the plan into action: they're going to do dirty things, terrible, terrible things. It's going to be over in two days. Please believe me." The wide white steps lead down into a beauti-fully kept garden, where a calligrapher is busy at work on a series of huge banners: IRHAL! IRHAL! IRHAL! Leave!

An hour later in the sky above Tahrir, helicopters circle and tilt, circle and tilt, and on the ground we tilt right back at them, all of us, waving and laughing and holding up our banners for the men in the machines to read.

Mubarak has extended the curfew—but the Midan is teem-ing with hundreds of thousands of people, and more and more are coming in. He announces a cabinet reshuffle with General Ahmad Shafiq as prime minister—and Tahrir chants: "The peo-ple demand the fall of this regime." Yesterday, when he appointed Omar Suleiman as his vice president, the Midan roared: "No Mubarak / No Suleiman / No more *umala amrikan*," agents for America, and on the front of the papers this morning, Mubarak and Suleiman going through the swearing-in ceremony look irrel-evant, even unreal. This is what's real; what's happening here: the citizens flooding into Tahrir, the cheers, the chanting, the waving banners, the sense that we are pushing against something that will give. We don't know when, but it will give.

So we carry on, we chant and we sing and we wave the flag, and then again we're all looking up at the sky because the air around us is growing dim and heavy and the sky darkens and darkens, and then the thunder comes. God's thunder. It rolls and booms above our heads. Again and again it comes, and then lightning cracks the skies open, and the deluge pours down on us. We stand in awe. Thirty minutes of rain fast and fat and furious, and then the sky, the air, the city clears. The sun comes out, and Tahrir sparkles and leaps to life. "Allahu Akbar" rolls across Cairo. God is with us; He has sent us a sign and has cleansed our skies of Mubarak's jets.

And Omar Robert, my older son, flies in. After a nail-biting interlude when they said the plane would not land in Cairo but would fly back to Athens, they changed their minds, and he arrives. It takes us two hours to get from the airport to Zamalek. The army has closed off the section of highway that runs past Mubarak's residence—even though he's in Sharm el-Sheikh—so we have to drive through side streets, and everywhere the Popular Committees have set up their barricades. Omar has his first taste of the revolution. We show IDs and licenses, and everybody thanks everybody. At midnight he goes down to volunteer for the barricade on our street. In a little while he comes back. "I have to have a weapon," he says, "and I don't fancy a kitchen knife." He roams the house looking troubled. Then, leaning against the hallstand, he finds what he's looking for. My son patrols our street armed with my mother's walking stick.

And I am left to remember the times I walked into this flat to find my sons chatting with my mother on the balcony, or in the kitchen being fed, and how we moved from my mother pushing their swings or watching over them by the pool to Omar driving her around the streets of Cairo and—a couple of times—to the little orchard by the Pyramids that she loved so much.

TUESDAY, 1 FEBRUARY

I shall park by the small building that I still think of as the Pocket Theater. In the mid-sixties my mother used to drag me here to see experimental productions of Beckett and Brecht and Aeschylus. I loved the Nile-side neo-pharaonic building in its grove of palm trees, and I liked being part of an evening activity, a "grown-up" activity. But after the already-too-long performances, there would be intense discussions as to whether Brecht should be rendered in colloquial Egyptian or modern standard Arabic, whether Shakespeare's sonnets had to rhyme in Arabic, whether Sophocles or Euripides was more useful for our times, whether you could—in a translation—add a phrase that changed no meaning but fixed the rhythm. I was *so* bored. But something stayed with me—something to do with, shall we say, believing that artistic endeavor matters—that it's worth arguing about, and that it can (should?) have an intimate relationship with the world it happens in. Something to do with responsibility.

There's no parking to be had. The space is crammed; in every nook and cranny there are BMWs, beat-up old Fiat 128s, sleek Mercedes, environmentally unfriendly SUVs, responsible Toyotas; everybody's parked and come to join the revolution. I find a spot down the alley by the Ahli Football Club, cross, and walk past the Andalus Gardens and over Qasr el-Nil Bridge. Families of four generations are walking into Tahrir on a brilliant, sunny Cairo day.

The entrance to the Midan is a tangle of tanks, barbed wire, soldiers, and people. Yesterday the twelve entrances to Tahrir were guarded and the sit-in secured by shabab from the Popular Committees. Today it seems the army's helping. At the Qasr el-Nil entrance, we hold up our IDs as one by one we squeeze through the narrow gaps between the tanks. It doesn't feel good. Soldiers stand above us as we squash ourselves through their hardware. But they look friendly, and on Sunday, after the air force buzzed us, the Supreme Council of the Armed Forces, SCAF, declared that the armed forces would never fire on the Egyptian people.[15] Battalions of people are continuing the charm offensive that started on Friday—they surround the tanks, lean on them, climb onto them, paint them, stick flags and flowers on them, throw their babies to the men manning them; every tank is overwhelmed, every officer and soldier is engaged in conversation, in photo ops. Last night there was a football match—the people versus the army—with a tank as the prize. The people won. They didn't get the tank. But an officer emerged onto the Midan, young, rugged, well-spoken and almost in tears. He made a speech urging us not to leave our positions until we'd got everything we wanted. He was lifted onto people's shoulders and carried round the Midan: "The people! / The army! / One hand! / The people! / The army . . ."[16]

I tell non-Egyptian friends, journalists, interviewers who ask that we're not Greece or Latin America; that the Egyptian army is very much part of the fabric of Egyptian society, and in both 1977 and 1985 it refused direct orders to fire on Egyptian demonstrators. An oath taken by every soldier is that he will never raise his weapon in an Egyptian face. The army says it will secure for us this space where we are carrying out our peaceful, democratic, young, inclusive, open-source, grassroots revolution. My parents' generation warns us; they send messages through their children, our friends: *Take care. Don't trust the army.* My sister quotes the proverb "Harras wala tkhawwensh"—Don't assume treachery, but be on guard! And in any case, what are our options?

Mubarak is holding on. The Dakhleyya is working against us; they have already killed at least 145 people, and news is filtering through of killings in jails, of bodies found on highways, of attempted robberies of state institutions, of arson—all conducted by men officially and unofficially on the payroll of the Dakhleyya. Next-door Libya's erupting, Sudan to our south is breaking apart, and to our east there is Israel, always Israel; Israel, which is declaring its concern for Mubarak and calling him a strategic asset—which we've always known and is a large part of our problem with him. And in between us and all this stands our army: our brothers and husbands and sons. They're not 400,000 men, and they're spreading themselves thin. Since the twenty-fifth, they've had to deploy rapidly through Egypt's twenty-six governorates, and now they have to be in the cities as well. And we believe that they're like the rest of the country: the very top levels were part of the regime and have made millions. The conscripts and soldiers are ordinary Egyptians making a meager living. The officers and middle ranks have the same wishes, fears, angers, ambitions, equivocations as the rest of us, and on the whole would rather not see Egypt on its knees and would rather not be America and Israel's scabby mongrel allowed to shelter and feed as long as it knows its place, and would quite like to have a decent country where we take responsibility for ourselves and work to make sure everybody can have bread, freedom, and social justice.

We know that the army collects a ton of U.S. aid. We know it represents about a third of the GDP of our country—that it is a massive business interest. We know that in the army, as in the government and the state and also outside our country, massive— fine, the biggest possible—interests do not wish us to do what we wish to do, do not want for us the lives we want for ourselves. But right now we have to take the chance that the balances within the army will keep it from harming us. Right now we need to deal with the other forces ranged against us, inside and outside Egypt. The forces that want our land and our location, our resources and our position, and our history and our quiescence, and that want us out of a number of equations in our region and the world. They fasten on to us and feed, they spoon out our brains, our health, and our will. And if we don't fight them off, we shall die not even the death that is a merciful release but the death that is death-in- life: we shall be condemned to a zombie existence where we are emptied of ourselves but continue to perform their "Egypt."

Bread. Freedom. Social justice. How many have come to today's millioneyya? The military say two million in Tahrir. Four million across Egypt. And all these millions look like people who've awakened from a spell. We look happy. We look dazed. We turn to each other to question, to reassure. A man asks, "How did they divide us? How did they make us frightened of each other like that?" Another man—with his hand on his son's shoulder—says to me, picking up the thread of a conversation we might have had: "Yes, really. I thought so badly of him, sitting all day at his computer. Now look what he and his friends have done. Respect. Respect." People have put up tents in the central garden. In one tent, young women are collecting footage of Dakhleyya torture. In another, people are stacking bottles of water and dry biscuits. I lower myself to the ground for a moment's rest and see I've sat next to the covered wife of a man in the shortened white thob and the white skullcap of the Salafis. I wonder if they'll mind. He sees my glance: "Are you looking at me because I have this beard and I'm smoking?" A wide smile: "I just couldn't afford razors. When he leaves, I'll buy all the razors I need." We all become instant friends. And I see old friends, too; as I wander the Midan, I bump into people I know are living in Brussels, in Doha, in D.C., in London. Everyone has dropped everything and come home. We're walking around wide-eyed, pale with emotion. We hug. "You, too? But of course you'd come," we say, and hug again. For a moment, Omar is next to me. "Would you have imagined the revolution would look like this?" he says. All the ills that plagued our society in the last decades have vanished overnight. Young men, who a month ago could have been thought a menace to any woman on the street, are chivalry itself. People offer each other biscuits, dates, water. People chat, people pick up litter. We revel in the inclusiveness, the generosity, the humor that come so easily to us. Students, businessmen, waiters, academics, farmers, civil servants, unemployed—we are all here together, all doing what we've not been able to do for decades: each and every one is speaking, acting, expressing themselves and insisting on being counted.

A group of some thirty fair-skinned young people are gathered by the central garden. They hand out leaflets written in Arabic, English, and French. They carry a banner that says: "The Khawagas [Western foreigners] who have made Egypt their home salute the revolution!"

The world's media are here. "I don't know if one should say this," a journalist says, "but it's like—it's like Woodstock." She looks worried, but if there'd been room, I'd have picked her up and waltzed. In an early morning interview, I'd reassured a worried BBC anchor that Tahrir was like carnival. Another journalist is in tears: "For thirty years we've been discussing revolution— and if a revolution can be 'good.' And—here it is; you've just done it." I see Jon Snow and Medea Benjamin. A man pops out of a tree with branches tied to his arms and performs a tree dance. Another improvises a stand-up routine as "the Indian Expert, Mr. Nana," coming to tell us how to run the revolution. Stages have been rigged up and bands are playing.

But there are also black ribbons flying and pictures, pictures, pictures of the young people who were killed by the regime in the last six days. Our shuhada.[17] Together, we pray for them the Prayers for the Absent: "And do not consider those who were killed in the path of Right as dead; for they live in the presence of their Lord, and they prosper."[18]

And the Midan feeds us, nourishes us: this is the Egyptian Museum that holds our ancestors, the museum that our shabab defended—the museum that bears witness to who we are. This is the Arab League—an example of the death-in-life that was to be our fate; we will breathe life into it. This is the plinthless space. What good fortune that no statue occupies this central space, that the absence of a leader is physically manifest in Tahrir, and our leaderless revolution is watched over, instead, from the boundaries, by Omar Makram, Simón Bolívar, and Abd el-Menem Riyad. And the roads that open out from it—Champollion to the great law courts and the unions, Qasr el-Eini to Parliament and the Cabinet Office and then to the great teaching hospitals, Tahrir Street to Abdeen and the Palace and then to the Citadel, Tal3at

Harb to town and Ataba and commerce and then the Azhar, Gala2 to the central railway station and then the Cathedral—and right next to you, running alongside you—the Nile.

In the novel I was working on before the revolution happened, there's a scene that was written in August 2007. "Mada" is talking to "Asya" about the museum:

> "You know," says Mada, "it's unbelievable. It's as if the city doesn't even belong to us. A soldier stopped me walking near the Museum in Tahrir the other day. In the center of Cairo. He said it's forbidden to walk here. I couldn't believe it. 'How d'you mean forbidden?' 'It's forbidden.' I pointed at a whole load of people walking into the Museum. He said they're for-eigners. I said, 'So I'm forbidden because I'm not a foreigner? Are you serious? What if I want to go to the Museum?' He said, 'Why should you go to the Museum?' I said, 'Haven't you noticed it's called the "Egyptian" Museum? And haven't you noticed this square is called "Liberation" Square? Do you know who it was liberated from? It was liberated from the foreigners, for us: the Egyptian people.'" "And what did he say?" "He said: 'You'll have to speak to the officer.'"

A great cry goes up from the square: "Irhal! Irhal!" Leave! Leave! Everybody is looking in the same direction: from the sixth-floor balcony of an art deco building, a long banner unfurls, falling gracefully down the front of the building. We read: "Leave! We want to breathe!" Holding it from the balcony is a young woman with streaming curly hair. She is jumping up and down and hold-ing up her hand in a victory salute. The crowd salutes back: "Irhal! Irhal!"

Tahrir is about dignity and image as much as it is about the economy and corruption. It hurts how much this regime has messed with our heads, divided us, maligned us to the world.

"They say we only care about a loaf of bread," a young laborer says. "We care about bread. But we also care about our dignity." Together, in the Midan, over the last four days, we have rediscovered how much we like ourselves and each other and, corny as it may sound, how "good" we are. I sneeze, and someone passes me a tissue. And all the time the chants continue, the demands are articulated, options for the future are discussed. It is not possible to say what will happen next. But I look around, and I know this won't stop. No one, nobody, not one of us, is going to step back into the nightmare.

An Interruption

EIGHT MONTHS LATER, OCTOBER 2011

"It is not possible to say what will happen next. But I look around and I know this won't stop. No one, nobody, not one of us, is going to step back into the nightmare." This is what I wrote eight months ago. And now, of course, we know what happened next: Hosni Mubarak fell on 11 February; we celebrated, and the world—you—celebrated with us. The Supreme Council of the Armed Forces, SCAF, with tanks on our streets, stepped forward, saluted our shuhada, declared its belief in our revolution, and promised to protect it and the people and the transition into democracy. We left the Midan.

But I need to pause while we're still there, in the Midan, to interrupt this account of the eighteen days, to tell you the ongoing story of our revolution. Because the story does go on; we have not stopped, even though we may have fallen off your—off the world's—television screens, for the moment.

This book is not a record of an event that's over; it's an attempt to welcome you into, to make you part of, an event that we're still living. And there are two problems in the writing of it. One is that while the eighteen days are locked into the past, the revolution and the fight to hold on to it continue, and every day the landscape shifts. The other is that you—my reader—are in a future unknown to me, and yet I want to tell a story that will ease the leap you need to make between where this book stops and where Egypt is as you read.

As I write, I think of you holding this book and reading my words, weeks, months, into the future, and I wonder what the reality that you are seeing will be. That reality is what we, today, as I write, are working, fighting, dying in order to shape.

These are the last few hours that this, my text and I, have together; the last few hours I have to write for you, to you. And it's hard to write because things keep happening, pushing my pen this way and that, or making me lay it down as I stare out the window and contemplate.

We've just had word that Alaa Abd el-Fattah, my nephew, Laila's son and Mona's brother, has been summoned to the military prosecutor to face a charge of "incitement and destruction." Alaa is twenty-nine, an IT man, an activist and blogger. He and his wife, Manal, like many of our shabab, like Omar, my son, had been living and working abroad and dropped everything and came home to work for the Egypt of the revolution. When Mubarak was deposed, Alaa and Manal decided the world was ready for their first baby. The first child of the next generation in our family will be born, God willing, on 24 November. Alaa is at a conference in San Francisco. And Manal received his summons to the military prosecutor earlier today, while she was painting the new nursery. So this morning, as I sit down to write, this is what's on my mind.

My family plays musical chairs with dwellings, and I find myself now, after four moves in thirty years, in possession of the flat in Zamalek where I grew up. When I lift my eyes from my desk—my mother's desk, her card still there, in the corner under the glass by my right hand—when I lift my eyes, there's the view that used to meet them when I was studying for my university exams, and before that, for my finals at high school. The view is unchanged except for the 15 May Overpass that runs about a hundred meters to my left. Under it are the traffic lights at the intersection of Shagar el-Durr Street where in '67, as the military were preparing for the war with Israel that they would lose with such catastrophic consequences, they crushed my uncle, Khalu, in his Citroën between two massive trucks. So I stare out of the window and I think about civilians and the military and how Khalu, though he was an only son and so not conscripted, lost an eye, an arm, and a career to them anyway and, in the end, was killed by an infection that entered his brain through an unhealed crack in the skull, a crack that happened in that accident twenty-eight years earlier. I think of Sally, my best friend, and how we sat in this room soon after we met on our first day at university, and she told me that her fiancé, her cousin, serving his conscription, had been captured by the Israelis in Sinai in the war. He was never heard of again.

I think about civilians and the military and how this year and within the revolution, our army started, on 28 January, to grab and beat civilians, and to detain them and subject them to military trials. Six thousand two hundred and thirty-five young people are serving military sentences now. Another twelve hundred and twenty-five are carrying suspended sentences. The army picked up a few here and a few there at every one of the "incidents" that have punctuated our lives since February, culminating, for the moment, in the events at the Israeli embassy on 9 September and the events at Maspero on 9 October.

On 11 February it seemed that we had emerged into a clear open space and that our progress would be swift. Now, eight months later, our landscape is more ambiguous, more confused. I try to describe it, and big, dramatic clichés crowd into my head: the Forces of Darkness, the Battle against Evil. But clichés can also be true descriptions. Hosni Mubarak threatened that it was either him or chaos. Not because that was the natural order of things, but because if we chose not-him, the forces that he represented would work to create chaos. Mubarak and his family were the packaging, the casing that held the Forces of Darkness together, that utilized them, through his National Democratic Party, his security apparatus, his corrupt government, and the corrupt elite inserted into almost every leadership position in the country. Now the casing's been smashed and the Darkness is out there, unchanneled, panicked, rampant, twisting into every nook and cranny as it seeks to wrap around us again.

On 11 February, SCAF became de facto president, but it kept in place the cabinet appointed by the deposed president, and on 26 February the Military Police attacked protesters who were demanding its resignation. On this occasion the army apologized—and appointed Essam Sharaf and his cabinet—but it had taken several young people into military detention, and a path was set. Not one step or procedure that should have followed on automatically from the success of the revolution and the removal of the head of the regime was conceded without a struggle, without protests and demonstrations and sit-ins. And each one of these was punished more severely than the last.

The slow pace meant that the "remnants" of the regime had time to collect themselves, to organize. Mubarak's sons were in jail, but they still had their cash and their connections and their mobile phones. Zakareyya Azmi, Mubarak's chief of staff, lived a normal life after his boss fell, with daily access to his office for two months before he was arrested. Omar Suleiman, Mubarak's last-minute vice president and long-term head of intelligence, continues very much at large and is even being proposed by SCAF from time to time as a serious candidate for the presidency. If twenty corrupt politicians/businessmen are being tried, fifty more are still free. The decapitated regime is still strong, it's fighting for its life—and possibly growing a new head.

Its weapons have always been cash and coercion. For coercion, it used its 1.5 million–strong security apparatus—plus the estimated half million or so baltagis. The minister of the interior, Habib el-Adli, was arrested in February, but SCAF has allowed no one to examine, punish, or rehabilitate the security establishment, so the country is full of armed and disgruntled police and baltagis, short of cash and ready to be used. The regime is still rich. And the old alliance between the regime and the security establishment is still in place.

And so we, the citizens, resort to the law courts and to direct action. Citizens file legal cases to place barriers between the regime and its money: cases against individuals, against companies, against transactions. Citizens propose ways forward for employment, education, agriculture, the Dakhleyya; a few days ago a group of professionals announced their detailed blueprint for its restructuring and reform. Other citizens sue it for murder, terrorism, and torture. And the shabab periodically besiege it and spray graffiti portraits of the murdered shuhada on its walls. Meanwhile we have no effective security, and a sizable number of our police force are working with paid criminals—attempting to cause chaos and disruption.

When SCAF promised to "protect the revolution," we assumed that this meant protect it against its declared enemies: the Dakhleyya, the remnants of the old regime, and the influence of the outside forces that wished it ill; that the military would hold the state in place as we, the people, went through the process of electing a parliament and a president to whom SCAF could hand over power.

We assumed that SCAF would want a guarantee that its members would not be tried for corruption, and perhaps would want an agreement about the position of the military in the future. This could have been something to be negotiated. Quite soon, though, it became clear that SCAF's policy was to conduct a war of attrition against the revolution and the revolutionaries.

Why?

You, my reader, are better placed to answer this than I. From where we are now, we can only guess at where they think they are leading us, and our dominant guess is that SCAF wants the old regime to continue, but with some cosmetic changes, maybe completely new faces. Its members would prefer not to have to impose an overtly military dictatorship to do this. So they will let the elections for Parliament happen, but they will work—have been working—to ensure that the elections do not deliver a "revolutionary" parliament. Then they will insist that the constitution is written before we elect a president. They will remain acting president and will veto any real moves to change the system and deliver on the aims of the revolution. They will also intervene strongly in the writing of the constitution—maybe to give the military a constitutional role overseeing a civilian government.

These are only guesses.

As I write now, we are supposed to be heading for parliamentary elections on 28 November. But SCAF is talking of eighteen months before it hands over power to a civilian president, while all the political forces in the country (apart from the remnants) insist that six months is their ceiling. Meanwhile, paid advertisements by remnant MPs have appeared in the state press inviting SCAF to declare martial law.

The SCAF generals, and Field Marshal Tantawi, repeatedly inform us that they "took a decision" not to shoot us during the revolution. Yet Tantawi has testified in court that Mubarak never gave him an order to shoot the revolutionaries. We know that the military conducted a poll among the field officers very early in the revolution and learned that officers would refuse a direct order to shoot at the people. We also know that the military were completely against the Mubarak plan to insert Gamal Mubarak into the presidency.

It seems, then, that the SCAF generals discussed among themselves, of their own accord, whether to shoot us, and decided not to because they feared a mutiny in the army. In any case, we were getting rid of Gamal Mubarak. They didn't like to see Hosni Mubarak himself go down, but they've been making his fall as gentle as possible. And meanwhile they've been gradually getting their officers used to harming us.

Our story—since SCAF, with tanks in the streets, stepped forward and promised to protect our revolution—has been a story of SCAF impeding, delaying, blocking every practical aspect of the revolution, every possible step toward achieving the goals of the revolution, while paying florid lip service to "the Glorious Revolution of 25 January." It has been a story of SCAF attempting to close down the public space so hard won by the people. And it has been a story of the people taking the revolution into the workplace: strikes and unionization in factories and hospitals, strikes for elections and transparent budgets in universities—ports, banks, law courts, schools. Since there's no "government of the revolution" making a plan that includes everybody, everybody's trying to act out some aspect of the revolution in their own sphere. And whenever possible, SCAF has held up the process. Court judgments to return fraudulently sold national assets, needing presidential ratification, are left unsigned. Officials who negotiate deals with factory workers are fired. A law to impose a five-year ban on remnants running for office is blocked. And more and more and more.

And so it has been a story of escalating confrontation between the revolutionaries and SCAF. Instead of "The people! / The army! / One hand!" it's become "Down! Down with the rule of the generals!"

↗↗↗↗

The incidents that mark our progression down the route of confrontation over the past eight months can be generally grouped under the headings "internal" and "external." The "external" incidents focus on the Israeli issue. The "internal" ones focus on division; and to the Mubarak agenda of dividing Muslim from Christian, Islamist from non-Islamist, Egyptian from non-Egyptian, and rich from poor, SCAF has added civilians from the military. Even though it was the people's anger on behalf of the army that led them to protest in front of the Israeli embassy on 20 August when Israeli forces killed three border guards in Egyptian Rafah and wounded three more—all of whom were later to die of their wounds.

Protesters headed to the Israeli embassy to demand an apology, the dismissal of the ambassador, and the lowering of the flag. Essam Sharaf's government did nothing except ask the Israelis for an explanation. The Israelis refused to apologize. The Israeli embassy is on the sixteenth floor of a residential apartment block. At dawn on the twenty-first, a young house painter climbed to the sixteenth floor, took down the Israeli flag, and raised the Egyptian. The crowds celebrated with fireworks and music.

This was not the first time the shabab had demonstrated in front of the Israeli embassy.

Egypt had celebrated when Nabil el-Arabi—in his brief tenure as minister of foreign affairs—opened the Rafah border and brokered a peace between the Palestinian Authority and Hamas. But a few days later, on Nakba Day on 15 May, while people across the world marched in support of the Palestinians, the Egyptian army stopped Egyptian buses crossing into Sinai; SCAF would not allow a peaceful march to Rafah. So the march went to the Israeli embassy—where it was attacked by the Egyptian Military Police; young men were ordered to kneel on the road in front of the embassy and to repeat the chants of Tahrir and were beaten while they did so. Many young men were taken into military detention, and one, Atef Yahya Ibrahim, was shot in the head. He was twenty-two. He would remain in a coma for five months—then die.

The symbolic victory won by "Flagman" on 21 August was quickly dampened when Sharaf's government, in a brilliantly obtuse move, built a gray fortified wall—reminiscent of the Israeli apartheid wall—on University Bridge facing the entrance to the embassy block.

Friday, 9 September, was dedicated to "Realign the Revolution." After songs and speeches all day in Tahrir, the shabab marched to the symbols of the entities they wanted "realigned": the Supreme Court building, the Dakhleyya, the Radio and Television building in Maspero, and the Israeli embassy. The marches were all peaceful, and they were all to demand changes in government policy. At the embassy, they dismantled the brand-new wall. Then several young men climbed the building and brought down the new flag that had replaced the Egyptian one.

What happened next is still under investigation. But what all the stories agree on is that neither the army nor Central Security—and both were present from the start—tried to stop the group that went into the building and broke into the apartment used by the embassy for storage. Only after papers had been thrown out of the windows did the army and Central Security suddenly act. They detained twenty-six people, injured 1,049, and killed three: Mustafa Hasan, twenty-four; Ala Salem, twenty-three; and Ragab Hussein, also twenty-three. Next day they came back and detained a further ninety-two people who happened to be in the area. All the detainees are being court-martialed. In an effort to support them, twenty-one political groups have claimed responsibility for the "embassy events."

Our issues with Israel are issues of sovereignty and of running Egypt in Egyptian interests—both prime movers of the revolution. Until we have a government that we trust with our sovereignty and our interests, the shabab will be again and again put in the position of protecting them. And this will be represented to the world as "chaos" and "irresponsibility." And it will be presented to the army as the shabab being careless of them, cavalier in pushing them into a new war. And a new wedge will be driven between the people and the army.

Consolidating this dangerous division, a new alliance is forming. The military and security establishments, long played against each other by Hosni Mubarak, are coming together. SCAF has refused any restructuring of the Dakhleyya; it declared the disbanding of the Central Security Forces, which then reappeared as the "Anti-Riot Police," and it renamed the State Security Service the "National Security Service." This alliance also embraces state media; the building in Maspero was always protected by the Presidential Guard, and it uses and is used by the remnants—whom SCAF has refused point-blank to remove from any field of public life.

And the tired tactics of the Mubarak era are very much in play: the attempts to sow division, to make people afraid of each other, of foreigners, of "outside forces," of "infiltrators"; the harping on the need for "stability," the need to not frighten investors, to not "suliy" Egypt's image abroad, the need to respect the state and its instruments.

Security's tactics are familiar to us: find a fault line and wrench, spread rumors, use cash, insert agents provocateurs—and then attack. And we've been finding their fingerprints everywhere in the military's dealings with the revolutionaries. Looking through our diaries, we agree that the tactical marriage of police and army began with the events of Abbaseyya on 23 July and consolidated in the period till the breakup of the Tahrir sit-in on 1 August.

23 JULY 2011

"This is the hospital where you were born," my mother would say whenever we drove past it. And I'd be mildly annoyed. "I know. You've been telling me since I was born." As I grew older, I made a joke of it. Sometimes I'd get in first, "Mama, Mama, what's this building?" She'd peer over her glasses, then frown at me: "It's the hospital where you were born. And you're being silly." My mother didn't much like being teased. Except by her grandchildren. Well, now that she's no longer here to say it, I think it. Always. At this junction. Always, always, always. This is the hospital where I was born. Soon I might start saying it to my children. Maybe I already do. Now I say it to Sherif Boraie, the friend with whom I'm driving in pursuit of the march: "This is the hospital where I was born."

The march left Tahrir at five, aiming to go through the Abbaseyya neighborhood to the Ministry of Defense on the airport road. There we would hand in our list of demands. Five months after our glorious, wonderful, successful revolution, we continue to protest and hand in demands—now to the Supreme Council of the Armed Forces, our acting president. SCAF members have been dragging their feet on every issue on which we need to move quickly: a schedule for elections, cleaning up state radio and television, reforming the Dakhleyya. And they've been arresting young people on a variety of charges and summarily trying them in front of military courts. There has been a sit-in in Tahrir since the eighth. The demands are a clear job description for SCAF and a detailed schedule for elections to Parliament and the presidency: we want the police officers accused of murder and intimidation by the families of the shuhada arrested; and we want the court-martialing of civilians to stop. Today we're taking these demands to SCAF.

And we have the now-standard paragraph demanding that SCAF and the cabinet time-table a start on establishing social justice programs such as minimum and maximum wages, reexamining the budget, and developing employment policies and pensions and national insurance systems. We know they won't do this; this will be the work of our elected government, but we have to keep the demands on the table. And we have to make sure we get to elect a government.

A statement on Thursday counted the revolution's recent gains: the cabinet reshuffle, the decision to hold the Mubarak trial openly, and the decision to allocate courts to the trials of regime bosses and people accused of murdering the young revolutionaries. All were wrenched from SCAF and the cabinet through escalated protests and sit-ins.

Today's march was planned to coincide with the anniversary of the revolution of 1952, to remind SCAF of the celebratory phrase, the mantra everyone was repeating in February: "In 1952 the army revolted and the people supported the revolution. In 2011 the people revolted and the army protected the revolution."

The march left Tahrir at five, but Sherif said he was driving in order to carry water and biscuits and stuff. Sherif is a publisher of exquisite books. Since the revolution began, he's been the "father" of a core group of activists, looking out for them, supporting them, and often underwriting their projects. I ride with him, and we zigzag through Downtown and arrive at the Gala2 junction, where we see our friends marching past us as we sit in the traffic jam. And facing me, across the march, is the Gala2 Hospital. It's the hospital where I was born.

He was twenty-six and she was twenty-three, and I was their first child. They were living in Shubra and they were poor, because even though they had both graduated with distinction, they couldn't get proper jobs—and certainly not in their university, Cairo University, which was what they wanted more than anything. Except to be together. The university was not allowed to appoint my father because when he was nineteen, he'd joined a Communist group and been jailed for a year. My mother had graduated from the English department, and you couldn't be appointed to the English department unless you were English. Or at least British. So he had a clerical job in Fisheries, and she taught at primary school. They were poor also because both their families had objected to the marriage, and even though the families had come round and were eager to help the young couple, the young couple would have none of it and insisted on living on their own resources. So they rented a flat in Shubra at the very very end of civilization, and my father worked on his M.A. (*Al-usus al-nafseyya l-el-ibda3 al-fanni*—Psychological Factors in Artistic Creativity— which became a classic) and my mother on her stories (which sit, unfinished, in a cupboard in my living room), and they agreed they couldn't manage kids yet so they tried to abort me, but I wouldn't let go; I hung in there till we were over the first three months and my mother surrendered and knew she had to have me.

She had me on the trolley in the reception courtyard of the Gala2 Hospital fourteen months after they married. The doctor who admitted her looked and said, "You have a long way to go," and she said, "No, the baby's coming." And out I came, in this hospital, at the midpoint between my mother's family home in Ataba and the flat in Zamalek that we were to move into seven years later—the flat where I'm writing now.

Depending on the point my mother was making, this was a story about how I was always in a hurry, or it was a story about how she always got things done in record time. She had me in an hour, and she had my sister in the middle of the Ph.D. that she finished in two and a half years. She wrote the last chapters pregnant with my brother, my sister levering herself up against her legs to toddle off into trouble. But that was in London and in another story.

Here, in the Cairo story, the 1952 revolution happened, and the two young graduates were appointed to Cairo University, traveled abroad to study further, and returned to set up the main geographical axis of my Cairo life: Zamalek/Ataba, Ataba/Zamalek. A straight line across Abu el-Ela Bridge, through Boulac, past the wonderful ruins of the Khedivial Stables with the carved horses' heads, past the hospital where I was born, past the magnificent High Court, through Fouad Street with Downtown unfurling on both sides of it, past Midan el-Opera, and past the National Theater and the Ruwei3i, and into the passage under my grand-father's house—which is where my brother was born. Not in the passage—in the house, with Toufi looking after my sister and Khalu playing distractingly noisy games with me on the stairs till the doctor left and I went inside and found my mother in her pink chenille dressing gown with baby Ala in her arms. "Each one of you was unwanted," she would tell us, "till the moment I held you in my arms—and then each one could not have been more beloved."

And now the traffic has moved, and we're driving through Ramses Street and past the Coptic Hospital until we're right behind the three thousand or so people in the march; behind a boy in a lime-green T-shirt with a Dolce & Gabbana logo. I catch a glimpse of Mona, one hand holding a phone to her ear, the other distributing leaflets: "No to Military Trials for Civilians." Marches that went out in Alexandria and Suez on Thursday were fired on. There were arguments throughout yesterday and today about whether this march should go ahead—but the general feeling among the shabab was that we have to keep up the pressure on SCAF. So even those of us unsure about this particular march are here to support and to witness. In the street, we are back to the instigator chants: "Why why why so quiet? All we want is your rights." Again there are the people on the balconies, watching us, but now mostly impassive. The street tries to carry on with its life.

After the Cathedral and by Ein Shams University Hospital, we park. We load bags with water bottles and join the march through Abbaseyya. We walk. Maybe four hundred meters or so, and suddenly we concertina into the people ahead of us, and the cry is coming from the front: "El-geish el-geish"—the army has closed off the road. We're at a dead end. We all press forward anyway to see the army. At the bottom of the access road to the airport overpass, the road is blocked off with thick coils of barbed wire, and behind the wire there are three lines of Military Police, each man cradling a gun. Behind the men there are the tanks. To our right there are people's houses and one narrow lane passing between them; to our left, the iron railings of al-Fat7 Mosque, then the grounds of the University Hospital—at the other end of which we'd parked. The mosque has closed its gates, and a line of soldiers is deployed inside its railings. An imam is holding on to the gate and remonstrating ferociously with the soldiers. People say he's the imam of the mosque and has somehow been locked out. We've come to a stop but there's that seething milling about when a crowd can't get to where it wants to get. The shabab at the front are nose to nose with the soldiers across the barbed wire. It's a standoff, and we don't know what to do. I think a lot of the shabab are actually willing, now, to take on the army. But we won't let them. We chant: "The army's ours / The council's not."

This morning SCAF issued Statement Number 69. It accused one of the most active movements of the shabab, the 6 April Movement,[1] of "special agendas" and of trying to make trouble between the people and the army. SCAF denied that the military used violence in Suez or any other city and urged "The People" to confront this "suspicious plot to destabilize Egypt . . . with all strength." And General Hasan al-Ruweini, the commander of the Central District, i.e., Cairo, who had just boasted that he'd started several rumors in Tahrir during the eighteen days, has warned on TV that "the people from Tahrir will be coming into Abbaseyya from three directions armed with weapons and Molotov cocktails." So the citizens of Abbaseyya are waiting for us, and they're expecting trouble, and because the army has closed the road and we can't move forward, they fear that we will start a sit-in on their doorstep. They stand in windows and on balconies watching us. We stand in the streets and chant: "Friends and neighbors / Abbaseyya / Our protest is selmeyya." But the feeling around us is not positive.

The first stones come from a group of men who've emerged from beside the army line. Then they come from balconies and roofs. The men on the roofs are in string vests. We can't really look up because the stones are flying at us. After the first shock, our young men start to pick up stones and hurl them back. At first some of us rush up and disarm them. "Selmeyya! Selmeyya!" we shout again and again—peaceful, peaceful. But very soon, as the rain of stones gets thicker, and as the stones start to come from the side street as well, it isn't possible to stop the shabab. A mother holds on to her son, who's trying to break free and run to the front lines. He's about ten or eleven. Quickly we're four adults holding him back: *Stay here and be a man. Protect your mother!* A car on the side street bursts into flames. People retreat from their balconies and close their shutters.

I watch our shabab surge toward the mouth of the side street. Leaders try to stop them: defending our position on the main road is one thing, but pursuing people into a neighborhood is another. The buildings are now completely shuttered. All the fighting is in the side street, and it rages on. The army stands behind its barbed wire, cradling its guns and watching. Two young men run out of the side street carrying a third with blood on his face. They run past me, away from the army lines, about thirty meters along, and lay the boy down by the side of the road. Almost immediately a young woman bends over him: a doctor.

A stone lands by my feet. I pick it up. It's not a stone but a chunk of thick ceramic tile. When I hold it in my hand, feel its weight, its jagged edge, I suddenly feel what its impact would have been on my head. I suddenly, for the first time, feel vulnerable, recognize that I'm standing in the middle of the road with tiles and stones hurtling round me. I start to move, but that seems worse, like I'll actually run into one of them. I stop. I'm uncertain.

Then I feel two hands take hold of me; one presses my head down, and the other holds my arm above the elbow. A familiar rasping voice I'd heard often in the Midan says, "Keep your head down, *ya doktora*. Bend." His hands propel me forward, and I feel my speed double with the energy of the friend who's pushing me to safety. I think, This is like planes refueling in midair. I stay under the tree where he's put me and watch the street. Sometimes I see Omar. Sometimes I see Alaa or Mona or Sherif or other friends. Laila is at the front near the army, where a line of young men stand glaring at the soldiers, taunting them. Stones land and skitter on the asphalt. Young men run backward and forward carrying other young men and sometimes women. Sometimes a stone catches one of the young men, and he staggers as he carries his wounded comrade to the makeshift emergency clinic at the side of the road. There are two doctors there now and a crowd around them, fanning the boys who lie on the ground, pouring water over them, trying to call in ambulances and medical supplies over the phone.

I sit on the curb under the tree. I don't know what this is about. SCAF is officially meant to be preserving order and running the country—never mind protecting the revolution—so what's its problem with receiving a set of demands? What's the worst thing we could have done? Chant in front of the Ministry of Defense. Why the baltagis and the stones? Since when does the army use baltagis and stones? This is a disaster; people are getting hurt. And we're losing neighborhood support. I grab Alaa for a second as he passes. He says we put out the car fire. They're telling us it's the army on the roofs, not the locals.

The mosque has opened its gates, and the imam has gone inside. Sherif and other people come to my curb. There's talk of retreat, of pulling the shabab back from the side street and marching together back to Tahrir. Then people come running up from the rear: we're surrounded; there are Central Security Forces, and they're blocking the road we came from. We all run down to look. Central Security is meant to have been disbanded, but here they are: the black-uniformed phalanxes, the helmets, the visors, the shields. And behind them the muscled toughs in civilian clothes. I watch the first Molotov cocktail crash out from behind their lines.

Word of the Central Security trap behind us has reached the shabab facing the army. Their chants rise to a roar, and they grab the barbed wire and start shaking it. The soldiers raise their guns, and I run up so close that I can see the anger in their eyes—anger and threat. I'm struck with fear for the young men. I think the soldiers would like to shoot them. Then my sister steps forward out of nowhere and with her two older women, one with a hijab and one without. They shove several young men out of the way, and they're standing in front of the soldiers with their arms spread wide. "Shoot us then," they say to the soldiers. "Shoot the women. Shoot the mothers of Egypt. Shoot your mothers."

The shabab are running out of the side street and racing down the road to face up to Central Security. It's gone dark. Stones, stones and Molotovs, and then the tear gas explodes in the middle of the road. Alaa runs past me, and I grab hold of him again. I daren't speak to Omar, but I can speak to my nephew: "*Habibi*, this is about nothing. Nothing. What's to win?" Sherif is checking a way through the hospital grounds. We have to leave. We can't leave. But this isn't Tahrir; this is about nothing. "I know," he says. "But we can't leave while one person stays. It's okay. We're trying to collect people." I don't believe him. I believe that it's become a point of principle: if Central Security or the baltagis attack the shabab, the shabab have to win. They can't afford to lose a battle. But what if someone dies? What about the boys lying in the road? What if one of them dies?

Sherif says stones are being pitched from inside the hospital grounds; the baltagis are in there. The mosque's loudspeaker bursts into life. The imam is pleading for peace. He demands that the army protect the shabab from Central Security and the baltagis, that they open a path for people to leave. There's an ambulance now in the middle of the road. One half of a young man is hanging out of it, and several young men are strewn on the ground by the wheels; their comrades lean over them, fan them, stuff clothes under their heads. The imam calls for prayers, and miraculously all is quiet for the duration of evening prayers. Then the gas comes again. The imam pleads angrily through the loudspeaker with the army: "Open a path. Open a path for the shabab. Let them pass in safety. . . ."

It's dark, and the air is smoke and gas. From the army side, there's silence. From the Central Security side, there's a constant roar and flames and the pop of gas canisters. From the mosque, the exhortations continue. I'm sitting on the ground by the ambulance. My scarf is over my nose and mouth, and I'm pulling in shallow burning breaths. I don't know where anyone is. I can no longer open my eyes.

Omar has his arm round my shoulders and is rushing me through the alley that's been opened by the mosque. Inside the circle of his arm, I run with my eyes closed. What breath I have I use to curse. He conserves his.

9:00 P.M.

Back at the sit-in at Tahrir, we're subdued and angry.

One of our friends is missing. His brother says he was taken by baltagis. Many people have been injured. Two are critical. One of them, Muhammad Muhsin Mustafa, a twenty-three-year-old activist from Aswan, will die of his injuries on 3 August.

Everyone swears the sit-in will continue. Everyone is coughing and exhausted. We know now that the Central Security Forces are back and that the army is working with them and with the baltagis. On the news, they're saying we went to Abbaseyya armed with Molotovs and attacked the army. The *10pm Show* calls me, and down the phone I give my account of what happened.

11:00 P.M.

At home I find a mountain of laundry on the kitchen floor. Shukri, who used to be my mother's driver and right hand and is now Sohair's, has brought down all the linen and towels and cushion covers from my mother's summer house on the coast. They need laundering. He's had the house sprayed against flying insects and checked the electricity and plumbing. Normally we do all this in late May and get the house ready for use. My mother used to go up, and we'd all come and go till September. The laundry is in the middle of my floor. I put the first load into the machine. I don't know if any of us will go up at all this summer.

SUNDAY, 24 JULY

Rabab el-Mahdi phones with an initiative to pull together all the "revolutionary political forces" to cooperate for the protests called for Friday the twenty-ninth; it's the only way we can pressure SCAF. Rabab is a young academic and activist and special in that she's liked and trusted by the Islamists despite not being one herself. Friday will be to ensure we all speak with one voice, she says. *And about time, too,* I think. The leaders of the political forces are like cells gone mad; they swim around frantically, they divide, they coalesce with other cells, then divide again; they accuse each other of not being cells at all.

You could say that this is normal, healthy: people are working out what they believe in and stand for—and they're not used to working together politically because anyone who tried to work together politically over the last sixty years was destroyed. So the revolutionary forces are really doing what they're meant to do, and our society is engaged in a process that will take time.

But we don't have time. Because the remnants of the old regime are gathering strength.

So what do we want? We want to pressure SCAF for a timetable for the elections. And we want everybody to agree that the elections should be held soon, and for no one to give SCAF any excuses to delay them, and we want measures put in place to ensure that they're free and fair. Meanwhile we want to safeguard our world till the elections and to try to move on some procedures that would at least indicate that we're heading in the general direction of the revolution's goals. We could, for example, cut part of the fuel subsidy to the cement industry, bring down their profits to 50 percent, and use the seven billion annual saving to institute a 700-pounds-a-month minimum wage. I'm ashamed even to write down "700" when we know the real minimum wage should be 1,436 pounds a month. But there we are: this is a revolution that's chosen to work peaceably and legally—and it's paying a price for peace and legality.

But everyone absolutely has to speak with one voice. Rabab says she has the leaders from the Ikhwan, the Salafis, and the Liberals. We have the Left and the Progressives. Everyone has agreed that Ibrahim al-Moallem of Shorouk should host it—because he has a lot of power and has maintained the same friendly distance from every faction. And that I should moderate—because I've no power at all and have no relationship with any faction.

I make lots of phone calls for this initiative. Our great problem, our maximum vulnerability, is the rooted, knotty, gnarled suspicion between the Liberal and the Islamist political currents.[2] The Liberals will remind you that the Ikhwan had declared in January that they would not join the revolution, that the Salafis held that rising against a ruler was a sin and they would live pure lives without touching politics. But that was the leadership. The shabab had all come together in Tahrir. Through the eighteen days, Liberals, Progressives, Salafis, Ikhwan, Leftists, Gama3at, and those with no affiliation, just the desire for a better, cleaner, happier life, had rebelled together, broken bread together, talked to each other, slept in the same place, defended the Midan, and finally died together—and they had discovered the vastness of the common ground they shared and the myriad meeting points between them and how much work they needed—and wanted—to do together. Many had begun to change, and to note and welcome the changes in themselves and others as they found this ground. But Mubarak fell, and we all went home and the old leaders all started pulling their shabab back into line. Some couldn't go back and broke away—became, as it were, homeless in Tahrir. Some tried to form new groups, and some tried to form coalitions between groups, and some stood alone and spoke truth. Everyone was madly busy. No one had control of anything.

But I make the many phone calls anyway, and we set up the meeting for Tuesday.

And I manage to catch my younger son, Ismail, at home in London, for a few minutes on Skype and to make more inroads on the washing mountain before I fall asleep on the sofa, waking only when Omar comes home from Tahrir while the mosque is calling for dawn prayers. I stumble to bed and sleep till late. I think this is the aftermath of yesterday's events.

MONDAY, 25 JULY

Monday morning at the Gezira Club with my father and my sister, as usual. Mr. Muhammad Adel, one of my father's caregivers, has his right index finger in a big bandage. He is very ambitious and enterprising. His latest venture is a butcher shop. He put his finger in the mincer, and it cut off the tip.

My father is eighty-six. He still runs his research projects, his committees and his clinic, and teaches once a week. He does this through having lots of support and being extremely organized. For the last decade, he's also been writing monthly articles with titles like "Psychological Health in the Absence of Democracy." The revolution has straightened his back and pumped up his voice. He is advising the activists of his college about the upcoming university elections. I think he is—in an out-of-the-self kind of way—living the happiest days of his life.

When he leaves, Laila and I confer about the coalition meeting tomorrow.

3:00 P.M.

Forty-seven Ramses Street, to give a witness statement to TV channels about the events of Abbaseyya.

I meet the mother of military detainee Ahmad Gabir Mahmoud (detained and tried 3 February, sentenced 9 February, moved to el-Wadi el-Gedeed prison 17 February). He was picked up from Hamad Mosque in Faisal Street, not in Tahrir. Accused of throwing Molotov cocktails and breaking curfew. Sentenced to five years. He is nineteen years old. His friend Muhammad Amin Gamal: same case, same treatment. They are both at secondary school, agriculture. "They create criminal records for the shabab," his mother says. "They all had clean records before this. Now each one has a criminal record. Even sixteen-year-olds. Why are they doing this to us? I'm demanding justice for my son. We walked peaceably all the way from Tahrir to Abbaseyya to ask for justice. We broke nothing, we weren't disorderly. All I want is justice for my son."

There are at least eight thousand mothers like her—and that's not counting the mothers of the martyrs, the shuhada. . . .

The young woman speaking before I do is a tour guide who'd been detained in an armored personnel carrier. The military found twelve dollars on her and accused her of being a foreign agent. They ripped off her hijab and beat and tasered her inside the truck and eventually said they would "give her another chance" and let her go. She speaks very clearly and confidently. I cannot believe we are back to this.

All afternoon, phone calls about the meeting tomorrow.

8:30 P.M.

Meeting in Simmonds Café with Mr. Hasan Ali, Abu Muhab, the father of the shaheed, the martyr, Muhab Ali.[3] He has his daughter, Rahma, with him. She sits silently by her father, giving me small, encouraging smiles when I look at her. They are the saddest smiles I have ever seen. Her brother was her best friend, two years older than her. She's just sat her school finals. She hasn't done very well. Yes, we all agree it would be best for both the revolution and the families of the shuhada if the Tahrir sit-in is suspended—not called off, just suspended. Everybody's tired and the weather's so hot and there's no progress and ordinary people are getting annoyed at the closure of the Midan to traffic. The calls to escalate the sit-in are worrying. Decisions are not taken collectively; every group has leaders, but there's no joint leadership. But we need a strategy to suspend. The families won't leave with nothing. They're being harassed, and they want the men, the officers, harassing them, the officers who killed their children, put away.

Abu Muhab and his son were together in Tahrir. They left when the army went into the streets because, he said, he'd lived through the bread riots in January '77 and didn't want his son exposed to the military. They went home, and Muhab couldn't find his memory stick, so he took his hard drive to go to a friend and download material. He'd changed into joggers and flip-flops and just popped out to his friend's. There was a small local protest on the traffic island at the top of the road and he joined it, and there they shot him twice in the neck and he died.

Abu Muhab used to represent a pharmaceutical company. Since 28 January, he has dedicated himself to Muhab and the revolution. He says he was responsible for Muhab's politicization. I say we bring up our kids to do what's right. Beyond that I'm silent. I cannot—don't want to—imagine losing a son. He says, "God has honored Muhab with martyrdom and honored me with being his father. He died for the revolution, and I will live for the revolution."

Khaled Abd el-Hameed joins us. He's getting married in a week—to a young Palestinian woman named Tahrir! He too wants to suspend the sit-in, but he's worried about suspending on a promise. "At least let's try to get two concessions on paper," he says. We look at yesterday's demands. Abu Muhab gives me the names and stations of the officers accused by the families: in Marg, Embaba, Alexandria, and Matareyya. Abu Muhab says his greatest sorrow is not for his son, and not for all the martyrs; they live with God and prosper. His sorrow is for what's to come. He says ninety families have bought arms, and if they're not given satisfaction soon, they will use them. "They need something," he says. He says, "I don't know who killed my son, but some of them know who killed their children. And all of us know who's still terrorizing us and pressuring us; their names are right here. Arrest these officers. Put them away for their own safety pending trial."

I go home and hang out some more washing. More phone calls. Alaa is on ONTV. Waleed Tahtawi phones in to the program. He's the brother of Ibrahim Tahtawi, who was killed on the twenty-eighth. And of Hoda Tahtawi, who was shot on the twenty-eighth and died yesterday. He says he wants to understand why this is happening. Why his brother and sister had to die. How the person who killed them lives with himself. What he feels when he looks at his mother knowing what he's done to other people's mothers.

He says he has received offers of money and death threats to sign that his brother died of heart failure. He says he's had to sleep away from home for the last ten days because of the threats. He's being pressured not to submit his sister's body for an autopsy. It's difficult enough to take the decision to have Hoda's body cut up—but to be threatened and offered bribes to go back on the decision is too cruel. The worst of it, he says, is not what happened to us or what happened to the other families—the worst is what's to come.

Nahla Hetta calls me. Physician, activist, entrepreneur, she's a friend of Amr Helmy, the new minister of health, whom Prime Minister Essam Sharaf has delegated to deal with the revolutionaries and the families. Amr Helmy is a "people's choice." She's just met with him and given him the list of demands. He's going to try and push for them over a cabinet meeting scheduled for tomorrow and the day after. Then he'll meet her on Wednesday at five. She wants to take someone sensible from the shabab in Tahrir who will listen to what Helmy brings back from the meeting and whom we trust to evaluate his results and tell him what more is needed. "I am so tired," she says. "What must we do?"

TUESDAY, 26 JULY

Eleven a.m. meeting hosted by Ibrahim al-Moallem at Shorouk. We got everyone round a table, and we've hammered out a deal to issue a statement on the aims and demands of the revolution. There will be joint organization of Tahrir on Friday. The six officers whom the shuhada's families want arrested will be outed in the Midan. No statement will be made now on the sit-in, but they'll aim to suspend it—or at least open the Midan to traffic—from Saturday. The announcement will be made by the shuhada's families.

I wonder how many other groups are meeting like this. Trying to get people together, to push for unity. Tens. Hundreds maybe.

6:00 P.M.

We have a draft of the statement, but our work is foundering on the phrase *al-Irada al-Sha3beyya,* "the will of the people." The Liberals are adamant that the phrase has been co-opted by the Islamists, and they won't gather under it. The Ikhwan insist on it. The arguments get more and more detailed; they're to do with past experience and with what each group suspects of the other's intentions. The Liberals will not sign.

The committee coordinating on the ground seems happy working together despite the problems.

Where is all this tiredness coming from? Beyond seven o'clock, I drag myself around like a wounded creature.

WEDNESDAY, 27 JULY

Nahla calls to tell me she's met Amr Helmy with a delegation of families of the shuhada and the injured.

A Liberal friend phones and spends an hour telling me how the Islamists will double-cross us.

Abu Muhab calls and asks me to apologize to Nahla for the behavior of the families in the meeting with the new minister. I call Nahla, and she says they were concerned and upset but they'd behaved just fine. (In September, Mona will tweet about how the mother of a recently detained young man called her back to apologize if she'd been somewhat abrupt.)

Amal comes round with her tiny little baby, Amina. We put my mother's quilt on the living room floor and play with Amina. My brother comes round and joins us on the floor.

I finish the last lot of laundry for the coast and send it off to be ironed.

THURSDAY, 28 JULY

Wake up to a group e-mail from Laila repeating her testimony about Amr el-Beheiri, the young protester who was taken by the military in the small hours of 26 February minutes after she'd already saved him from them once. A military tribunal convicted him of possessing arms and sentenced him to five years.

Write and file my column. Use half of it for Laila's statement. Stay sitting at my mother's desk. I have cleared one drawer, the top left one. I cheated, because I just moved what was in it to the other drawers without looking. Now I reach and open another drawer, and there, lying on top of everything, is an old *London Review of Books* with two of Ian's poems. Two of my late husband, Ian Hamilton's, poems. I close the drawer.

I make, and receive, many phone calls about tomorrow. Everyone says it's all under control. It's looking good. We'll all be out there and prove we can work together, just like in the eighteen days.

6:00 P.M.

Sohair drops by for tea.

The ironing man delivers the linen.

Shukri is driving Sohair to Alexandria tomorrow so he'll go to the coast and drop it off.

9:30 P.M.

Cannot carry on. Shower and get ready for bed.

10:00 P.M.

I can't go to bed without checking on the Midan.

10:30 P.M.

The shabab guarding the entrance are three lines deep. They are courteous and welcoming as ever as they check my ID, my bag. Women pat me down.

Omar is rigging up his screen as he's been doing at ten o'clock every night since the sit-in began. He has three street-kid helpers, and a tea man has set up his stall near the screen. He and Khalid Abdalla, Tamer Said, and Ziyad Hawwas (part of the Mosireen[4] Collective) have established "Tahrir Cinema"[5] together with Lara Baladi. They've hand-built the large screen and borrowed equipment from home and family. Every night they show footage, clips, film from the revolution. From the first night, it became clear that the material was new to a lot of people: Cairenes had not seen the films from the provinces; people from other cities visiting Tahrir had never seen footage of the action to take the Midan, or the vast protests sweeping into the center from every part of the city. Within hours the cinema became an exchange point for material that volunteers quickly reproduced. Soon they were inviting guest curators to show their films or footage. A young Libyan came and showed a film. Tahrir Cinema was performing the function that the Egyptian state media had been too cowardly or too complicit to perform—even after 11 February. The cinema also helped stage TweetNadwa—the first nonvirtual meetings of the Egyptian Twitter community.[6]

Now the big handmade screen is up, and people are starting to gather and sit on the mats. I go for a walk and to check things out.

And I find something is different. We've always had posters of the shuhada. Now there are also images of "The Hated." I stand and stare at posters of the Mubarak family, of their associates who became symbols of corruption, of the artists who stood against the revolution in its early days. And I think how the delay, the unwillingness of SCAF, the ineffectualness of the older leadership, the failure of the shabab to come forward as one coherent unit—are all conspiring to push the spirit of Tahrir away from the miraculous and into the mundane. But the tents are all there, in the central garden with the absent plinth in the middle of the Midan, each tent bravely displaying its banner and its exhausted revolutionaries. Even at this hour, the weather is clammy and hot. People everywhere pick up conversations, mostly about what they think might happen tomorrow. I keep talking about unity and agreement and how all the "patriotic forces" have agreed to work together. Any tentative mention of suspending the sit-in or moving the tents to the side is referred immediately to the shuhada families; Tahrir has centered itself on the murdered and the wounded.

Mosireen's screen comes alive with the battle for Qasr el-Nil, the battle for Mansourah, and some new footage from Suez. Then we see footage from Saturday, from Abbaseyya. A young man in the audience tells how he went back next day, and people told him the men on the roofs had been soldiers who'd taken off their uniforms, and that baltagis and stones had been bused in from the Wayli district close by. Hundreds of people are watching; they sit on the ground, they stand in a great semicircle. An activist from Qena says people there have to see this material. Someone from Beheira says they need to see it, too. State media are telling people the revolution's succeeded and everything is fine and on course and needs to be left to the authorities. They're telling them that anyone still in Tahrir, anyone who hasn't quieted down and gone back to their pre-January lives, is a traitor or a baltagi or misled and will cause the downfall of the country. They're brainwashing people, they say, and people have grown tired and want to believe them. So the young cinemateers burn CDs on the spot and distribute them to whoever asks.

And as I write this, it occurs to me that the shabab, Omar and Tamer and Khalid, should have asked for donations, just one pound, whatever anyone could afford. The suspicion that there is "funding" for this revolution is taking hold. As the regime was pushing the lie in January and February, so SCAF and the state media are pushing it now. We must be careful of looking as though we think ten pounds is nothing.

I sit on the curb with my sister and Ahmad Seif watching the films. Ever since Omar and his friends set up this screen, I get a hint of that pleasant summer cinema feeling when I come to Tahrir at night. One day, when the revolution is safe, they can start showing the big classics. Revolutionary still, but structured, and of a satisfying length. *The Battle of Algiers*, perhaps, and *Z*, and *el-Ard*. For tonight we watch the footage, and we also watch coaches arrive from the provinces. Each coach delivers thirty or forty men, mostly in shortened white thobs and white skullcaps, mostly with beards and no mustaches. Salafis. They walk in orderly lines, find sheltered spots on the peripheries of the Midan, and lie down and sleep.

FRIDAY, 29 JULY, MORNING

Twitter is ablaze with news of Islamist banners going up, then being taken down. And then with news of Salafi phalanxes hitting the Midan.

Rabab calls and says Salafist banners went up, but the Ikhwan persuaded them to take them down. The joint organization is working.

Rabab calls again and says I must not go into the Midan on my own; the Ikhwan say they can no longer control the banners or the slogans. "Don't go in," she warns, "you may never come out. Come to Beano's by the American University—we're all there."

A friend phones and says that the Salafis have been going round the villages in tok-toks telling people an important thing is happening in Tahrir, and they're busing them in. ("Three pounds a ticket," I hear next day, "from any part of Egypt to Tahrir.") Whenever anyone describes people as "going around in tok-toks," I suspect them—perhaps unfairly—of classism, because tok-toks are the transport of the poor and the provincial.

I arrive in the area as Friday prayers are ending. I catch the Prayers for the Absent. They feel different. I can't quite put my finger on it, but it all feels more down to earth and practical. None of the emotion I'm used to on the Tahrir Fridays.

I enter the Midan from Muhammad Mahmoud Street, passing Beano's but electing to throw myself into the Midan and see what happens. I do not need protection to be in Tahrir.

Well, the crowding is like nothing I've ever been through before. In the fullest days of the Midan, when a woman needed to move through the crowd, there were always men who miraculously formed a human cordon that created a passage for her. Or there were lines of people on the move, and you took your place among them. Here it's like some terrible crush at a bus stop. A heaving and surging without getting anywhere. People behind trying to push past you. Men, it's true, try not to push you and try not to touch you, but it's hopeless. I am hemmed in with the crowd behind the platform on which Sheikh Safwat Hegazi is speaking. He stands on the massive stage with his mouth to a dozen microphones, and one minute he's shouting, "Muslim / Christian / One Hand," and the next minute he's shouting, "Lift your head up high / You're a Muslim."

The crowd surges this way and that, trying to move from behind the platform. Street traders who've pulled up their stands for prayer time are pushing them out again—against the mass of people, penning us against the platform. Men on the stage throw bottles of water into the crowd, but throw them so high and so far that I'm sure you'd be hurt if you were hit by one. A bottle just misses my head, and I cry out. Sheikh Safwat is screaming into the microphones; he praises the army and SCAF. I remember reading somewhere that in these crowd situations you should stop trying to walk; just make sure you don't sink and get trampled. Allow yourself to be carried by the crowd. I try. I had thrown a scarf over my head during prayers, and now it's been dragged off and is throttling me, and I can't raise my arms to loosen it from my neck or drag it back on to my head.

Sheikh Safwat is yelling in great triumph that *iftar* on 5 Ramadan, next Friday, will be in the Midan: "We shall break our fast in Tahrir! We shall pray the Tarawee7 in Tahrir!" He is practically sobbing with emotion: "Then they'll know who we are!" I don't understand what enemy territory he's capturing. People have always broken fast in Tahrir. Tarawee7 have always been prayed in Tahrir. Omar Makram Mosque, in the heart of Tahrir, is the funeral mosque of choice for Cairo. It's not like he's taking the believers to Jerusalem. To be fair, the crowd is not responding to his decibels with corresponding enthusiasm. And there, I've got it, the difference that's been eluding me between this Friday and all the others: it's as though these hundreds of thousands in Tahrir today are—kind of—tourists. I don't feel an energy coming from them, a wish to make something happen. Their purpose is to be here, and here they are. I feel their bodies pushing against me but not their will. But I see the Saudi flag flying in Midan el-Tahrir.

The knot of the crowd that I am in gets beyond the stage, and

I shove and shoulder and elbow my way out of the crowd and out of the Midan and into the mouth of Tahrir Street. It's still massively crowded, but there's room to walk of your own volition. Groups of men and families wander along the street. Many, many of the men are in the white thob and the white skullcap and the beard-but-no-moustache. I walk toward Midan Bab el-Louq. For the first time ever, I walk down this street and forget to even think about drinking a glass of carob juice at the shop on the corner. We used to come specially. Park and honk, and the guy would come out with the big glasses of light red-black liquid on a tray. Now I walk past the entrance to his shop and the street of the Mosque of the Servants of the Compassionate in a semidaze. Groups of people, mostly men, are drifting along the street, looking around like they've never been here before. I remind myself that this is their capital as well as mine.

My back hurts. I find a raised shop doorway and sit down. I might as well be in an alien city. Groups are making themselves comfortable on the pavements. They spread newspapers on the ground and serve food on them out of plastic bags. What conversations I hear are not political at all: he said, she said, money, family, detailed, personal . . . I lean against the shop window and wonder if somebody will ask me to leave.

My younger son rescues me; Ismail phones me from London and says, "Where are you exactly? What's it like?"

"It's their country, too," I say. I'm saved. I get up and dust myself down and describe it all to him as I walk away.

I walk to Sherif's place. He makes me tea, and we sit silently in his air-conditioned study staring out at Midan Abdeen.

2:00 P.M.

Nahla Hetta calls. Can I meet her in Amr Helmy's office now?

I walk up to the Ministry of Health. Helmy says there's been a decision that the Midan must be opened; the sit-in has to end.

Nahla and I tell him the shabab want to suspend, but they won't abandon the shuhada's families. The families are exhausted, but they say they're still being pressured and threatened to make them change their testimonies and drop their cases.

He says he's allocated Agouza Hospital to receive the injured, and he will put a wing there at the disposal of the families; if they suspend the sit-in, they can stay there. We say they really need to see some officers taken off the streets. We have their names.

He says this is serious: SCAF is determined to clear the Midan.

He also says he's looking for a young, revolutionary doctor to be in charge of the injured and the families at Agouza. I put him in touch with Hoda Yousri, the young doctor I'd met in Tahrir the night Mubarak didn't leave.

3:00 P.M.

Nahla's car smells of mangoes. It's just brought back a crop from their farm. Which reminds me that I have to go and collect our fruit as well, from my mother's little orchard, and check on the repairs to the roof. I should really go before Ramadan starts.

We sit in Café Riche, just off the Midan. Sooner or later everybody stops by Café Riche. At a long table in a side room, I see my brother and Ahmad Seif in a meeting with their Initiative to Restructure the Security System. Judge Ashraf al-Baroudi, the revolution's favorite for minister of the interior, is with them. Omar

is at another table with his group, and Sherif at yet another. Today
Tahrir is operating out of Café Riche. Nahla and I have meetings
with several people about the conditions for suspending the sit-in;
a compromise suggestion is to move the tents of activists who want
to stay and place them by the Mugamma3 near the tents of the
shuhada families. To consolidate and tighten the sit-in, vacate the
central garden and allow the Midan to open. Most people accept
that three weeks is long enough to close down the central *midan*
of the third largest city in the world, and that they need to take
account of the residents and business owners and shopkeepers of
the area who're getting fed up. This compromise would allow the
physical manifestation of solidarity with the shuhada families to
continue, keep a symbolic presence in the Midan, and undermine
the theory—fast becoming popular—that the Tahrir sit-in is
responsible for all our ills, from the Cairo traffic jams to the state
of the economy. At four o'clock we seem to have reached agreement, and we write a draft announcement. Abu Muhab goes to
have a final word with the families. We alert the newspapers and
phone ONTV, al-Jazeera, and al-Nil. Their crews arrive and set
up. Abu Muhab does not come back. We phone him, and he says
they're still in discussion. Time passes.

At six the Salafis pack up and get into their coaches. We're back
in possession of Tahrir. Some shabab put on plastic gloves and
start collecting the mountains of litter left behind. We find Abu
Muhab in the families' encampment near the Mugamma3. There
are no lights. People are standing in clusters, arguing, shouting.
Abu Muhab holds my arm, steadies me: it's dark and hot and the
ground is treacherous. Judge Baroudi appears and begs everyone
to understand the importance of unity, of working together. They
listen, then resume arguing. Strong voices argue for suspending.
Strong voices retort that the closure of the Midan is the only card
they have. I think people don't want to go home and pretend their
lives are normal when their kids are dead. They need to remain in

an "exceptional" state. A woman faints. A young man on crutches tells me he's one of the "injured." He says they're offering him ten thousand pounds. "And what happens to me when they're finished?" he asks. "I don't want money. I want a job." Abu Muhab gives me a folded sheet of paper. It's the draft announcement. Rejected. I phone the TV crews: we don't have an agreement. The sit-in will remain.

SUNDAY, 31 JULY

I steal three hours to go to the orchard. Osta Ashraf has laid palm branches down for the section of ceiling that's collapsed. I climb onto the roof to see his work from above. He urges me to walk on the branches, to jump up and down; the branches, he tells me, are stronger than steel. We're not using a teaspoon of cement in this work. It is so pure, so peaceful, up here that I don't want to come down. If I angle myself. I see nothing except a sea of palm trees. And just beyond them, the Pyramids.

When I leave, I'm loaded with mangoes, limes, mulukheyya, and mint.

MONDAY, 1 AUGUST/1 RAMADAN

I see the tweets at about one o'clock: "Tanks moving into Bab el-Louq. Must be heading for Tahrir."

"We have to open the Midan."

"We have to open the Midan now."

I phone Sherif. He's seen the armored personnel carriers rolling out of Abdeen and is on his way.

I get to Qasr el-Nil Bridge and run into the battalion arriving to control its mouth into Tahrir. They're maybe fifty men. They feel like army—tall and well built and disciplined—rather than police or Central Security, but they're in black. They're carrying long, rough wooden sticks. They're almost forcing cars to drive through Tahrir; they bang on cars that want to turn right at the end of the bridge and push them toward Tahrir—until a boss soldier says to let cars turn right if they want.

The Midan is a massive wreck, a giant tip. They've demolished our small city. Abbaseyya was the first cooperation between the military, the Dakhleyya, and the baltagis. Today is the tryout for the Anti-Riot Troops, the new name for Central Security.

On Saturday, in the burning midday sun, Nahla and I and Abu Muhab stood with ten young people, at an impasse, between the Midan and Amr Helmy's office in Parliament Street. The shabab said, "We can't leave as long as some families and some activists won't go; we can't abandon them."

"So don't abandon them. Move your tents closer to them, and open the Midan."

They wanted to but said there were a few who took a hard line and insisted that the closure should continue.

"Who are these few? Can we talk to them?"

They were mainly independents; they'd become responsible for manning the accesses to the Midan. Some were young activists who'd worked on various campaigns for months; others were new but had worked hard and contributed to protecting the Midan for the last three weeks.

"Please, would some of you—or, better still, the hard-liners—come and talk directly to Amr Helmy?"

They said that for the hard-liners, even that would be treachery. "Please help us maintain unity," they begged.

On Sunday we continued our failed shuttle diplomacy, crowning it with three unprofitable hours with the deputy public prosecutor.

Now the Midan is overrun with soldiers. It's like a scene in a film when an army's been through an enemy village: everything's razed to the ground; the military pass through, and the tents, the flags, the banners, the billboards—everything is transformed into rubbish. Military and Central Security (or, now, Anti-Riot) soldiers are on the move everywhere. Some civilians try to reason or object; some of the families try to go back to their positions; some of the passersby make a point of showing support for the soldiers. We see young men being pushed by soldiers toward tanks, and we see soldiers deliberately breaking up unresisting chairs and tables. Some of the "hard-liners" who'd prevented the shabab from opening the Midan are wearing the vests and headgear of the military over their civvies and chatting comfortably with the soldiers.

The Tahrir Cinema screen is on the ground, broken up by our army, the cables cut and tangled. I see the screen on the ground, then I see a child dragging a blanket behind him and crying. Then I see other children—children for whom the Midan had brokered a truce with their cruel lives and who'd found shelter in the central garden between the tents; the revolutionary shabab had held classes for anyone who wanted to learn to read or write, shared their food with them, and given them responsibilities: the children had spread mats and connected wires and held lights and cameras. All this in ruins now.

I spot Mona and Sherif and other friends on the Hardee's corner and join them. They've just got news of several activists detained by the military. We call our human rights lawyer friends and report what we've seen. A loud voice demands, "Who are these people? Are they Egyptian? Why are they using their phones?" There's something theatrical about the voice, but the atmosphere is suddenly tense. Mona says of course we're Egyptian.

"What are they doing?" voices shout. "Let's see the phones!" "Mind your own business! Move away!" Mona, Nazli and others are shouting back. We're actually scuffling, or being scuffled; somehow we're in a crowd, we're being pushed with shoulders and chests, we're pushing back.

A man looks at me and shouts: "What's this one? Look what she looks like!"

I'm taken by surprise. "Me?" I ask. "Yes, you. I heard you insulting." "Insulting who? Tell me, who did I insult?" I'm shouting at the top of my voice, but it's not carrying as I thought it would. I do it again, above the jostling and pushing and yelling: "Who did I insult?"

His eyes flicker, then he stares straight at me: "I heard you insult the Egyptian people. Yes, you. I'm here and I'm a witness against you—"

My focus narrows right down: I don't know, see, hear anything that's happening around me, it's just me and him: "Me? I insulted the Egyptian people, you son of a . . ." I hear my voice yelling and swearing, and I think I lunge at him. Then there's a military chest in my face and a body of soldiers between us, and the crowd and the military are hurrying us out of the square "for our own good" while we remonstrate: "But did you hear what they said? Did you hear—"

They pushed us gently. Gently out of the Midan. But the next day, when the families tried—not to camp, but just to break their Ramadan fast in the Midan, they were not so gentle.

TUESDAY, 2 AUGUST, MIDNIGHT

At Agouza Hospital, taking the testimony of Mustafa Mursi, sixty-two, veteran of the Egyptian army, father of the shaheed Muhammad Mursi, shot and killed in Marg.[7]

Mustafa Mursi is on a hospital trolley. His shirt is bloody. He refuses to take it off and says he will return to Tahrir wearing it.

He is accompanied by others from the shuhada's families. They confirm he was beaten by the army earlier tonight just after iftar.

Mr. Mursi has a cracked rib and collarbone and bruises to the head and legs, and dizziness. He is diabetic, suffers shortage of breath, and has shrapnel in his leg from service in the 1973 war. He speaks clearly but with frequent stops to catch his breath. He holds up the photograph of his son throughout the testimony.

I said [to the officer] we're going home, son. I was army too and I fought in '73. Swearing and cursing all of them. [Hitting me] on my head and on my chest till I collapsed. They took my son's photo from my chest and threw it on the ground and trod on it. I know them, the two officers. Army. One in camouflage, one in plain. I'll hunt them down. God willing. And I'll hunt down those who killed my son.

I was just saying to them that I am a man who—I am a man—I—my son. My son is now with the Just who never treats anyone unfairly. God forbade Himself injustice. He forbade Himself injustice, but the rulers of Egypt and the corrupt regime in Egypt is unjust. But God is with the downtrodden. I want to follow my son because he's with the Just. Up there. Here, in the world of Egypt, there's no respect for humanity, or for age. The revolution came to clean the land of Egypt. But we still have a corrupt regime. Field Marshal Tantawi—we pray that God forgives him. We pray that God may guide him to the right path. If they wanted to control the situation, two words would do it: *Arrest the officers who killed our children, and the snipers, and try them.* Egypt would straighten out, and the wheel would turn again. But they don't want to. Why? Because there's something in their hearts. Truly. I wish each one of them would sit with his conscience and with God and look into his heart. I hope they do it for the common good.

My heart won't cool until the people who killed our children are arrested. I'm not asking for any of that stuff—they're saying we'll give them this and that. What we have is enough. We lived under injustice and never harmed anyone and what God sent us was enough. But you see murderers and bribe-takers—my son, God knows, before he met God he knew Him well. He knew God. He's in the third year, Information Systems. His name is Muhammad Mustafa Muhammad Mursi. The Marg officers killed him and smashed his head. I'm over sixty now, and we've never harmed anyone. God knows I speak the truth. All we want is that the officers who killed our children are arrested.

The army took me by treachery. I was going home. General Ruweini, when we met him, he said we'll stand by you, yes, stay in your tents. And we'd just arrived at our pavement, and the army came and beat us and pulled down the tents on top of the shuhada's mothers who were preparing food to break the fast. They beat me with such cruelty and such stupidity that I got dizzy and fell. My chest is cracked from how hard they hit me. But God is present. God is here. With us.

OCTOBER 2011, AGAIN

For weeks through August, Central Security Forces occupied the central garden of the Midan. And in September we found out that the regime had been planning to sell Tahrir. They'd been planning to sell the central public space in our capital to a hotel chain, to a foreign hotel chain, because "Hosni Mubarak's government was worried about large gatherings and protests . . . in central Cairo."[8]

I'm not surprised because we knew that everything was up for sale: land, monuments, islands, lakes, beaches, people's homes, antiquities, stretches of the Nile, natural resources, people, sovereignty, national parks, human organs, gold mines, the wealth under the ground, the water in the river, the labor of the people—everything. And yet every time we come across a specific transaction, a specific target, we're gripped again by that surprised horror: They would sell *what*? And it's no use saying, "Well, but we knew they were venal beyond venality, treacherous beyond treachery"—you still feel your heart thump, and the pain in your stomach, and the shiver down your spine: They were going to sell *Tahrir*?

But they would do anything . . . one never really believes that, though, but they would, yes, they would. What could be worse than trying to provoke conflict, war, within the community? That's what the regime has been doing between Muslims and Christians for more than thirty years. And that's what we detect again in what happened in Maspero.

If I had been in Cairo, I would have been on that march on 9 October when thousands of Egyptian Christians and their Muslim comrades demanded the long-awaited "Unified Law for Houses of Worship." But I was in London and sat watching it on fragmented screens: setting off from Shubra, walking, chanting, the people within it, old and young, talking, even laughing. I felt the tension as it drew close to Maspero and then the great explosion of energy and noise and movement: the shooting, the armored personnel carriers zigzagging among the people, hitting them, running them over, dragging them along. I heard the anchor of Channel 25 screaming as the channel was attacked, while state TV tried to incite Muslim viewers with reports of soldiers killed and "Christians attacking the Egyptian army." Twenty-one civilians were killed that night, rising to twenty-eight later. And fourteen hundred wounded.

At my kitchen table, I followed Alaa's heartbroken tweets from the morgue: "Mina's body is here Mina my comrade I can't believe it," "We lost you as you fought for our country may your soul be safe Mina Danial my friend," "I went in and saw them 17 pure bodies and Mina shining in their midst how shall we ever forgive ourselves." But what Alaa and the shabab then did was remarkable: from the morgue of the Coptic Hospital, they took on the entire system. In the face of the priests pushing for a speedy burial and the hospital administration issuing death certificates from "natural causes," they persuaded the stricken families of the shuhada to demand that their children's bodies be cut open. Activist lawyers pressured the public prosecutor to order autopsies. They fetched—bodily—the coroner and his staff and persuaded them to carry out the autopsies in the presence of physicians—like Mona Mina—whom they trusted. And then they made them sit individually with the families and read and explain the reports to them. The hospital morgue had only three drawers, so all the while they treated the bodies of their comrades with ice and fans, and they treated the anger, grief, and suspicion of the families with tears and embraces and explanations.

Back in Cairo, I went to visit the wounded at the Coptic Hospital—and they told me again about Alaa and his friends, Mina's Muslim comrades, who made sure the Christian shuhada were not hastily buried with their blood unaccounted for.

And now Alaa is summoned by the military prosecutor to answer charges of "incitement and destruction."

I can hear Omar on the phone at the other end of the flat, on the balcony where my nanny, who could not read or write, told me stories and gave me lessons in narrative. It used to amuse me that Omar would be working there on a script. These days he works on material for the independent cinema he and his friends at Mosireen are planning to set up—but right now he and Mona are working to put everything to do with the No to Military Trials for Civilians campaign on one website.[9] Back in February, Mona created and spearheaded this campaign, and now she and Omar have their heads together over its papers, as they used to have them together over summer plans when they were younger.

Mona was always the good child, the one who laid the table and helped the smaller children. As a young scientist over the last year, we watched her care for her—"genes"? The things she was growing in the lab that she had to check on every three hours. Serious in her white coat and her spectacles, her hair bunched up, her earrings a gentle, time-keeping pendulum. And then there she was in the revolution—her effervescence stilled into seriousness. And now she peers into her laptop and answers her phone and the campaign in hand now is for her brother when he comes back from San Francisco. Our children.

For twenty years it was school year in England and holidays in Egypt. We would come back, and all the children would fall in together as though they'd never been apart. I built a *diwan* in the playroom, a wide bench that ran the four meters from wall to wall with a window behind it. I furnished it with a giant mattress and bright cushions, and they all gathered on it to talk and play and watch movies and eventually fall asleep in a tangle like a litter of kittens. They ran together in Ataba, in Zamalek, at my brother's and my mother's and the little orchard and the house on the coast. And the first question every grown-up arriving at one of the houses asked would be: "Where are the shabab?" Toufi fed them and embroidered their initials onto their school uniforms, my mother gave them books and listened to them, Lulie treated their cuts and colds, Laila helped with science and maths, Sohair was their confidante, and my brother and Ahmad Seif were the still reference points who made everything special by their presence. And every child had their personality and their role. Alaa was the Guru, who had a detailed and passionate opinion about everything. Omar Robert was the Lord of Games and quizzes and mischief. Mona was the Good Child and the Romantic. Salma

was the Organizer, the one who bought tickets and got the family
to things on time. Mariam was the Princess, born to be served.
Ismail Richard was the Healer; a smile or hug from him made the
world your friend again. And Sanaa (Laila's youngest daughter)
was the Dreamer, whose off-the-wall comments became family
lore. And now they're all working for the revolution. And tonight
Mona and Omar are preparing the campaign for Alaa and the
newspaper on their table headlines a statement by the Chief Judge
of the Military Judiciary: "It is illegal to demand that civilians not
be tried in military courts."

What is legal and what is not? The Supreme Council of the
Armed Forces, SCAF, makes up the rules as it goes along. The
right to protest is enshrined in law, it says. But protesters in front of
the Israeli embassy are brutalized and hauled off to military trial.
And every one of the incidents that have marked the last eight
months has registered a worsening of the relationship between the
people and the army.

〜〜〜〜

The big question for us now—the question to which you know the
answer and I don't—is, will we have the parliamentary elections
scheduled for 28 November? Many of us think the Maspero event
was meant to cause enough civil unrest to give SCAF an excuse to
declare martial law and postpone elections. It didn't work because
Muslims did not respond to the incitement from state radio and
television. Will it work next time? Will there be a next time?

"Not one of us is going to step back into the nightmare," I
wrote eight months ago. But the nightmare chases us, surprises us,
attacks us. So far we have beaten it back.

And the thought is starting to take hold that maybe even elections will not lead to where we want to go.

We are not alone. We were never alone; the feelings, the prayers, the messages that came pouring into Egypt from every place on earth during those eighteen days of Tahrir lodged in our minds and in our hearts and affirmed every minute what we knew already: that the freedom we sought was the freedom the people of the world wanted, for us and for themselves. And what has been happening across the planet since has confirmed and reconfirmed our belief. The first placards raised in Wisconsin, the street signs invented for the City of London, the words we hear from Tokyo to Wall Street, the chants in Oakland, California—all echo the call from Tahrir and Tunis: the people demand the fall of this—entire—regime.

6 october bridge

MASPERO

flyover

FIELD HOSPITAL

EGYPTIAN MUSEUM

Corniche

TAHRIR CINEMA

ARAB LEAGUE

ANDALUS GARDENS

qasr el nil bridge

OMAR MAKRAM

MOGAMMA

qasr el nini street

AV

patian

CENTRAL
CAIRO

250 YARDS

250 METERS

TALAAT
HARB

CAFE
RICHE

Tahrir street

FIELD
HOSPITAL

mohamed mahmoud st.

ABDEEN
PALACE

MINISTRY
OF
INTERIOR

st. street

LAZOGHLI

N

The Eighteen Days Resumed

1 FEBRUARY–12 FEBRUARY 2011

It's getting cold. But there's been an announcement that Mubarak will speak. We're hoping that he'll resign, and everyone wants to celebrate with everyone else when it happens. So we stay. We talk and walk and discuss and chant and shiver. They say he'll speak at 10:00, then 10:15, but it's 11:00 when he starts. There's no screen, but loudspeakers are rigged up to lampposts, and everyone quiets down. And we cannot believe what we hear. Hosni Mubarak has simply not understood what has happened. He talks of how some decent young people have been "led astray" and are being used by unnamed "political forces," of how we're "living together through these painful days." He's suddenly aware of everything that's wrong and pretends that his regime, which has been de-developing Egypt for thirty years and stealing the bread from our mouths, is now suddenly equipped to "respond to the demands of our young people." He's going to create jobs and respect the law and run clean elections and put the police at our service, and all he wants is a chance to end with honor his service to his country. The second he finishes the call rises stronger and more determined than ever: "Irhal! Irhal!"

2:00 A.M.

I want my mother. I am cold and shivery and I. Want. My. Mother. I cannot tell you how many people in the Midan have said to me, Can you imagine if your mother were alive today? How she would have enjoyed this? I want to ring the doorbell and find her in the living room surrounded by newspapers with the television on loud. I'll turn it down, get some food from the kitchen, and sit beside her and tell her everything that's happened. I want her to be astonished and amazed and indignant and tickled. I want her to interrupt and interject and laugh and question. I want to talk to her, and I want to see her face.

Every night as I've left the Midan, I've thought for a moment I was on my way to see her.

Many years ago, with her living in Cairo and me living in London and the telephone an open line between us, I realized that things I did, or things that happened, never became completely real to me until I had told them to her; until she knew them, too. And I so want her reality imprimatur, her seal, on everything that's happening, everything we're doing now.

Her last summer, 2007, I was sorting out her library while she lay on the sofa watching me, facing the French windows onto the balcony. And at one point I glanced at her, and she had this curious expression, like in a movie when people see a UFO. And I went over and took her shoulder: "Mama, Mama? What is it?" And she kind of shook herself and came back to me and said, wonderingly, "Do you know? I thought I saw a massive storm rolling toward us." She paused. "I'm worried about el-balad"; the country, Egypt.

My mother always had solutions. She always knew what people should do better than they knew it themselves—and told them so. But she was stumped by our condition.

She was worried for our world. And I was worried for her. Ever since I can remember, I've been terrified at the thought of the world without her. That summer she seemed different, less combative, gentler. She'd had mobility problems for a few years. And I think she decided it wasn't going to get better. And she was—loosening her hold. I asked her not to. I really did. And she said gently, "So should I be an old lady in a chair forever?" And

I said, "Yes. Yes. You've always done things for us, not for you. Do this for us." And she laughed and said, "Okay, okay, don't fuss." But I worried. I made her have a brain scan. I was utterly surprised when she submitted. It came out fine. I arranged for an old friend of hers, a psychiatrist, to come and visit. She was vivid and happy, and I'd swear there was a moment when they were flirting. But then they were both quiet, and after a bit he said, "What is it you're worried about? Are you worried about Mustafa [my father, who'd just been ill]?" She said no, he has excellent care—and we're all there for him. "Are you worried about yourself?" No, my children and grandchildren are all around me. "What then?" I'm worried, she said, about el-balad.

When she was six months pregnant with me, her mother told my father he had to make her walk a kilometer every day. The Church of St. Thérèse, la Rose de Lisieux, was half a kilometer from their home in Shubra. So every evening my mother and my father walked to St. Thérèse and back. She told me this when, many years later, my car broke down in front of the church, and I came back amazed at the hundreds of little notices of thanks, the gifts that had been left for the saint on the walls of her church by Muslims and Christians whom she'd healed. There was even one from my favorite singer, Abd el-Haleem. So that summer, when I had to go to Shubra to buy a noticeboard, I went into St. Thérèse and said a little prayer.

But my mother slipped away one night while I was in London. All it took her was fifteen minutes.

Just two weeks earlier I'd seen her and my two boys sharing the massive diwan in the living room, and Omar was reading to her, for a treat, her choice of poem. It was a toss-up between Pope and Byron, but she went for Pope. I used to be unable to gaze full-on at that image of her laughing and repeating choice phrases. Now, for some reason, I can do it. These days I see her constantly, look-ing surprised, looking delighted, looking up every time one of us walks into the room: "What's the news? Fein el-shabab? Where are the young people? What are they doing?" And I tell her: "Mama, you would be so proud of them, of your grandchildren, and of your students and the children of your students. Of all our young people. They are out there: and they are so many."

WEDNESDAY, 2 FEBRUARY

Aches and shivers. Sore ear, nose, and throat passage, and those nightmare suites of consecutive sneezes where you don't have a second to gasp for breath. By the time nine sneezes in crescendo have pumped the air out of me, I am collapsed on a chair in the hall, glad to be told to stay at home and do "media work" rather than go to the Midan.

I knew something was wrong as soon as I woke up. There were car horns. It had been so quiet and peaceful for the last few days that we'd started to see the bats once again flitting in and out of the fruit trees at dusk. And this wasn't even the normal noise of Cairo traffic; this was aggressive, patterned, and constant.

Out of my window I can see bands of people marching across 15 May Overpass, and I realize, even before I see the banners, that these are the "other lot," the pro-Mubaraks. My immediate thought is that they have a right to march. My second is that they're not actually freely expressing their opinion. They are regimented: each band of fifteen or twenty men (always men) accompanied by a honking car; even from this distance, they lack the civility, the friendliness of the protests: they carry sticks, they make provocative gestures at the street, they have obvious leaders, "stewards" even, marshaling and directing them. The banners they carry are the uniform, professional banners we've grown used to seeing at election time.

Why am I taken by surprise? Because we need to believe that

the whole country wants to get rid of the regime? Why am I dis-heartened? Because I thought the regime had vanished forever after the twenty-eighth and now it looks like it will fight back—and on the streets, which should now belong to the revolution? Because I'm ill?

I am ill. Layers of jumpers, woolly socks, and a hot-water bottle to hug. Boxes of tissues. But it doesn't feel right to just lie down and take it easy; we all have to be useful. The novel I've been working on (and off) for the last several years has gathered itself into a cold little knot in the corner of my mind: is my novel obso-lete? My characters, discussing the state of Egypt, the state of the world, acting, working, loving—are they dead? If I think about it, I'll be racked with guilt and self-blame that I did not finish it two, one, half a year ago, when I could have, and then it would have been part of what's happening now, it would have been part of the great turmoil of ideas and discussions that are taking place. But no-o-o-o, no: I procrastinated. I did a million other things when I could have, should have, been writing, and now my poor novel struggling to be born has been left behind, unrealized, unfinished, aborted, irrelevant, stillborn—okay, this is not what I should be thinking about. So work on PalFest instead. The Palestine Festival of Literature, my other baby that took me away from the novel these five years. This year's festival is due to happen in under ten weeks, and still the money is not in place. So, cough and sneeze and write to a potential funder. And cough and sneeze and write to another potential funder—

Omar calls from Tahrir to say that something's different. There are no civilians on the checkpoints, and the military are not searching people or bags or looking at IDs anymore.

I keep an eye on al-Jazeera as I try to work, and suddenly I realize that what I am seeing on the TV screen in the corner of my living room is a camel and horses galloping into Tahrir—yes, indeed: a camel with a colorful tasseled saddle and stirrups—a

Pyramid camel, in fact, decked out to attract tourists and to pose for photographs, and his bright tassels are tossing about, and the horses are prancing and dashing, and people are running and circling round them, and without taking my eyes off the screen, I try to call Omar, but I can't get through, so I call my sister, who has just got in from the airport where she was collecting Alaa, her son (named after my brother), and Manal, his wife, who are coming home from South Africa to join the revolution. She is so happy; I get her typical big laugh that doesn't end when she starts to speak but runs through her words so sometimes you have to ask her to repeat what she's saying—but this time she's so happy and there's so much background noise that she's shouting loud and clear: "It's okay, it's okay," she shouts and laughs. "They attacked us with horses and camels, but we've captured them, and the kids are having rides on them in the Midan, and everything's fine, and Alaa and Manal are with me."

My sister is a force of nature, a rebel child who became the backbone of the family, a brilliant mathematician who dedicated her professional life to saving her students, intellectually, morally and physically; a radical Romantic who has spread her sheltering wings over friends and family and brought up three children who've shone like comets in the skies of our revolution. Over the years, I've tagged along with her to protests—outside the central police station in Garden City, on the steps of the Journalists' Union, Downtown, at the Courthouse in Alexandria—always trying to edge nearer to the center, always cordoned off, blocked by Central Security that was always at least five times our number. I once asked whether she wasn't afraid. And the answer came back simply: no.

Once, on a protest near the university, one of her most brilliant students, fresh back from Britain with a Ph.D. earned in record time, was jostled and pushed, and his glasses were knocked off his face. He got down on the ground to find them, and a Central

Security soldier, smelling blood, moved in on him and Laila just hurled herself between her felled student scrabbling for his spectacles on the ground and the booted kick swinging for his head. "You animal!" she yelled at the helmeted, shielded, jackbooted soldier. "You animal! Have you any idea what that head is worth?" And later, laughing over coffee: "All the years and the effort I put into that boy, and the bastard was going to finish him off for me in a second!" My sister makes a personal investment in everything and everyone who crosses her path.

I nurse a fever, take lozenges with cortisone for my throat, try to write. Egyptian state TV is lying so shamefully, I cannot watch it. We should have taken Maspero on the twenty-ninth, I think for the hundredth time. I follow news on satellite channels and Twitter. The people who last night were listening to music in Tahrir and debating modes of government—my nieces and nephew, my son, their friends, and all the shabab and everyone who has come to the Midan because they want a better life for their country—will now be putting their bodies on the line—again. It's all they have. The Mubarak baltagi militias have sticks and stones, and swords and chains, and dogs and trucks. And the military stand by and do nothing. On the news, I can hear thousands of voices raised in the angry chant: "Wa7ed, etnein, / el-geish el-Masri fein?" One, two, / Army, where are you? And then again: "Selmeyya! Selmeyya!"

〃〃〃〃

Alaa, my nephew, was taken into administrative detention in 2006 for supporting the Egyptian judiciary's move for independence. The regime kept him for forty-five days. He was in Tora, the same jail that had held his father, Ahmad Seif, for five years in the early eighties for leftist political activism. My sister could not bear to visit him. She, so definite and loud and—*there*, she went quiet and blurred and lost. Our nanny, Dada Ziza, old, and wrinkled and losing her sight, berated her in her distress: "Are you happy now? Content? You brought him to this. Every day protests, protests and big talk. Now we've lost the boy because of you." And Laila didn't even answer. Until he came out of jail, no one could comfort her. Now he's back from his job in South Africa with Manal. The revolution is in full swing. Ahmad Seif is running the amazing team at the Hisham Mubarak Law Center (HMLC) and they're at the heart of the practical and legal support for the revolution. Mona is doing her brilliant lab work and her brilliant communications work. That just leaves Sanaa, seventeen, who lives in her head but who's also in the Midan with her friends: taking notes, collecting information. She still has her school finals to get through. Later tonight, she and her friends will take refuge from the fighting in an apartment high up above Tahrir. Over the hours they will transform into the editorial board of *el-Gurnal*, the first independent newspaper to come out of the Midan.

I call Omar, and he says the baltagis are attacking, and there are battles at three entrances to the Midan, and the shabab have formed defense lines. He says that they can see trucks driving up behind the attackers.

There is one useful side to all this: it will nip in the bud any sympathy that started up for Mubarak after the show we were treated to last night. Once again the regime displays its banality; unable to come up with any move that is decent or innovative, it resorts to its usual mix: last night it serves up a sentimental tearjerker, then it can't even wait for its possible effect but gets right back to obtuse brutality. It is its nature.

Mubarak's baltagi militias attack Tahrir from Qasr el-Nil Bridge in the west, from four streets on the eastern side, and from the main northern entrance that runs alongside the museum. The shabab's first act is to secure the Midan's entrance from Tahrir Street, to protect the little field hospital in the Mosque of the Servants of the Compassionate. The army makes sure to block off one street, Qasr el-Eini, which leads to the ministries and the Cabinet Office. Other than that, it stands aside.

All day long the baltagis swarm the entrances, and the shabab beat them back. Midan Tal3at Harb becomes the baltagi head-quarters for the day, and the whole of Downtown is the scene of running battles as the baltagis retreat from the entrances, regroup, and attack again. For several hours, the periphery of the Midan is a fierce battle zone, while in its heart children have rides on the captured horses and the Midan lives the life it's developed over the last four days. The Battle of the Camel: the same tactics that have been used against us, against every protester over the last five years, the same tactics used at the last elections to scare voters off the streets, have reappeared and with redoubled viciousness. This is the regime that promises to listen to the people and use the com-ing months to put in reforms.

Their next trick will be to say that the young people in Tahrir are "foreign" elements, that they have connections to "terrorism," that they've visited Afghanistan, that they want to destabilize Egypt. But by now the whole world knows what Ali-who-couldn't-speak always knew: that this regime lies as naturally as it breathes.

Omar calls, and I can hear the roar of chaos in the background, and he says, all bored and laconic: "Could you talk to this officer who's trying to take me away and tell him I'm Egyptian and I'm your son?"

"Yes," I say. "Hello?"

I hear a man's voice saying: "I'm not going to talk to anyone. I want you to come with me—"

And then Omar: "You said you'd talk to any relative who—"

"I'm not talking to anyone. I suspect you—"

"Hello! Hello!" I shout.

"We have been arguing for half an hour, and you finally said—"

"I'm an officer in the army, and I suspect you—"

"Hello! Talk to me!"

"Talk to my mother."

"And I suspect you—"

"Talk to ME! TALK TO ME!"

"It's okay. Leave it," my son says into the phone, and the line goes dead. I keep calling him back and getting unavailable.

〳〳〳〳

An hour later I call and get him. The noise in the background is intense. "What happened?" I shout.

"With what?"

"With the army?"

"It's okay, it's okay. I got rid of him. People helped."

7:00 P.M.

Channel 4 News' fixer calls and says they can't send the car they'd promised to take me to the studio because they can't accept responsibility for my safety.

The studio they're using is between the Ramses Hilton and the Radio and Television building, with the entrance in the alleyway running behind the Maspero Corniche. On a normal day it would be a twenty-minute walk from my house.

9:00 P.M.

I know it must seem strange to the garage chaps. I appear out of the darkness, and they have to move cars to clear a path for mine to leave. I apologize. The garage entrance has no gate, and so they've blocked it with a massive black SUV. It has to be moved for me to drive out and will have to be moved again for me to drive back in. I'm putting them to a lot of trouble. "Work," I say, and make a helpless little flutter with my hands. In other words: I am not a mad person driving out into the night in the middle of a blackout and a curfew on a whim.

And so I drive through two neighborhood checkpoints—they apologize for the inconvenience they're causing me, I thank them for the security they're providing—and on to 15 May Bridge. A man on the approach to the bridge taps on my window.

"There's trouble Downtown," he says. "Don't go."

"I have to," I say. "Work."

"Well," he says doubtfully, "take care."

/ / / /

From the bridge, I glance down at Maspero and see that the tanks are still in place around the R&T building. I pass my beloved derelict Khedivial Stables with the horses' heads, which seem even more weird and ghostly tonight. I'm asking myself if two minutes on the news in the UK is worth this. But that's not why I'm doing it, really. I'm doing it because I want to be closer to whatever's happening in Tahrir. And because I will not be stopped from moving around my own city. This is the route I used to walk with my nanny when I was eight. Before they put up this overpass. When we used to walk across Abu el-Ela Bridge to buy fresh chicken, and to buy salted fish for Shamm el-Neseem. And later with my friends to walk into town, to the shops and the movies. I miss the old iron bridge, and I hate this overpass, but I won't be made into a frightened stranger ten minutes from my home. I descend into Boulac.

The spookiest thing is the absence of people; how the streets are deserted. Cairo streets are never empty. There are always people walking, men sitting outside their shops, youths loitering, people spilling out of coffee shops and juice shops, gathered around food stalls. Even in the dead hours between three and five in the morning, there will be street cleaners and nightwatchmen and men sitting in the doorways of greengrocers' and bakeries and pharmacies that stay open all night. In winter, they're often huddled around a small fire in a brazier. First-time visitors to the city always think something extraordinary is happening, a fiesta perhaps, to bring all these people out onto the streets. Me, I've never been in an empty street except in London or Washington, D.C. Now the emptiness spooks me. I resist locking my car doors.

There's a barricade at the intersection with Gala2 Street. The young men guarding it look rougher than the ones back in Zamalek. Actually, I'm not sure whether they're Popular Committee or State Security in civvies or even baltagis. But I open the window and show my driver's license and ID, and they wave me through.

Boulac rose against the French in 1798. The French captured one of the leaders of the revolt, Mustafa el-Besheiti. They put down the revolt, shelled the neighborhood, and laid Boulac waste. Then they released el-Besheiti to the people, and the people killed him.

I pass the hospital where I was born and park just before the Ramses Hilton. There are three other cars. The man looking after them says it'll be ten pounds now because it's so dangerous. I don't know if he's the regular guy who parks cars or a baltagi; how can you tell? I'll assume everyone is a good person until I'm proved wrong. Not a hundred meters away, the battle rages. My sister and her children are there. My friends are there. My son is there. I'm sure he's balanced on something high so that he can get a good view for his camera.[1] I shut the image out and phone the fixer, and she says she'll come and get me and not to walk alone. I walk anyway and meet her and two young men, and they take me into the building down through the garage and up the back stairs because the normal entrance is locked and barricaded. Upstairs it's buzzing: several stations are broadcasting out of the flat, every studio is working, and—no big deal—many people have made it here.

Tomorrow the baltagis will arrive on the doorsteps of this and every studio in the neighborhood, and they'll give them a choice: close down, or we'll smash all your equipment. But tonight the studios are telling the world what's happening over there in the Midan.

And what's happening is one of the decisive battles of the revolution. The regime's forces have been pushed back from Qasr el-Nil and all the eastern entrances and now, at ten p.m., are concentrating their attack on this northern approach to Tahrir, the wide road that runs out of Midan Abd el-Menem Riyad and then is flanked on the east by the Franciscan School and some residential buildings, and on the west by the museum. And crossing over the road is a section of 6 October Overpass. The shabab have captured some baltagis, and their IDs showed them to be Central Security soldiers. Anyone they capture, they copy their ID, then turn him over to the military. Now the shabab have beaten the regime's force back from the road itself, but it's taken up position on the overpass—and it has men on the roof of one of the higher apartment blocks by the school. The shabab can see these people. What they can't see are the snipers positioned on the roofs of the museum and the Hilton. But from time to time, they spot a green laser beam shining into their lines. And they suspect that this means snipers.

From the overpass and from the roof, the regime hurls its usual missiles at the citizens: stones and shards of ceramic and marble, bottles and Molotov cocktails. Fireballs land in the midst of the crowd below. The shabab gain access to the roof of the next-door building. Stones and Molotovs are exchanged roof to roof, but the regime has the advantage: it has the higher roof. And on the overpass it is using ambulances and Central Security trucks and civilian minibuses to bring in new cargoes of fighters and ammunition.

The battle is fought across the statue of the shaheed Abd

el-Menem Riyad, the chief of staff of the Egyptian army during the War of Attrition with Israel. Riyad was killed by an Israeli shell, with his men, in Trench No. 6 by the Suez Canal, on 9 March 1969. "A leader's place is with his men," he had said, and now his face is turned toward the citizens defending the Midan.

The citizens have fallen into battle formation. Older people are the supply lines, and they tear the corrugated metal fencing from the mysterious building site next to them and the stones from the pavements. Runners pile the stones into blankets and run them to the front. The shabab on the front line pitch the stones and hold up a shielding wall of corrugated iron. They can't see past their shield so they follow the directions of a maestro standing farther back, high up on the burned-out shell of an armored personnel carrier. A few meters behind the front line, another line stands. These are the substitutes. When a "forward" falls, a substitute takes his place. And a few meters behind the substitutes are three lines of the next "forwards." At a signal, they will step in to give their friends a rest. In the middle of the lines, groups stand on the tops of upturned vehicles; they keep the flag flying and the information flowing. Rations of water and bread pile up. The first lot of crash helmets to be brought in is given to the young women paramedics and the women doctors and nurses giving emergency treatment behind the lines. Bad cases are rushed across the Midan to the field hospital in the Mosque of the Servants of the Compassionate. Anyone who's not busy drums. A loud, energetic, rhythmic drumming drumming drumming on the metal sheets. This is the sound of the citizens, the voice of the revolution. They keep it up all night long. It tells any approaching regime baltagi that the shabab are awake and waiting, and it helps to keep everybody going; it says we're here, we're here, we're undefeated.

On the twenty-fifth, the first day of the revolution, when the regime choked Tahrir with gas and attacked the first waves of protesters with truncheons and shotguns, people found refuge in residents' flats nearby. My friend Ghada Shahbandar eventually decided she would leave her refuge, and a young man volunteered to accompany her to her car. On the steps he told her he was a butcher and had looked at his knives that morning and considered. "But then," he said, "I reckoned we really wanted to keep it selmeyya, so I didn't bring any." He held her arm to run her to her car, and as they ran, he was taken. "I tried to hold him," she says, "but they took him. In Talʒat Harb Street. He was on the ground, and five men were kicking him. Baltagis." Every few meters, she said, there would be a group gathered around a fallen young man kicking his head in.

On the twenty-eighth the regime was taken by surprise. They had not expected to be so comprehensively beaten in Cairo, in Suez, in Alexandria. Now they've regrouped, and they're back. Not with official forces but with their paramilitary thug militias: the baltagis, and some of their soldiers and conscripts in baltagi-type clothing. Later we will discover that one of the organizers of today is the National Democratic Party member of Parliament for Nazlet el-Semman, the neighborhood at the foot of the Pyramids where many of the camelmen and horsemen live. He is also the owner of the massive Ceramica Cleopatra, from whose factory floors come the shards that are splitting our heads open.

The army could stop all this in a minute. It doesn't. At one point a sole officer fires his gun into the air.

I finish my broadcast and hesitate. The shivers and aches are worse. But the battle for Tahrir is taking place not a hundred meters from where I'm parked. Somewhere in there my nieces are manning communications with the outside world, my son is filming the battle. But to go in, I would have to somehow cross the battle line. I phone one last time: Is there anything any of you need? No. What should I do? Go home. Now.

Jon Snow walks me back to my car. How many ways can this government disgrace itself? Would they destroy the country rather than leave?

On Monday the seventh there will be a TV interview with Tarek Helmy, our top heart surgeon. He will say that he's not a revolutionary but had gone into Tahrir tonight because his son was in the sit-in and he wanted to see it for himself. He got caught in a fight between two groups of young men and stepped forward to talk them down. And, just as he thought he'd made peace, stones came flying from the back lines of one group. He shielded himself with a corrugated iron sheet and watched, and he said he had no doubt then who was on the side of right. He said one side fought with courage, and the other, where the peace-breaking stones had come from, was both brutal and cowardly. He said he'd phoned his hospital and asked for medical supplies. His son-in-law filled a car with everything you needed for a field hospital and drove it across Qasr el-Nil Bridge—and the baltagis stopped him and beat him up. They emptied the car. Till that point, he said, he'd thought, *Okay, they have their wounded, too.* But then, he said, they threw all the medical equipment, all the supplies, into the river. He knew then that he would not leave Tahrir till the revolution had been won.

I drive back. I take my time. The streets are dark, but I've gone out and done my thing, and the shabab are holding Tahrir. If we, the pro-democracy movement, win this battle, the spirit that inspires Tahrir will pervade the country. In the Midan, every shade of the political spectrum is represented. The Left is here, and the Liberals. The Muslim Brotherhood, the Gama3at Islameyya, and the Salafis are officially not joining, but their shabab have rebelled, and they're with us, too, making up an estimated 10 percent of the people in the Midan. Our society is rich and complex and varied, and we revel in it. The people here are so way ahead of their government. If you could see the kids on the street telling you that the regime wants to pin the responsibility for this movement on the Islamists in order to scare the West. If you could see the small field hospitals with their volunteer doctors—mostly young women—and the medicines pouring in from well-wishers. If you could see the young men, with their jeans worn low and the tops of their colored boxers showing, form a human chain to protect what the people have gained over the last week in the streets of our country. If you could see my nieces hanging banners from balconies . . . you would know beyond a shadow of a doubt: Egypt deserves its place in the sun—out of the shadow of this brutal regime.

THURSDAY, 3 FEBRUARY

I've woken up much better, and the Internet's working, although it's slow. Our mobiles work, but we can't send messages. The only messages that come through are from SCAF, urging us to behave responsibly! Everyone phones to check up on everyone else. The grocer calls to ask if we need anything, and we ask for bread, milk, tea, eggs, biscuits, cheese. . . .

Lulie is staying with me. We have breakfast, read the papers. I slowly answer some e-mails. Then we get the phone call with the news about Ahmad Seif, Laila's husband, and I send out a last message before we leave the house:

DATE: THU, 3 FEB 2011 13:05:47

A good friend just saw 8 to 12 people being dragged out of No 1 Souq el-Tawfikeyya St and bundled into a civilian microbus while a military police vehicle waited near by. The people were being beaten and the street had been told they were "Iranian and Hamas agents come to destabilize Egypt" so the street was chanting against them. No 1 Souq

el-Tawfikeyya St is the home of the offices of the Hisham
Mubarak Legal Center, the Center for Social and Economic
Rights, and the 6th April Youth.

And, btw, my brother-in-law, the lawyer Ahmad Seif, *is*
the Legal Center.

Please get word out to as many news outlets as you can.

I call Ismail in London to make sure he's got the e-mail and will
get it out. I call my sister, and we arrange to go into the Midan
together, to meet by the Andalus Gardens. Then we head out.

As we park, we meet relatives and friends. Everyone walking to
Tahrir is carrying something: blankets, bottles of water, medical
supplies. Lots of us are taking mobile charge cards for the people
in the sit-in. As we get to the middle of the bridge, three men
come toward us, and we know straightaway they're not friends.
We automatically form into a tight unit. They're grabbing at the
blankets and the first aid bags and shouting that we have to be
searched, that these things have to be delivered to an "official station." We shout louder. In fact, we scream as we beat them off:
"Get away from us! Get away from us!" This is the first time I've
screamed in the street. We're holding on to our supplies and on
to each other, and we keep moving. My sister hits the man who's
trying to grab her bag. She has even less patience than usual today
because of Ahmad Seif and his comrades. We have no idea where
they've been taken. My sister says Ahmad had told her that if this
happened, we should not spend time looking for him but should
concentrate on holding Tahrir, on making the revolution work.[2]

The men snatch at our supplies and call us spies and whores.
Activists run forward from the Midan to help us, and we reach the
shabab's checkpoint, where they thoroughly and politely search
us: men by men, women by women. Two army soldiers stand by.
A young activist asks us to give the soldiers two blankets; he says

the men have been there for two days with no cover. The soldiers demur but eventually take the blankets.

In the Midan the mood is sober, determined, indignant. The disinformation, the smears being spread by the government, is hurting—perhaps more than the wounds and bruises so many people are carrying. That this regime should dare to say that the protesters are agents of Israel, Iran, and Hamas—suddenly able to put aside their differences and work together—beggars belief. This is what people are talking about. This, and the insult of being attacked by thugs on camels and horses, and that women leaving the Midan yesterday were roughed up, insulted, and robbed. And that there's no turning back.

I'm supposed to do a TV interview at 6:30. I phone the recording studio at 4 Gala2 Street, and they tell me they're closed. "They came round," they say, "with sticks. And threatened to smash everything up if we didn't close."

I go to look at the front line of yesterday's battle. The pavements are broken up, and the corrugated-metal sheets are stacked in case they're needed again. "Don't assume treachery, but be on your guard": men lie on the treads of the army tanks to prevent them moving. The regime's baltagis have been beaten back, but they're regrouping on the overpass. Lines of young men with linked arms protect the entrance to the Midan. The clinic that was set up when the baltagis were beaten back hums with activity. Doctors in white coats change dressings on wounds, take details. Two lawyers—in their legal court gowns—take statements. A woman sees me writing and comes up. "Write," she says, "write that my son is in there with the shabab. That we're fed up with what's been done to our country. Write that this regime divides Muslim from Christian and rich from poor. That it's become a country for the corrupt. That it's brought hunger to our door. Our young men are humiliated abroad while our country's bountiful. Be our voice abroad.

Tell them this is a national epic that will be taught in schools for generations to come. We've been in Tahrir since Friday, and the whole Midan was sparkling. Look what they've done to it! But look! Look at that microbus: twelve people on it at all times, and the banners never came down, and the flag never stopped waving. The army stopped the ambulances from coming in, but these young doctors—they sewed up the shabab on the pavement. My son, it took an hour to dig out the pellets from his legs. And then he went back in—" Everybody, everybody here has become an orator. We have found our voice.

The regime has rid itself of one of its central pillars: Habib el-Adli, the minister of the interior, is under house arrest. A new general takes over the ministry, and we get news that thirty-nine more people have been kidnapped. Among them seven of the young organizers of the revolution—kidnapped from the street after a meeting with Muhammad el-Baradei. A friend phones to say many Egyptian Christians have declared three days of fasting: fasting for victory.

My sister comes up with her friend and colleague Hani al-Hosseini. He has blood running down his face. He says he was detained by the military, who refused to believe he was a university professor and beat him up. He says they dragged him into the Egyptian Museum, and there are people there tied up and being beaten. We set about forming a delegation; we find two friends, MH and a surgeon, and our group of five walks up to the tanks by the museum and requests to speak to the officer in charge. A brigadier comes to talk to us. He's totally wooden and persistently denies that anything is going on in the museum. We give him an out by suggesting maybe it's going on without his knowledge. He doesn't like this. We say if he goes in and comes back and gives us his word that there's no one in there, we'll believe him and go away. He says he will, but he doesn't move. Eventually I make a little speech about dignity and iconic buildings and how shameful it is that the Egyptian army should be torturing people inside the Egyptian Museum. His jaw tightens, and he says: "They're not inside the museum; they're in the garden." We go and give statements to the lawyers in the field hospital.

Later we're to find out that the museum was, in fact, used as a holding station for detainees, and they were mistreated. Rami Essam, who became famous for his guitar-accompanied songs in Tahrir, had burns and stripes on his back from the hours he spent there. He was released, but many others went from the museum to military trials and are now in jail.

FRIDAY, 4 FEBRUARY

Morning, and I'm leaving for Tahrir. My family is already there. Omar phoned and said it's fine: the checkpoints are back up and everything's orderly.

It's become a tradition: Friday and Tuesday we get at least a million people out on the streets. Last Friday, the twenty-eighth, was the Day of Wrath, today is the Day of Departure—Mubarak's, we hope. It's also become a tradition that Friday (Muslim) prayers in Tahrir are followed by (Christian) Mass—with everybody joining in both sets of "Amens." This is the first time I am moved by a Friday sermon. Sheikh Mazhar Shaheen, the young imam of Omar Makram Mosque, speaks what's on people's minds and links our actions to spiritual values. He addresses his sermon to "Egyptians" and he speaks of "Christ's example." He ends by praying to God to "make us stand fast. Restore our rights. We want not war but peace. Bear witness that we love Egypt and hold the dust of this land dear. Restore our dignity. Unite us and let not our blood be spilled." Our great communal "Amens" roll through the Midan.

The questions that are being settled on the streets of Egypt are of concern to everyone. The paramount one is this: can a people's revolution that is determinedly democratic, grassroots, inclusive, and peaceable succeed?

4:00 P.M.

Delegations from many Egyptian cities and governorates are here. The regime has stopped the trains running, but people have got here anyway. The flags and banners of Alexandria, Assiut, Beheira, Herghada, Port Said, Qena, Sohag, Suez, and others are flying. The chant is "El-shar3eyya m'nel-Tahrir." Legitimacy comes from Tahrir.

8:00 P.M.

The baltagis have stayed in the side streets. The Midan is well defended and has provided all day—as in the other days of peace we've had—a space for debate. Many ideas for moving forward are being articulated and discussed. Older people are still hopeful of democracy, of clean elections, the representative government they've longed for all their lives. Some of the shabab argue that we're beyond—the world is beyond—the old forms of democracy; that for the last twenty years every movement with energy has come from outside the traditional frameworks; that the static structures of the nation-state and the fluid power of capital cannot coexist without leading to repression. What we have in Tahrir is the opposite of a vacuum; we have a bazaar of ideas on the ground. We are full of hope and ideas, and our gallant young people are guarding our periphery.

SATURDAY, 5 FEBRUARY

Rushing around. Word is that people are being snatched from the fringes of the Midan. Two young women activists were taken by baltagis, but they were freed by two army officers and taken to safety in an ambulance. Six activists have disappeared.

I wish I could stay in Tahrir all day. I'm doing so many interviews, I seem to be talking all the time. I'm tired of my voice. And I can hardly get it out anyway. Thank goodness there are no traffic rules and no traffic police anymore. I just drive the shortest way, park anyhow, run in and speak, then out and start all over again.

I get a transcript of our friend Maysara's testimony. He was snatched by baltagis in Tal3at Harb Street, but it was the military who beat him up—in the museum. And he was moved around other locations and beaten up—in an ambulance. He says they weren't all vicious, and he says they really think the revolution is being pushed by paid outside forces.

I also get a chronology, a history of our new vice president and longtime head of Intelligence, Omar Suleiman. It details his extensive, personal involvement in rendition and torture. The Midan, of course, knows everything: "No Mubarak, No Suleiman / No more agents for the *amrikan*."

There's no news yet of Ahmad Seif and his colleagues. Or rather, we know that they're detained by Military Intelligence, but that's all we know. While they were being taken, one of them left his mobile on, and a transcript has come out of what was heard. Again, the accusations were all of being spies and traitors: "If you walk out on the street now, the people will kill you: they know what you are."

I know that if I could go to the Midan for a bit, I would feel better and my spirits would rise. But I can't. I finish with the BBC Arabic and race home just ahead of the team that's coming to do an interview for an Indian TV channel.[3] I had suggested I could go to their hotel, but they said they'd been threatened and the hotel had been told not to let them film. I'm uncomfortable, but I welcome them in, and two minutes later my doorbell rings again. It's the concierge's daughter, and she wants to know who the two women are who just came up. I stare: "They're my guests." "This is your home," she says, "and you must do as you please. But the plainclothes have been round, they're asking who lives in each flat, and they're asking about foreigners and about media people, and we have to report to them if foreigners or media people come round. How long are your guests staying?" "They'll have their visit and leave," I say. I close the door, and I make tea. I call Omar, and he says we should sleep at my brother's. When the interview's over, I ask the two journalists to wait. I throw a few things into a bag and leave with them. This flat has been my home, on and off, since I was seven. Now I feel uncomfortable and alien in it.

The garage attendant has to move the SUV again. I apologize and say I hadn't meant to go out again; family emergency: I won't come back tonight. But then it's time for the *Democracy Now!* interview, and I no longer feel comfortable giving it while I drive; I feel I need to be alert to the street. I sit in the dark garage and talk to America for an hour.

TUESDAY, 8 FEBRUARY

There's a small, cracked, black and white photograph that shows my father's family deployed on one of the narrow terraced lawns of the Andalus Gardens. Something keeps bringing me back to this picture: my grandmother, in a demure dark coat, sits with her legs tucked under her, her two daughters one on either side of her. My small father, his hands in the pockets of his short trousers, stands a little apart, in that borderline aloof, slightly arrogant positioning that he is to maintain throughout his life. They were on that step over there, just across from where I'm sharing a sunny bench with Omar.

We're only here briefly, my son and I; a fleeting moment, captured when I said, as he walked me from my car to Tahrir, "Could we go in here for a moment? I don't think I've been since I was ten." "Sure," he said, glancing quickly at his mobile. We clasp our glasses of hot tea and share—though we shouldn't—a cigarette. A limestone Ahmad Shawqi, Prince of Poets, sits pensively to our right. The Nile runs behind us and the sun shines upon us, and we speak of concerts and screenings that could happen in this space. Because everything is possible now; such is our confidence. It's just a matter of time. Hours—perhaps.

For the last twenty years, my main feeling as I pass the Andalus Gardens has been dread; dread that one of the regime's intimates would be able to commandeer it and "develop" it as they've done with so much else in the country. I would search for telltale signs of impending brashness and be relieved to see the dusty old municipal noticeboard still in place. Today the dread has evaporated; suddenly I'm thinking what a great place this will be for music in our new, recovered city.

Omar is answering phone calls. If I get up from this bench and run down the nine steps that dip through this charming amphitheater, and through the narrow fountained rectangle at the bottom, and up another—maybe six—steps on the other side, I'll be right there where my grandmother sits, where my father stands. A cracked black and white photo. Since I was a child, I've been intrigued by it: there's the garden, so distinctive, familiar, unchanged, except that there also is my father, as small as me, a million years ago. Other pictures exist of my father in a Boy Scout uniform in the desert, or with his family posed against the Pyramids, or against a river backdrop. But these things were given, permanent parts of life; you knew you shared them with the whole world since the beginning of history. Is that it, then; that this small, urban, constructed, specific part of my neighborhood should be so unchanged, when change has so marked the four people photographed against it? My grandmother, Neina, old and strict ever since I knew her, and yet—here's a memory: I'm loitering behind her in the kitchen of the Abdeen flat while she whips up a treat for me at the cooker: *sadd el-hanak*, the "mouth-stopper"; flour and brown sugar fried quickly in butter and arranged in spoon-shaped petals on a china plate. I eat it on the small balcony where, angled sideways, I can see the palace that's also pictured in the schoolbook on the table in front of me. There are the iron railings, and behind them the low, far-flung building, and in between the railings and the palace, the courtyard—empty now, but in my book it's teeming with people: on the left stands the Khedive Tewfik, flanked by Sir Charles Cookson and Sir Auckland Colvin, on the right and facing him a melee of troops of the Egyptian army, on horseback and on foot. At their head stands Ahmad Orabi Bey in military uniform, in the act of sheathing his sword. The caption reads: "We are slaves to no one and will be inherited no longer." 1881. That's 120 years ago—and we're saying it again today.

EARLIER

I woke up to voices sounding as though they were with me in the room:

"The army'll stage a coup—"

"They don't need to. They'll wait and take it peeled and ready—"

"Suleiman is army—isn't Suleiman army?"

"Enough military; we've had a bellyful of military—"

"A parliamentary republic—"

"No, no. Egypt has to have a president—a leader—"

In Zamalek I'm on the sixth floor. Here, at my brother's, I'm on the second. In Wimbledon I sleep on the ground floor, but there's never anyone talking outside. Except if they're drunk in the middle of the night and the police come.

Bright sunlight. I get out of bed and look out the window: cigarette smoke rising, keys jingling, a group of men by the front door. I can't get over these open discussions of politics you hear everywhere now. Not just in the Midan but everywhere, the conversations you overhear are political: systems of government, education, public versus private ownership . . . what weight of repression was keeping all this down?

I glance into Mariam's room: a whirlwind of shoes, hairbrushes, tops, necklaces, on the floor, the bed, the chairs; ribbons hanging from mirrors, silver cups on bookcases, hundreds—well, tens—of medals, cups, trophies. Salma's is just the same, with a few extra Egyptian flags: you don't know whether you're backstage in a theater or in a club locker room.

〜〜〜〜

I like being at my brother's. Apart from having to stop by Zamalek to pick up clothes or papers—or hairbrushes or necklaces—I like being here; back in the heart of a noisy, argumentative, varied family with lots of friends in and out.

The living room has last night's tea glasses, chocolate wrappers, and orange peel. The cushions are still squashed and scattered from where we sat: my brother in his armchair, Sohair next to him in her upright with the back support, Omar—having inherited from Khalu the ability to simultaneously sleep and participate—stretched out full length on a commandeered sofa, the girls on floor cushions, me perched on the arm of a chair, near the exit, always only there for a minute and about to go and work.

Ahmad Seif and his colleagues from the Legal Center had been released unharmed, the shabab of the Popular Committee were on the barricades outside, my sister and Mona, Alaa and Sanaa were in Tahrir, and we watched heart surgeon Tarek Helmy's testimony about Wednesday's battle reel in anybody who hadn't already been captured by Wael Ghonim.

Ghonim had gone straight to the *10pm Show* TV studio after eleven days in detention, eleven days blindfolded and under interrogation. He looked haggard, and he was twitchy with tension. They'd snatched him from Tahrir on the twenty-eighth.[4] He spoke of how for eleven days his parents and wife hadn't known where he was. He cried and collected himself and spoke again. He hadn't wanted it known that he was the admin for the Khaled Said Facebook page, which had got people into the streets on the twenty-fifth. But he'd been outed now, and he had something to say. He started with the shuhada: "I want to say to all parents whose children have died—they are shuhada with God. I want to say we never thought we'd—even break anything, let alone kill a person." And when the anchor showed the images of Eslam Beker, Hussein Taha, Ahmad Ihab, Seifallah Mustafa, and Muhammad Abd el-Menem, he ended, in tears, with the shuhada: "To every mother and every father whose child has died: I swear it's not our doing. It's the doing of the people who held on to power and wouldn't let go."[5] Overcome and weeping, he stumbled off the set. But he'd done enough; he'd spoken with passion about the allegiance of the shabab to Egypt: "We are not traitors—we love Egypt. Don't treat us like we're being pushed by someone." He'd stated again the big aims of the revolution: to restore dignity and a sense of belonging to every person, to end corruption, and to run Egypt for the benefit of its citizens. He'd begged us to "put aside the past for a while and think what we'll look like in the future." And he'd restated what we all knew we needed: a new security apparatus, a new constitution, and a transitional government formed by the head of the Constitutional Court moving toward free and fair elections. He sounded like every young protester on the streets of Egypt; this was an authentic voice of the revolution arriving on the TV screen, and we knew it would carry to those who had started to lose heart and to those who, until now, had been unsure.

The day before, Sunday the sixth, the regime had sent out messages: state radio and TV pumped lies into the ether: drugs and "bad things" were happening in Tahrir, the economy was collapsing, the country was witnessing a total breakdown of law and order, the president had promised to consider all legitimate demands, and now the good shabab of Egypt were being led astray by infiltrators from Hamas, from Iran, from Israel, from America—and they were leading the country to its destruction. The new minister of the interior inspected the Central Security Forces barracks on TV and talked of redeploying them. State-run organizations resumed work, and banks opened. The message was, *Okay, we got the message: now, everything back to normal.*

So there's a call for another millioneyya today. I'll go to Tahrir for one o'clock. Meanwhile I'm producing copy and doing phone interviews at Sohair's dining room table. Everybody's gone to work, and Omar's gone to Tahrir. Um Nagla has arrived, and she's clearing up around me, practically dusting my keyboarding fingers, so I stop typing, and she tells me how people are worried because there's no police on the streets, so I remind her what the police on the streets used to do to people, and she agrees but she would still like police on the streets—good police. Well, that's one of the things this revolution is about: good police. And a fair chance for everybody. And health care, she says: her husband was as tall as the door and worked all his life, and when he fell ill, there was nothing. Except for good people who helped her—"yes, indeed." I'm on my soapbox: "Your husband. No health care, no cover. And how come you don't get a pension for all the years he worked? So God's given you health and you're able to go out to work. But what about people who can't work? What should they do? And your daughter, didn't she work in a textile factory? Six days a week, twelve hours a day, for thirty-five pounds a week? Tell me what you can buy for thirty-five pounds. And your son: he's working at a gas station. What do they pay him? Nothing. That's right. They give him access to drivers who'll maybe give him tips. You've tried to educate all your kids. Did they get an education? Is Ali staying on at school? No. Why? So what is a government for? Is it there to steal the bounty of this country, the sweat of its labor—"

"God will punish them," she assures me. "God is with you. Ali says the income of the Suez Canal alone would pay off all our debts. *Yalla*, I'll let you work." She escapes into the peace of the kitchen, and I hear the radio start up: *and I never knew . . . before today-ay . . . that eyes could betray . . . in this way . . . and I never knew . . .*

〃〃〃〃

Today will be critical. Yesterday Tora Cement and Suez Textiles came out on strike. We're hoping the "back to normal" strategy will backfire and that once people get back together in the workplace, they'll decide to join the revolution. My sister says the academics are going to march. And there will be others.

EARLY AFTERNOON

The entrances to the Midan have been narrowed even more. Sunday night the army tried to move its tanks a few meters into the Midan and fired into the air when people stopped it, and there's a rumor that last night, too, they tried to move. Now they're completely surrounded. People have spread mats and newspapers on the treads and are lying on and around them.

But once you're inside, the Midan is amazing. Even the light in here is different, the feel of the air. It's a cleaner world. Everything's sharper, you can see the leaves on the trees. Badly lopped, they're trying to grow out. Everyone is suddenly, miraculously, completely themselves. Everyone understands. We're all very gentle with each other, as though we're convalescing, dragged back from death's very door. Our selves are in our hands, precious, newly recovered, perhaps fragile; we know we must be careful of our own and of each other's.

The Midan is sparkling clean. The rubbish is piled neatly on the periphery, with notices on it saying NDP HEADQUARTERS. The fence of corrugated iron stands again around the mystery building site and screens newly constructed washrooms. Lampposts have put out wires so that laptops and mobiles can be charged. The field hospitals provide free medical care and advice for everyone. A placard reading BARBER OF THE REVOLUTION guides you to a free shave and a haircut. A giant transparent wall of plastic pockets has gone up. The shabab sit next to it. People tell them jokes, and they draw or write them and slot them into the pockets; a rising tide of jokes and cartoons. A Punch and Judy show is surrounded by laughing families. A man eats fire. There's face painting and music and street theater and a poetry stand.

On Sunday at Christian Mass and Muslim prayers, we all pray together for the young people the regime has been killing since 25 January—and before. Then, in the evening, there is Omar Suleiman: we watch the veteran intelligence boss interviewed by Christiane Amanpour. Earlier in the day he met with sections of the older "political leadership," including the Muslim Brotherhood. But he assures Amanpour that we, the people, don't yet have "the culture of democracy," that the "Islamic current" is pushing us, that the "other people who have their own agenda" are pushing us, that the Internet and social media have "facilitated" our young people "to talk all together but is not their idea [*sic*]; it comes from abroad."[6] Again he confirms: in the eyes of the regime, we simply cannot be self-propelled. The most we can be is a handcart, and anybody can throw their rubbish into us and trundle us along. The country falls on its back and kicks its legs in the air with laughter as he intones, yet again, for his American audience, that el-Baradei "has links" with the "Brother Muslimhoooood" and that "the Brother Muslimhoooood" are pushing us. Why, we ask, does he speak in English at all? Why don't these people respect themselves even if they don't respect us? We watch the old torturer, stiff with formality and self-belief, clinging to his simple conspiratorial concepts, holding himself rigid against the tide, the tsunami of us in the Midan and in the streets, his thumbscrews and cattle prods for the moment useless. When he says his message to us is "Go home. We want to have a normal life," the streets answer with one voice: "Mesh hanemshi / Enta temshi!" We're not going / You go home!

And then, in the Midan, there is a wedding, and then more music, and everywhere there are circles of people sitting on the ground talking, discussing; ideas flow from one group to the other, until the most popular find their way to one of the four microphones on the stages. I pause by one group, and they immediately invite me to sit. People introduce themselves before they speak. Three civil servants, a teacher, a house painter, two women who work in retail. They talk about what brought them to Tahrir. In the end, the house painter says, it comes down to one thing: a person needs freedom.

There's word that a cold is spreading; people have been sleeping out for twelve days. Everyone coming in brings vitamin C. A travel agent has emptied his office so that it can be used as a clinic. A call's gone out for tarpaulins. People go to check on the

Dakhleyya: the tanks that rescued it from the shabab are still protecting it. The police have locked themselves in and are to be seen
crowded behind their windows staring out into the street.

Tahrir is teeming, and people are still flooding in. There's an
excited buzz as news comes that a march of ten thousand workers is on its way. Laila phones: about five thousand academics are
coming along Qasr el-Eini Street; the army has taken down the
military barricades at the entrance to Parliament Street and made
them go through it and enter Tahrir from Muhammad Mahmoud
Street. I walk across to meet them. I've bought fresh mint from a
child in the street and brought it and biscuits into the Midan. The
courtliness with which people accept the offer of a biscuit! The
dignity with which the hungry try to decline! The bow! The hand
on the chest! We're all princes here, our manners are impeccable. I
walk through the crowd holding a spray of fresh mint in my hand,
and nobody thinks it strange; they smile and help themselves to a
sprig and hold it to their noses. People move between the different
stages and the different speakers, and people pose by the tanks,
and people kiss the soldiers. By the time I get across the Midan
to meet them, my sister and aunt are sitting on the curb at the
American University corner. A Salafi family sits next to us, and
we exchange cakes. My sister says she's going back to check on
Parliament Street because "we've left a couple of thousand people
to take it over."

Lulie and I sit side by side on the curb facing the Mugamma3
building. Lulie had a small medical "event" a few years ago, and
there's a slight drag to her left leg. She is, like all the women in
my family, gallant and raring to go—except her body's starting
to block her. My mother, to stop the war on Iraq, marched from
Charing Cross to Hyde Park in and out of her wheelchair, and I
saw the pain in Toufi's knees bring tears to her eyes as she insisted
on climbing yet another set of crumbly stairs to visit yet another

woman in the Productive Families project. Lulie and I give our bodies a short break on the uneven curb, and we're both thinking about Toufi because for us the Mugamma3 building, there, across the road, is Toufi.

That massive curve, like the beginning of an embrace; you step into it and into a different, darker universe: a huge lobby funnels upward into a massive galleried tunnel soaring up eleven floors and swirling with solid noise, its air heavy with thousands upon thousands of forms and applications and stories and desks and chairs and paper clips and complaints and carbon paper and filing cabinets and cupboards, crowds of people are in a permanent stampede crossing and recrossing the giant lobby trying to find the right staircase the right corridor the right lift and me with my hand in Toufi's waiting in line for the narrow lift that will, amazingly, carry eight people plus me uncounted up to the seventh floor and her office. All the government departments that deal with actual people are in this building, and Toufi works in Social Affairs but she doesn't really do her work in the office but out in the city.

Sitting on the curb, outside the building, I can feel the noise and bustle and jokes and ribbing of the crowded offices, people squeezing past each other to get to their desks, files files files everywhere, the hunt for someone's missing chair stolen by another office, the maps of the city on the walls as everyone in Outreach sets their routes for the day and yells at the "buffet" for their coffee and assembles their cases and finishes their paperwork. We'd always stop by the department boss; tall, gentle, graying Uncle Rashad, whose face I can, oddly, see very clearly as I write these words. He had a smile that only crinkled the lines around his mouth a little bit but filled his eyes. And his eyes and eyebrows were very black, like my grandfather's. He stooped, but maybe that was because I was so small. And everybody would disperse into the streets of Cairo: Tante Zeinab, plump and fair and red-haired and loud and always in the highest of slingbacks, Tante Kawthar, dark, green-eyed, and a little sad. And Toufi, with that swing to her cropped hair and her full skirt and me holding on to her hand. They dispersed into the streets to make good things happen. We walked through alleys too narrow for cars, and we came to the "sa7at sha3beyya"—the People's Spaces—and wherever we went, the kids and the staff were busy around her, and Toufi watched the boys play football and looked into the arts and crafts room and admired the woodwork or sat down to give a quick demonstration of hemming or a neat blanket stitch. She looked at papers in the admin office, and sometimes there was a small musical performance or a play. The high point of the year was the Sa7at Sha3beyya Exhibition, where the great Cairo stadium filled with the kids and their families. President Nasser attended these, and I remember one show ending with a young girl draped in the flag of Egypt holding up a torch while everyone sang around her. This must have been before February '58 because the flag was the green one with the crescent and stars.

My sister says that Nasser is all the proof anyone needs that the "benign dictator" scenario can never work. No one could have been cleaner than him, or more on the side of the disadvantaged, yet he set in motion the practices, the systems, that led, finally, to Mubarak's regime. Omar says, isn't "a girl draped in the flag of Egypt . . . etc." a typical fascist image? I say surely it's fascist only if you're powerful? We'd just got rid of the king in '52, the British in '54—and then were attacked by Britain, France, and Israel in '56. Can't we be allowed a girl in a flag?

Time passes, and I am in those narrow streets again, Toufi heavier now, her hair gathered under a gray bonnet, holding on to my arm over the extra bumpy bits or the bits where we have to balance on narrow ridges between stagnant puddles. We go through entrances and up stairs where we can't avoid brushing the walls with our shoulders even though we walk in single file, and we sit in tiny rooms taken over by the fabrics and the sewing machines that Toufi has, in part, come to see have not been sold or pawned.

Toufi knows the names of all the small children who come and
lean against her and knows which fathers, husbands are in work,
out of work, invalided, dead. She listens to the women and looks at
their hems and buttonholes and seams and makes sure the leaders
of the Productive Families project are delivering linen and thread
and collecting finished work and paying cash, and she sees which
women are ready to move on from sewing to cutting and who
wants to do a refresher course at the local center—which is where
we go next to check on the preparations for the Productive Families Bazaar: the current high point of the year. The bazaar is held
nationwide, but the main one is in Cairo and inaugurated by Mrs.
Mubarak, and by the time the ceremony's over, the best pieces
have all been reserved by Mrs. Mubarak's train of ladies in power,
to be collected by their drivers next day and never paid for. One
year Toufi quietly sold off the best pieces ahead of the bazaar—
some pieces went to foreign friends who willingly paid three times
the asking price, and the money went to the women in the narrow
rooms. And word came that if the project could not produce its
usual level of work, it would be closed down. So the Productive
Families limped along, with its well-wishers buying the indifferent
stock and the old-style leaders, Toufi, Tante Zeinab, etc., raising
and donating money to keep it afloat.

"Khalas," I say to Lulie, "no one's going to rob the Productive
Families anymore."

"My sister, *habibti*," she says, "this city used up layers of her.
Her legs, her soul."

We observe the Midan, heaving with bodies, with chants, with
flags, with freedom. But where I could see my mother wide-eyed
with wonder and delight, I could only see Toufi cautious, skepti-
cal, a little grim, to be honest. A kind of *this is all very well but
where's it leading?* "Come on, Toufi, it will lead to clean, honest,
transparent government—why not? We'll have clean elections. A

government that's accountable to the people, to Parliament . . ." I hear her typical phrase: "Let's hope so."

LATER

Tahrir has spread into Parliament Street. The Qasr el-Eini entrance to the street is a swarm of red berets as the Military Police, wrong-footed, move to block it again. People are streaming in from the bottom end of the street—reinforcements for the two thousand academics. A group of men get as far as the soldiers and sit down at their feet. One man, large, fiftyish, eases himself onto the tarmac, glances up at the soldiers, and comments good-humoredly: "Here we are. Maybe I've sat down on my grave."

Blankets and carrier bags of bread and dates and water are already being stacked by the Parliament walls. We watch the figures moving behind the windows of the Cabinet Office and the Ministry of Health. Two shabab start spraying graffiti on the wall of the Cabinet Office. A cleaner comes out and tells them he's going to have to stay up all night cleaning it. They apologize and put away the spray cans.

Lulie and I sit on the low wall and lean against the railings. Seventeen days from now, on 26 February, at this same spot, Laila and Mona will see Military Police dragging away a badly beaten young man. My sister will rescue the young man from the soldiers and put him in a car that will take him home. Mona wants to keep him till they can take him home themselves, but she's overruled; he's so unwell he's better off going now. Ten minutes later he's taken from the car, and this time it's not possible to save him. Amr el-Beheiri will be tried for "possessing arms" and be sentenced to five years in el-Wadi el-Gedeed prison in the Western Desert.

But today we sit and watch the street fill up. We hear the cheers of the Midan as the workers' march arrives, and they bring news that Lafarge Suez and Cairo Telecom have come out. And now all the diffused noises and shouts and bangs and cries of the street get sucked and unified into one song: the drumming clapping chanting of the Ultras. The White Knights of the Zamalek Football Club and the Ahlawi of the Ahli Football Club, the guys who were at the front of the marches on 25 January and broke the police and Central Security lines. It's always a party when they get to the Midan, and now they're here to seal the takeover of Parliament Street. They drum and swing and chant their way up the road just in time to surround the black limo driving out of the gates of the Cabinet Office. Nobody tries to stop it, but we drum it on its way. And now people sit and talk, and some of the shabab want to occupy the Parliament building, Magles el-Sha3b: "This is the People's Council and we are the People," but the dominant opinion is against breaking into anything. They discuss marching on Maspero, since we're all now aware of the harm that state radio and television is doing us—but again the dominant opinion is not to break into the building and not to push a confrontation with the army.

I look back now at the spectacle of us, us the people, in all our variety, picnicking, strolling, camping, chanting, on the street of the ministries between our Parliament and our Cabinet Office; my aunt and I and a few thousand people are outside the railings. It would be dead simple to go in and occupy them both. And it's not fear that holds us back. How can these shabab be afraid after their attempt on the Dakhleyya down the road—when for three days they surged against that Fortress of Evil facing bullets and gas? Or after Bloody Wednesday, when they defended the Midan against cavalry and Molotovs and snipers and militias? No, we the people were implementing a doctrine of minimum force, minimum destruction. This was a revolution that respected the law, that had at its heart the desire to reclaim the institutions of state, not to destroy them. It was very clear who its enemy was: the Dakhleyya and State Security and the National Democratic Party. Theirs were the buildings the revolution torched. Even the common soldiers of Central Security were spared—because they were conscripts.

Would we have ended up in a better place if we had been more violent?

When we leave the Midan, we walk through two lines of shabab clapping and drumming and encouraging us to sing along: "We'll come tomorrow / And bring our neighbors / We'll come tomorrow / And bring our friends."

On Qasr el-Nil Bridge there are stalls selling grilled sweet corn, cold drinks, peanuts. Soon there will be candyfloss and rice pudding.

Driving home, I find the barricades manned by army soldiers alongside the shabab of the Popular Committees. But the soldiers are, for the moment, wearing the armbands of the committees.

FRIDAY, 11 FEBRUARY, NOON

Osta Ashraf is waiting, as arranged, next to the mosque just after the Pyramid underpass. He'd gently reminded me that life doesn't stop just because there's a revolution: "May God strengthen you all. Our country could be so good if the people running it feared God," then "And are you not thinking of coming out to see the land for an hour or so?" The Land! The Land is the little orchard-cum-palm grove near the Pyramids that my mother bought maybe twenty years ago. It's only about half an acre, but with this being Egypt, Kemet, the Land of the Black Earth, it produces in abundance dates and mangoes, limes and melons, and whatever vegetables are in season. My mother bought it from Hagg Kamal, a retired schoolmaster, and he continued to look after it for her. She came out every Friday afternoon, and they would sit on the stone verandah and talk leftist politics, and he would tell her jokes. Soon after my mother died, at eighty, Hagg Kamal, who was eighty-five, had a stroke. To receive his condolences for my mother, I visited him at home, and six months later Ala, Laila, and I were all there again to offer condolences in turn to his widow and family.

So now my mother's children have to look after the Land, and now the little house on the Land needs fixing, and Osta Ashraf is fixing it for us, and that's why he and I are driving along Pyramid Avenue on this Friday noon after prayers. I know I'm getting old because as we drive, I'm wondering, yet again, at the changes; at how this urban sprawl has taken hold in the short space of my adulthood. I take care not to gaze out the window and say, "Imagine . . ." But it really did used to be green fields on either side, the fields that fed Cairo.

"He's not gone," Osta Ashraf says.

"No."

"People were devastated last night."

"Yes."

"What's he waiting for?"

Which is indeed the question everyone is asking.

〃〃〃

We had been so sure. Wednesday had brought a rolling wave of strikes: in Kafr el-Sheikh in the Delta, thousands had besieged the governor's office, the workers of PetroTrade and the Co-op and three other oil companies came out against Sameh Fahmi, the minister for petroleum and mineral resources, the Water and Sewage Workers of Cairo came out, and the Garbage Collectors. The boss of the National Union of Journalists—a regime man—was thrown out of his office, and the younger journalists of the government mouthpiece, *al-Ahram*, issued the supplement *el-Tahrir*, in support of the revolution. Everywhere people had scented freedom.

Spokespeople and committees had for days been going off to meet with SCAF to propose presidential councils and interim cabinets, and on Thursday SCAF had declared it was in a state of "permanent convention" to monitor developments and plan how to "safeguard the nation, its achievements and its ambitions." The camera, lingering over the generals in their wood-paneled meeting room with the flags and the flowers, seemed to be underlining the absence, for the first time, of the Supreme Commander of the Armed Forces: Hosni Mubarak.

From the afternoon on Thursday, everybody was heading for the Midan. We were certain: today would be it. Time passed and passed. The clock on the Arab League building said 8:30. The Midan, all geared up to celebrate, held its breath.

I'm in front of the "Artists for the Revolution" stage. Like the hundreds of thousands around me, I'm bouncing, waving. West el-Balad (Downtown) are pounding the floorboards. There's no room to dance because we're squashed so close together, but everyone's bobbing and swaying and singing along. The uplifted hand of Omar Makram's statue blesses us all, and so does the half-moon, farther up, nestling—truly—in the fronds of a palm tree. Tahrir is bubbling, bobbing—and so's the whole country. Maybe the whole world. We're waiting. I know my family's in the Midan—but so are a million people. I know we'll all find each other eventually.

Nine thirty, and nothing's happened.

Tomorrow we shall learn that while we, the people, were waiting in Tahrir, our soon-to-be-deposed president was on the phone to his friend, the former defense minister of Israel, Benjamin Ben-Eliezer. For twenty minutes he complained that America was abandoning him and prophesied that "civil unrest" would not stop in Egypt but would spread to the whole Middle East and the Gulf.[7]

A hand on my shoulder, and it's my brother Ala. I've no idea how he's found me, but I hang on to his arm, and we work our way through the crowd, and we find Sohair, and she and I sit on the curb facing Omar Makram. Someone brings us tea, and we clutch at the glasses, cup them, expose as much as we can of our palms to their warmth. Ala is standing with a group of friends who're discussing whether we're actually in the middle of a military coup and the revolution is about to be turned into a sideshow. We need a figure, or a group, to step forward and claim the revolution, in Tahrir and with Tahrir behind them. The one individual who could conceivably do this is el-Baradei, but when he came to Tahrir, he couldn't take it and had to leave after fifteen minutes. He doesn't like crowds. Alaa, my nephew, and many of the young people have for days been trying to put together coalitions, governments. Sometimes they've consulted us, and we've sat in the street forming cabinets. But we're in a catch-22 situation: there is no mechanism for Tahrir to select and mandate a group to talk to SCAF. So separate "leaderships" are taking it upon themselves to do it. And the talks are private, which means that anyone who talks to SCAF now automatically loses credibility with the Midan.

We wait on the curb. We walk. We join an arguing group. Three young women come and ask if I'm me; they've seen me on television and think I'm "clean." One is a doctor, Hoda Yousri, the other two are in the final year of school and want to be journalists. They live in Ma'adi, and they've been collecting files on the people who were killed there on the twenty-eighth. They want a good contact in the media. Hoda also wants a contact who will help her help the injured. They say more than twenty people have been killed in Ma'adi and that the police were particularly vicious and let criminals loose on the people and started using live ammunition straight off. They say there was a sniper stationed near the house used by the Israeli ambassador, and he killed anyone who came within range. The young women have been collecting information from families of the dead and injured. They say the area around Gumhureyya Street is full of posters of shuhada as though you were in Nablus or Bint Jbeil. We exchange phone numbers as cries rise from everywhere to "Hush! Hush!"

Hush.

And unbelievably, he does not go. And unbelievably, he has not understood. And quite believably, he cannot change his game. In our millions across the country, we listen to him patronize the shabab, "speaking to you as a father," assuring them that the blood of "your martyrs," the young people his police and his thugs have killed—more than three hundred, we think—has not been shed in vain, promising us that he'll move forward and fulfill legitimate demands—people start angry chants, but the Midan shushes them; we listen intently. He trots out the tired old "I will not be dictated to from abroad" trope, and we stare at each other in disbelief; this person who's been doing America and Israel's bidding for thirty years will not be dictated to from abroad! When he declares his determination to carry on "serving" his country, we erupt: "Don't you understand? *Irhal* means depart!" He promises dialogue, waffle, constitutional changes, waffle, he talks about team spirit and safeguarding the economy, and the crowd yells: "Thief!" When, twelve minutes in, he starts on the "I was once young like you" riff, a great collective groan goes up, and when he ends with delegating presidential powers to the vice president, we erupt.

The Midan is furious and in tears. What will it take? I write: "By choosing this path, Mubarak is deliberately pushing Egypt further into crisis. He is putting the army in a position where they will soon have to confront either the Egyptian people or the president and his Presidential Guard. He is also ensuring that by the time the revolution is victorious, the military will be in a far stronger position than when all this started. We are on the streets. There is no turning back." People are on the move. Crowds move

to Maspero but still besiege the Radio and Television building
rather than breaking into it. And others start the long trek to
Urouba Palace, Mubarak's Cairo home.

〳〳〳〳

"He still doesn't understand," I say to Osta Ashraf.

"He understands," he says. "He's just obstinate."

I call Laila for news. She says that people, millions of people,
people who've never come out before, are moving into the *midans*
of all the cities, that Tahrir is full.

"This regime would rather see the country ruined than let go,"
Osta Ashraf says. He gets out of the car to open the gates of the
Land.

When I'm here, I leave the world behind. For a while. Except I
keep thinking about my mother. Wishing I hadn't so often wrig-
gled out of coming here when she asked me. What had I done
with those few saved hours anyway? Wishing I'd done this refur-
bishment while she was alive. But she would not have let me. She
was opposed to spending money "unnecessarily." But maybe she
would. And she always liked what I did when I'd done it. Oddly,
very oddly, I'd refurbished our *madfan*, our burial house, just
months before she went. I'd wanted to do it for ages, but I'd been
afraid it would be a bad omen—as though I were expecting it to
receive someone. And then, when my father was in hospital for a
while, I had his whole flat decorated and all the furniture reuphol-
stered and restored for when he came home, and I thought that
was so life-affirming that I could afford to slip in the *madfan*. We
gave it a ceiling of pharaonic blue with a band of gold running
between it and the cream walls. We polished all the stone and
brick and marble and bought new plants and put fresh netting
on the windows. And five months later my mother was buried
there.

Osta Ashraf is holding the gate. He's always so neat and clipped and pressed, he could have stepped out of a fifties schoolbook. He wants me to decide how to align the floor tiles. The house is crooked, and whatever we do they'll look slightly off anyway. What I'd like to do is align them to the center and have them be off at the various walls. But the tiler says that can't be done, so I choose, haphazardly, a wall in the kitchen and say we'll align to that.

I go up the ladder to the roof and sit. The Pyramids are there, just beyond those trees. We used to come out to the Pyramids at least once a month. We'd run around in the desert, measure our height against the huge rocks of the lowest rung of the great Pyramid of Khufu, attempt a bit of climbing, and have tea in the King's Lodge. (The king, Farouk, had "lodges" at the Pyramids, Helwan, Fayyoum, all the beauty spots of Egypt, and the 1952 revolution turned them all into cafés for the people.) And always, always, we would stand at the edge of the plateau, looking down toward Cairo, and marveling at the definiteness of the line between the desert and the green valley; the line this little bit of an orchard is on; the line I'm standing on now.

I need to go to our *madfan*. I've not visited for a while. My mother, Toufi, Khalu, my grandfather and grandmother—all there. When Omar made his first film, *Maydoum*, he shot a scene in the *madfan*. They hung up white sheets to reflect the light and weighed them down on the roof with bricks. And a brick came loose and crashed onto his head. Forever now, in bright sunlight, superimposed on the marble sarcophagus of those whom I love but see no longer, I see my son, slowly crumpling to his knees, on his face a look—not of fear or of pain but of intense and interested surprise. Before the blood started making tracks down his face.

I climb down and discuss the roofing. We'll roof the house with dried palm branches. This will be the Big House, the playground and memory-former of the coming generation of our family. Amal,

Lulie's daughter, has given us Amina. Maybe Alaa and Manal will follow. And the others, too. Soon.

Hamed, who looks after the Land, makes me walk to the crumbling end wall. The neighbor children climb over it and steal the fruit. He wants me to rebuild it. I haven't the heart to tell him that the fruit he sends us is so plentiful that, even after it's distributed among the whole family, sometimes a few pieces will rot at the bottom of the fridge. I don't mind the children stealing it. I can't tell him that, though, so I say let's not do the wall just yet; enough expense doing the house.

We walk through the Land and pick juicy limes off a tree. Hamed shows me a palm that's collapsed. Why? Its time had come. "Look at the grace of God," Osta Ashraf says, "a palm tree, even when it rots and falls, will fall into a clear space so it hits nothing." Hamed agrees: "A palm tree will never cause harm."

4:00 P.M.

" 'Bye!"
  " 'Bye!"
  " 'Bye!"

The afternoon is a series of 'byes and doors slamming as Sohair, my brother, Salma, Mariam, and the assorted friends and family who've been in the house go off to Tahrir. I sit at Sohair's dining table and work on the copy that I'm to complete and file the minute Mubarak has spoken. Will he leave?

I am ready to go the minute I've filed. We've all perfected routines, routines and costumes born of five years' experience with baltagis and Central Security. Mine is cotton trousers with zipped pockets over leggings. Actually, the "cotton trousers" are the pants Egyptian farmers and laborers wear under their galabeyyas. They're wide and loose but with fitted cuffs. They have zipped pockets and drawstring waists, and they come in all sizes in beige, gray, navy, and white and sell for twenty-five Egyptian pounds. One pocket for my ID card, the other for cash and mobile, a shoulder bag for water, notepad, pens, scarf, and tissues. A tight T-shirt with a loose shirt on top and then a looser cardigan. The layered look—so if you're grabbed, you can shed clothing and not be naked. An elastic band for the hair, shades, cotton socks, and flat shoes, and you're ready for anything.

The phone keeps ringing. London, Montreal, Delhi, Dublin, the world wants to know how it feels to be in Tahrir, and I keep saying I don't know because I'm not there. But over a million people are.

I'm writing and pacing. Writing and hedging. Will it be a piece about how we're free? Or a piece about how we're waiting, holding on? Pacing and answering the phone. Keeping an eye on the TV. Tahrir is the center of the universe, and it's ten minutes away, and I'm not there. I go out onto the balcony. The street is deserted. The bats flit in and out of the mango trees. I write another paragraph. Pace and check my bag and pockets.

6:00 P.M.

It happens. A brief statement delivered by Omar Suleiman look-ing even deader than usual, with a scowling, heavyset man in the frame behind him: Hosni Mubarak has stepped aside; the armed forces are in control of the country. My heart is pounding, and my hands are freezing. I'm so—so full, I think I shall burst. I rush back to the table and look at what I've written. I can hardly read, but I know it won't do. I sit down, screw my eyes shut, and take several deep breaths. Then I start again:

"In Tahrir Square and on the streets of Egypt the people
have reclaimed their humanity. Now they will reclaim

their state. . . . As of this minute there is no embezzling
president, no extraordinary-rendition-facilitator
Vice-President, no corrupt Cabinet, no rigged Parliament,
no brutal emergency laws, no—regime! We have entered a
new phase. For two weeks the people have been chanting:
'The People! / The Army! / One Hand!' We will now work
to make this true in the most positive way possible: that
the army will guarantee peace and safety while we put in
place the civilian structures that will help us to articulate
how we want to run our country. . . . In Tahrir I had met
two women in the last stages of pregnancy. They were due
to give birth any day and they wanted to give birth in a free
Egypt. Now they can have their babies. . . . The world has
been watching this struggle between a tenacious, brutal and
corrupt government, using all the apparatus of the state,
and a great and varied body of citizens, armed with nothing
but words and music and legitimacy and hope. The support
of the world came through to us loud and clear, and what
has happened here over the last two weeks will give voice
and power to civilian citizens everywhere. . . . Our work
will begin now: to rebuild our country in as exemplary
a fashion as the one in which we've won it back. To
remember our young people who died that this night might
happen and to carry them forward with us into a future
good for us and good for our friends and good for the
world . . . Look at the streets of Egypt tonight; this is what
hope looks like." Press SEND.

I emerge from Mesa7a Street straight into a traffic jam in
Midan el-Gala2; everybody's trying to get to Tahrir. I sit with my
windows open to the drumming, the happiness. It's a party; joyful
cries ring out constantly, people are dancing and jumping up and
down on the traffic roundabout, dancing on the roofs of their cars,

handing out candy. A man walks around with a tray handing out wedding sherbet. Kids are climbing lampposts to wave their flags from the highest point possible. I call my sister, my father, Omar, Ismail, Lulie. I call Osta Ashraf: We've done it! We've done it! We've done it! We've done it! We only inch forward from time to time, but we don't mind.

You can hardly see the lions on Qasr el-Nil for the kids climbing onto them. All the mobiles are held high; everybody is being photographed in the moment. I'm part of the surge of happy humanity flowing across the bridge. Beneath us, our river, alight with sparkling lights, with fireworks, with song. Then, Tahrir.

You breathe deep when you get to Tahrir. A steady roar rises from it, and there are more fireworks, and a million flags are waving and banners fly: "No More Torture!" "Welcome to Tomorrow!" "Congratulations to the World!" And as I walk into the Midan, the song that welcomes me from every loudspeaker is Abd el-Haleem's 1962 "bel-Ahdan": *In our a-arms, in our a-arms, in our a-arms, in our arms our lovely country in our a-arms* . . . The last time I heard this song was in 2005, in the great auditorium of the Opera House, and the whole auditorium wept in desolation; now I see us all here: we're crying and laughing and jumping and hugging and singing, and then "Watani Habibi" comes on, the pan-Arab anthem that's been forbidden for decades, and everyone knows it by heart and roars along:

> *In Palestine and the rebellious south*
> *We'll bring back your freedom for you*

and more gently,

> *We're a nation that protects not threatens*
> *We're a nation that maintains not destroys*

and now the Ultras are circling the Midan, their energy like an electric current fizzing off the walls of the Arab League. "Everyone who loves Egypt / Come and help fix Egypt," off the Mugamma3 building, "We'll get married / We'll have kids," off the Egyptian Museum, "Lift your head up high, you're Egyp-tian. Lift your head up high, you're Egyp-tian. Lift your head up. . . ."

And in the center of the Midan a stillness. The pictures of the murdered. The shuhada. Sally Zahran, massive blows to the head, glances upward and smiles. Muhammad Abd el-Menem, shot in the head, his hair carefully gelled. Ali Muhsin, shot, carries a laughing toddler with a big blue sea behind him. Muhammad Bassiouny, shot, lies back with his two kids. Muhammad Emad holds his arms open wide and wears a LONDON T-shirt. Islam poses against the Nile. Ihab Muhammadi smiles, but his eyes are thoughtful . . . and more, 843 more. In the triumph and joy and uncertainty of the moment, they are the still center; the young people, the shabab, who walked into the Midan in peace, to save their country and to save us. Our future has been paid for with their lives. There is no turning back.

REVOLUTION II

Eighteen Days
Were Never Enough

OCTOBER 2012

Khaled Abd el-Fattah, Alaa and Manal's son, was not after all—born on 24 November. He was born on 6 December. In the pause between the battles of Muhammad Mahmoud Street and Parliament Street, our family acquired the second member of its new generation, my father his first great-grandchild. And our small corner of the revolution moved into Manal's fifth-floor hospital suite on Roda Island. Omar filmed the baby and the family, edited footage of Alaa in court, and uploaded. Mona typed and tweeted and phoned; the army had taken more prisoners in Muhammad Mahmoud, and the campaign against military trials for civilians was busier than ever. Sanaa worked on her newspaper and the Midan tasks that had fallen to her. The baby's two grandfathers gave media interviews. When Ahmad Seif held the baby, he told the TV cameras that he was going to start a campaign for his right to retire and spend his remaining time playing with his grandson. Laila said if there had to be interviews, they should be done outside, in the street.

The river here is the widest it gets in Cairo, wide and placid, and on this quiet street it's hard to look around and believe a revolution is taking place. Hard to believe the degree to which every space, every concept is being contested, being transformed. But step back into the bustle of our rooms, and it all starts up again. Manal's girlfriends and Khaled's two grandmothers are in and out of the inner room that's being kept quiet and separate for mother and baby. Occasionally Manal comes out to join us. Even in our loving midst and with Khaled in her arms, there's an aloneness about her. We show her the lobby filling with flowers and cards and wishes and chocolates and flags and miniature cardigans with

MY DAD'S A HERO knitted onto them. And Khaled's dad is still in jail.

Alaa, as I wrote back in October 2011, had been summoned by the military prosecutor to answer charges of "incitement and destruction." The summons had arrived at his home on Saturday October 22, while he was on his way to give a keynote speech at a software conference in San Francisco. He came home a week later and sat up late into the night with Manal and his sisters and parents discussing the courses of action open to him. When he presented himself at the military prosecutor's next morning with his father and twenty volunteer lawyers, Alaa had decided to take the most radical course: he told the prosecutor that he did not acknowledge the legitimacy of the court and would not submit to the investigation. Civilians should not be tried before military courts, he said. Also, since the military themselves were an accused party in the Maspero case, they could not bring the case, prosecute it, and judge it. The prosecutor jailed him pending trial. The lawyers argued that he had come back from abroad to stand before the court, that he had a known address and family, and that his wife was due to have their baby soon—he wasn't going to run away. But the military locked him up anyway. They locked him up for the maximum they could: fifteen days renewable.

Alaa had arrived at the Maspero protest after the killing stopped. And he had been in jail when both Muhammad Mahmoud and Parliament Street happened. When Ahmad Seif was asked—again on television—how he felt about his son being in jail, he said he was fine with it: "This way they can't gun him down on the street. I wish they'd take my daughters, too."

His daughters, Mona and Sanaa, were both beaten up by the military in the events of Parliament Street. With the stitches fresh in her head, Sanaa wondered on TV, "Why do they still do this? They drag the shabab away and beat them and the minute they let them go they're back in the protests. Don't they see that it's useless?"

Well, no they didn't. For a long time. Perhaps they still don't. Perhaps that's one of the characteristics of power: its belief in itself is unshakable. Or perhaps they have no option; if they are to prevail, to survive, they have to use violence. Maspero, we now see with hindsight, was one stop in a sustained military campaign that SCAF fought against the revolution.

It had started, though most of us didn't see it, on 28 January 2011, the Day of Wrath, when Salma, Mariam, and I, holding our ground with thousands of our fellow citizens at the Qasr el-Nil entrance to Tahrir, had heard the cry "The Army's here!" and rejoiced at the arrival of the red berets of the Military Police—an affirmation that the Ministry of the Interior was in retreat. But just along the Corniche, possibly just meters from us, a young student was being dragged from his car and beaten—by the military. They tasered him and cracked his head open and kept him in a military jail for sixteen days. And there were others, many others,[1] but, at that point, we had no channels of information to tell us what was happening. Then, on 2 February, at the Battle of the Camel, we watched the military block the approaches to government buildings and then stand by while the regime's baltagis attacked us. On the third we had the first intimation that they were using the Egyptian Museum as a detention center. On 11 February Mubarak stepped down, and General Muhsin al-Fangari read the famous SCAF statement promising to safeguard the revolution and—the icing on the cake—performed a military salute to the souls of our shuhada. Two weeks later Military Police attacked demonstrators in Tahrir with sticks and tasers. They apologized next day for the "unintended clashes between military police and revolutionaries" and promised it wouldn't happen again, but they had detained Amr el-Beheiri and nine others, and they tried and sentenced them to jail—the event that gave birth to the No to Military Trials for Civilians campaign. The military continued to fight the revolution; the places zoom by, the dates gather speed: on 9 March they attacked Tahrir and arrested a hundred people, among them eighteen young women who became the victims of the infamous "virginity tests." (One of the young women, Samira Ibrahim, later took them to court and became a national heroine.) On 9 April the army hit Tahrir again to retrieve fifty of its own officers who had joined the revolution. The officers were in the central garden, and the shabab formed cordons round them, but the army attacked heavily. Two people were killed, the officers were arrested, jailed, and subjected to a program of "re-education." Five of them remain in jail as I write. One, Muhammad Wadie, is a Special Operations commander, a demolition expert; he's also a guitarist and a poet and smuggles his work out of jail.[2] On we go: the Israeli embassy I on 15 May, the Balloon Theater on 28 June, Abbaseyya I on 23 July, Tahrir on 1 August, the Israeli embassy II on 9 September, the Ministry of Defense on 30 September, Maspero on 9 October, Muhammad Mahmoud on 19–24 November, Parliament Street on 16–22 December, Port Said on 1 February (2012), Mansour Street for the next few days, and Abbaseyya II in May.

These events mark the road that has taken us to where we are now: on the first anniversary of the Maspero massacre with thousands taking part in a march of remembrance, vowing not to forget and not to let go.

Now, in October 2012, Egypt has an elected president—who was the first and real choice of only 5 million out of an electorate of 52 million. We have no parliament because it's been dissolved. We have a committee writing the Constitution—but it too might be dissolved because it was elected by the dissolved parliament and, in any case, no one likes the draft articles it's floating. We have a judiciary that's been widely discredited, a police force that's furious and out of control, its long-standing baltagi militias unpaid and unhappy. And we have a political leadership that seems chronically dysfunctional.

Meanwhile the revolution is determined to push toward its declared aims: bread, freedom, social justice. It is also determined to establish its narrative of what happened from 25 January 2011 until the elections of June 2012 and beyond. And vital to both these aims is the need to hold on to the transformations that have taken place in our cities and in ourselves.

Across the country people's landscapes have been changed. In Cairo a new map has come into being; the names of its spaces resonate with new significance and new energy.

MASPERO, 9 OCTOBER 2011

The French Egyptologist's name that had come to mean state radio and television now means 9 October and the military lying in wait by the Radio and Television building to open fire on the vanguard of the unarmed—mainly Christian—protesters who were marching from Shubra to Tahrir. It means armored personnel carriers zigzagging through the panicked crowds smashing into people, dragging them along, running them over. It means State Television itself plumbing new depths of baseness as it urges Muslims to go out and attack Christians to "protect the Egyptian army." Maspero means a young man in a red lumberjack shirt throwing himself on the neck of a commanding officer watching from the sidelines. (Was that officer Hamdi Badeen, the chief of Military Police, at this very moment retired with honors to be Egypt's military attaché in Beijing?) The young man begs him, pleads with him, in his despair he slides down the officer's body till he kisses his feet, imploring him to stop the killing. Maspero is the morgue in the Coptic Hospital and someone's mother screaming, her eyes still wide with disbelief. It's Vivian's grief-stricken face turned to the sky as she presses Michael's cold hand to her heart.

Maspero is Mina dead.

Mina Danial was twenty-three and had the widest smile. Mina Danial had a passion for Egyptology. Mina Danial refused to be ghettoized into "Christian affairs" but insisted on the struggle for everybody's rights. He'd been among the hundreds wounded on 28 January and in Maspero they murdered him with one bullet to the chest in the first few seconds of the killings; the bullet went through lung and liver. Now Mina manifests in varied ways. His stenciled face was the first to appear after Khaled Said's on the walls of the revolution. And in Muhammad Mahmoud, we saw for the first time that same stencil, on a square of red fabric, flying under the wing of the Egyptian flag that danced in great arcs and circles in the smoke of the guns and the tear gas.

Mina's banner appeared when we most needed it. This double flag, the large Egyptian one fluttering over the red square with the now-familiar face and the legend "We are all Mina Danial" became an immediate icon, transforming into myth even as it was real and palpable in our hands—even as the bit of fabric grew tired and tattered. Throughout the year, Mina's banner appeared at the darkest points of our confrontations with the military, at the protests outside Parliament, at the heart of the strikes. It spoke of a courage and gallantry that could never be defeated. It lifted our spirits and put courage in our hearts, because where we saw it rise, we knew that around it, under it, there were kindred spirits and a space that was human and humane and inclusive and clever and free. And Mina's banner appeared in Cairo and Luxor, in Alexandria and Aswan; everywhere where people were expressing an idea of freedom and dignity, social justice and inclusiveness, the red banner with Mina's stenciled face under the Egyptian flag was there.

And the same stencil, surrounded first by a garland of flowers then by a geometric arrangement of lotus, heralded an eruption of innovation in graffiti, the art that—together with poetry and music—most expressed the revolutionary moment. Then Mina was the first shaheed to appear in a full-length portrait—he appeared one night on the wall of the Mugamma3 Building and was soon joined by other young shuhada posed together in a comradely group: Khaled Said, Ali Taha, and Rami al-Sharqawi. A few days later we were dazzled by a larger-than-life freehand portrait of Mina sitting cross-legged on the ground, two huge angel wings springing rainbow-colored from his back.

Maspero was the consolidation of SCAF and the Dakhleyya working together against the revolution. We'd seen their first simple cooperation in Abbaseyya I; now we saw them plotting, daring to kill several people in one event, trying to turn sections of society against each other, deploying state radio and TV to spread lies, silencing independent reports, and co-opting the leaders or elders of the targeted group—in this case, the priests who tried to bury the bodies without proper autopsies. Maspero was also the coalescing of a core revolutionary front that understood that the regime had not fallen with the departure of Hosni Mubarak and that rejected all initiatives or procedures with any connection to the current rulers of the country—the military.

/ / / /

At six o'clock on a cold, dark night in early November, Laila and I are walking fast on a narrow pavement by the river in Muneeb, in the southernmost part of Cairo. There's a loud and constant roar of traffic. This is the road that connects Cairo to Upper Egypt, and giant trucks are roaring past us, swirling up dust and exhaust fumes. Our old nanny, Dada Ziza, lives a few narrow lanes off this road. It's 3 November, and we'd been sitting in crawling traffic on the Ring Road for two hours, so we decided to get out of the car and go and visit her as we do at the beginning of every month. We're marching along in silence, because of the noise and because the military prosecutor has just renewed Alaa's imprisonment on remand for fifteen more days and there's nothing to say right now.

Alaa had refused to recognize the authority of the military court, and the military prosecutor had decided to jail him. They'd sent him to the Appeals prison in Bab el-Khalq. Next day three thousand people marched in support of Alaa, from Talʒat Harb to Tahrir, down Tahrir Street and through Abdeen to the prison. There a battalion of Central Security Forces faced us, and we could see more down the side streets. As our chanting and drumming grew louder, the roof of the prison was filled with plainclothesmen peering down at us. We stood for two hours chanting for Alaa and all the shabab held by the military, then we wound back into town. We chanted and distributed stickers and talked to people. Once again we were reclaiming our streets—and waiting to see what effect we would have.

Over the days protests were staged, graffiti appeared, poems were written, leading figures in the country contacted us to assure us that they expected SCAF to let him go soon. And Alaa stayed in jail.

So today we'd been in S28: the Military Court, way out in the Fifth Tagammuʒ on the southern section of the Ring Road. We got there at ten in the morning and joined the group of fifty or so of Alaa's comrades chanting outside the court. At midday the military took our IDs and mobiles—that's to say, the IDs and mobiles of the family and the lawyers—and let us in. We waited in a large courtroom. Thirty-two young men wearing the white training suits of prisoners on remand came into the room. They were handcuffed to each other. One of them was Alaa. He was handcuffed to a guard, and he was smiling at us and already talking to us, telling us quickly about the other prisoners, who they were, and the ways in which they were being set up. The lawyers started moving among them, taking names and contacts, so officers came and took us away and into a courtroom on our own. They took the handcuffs off Alaa, and the guards went and sat at the back of the room, and we all sat round him, Manal on one side and Laila on the other, Sanaa and me opposite. His father moved between the family group and the lawyers. Laila kept her hand on her son all the time. Occasionally she would rest her head, for a brief moment, against his shoulder. They had cut his long hair but allowed him to choose the barber. He was shorn and beautiful. He talked about the terrible conditions in the Appeals jail, about the men held there unjustly, about his take on what was happening. He asked me to deliver a message to Amr Helmy, the new minister of health: *The Appeals jail is crammed with injured people. Their injuries, untreated, will affect them for life. This doesn't need to happen; they can be treated well and seriously in jail.*

When the court came in, we stood up. Alaa was asked to stand in front of the bench. The military prosecutor read out the list of charges:

1. Taking by force weapons belonging to the Armed Forces.
2. The deliberate sabotage of the property of the Armed Forces.
3. Attacking public officials of the Armed Forces in the course of their duty.
4. Using violence and force against the Armed Forces.

The judge asked for Alaa's lawyer, and twenty-three lawyers stepped forward, men and women from the Revolutionary Socialist end of the political spectrum right through to the Liberals, the Brotherhood, and the Salafis, all in solidarity. Seven of them made statements, and when they'd finished, Alaa said that he would like to speak. He reminded the court that he had been imprisoned on remand for forty-five days back in 2006 when he'd supported the Judiciary's bid for independence; he had no doubt that his imprisonment now, as then, was meant as a punishment. He pointed out Manal; surely his place—in the last days of her pregnancy—was at her side? He listed all the reasons why the authorities could be certain that he would present himself to the court when required. He spoke naturally and courteously and with such genuineness that I was sure that they would let him go.

They adjourned. And we encircled him again, and our lawyer friends brought us tea and biscuits, and it felt like one of our normal family gatherings except for Laila sticking so close to her son. And then suddenly our little group fragmented, and there were shouts—"Quick!" "Move!" "Down the stairs!"—and we were jumping out of our seats, and a tight posse of soldiers was moving away fast, and in its center was Alaa, and we were all running after him, and Manal couldn't run but her arm was stretched out, and she was holding a book and shouting "His book! His book!" and someone, it might have been me, grabbed the book from her and tore down the stairs because now the most important thing in the world was to give Alaa back the book he'd brought with him, the book he was in the middle of reading. So we hurtled down the stairs and out into the sunshine and saw him being bundled into a military transport and threw him his book, and they locked him in. We stood around calling, "We're still here. Can you hear us?" And he said, "Yes. Get information about the others." So we went to the other young prisoners: "I don't even know what I'm being charged with," "Don't forget us," "Your campaign is our only hope," "Do you have any campaign stickers?" And suddenly again the shouting: "The building's shutting down. Everyone out. Out. Quickly. Out." From inside his solitary transport, Alaa called out to us to find a way to let him know the decision of the court.

Because that's how they did it, you see. They waited and waited for the phone call that was to instruct them what their decision would be. Then they grabbed their prisoner and locked him up, dispersed family and lawyers onto the street, and announced their decision to an empty courtroom. And when we were in the car, crawling in the traffic on the Ring Road, one of the lawyers called Laila and told her the military were keeping Alaa for another fifteen days.

Now, as we walk, Laila is saying something. I lean toward her, shout into the traffic: "What did you say?"

"I'm going on hunger strike," she shouts back. "From tomorrow."

We stumble headlong on the ruined pavement, the trucks thundering past us, and she shouts that she believes they have it in for him and she's going to pull out all the stops. Total hunger strike, nothing but water. I say, "You can't look like you want special treatment for your son." No, she says, she's going to fast until the whole Maspero case is removed from the military and referred to a civilian court. A friend said once that when the sky's about to fall and crush us, Laila Soueif appears and holds it up. And this is what she's doing; she's trying to keep a terrible evil away from her son and the other young men in the white training suits. I'm at a loss. I say, "Should I join you?" She says no—or not yet, anyway. I say, "Is there a chance you'll die?" She shrugs. I say, "You won't tell Dada Ziza, will you? Because it'll kill her—after she's killed you first."

〜〜〜〜

Mona's blog three days later:

Sanaa goes for a nap in the car. My uncle goes to buy us some cartons of juice. My dad and Tante Sohair (my uncle's wife) sit on the kerb solving a sudoko together. Tante Ahdaf drags a chair away from the shade and suns herself while she writes on her laptop. Mama and Manal read the newspapers and mark every item connected to Alaa. Azza and Rasha have vanished for the moment. I'm chopping up a salad. My cousin, Omar, is filming all this. This was not a scene at the club; this was the first day of Eid on the pavement opposite the wall of Tora Istiqbal Jail. It could look strange to a lot of people, but to my weird, wonderful family it was totally normal.

It was the Eid and every prisoner was allowed an extra visit. And so we'd become one of the many thousands of families spending their Eid morning camped outside the gates of a jail that holds a loved one.

We'd come to visit my brother. All jails permit a maximum of three blood relations to visit at any one time, but we're a family that loves to crowd together and make a lot of noise so eleven of us came along and were so surprised when they wouldn't let us all in!

When they wouldn't let us all in, we formed an assembly line to pass the bags we'd brought him to each other, through the security scanner, and to the rest of us till they got to the soldier at the door. Two young officers stood at a distance watching: pillows, blankets, soaps, shampoo, fruit and vegetables, fruit and vegetables, books, books, books—they intervened. They had the books carried over and bent to look through them: novels, graphic novels, comics—one of them looked up at me and Sohair, his face alive with interest: "Who is it you're coming to visit?"

"Alaa Abd el-Fattah."

His face broke into a wide smile. He turned to his colleague: "Didn't I tell you?" And back to us, still with the big smile: "You are very welcome here. I knew it! Who would be bringing these kinds of things to jail? You can't take them in, though. They're too many." We negotiated. Half the books went in, the other half we took back, for next time.

~~~~

As the days passed, the list of charges against Alaa grew. He was charged with destroying an armored personnel carrier and stealing the weapons it was carrying. A witness was found to say she'd seen him do this. She was the mistress of a general who was the former head of psychological operations in the Armed Forces. When Laila asked—in an open letter in the papers—why the army hadn't raided Alaa's house if they believed he was in possession of a mini-arsenal of automatics, why they had waited till two weeks after Maspero to summon him, another witness came forward to say he'd seen Alaa run away with the weapons and throw them into the Nile.

~~~~

Alaa's article, "Your Solidarity Is Not Enough," smuggled out from jail and published in *Mamal and Alaa's bit bucket free speech from the bletches* on November, urged everyone, of every political color, to take to the streets on the eighteenth, to remove legislative power from the hands of SCAF, and to insist on elections on the twenty-eighth and a swift handover of power to the elected Parliament. No one knew how he smuggled out his articles. Manal, Laila, and Mona went to Tora jail every visiting time. Sanaa did a food, newspaper, and laundry run every day. Ahmad Seif, unwilling to use the family allocation, visited his son as his lawyer. On the eighteenth, *Shorouk* published Alaa's "The Hostage State," in which he added his voice to those insisting that the Constitution must not be written under the supervision of SCAF.

SCAF had gathered around itself a collection of old politicians, judges, academics, and experts various. I would not accuse them of betraying the revolution; I think that for them the revolution had been an excellently useful event to sweep away the Mubaraks. But now that that was done, it was time for order to be reestablished. For them, it was always the state that mattered, not the people. They could not see "a people" operating outside the known and accepted framework of the state—they saw us as a mob, mindless, and bent on chaos. It was natural for them to gather around the military, around SCAF, the one pillar of the state that seemed unshaken. Perhaps it was even their consciences that guided them to help SCAF fight the revolution.

Since August the leaderships of all the political forces—the Left, the Liberals, the Salafis, the Muslim Brotherhood—had been holding meeting after meeting trying to reach an agreement on basic principles to govern the Constitution. SCAF too had been doing its work, and a document produced by Dr. Ali al-Selmi was the military's contribution to the debate. It proposed that it was now SCAF—not the people or their representatives—who were the "protectors of revolutionary legitimacy." And it gave SCAF authority over the larger part of the country's budget and sole authority over military budgets and over any legislation that affected the military.

For most people, the "Selmi Document" was proof that SCAF was trying to steal the revolution, and that it was getting help from sections of the judiciary and the old political elite. The country was in an uproar.

Alaa's "Maybe I'm Confused" is representative of the concerns of the street; it engages with the processes of elections and constitution writing but knows that these are, finally, the instruments, not the aims, of the revolution. Alaa calls on his friends and supporters to carry on working on several fronts. He urges them to join or create neighborhood or workplace Popular Committees to protect the revolution; to join campaigns like No to Military Trials for Civilians; to organize TweetNadwas; to investigate and publish information about the remnants of the old regime; to support the electoral campaign of "The Revolution Continues"—the group of parliamentary candidates coalescing around the revolution's aims of human rights and social justice; to follow up the initiative to set up a People's TV Channel and the Let's Write Our Constitution project. All this, and to not abandon direct action but to join the millioneyya called for on the eighteenth.

The eighteenth had been declared the Millioneyya of One Demand: *tasleem al-sulta*, the handover of power—by SCAF to an elected civilian body, by April 2012.

MUHAMMAD MAHMOUD STREET, 19–24 NOVEMBER 2011

There are an estimated eight thousand people that the police, the military, and their baltagis have injured to a point where they are not able to resume their normal lives. Sami Emile is a young geographical surveyor. He had just married the woman he loved, a lawyer. They owned their apartment. His life was set. The army smashed his leg, and he now drags it behind him and has to pay for the physiotherapy that just about keeps it from withering away. I met him at the Coptic Hospital when I went to visit the Maspero injured. His leg had been smashed—not in Maspero but in an earlier clash with the military in March. He was just visiting. He was incredibly gentle. Soft-voiced. His eyes kept filling with tears as he asked why. Why was all this happening? As I was leaving, an older man who was very ill with a bullet in the stomach called me over. I sat bent close because he was whispering to me. He said, "If you can do one thing, do it for Sami. He's the one who needs it most."

Another: Randa S. is a nurse. The doctors in the field clinics always got her to do the stitching because she was so good at it. On 28 January she was suturing the heads of the shabab, and a Central Security Officer beat her so badly that she was paralyzed. In fact, he would have killed her, but she stabbed him in the hand with her needle. She's in the rehabilitation unit at Agouza Hospital—the one where we took Abu Mustafa's testimony on 2 August—and she's giving them hell. She's in a wheelchair but has got back the use of her arms, and she plays revolutionary music and organizes her fellow injured.[3]

Some of the injured are still fighting, and some are broken, but all need long-term provision. They need a plan; they need jobs that they can do and that can support them. The majority of them are responsible for households. One of the things that this revolution has revealed is how many young people—young men especially—support parents, how many have dead fathers and look after their mothers, how many fund their sisters through college or weddings and need to see them settled and safe before they can carve out their own lives. A lot of their injuries—particularly the people shot in the eyes—could have been rectified. But after they were given emergency treatment in the field clinics, they—if they were lucky—went into our abysmal public hospitals. Many doctors opened their clinics and treated people for free, many doctors came from abroad to help, but there was no system in place to ensure that patient and doctor found each other. In fact, there was no official will to take care of them at all. What care some got was philanthropic, through individuals and civil society actions. The government, under SCAF, was content to issue statements—crass at the best of times—about compensating people to the tune of X for a leg and Y for an eye, or—with more enthusiasm—about how imposters were trying to take advantage of the government's generosity and posing as injured.

Some of these injured had started a sit-in in Tahrir on Friday, 11 November, to demand that the government give them medical and practical provision. General Fangari of SCAF—he who had performed the military salute to the shuhada in February when the military promised to "safeguard the revolution"—now scoffed: *Let them go to the Midan with their demands. See if it'll do them any good.*

A week later, on Friday the eighteenth, hundreds of thousands of us went into Tahrir to insist that elections had to happen on the twenty-eighth and to demand that SCAF set a date for a handover.

Manal was one week away from the due date of her baby, and despite everything—despite Alaa in jail, her furniture in cargo from South Africa, her flat topsy-turvy, and the nursery unfinished—she was radiant. Laila was on day fifteen of her hunger strike, and people—hundreds of people—came up to talk to her, to put their arms round her shoulders, and to kiss her head. I stayed close by, pestering her with my concern. "Listen," she said, "I really feel the same as in the days when I used to eat." Fifteen days without food, and the only change I could register was that her voice was more quiet. She submitted to some organ function tests set up by Lulie, and they seemed okay, but I was worried. I tried a tangential approach: "Isn't it hard for Alaa knowing you're on hunger strike?"

"No," she said. "That's our relationship: we trust in each other's strength."

And it was Alaa's birthday: today he was thirty. His friends brought a giant birthday cake to the Midan, and we all lit sparklers and sang happy birthday to him in front of the Mugamma3, in the area where once again the families of the shuhada and the injured were congregating.

Tahrir was back. SCAF's attempt to control the writing of the Constitution had galvanized everybody, and the call to protest had gone out from all the parties, the coalitions, and the movements. The Midan and the streets surrounding it were full, spirits were high, people were in a good humor, the Ultras were out in force, and the sky was lit up with their fireworks. The plan was

that everyone would leave at the end of the day, and most people
did. But as usual, when the shabab are in a position where they feel
they'll be abandoning the injured or the shuhada families, some
of them can't do it. Around two hundred people decided to stay.

Next day, Saturday, Central Security Forces moved. They tore
down some tents of the sit-in and set fire to the others. They beat
the injured. Supporters rushed in to Tahrir to help fight them off,
and by nightfall, when I went down to the Midan, there was gun-
fire and smoke and tear gas and hundreds of Security Forces with
guns and sticks and hundreds of protesters hitting back at them
with stones. The military stood by. From time to time they covered the Security Forces.

The Security Forces always entered Tahrir from Muhammad
Mahmoud Street; this is their route from the Ministry of the Inte-
rior in Lazoghli, some seven hundred meters away. So it was on
Muhammad Mahmoud that the protesters intercepted and even-
tually managed to stop them. For four days the shabab protected
Tahrir and held off the Security Forces in Muhammad Mahmoud.
The battle was presented by state media as "revolutionaries and
baltagis try to storm the Dakhleyya building," but what the shabab were doing was once again protecting the Midan—unarmed.
Fifty meters was the distance between relative normality and war.
And the shabab taking a break from the front told us that soldiers
had waved and indicated "peace" so they could change shifts and
attack them again, and they told of the attacks breaking the traditional prayer-time ceasefire. A residential block caught fire, the
shabab climbed to help the people inside, and Security shot them
as they climbed. I learned later that Omar had come within inches
of being shot when he and Aida, another young filmmaker, were
trapped against a doorway in Falaki Street trying to hide from
approaching soldiers. He turned his back to the street and covered
her with his body, and they heard the soldiers come closer and
closer till they came to a stop next to them. As they heard the

clicks of the shotguns, she leaped out from behind him shouting, "A girl! There's a girl! I'm a girl!" and the soldiers didn't shoot.

At six p.m. on 23 November, I wrote:

I've just read this tweet: "Eat a good breakfast. Take a ruck-sack with a gas mask and swimming goggles. Write your name on your arm. Write your details into a message on your mobile. And go to the Midan."

Tuesday was declared a day to "Save the Nation," and people across the country once again demanded the abdication of SCAF. Tuesday night as the news cameras concentrated on Tahrir, the Army and Police were attacking citizens in other cities: in Alexandria, Assiut, Aswan, Damietta, Ismailia, Luxor, Mahalla, Mansoura, Sohag and Suez. And yet, of course, in this age of televised spectacle it was the images of Tahrir that were most relayed: Midan el-Tahrir teeming with citizens, decorated with flags, and clouded with tear-gas.

All day that Tuesday thousands had poured into the Midan. In the small hours of Sunday the little field hospital in the small mosque of Ibad al-Rahman had been pleading for a stethoscope, a blood pressure gauge, betadine, cotton wool. By Tuesday afternoon there were seven field hospitals around Tahrir stockpiled with equipment and medicines— all donated by the people coming in. Omar Makram Mosque and Qasr el-Doubara Church cross-referenced specialisations. On a wall between them someone had written: "We are the Midan: A Church, a Mosque and a Parliament."

On Tuesday two hundred young doctors walked in to the Midan together in their white coats and distributed themselves among the hospitals—in a few hours one of them had been killed.

The revolution is using what it learned back in January/
February and adding to it. Signposts, information,
directions. Young men on motorbikes ferry the injured
from the front lines to the field hospitals. The spontaneous,
organic organization is breathtaking. And the creativity:
when Malek Mostafa—a popular, newly married young
activist had his eye shot out by the Army, one of the great
bronze lions on Qasr el-Nil Bridge suddenly sported an eye
patch.

In a flat on the 10th floor above Tahrir we were weeping
under our gas-masks, the smell was so strong.

The protestors are unarmed. When the Army/
Police attack them they fight back bravely, using stones
from the street, lobbing back gas canisters, keeping up
a constant chanting and a constant drumming on the
metal lamp-posts and street-signs, occasionally shooting
fireworks. The Midan is well aware of the contrast between
their drumming and fireworks and the deadly thud of the
teargas canister and the treacherous silence of the sniper.

We're saying these are "ayyam el-farz"—the days of
sorting. The situation is very intense. Just now, at that
flashpoint on Muhammad Mahmoud where a truce was
brokered at 3 and broken at 5, the Army/Police have shot
the protestors at sunset prayers. The field hospitals in Qasr
el-Doubara Church and Omar Makram Mosque are calling
for neurologists; the motorbikes have brought in 50 cases in
the last 10 minutes—[4]

In the events that radiated across Egypt from Muhammad
Mahmoud Street, 3,800 young people were injured and 42 killed
in Alexandria, Cairo, Ismailia, and Marsa Matrouh. Ahmad Surour was one of them, killed on the morning of the twenty-sixth,

when a police car hit him and dragged him fifty meters down the street. His mother: "When they knocked on the door they said he's just injured in hospital I said he's in the morgue. I know my son. My son won't be laid low except by death. At the [Israeli] embassy he took two bullets and he never flinched. He kept them. Last night I told him: Enough. Enough! You're lucky nothing's happened to you so far. He said how can we be men and leave it now? My son. He helped everyone, he would help the stones on the ground if they asked, and now they've killed him."[5]

Forty-one more mothers lost their children over those four days. The young dentist, Ahmad Harara, who had lost one eye on 28 January, lost the other on Muhammad Mahmoud. Friday the twenty-fifth was declared Shuhada Friday and Last Chance Friday. An unprecedented number of citizens filled the Midan to repeat their demand for the immediate abdication of SCAF and the handing of power to an interim president. No waiting till April now. The street would accept any one or combination of three presidential candidates: Muhammad el-Baradei, Abd el-Moneim Abu el-Futtouh, Hamdein Sabahi. Chants and banners demanded the trial of Hamdi Badeen, the head of the Military Police. The anger and demands of Tahrir were replicated across the country.

But in Cairo, two alternative protests appeared. The Muslim Brotherhood declared against Tahrir and set up its own protest, at the Azhar, the seat of Sunni Islam in Fatimid Cairo. (The grand imam of al-Azhar, for his part, stepped away from this and sent a representative to Tahrir to demand the trial of the murderers of the shabab.) The Brotherhood named the day al-Aqsa Friday. The al-Aqsa—Islam's third holiest mosque—has been under periodic Israeli attack for years, but the Brotherhood claimed they just happened to choose this Friday to show solidarity for the beleaguered mosque. The Palestinians were quick to denounce the naming and accuse the Brotherhood of cynicism and of using the Palestinian cause to undermine the Egyptian Revolution. And in Midan el-Abbaseyya, near the Ministry of Defense, the first demonstration in support of SCAF appeared. This gathering of a few hundred, presented by state TV through close-up shots as the equivalent of Tahrir, became the nucleus of the campaign for the military's candidate, Ahmad Shafiq, in the presidential elections. Some Abbaseyya residents said the "protesters" were mainly police and army conscripts in civilian clothes.

On Muhammad Mahmoud, the army piled up great cement blocks in the middle of the street. As with the Israeli-style wall they had built in May at the end of University Bridge, they now built one cutting across the middle of Muhammad Mahmoud, truncating the street. To protect, they said, the Ministry of the Interior from the revolutionaries. And the street miraculously transformed itself, from a somewhat characterless thoroughfare connecting Midan el-Tahrir to Midan el-Falaki, it became the spiritual home of the revolution. People came to look, to see the wall the army'd built, to take in the place where so many had fallen to protect Tahrir. A group of young artists came up from Luxor, and Mina Danial's cross-legged angel appeared. Then groups of angels in gas masks rose from the pavement into the wall of the American University downtown campus. Pharaonic scenes, Muslim symbols, poetry, and Coptic icons—great vivid murals bloomed onto the walls. In December, when Sheikh Emad Effat fell, he reappeared on the wall of the Greek School luminous with energy. Angel wings burst from his shoulders, and from his extended hands flowed the Quranic verse "And they said Lord, we obeyed our masters and our elders and they led us astray. Lord, double their torment and curse them forevermore."[6] Later in February, when the Ultras fell, it was here that they were celebrated. The street grew plastic chairs and modest tea stands. People sat with their friends, their books, and their laptops in the company of the shuhada. The colors from Muhammad Mahmoud spilled over into Tahrir and into Downtown. General Muhammad al-Batran—killed by the police in January 2011—appeared in his police uniform with angel wings and so entered officially into the ranks of the revolution's martyrs. Through the dark, cold winter, the walls on Muhammad Mahmoud erupted into huge images of celebration, lamentation, and commentary. The army dismembered Downtown with six more walls, and all the walls they built were turned into views from submarines, fantasy beaches, trompe l'oeils, and miragelike street scenes.

They were beaten. Just as they were beaten on 25 and 28 January, the Security Forces were beaten in Muhammad Mahmoud and retreated behind the walls the military had provided. By the end of the Battle of Muhammad Mahmoud, SCAF head Muhammad Hussein Tantawi had pledged that elections would start on the twenty-eighth as scheduled; he had accepted the resignation of Essam Sharaf's cabinet, and he had transferred the Maspero case from the military to the civilian courts. My sister ended her hunger strike. All talk of the people and the army being "one hand" was over, and it became mainstream to chant "Yasqot yasqot 7ukm el-3askar"—Down, down, with military rule.

✓✓✓✓

I keyed my ID number into the election website and found my electoral number and polling station. I keyed in my sons' and Um Nagla's and got their electoral numbers and polling stations. I felt as though some corner had been turned. There were almost forty thousand polling booths across the country, and people filled them: not the 80 percent plus who'd turned out for the referendum in March, but close to 60 percent.

Our polling booth was right by our house, in the school next to the pharmacy where I'd talked with Sitt Karima late on the night of Friday, 28 January, the school I'd never been inside before, the rival to my own school just down the road. On 28 November I took my place in the line waiting to vote. Many of us were in black for the shuhada, and in Zamalek the mood was one of determination to not let the Brotherhood in rather than to celebrate the democratic process. But we were out there, going into polling booths and voting, and no one was beating us or stopping us, and there were arrangements in place to make sure the vote we cast was counted.

But by voting, were we honoring the shuhada of Muhammad Mahmoud and Maspero? Or were we disrespecting them? The progressive Left split. The group that had decided after Maspero that SCAF had lost legitimacy to run elections and run the country was hardened in its resolve to boycott after the killings in Muhammad Mahmoud. Many joined them. They believed that by taking part in elections, people were according the military the legitimacy they had forfeited, and since the military had shown themselves to be against the revolution, by voting people would be, in fact, impeding the progress of the revolution for which the shuhada had died. But the majority still felt that elections could be a way of getting rid of the military and moving forward.

Personally, I do believe that it would have been best, it would have been more true and honest, if every one of us had boycotted the elections, if we had all stayed home and sent a vote of no confidence to SCAF and made their position untenable. But the boycott would have had to be total, and the country leaned toward dialogue, and the people in general preferred to avoid the shedding of blood on the way to their goals.

The elections did not conform to the arrangements laid out in SCAF's Constitutional Declaration, which had stipulated that two-thirds of the seats would be contested by parties and one-third by independents. When it came to it, the parties were allowed to contest all the seats, with the independents contesting their third only. (After the elections, a case was, in fact, lodged with the Constitutional Court charging that the elections had contravened the law.) This gave an unfair advantage to party candidates, and the only parties with a real presence and real organization were the Muslim Brotherhood ("Freedom and Justice") and the Salafis ("al-Nour," the Light). The Liberal parties had been too busy campaigning for elections to be postponed until after the Constitution was written to organize or acquire a presence on the street. The Left—while very high profile in the campaigns and initiatives and struggles that fed the revolution—was disorganized and had absolutely no funding but scrambled at the last minute to field young candidates under the slogan "The Revolution Continues."

When the results came in the Muslim Brotherhood had won 47 percent of the vote and the Salafis 24. The Liberals got 15 and the Left got 4. The heartening surprise was that not a single candidate believed to have a connection with the Mubarak regime was returned. And that when people managed to find a candidate from the revolution, they voted him in.

PARLIAMENT STREET, 16–22 DECEMBER 2011

On November 24 Tantawi announced his choice of Kamal el-Ganzouri as prime minister. Ganzouri had, from 1996 to 1999, been Mubarak's prime minister, and the appointment was greeted with whoops of derision. Accounts of the rash of massive and unpopular sell-offs of national industries that he had brokered during his tenure exploded in the media. I was crossing and recrossing the Midan all day to al-Jazeera, CNN, the BBC—and I didn't hear a good word for him anywhere. By evening, young revolutionaries had set up their tents outside the gate to the Cabinet Office in Parliament Street to stop the new prime minister gaining access. So now, while elections were being held across the country, a new sit-in started in Parliament Street, besides the continuing sit-in in Tahrir.

On August 1, when the military broke up the July sit-in, they had occupied Tahrir. Soldiers stood to attention all day in the blazing August sun—just as they used to stand along the sides of roads when Mubarak traveled on a Cairo street. They kept it up for a few weeks, then withdrew and turned instead to the slyer methods of democracies. If Tahrir was our Holy Grail and the symbol of our revolution, we could have it. Its electricity would remain disconnected, its traffic lights wouldn't work, and it would never be cleaned. It would be infiltrated, and drugs would be found there. Baltagis would make trouble with business owners and residents, and state media would talk about how scummy the revolution had become, how prostitution and drugs were rife in Tahrir, how the people there were no longer the "honest shabab" of January but baltagis and agents of foreign enemies. Discredit Tahrir, discredit the revolutionaries, discredit the revolution—while pretending to honor them all.

And the message was getting through to the people: the Midan was being held responsible for the worsening of the economy, for bad security, for traffic jams, for everything. We tried to end the sit-in and to mount a PR and information campaign for the Midan. We tried to enact the vision of the revolution in the small encampment near the Mugamma3. One tent became a walk-in clinic; another became a play center. We held meetings with veterans of societies that worked with street children to see what we could offer the children. The flags of different cities flew above us. We asked a calligrapher for five huge banners that spelled out the demands of the sit-in: as usual, support for the injured, restructuring the Dakhleyya, and restructuring state media, and now also an investigation into the Muhammad Mahmoud killings and rejection of Ganzouri's retro cabinet.

But Tahrir was becoming chaotic. Fights broke out between "revolutionaries" and street vendors, groups accused each other of being infiltrators, and no one was sure who was securing the space. Rubbish was not collected, and the area around the Mugamma3 smelled of urine. Strange characters appeared, with aides-de-camp and followers, and commandeered spaces where they presided over mobile-laden tables. Mona discovered a "prison" in Tahrir where some alleged thieves were being held. My sister and Sanaa and Sherif Boraie went to the rescue, argued through the night with their captors, and set them free. But the practice had started and would continue. It became one of Sanaa's self-appointed tasks to sit vigil with prisoners to make sure they weren't harmed. Sometimes she was able to negotiate their release, and sometimes not. Sometimes the bosses in charge of them released a few as a gift to her. The quantities of medicines left over from the field hospitals and stored in Omar Makram Mosque became a problem; some people claimed that the mosque was trading in them, while others said no, it was using them to pay off baltagis who were protecting it. Mona Mina took a team of young doctors and went in and did a stock-taking of everything that was held, and a decision was made to remove the medicines to the Doctors' Union.

The street now wanted the Midan opened. Again and again Abu Muhab and the activists among the injured and the shuhada's families tried to end the sit-in, or to contain it in the area by the Mugamma3 so that the traffic could flow through. And again and again they were overruled by self-styled "security." We felt that the same scenario that had happened in July was playing out again. Once again it came down to individual efforts to get vulnerable people out of the Midan and into the Parliament Street sit-in. While sitting on a pavement by the Qasr el-Eini entrance waiting for the ladder we were going to use to hang up our banners, I watched a friend, media figure Buthaina Kamel, try with a small band of followers to open the cordon blocking the Midan, and a young woman leaped up out of nowhere to hit her in the face.

Sitting there on that pavement, I got talking to a young man who said his name was Hasan. He was here with his friend, Mahmoud. They were from a village on the southern periphery of Cairo and had been friends since they were three. They'd shared a wedding and now each had two children. Neither young man could read or write, and Hasan had broken his leg when he was fourteen, and it hadn't mended properly, and sometimes the pain made him cry like a child. But they'd worked hard at anything available and eventually got enough money to rent a coffee shop, which they ran together. In the last months business was bad, and the coffee shop owner had raised the rent by 20 percent. They struggled but couldn't pay. They gave up the lease and hired themselves out as day labor, but wages were down to fifteen pounds a day (that's three U.S. dollars), and a house couldn't survive on less than twenty. They'd had to move back in with their parents, and they were embarrassed. "My father worked all his life to support me," Hasan said, "and now he has to support my children, too?" So they'd both left home last week and come to join this revolution that spoke of social justice and the right of everyone to work for a decent life. It also promised health care for everyone—Hasan had been told that he needed a scan on his leg and that it cost 750 pounds. So here they were, standing on the periphery of a dark Tahrir, ready to do the revolution's bidding. I was certain that within days these two young men would be either dead or added to the twelve thousand in military jails. I persuaded them to come with me to Parliament Street, vouched for them that they were not baltagis sent to infiltrate the sit-in, found them blankets, and got them on the rota for the meager bits of food that were being distributed from time to time. All across the Midan, other people were doing the same.

The Parliament Street sit-in was in much better shape than Tahrir; it was contained, and it focused on what it was there to disrupt: SCAF's new cabinet. It had an entrance at either end of the street, and between them, in a row down the center, the protesters had arranged cardboard coffins bearing the names and pictures of the shuhada of Muhammad Mahmoud. There were debates and discussions, musical rehearsals and manifestos. Eskenderella came and played. One night they tried out an early version of a new song. We made them sing it twice so we could all learn it and sing along. The military inside the Parliament compound came closer to the railings, and the band reoriented themselves so the soldiers could hear. When the band left, the shabab and the young officers tried to talk to each other, but the shabab were bitter about their murdered friends, and the military were adamant that any activity other than elections was destroying the country and that the shabab were being misled by a "third party." Their superiors called them back from the railings.

Manal was there that night—the night Eskenderella played to the Parliament Street sit-in. She was supposed to have gone in for a cesarean section and kept postponing it in the hope that the civil court would set Alaa free. But on December 6 she checked into hospital, and Khaled was born, and once again a birth in our family was linked to a jail. A few days after giving birth to me, my mother had held me up outside the Citadel Jail so her brother, who was imprisoned for belonging to a leftist group, could see his new niece. Now Manal rose early from her confinement and took her newborn child to prison to place him in his father's arms. And as I had gone with my sister in '86 when she went to show Mona to Ahmad Seif, so Mona went with Manal to show Alaa his baby. Alaa had thought it would be at least a week after the birth before Manal would risk coming to see him. Mona writes that when, from far away, he saw his wife and the bundle in her arms, Alaa started to leap up and down. I had seen him leap up and down with the agony and the anger of Mina's death, and I'm glad to have this other image: of my nephew jumping with joy at the arrival of his son.

On the ninth he wrote:

On his third day of life Khaled visited me for half an hour. I held him. My God! How come he's so beautiful? Love at first touch! In half an hour he gave me joy to fill the jail for a whole week. In half an hour I gave him love I hoped would surround him for a whole week. In half an hour I changed and the universe changed around me. Now I understand how I will resist: my prison cannot stop my love. My happiness is resistance. Holding Khaled for a few moments is carrying on the fight.

I was not alone for a second in my resistance; I'd become used to receiving telegrammed tweets in my jail: congratulations for the Eid and for my birthday, I also got congratulations for the return of the revolution to the Midan. But Khaled was something else! A huge amount of telegrams, most of them from people I don't know and might never have the honour of meeting; they wrote to tell of their joy at Khaled's arrival and their love for him. They wrote introducing themselves, the names of the members of their families, their addresses, their jobs, their cities. They wrote that Khaled has family in hundreds of homes everywhere in Egypt. . . .

Half an hour in which I did nothing except look at him. What about half an hour in which I changed him? Or half an hour in which I fed him? Or half an hour in which I played with him? What about half an hour for him to tell me about his school? Half an hour for him and I to talk about his dreams? Half an hour to argue about whether he should go down to a protest? Half an hour for him to give me an impassioned speech about the revolution and how it will free us all? About bread and freedom and dignity and justice? Half an hour for me to feel proud that my son is a brave man carrying the responsibility of a country before he's of an age to carry the responsibility of himself? How much happiness in half an hour like that? In that last half hour the father of the shaheed spent with his son?

Prison deprives me of Khaled except for half an hour. I'm patient because we shall spend the rest of our half hours together. Why is the father of the shaheed patient?

The shaheed is immortal, in our hearts, in our minds, in history, and in paradise. But does his immortality bring happiness to his father? His heart will burst with love for the remaining half hours of his life. Will he pour out that love into the arms of history? I am resilient as I wait for my release. What does the father of the shaheed wait for?[7]

On December 15, I went home at midnight. There had been a debate at the Parliament Street sit-in, and then I'd stopped at a meeting in Tahrir. A lawyer/activist friend had managed to bring together a group semirepresentative of the Midan, and we were formulating a statement that basically declared the Midan open. We thought that if the shabab were unable to actually open it, the statement would at least mean that the revolution could no longer be blamed for keeping the Midan closed. I took the document home to key it in, hone it, and format it, and it was about three o'clock when I sent it back to the group to send on to the media. I flicked on Twitter one more time before I switched off my laptop.

Within twenty minutes, I was parked and hurrying down Parliament Street. Young men tried to stop me. "There's trouble down there." "I know. That's why I'm going." I get to the trouble. In the dark street about fifteen young men are hurling stones and insults into the railings of the Parliament compound. They're in T-shirts and singlets, sweaty, sooty, and very angry. Behind the railings, out of the reach of the stones, armed soldiers watch them. The young men have set up barricades either side of their small group. A few fires burn on the road. There's no point hurrying anymore. Some older men are standing at the periphery, watching, and I stand with them. A young man breaks off from the group. He's scanning the ground and finds what he's looking for almost at our feet. He squats down and starts breaking up a loose paving stone. I start talking: "What are you doing? What's the point in what you're doing?"

"Go home, ma'am." He doesn't even look up.

"But what's the point—"

"Go home, ma'am. It's dangerous here for you."

"You can't even reach them—"

"Because they're hiding—the cowards—"

A man joins us, adds his voice to mine: "What you're doing is useless—"

The young man starts gathering the stones he's broken, loading them into his arms. He's glistening with sweat and soot, and he's tied a white bandanna round his head: "So what should we do?"

"Move away from them. Don't put yourselves in pointless—"

"You didn't see him," the young man says. His glance takes us in properly for the first time. "You don't understand. You didn't see him. They gave him back to us finished. Ruined."

With his armful of stones he lopes back among his friends and starts hurling.

"Him" was Abboudi, one of the Ahli Ultras. It was said that his father was rich and owned many shops downtown, and that Abboudi had broken away from him and joined the revolution. And in the sit-in on this street, he had become a leader. This evening, at this spot where the young men are attacking the shadowy soldiers, he'd challenged an officer standing beside an unmarked white vehicle. He'd told the officer that he believed this was the vehicle that had been used to kidnap several activists over the last few days, then soldiers surrounded him and dragged him into Parliament. Two hours later they threw him out. Finished. Ruined.

Abboudi's friends hurl stones, and the soldiers watch from the shadows. I step back. A young woman comes running up and asks if anyone has a car—there's an injured kid who should be taken to hospital. I run back with her. We get the kid into the back of my car, and a young doctor comes too. We get to the back entrance of Qasr el-Eini hospital, but the boy panics and won't go in: "Just back up. Back up. I'll get off here." The doctor tells him he thinks his leg might be broken. "I'm not going in. They'll kidnap me. I'll get out here. I'll get someone." We leave him leaning against a wall, fumbling for his phone, and drive forward again to the hospital.

Dim lights. Dirty green walls. Misery. The main teaching hospital of Cairo University. The clerk at reception has closed his admissions register and is swearing he won't work and he won't be blamed for Security taking away people wounded in Tahrir. "What do they still want?" he shouts. "A prime minister's been named. Why don't they calm down and let him do his work?" In the corridors, patients are wheeled about on tilting, rusty wheelchairs; ordinary people, needing repair. Rasha Azab comes toward me, one of the bravest of our young activist journalists: "You've come to see Abboudi? Come. He's bad." I follow her. Abboudi is on a bed in a room teeming with people. His friends are all around him. His ears are torn, his eyes are sealed shut, his face is caked with blood. It's so swollen that it doesn't even look like a face.[8]

A personnel carrier is in the ambulance driveway. The soldiers in it stare at Rasha and me as we leave. We stare back. We stop at the all-night pharmacy on Qasr el-Eini Street to get some dressings and painkillers and antiseptics. We figure the field clinic at the top of Parliament Street is going to need them. I've been to this pharmacy before, so the pharmacists give me a 10 percent discount and ask for news. I think it's strange that they need news of what's happening a hundred meters down the road, but I tell them anyway. We drive down Qasr el-Eini with men flagging us down to tell us there's trouble. "We know," Rasha keeps repeating, "we know. That's why we're going there."

This was the opening salvo in the attack on the Parliament Street sit-in. Later on, on that Friday, 16 December, Sheikh Emad Effat, a beloved presence in the Midan and a high-ranking researcher and academic at al-Azhar University, is shot dead. Alaa Abd el-Hadi, in his fifth year of medical school at Ein Shams University, has been providing medical help in Tahrir since the beginning of the revolution. When news of the trouble in Parliament Street broke, he writes on his Facebook: "I'll go see what's happening. May God protect us all." Alaa is trying to help Sheikh Emad when he is shot. His mother, worried about him, phones. A stranger answers her son's phone and tells her to "bring someone with you and come to the hospital." She says, "We got to the hospital and I heard them say go to the morgue and I fainted. I never saw my son again."

The Parliament Street events last for five days. In my Arabic weekly column in *Shorouk*, I write:

Blood runs down the streets of downtown. At four o'clock every morning the valiant Egyptian Armed Forces swoop down on Egyptian civilians in the heart of our capital, they kill and wound and kidnap, then retreat behind the cement walls they've built in the streets that lead into Tahrir; they rest and regroup and get ready to attack again.

Over the course of the week, we've seen the military seduce the shabab into a small war, angering them with insults and gestures from behind railings and from the tops of roofs, pelting them with stones and bricks and Molotov cocktails and furniture and china and oil paintings and glass panes—as well as their more traditional missiles of bullets and buckshot and gas canisters.[9]

We've seen the vicious beatings of young men, and young women being dragged to places of detention inside the Parliament and the Consultative Council buildings. We saw them come out beaten and electrocuted, one of them with the letter T carved into her head. And we saw the burning and the attempted burning of public buildings like the Egyptian Academy, and the military hurling bricks at the shabab trying to save the books.

Then there was the spectacle that went round the world in seconds: the young woman separated from the young journalist she was talking to. He gets beaten, and we see a soldier jumping on his fallen body more than once. She is dragged along, her clothes lifting off her. A soldier's foot thumps into her blue-bra'd breast. We see an older woman beaten by soldiers when she tries to help her.

At seven o'clock on Monday morning a thread, a line, a fifty-meter trail of blood: the fifty meters along which Muhammad Mustafa bled as his comrades of the moment raced to carry him to help. Muhammad Mustafa, a student of Engineering at Ein Shams University, whom the soldiers of SCAF shot, now lies in the Hilal Hospital. A fifty-meter trail of blood; the shabab marked its path with stones then someone filmed it. A simple, truthful action, awesome in its symbolism, clear in its message: Blood is dear; every drop of it has a price.[10]

Both Sanaa and Mona are taken into Parliament and beaten. One piece of footage shows a young woman doctor, Farida al-Hussi, being hunted down. I've watched it again and again, and each time I see an image of a hunted deer falling in slow motion.

Another: Ghada Kamal. Another: Azza Hilal. Each one of them, as soon as she is released, gives her testimony on television—on the private channels that have somehow become the forum for the revolution. And a few days later, Hend Nafe3, a student at the University of Banha, becomes famous when she throws Tantawi out of her hospital room. The military had beaten her up and given her a massive head wound. Then, in that strange way they'd developed, they gave her medical treatment: they took her to hospital, handcuffed her to a bed, and sewed up her head with twenty-five stitches.[11] "Her face was as badly bruised and swollen as Abboudi's—her whole body was bruised. And then Tantawi comes to visit the wounded in hospital. The state TV producers choose to start with her. The cameras come in first and set up their angles to capture Tantawi's entry, but Hend ruins the whole show by screaming her accusations at him as he comes in.

On 19 December SCAF hold a long press conference in which they deny every accusation leveled at the military and repeat again and again the claim that a "third hand" or an "invisible party" is working methodically to create division and destroy the state.

The same day a coalition of groups and campaigns—6 April, No to Military Trials, Mosireen—and others hold their own press conference where they present documentary footage and witness statements to prove that SCAF are lying. Anger and grief fill the room. A young activist, Lina, shaking as she speaks, holds up the blood-soaked cloth with which she tried to stop Muhammad Mustafa's wound. From this is born "Kazeboon" (Liars), a people's street campaign against the military. The Mosireen collective—and eventually others—will create footage and post it, and activists will download and screen it. It is a great exercise in utilizing cultural commons. Nobody owns or runs the campaign. Individuals will hear of it, form a group, download material, and screen it. The screenings are sudden and unannounced, they take place in densely populated areas and on the walls of public buildings across the country. Sometimes fights break out. But the movement will grow and gain immense credibility and be crucial in stripping the military of popular legitimacy.

And on Tuesday three thousand women march through Downtown. In the first months of the revolution, we refused to highlight gender issues; even radical feminist groups insisted that the struggle was to create a society in which there was no discrimination on *any* basis, including gender. Now, in the face of the images of women being beaten, dragged, and stripped, in the face of the methodical return of harassment on the streets and the news of the "virginity tests" carried out in military jails, we are marching as women, and our challenge to the existing powers is clear: "Where's the field marshal? The women are here," "Where's the Brotherhood? The women are here!" "SCAF stole our revolution / The women of Egypt will bring it back!" Men, trying to be helpful, link arms around the march, so the massive bloc of women is moving in a kind of protective noose of men. At one point the men, bursting with emotion, start a self-castigating "Where were the men? The women are here!" After they repeat this a few times, the women thunder back their comfort: "Muhammad Mahmoud will bear witness / our men there fought like lions." The women's march is brilliant in its subtlety. It is a demonstration of womanpower, but it seeks to enlist and implicate men, not to alienate them. "Beat me! Strip me!" we chant, "my brother's blood will cover me." For we never lose sight of one fact: the overwhelming majority of the murdered are male. Like Muhammad Mustafa. Like Alaa Abd el-Hadi.

In the years leading up to January 2011, when the 9 March Movement—one of the many movements whose separate campaigns came together in the revolution—was calling for academic independence and administrative transparency in the universities, Ein Shams University was famous for the corruption of its administration. When, for example, the movement won a court order banning police from the university campus, the administration set thugs wielding bicycle chains on the faculty to teach them the value of the police. After the revolution, therefore, Ein Shams was very quick to revamp its articles and run proper elections. Its first elected president was Professor Alaa Fayez, a celebrated pediatric surgeon who was known to be pro the revolution and pro his students. When Alaa Abd el-Hadi was killed trying to tend to Sheikh Emad Effat in Parliament Street, the new president consulted with the student union, and the university mobilized. Two professors from the medical school attended the autopsy. The dean of the law school filed a case of murder, and Professor Fayez himself described on TV how the bullet entered Alaa's body below the heart and exited through his skull—indicating that his killer was extremely close to him. The university organized buses for the students who wanted to attend their friend's burial and the president and professors attended the funeral.

The walls of Ein Shams Medical School flanked the events of Abbaseyya I in July 2011, and the Security Forces used its grounds as a base from which to attack the protests. In April 2012, during the events of Abbaseyya II, Professor Fayez will discover that the medical school grounds are once again being used by Security Forces to launch attacks on protesters. He will order the grounds shut down. Next day, on May 1, on his way to inspect new university buildings, his car will be hit by a truck coming from the opposite direction on the ring road. His driver and secretary will sustain massive injuries, and he will be killed instantly.

But this is all to come later, in the run-up to the presidential elections. And later yet we'll learn that the university is used as a trade hub for drugs and small arms.

Back in December 2011, we go down every day to the intersection of Parliament Street and Qasr el-Eini Street, where soldiers of the Egyptian army have commandeered the roof of the Cabinet Office building and, from that vantage point, pee on Egyptian citizens, where the army pelts the citizenry with the embossed china place settings of Parliament and ceremonial shields from its walls. Once a metal filing cabinet comes crashing down. Glass panes are common. A lot of the time the army fights street children, whom the revolutionaries try to hold on to, to hold back. "Every couple of days the government takes me," a child says, "they take the money I've made and do bad things to me." He says he is twelve, but he looks more like eight. They all look small, these kids, because they're undernourished and because they can't ever sleep properly so they can grow.

By the end of "Parliament Street," seventeen more people have been murdered, and a further nine hundred seriously injured.

END OF 2011

On 15 December a civil court set free all the young men detained by the military in the Maspero case—all except Alaa. The next time Alaa appeared in court—ten days later, on the twenty-fifth— he was released. And the judge ordered that a charge of perjury be brought against the two people who had borne witness against him. I was in London, doing Christmas and Boxing Day with Ismail Richard and my London friends. Omar texted, "He's out," and I raced back on the twenty-seventh. On the last day of the year, we held a belated Seventh Day party for Khaled.

We swept and cleaned the house I'd refurbished in my mother's orchard. We laid out tables and chairs and strung up colored lights and strings of Egyptian flags. We set up a barbecue, and all our family and friends and friends of friends came and brought lots of food. We played music and danced and carried Khaled in a satin-lined sieve into every room and into all the dark corners so he would know his way around and know there was nothing, ever, to be afraid of, and we sprinkled the seven seeds in his path so he would always have plenty, and we sang to him the old instructions to obey his mother and his father and added that he must never ever obey SCAF or a government. My mother's orchard was teaming and buzzing and radiating love and light. And just before midnight, we all drove to Tahrir—the biggest family home in the world. And despite the dark days, Tahrir was full of hope and joy, and there was music and song and a church choir and people all the time gathering round Alaa and talking talking talking about the future and about what we need to do.

And while we were in Tahrir and unknowing, two men showed up and parked their motorbike and went around waking up the people in the houses near our orchard and questioning them about who'd been to our party and what had been said and sung and chanted. They went round to 3amm Hamed's house, but his wife wouldn't let him come out and speak to them because he has a weak heart and a strong temper. So she parried them and held them off and in the morning called Shukri who told Sohair who told me. Next day Alaa and Ahmad Seif and I went back to the orchard and talked to our neighbors and paid a visit to the local police stations, where we told the superintendent that we'd be happy to answer any questions he had and there was no need to send plainclothes round to inconvenience our neighbors. He was adamant he knew nothing about the two men. We asked if someone could operate like that in his district without him knowing? He said yes.

From jail, Alaa had written:

We need to be vigilant: they do not kill us to restore their state; they kill us because killing and jailing are normal behaviors in their state.

Remember their state: it wasn't only the police of their state who let us down; didn't the deans of their colleges run over our children? Didn't their bakeries and gas depots let us down? Were we not abandoned by their "wheel of production" that lavishes millions on the director and the consultant even when it's standing still but can't spare a crumb for the worker even when it's turning? Were we not let down by their state's economy that closes down the textile factories while the cotton is piled high in the farmers' homes but keeps the fertilizer plants pouring poison into our river? Were we not let down by its football clubs that permit their Security to brutalize the fans if they cheer too noisily but intervenes to shield players when they carry guns? We are let down by all their state's institutions and every leader in it, and tomorrow we will be let down by its parliament and its president.[12]

/ / / /

The Second Palestinian Intifada at the end of 2000 brought Egyptians out onto the streets. The next great protests came in 2003, against the attack on Iraq. We came out in protest at the rigging of parliamentary elections in 2005 and to support the judiciary in its fight against the regime in 2006. After that we never quieted down. The protests over the six years preceding the revolution were big industrial strikes, as in the textile factories of Mahalla, or else were initiated by the secular branch of the national movement: the Kifaya Movement, the civil and legal and physicians' groups, university students and faculty, small leftist parties, farmworkers, and the professional syndicates. A repeated pattern was that the secular organizers of protests—fully aware of the numbers that the Brotherhood commanded—would try to persuade them to make common cause against Mubarak's state. Time and again meetings would be held, the Brotherhood leadership would commit to putting large numbers on the street—and then the numbers wouldn't show up. Or a couple of thousand Brothers would come out and then vanish at five o'clock, leaving their secular comrades to be beaten up and detained by government forces and baltagis. Some individual Brotherhood members always acted according to their conscience, and some—like Muhammad Abd el-Quddous at the Journalists' Union—played a crucial part in nurturing the burgeoning protest movement, but they were acting outside the remit of the Association. Some younger Brothers came to feel over the years that they could no longer adhere to the principle of obedience that the Brotherhood exacted and went through the trauma of breaking away. But on the whole, the Islamist branch of the national movement did not have an appreciable input into the street dynamics that ultimately became the revolution of 25 January.

On 25 January young Salafis and Brothers did not wait for directives but simply and naturally joined the marches into the centers of their cities. And they were there again on the critical marches of the twenty-eighth. Their leadership did not announce a clear position with regard to the revolution, but when the attacks on Tahrir started on 2 February, the Day of the Camel, the leadership mobilized its network, and Brothers poured in from the countryside to protect the revolution in Tahrir.

But from 11 February, when SCAF and the military took overt charge of the country, the leadership of the Islamist current tried to pull back their young members from street action. Just as they had never been keen on confrontation with Mubarak, now they were clearly not keen on confrontation with the military. The worst manifestation of this was in the four days of Muhammad Mahmoud. The absence of the Brothers and the Salafis from the street, the fact that they stayed home while the Security Forces attacked Tahrir and killed young people who thought they were comrades, left a bitter taste in every mouth.

To the Islamist leadership, the revolution had become a matter of politics and elections and gain, and the Brotherhood, the Salafis, and the Gama3at leadership—now released from jail—swung into political action. The Brotherhood set up the FJP, the Freedom and Justice Party, the Salafis formed the Nour Party. Organization mattered, and numbers, and experience. The Salafis had numbers, the Brotherhood had numbers and organization and experience. Both were present in towns and villages across the country, and both had a membership that did what it was told. Together, as we've seen, they took home 71 percent of the vote.

REVOLUTION, YEAR TWO: 2012

On 23 January 2012 the elected Egyptian Parliament sat for the first time. The country expected it to start acting in the interests of the country. To legislate, for example, for a minimum wage. To act against remnants of the Mubarak regime that were still in position and working against the revolution. To order serious investigations into the murder of protesters and legislate to protect civilians from the military. To start work on legislation for human rights. To deal with the Ministry of the Interior. In other words, we expected and demanded that our elected representatives should start the country moving seriously toward "Bread, Freedom, Social Justice" through the legislative channels now in their power.

The country also expected Parliament to recognize the exceptional circumstances in which it had been elected and to rise to them. We had succeeded in protecting the new constitution from being written under the influence of SCAF; now we were entrusting Parliament with choosing the founding committee that would draft that constitution. For ten months the Islamists had refused to commit to any joint document of "governing principles," protesting again and again that they understood that the constitution had to be a document that spoke for the nation as a whole, not the particular group that happened to be in power. We expected them to grab this opportunity to show good faith and choose a founding committee that was balanced and serious and popular and representative.

So on 23 January, to remind their representatives of all this, thousands of citizens marched toward the Parliament building from different points in the city. Ultimately, the message they were bringing to their representatives was that they should remove SCAF and act as the legislative body of the revolution. If they acted for the people, the people would be their protection and their support. Workers marched from the trade union headquarters. No to Military Trials for Civilians marched from the Supreme Court. Just Retribution [for the killers of the shuhada] marched from the Shaheed Abd el-Menem Riyad Square. I walked in the artists' march from the Opera House. Not one of us managed to reach Parliament. The military had put up an artful series of barricades to protect Parliament from the people: walls, barbed wire, railings, and hundreds of Security Forces.

On 25 January, the first anniversary of the revolution, millions marched across the country calling for the transfer of power to Parliament and declaring "the revolution continues." The Islamist representatives so badly didn't want to hear this message that they encircled the building with a cordon of young Muslim Brothers, drafted in from the countryside, who stood ready to beat us off with sticks and belts. In Tahrir fights broke out between protesters and Islamists. The Islamists' position was unshakable: demands for the transfer of power to the Parliament where they held 71 percent of the seats were a conspiracy to cause a rift between them and the military. The Brotherhood was staying close to power—as it saw it. They did not even seem to recognize that *they* had become the power. They certainly didn't think that we, standing outside in the street, were the power—or at least we were not the power they wanted to align themselves with. Parliament had declared for SCAF.

So the revolution declared the twenty-seventh of January the Second Friday of Wrath. We marched from the four corners of Cairo to Tahrir, and at the mouth of Qasr el-Nil Bridge some of us diverted toward Maspero. Kazeboon projected one of its bloodiest documentaries directly onto the walls of the Radio and Television building. When the lights came on in the windows of the Ministry of Foreign Affairs next door, they spelled out "Thawra": Revolution! Cheers rang out in the street as the message of the activist/diplomats registered. The protesters in Maspero settled down for a sit-in. We would concentrate on the state's media machine and the Parliament. And despite the fact that a representative legislative body was now in place, we still chanted "Down, down with the rule of the military!"

PORT SAID, 1 FEBRUARY 2012

On 28 January the Cairo-based premier league football club, Ahli, played the Arab Contractors Club in Cairo Stadium. The Ahli supporters, Ultras Ahlawi, as you remember, together with their traditional rivals, Zamalek White Knights, had been at the front of the marches that broke police lines in the first days of the revolution.

Ultras Ahlawi were formed in 2007 and from the start had a problem with the police. They were the unofficial fan base of the club, and the police made a point of harassing them and would often round up groups of them and keep them in cells to prevent them attending a match. In July 2010, after a particularly fierce clash with police, they went on strike and stopped supporting their teams. When the Ahli football club board asked them to return to the stands, they demanded protection from the police—which the club tried to ensure. So when the revolution broke out, they were there for it.[13] They roused the Midan and gave it heart, and their cheer for freedom—four short claps and then "Horreya!"—became a punctuation mark for the chants during marches and sit-ins.

Muhammad Mustafa, who'd been killed in Tahrir, and Abboudi, who'd been brutalized in Parliament Street, were the latest Ultra victims of the police and military. Playing the Contractors football club on 28 January, Ultras Ahlawi raised their martyred friends' images and sang against the police throughout the match.

He was a failure
all through high school
just scraped through
fifty percent.
With brib'ry now
the man's a scholar
got a degree
from a hundred schools.
You raven nesting
inside our homes
why d'you ruin
all our pleasure?
We won't do
what you want.
We don't want
to see your face.
Frame us, frame us
lock us up, jail us.
That's the way

of the police.
Catch me, call me
international terrorist.
I play with fireworks
and sing for Ahli
and
freedom . . . freedom.

On Wednesday, 1 February, there was a meeting at the Saqia Culture Wheel in Zamalek to discuss the unpromising performance of Parliament so far, and to develop a strategy to influence the formation of the Founding Committee for the Constitution. We'd taken our seats; I was between Alaa my nephew and Ibrahim al-Moallem, and we were chatting and the meeting was just gearing up when Ibrahim got a message on his phone. Ibrahim (my publisher and the boss of Shorouk publishing and *Shorouk* newspaper) used to play water polo for Ahli and for Egypt, then sat on the board of the Ahli; he's been affiliated with the club all his life. That night the Ahli were playing Port Said FC in Port Said. Ultras Ahlawi had gone up to support, and nobody doubted that Ahli would win. As it happened, they didn't; they lost by two goals to nil.

But the message Ibrahim got was that there was trouble in Port Said and an Ahli supporter was hurt. "But why?" he said. "Port Said won." In the time it took him to say the words, another message came through: three supporters had been killed. And instantly another message: the number of suspected victims was now being put at eighteen. "What's happening?" he kept repeating. "What's happening?" We got out of the hall and stood at the entrance to the Saqia, under 15 May Overpass, meters from my home, and I watched him and Alaa on their mobiles. Twenty-seven supporters dead—no, thirty-six supporters . . . As the numbers rose, we raced to his office at *Shorouk* and switched on all the monitors. People crowded in. The screens and the telephones were registering the rise and rise of numbers.

At midnight Alaa and I left Ibrahim in his office and headed to Cairo Railway Station in Rameses to wait for the train that was bringing the Ultras home. Hundreds had had the same impulse, and there was a mass of people arriving at the station. The huge hall echoed with chants. Just before the revolution, the regime had once again surpassed itself and redecorated the beautiful, austere building with garish gilt pillars and giant metal plants. The scaffolding was still in place, and now it was covered in young men. They were on the scaffolding, on the stairs, the escalators, the balconies. The hall was full of mothers, shabab, sympathizers. It was an ocean of waving flags. At three in the morning, the train chugged in; a third-class train, it had taken five dark and cold hours to make the journey from Port Said. Hundreds rushed to meet it. The train arrived at the platform submerged in people; people on top of it, clinging to it, walking alongside it. The chants died down when the young Ultras who'd been on the train appeared. They looked pale and shrunk, their clothes were torn and bloody, and their heads, arms, and legs were bandaged. They leaned on each other and limped. Some were carried.

Seventy-two young men had been killed.

Mysterious buses had arrived at the stadium, their passengers allowed in without tickets. The governor and the chief of police, both of whom attend all Port Said Club matches, were absent from this crucial one. As the match ended, all the lights went out. Security Forces parted to let groups of men through, and they rushed the away team's terrace. Ahli supporters tried to escape but found the gates soldered shut. Some young men were killed with a quick snap of the neck; others were thrown from the top of the stadium.

We said it in the stadium and we sang it to the crowds:
In Port Said the victims were betrayed before they died.

> *They plotted hard against us they were vicious they were mean,*
> *They murdered our best mates and they murdered all our dreams.*

We somehow couldn't quite believe it. In towns and villages, thousands gathered to bury their friends and mourn them. The Ultras cut across class, profession, geography.

> *Hey SCAF, hey bastard Council,*
> *What were you paid for the martyr's blood?*

Tantawi sent a military plane for the players. In a brief appearance on national television, he said, "I don't understand why the people are letting this pass. Everybody has to take part." Once again the authorities were trying to instigate people against each other. For days the media tore into Port Said's "heroic" label—earned when the city bore the brunt of Britain, France, and Israel's attack on Egypt in 1956—and painted it as a place of evil. The people of Port Said went on protests, described how they had tried to get to the visiting fans but were blocked by Security. An investigation was started.

Ultras flags and banners flew in every street. Wherever there was an injured Ultra, his friends were camped outside his door. Ultras White Knights Zamalek joined Ultras Ahlawi in protest marches, and their banners flew together.[14] Groups of young people gathered outside the homes of murdered Ultras to sing Ultra songs while artists painted their images on the surrounding walls.

In the midst of the grief and the anger, the young men began appearing as angels on the walls of Muhammad Mahmoud. Anas, fourteen, the youngest Ultra, who'd skipped off to the match behind his parents' backs:

> *I'm wearing a red T-shirt*
> *And headed for Port Said*

Came back my shroud was white
And in my country I was martyred

Kareem Khuzam, whose father soon died of a heart attack:

Paradise for the martyrs
And the revolution's born anew

Amgad Aslan, Hasan Taha, Islam Tolba, Basem Osman, Muhammad Ghandour . . . seventy-two young men.[15]

DOWNTOWN

From dawn on 2 February, the streets around the Ministry of the Interior became scenes of running battles. The shabab threw stones and fireworks, the police shot live ammunition, and the army started replicating the wall it had built in Muhammad Mahmoud in November. Seven walls in a small part of downtown Cairo: Qasr el-Eini, Sheikh Rihan, Mansour, Noubar, Falaki, Muhammad Mahmoud. Cement walls, barriers, barbed wire. The walls blocked traffic and irritated residents and antagonized the shabab, but most important they provided cover for the police and army officers when they went out hunting. Now they could come out to the middle of the street and shoot at the shabab in comfort, their backs covered. The shabab pulled down one wall with nothing but steel levers, rope, and coordination.

Once again the small field clinics appeared. Once again the smoke and the tear gas and the crowds and the motorbike ambulances carrying the wounded wedged between two riders. Some newly elected parliamentarians proposed a law to officially allow the troops to shoot protesters. Others threatened to go on hunger strike until the shooting stopped.[16]

On the street the protesters this time looked poorer, less privi-leged. Laila Soueif and Hani el-Hosseini established a roster so that "an adult of standing" was always there to bear witness. A young man stopped me in my tracks. "Don't step here," he said, "not here—" He had his arms spread out wide, protecting a patch of pavement, about one square meter, and as people surged and heaved with the shooting and the stone throwing, he held every-one off from stepping on that square meter. "Someone died here," he kept saying, "Someone died here. Don't step on his blood."

On the fourth a Mothers' March headed for Parliament. Practi-cally every Egyptian woman I've ever known was there; we ranged from women of eighty to girls of fourteen. We crowded the railings and called, "Give me back my country. Give me back my son." An army officer came out, a paratrooper, flanked by his men, his eyes behind shades, and said, "What do you want? They're dead. What do you want now?" Some parliamentarians came out to where we could see them; they were the independents, and they were wear-ing the yellow scarves of No to Military Trials. Security men were busy taking photos of us. Lulie stuck out her tongue at the camera.

In the evenings, visored officers went well into the streets to shoot at people. Mosireen were out there filming, finding cover wherever they could and filming. Salma Said was sheltering behind a metal electricity box. As she peeped round the side with her cam-era, an officer shot at her. Within hours, as she was lying in hospi-tal, Mosireen had put out a film on YouTube: a girl's face with five buckshot pellets: one in the right cheekbone, one four millimeters below her left eye, the third by her nose, and the fourth and fifth in the dimple of her chin. An X-ray image of a leg powdered with thirty-three pellets. She tells the story from her bed. The masked soldier had seen her filming and shot. He hit her in the face, and she fell. He shot her again as she lay on the ground. And he shot the third round as the shabab lifted her and ran. More than fifty pellets were embedded in the young woman.[17]

ABBASEYYA, 11, MAY 2012

Through the rest of February, through March and April, there were constant marches and protests. People tried to implement the aims of the revolution in their own lives and workplaces. The students organized, and so did schoolchildren, teachers, doctors, and workers. New independent syndicates and unions were formed. People worked on the campaigns to end military trials for civilians, to expose the lies of the military, to reform the Dakhleyya. The universities held elections and installed new deans and presidents. Everywhere there was movement. The street demanded that the military step down, but Parliament did not step up to the demand. The majority parties were too busy dividing up the house committees among themselves and trying to form the Founding Committee for the Constitution. The first committee they formed was so clearly both biased and below par that they had to dissolve it and start again. The second one was still flawed, but it countered that it would have satellite committees, and advisers, and groups to collect input from the people everywhere.

And the country was heading for the last "procedural" hope of pushing the revolution forward: the presidential elections. Political parties were formed. Coalitions came together and disbanded again. Candidates put themselves forward, and supporters campaigned to get them the endorsements they needed. The revolution's dream ticket was a coalition of Muhammad el-Baradei, Hamdein Sabahi, and Abd el-Moneim Aboul Fotouh, but we could not get them to work together. El-Baradei even withdrew from the contest altogether. The Elections Committee disqualified the old intelligence chief, Omar Suleiman, and the Muslim Brotherhood boss and millionaire businessman Khairat el-Shater. But it refused to disqualify Mubarak's last prime minister, Ahmad Shafiq. Salafi candidate Hazem Abu Ismail was disqualified because his mother had held an American passport. His supporters refused to accept the committee's decision and held demonstrations at the military's Cairo headquarters in Abbaseyya. The demonstrations turned into a sit-in. When they were attacked by baltagis, people who would never have voted for Hazem Abu Ismail went to help.

Atef el-Gohari was one of the revolutionaries who went to the aid of the Salafis. You can see a video of him speaking in Tahrir, surrounded by children: "What's most important," he says to them, "is that shabab have died; they've died for justice."[18] He says it in that voice with the built-in rasp I'd recognized when he ran me to safety in Abbaseyya in July; the voice I'd heard so often in the Midan: "Ezzayyek ya doktora?" Do you need anything? And I'd known that if I did need something, he'd find it for me. Another video clip shows him handing out breadsticks from a plastic bag during Muhammad Mahmoud. "Anyone hungry?" he calls. "Anyone hungry?" The Midan, the revolution, had been Atef's personal responsibility. He'd gone to Abbaseyya to help keep the peace, to help protect the protesters, even though he was totally against their ideology. On 3 May, on their last killing spree before the presidential elections, the army murdered him. You can see a photo someone's posted of him with his mouth and chin and throat blown away.[19]

THE PRESIDENTIAL ELECTIONS, MAY 2012

A tweet on Wednesday, 23 May: "Intermission for the Elections, then we continue the Revolution."

You could say that more than half the population boycotted the elections. The 80 percent of the electorate that had turned out in such orderly and optimistic fashion to vote in the March 2011 referendum had seen how that exercise had been used to consolidate the grip of the military and divide the country. The 54 percent who had persevered and voted in the parliamentary elections had watched in dismay for four months as Parliament anxiously tredded water and bickered. The revolutionary core that had refused to take part in the elections for Parliament after the army killed protesters in Maspero and Muhammad Mahmoud had gained strength after the killings of Parliament Street, Port Said, Mansour Street, and Abbaseyya II.

The turnout for the first round of presidential elections was 43 percent.

One little pocket of revolutionary activity was the candidacy of Khaled Ali, the young lawyer who was the one candidate truly born of the revolution. Ali only got some 130,000 votes in the end, but he provided a nucleus for an innovative and radical revolutionary group. Working on his campaign, they developed a small network of professionals who put together a detailed economic and social program for the country. This program now provides the basis of the positions of the secular Left in the national discussions we insist on having.

Of the top five candidates, three were very clear in their backgrounds and ideologies: Muhammad Morsi was the candidate of the Muslim Brotherhood and the Islamists in general. Ahmad Shafiq was the candidate of the Mubarak regime remnants and the military. Hamdein Sabahi appealed to seculars and Central Left. The remaining two were more ambiguous. Abd el-Moneim Aboul Fotouh was a veteran of the Brotherhood leadership but had recently fallen out with them, and his international and economic politics seemed well to the left of Morsi and the Brotherhood in general. And Amr Moussa was a statesman of the old regime but famous for being at odds with it, and he had been very careful to publicly support the revolution—although in a "but finally we have to be sensible" kind of way.

The military, the remnants, and the Islamists commanded networks and practices and funds well beyond anything remotely available to the others, but even so, the results of the first round were

Muhammad Morsi: 5,764,950 (24.78 percent)
Ahmad Shafiq: 5,505,327 (23.66 percent)
Hamdein Sabahi: 4,820,273 (20.72 percent)
Abd el-Moneim Aboul Fotouh: 4,065,239 (17.47 percent)
Amr Moussa: 2,588,850 (11.13 percent)

The inability of the candidates of the Left, Sabahi and Aboul Fotouh, to work together cost us the elections, and the two powers heading for a run-off in the first elections after the revolution were the Muslim Brotherhood and the Mubarak regime.

There was a maelstrom of political activity as Shafiq made triumphal appearances and gave presidential addresses. Hamdein Sabahi charged that nine hundred thousand of Shafiq's votes had been fraudulently obtained. Morsi wooed the various secular parties and coalitions and made them sweet promises about how he would be the president of all of Egypt, not just of the Brotherhood.

Hours before the runoffs, SCAF issued a new law giving military forces the right to legally detain civilians. At the same time, the Constitutional Court decided that this was the moment to consider the four-month-old charge that the parliamentary elections in November had contravened SCAF's Constitutional Declaration. They found for the charge and announced Parliament illegitimate.

For the non-Islamist revolutionaries confronted once more with the ballot box, the choices were terrible. You could either vote for Muhammad Morsi, or you could spoil your ballot. And if you spoiled your ballot—or boycotted—and Ahmad Shafiq won, how would you live with yourself? After everything we'd done, after our friends had been killed and maimed, after so many lives had been ruined—and also after the freedoms and the gains and the new spirit we had achieved—we would have allowed the regime to come back. But if we voted for Morsi—if we betrayed the shuhada of Muhammad Mahmoud and Parliament Street, if we forgot the cordons round Parliament and the commandeering of its committees, if we forgave the nonsense spoken in the Islamist Founding Committee for the Constitution, we would still be voting for a religion-based party, and an economically and politically conservative one to boot. But then the Islamists had also been part of the revolutionary current, the current for change, and their young people had shown an ability to be open, to be persuadable—and to make us listen. The trajectory of history suggested that we had to pass through an Islamist phase sooner or later—maybe we'd be able to come up with a different model for that, an Egyptian model. And Morsi would not allow people to be shot on the street, would he? While Shafiq would. Ahmad Shafiq would come in precisely to make sure people were shot on the street, to make an end of all this nonsense and get right back to business as usual—with a new set of faces, more agreeable to the military.

As for "freedoms" there probably wouldn't be much to choose between the military and the Islamists. Around fifteen million people had voted the Islamists into Parliament, and only five million had come out and voted for Morsi. Maybe by the next elections we would vote them out. At least with the Brotherhood there would *be* next elections—or would there? Well, with Shafiq there certainly wouldn't. Every day of these past fifteen months, everything each day had held, everything each day had meant, would all be for nothing. For worse than nothing: Egypt would have voted to bring in a corrupt military dictatorship.

I stood behind the curtain with the pen in my hand. I had been all set to write "The Revolution Continues" right across the ballot. But I put my tick in front of Morsi's name and went home ill and miserable.

Close to three million extra voters took part in the runoffs. And almost one million people could not stand the choice and ruined their ballots. Muhammad Morsi was returned with 13,230,131 (51.73 percent). Ahmad Shafiq got 12,347,380 (48.27 percent) and fled Egypt for the Gulf.

What everybody pointed out, when the results came in, was that the difference between the votes in the first and the second rounds, the extra 7.5 million who voted for Morsi and the extra 6.8 million who voted for Shafiq, were not voting for either man or his program; they were voting because they hated or feared the alternative. Finally, more voters hated SCAF and the old regime.

✓✓✓✓

We will not forgive. Every minute of every day was an opportunity for the military to do the decent thing: even to secure what ill-gotten wealth they already had and still do the decent and the honorable thing and help preserve our bright, shining revolution and the new retrieved spirit of our people. And instead SCAF and its army targeted and killed and imprisoned and tortured and insulted and degraded. We will not forget, and we will not forgive.

AND NOW?

Once again, as I write the last words of this text, at the end of November 2012, I've no idea what will be happening in Egypt as you read it.

In November 2011, Muhammad Mahmoud Street became the place we went to for emotional and spiritual sustenance. We would sit surrounded by the graffiti that had been midwifed by the terrible events that took place here, the drawings and texts that rose above this street to create an art that spoke of our shuhada every-where, and that spoke to us of Egypt and of the revolution and reminded us what it was we were fighting for.

Ten weeks ago, late at night on 18 September 2012, govern-ment workers protected by Security Forces descended on Muham-mad Mahmoud and started erasing the graffiti. People gathered and protested. Soon the Presidency, the Ministry of the Interior, and the municipality all denied ordering the erasure! Meanwhile the brushes and paint had come out again. Next day a mischie-vous face with a shock of black hair appeared; the young man was laughing and sticking out a long green tongue. Within days a whole new set of graffiti went up.

Who owns the wall on Muhammad Mahmoud? Who owns the city? Who owns the revolution? The country? This is now the struggle.

On Friday, 12 October 2012, there was a call for a Friday of Accounting. Muhammad Morsi had been president for one hun-dred days; so how well had he done? Thinking in terms of two sim-ple axes: an Islamist/secular axis, and a conservative/progressive axis, we knew which pole Morsi came from; how far had he moved toward the other? And did he look like he was heading for some balance? There were always going to be two tests: whether he had managed to rise above party politics and be a president for all of Egypt; and whether he was guiding the country toward the aims of the revolution: Bread, Freedom, Social Justice.

"Bread": The world is now debating the ideology of economics. The Occupy movement in the United States and the protests in Britain, Spain, and Greece are all about the ideology of economics. In Egypt, we find that the economic ideology of the Brotherhood is not very different from that of the Mubarak regime; essentially a free market, capitalist ideology that favors the corporation over the citizen and the rich over the poor. Where it differs is, possibly, in its attitude to the poor; where the Mubarak regime discounted the poor, the Brotherhood sees them as objects of charity—and useful foot soldiers.

But the revolution demands a radical restructuring of economic power relations in the country.

At the moment the most visible argument is over loans from international financial institutions. The Morsi government is negotiating a loan from the IMF. It is deeply unpopular; people know that even if the overt terms of the loan are favorable, its underlying requirements will lead to more privatization and less public spending—while the country is looking for more public ownership, more public spending, and big developmental projects to utilize Egypt's enormous, underused human resources.

Social justice: while no political party will declare itself to be against social justice per se, the question is how this "justice" is to be defined, and how it is to be achieved. The Egyptian revolution wants every child to be born into equal opportunity. And for this you need good free education, universal health care, good public transport, and affordable housing. All this is achievable if you privilege the poor and the majority, if you think in holistic terms of a sustainable way of life for ourselves and our planet.

Freedom: The report put out a few days ago by the al-Nadeem Center for the Rehabilitation of Victims of Violence makes for terrible reading. The shootings, torture, and detentions continue. Not one of the hundred days of Morsi's presidency has been free of some human rights violation by the state.

Muhammad Morsi has not enthroned our shuhada in a place of honor at the heart of revolutionary Egypt—even though his first visitor at the presidential palace was Khaled Said's mother. He has not set in place an emergency commission and fund to support the injured, even though he has instituted a fact-finding committee to investigate their issues. He has hosted a delegation of American businessmen that included every major arms manufacturer in the industry. He has not adopted any of the existing initiatives to restructure the security establishment, and people are still dying under torture in jails and police stations, but he has retired the top generals of SCAF. Whether the medals he gave them will make them immune to prosecution for murder remains to be seen.

In Tahrir, on 12 October 2012, the people raised the following demands:

1. Re-forming the Founding Committee for the Constitution to achieve more balance. We need more women, young people, Christians, seculars. The Constitution is a constitution for all Egyptians.
2. Restructuring the Ministry of the Interior, the Dakhleyya.
3. Providing justice for the shuhada and the injured.
4. Instituting minimum and maximum wages.

So what has changed? Well, us, and the way we see our problems. We see now that we were never going to clean out the residue of forty years of degradation and corruption in eighteen days, or a year. The failures of our state and the ills of our society are coming out for all to see. And this is necessary if we are to put things right. We're finished with smoke and mirrors. We see that we are divided, and that we have to make a huge and imaginative effort to forge a new common ground. We see that our institutions are hollowed out and that we have to clean and rebuild them. We see that we have to clean out the corruption that has eaten into every aspect of our public life. But we see that there are very many good people among us who are dedicated to bringing about the change the revolution demanded. And we see that even though the state is more or less failed, Egypt itself continues to function. Real crime rates have not gone up, shops are open, and people still crack jokes and sit in cafés and take the air on the bridges. This is a testament to the amazing solidity of our society.

As I write these words, in late November 2012, the revolution itself is in many places. Here are some of them:

1. Gaza: while the new Israeli attack on Gaza ("Pillar of Cloud") was under way, five hundred Egyptian activists traveled to Rafah and sat on the border until they were allowed through.[20] They talked with our Palestinian neighbors, gave blood, shot footage, and collected lists of needed medicines . . . this could not have happened any time in the last forty years. Now the people of Egypt will stand—literally—by Palestine.

2. The Nile University in Cairo has been fighting an unfair takeover of its building by the government, which had decided to gift the building to the Egyptian Nobel laureate, physicist Ahmad Zuweil. The students and faculty took the case to court, conducted a sit-in for over two months, on the pavement outside their university, and held classes and exams right there, on the street.[21] Two days ago the judge found for the university. They will keep their building.

3. Qorsaya is a lovely island in the Nile at the southern end of Cairo. It's a farming island, marked by Gamal Mubarak's "Cairo 2050" development project, which would have got rid of the thousands of people living on the island and turned it into a luxury development. This project and several like it were paused after the revolution. Now they seem to be starting up again. But the people won't have it. Three days ago they fought off the army trying to take a piece of the land.[22]

4. In every hospital in Egypt, the doctors have been on strike for sixty-five days now. They demand transparency, an allocation of 15 percent of the country's annual budget for health care, and the tools with which

to deliver decent health care. In a desperate attempt to
get the government to pay attention, they've emulated
the football fans and created Ultras White Coats,[23]
they've appropriated the Ultras' songs (but made them
less rude), and now they bring the streets alive at their
protests.

There is not a day that passes without a spontaneous public
protest of some kind. Workers protest the manipulation of their
factories and the denial of their rights. Mothers protest the absence
of vaccines. Doctors protest the lack of equipment and resources
in hospitals. The work of the revolution now is to attach itself to
each one of these actions and so to politicize them and draw them
together.

Only connect.

And the connections are happening. Not just within Egypt, not
just among the Arab peoples, but across the world. When Wisconsin was first to raise the Tahrir banner in its own protests in early
2011, Tahrir revolutionaries ordered a delivery of pizza to the protesters there. The protests in Spain last month used the rhythms
of the Egyptian chants. In Egypt we're watching Greece carefully. And across the world, hundreds of thousands of civilians are
marching for Palestine. As the systems that oppress and exploit the
people have become global, so our resistance is becoming global.

None of us is alone.

REVOLUTION III

Postscript

31 July 2013

I am writing this by the sea, waiting for Armageddon. Hoping it won't come.

We have persuaded ourselves to take three days out of Cairo; away from the jingoism and army-worship of a Tahrir where we don't, for the moment, feel we belong.

Everything here, seventy kilometers west of Alexandria, at my mother's beach house, is unchanged. The sand is impossibly white, the sea many, many blues. When from the road I first caught sight of the colors, I felt as if I were slipping back into the past. But Khaled is not the past, and he's here: eighteen months old, stepping determinedly through the sand, staggering a little, pointing, beaming smiles into our faces, picking up shells and the plastic covers of juice cartons with heartbreaking delicacy. His father, Alaa, still has a variety of court cases hanging over him—new ones brought by the Muslim Brotherhood (MB) government joining the old ones brought by the military—but right now he's waist high in the gentle waves, settling his son into the bright yellow swimming ring Manal is holding out for him.

Ahmad Seif is reclining in the shade of the wide bamboo parasol. He's getting stronger every day after the heart attack that nearly killed him two months ago. The blue kite he's been teaching Khaled to fly bucks and rears and dives up above our heads, tethered to the rim of the parasol.

Back in Cairo, hundreds of thousands of Muslim Brothers and

their supporters are camped out at two ends of the city: northeast at the Rab3a junction on the road to the airport, and southwest in the piazza between Cairo University, the zoo, and the botanical gardens. They have been there for thirty-three days and they say they'll stay until Muhammad Morsi—deposed by the armed forces by popular demand on 3 July—is reinstated as president. A week ago, General Abd el-Fattah el-Sisi, Commander of the Armed Forces and minister of defense made a brief speech requesting the Egyptian people to "mandate" him to "deal with terror"— that is, to end the Brotherhood sit-ins and protests. People poured onto the streets to shout and sing the mandate he'd asked for; effectively a blank check. Fighter planes drew hearts in the sky.

Yesterday, the minister of the interior, General Muhammad Ibrahim, announced that the police and the army intend to break the sit-in in the coming four days. The police general is one of the remnants of Morsi's government in the new cabinet.

Morsi himself is being held at an unknown location—but was visited the day before yesterday by representatives of the European Union who found him to be well and defiant. Many of the Brotherhood leadership are in detention. Four, including the head of the Association of the Muslim Brotherhood (the AMB), Muhammad Badi3, are inside the Rab3a sit-in with warrants out for their arrest. AMB supporters are organizing marches throughout the country. Where they clash with citizens, people die. The country is awash with weaponry that's been flooding in through our western border since the fall of the Qaddafi regime in Libya: automatics, machine guns, RPJs. In Sinai, a low-intensity war is being fought. The AMB has said that Sinai will not quiet until Morsi is back as president.

The entire world is debating whether what happened in Egypt one month ago was a military coup or a political procedure, legitimate because it expressed the will of the majority of the people—

the millions who went out onto the streets on June 30 to demand early presidential elections.

The Brotherhood's failure to rule Egypt was spectacular; in the space of twelve months they lost everything they had worked toward for more than eighty years. They did this by demonstrating, again and again, that the only real project they had was their own empowerment. It started in November 2012 with Muhammad Morsi issuing a constitutional declaration giving himself absolute powers. He had to retract it a few days later, but by then he had pushed through the founding committee that would write the constitution and had appointed his public prosecutor. Then the country watched as the new elected president and his cabinet allied themselves with the enemies of the revolution. The Ministry of the Interior, the Dakhleyya, was courted and honored and got pay raises—as did the military. Morsi and his cabinet busied themselves with overtures to Mubarak's jailed or fugitive business elite, to the International Monetary Fund, to the Gulf countries, while ignoring the growing number of industrial and social protests sweeping the country. Soon, factory sit-ins were being broken up with police dogs, and young activists were vanishing from the streets and showing up at the morgue.

The president seemed to have no economic policy apart from soliciting loans from international lenders and donations from the Gulf; certainly nothing that might start moving the country toward the social justice that was one of the declared aims of the revolution. During the one year of his presidency the country saw more than seven thousand protests. His government paid no attention.

A group of young people came up with the "rebel" campaign: an A4 sheet of paper declaring "I, as a member of the AGM of the Egyptian People, withdraw confidence from the president and call for early presidential elections." People everywhere downloaded the statement, printed large numbers of it, and went out to solicit signatures. The campaign went viral.

At a mass rally, Morsi sat unmoving through hate speeches against Shia Muslims. Days later citizens murdered four Shia men in a village not forty minutes from downtown Cairo. Attacks against churches and Coptic citizens increased in provincial towns. For the first time in its history, the papal seat, the Cathedral in Abbaseyya, came under attack. And the president officially encouraged young men to go to "holy war" in Syria.

The purpose of democracy is to ensure that the people most affected by decisions get to make the decisions. The people saw the president steering the country to disaster. When, in the final days of his rule, Morsi appointed a round of county governors— all connected to the AMB—citizens prevented them from entering their offices. Armed AMB men confronted protests and people were killed in clashes on the street.

The MB insisted that when the Egyptian people elected Morsi president they entered into an unbreakable contract to keep him for four years. The protesters, on the other hand, said that Morsi had been elected on the basis of a stated commitment to the goals of the revolution and promises he'd made—and that he had honored neither.

But the constitution that the MB had pushed through did not describe a procedure to get rid of a president. So the people invented one: millions of endorsements to "rebel" and possibly twenty-five million people on the streets on 30 June.

On 30 June, across the whole country, Egypt staged gigantic protests. Once again we dominated the world's TV screens. How many millions? Was this the biggest mass action humanity had ever known? What about 1917? It's now said that the "rebels" were contacted quite early on by Egyptian intelligence and the military, that the path of their campaign was maybe smoothed, but there's no doubt that the campaign tapped into a deep and growing anger in the country.

That Sunday afternoon I sat on the curb at the Roxy intersection in Heliopolis watching the marches coming from every district of Cairo toward Morsi's seat at the Ettehadeyya Palace. People streamed by on both sides of the eight-lane road. Hour after hour they didn't stop. In the provinces the streets of one town after another filled up. Tahrir was fuller than it had ever been. Once again the Egyptian people had taken to the streets to drum a president out of office.

But there are differences between July 2013 and January/February 2011. The revolution, raising the banner of "Bread, Freedom, Social Justice," is against corruption, injustice, and brutality. In Revolution I, Mubarak's ruling National Democratic Party (NDP) was the known and declared enemy, as was the security establishment. The military was an unknown quantity that—in the optimism of our hearts—we might believe would protect the country in the process of transition.

The twenty-nine months between then and now have taught us a great deal. We've learned the extent to which our institutions are hollowed out. We've learned that large sections of our judiciary are crooked and partisan. We've seen the bankruptcy of the political elite that was considered the opposition to Mubarak. And the military, under the leadership of the SCAF, has demonstrated its devotion to its business interests and its murderous contempt for the people. These lessons have been learned the hard way, with young people losing friends and limbs and eyes. Getting rid of SCAF was Revolution II.

In June 2012, when we were in the terrible position of having to choose a president who was either an MB candidate or a military remnant of the Mubarak regime, I wrote: "The revolution will continue because neither the old regime nor the Islamist trend in its current form are going to deliver 'bread, freedom, social justice.' Neither of them are going to validate the sacrifices made by the 1,200 young people murdered by the regime, the 8,000 maimed, the 16,000 court-martialled" (*The Guardian,* 17 June). One week later, having listened to Morsi's promises, I allowed myself to hope: "Maybe, maybe, we have voted in a president whom we can support, or oppose with honor—without being shot" (*The Guardian,* 25 June).

Well, the shooting didn't stop when we got rid of SCAF, neither did the torture; Jeeka, Christie, el-Husseini Abu Deif, Muhammad el-Gindi, Muhammad el-Shaf3i are just a few of the young activists the country lost to the Morsi regime.

The economic situation worsened and Morsi outdid Mubarak in opacity and cronyism. And, on top of that, his regime was inefficient to a point of danger. A view of the situation in Sinai, our relations with Africa and with Syria, pointed to big disasters ahead. And so, one year into Morsi's presidency, we arrived, on 30 June, at Revolution III.

In Revolution III the whole country—the revolutionaries, the Dakhleyya, the "deep state," the "sofa brigade," and the remnants and supporters of the Mubarak regime—united against the Muslim Brotherhood. And so, on 30 June, revolutionaries who'd been steadfast for two years found themselves in bizarre company: the previous head of State Security led his own anti-Brotherhood march; there was a march of police in uniform; we saw protesting police officers chatting easily under the white banners of young men murdered by the police over the course of the preceding three years; a police band played on the stage in Tahrir. And although some voices were raised in an anticipatory reminder: "Down, down with military rule," the dominant chant was "The army, the people, one hand!" The people were calling on the army to step in—to be the executor of the people's will.

The people are, until now, insisting on treating the army as their own. People want to believe that the military has learned its lesson and doesn't want to rule. That it got what it wants in Morsi's 2012 constitution and, even if it's amended, no one will touch its interests. That Tantawi and the baddies are no longer in SCAF and that General Sisi will simply oversee another set of elections.

So, will the generals look after Revolution III better than they looked after Revolution I? General Sisi was, after all, part of SCAF and in charge of military intelligence.

Many of us now fear that Revolution III is in grave danger of being co-opted by the enemies of Revolution I. We point out that Revolution III is not against Morsi and the MB as such, but against the continuation of the policies that marked the Mubarak era. That we're in danger of the old regime slipping on yet another mask, slipping into power. But the sentiment of the people is: get rid of Morsi first and deal with the rest later.

Could we have waited for parliamentary elections and trusted that the dismal performance of the presidency over the preceding year would vote the MB out of the majority? The worry was that the government had been busy redrawing electoral districts to favor the MB, and that a large portion of the judiciary (who would have overseen elections) were MB supporters. And in the long tug of war between the presidency and the Constitutional Court over the election law, no one was sure when the elections would actually be allowed to happen.

When people protested on the streets, Morsi chose to fight back by shooting at them. As late as 29 June if he'd appointed a prime minister from outside the MB, people would have given him another chance and the Brotherhood would still have had a seat at the table. Now we were back to standing vigil at the morgue, clocking the murdered as they were carried in and fighting with the coroner to let parents check to see if their children were in

his fridges. Graffiti on the Ettehadeyya wall says THE LEGITI-
MACY OF YOUR BALLOT BOX IS CANCELED BY OUR
MARTYRS' BOXES [COFFINS]. GO!

But today, 31 July, the MB in their thousands are marching
through the streets of towns and villages to support the sit-ins and
support the man they still count as their president. The rest of the
country is determined to keep the MB out of power and out of
office. The media are baying for blood. The armed forces and the
Dakhleyya are weighing their options. No one knows how much
room for maneuvering the one-month-old cabinet really has. No
one knows how far General Sisi's ambitions extend.

There is a core, a resolute core, that does not lose sight of the
aims of the revolution—bread, freedom, social justice—and what
these bring of human dignity; that knows that what the people
will finally demand is the administration that will put them on the
road to achieving these aims. And that the people—even if they
digress onto a side street—will return to insist on their original
path and their essential aims.

But for the moment, we figure we can take three days off at the
beach. We recuperate, cook, fly kites, and play with Khaled. Sun
and sand and sea and wind. Soon, we'll be back on the streets,
helping our revolution on its difficult path. And when you read
these words, many months from now, maybe we'll be farther
down the road toward its great, human aims.

Meanwhile, it does no harm to repeat, now and always:

Down, down with military rule.
Down, down with the rule of the Brotherhood.
As long as human blood is cheap / down, down with every
    president.
And glory to our martyrs forever.

A BRIEF AND NECESSARY HISTORY

1517

The sword-wielding Mameluke kings of Egypt were defeated by the Ottoman Turks' state-of-the-art cannon and gunpowder. Egypt was subsumed into the expanding Ottoman Empire and ruled from Istanbul.

1798

Ottoman decline and the growing British Empire in the East tempted Napoleon to invade Egypt, but his expedition did not last long. By 1801 a combination of British, Ottoman, and Egyptian forces had expelled the French. The Ottoman force was led by an Albanian/Macedonian soldier/adventurer, Muhammad Ali.

1805

The Ottoman Sultan, Selim III, under pressure from Egyptian notables, including Sheikh Omar Makram, appointed Muhammad Ali Pasha "Viceroy of Egypt," to rule it on behalf of Istanbul.

Muhammad Ali created a comfortable margin of autonomy for himself and embarked on a massive modernization program. He retained French officers to help build a modern army, set up arms and munitions factories, seized all agricultural land and made it Crown Property, and instituted a centralized agricultural program supported by massive public irrigation works. He put in place a modern education system and in 1813 started sending hundreds of young men to study in Europe. In 1821 he set up the Boulaq printing press—which is still the state printer—and started an economic boom based on agriculture and industry. He forbade the removal of antiquities from Egypt and created the Egyptian state bureaucracy to run the country's administration. In the twenty years of his reign, Egypt's population doubled and her society became more diverse and mobile. On behalf of the sultan, he put down rebellions in the Arabian Peninsula and Crete and expanded into the Sudan. But Muhammad Ali saw Egypt's strategic depth in Palestine and Syria and in 1832 he acted; the campaign of Ibrahim Pasha, Muhammad Ali's eldest son, swept through the cities of Palestine, Lebanon, Syria, and Anatolia and paused at the gates of Istanbul itself. The European powers, however, were unwilling to see a strong Egyptian state replace a weak Ottoman one. Britain, Russia, Prussia, and Austria treated with the new young sultan Abd el-Meguid I and in 1840 forced Muhammad Ali to limit his ambitions to Egypt in return for a pledge that his rule there would become hereditary.

1863

Ismail, Muhammad Ali's grandson, took up the next phase of Egypt's modernization. He established elected local councils and a house of representatives. He dug the Suez Canal (naming its cities Port Said and Ismaileyya for his uncle, Said Pasha, and himself). He built Abdeen Palace and made it the seat of the ruler instead of Salahudin's Citadel. He lit the streets and pumped water into houses and, with his formidable minister of public works, Ali Pasha Mubarak, he laid out downtown Cairo—stretching from Midan el-Ataba, where he built the Opera House, to Midan el-Ismaileyya (now Midan el-Tahrir) and Qasr el-Nil Bridge. They dug canals and increased the area of agricultural land, built factories and energized trade, introduced state education for girls, and set up the National Library (1870) and the National Archives.

And along the way, Ismail incurred massive debts from European bankers. Books have been written about the issue of Egypt's debts, but in any case, in 1876 Ismail was forced to accept British and French supervision over Egyptian affairs to ensure repayment. In 1879 he was forced out of Egypt, and his son, the much weaker Tewfiq, was instituted as khedive of Egypt.

The issue of the debt and foreign dominance of Egyptian affairs was one of the triggering factors behind the revolt of the Egyptian army under the leadership of Orabi Pasha. But the revolt spread to demand a functioning parliament overseeing the cabinet, a strengthening of the army, and a review of the administration of the new Suez Canal by representatives of France and Britain.

1882

The Khedive Tewfiq asked his debtor friends for help. Britain invaded, declared Egypt a "protectorate," and exiled Orabi and his fellow rebels.

Now Egypt had two masters: the khedive, representing the Ottoman sultan, and the High Commissioner, representing Britain. When, in the First World War, Ottoman Turkey lost to the Allies and was stripped of her empire, the Egyptian national movement united against the British occupation and rose up in the celebrated but ultimately unsuccessful Sa3d Zaghloul revolt of 1919.

And since then the national movement in Egypt has developed

in two branches: the modernizing liberationist secular movement, which sees the future of Egypt as an independent nation-state; and the tradition-based movement, which does not see Egypt standing alone but envisions it as part of a powerful Muslim *ummah* (nation)—along the lines of the Ottoman or the Abbasid states—with a caliph at its head. This Islamist trend was articulated into the Association of the Muslim Brotherhood by Hasan al-Banna in 1928.

1952–1981

Nasser's 1952 revolution threw out both the king and the British. For some, it was a military takeover, hijacking and aborting decades of civil action that were just about to bear the fruits of liberation and democracy. But the revolution—even though it dealt harshly with the first strikes that confronted it, executing two young labor leaders, Khamees and Baqari in August 1952—was embraced by the bulk of the people; they felt that it was on their side. The revolution tried at first to work with the statesmen of the ancien regime, with the Americans and with the Islamists, but it soon found that it had to follow its own track. It quickly declared for the secular nation-state, for social justice and modernization, and for "positive nonalignment" in foreign policy. From 1954 onward, the Muslim Brotherhood was the state's internal enemy; its members were jailed, tortured, and driven into hiding or exile. Growing up in the sixties, I—and my generation, I think—were aware of the Brotherhood only as a "historic" reactionary faction.

The period from 1954 to 1967 is often likened to the Muhammad Ali period in its emphasis on modernity and development, centrally planned and orchestrated by a powerful state. Its progress was halted and its faults exposed by the Naksa, the defeat in the Six-Day War with Israel in 1967. Within weeks, though, we felt that the state had taken the terrible lesson to heart and was moving toward more serious openness and power sharing.

But in September 1970 Nasser died, and Anwar Sadat took over as president of Egypt. Sadat's overall project was to remove Egypt from the nonaligned camp and plant it firmly under the American umbrella, to adopt free market capitalism, and to make peace with Israel. To do all this, he needed to discredit the Nasser era and disempower the Left, the Nasserists, and the Progressives. The instrument he chose was the Muslim Brotherhood.

Sadat encouraged and nurtured religio-political groups, promoted religious discourse in public life, and clamped down on protest. Elections in student unions and in the professional syndicates were rigged to bring in Islamists. The Brotherhood, although never legalized, became a major social force, offering health and education services at a time when the state—cutting public spending—was allowing the running down of both. The MB set up businesses and started amassing wealth and running philanthropic projects.

Many in the Islamist current, however, did not agree with Sadat's policies—in particular his foreign policy and his closeness to the United States. Meanwhile his "open door" economic policy sent inflation soaring, introduced high-level corruption, and failed to bring in foreign investment in any area beneficial to ordinary citizens. Egypt started to borrow heavily from international financial institutions; the loans were twinned with "reforms" and restructurings that closed down industries and exacerbated the hardship already caused by inflation. Opposition to Sadat grew among both secular and Islamist circles. In January 1977 we saw bread riots—which the military refused to crush.

When Sadat signed the deeply unpopular Camp David Accords in 1979, Egypt—with that stroke of his pen—lost its standing in the Arab and the nonaligned worlds and became a pariah state. That same year the CIA and MI6 started running U.S. national security adviser Zbigniew Brzezinski's campaign to fund and arm radical Islamist forces. The campaign was designed to support volunteer fighters against the Soviets in Afghanistan (among whom were Osama Bin Laden and Ayman al-Zawahiri), but its effects spilled over into the entire region. The Muslim Brotherhood itself remained nonviolent, but various militant groups—known collectively as the Gama3at Islamiyyah (Islamist Groups) splintered off from it. It was one of these that assassinated Sadat in 1981.

While that assassination was not generally disapproved of, the wave of bombings that followed it and destabilized the country was deeply unpopular. So much so that in the mid-nineties the imprisoned leadership of the Gama3at issued a closely argued thesis from jail announcing an official, one-sided cease-fire in its battle against the state.

On Sadat's death, Hosni Mubarak became president, and it was during the first years of his presidency that the third of the Egyptian Islamist clusters came into being: the Salafis. Inflation and the drop in living standards experienced by the middle classes during Sadat's rule had sent many Egyptian professionals to look for work in booming Saudi Arabia. These expats, when they came home, brought with them not only petrodollars but Saudi Wahhabi puritanical ways of thought and behavior. Sadat's promotion of religious discourse in the political sphere had also allowed Saudi dollars to fund Egyptian preachers in Egyptian mosques. Wahhabi-influenced returnees came home to find Wahhabi-preaching mosques, and so the Salafi movement was born.

1981 TO 2011

Mubarak's policy was fire and iron against the Gama3at. Even though they had renounced violence, they remained in jail until the revolution of 25 January.

The Salafis' position was that they retreated from society, mixed only with Salafis, and tried to live an ethical life that followed the example of the earliest era of Islam, the time of the Prophet and his Righteous Successors, ending with the death of Imam Ali in 40AH/A.D. 661. They would not engage in politics, and they held that rising against "those who have been given dominion" was wrong. Nevertheless, Mubarak's police persecuted them and jailed them. Two of my sister-in-law Sohair's nephews are Salafis. They're French-educated, and they used to write pamphlets about Islam in French and hand them out free to tourists. For this they served five years each in administrative detention. Every time a court acquitted them, they would be detained again within days. The first time their mother went to visit them, she discovered thousands and thousands of young men held in Damanhour jail. The jail was under the control of the chief inmate, Abboud el-Zomor, one of the conspirators in the assassination of Sadat and the author of the cease-fire tract—and it was more or less a training camp for Islamist militants.

As for the Brotherhood, it continued to be banned as an organization, but its members and Mubarak enjoyed an ongoing flirtation. Sometimes he had them detained and imprisoned. Sometimes he allowed them to run for Parliament as independents, and they, in turn, agreed to contest only a limited proportion of seats. Meanwhile they built a formidable war chest and a remarkable organization on the ground with representatives in every town and village and cadres and foot soldiers, every one of whom took an oath to obey only his local leader.

The Mubarak strategy was to control the Islamists but keep them as the bogeyman with which to scare the West and the Gulf; they were the "mad bearded ones," the "militant suicide-bombing America-haters" who would take over Egypt if his regime did not get the support it needed to remain in power. Egypt would join the Iran-Hezbollah-Hamas gang—and where would that leave

Israel? The aid, the arms, the joint exercises, the loans kept flowing in, and the cash kept flowing out—to Swiss bank accounts, real estate in London, companies in Cyprus. And Egyptians got poorer and more desperate.

The non-religious opposition to the Mubarak regime acquired a visible presence in 2000 with the Palestinian Intifada. It gathered pace with protests against the war on Iraq (2003), then protests against the rigging of Egyptian elections (2004 and 2005). These were the first stirrings of what finally became the Revolution of 2011.

ACKNOWLEDGMENTS

I want to thank LuAnn Walther, my editor at Pantheon, first for making me write the 2012 part of this book and then for her patience while I struggled with it and with the circumstances surrounding it.

I thank Alexandra Pringle, my editor at Bloomsbury, who phoned me in Tahrir in February 2011 to tell me the moment for this book had come. Without her tenacious support and subtle judgment I don't think I'd have completed it.

Since 2000, the *Guardian* newspaper has been the British home for all my reportage and commentary on Egypt and the Arab world. That space has been of central importance to me at every level. I thank all the editors I've worked with there.

My Egyptian publisher, Ibrahim al-Moallem, and his editorial team at *Shorouk* newspaper bullied me into producing a weekly column. It's thanks to them that I've found my Arabic writing voice (hand?), a whole new audience, and the opportunity to serve the revolution.

I thank: always my agent, Andrew Wylie, and my friends at his London office; my dearest friend and guardian angel, Susan Glynn, for reading drafts—always with my best interests at heart; Ismail Richard Hamilton, my younger son, and my family and friends who had to put up with having overlong out-of-context bits anxiously read out to them at inappropriate times.

Finally, Omar Robert Hamilton, my older son. His critical acumen, forceful opinions, artistic sensibility, and thoroughness have been invaluable as I've struggled to produce my first sustained piece of work since the loss of my husband, Ian Hamilton; my mother, Fatma Moussa; and my friend and mentor, Edward Said. I am incredibly grateful to have him.

NOTES

1. "At 22:34 UTC (00:34 a.m. local time), Renesys observed the virtually simultaneous withdrawal of all routes to Egyptian networks in the Internet's global routing table. Approximately 3,500 individual BGP routes were withdrawn, leaving no valid paths by which the rest of the world could continue to exchange Internet traffic with Egypt's service providers. Virtually all of Egypt's Internet addresses . . . unreachable." http://gizmodo.com/5746121/how-egypt-turned-off-the-internet.

   All links given are live at time of publication, but if a video has been removed, just search YouTube with keywords; somebody will have posted a similar one.
2. http://www.youtube.com/watch?v=hWplni-sWzs.
3. Throughout the nineteenth century, one of the many theaters to host the drama of British-French rivalry was archaeology—and the stealing of antiquities—in Egypt. Successive Egyptian governments of the period consistently favored the French. Three of the most important streets in the part of Cairo established by Khedive Ismail in the late nineteenth century are named after Frenchmen who made radical contributions to Egyptology. Jean-François Champollion (1790–1832) published his translation of the 7agar Rasheed (the Rosetta Stone) hieroglyphs in 1822. Auguste Mariette (1821–1881), for whom, in 1858, Khedive Ismail created the post of Director-General of Excavations and Antiquities, started the institutionalization of archaeology in Egypt. His sarcophagus rests in the garden of the Egyptian Museum. And Gaston Maspero (1846–1916) succeeded Mariette Pasha as Director-General of Excavations and Antiquities from 1880 to 1886 and 1899 to 1914. In 1902 he superintended the move of the Egyptian Museum collection from Giza to its new (and current) home. He is present in Shadi Abd el-Salam's 1969 film *Al-Moumya* (The Night of Counting the Years).
4. *Shabab* derives from the root *sh/b*, "to grow." I love the word; it carries the

same emotional load as *youth* with an extra dash of vigor, and it's both classical and colloquial in all Arabic dialects. It's unusual in that in its colloquial use it's plural without a gender marker. It also carries with it lots of words having to do with the progress of age: *shabba* ("he grew up"), *shaba* ("he grew old"; literally, "his hair grew white"), *shayb* ("white hair"), *shayeb* ("an old man with white hair"—generally used only if he's done something not befitting his age). Unpackaged, it carries the signification of "people, men and women, who are at the youthful stage of life with all its energy, hope, optimism, vigour, impulsiveness and love of life, and who are acting communally, together."

5. Diplomatic car runs over protestors 28 January 2011, http://www.youtube .com/watch?v=3luSbFP60a8.

6. Protestors comfort Central Security Soldiers 28 January 2011, http://www .youtube.com/watch?v=k8jrDxLs3lE&feature =related.

7. Muhammad Lazoghli, the man whose statue stands at the center of the *midan*, was a young soldier who came to Egypt with Muhammad Ali at the beginning of the nineteenth century, to re-establish Ottoman rule after the withdrawal of Napoleon. They say he was the brains behind the Citadel Massacre, which got rid of the remnant leaders of the old Mameluke era. His life's work was to set up a modern Egyptian state in the face of a for-the-moment-defeated French imperialism. He served as minister of defense, minister of finance, and first prime minister of Egypt from 1808 to 1823, and his statue—statesmanlike, bearded, robed—was sculpted many years after his death and posed for by an Egyptian water carrier who resembled him.

8. Ahdaf Soueif, "Egypt Tortures for US, So Why Not on its Account?," *Guardian*, 9 March 2006. "Over the past three decades, such arrests, detentions and kidnappings have become fairly common. People disappear. Friends hunt for them. Usually they are in the State Security Intelligence Bureau in Lazoghli Square in Cairo. They are generally held long enough to extract a confession. Their treatment ranges from insults, threats and beatings to fairly evolved methods of torture. Sometimes the person is not required to confess to anything; they are given a warning and let go. Sometimes the person dies. Mostly, they are sent to jail to await trial.

"Human rights cannot be regional. The rule of law cannot be selective. Guantánamo, Belmarsh, Lazoghli and Facility 1391 in Israel are part of the same configuration; they stand together or—one hopes—fall together."

9. Snipers on the roof of the Ministry of the Interior, Cairo, 29 January 2011, http://www.youtube.com/watch?v=V5kJholiV-8.

10. http://en.wikipedia.org/wiki/Hisham_Mubarak_Law_Center.

11. Aziz el-Shaf3i and Rami Gamal, Ana ba7ebbek ya bladi, http://www.youtube.com/watch?v=btXZMh5tHDA.

12. Khaled Said was a young man killed by police in a cybercafé in Alexandria on 6 June 2010. Because he was an "ordinary" young man—i.e., middle class, and neither a criminal nor an activist—and because his brother managed to get a photo of his face disfigured by his beating, he became a rallying point for the opposition to police brutality in Egypt.

13. Protestors in Tahrir chant "Hosni etgannen" (Hosni's gone mad), http://www.youtube.com/watch?v=U94PCrdHG4w.

14. *Millioneyya*: adding the suffix *eyya* to a noun makes an adjective. So *selm* is "peace" and *selmeyya* is "peaceful"; *millioneyya,* in this case, is a million-person event.

15. The story went that on 31 January, the day the F-16s buzzed Tahrir, Mubarak had ordered the army to attack the protesters, the hundreds of thousands of Egyptians in the streets and *midans* of the country. The story continued that the army had already conducted a poll among the middle-ranking officers, the men in the field who would have had to fire on the protesters, and learned that if the order came to shoot, the officers would refuse. So when given the order, Field Marshal Muhammad Hussein Tantawi had said, "I can't do it, Mr President." Field Marshal Tantawi later (in October) testified that he had never received such an instruction from Mubarak. This left open the question why army spokespeople repeatedly boasted that the army had not attacked the revolutionaries.

16. An officer in the Egyptian army joins protestors in Tahrir, http://www.youtube.com/watch?v=bdaXYtbIEVg.

17. *Shaheed*—plural *shuhada*—means "martyr." The root *sh/h/d* is "to see" and "to bear witness." A witness, for example in a court case, is a *shahed*. Being a *shahed* is only part—a temporary part—of a person's identity or function. A *shaheed* is someone who bears ultimate witness; someone whose sole function now is to bear witness.

18. Quran, chapter 3, verse 169.

AN INTERRUPTION: EIGHT MONTHS LATER, OCTOBER 2011

1. One of the major protest groups, named after a massive strike by Mahallah textile workers in 2008, where several people were killed by the police.

2. The first great quarrel among the "patriotic political forces" after the revolu-

tion had been run under the heading "The Constitution First." When SCAF
announced the transitional program for the country, it was as follows:

1. Election of the two houses of Parliament
2. Parliament chooses a "founding committee" that writes the
   constitution
3. Election of the president

All the political forces rushed off to create parties; some activated existing
parties that were in various conditions of decay or discreditation or division.
One group saw the need to create a coalition of civilian forces to negotiate
with or confront or in any case be the civilian voice of the revolution addressing SCAF and the world. They called the First Conference of Egypt on
7 May. It was attended by some five thousand people and was as close to
broadly representative of Egypt as you could get—except that the Islamist
currents were represented only by some of their shabab who were already
moving away from their mainstream. On the economic front, the conference aligned itself with sustainable development and social justice and a
more equitable distribution of wealth. It presented a strong paper on the
constitution—almost a draft document. And it declared the formation of the
National Council.

The first meeting of the National Council was convened on 7 June, and
by then it was already defined by one main feature: it was calling for change
of the SCAF schedule already agreed by the people in a referendum. Its position, put forward by some powerful lawmen and -women, was, How can we
have elections without a constitution? The constitution is the foundation of
everything. How can you start to build without a foundation?

But putting the constitution first would mean

1. Throwing out the results of the referendum, the first democratic
   exercise the country had engaged in, and whose results (agreeing to
   SCAF's schedule) represented "the will of the people."
2. Postponing elections, thereby giving the secular parties more time to
   organize and to try to catch up operationally with the Ikhwan (the
   Muslim Brotherhood), who had much more presence on the ground.
3. Removing the possibility that the constitution would ultimately be
   written by a founding committee chosen by a parliament with an
   Islamist majority.

Putting the constitution first would also mean keeping the country in limbo
by maintaining the military in power for longer and postponing stability and

an accountable government. The Constitution First campaign split the country into

1. Some powerful secular figures and new parties insisting on putting the constitution first.
2. Islamist figures and parties insisting on respecting "the will of the people," as expressed in the response to the referendum, and abiding by the SCAF schedule.
3. Figures (mostly non-Islamist) who said that in an ideal world it would make more sense to write the constitution first, but in our current circumstances, with the military seizing more power every day, the cabinet weak and paralyzed, and the revolution stalled, it would be best to move toward elections and an accountable government and write the constitution later. This group was also unwilling to discredit the first democratic exercise the country had gone through—the referendum.

Eventually, Group 1 came up with the idea of putting forward (a) proposals for the selection of the founding committee that would write the constitution—to ensure that it was representative of the country as a whole and not just of whoever happened to have a parliamentary majority at the time; and (b) a document listing a set of "constitutional principles" that everyone could agree would frame the constitution.

Many individuals and organizations started putting forward proposals and ideas. This activity took away from the support for Constitution First and so, eventually, Group 1—without officially renouncing its position—started putting forward its own proposals.

By then, however, their distrust of and dislike for the Islamist trend had become so obvious that the Islamists, Group 2, announced that even these ideas were an attempt to subvert "the will of the people" and that it was firmly against them and would not bind itself to any pre-constitutional documents or agreements whatsoever.

3. *Shaheed*: "martyr." See note 17 above.
4. *Mosireen*: "determined." A pun on *misriyyeen*, "Egyptian." A group of independent filmmakers who have set up a collective media center. See their website at http://mosireen.org.
5. Blog from Tahrir Cinema, http://www.cinerevolutionnow.com/2011/07/tahrir-cinema-needs-you.html.
6. http://literaryrevolutions.wordpress.com/2011/07/19/tweetnadwa-real-hope-for-egypts-future/.

7. Testimony of Mustafa Mursi, http://www.youtube.com/watch?v=ilyJAAw G74U.

8. Ahmad al-Musallami, "Al-Tabaa al-Oula," Dream TV, 17 September 2011.

9. http://en.nomiltrials.com/2011/10/egypt-end-military-trials-for-civilians.html.

THE EIGHTEEN DAYS RESUMED: 1 FEBRUARY–12 FEBRUARY 2011

1. Omar Robert Hamilton's film of Bloody Wednesday, http://www.youtube .com/watch?v=jx33QyWZo2s&feature=youtu.be.

2. Eyewitness report from the Nadeem Centre for the Rehabilitation of Victims of Violence, https://alnadeem.org/ar/node/346: "On the 3rd of February 2011 at about 2.30 p.m. an individual claiming to be the Azbakeyya investigation inspector broke into HMLC ordering everybody there to sit on the floor. He was followed by a Military Police lieutenant accompanied by two Military Police officers where the former stood on a chair and shouted: I have orders to shoot anybody who moves. A huge group of thugs then entered the centre accompanied by an intelligence officer. They searched the place, destroyed files and stole some of them, destroyed desks and took papers and CDs, searched personal bags of staff all the while throwing obscenities and accusa-tions of destroying Egypt and conspiring with foreigners.

"After six hours of insults, verbal abuse, accusations of treason and tying the hands of staff members with leather strings the detainees were taken to the central administration of the Military Police in Khalifeh el Maamun in Heliopolis where their names were taken and photos and videos taken of them. They were then transported to some headquarters in Madinet Nasr, assumed to be one of the headquarters of Military Intelligence, where they were interrogated while blindfolded. They were released three days later.

"As for the centre, windows, doors, desks, drawers and file cabinets were destroyed. Two computers, a printer, fax machine, router and a scanner disappeared."

3. Barkha Dutt interviews Ahdaf Soueif, Shahira Amin, and Heba Fatma Morayef, http://www.3quarksdaily.com/3quarksdaily/2011/02/the-women-of -tahrir-square.html.

4. The abduction of Wael Ghoneim, http://www.youtube.com/watch?v=rgLlx Oqi1Hg.

5. Wael Ghoneim weeps over the shuhada, http://www.youtube.com/watch ?NR=1&feature=endscreen&v=crGZmVmULp4. These are the references

for the young shuhada shown in that program. "Lan-nansahom" means "we shall not forget them": https://www.facebook.com/AlShaheed.EslamBeker; http://www.lan-nansahom.org/#!martyr;698; http://www.lan-nansahom.org/#!martyr;542; http://www.lan-nansahom.org/#!martyr;759; http://www.lan-nansahom.org/#!martyr;986.

6. Christiane Amanpour interviews Omar Suleiman, http://abcnews.go.com/ThisWeek/video/omar-suleiman-crisis-12852023.

7. http://www.haaretz.com/news/diplomacy-defense/mubarak-slammed-u-s-in-phone-call-with-israeli-mk-before-resignation-1.342831.

EIGHTEEN DAYS WERE NEVER ENOUGH

1. http://www.nomiltrials.com/2011/03/diaries-of-citizens-under-rule-of.html.

2. Officer Muhammad Wadie singing on his birthday, http://www.youtube.com/watch?v=1qfKpLJdZow.

3. Randa S., disabled in the revolution, observes elections from her wheelchair, http://www.youtube.com/watch?v=3qvKoomVfRA.

4. Ahdaf Soueif, "Ahdaf Soueif in Cairo: 'By early evening it was clear that this was Revolution II,'" Guardian, 23 November 2011.

5. Ahmad Surour's mother, http://www.youtube.com/watch?v=8pfcFGfErvI&feature=related.

6. Quran, chapter 33 (al-A7zab), verses 67 and 68.

7. *Shorouk,* 19 December 2011.

8. Abboudi's story, http://www.youtube.com/watch?v=Vop7OAKV660&feature=fvst.

9. The army above the people, http://www.youtube.com/watch?v=3a8akplbudQ&feature=fvst and http://www.youtube.com/watch?feature=endscreen&NR=1&v=bgG6ugMZkkg.

10. *Shorouk,* 21 December 2011.

11. It's later revealed that medical military personnel had orders to treat protestors without anaesthetic. The report of the Fact-Finding Commission on the Huhad and the Injured, as yet unpublished.

12. *Shorouk,* 9 December 2011.

13. Ultras in metro station on the way to Tahrir chanting against the military and police on 27 January 2012, http://www.youtube.com/watch?v=CatbTdWMzoo.

14. Ultras anthem, "The Sun of Freedom," http://www.youtube.com/watch?v=UmHHU4fQ7ps.

15. Ultras anthem, I was in my red T shirt, http://www.youtube.com/watch?v=UD Vv2esX560.

16. Summing up of the Ultras' massacre, http://www.youtube.com/watch?v =YqPMuFwqPZw.

17. Mosireen film of Salma Said, http://www.youtube.com/watch?v=7JhA4jI v4bk.

18. Atef el-Gohari speaking in Tahrir, http://www.youtube.com/watch?v=MM Jn3FgJYLo.

19. Atef al-Gohari after his shooting, http://kenzo2010.blogspot.co.uk/2012/05/ blog-post_8224.html#.UbwpgPbACzs.

20. Egyptian solidarity convoy visits Gaza, http://www.youtube.com/watch?v =zPG474zBvko.

21. http://blogs.nature.com/houseofwisdom/2012/10/nile-university-students -discuss-their-dissertations-in-makeshift-tents.html.

22. Army versus Qorsaya, http://www.youtube.com/watch?v=g6PZcY6Qtu8.

23. Ultras White Coats hold a "funeral" for the Ministry of Health, http://www .youtube.com/watch?v=0CAuQshLEiA.

A NOTE ON THE TYPE

This book was set in Adobe Garamond. Designed for the Adobe Corporation by Robert Slimbach, the fonts are based on types first cut by Claude Garamond (c. 1480–1561). Garamond was a pupil of Geoffroy Tory and is believed to have followed the Venetian models, although he introduced a number of important differences, and it is to him that we owe the letter we now know as "old style." He gave to his letters a certain elegance and feeling of movement that won their creator an immediate reputation and the patronage of Francis I of France.

Typeset by Scribe, Allentown, Pennsylvania

Printed and bound by Berryville Graphics, Berryville, Virginia

Designed by Maggie Hinders.

ALSO AVAILABLE BY AHDAF SOUEIF

THE MAP OF LOVE

Shortlisted for the Booker Prize

At either end of the twentieth century, two women fall in love with men outside their familiar worlds. In 1901, Lady Anna Winterbourne, recently widowed, leaves England for Egypt, an outpost of the Empire roiling with nationalist sentiment. Venturing out of the British expat comfort zone she finds herself enraptured by the real Egypt and in love with an Egyptian patriot, Sharif Pasha al-Baroudi. Nearly a hundred years later, Isabel Parkman, a divorced American journalist and a descendant of Anna and Sharif, goes to Egypt, taking with her an old family trunk. The notebooks and journals she finds in the trunk will reveal her ancestors' lives and will profoundly transform her own.

'A magnificent work, reminiscent of Marquez and Allende in its breadth and confidence'
GUARDIAN

'A vivid and passionate love story'
SUNDAY TELEGRAPH

'A moving exploration of how love is, in the end, a political act, especially when individuals come from different worlds'
INDEPENDENT

BLOOMSBURY

I THINK OF YOU

Stories from *Aisha* and *Sandpiper*

In these selected stories, Ahdaf Soueif writes about love and displacement in prose that is delicately nuanced and acutely observed. These are achingly lyrical stories, resonant and richly woven. But they always retain an edginess as they explore areas of tension – where women and men are ensnared by cultural and social mores and prescribed notions of 'love', where the place you are is not the place you want to be. She delivers her characters with infinite tenderness and compassion as they inhabit a world of lost opportunities, unfulfilled love and remembrance of times past.

'There is lively, lucid writing here, vivid description and sharply observed dialogue'
THE TIMES

'A fetching and original talent'
HERMIONE LEE, OBSERVER

'Highly unusual and richly impressive . . . The author weaves a circle round us thrice with the touch of a born sorceress'
GUARDIAN

BLOOMSBURY

IN THE EYE OF THE SUN

Set amidst the turmoil of contemporary Middle Eastern politics, this vivid and highly-acclaimed novel is an intimate look into the lives of Arab women today. Here, a woman who grows up among the Egyptian elite, marries a Westernized husband, and, while pursuing graduate study, becomes embroiled in a love affair with an uncouth Englishman.

'Something of a landmark . . . a bold and important work. [This] is the first novel I know of that successfully renders an Arab, Egyptian Muslim reality in English. A tour de force'
LEILA AHMED, WASHINGTON POST BOOK WORLD

'Raw, accurate, searing . . . Soueif [is] one of the most extraordinary chroniclers of sexual politics now writing'
EDWARD SAID, TIMES LITERARY SUPPLEMENT

B L O O M S B U R Y

MEZZATERRA

Fragments from the Common Ground

Ahdaf Soueif is one of the finest commentators of our time. Her clear-eyed reporting is syndicated throughout the world, and these essays, written between 1981 and 2004, are collected here for the first time. They are the direct result of Soueif's own circumstances of being, as she puts it, 'like hundreds of thousands of others: people with an Arab or a Muslim background doing daily double-takes when faced with their reflection in a western mirror'. Whether an account of visiting Palestine and entering the Noble Sanctuary for the first time, an interpretation of women who choose to wear the veil, or her post-September 11th reflections, these selected essays are always perceptive, fearless, intelligent and necessary.

'Soueif is a political analyst and commentator of the best kind'
LONDON REVIEW OF BOOKS

ORDER BY PHONE: +44 (0)1256 302 699; BY EMAIL: DIRECT@MACMILLAN.CO.UK

DELIVERY IS USUALLY 3–5 WORKING DAYS. FREE POSTAGE AND PACKAGING FOR ORDERS OVER £20.

ONLINE: WWW.BLOOMSBURY.COM/BOOKSHOP

PRICES AND AVAILABILITY SUBJECT TO CHANGE WITHOUT NOTICE.

WWW.BLOOMSBURY.COM/AHDAFSOUEIF

BLOOMSBURY